Praise for

EUROPE by EURAIL

"If a trip to Europe is coming up, and you plan to use the excellent train system, pick up a copy of the new edition of *Europe by Eurail*. . . . The book covers all countries that are a part of Eurail and gives suggestions for side trips by train out of the major cities."

—*New York Post*

"A hefty tome that preaches the base-city gospel passionately."

—*Travel & Leisure*

"A traveler armed with the book . . . can easily get just about anywhere in Western Europe."

—*Columbus Dispatch*, Ohio

Also by George and LaVerne Ferguson
Britain by Britrail

EUROPE by EURAIL
How To Tour Europe By Train

Twenty-Second Edition

written by
George and LaVerne Ferguson

edited by
Christina DiLorenzo
and
Stephanie Bell

A Voyager Book

The Globe Pequot Press

Old Saybrook, Connecticut

Cover photo courtesy of German Rail/DER Tours
Cover inset photo © Charlie Westerman/Liaison International
Cover design by Laura Augustine

ISSN: 1081–1125
ISBN: 0-7627-0109-9

Manufactured in the United States of America
Twenty-Second Edition/First Printing

Contents

Europe by Eurail Team

Europe by Eurail has always been a thorough, friendly guidebook, as proven by its continuing best-selling status. But it began as a labor of love.

George Ferguson, a test pilot with the Eighth Air Force during World War II, was closely connected with railroads and travel all his life. He was born 20 minutes after his mother left a Washington-to-New York Express train and spent his childhood growing up alongside the Baldwin Locomotive Works on the "Pennsy" main line. His international experiences began with the U.S. Air Force and later as an international coordinator for a large research organization. His first European train experience as a young man was aboard a vintage 1918 Forty-and-Eight freight train (40 soldiers and 8 horses), a long way from the comfort and speed of today's modern European trains that he loved so much.

George and **LaVerne Ferguson** co-authored this comprehensive rail guide for 21 editions. George's life-threatening illnesses, however, prevent him from participating in this and future editions. But before leaving the team, he wanted to ensure that accurate rail-travel information would continue to be available. LaVerne has established an international staff dedicated to being on track with the latest rail information.

LaVerne brought her love for travel to their writing team, having dreamed of traveling the world since childhood. She pursued her goal through higher education at Ohio State University and by living in and traveling throughout Europe.

Aware of the need to provide easier access to European rail information and rail passes for travel, LaVerne and George started Rail Pass Express, Inc., a company based in Columbus, Ohio, designed to provide travelers with the information resources and rail travel products necessary to pursue the itineraries and concepts outlined in *Europe by Eurail* and *Britain by Britrail*.

LaVerne is president of Rail Pass Express, Inc., and director of the international research and writing team. Her extensive technological editorial background; her academic background in English, world history, and communications; and her experience in research and development for an international corporation add substance to her 22 years of experience in traveling the rails throughout Europe. LaVerne also has extensive experience in creating and custom-designing European tour packages and itineraries for individuals and groups.

LaVerne's powerful team of professional researchers were instrumental in producing this edition. They, too, share in LaVerne's enthusiasm for the exciting world of European train travel—its comfort, high-tech speed, and continuous adventure.

Stephanie Bell and **Christina DiLorenzo** maintain an extensive European rail research library. Stephanie employs her excellent editorial and research skills on the Ferguson guidebooks. Christina studied international marketing in Milan, Italy, and implements her tri-lingual skills to scrutinize specific marketplaces and design rail pass opportunities for North American travelers heading to Europe.

Sheila Clowes investigated and updated key changes in rail station facilities and operations in Europe.

Mary DiThomas, director of Rail Pass Express operations in Dallas, Texas, analyzed European rail network infrastructures and how they impact travel.

Mary Kish is general manager and director of operations for Rail Pass Express and Ferguson Rail Publications. Mary's managerial capabilities and ingenious business acuity keep everyone on the right track and moving in the right direction.

Sandra Lambert shared her expertise of Ireland, Portugal, and Spain in this edition. Sandra has an extensive academic background and lives abroad six months out of the year. She writes for various American and European publications.

H. Milton Peek, whose international expertise stems from his experiences with the U.S. Department of State, is a true detail man who explored and reported on new trends in rail travel throughout Europe.

Kevin Siegmann, a graduate of Ohio State University's top-ranked Industrial Design Program, is Graphics/Systems Designer for Rail Pass Express. He designs and maintains the award-winning web site that contains *Europe by Eurail* information for its online readers, an extensive European rail-related database, and a secure online ordering system for European rail travel products. The site is found at http://www.eurail.com

William Stafford, Ellie Byrnes, and **Matthew Palma,** rail scheduling experts at Rail Pass Express, meticulously deciphered complicated timetables in order to choose the best and most convenient trains for *Europe by Eurail* day excursions and rail connections between base cities.

Research assistants on *Europe by Eurail* and other rail-travel experts at Rail Pass Express include **Colleen Beader, Laura Biemel, Karen Cherdon, Susan LaMarche, Erin Robinson,** and **Jerry Theodoropoulos.**

Invaluable research correspondents include **Major Robert Bean** (Germany), **Margaret Keith** and **Benoit** and **Simone Drillon** (France), and **Jerry D. McNamee** (Ireland and Northern Ireland).

Invaluable contributions also were made by the many resourceful tourism officials and travel partner professionals throughout the European community, including **Heinz Wisner, Barbara Schmidt**, and **Cathy Featherstone** of **DER Travel Services**; **Alan Wissenberg** of **EurAide**; and **Shay Dempsey**, an Irish entrepreneur whose insights helped to provide a new view of the Emerald Isle.

Introduction

"To travel by train is to see nature and human beings, towns and churches and rivers, in fact to see life."   —Agatha Christie

This all new edition of *Europe by Eurail* is reflective of the "new" Europe and the new energy and exuberance of its rail system. It's dynamic, futuristic, and it's on the move—accelerating into the millennium with the high-tech boldness and immense speed of the world's finest transportation system.

Train travel is an enigma for most non-Europeans who have either forgotten or have never had an opportunity to learn what travel by train is like. Europe by Eurail takes the puzzlement out of European rail travel—like having a friend along who takes you by the hand and shows you how to use the world's finest transportation network to see and learn about European life and culture. Toward that end, it provides specific, pragmatic information with step-by-step directions.

Europe by Eurail is a train traveler's how-to guidebook. It is not a hotel/restaurant guide, but rather tells you *how* to locate them. Certain hotels and restaurants do occasionally gain mention, however, especially if they add to the graciousness and enjoyment of a train trip or a stay in a city. *Europe by Eurail* deals primarily with the necessities of train travel in Europe and offers guidance for appreciating the educational and cultural sites and events that abound along the right-of-way of the Continent's magnificent rail system, Eurail.

"See Europe by Train" has been a favorite slogan of Europe's railways for decades, but never has it been as full of meaning as it does today. You will never be bored traveling on a high-speed train because rail travel is still leisurely enough to fully enjoy the constantly changing scenes of hills and hamlets, farms and forests, and cities and countrysides that make the European landscape fascinating. Each country has its own special attractions to offer rail travelers as they speed through, ensconced in comfort and free from worry. Added to the passing scenes is the opportunity for leisurely dining and drinking while chatting with fellow passengers, most of whom are the Europeans you hoped to meet.

Travel by train in Europe is a unique and pleasurable experience. All aboard—and take your imagination with you.

WHY EURAIL?

Many visitors to Europe fail to realize that **Eurail,** the European rail network, can take you to practically every nook and cranny on the Continent, so they insist on renting a car. At first glance, those European fly-drive packages might appear enticing, but the more you investigate them, the less appealing they become.

Consider that the number of European road traffic fatalities is more than four times that in North America, and that watching the road ahead is not really what most folks go to Europe to do. Most European automobiles are small, compact vehicles. That four-passenger economy car you're thinking of renting could never carry four passengers *and* their luggage—so, bring on the Mercedes at three times the price and double the gas. Prepare yourself for another shock—the price of gasoline in Europe is about three times that in the United States, and gasoline stations are not nearly as numerous as they are stateside.

Another very important facet of a fly-drive package is the VAT (value added tax), which ranges from 6 to 33 percent in European countries. In some countries, foreign tourists are eligible for refunds on certain purchases, but there are no VAT refunds on car rentals. Reference to the VAT may be tactfully avoided in car-rental information or perhaps hidden in the fine print of the terms. Whether or not it's hidden, after determining the low, low cost of a rental car with unlimited mileage privileges (which also includes the privilege of buying unlimited gasoline), don't forget to multiply the bottom line by the VAT of the country and add that figure into the equation.

Another item frequently overlooked is insurance. To assure yourself of the minimum personal insurance protection, plan to add several dollars a day for that coverage. By now, you will realize why Europeans park their cars and ride the trains.

One key reasons for going to Europe is to mingle with Europeans. Traveling day after day in a motor coach filled with other American tourists or riding for hours in a small rental car with your spouse helping you navigate and the kids crammed in with the suitcases are not, in our opinion, the best ways to mingle. Europeans use their trains. They will be sitting next to you or across from you in the diner. You will be sharing the same experiences, so conversation will come easily. It's a great way to make new friends, and the kids can eat, get a drink, or go to the bathroom just as often as their little hearts desire.

Trains have always held an aura of romance and charm about them that cannot be experienced in any other mode of transportation. The mere mention of *The Orient Express*, for example, sparks visions of glamour, intrigue, mystery—and sumptuous dining. Although many of the original famous trains have been replaced by high-speed, high-tech international express trains, that special thrill of rail travel is still there.

The Europeans know how to run a railroad. The Eurail network connects more than 30,000 cities, villages, and hamlets with more than 90,000 daily train departures on more than 100,000 miles of track. That's awesome—and the system is getting faster, more efficient, and more elegant. Unlike the airlines' sardine-like accommodations, European trains are comfortable, stylish, and loaded with amenities to please the tourist and business traveler alike.

Best Way to Use the Eurail Network

Originally, the idea of purchasing a pass for unlimited travel by train within a specified time period, for example, 1 month, on the **Eurail** system was a simplistic one. One type of rail pass, a **"Eurailpass",** was offered to non-European residents as a way to encourage independent travelers to use Europe's rail network.

Although today's European rail passes encompass a wide variety of options, time periods, and countries, using a pass is still the most economical, convenient, and flexible way to get the most out of the European rail network. A point-to-point ticket enables you to travel from one point to another but does not provide the flexibility to change your plans.

Rail passes, on the other hand, provide unlimited rail travel each day within a specified time frame. They eliminate the hassle of standing in long lines to purchase tickets, and they can save you a bundle of money if you make long or frequent journeys.

For details on the various kinds of European rail passes available to non-European residents, please consult the **Europe's Rail Passes** section later in this introduction, or contact Rail Pass Express, Inc., 2737 Sawbury Boulevard, Columbus, Ohio 43235 USA; (800) 722-7151, (614) 889-9100; Internet: http://www.eurail.com.

Remember . . . Purchase your rail passes before leaving for Europe!

Base City–Day Excursion Concept

In 1976 *Europe by Eurail* first launched a new concept for comfortable, hassle-free train travel by combining the economy of a Eurailpass with the Fergusons' "Base City–Day Excursion" method of touring Europe. Now in its twenty-second edition, Europe by Eurail has been rewritten and modified to produce a most useful tool for travelers using any type of rail pass that allow you to access the 17-country Eurail system.

Europe by Eurail identifies base cities throughout Europe in which you can stay in comfort and from which you can make numerous day excursions to interesting places, returning each night to the same hotel room. This concept eliminates the hassles of daily packing and unpacking. This more relaxed approach to rail travel is not only an enjoyable way to visit Europe's great cities, but it also affords the time to see and do a delightful variety of things outside major cities.

Speeding into the next century, the "Base City–Day Excursion" concept combined with the appropriate rail pass provides greater flexibility to see more of Europe at its best—by train. Many of our cost-conscious readers modify the concept by using the less expensive suburban area of a major city or one of our day excursion points as their "base." With any one of the various types of Eurail passes available today, it's easy to modify our comfortable rail travel concept to suit your budget and itinerary. Combined with a rail pass and a current copy of *Europe by Eurail,* you become your own tour guide, packing and moving on only when you want to. For the experienced traveler or the novice, it's the only way to go.

HOW TO USE *EUROPE BY EURAIL*

Europe by Eurail takes a pragmatic approach to European rail travel by providing explicit walking directions and explanations based from rail stations. For example, a bewildered tourist standing on a train platform in one of Brussels' *three* train stations needs practical, no-nonsense information—in a hurry:

The Grand'Place? How do I get there?

Where's the tourist information office?

Europe by Eurail leads you with specific directions: "To reach the Grand'Place from Gare Centrale (Central Station), walk down hill in the direction of the Town Hall's spire until you reach the square. The tourist office is to the right of the spire when you are facing the Town Hall."

You do not have to be a geographer to use *Europe by Eurail.* It is conveniently arranged alphabetically—first by country, then by Base City. Rail system maps accompany each country chapter.

Europe by Eurail picks up the traveler disembarking from the train on arrival from another base city (or at the airport if it is the traveler's entry point to Europe) and leads him or her *step-by-step* through the essentials of European rail travel.

Country sections explain what types of tourist rail passes are accepted, what kinds of bonuses are available, and provides specific information about rail travel within that country. These sections also list each country's tourist information office locations in North America, their telephone/fax numbers, and, where applicable, internet site addresses.

Some base cities have a single station; others have multiple stations. Under **train station descriptions** are the subsections concerning

- Exchanging money and using ATMs
- Locating tourist information
- Luggage facilities
- Securing hotel accommodations
- Train information and reservations
- Rail pass validation

Base city **tourist information offices** and **hotel reservation informa- tion** are listed with addresses, telephone and fax numbers, internet web addresses (if available), hours of operation, and, of utmost importance, how to reach the offices from the rail station.

Connections from each base city to others are listed at the end of each base city section. Not all base cities can be reached from another in the same day, although most can.

Sightseeing, attractions, and **special tour** information section for each base city provides a general introduction to what to see and do and how to do it.

Day excursions begin with the distance and average train time and include train schedules to/from the base city. Trains departing a base city are usually in the morning and trains returning from the day excursions are usu- ally in the late afternoon or evening.

A brief history and highlights of each day excursion enable you to decide which ones are of the most interest. Then, *Europe by Eurail* again provides *step- by-step* directions on how to get from the rail station to the tourist informa- tion offices and to the day excursion sights and attractions.

Special Features

Special features in the Appendices of this edition of *Europe by Eurail* include
- **Sample 15-Day Itineraries**
- **International Calling & Dialing Codes**
- **Glossary of Rail Terminology**—in four languages
- **Pictographs**—Symbols that identify places and things by a uniform sign. Study the pictographs before leaving on your Eurail trip.
- **Point-to-Point Fares**—Cost of a single train trip between base cities to aid in determining if a rail pass is more economical than purchasing sepa- rate tickets. Nine times out of ten, a rail pass will come out dollars ahead.
- **Euraide Offices and Locations**—Where to get help if you have a prob- lem with your rail pass.
- **European Tourist Offices in North America**—Where to get advance destination information
- **U.S. Passport Offices**
- **Toll-free Airline** and **Hotel numbers**
- **Tear-Out Reader Card**—We want to know more about our readers' travel needs and we appreciate any comments and/or suggestions. We'll send you additional information about any special promotions and dis- counted rail travel in Europe—FREE! Please answer the questions on the card and mail it to **Rail Pass Express, Inc., 2737 Sawbury Boulevard, Columbus, OH 43235.** Or, if you have internet access, e-mail us at **ques- tions@eurail.com.**

EUROPE'S PASSENGER TRAINS

Many European trains run at speeds in excess of 100 mph, and the high-speed French **TGV** (*train a grande vitesse*, or train of great speed) *Atlantique*, which normally cruises along at 186 mph, holds the world's speed record at 320 mph. The basis for high-speed rail traffic is a flawless rail bed, and Europe's rails sing as trains move smoothly enough to permit dining without fear that the next curve might slosh your coffee. Most rail lines throughout western Europe today are equipped with endless, welded track. The old "clickety-clack" of the track, regardless of its nostalgic value, is gone forever.

Europe's passenger trains range from the sleek, high-speed, high-tech **AVEs, Eurostar**, and **Thalys TGV** international express trains, running on the main lines to the perky little omnibus rail cars that ply the suburban lines. In between are national **InterCity** and regional trains that provide express services within a country's borders. The newer trains include a whole stable full of various passenger car (carriage) types, including plush compartment interiors, comfortable seats, and businesslike amenities. Each of the new double-deck TGVs, for example, can carry 545 passengers and features telephones, a children's play area, and computer hook-ups.

Germany's **InterCity Express (ICE)** service provides cars with increased leg room, headphones, and even some video systems built into the seat backs. Italy has not only a "tilting tower" (the Leaning Tower of Pisa), it also has "tilting" trains, termed *Pendolino*. You can sit back and relax with complimentary snacks and an espresso while this comfortable train whisks you to your destination at an operating speed of 155 mph. And, the powerful dual-voltage **Cisalpino** trains, the world's first international tilting trains, easily climb the mountain routes between Italy and Switzerland.

The British-Belgian-French-modified TGVs, known as "Eurostar" trains, connect Britain with continental Europe. Connecting through London and the English Channel tunnel (Chunnel) to Paris, Brussels, Amsterdam, and Cologne (Koln), the Eurostar trains make the British connection between London's Waterloo International station in the city's center and Paris' Gare du Nord station in under 3 hours. Even the airlines can't get you there any faster if you consider the amount of time it takes from city center to the airport, going through security and customs, and then transportation from the arrival airport to city center.

Europe's Night Trains/Hotel Trains

Although we usually advocate going to Europe to see it, not sleep through it, today's European overnight trains provide a most comfortable and convenient means of transport over long distances. And there's an aura of romance on Europe's luxurious hotel trains.

There is a great variety of accommodations on night trains, ranging from

sleeperettes (comfortable reclining seats) to the new luxury hotel-style trains complete with a hotel lobby area and concierge. Traditional night-time trains usually do not have full restaurant service, but the steward can provide drinks and snacks. They are normally comprised of standard sleeping cars, **couchette** cars (with four berths per compartment in first class and six berths in second class), and regular seats. The couchette cars usually offer washrooms and toilets at the ends of the cars. You get a place to lie down, a blanket, and pillow.

EuroNight (EN) trains are usually air conditioned and provide additional comfort and services with the same basic facilities as the traditional sleeping car trains. EN trains complement EuroCity day-time trains and offer a wash basin with soap, towels, and a power plug; a real bed with sheets, pillows, and blankets; a complimentary mineral water and snacks and complimentary continental breakfast served in the cabin.

For luxury, comfort, and privacy, Europe's high-tech, high-comfort hotel trains are top of the line—InterCity Night (German Rail), CityNightLine (based in Switzerland), and Trens Hotel (Spanish Rail). An InterCity Night cabin contains its own private shower, toilet and wash basin, and beds are aligned in the direction of travel. Popular routes include Berlin (Charlottenburg station)–Munich and between Berlin–Dortmund, Essen, Dusseldorf, Cologne (Koln), or Bonn. Rail pass holders receive about 50 percent discount on cabin rates.

CityNightLine trains feature high-quality, double-decked, hotel-style sleeping accommodations and single-level sleeperette cars. Luxury Category A provides spacious compartments on the upper deck with one or two wide beds, shower, toilet, and panoramic windows. Rail pass holders receive about 30 percent discount. For budget travelers, Category C has large reclining seats with a canopy containing a reading lamp to enhance a feeling of privacy. Rail pass holders pay only about $20. CityNightLine routes include Berlin–Zurich, Zurich–Vienna or Hamburg, and Vienna–Cologne/Dortmund.

The tilting Spanish **Trens Hotel** trains operate within Spain and internationally into Portugal, France, Italy, and Switzerland. The Gran Clase sleeping cars include private toilet and shower facilities; Turista Class offers four-berth compartments; or for economy, choose the sleeperette seats. Trains carrying the Gran Clase cars include the famous Pablo Casals (Barcelona–Geneva, Bern and Zurich), the Antonio Machado (Barcelona–Seville/Malaga) and the Lusitania Express (Madrid–Lisbon).

Generally speaking, the least expensive trains with sleeping accommodations are in Southern and Eastern Europe; Northern and Central Europe are the most expensive. The sleeperette, or reclining seat, is the least expensive type of accommodations and Luxury Class on hotel trains is the most expensive.

Remember: Rail passes do not cover the costs of sleeping accommodations; in most cases, however, they do provide a discount.

Train Reservations

Many trains require seat reservations, especially international and long-distance express trains including TGVs, Eurostars, many ICEs, InterCity and EuroCity trains, Cisalpino and Pendolino trains, and specialty sightseeing trains such as those in Switzerland (*Glacier Express, Bernina Express, Crystal Panoramic*, and *The William Tell Express*).

A computerized reservation system linking the Eurail routes is available in every major rail terminal in Europe. Check the train departure board—if there is an **"R"** next to that train, then seat reservations are mandatory, and you should not board without one. Seat reservations for TGVs and many other types of trains can be made at automatic reservation-ticket dispensers in the rail stations.

Seat reservations in Europe cost about $5.00 each, and this cost is *not* included in a rail pass. Advance seat reservations can be made from North America, but they are considerably more expensive and non-refundable. If, however, you choose to make seat reservations from North America, you can make them through the same place you purchase your rail pass.

The farther south you travel in Europe, the more important it becomes to have seat reservations. *Always* have seat reservations when traveling in Italy and Greece. Seat reservations are not, however, accepted for most local trains, nor for trains traveling *within* the borders of Belgium, the Netherlands, Luxembourg, or Switzerland.

To assure that you receive the proper reservation,
- Determine the day and date of your travel
  NOTE: Europeans reverse the order of the month and day when writing dates, i.e., June 15, 1998, appears as 15/06/98 and not as 06/15/98.
- Check the train schedules posted in the rail stations for the train number, its departure time, and arrival time at your destination
- Print this information on a piece of paper, starting with the date, the train number and the departure time. Draw a short arrow, and then add the arrival time of the train and the name of your destination.
- Indicate the number of seat reservations required.

Your seat reservation will identify the class of travel (first or second), smoking or non-smoking, car number, and, in most cases, the seat number(s).

Plan to be on the train platform several minutes prior to scheduled departure. European trains stop only for a short time at intermediate stations to let passengers on and off, and stops of only 1 or 2 minutes are usual. To save a lot of scurrying around when the train arrives, **check the illustrated train composition diagrams** displayed on the platforms to determine the approximate positioning of your train's first- and second-class coaches.

Then, as your train approaches, look for either a large number **"1"** on or near the doors; or a yellow stripe above the train windows to indicate first class cars if you have a first class rail pass and/or first class seat reservation. Second class cars are indicated with a large **"2"** on or near the doors.

Train Schedules

Every European rail station has train arrival and departure times prominently posted, usually by huge digital display boards. The printed ones posted are easily recognized by their background color—departure times are printed on yellow; arrival times on white. Intermediate stops, train platform and track numbers are posted as well. In case of discrepancy, the digital display boards take precedence. Although the time schedules may change, the track numbers seldom change.

Schedules are listed chronologically in **24-hour time** from 0001 (1 minute after midnight) to 1200 (noon) and to 2400 (midnight), i.e., a departure time of 1843 would be equal to 6:43 P.M.

Train information and reservation offices in the stations also provide printed mini-schedules listing rail services between two specific points. They're free. These offices have national and international schedules as well.

Train schedules presented in this edition of *Europe by Eurail* are updated to press time. They are, however, for planning purposes only. When purchasing a rail pass, you are entitled to receive a free Eurail timetable and map of the major rail connections. For detailed itinerary planning, purchase a ***Thomas Cook European Timetable,*** which is printed monthly. In North America, the timetable may be purchased from some travel bookstores or from **RailPass Station BookShop,** (800) 722–7151; Fax: (614) 764–0711; via secure Internet: http://www.eurail.com. Elsewhere in the world, write to Thomas Cook Ltd., Timetable Publishing Office, Box 227, Dept. E, Peterborough, PE3 6PB, England. In Europe, the Thomas Cook European Timetable can be purchased at the company's main offices in major cities.

Train Splitting

When international trains in Europe have multiple destinations, sometimes passenger coaches are "split" en route. To make certain you end up where you want to be:

- **Check the train sideboards** displaying the departure point, stops en route, and the final destination
- **Announce your destination** to the conductor as he or she checks your rail pass
- **Stay in your seat** when the train halts at a terminal for "splitting" the coaches. Since the splitting process occurs quickly, if you are in another part of the train you could easily end up at the wrong destination—sans suitcase and your fellow travelers.

The "Chunnel" and Eurostar Services

In 1888, Louis Figuier proclaimed that "linking France and England will meet one of the present day needs of civilization." On May 6, 1994, England's Queen Elizabeth II and France's President François Mitterand brought Figuier's words to life and inaugurated a new era in European train travel—the linking of England and France via a tunnel that runs underground and under the English Channel. More than 17 million tons of earth were moved to build the two rail tunnels (one for northbound and one for southbound traffic) and one service tunnel.

The Chunnel has proven to be one of the world's largest undertakings. The project cost more than $13 billion and took seven years to complete. Napoleon's engineer, Albert Mathieu, planned the first tunnel in 1802, incorporating an underground passage with ventilation chimneys above the waves. For obvious reasons the British were nervous. Later, in 1880, the first real attempt at a tunnel was undertaken by Colonel Beaumont, who bored 2,000 meters into the earth before abandoning the project. When work on another tunnel began in 1974, the Beaumont tunnel was found to be in good condition. Construction of the current tunnels began in 1987 and are 38 kilometers in length undersea and have an average depth of 40 meters under the seabed.

Operated by British Rail, the French (SNCF) and Belgium (SNCB) railways, the Eurotunnel provides three different types of service between England and the Continent. Eurostar provides passenger service, and Le Shuttle provides automobile, coach, and lorry service between Folkstone and Calais. International rail freight rounds out the list.

Eurostar service is offered from London's new Waterloo International Eurostar Terminal to Paris' Gare du Nord or Brussels' Midi stations, in either direction. Travel times from London to Paris are reduced from more than five hours to three hours; Brussels is only three hours and fifteen minutes away, thus making a European Capitals tour nothing more than a day excursion. *Eurailpass* holders receive a discount on Eurostar tickets. Eurostar also serves Lille and Calais in Northern France and Ashford, Kent.

In the future, services will be expanded to include Eurostar originations from Glasgow, Edinburgh, York, Manchester, Birmingham, and other cities linked to Paris and Brussels in either direction. These direct daytime Eurostar Regional Services will reduce travel times from Edinburgh to Paris, for example, from more than twelve hours to about nine hours. At press time, plans include adding European Night Services for those wishing to arrive in Paris or Brussels in time for breakfast. Included in the night services will be services from London to Amsterdam, Dortmund, and Frankfurt, Germany. Both seated and sleeper accommodations will be offered for overnight departures with on-board catering and luggage storage compartments.

The Eurostar Trains

The sleek Eurostar trains *(Trans Mache Super Trains)* each carry 794 passengers (210 in first class and 584 in second class) and reach speeds of 200 miles per hour in France, 100 miles per hour in England, with speeds through the Chunnel of 80 miles per hour. The train is based primarily on the TGV but was redesigned to accommodate the three different voltage types encountered en route. The trains are accessible to handicapped passengers and provide sufficient storage for luggage.

You are required to arrive at the Eurostar terminal at least twenty minutes prior to departure. After check-in and passing through the security and passport control you will find a boarding area lounge, cafeteria, bar, and shops.

Those taking advantage of a trip from Paris or Brussels to London on a Eurostar train are in for a treat. The trains offer the comfort and amenities comparable to few trains in the world. From departure you're in store for a smooth, quiet ride, and even when you enter the tunnel, the only noticeable change is the sudden darkness. Those concerned with changes in air pressure needn't worry. Air flow through the tunnel is regulated to minimize changes in pressure and few passengers, if any, notice discomfort.

Eurostar staff are multilingual and are available to provide assistance from the minute you enter the terminal to the minute you exit the platform. You'll notice them right away, dressed in navy blue uniforms with accented yellow scarves or ties. If you have any questions, don't be shy—they're there to serve you, and serve you they do.

Passengers traveling first class are treated to an on-board meal ranging from breakfast to dinner, depending upon the time of day. Second-class passengers won't starve either, as a buffet car and roving refreshment cart services are available at nominal costs.

EUROSTAR PASSENGER TIMETABLE

LONDON–BRUSSELS

Monday-Friday			Saturday			Sunday		
Train #	Depart	Arrive	Train #	Depart	Arrive	Train #	Depart	Arrive
9110	0653	1126	9110	0653	1126	9118	0843	1344
9118	0857	1344	9118	0857	1344	9186	0943	1434
9186	0957	1434	9186	0957	1434	9130	1140	1826
9130	1153	1626	9130	1153	1626	9142	1440	1926
9142	1453	1926	9142	1453	1926	9154	1740	2226
9152	1719	2226	9154	1753	2226	9158	1840	2324
9158	1853	2324	9158	1853	2324			

BRUSSELS–LONDON

Monday-Friday			Saturday			Sunday		
Train #	Depart	Arrive	Train #	Depart	Arrive	Train #	Depart	Arrive
9113	0735	1039	9113	0735	1039	9119	0852	1139
9119	0852	1139	9119	0852	1139	9127	1052	1339
9127	1052	1313	9127	1052	1313	9133	1235	1539
9133	1235	1513	9133	1235	1513	9145	1538	1839
9145	1538	1839	9145	1538	1839	9187	1753	2039
9187	1753	2039	9187	1753	2039	9163	1955	2239
9163	1955	2239	9163	1955	2239			

LONDON–PARIS

Monday-Friday			Saturday			Sunday		
Train #	Depart	Arrive	Train #	Depart	Arrive	Train #	Depart	Arrive
9078	0550	1014	9078	0550	1014	9004	0640	1120
9004	0657	1120	9004	0657	1120	9008	0740	1214
9008	0753	1214	9008	0753	1214	9012	0840	1308
9012	0853	1308	9012	0853	1308	9016	0940	1408
9016	0953	1408	9016	0953	1408	9024	1143	1614
9020★	1053	1505	9024	1157	1614	9028	1240	1720
9024	1157	1614	9028	1253	1720	9032	1340	1811
9028	1253	1720	9032	1353	1811	9036	1443	1914
9032	1353	1811	9036	1457	1914	9040	1540	2008
9036	1457	1914	9040	1553	2008	9042	1543	2011
9040	1553	2008	9044	1653	2114	9044	1640	2114
9044	1648	2114	9048	1757	2229	9048	1743	2229
9048	1748	2229	9052	1857	2314	9052	1843	2314
9052	1857	2314				9056	1940	0005
9056★	1953	0005						

★Friday only

PARIS–LONDON

Monday-Friday			Saturday			Sunday		
Train #	Depart	Arrive	Train #	Depart	Arrive	Train #	Depart	Arrive
9007	0710	0920	9007	0710	913	9011	0810	1043
9011	0810	1043	9011	0810	1043	9015	0910	1139
9015	0910	1113	9015	0910	1113	9019	1013	1239
9019	1013	1213	9019	1013	1213	9023	1113	1339
9023	1113	1339	9023	1113	1339	9027	1213	1439
9027	1213	1413	9027	1213	1413	9031	1310	1539
9035★	1413	1613	9031	1310	1539	9035	1413	1639
9039	1510	1713	9039	1510	1713	9039	1510	1739
9043	1607	1843	9043	1607	1843	9043	1607	1843
9047	1710	1913	9047	1710	1913	9047	1710	1939
9051	1818	2043	9051	1818	2043	9051	1818	2043
9055	1910	2113	9055	1910	2113	9055	1910	2139
9059	2013	2243	9059	2013	2243	9059	2013	2243
9063★	2107	2316				9063	2107	2339

★Friday only

Note: 1998 schedule not available at press time. For current schedule call (800) 722-7151 or visit http://www.eurail.com/eurostar.

EUROPEAN RAIL PASSES

A point-to-point ticket is, of course, good for travel from one point to another. It does not, however, provide flexibility nor economy if you are making several trips, especially any over long distances. You can, however, consult the fares between major cities listed in the Appendix of this edition or visit our more extensive point-to-point fares database on our web site at **http://www.eurail.com** to add up the cost of your journey and then compare it to the cost of a rail pass.

Today's rail traveler has a wide choice of rail passes available, from the seventeen-country Eurailpass to regional passes encompassing groups of countries and individual, or national, country passes.

A comprehensive list of prices and types of rail passes is listed in the Appendix of this edition and on our web site.

What is a Rail Pass Day?

There are many different types and price ranges of rail passes available that provide *unlimited* rail transportation for a specified number of days. A "rail pass day" runs from midnight to midnight during which it is possible to make unlimited journeys.

Rail Pass Validation

You have 6 months from the issue date of the rail pass (the date that is stamped on your pass) in which to begin using it. Prior to boarding your first train in Europe, present your pass for validation at the rail station. Allow for a little extra time for the validation process, but once your pass is validated, that ends standing in line to buy another ticket—a real convenience.

- Do not make any entries (such as filling in your passport number) prior to validation.
- Although it is not a part of the validation process, write the starting and ending dates of your pass validation period on a piece of paper and hand it to the clerk along with your pass and passport. (Remember that Europeans write the day before the month, as in 10/07/98 would mean July 10, 1998.)
- Be certain the clerk agrees to the dates before he enters the validity period on your pass
- Double check the validation dates before accepting the pass. If an error is made either in the dates or your passport number, have it corrected immediately.
- The clerk then enters your passport number and stamps the pass.
- Sign the pass only after the rail official has asked you to do so.

Once validated, your pass is neither refundable nor replaceable.

Pass Protection Program

Guard your rail pass with the same attention you give to your cash, traveler's checks, and passport. Lost or stolen passes are not refundable; Rail Pass Express offers a pass protection program that reimburses its clients in full for the unused portion of the rail pass, and the cost is only an additional $10 per pass.

Eurail Passes

There are two basic types of Eurail passes—consecutive-day and flexible passes. **Consecutive-day passes** are valid for an unlimited number of rail journeys during the number of rail pass days you purchased, which constitutes the pass's "validity" period. As an example, if you purchased a 15-day Eurailpass and took your first train trip on January 1, your pass would be valid for use as many times as you want in any of the 17 countries listed below until midnight on January 15. We call it the "tick-tock" pass.

Consecutive-Day Eurail Passes

Eurailpass

Unlimited **first-class** rail travel (some trains may require a special supplement) throughout any or all of **17 countries**:

Austria	Germany	Luxembourg	Sweden
Belgium	Greece	Netherlands	Switzerland
Denmark	Hungary	Norway	
Finland	Ireland	Portugal	
France	Italy	Spain	

Choose from these validity periods: **15 days, 21 days, 1 month, 2 months**, or **3 months**. It also provides access to many steamers, ferries, and buses, either entirely free or at reduced rates. (Eurailpass bonuses are detailed in each country introduction in this edition.) Go as you please; stop where and when you want. It's an excellent value for anyone visiting several countries.

Eurail Saverpass

Unlimited **first-class** rail travel for 2, 3, 4, or 5 people traveling together in any or all of the above-listed 17 countries with the same privileges and choice of validity periods as Eurailpass.

Eurail Youth Pass

For those who are still **under age 26** on their first day of train travel, this pass provides unlimited **second-class** rail travel in any or all of the above-listed 17 countries. It entitles you to the same privileges and choice of validity periods as the first-class Eurailpass, except it is valid for second-class travel only.

Flexible Eurail Passes

Flexible-type Eurail passes provide exactly what the "Flexipass" name implies—flexibility. The Flexipasses work especially well if you plan to stay in one place and not travel for a few days. You choose the number of travel days that can be used at any time within a 2-month validity period. Thus, while you're not traveling, your rail pass is not "ticking" away. All of the Flexipasses that are preceded by the word "EURAIL" cover any or all of the 17 European countries listed above.

For example, if you purchase a 5-day Europass, you will have 5 boxes on your pass in which you write the dates of the days you will use the train. We recommend that you write in the date *on* the date that you travel, rather than in advance, just in case you want to change your travel plans at the last minute.

Eurail Flexipass

Unlimited **first-class** rail travel in any or all of the above listed 17 countries. Buy either 10 or 15 travel days and use them within a 2-month time period.

Eurail Saver Flexipass

Unlimited **first-class** rail travel for 2, 3, 4, or 5 period traveling together at all times in any or all of the above listed 17 countries. Purchase either 10 or 15 travel days to be used within a 2-month validity period.

Eurail Youth Flexipass

Unlimited **second-class** rail travel for passengers under age 26 on their first date of travel. Purchase either 10 or 15 days of travel.

Eurail/Drive Pass

Designed for those who utilize the rail network for most of their travels but who occasionally want an automobile to explore the local countryside. Includes 4 days of unlimited first-class rail travel throughout the 17 Eurail countries and 3 days of car rental vouchers that can be used at any time, and not necessarily consecutively, within a 2-month period. You can purchase up to 5 additional rail days and up to 5 more car days.

Europass

If your Eurail travels will be limited to **Germany, France, Italy, Spain, and/or Switzerland**, consider this "design-your-own" flexible multi-country pass for unlimited **first-class** rail travel. Choose any number of rail travel days from 5 to 15 to be used within 2 months. As with the other Flexipasses, the travel days need not be consecutive.

You can really get creative by adding up to 4 additional "zones" to your pass for additional fees (see the list in the Appendix for all prices):

Benelux Zone (includes Belgium, the Netherlands, and Luxembourg)

Danube Zone (Austria and Hungary)

Greece Plus (Greece and ferry crossing from Italy to Greece)

Portugal

Youth Europasses for unlimited second-class rail travel are available to those under age 26

Europass Drive

Similar in concept to the Eurail/Drive Pass but valid only in the same countries as the regular Europass. It includes 3 days unlimited first-class rail travel and 3 days of car rental vouchers. Additional car rental days may be purchased, but additional rail days and zones are not available.

TRAVEL TIPS

Planning Pays Off

Careful planning is the key to success in just about everything we do, and planning a Eurail vacation or business trip is no exception.

How Much? Perhaps the most important consideration of any trip, at least for most of us, is its cost. Can you afford it? How much will it *really* cost, including all those extras that seem to creep into a trip regardless of how well it was planned? Many vacations have turned into financial nightmares because of "unknown" costs. Reduce those "surprise" costs by purchasing your European transportation in advance. The Eurail system, in many instances, includes connecting transport, so about the only additional transportation costs would be for an occasional bus, taxi, or local tour ticket. Taxis are usually the most expensive means of transportation. Coupled with your air transportation ticket, purchasing a rail pass nails down total transportation costs long before your trip begins.

Use the public transportation systems whenever possible. In a base city, investigate the multiple-ride tickets and city transportation passes. They're inexpensive and frequently include all sorts of discounts for sightseeing and/or shopping.

Accommodations

There are several ways to regulate accommodations costs. You can set a budget—so much for a night's lodging and no more. This is about the only

way a traveler on the move can make it with no fixed itinerary and no knowledge (or care) of where they might be tomorrow. Of course, Eurail passes are
invaluable to this type of traveler. Can't find a place to fit your budget? Use
your rail pass and board a train to the suburbs where lower rates and more
vacancies usually exist.

Keep in mind that tourist information offices maintain extensive current
lists of all types of accommodations from hostels, bed-and-breakfast establishments or pensions, to 5-star luxury hotels.

The budget-minded traveler can write to the appropriate European tourist
offices in North America listed in the Appendix and ask for information
about budget accommodations. The plenitude of modestly priced lodgings
and inexpensive restaurants, even in Europe's most expensive cities, will amaze
you.

Those interested in international hostels must join the American Youth
Hostels. A junion (age 17 and under) membership is $10; adult (age 18-54),
$25; senior citizen (age 55 and over), $15; Family membership, $35. You may
purchase hostel memberships from Rail Pass Express, Inc., at (800) 722–7151.

We recommend having a confirmed accommodations reservation in your
European arrival city or wherever you will be spending the first night..

Not by Bread Alone

Oddly enough, the reader who exists on hamburgers and milk shakes back
home will find such a diet expensive to maintain in Europe. Europe abounds
in good, wholesome food. Practically every major railway station has a cafeteria where the food is displayed along with the prices. "Order the spaghetti
Bolognese," was the advice of one tourist official in Switzerland. "You can't
go wrong," he declared, and he was right.

Many of the railway stations have dining-room facilities and some even
have gourmet restaurants. Most European restaurants offer a tourist menu at
a fixed cost. Look for the MENU sign, posted outside, showing the prices and
food selections.

If you are puzzled by foreign menus, take heart. Many European restaurants
have menus that have been translated into your language. Although it might
take some of the "adventure" out of eating in a foreign country, it also might
save an embarrassing moment—such as ordering the poulet, which you recognize as chicken and ending up with a whole roasted chicken!

To help hold the food price line, determine if your hotel includes breakfast with the accommodations and if so, what kind of breakfast and how much
is the room without it?

On day excursions, pack a picnic-style lunch. Bread, cheese, pastry cold
cuts, fruits, soft drinks, and beer or wine—all are available from local shops. If
you give advance notice, perhaps the hotel will prepare a basket lunch for you.

For the most part, meals served aboard the trains are, naturally, on the expensive side. In many cases, though, the food is excellent and well worth the premium you pay for enjoying it as you speed along with the scenic countryside. Many trains provide buffet and cafeteria services, and you can usually count on a food trolley being aboard for drinks ad sandwiches. On some trains, such as the TGV Thalys, gourmet meals are served at your seat—airline style. One fact remains: The least expensive food aboard a train is that which you brought. Again, plan ahead and save.

How to Get There

Excursion fares are available in a multitudinous variety. Charter flights are usually money savers but some APEX (advance purchase excursion) fares can save even more. You can start with the toll-free numbers in the Appendix, or if yours is not listed, telephone the 800 directory service at (800) 555–1212.

We refer readers to their travel agents (the air experts) for airline information. Consider that on any given day there are more than 180 different fares on the same airline flying to the same destination.

What to Take and How to Pack It

The obvious answer is "as little as possible." In these days of wash-and-wear fabrics (and deodorants), there is no need to pack your entire wardrobe, lug it everywhere, use very little of it, and return home with longer arms. Unlike a motorcoach tour, the beauty of a Eurail tour is that you will not be seeing the same people day after day. Also keep in mind that for the most part, you will need to carry or roll your own luggage.

1. Take one medium-size suitcase, preferably one with wheels, and perhaps a shoulder bag.
2. **Thomas Cook European Timetable.** We recommend the *Thomas Cook European Timetable* as a part of your Eurail trip planning. An invaluable aid, it contains complete timetables covering every major rail route in Europe.

   The timetable is published on the first day of each month. The June-September issues contain summer train schedules. February-May issues contain advance summer-service supplement; October-May contain the winter schedules.

   When you purchase a Eurail pass from Rail Pass Express, you will receive a current *Eurail Timetable* of major rail connections free of charge, which may be sufficient for your pre-trip planning; if not, you can purchase a copy before departure from Rail Pass Express at (800) 722–7151 or on secure online at **http://www.eurail.com**.
3. **Money/traveler's checks, debit card, credit card.** Don't take more cash than you can afford to lose. Take a credit card and a bank debit card with you. You can use a bank debit card to obtain cash from your check-

ing account and the credit card for a cash advance or to charge hotels bills and large expenses, reserving cash for smaller items.

Use the convenience of ATMs (Automatic Teller Machines). The foreign exchange rate is better at ATMs, but they usually charge a service fee or $1.00-$2.00 for using a debit card and credit card advances are more expensive. The two largest international ATM networks are Visa/Plus and MasterCard/Cirrus. To find out which network your bank uses, look on the back of your card for the network logo. To find the ATM locations abroad for Visa/Plus, write to Visa International, 900 Metro Center Blvd., MI-9C, Foster City CA 94404 or access the website at http://visa/com/cgi-bin/vee/vw/products/atm/wrld.html?2+0; for MasterCard/Cirrus, call (800) 4-CIRRUS or its website at http://www.mastercard.com/Info/ATM-form.htm.

If you carry traveler's checks, cash them at currency-exchange offices in railway stations and airports. Banks often charge an additional fee and hotels and stores seldom give you the full exchange value. Since the fees are usually charged per check, carry traveler's checks in denominations of at least $100. Wherever possible, cash them at the bank or office of the issuing company.

Pick Pockets

Picking pockets is an art. The art is practiced frequently in Europe. Coat pockets are the main targets. Foil 'em by sewing on two medium-size buttons, one above and one below the pocket opening. Then, loop a piece of shoelace or strong string around the buttons when carrying any valuables in that pocket. Or, affix Velcro tabs inside the tops of your pocket. At least you'll be able to hear and feel it if someone else is in your pockets. Avoid carrying anything more valuable than a handkerchief in hip pockets. Purses should be the "fanny-pack" style. Shoulder bags should be worn with the strap placed over the head and across the diagonally opposite shoulder.

Don't let the thought of pick pockets alarm you, just be alert.

Jet Lag and What to Do about It

Jet Lag can seriously affect your European trip unless you understand it and know the means of dealing with it. The following explanation of what jet lag is, and some of the means of combating it, should prove helpful to any traveler planning a trip involving four or more hours of time change. The human body has numerous rhythms. That for sleep is one of them. Even without sunlight, as in a cave, the body will still maintain a twenty-four-hour awake-asleep cycle. The heart rate has another cycle, one that falls to a very low ebb in the early hours of the morning. Body temperature, which affects the mental processes, also drops during this time. Thus, if a traveler were transported rapidly to a location five or six time zones (hours) removed from the point of departure, even though it may be eight or nine o'clock in the morning at the arrival point, the traveler's body functions would be at a low ebb. Consequently, the traveler would feel subpar, and this feeling can persist for as long as three days or so unless something is done to correct it.

To cope effectively with jet lag, start varying your normal sleep-eat-work pattern a week or so before your departure. If you are normally up by 7:00 A.M. and in bed around 11:00 P.M. or so, start getting up earlier and going to bed later for a few days. Then reverse the procedure by sleeping in a bit in the morning and going to bed ahead of your normal time. Vary your meal times, possibly putting off breakfast until you can combine it with brunch at noon. What this erratic life style will do is to condition your body to begin accepting changes in its normal routine. In turn, when the big transatlantic change comes, it won't be as much of a shock to your system.

To lessen the effects of jet lag during your trip, avoid excessive drinking and eating en route to Europe. Set your watch to local time at your destination as you depart on your flight. When you do this, your eyes will begin to tell your body functions that there is something new going on, and you'll accelerate your adjustment to the new time zone. Exercise on the first day you arrive in Europe by taking a vigorous stroll; then take a long nap. Rest and relax through the balance of that day. Then on the second day, begin doing everything you normally do back home—but on European time. Above all, don't keep your watch set at the time back home. (How many times have you looked at your watch and then realized that you were hungry?) Respect jet lag and take these precautions in order to enjoy your Eurail vacation to its fullest.

Some current studies have shown the hormone melatonin to be useful in combatting jet lag, but as with any other over-the-counter drug, you should first consult you physician.

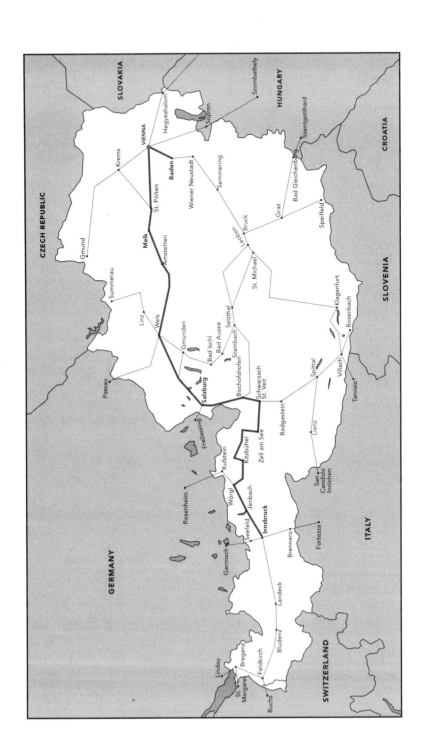

Austria

Austria's central location in Europe and its six international airports of the Imperial Cities—Vienna, Graz, Innsbruck, Klagenfurt, Linz, and Salzburg—make it a convenient gateway country for European travelers. Although German is the native language of Austria, most tourism officials speak English. With a smile on your face, try the informal German greeting, "Grus Gott," and ask slowly and distinctly, "Do you speak English?" A smile almost always elicits a cooperative attitude.

Austria is more than museums and antiques; it is also music, gorgeous scenery, and gourmet foods. Austria is a country where one can easily commit suicide with a knife and fork by overindulging in its temptingly tasty pastries and piles of *schlagrahm*—but what a way to go. We discovered why the *schlagrahm* (whipped cream) is so delicately delicious—it's the *real* thing—unlike the ultra-pasteurized concoctions found in the U.S.

Austrians say if you plan a seven-country trip in Europe that begins in Austria, you'll end up skipping the other six countries. Perhaps they are right. A rail excursion through the snow-covered Austrian Alps may influence you to do just that.

As the Austrian National Tourist Board succinctly states: "Austria is 1,002 years old. So far, so good." For more information and pre-trip planning tips, be sure to visit Austria's web site: http://www.anto.com or contact the Austrian Tourist Offices in North America:

New York: PO Box 1142, New York NY 10108-1142. Tel. (212) 944-6880; Fax (212) 730-4568.

Los Angeles: PO Box 491938, Los Angeles CA 90049. Tel. (310) 477-3332; Fax (310) 477-5142

Banking

- **Currency:** Austrian schilling (AS or S)
- **Exchange rate at press time:** 12.23AS = $1.00 U.S.
- **Hours:** 0800-1230 and 1330-1500 Monday-Friday; closing at 1730 on Thursday; closed Saturdays and Sundays. Banks in most airport and rail terminals are open 7 days a week, 0800-2000; until 2200 in Vienna.

Communications
- **Country Code:** 43
  For telephone calls within Austria, dial a zero (0) preceding area code.
- **Direct dial:** AT&T Direct: 022 90 30 11; Canada Direct: 022 90 30 13;
  MCI WorldPhone: 022 90 30 12; SprintExpress: 022 90 30 14

What's the best way to phone home? Telephone calls to the U.S. made from a private or a public phone at the post office cost AS 18 (about $1.50) per minute (rates for Alaska and Hawaii are higher). It may be worth your while to buy a green Telephone-Wertkarte for AS 50 (approx. $4.10) or the gold one for AS 100 (approx. $8.20) at a post office and make your calls from a card-operated pay phone. Collect and credit card calls are possible from Austria; special overseas operators can be reached by dialing 09 nationwide.

Avoid placing lengthy long distance phone calls from your hotel since hotel surcharges can be astronomical.

Rail Travel in Austria

The Austrian Federal Railways, or Osterreichische Bundesbahnen (OeBB), operates the 5,800 kilometer rail system and accepts the variety of **Eurailpasses, Europasses** (with purchase of **Austria Option** – see Appendix for list of Rail Pass types and prices) and the Austrian Railpass. The basic **Austrian Railpass** is valid for 3 days of travel within a 15-day period: $145 First Class; $98 Second Class; each additional rail day (5 maximum), $20 First Class, $14 Second Class. Purchase your rail passes prior to your departure for Europe. (See the Appendix for a detailed list of passes or consult the Rail Pass Express web site at http://www.eurail.com.)

A Eurailpass includes the following discounts within Austria:
- Boats between Melk, Krems, and Vienna v.v., operated by DDSG Blue Danube Schiffahrt—15 percent discount
- Wurm and Kock steamers on the Danube River from Linz to Passau (Germany)—50 percent discount
- Rack railroads Puchberg am Schneeberg-Hoschsneeberg and St. Wolfgang-Schafbergspitze—10 percent discount
- Rent-a-bike (130 stations)—50 percent discount.
- Steamers on Lake Wolfgang (Wolfgang See)—10 percent discount

Europass with purchase of the Austria option includes the above discounts (except rent-a-bike) and 10 percent discount on boats operating on Lake Constance (Bodensee) Lindau-Rorscharch.

Rail seat reservations cost AS 30; both national and international reservations may be made at any rail station. Eurail Aid Offices are located in Innsbruck Hauptbahnhof, Salzburg Hauptbahnhof, and Wien Westbahnhof (Vienna West Station).

Base City...

Vienna (Wien)

City Dialing Code: 222
International Dialing Code from Vienna: 1
Internet: http://info.wien.at

Arriving by Air

Schwechat Airport Telephone 70 07 22 31 or 70 07 22 32 (24 hours)
Located 19 kilometers from the city center Schwechat Airport is the home base for Austrian Airlines, which offers non-stop flights between the U.S. (New York) and Vienna and serves more than 30 other international airlines.

Airport-City Links: Trains run every 30 minutes from the airport into Wien Mitte and Wien Nord stations. The price to Mitte is approximately $7 U.S. and $10 US to Nord. During heavy morning and evening traffic, the train is the best way to go. At other times, we recommend the airport bus service which connects with the Westbahnhof (West Station) and Sudbahnhof (South Station), as well as with the city air terminal (Hilton Hotel). The fare is AS 70; time en route, 20 minutes. The bus-departure point is immediately outside and to the left of the arriving-passenger exit. Purchase tickets on the bus.

Arriving by Train

The Westbahnhof (West Station) and Sudbahnhof (South Station) are Vienna's major railway terminals. Westbahnhof is the gateway to Germany, Switzerland, and the rest of northern and central Europe; Sudbahnhof is the gateway to southern and eastern Europe. Wien Mitte and Wien Nord are commuter-type stations. For **train information** by telephone, dial 1717 (24 hours).

Westbahnhof has two levels. Arriving by train, you will be on top of the elevated level. The taxi stand is on the left as you leave the train platform. The main station concourse is at street level.
- **Baggage storage** located on main station concourse level. After descending on the escalator from track level, turn right and go to the far end of the concourse just before the station restaurant. The facility will be to your immediate right.
- **Money exchange** (*Exchange-Wechselstube*) located to the right of the escalators on the top level. Daily hours: 0700-2200.

- **Train information, reservations, and rail pass validation** may be made at *Reiseburo am Bahnhof,* located in the glass kiosk.
- **Sudbahnhof** is a three-level terminal with the train platforms located on the middle and top levels.
- **Money exchange** located in lower level immediately to the right of the main staircase. Daily hours: 0630-2200.

Tourist Information/Hotel Reservations

- Schwechat Airport, left of Customs in the arrivals hall. Daily hours: 0830-2100. Hotel reservations.
- Verkehrsburo Travel agency in the Westbahnhof (West Station). Daily hours: 0700-2200. Hotel reservations. Located in the glass kiosk to the left of the escalators.
- Verkehrsburo Travel agency in the Sudbahnhof (South Station). Daily hours: May-October, 0630-2200; November-April, 0630-2100. Hotel reservations.
- City center main tourist office: Karntner Strasse 38, Vienna 1 (behind the Vienna State Opera House). Daily hours: 0900-1900. Tel. 51 38 892. To get there by public transport take the U-bahn (underground) Line U3 to Volkstheater and on the Ringstrasse you can take tram 2, D or J for the two stops to the Opera House. From Sudbahnhof (South Station), only tram D will take you to the Opera House.
- Tourist information by telephone: 211 14-0 (Monday-Friday 0800-1600)

Getting Around in Vienna

Public transportation in Vienna includes the underground, trams, S-Bahn (rapid-transit intra-city trains) and bus service. Tickets are sold at Vienna Transport Authority sales offices (there's one in the Westbahnhof), at tobacconists, from vending machines in the underground stations, and even from reception desks in many Viennese hotels. Tickets are valid on all forms of public transport. A single-journey ticket is AS 20 (AS 9 for children; children under age of 6 years travel free). There are also 24-hour and 72-hour rover tickets at AS 50 and AS 130, respectively. Once you validate your ticket, you can travel anywhere in Vienna for the next 24 or 72 hours.

The most economical and convenient way to discover Vienna is to purchase the **Vienna Card.** For only AS 180, you not only have access to Vienna's entire public transport network for 72 hours, but you also receive discounts at more than 100 museums, sights, concerts, shops, theaters, restaurants, cafes, and *Heurigen* (wine taverns). Purchase the Vienna Card at tourist information offices, your Vienna hotel, or at Vienna Line (Wiener Linien) information offices in underground stations (for example, at Stephansplatz U, Karlsplatz U,

Westbahnhof U, which are open Monday–Friday 0630-1830 and Saturday–Sunday 0830-1600). Or, order one via your credit card from outside Vienna by calling 43 1 798 44 00 28. For Vienna Line information, phone 7909/105.

Sights/Attractions/Tours

The Vienna Tourist Guides can help you find a variety of ways to see Vienna, and one of the best ways to really get to know the city is on foot. Ask for the brochure "Walks in Vienna" and choose from sixty walking tours; each has a different theme spanning the spectrum from "Pure Hapsburg, The Hofburg and its Emperors" to "Chow-houses, Boozers, Brothels, and Other Houses of Ill Repute." The tours are booked through different telephone or fax numbers. Choose the tour you want and call or fax the number listed in the brochure for that specific tour. Private guided tours may also be arranged. For a real moving experience, tour Vienna by bicycle. Call Vienna-Bike at 319 12 58 to book your bike.

For a leisurely view of Vienna, take a cruise aboard the ship *MS Vienna* from the Little Danube onto the Big Danube. The ship departs from Schwedenplatz for a 1½ hour cruise to Reichsbrucke. You can return to the city via the underground or the *MS Vienna*. Departures are at 1000 and 1400. One way AS 120; round trip AS 170 (10 percent discount with Vienna Card; reduced rates for children). Ask the tourist office for the DDSG Blue Danube Ships' brochure detailing their cruise programs or call 588 80 222.

Vista of Vienna

The pace is slower in Vienna; Vienna developed the waltz and the city's tempo has moved in leisurely three-quarter time ever since.

Vienna's coffeehouses are oases of good living at a leisurely pace. Visiting them during your stay is a must. Our favorite coffeehouse happens to be the original one in Vienna, the **Sacher Café**, a part of Hotel Sacher immediately behind the Opera House. It has a semiformal but friendly atmosphere. By all means try the sugar tarts and don't miss the *Apfelstrudel* (apple cake). Expensive? Well, yes, but it's worth it.

The Viennese "invented" coffee. According to legend, in 1683 the Turks were defeated and abandoned their three-centuries quest to conquer the heart of Europe at the gates of Vienna. In their hasty departure, they left some bags of coffee beans behind. The local folks swarmed out of the city and carried the bags back behind its protective walls and began experimenting. A gentleman by the name of Kolschitzky evolved a clear brew—unlike the Turks who, to this day, serve it with the grounds—and the people of Vienna were so elated that they erected a bronze statue to his memory.

The Viennese like to eat well, and they take great pride and pleasure in giving their visitors every opportunity to do likewise. A dazzling array of eateries from stand-up snack bars and simple little pubs known as *Beisel* to ethnic specialties and gourmet restaurants. Since good food deserves good libation, try the tasty and strong Austrian beer or some of Austria's great vintages. These are bottled and aged; but young, fresh wine is rushed to the taverns, where locals and visitors alike consume it as though it might lose its freshness between sips.

Since Hungary accepts Eurailpass and Europass (if one has purchased the

Train Connections to Other Base Cities from Vienna

TO:	DEPART	ARRIVE	TRAIN NUMBER	NOTES
Amsterdam	1920	0940+1	EN 224/D 214	
Brussels (Midi)	0820	2055	EC 28/434	(1)
	1920	0921	EN 224	
Budapest (Keleti)	1007	1318	345	
	1435	1735	EC 63	
	1800	2046	EC 25	(5)
Hamburg	0820	1752	ICE 791/EC 23	
	1950	0752+1	IR 2489/EN 49	
Milan	1930(2)	0850+1	235	(3)
Munich	0550	1035	EC 16	(4)
	1530	2036	EC 62	(4)
Paris	0850	2222	EC 64	
	2028	1025+1	262	
Prague (Praha)	0710	1218	EC 70	
	1110	1621	EC 172	
	1525	2037	EC 72	
	2125	0341+1	202	
Rome	0730(2)	2105	EC 31	
	1930(2)	0928	235	
Zürich	0720	1626	EC 160	
	0920	1826	EC 162	
	2125	0625+1	EN 466	(4)

All departures from Vienna Westbahnhof. Daily departures unless otherwise noted. Make reservations for all departures.

(1) Transfer in Cologne (Köln) to train 434
(2) Departs from Vienna (Wien) Süd
(3) Departs at 2015 Friday through Sunday (train 1235)
(4) Supplement payable
(5) Transfer in Nürnburg

Austria/Hungary option), many Eurail travelers transit Vienna on through trains such as the *Wiener Walzer* without stopping. Take advantage of the frequent rail service and stop for a few hours in Vienna en route to Budapest. Baggage can be stored in the *Gepackaufbewahrung* (temporary baggage storage facility) in the Westbahnhof main concourse level.

Vienna is many things, but primarily it is music. Visit the State Opera, a preeminent point of European music, or visit the Strauss home where the *Blue Danube Waltz* was written. Thrill to the voices of the Vienna Boys' Choir, or marvel at the white Lipizzan stallions as they dance to music in the Spanish Riding School. Vienna is a memory that will waltz through your dreams forever.

Day Excursions From Vienna

Because of its location on the Danube River and the eastern reaches of the Alps, Vienna can offer some unusual day-excursion opportunities. Among them are cruises on the Danube or tours through the Vienna Woods and the Austrian Alps by train.

Express trains can whisk you from Vienna to Salzburg in time for lunch—followed by dinner—and still return you in time to slumber in your base city Vienna. Local trains can take you to Baden, one of the most famous sulfur-bath spas in Austria.

Day Excursion to
Austrian Alps Tour   VIA VILLACH AND SALZBURG
Depart from Vienna Sudbahnhof (South Station)

Distance by train: 541 miles (871 km)
Average train time: 14 hours, 40 minutes

The Austrian Alps probably provide more beauty than all of the man-made masterpieces in the world laid end to end. The fact that you can watch the splendor of their Alpine panorama unfold from the comfort of a train compartment makes this a most unusual and thrilling day excursion.

Take an adequate, large-scale map of Austria along, and try to select a day when good visibility is forecast. For the latter, your hotel should be able to provide a weather forecast, and an ideal map is the one published by Kummerly and Frey. You'll find it in newspaper kiosks or station newsstands.

This day excursion requires changing trains in Salzburg with the option of changing trains en route to Salzburg at Villach. The time between trains in

Vienna–Austrian Alps Tour

DEPART VIENNA SÜDBAHNHOF STATION	TRAIN NUMBER	ARRIVE VILLACH STATION	NOTES
0655	531	1150	(1)
0855	IC 597	1350	(1)
1055	IC 599	1550	(1)

DEPART VILLACH STATION	TRAIN NUMBER	ARRIVE IN SALZBURG STATION	NOTES
1200	EC 10	1446	(1)(4)
1400	IC 597	1646	(1)
1600	IC 599	1846	(1)

DEPART SALZBURG STATION	TRAIN NUMBER	ARRRIVE VIENNA WESTBAHNHOF STATION	NOTES
1710	IC 547	2035	(1)
1805	EC 65	2118	(1)(2)
1932	EC 161	2245	(1)(3)
2005	EC 17 "Max Reinhardt"	2315	(1)

(1) Daily, including holidays
(2) IC 65 train is the Mozart
(3) EC 161 train is the Maria Theresa
(4) EC 10 train is the Mimara

Distance: 541 miles/871 km.

Villach and Salzburg varies according to the schedule you select. Consider having lunch in Villach followed by dinner in Salzburg, thereby adding a culinary note to your excursion. Dining aboard also is possible, since all of the trains listed on the schedule haul dining cars.

The Alps in Austria are divided from north to south into three chains: the northern limestone Alps, the central high Alps, and the limestone Alps of the south. These chains are separated from each other by the great furrows that form the river valleys of the Inn, the Salzach, and the Enns in the north and the Drava and Mur in the south. The route we have selected for this day excursion takes you through all three alpine chains.

Even if the weather is good when you leave Vienna, the climate of the Alps varies considerably with differences in altitude. You can expect some changes in the temperature and visibility while en route. It is not unusual to enter a tunnel with the landscape bathed in sunlight only to emerge at the other end in a dark and foreboding storm.

Vienna is 580 feet above sea level. Leaving the city, the train moves along the edge of the Vienna woods. Before arriving in Bruck, you will get an occasional glimpse of the Raxalpe Peak (6,630 feet). This steep-sided limestone massif, due to its proximity to Vienna, has become very popular with city-based mountain climbers. Here, the train follows the first mountain railway (Semmeringbahn) built in Europe (1848-54), which runs between Gloggnitz and Murzzuschlag.

From Murzzuschlag to Bruck, the train parallels the Murz River through the last really mountainous pass leading out of the Alps and on to the broad plains fed by the Danube. Bruck lies at the confluence of the Mur and the Murz rivers in the pleasant setting of the Styrian Alps. After passing Unzmarkt, the peaks of the Zinken (7,255 feet) and the Greimberg (8,115 feet) Alps are visible. You then arrive in Klagenfurt, 1,472 feet above sea level. Summers here are extremely hot, for the town lies in a basin shielding it from the moderating effects of the Mediterranean.

Between Klagenfurt and Velden, the train passes along Lake Woerth before arriving in Villach. Leaving Villach and approaching the Tauern Tunnel (5 miles long), you will be able to view Mount Hochalm (11,020 feet). As you exit the tunnel, Edelweiss-Spitz (8,453 feet) stands guard on the left while Mount Gamskarspitze (9,296 feet) looms on the right.

After pausing briefly at Badgastein—the highest en route station at 2,838 feet above sea level—the train gradually descends into Schwarzach and parallels the Salzach River, which flows past Bischofshofen and the city of Salzburg. Your return train to Vienna arrives at Westbahnhof (West Station).

Day Excursion to
Baden
BATHS, CURES, AND CASINO

Depart from Vienna Sudbahnhof (South Station)

Distance by Train: 17 miles (27 km)
Average Train Time: 20 minutes
City Dialing Code: 2252 or 2258
Tourist Information Office: Brusattiplatz 3, A-2500 Baden
Tel: 0 22 52/445 31 ext. 59; *Fax:* 0 22 52/807 33.
Hours: May 1-October31, 0900-1800 Monday-Saturday; 0900-1400 Sunday; November 1-April 30, 0900-1230 and 1400-1700 Monday–Friday; closed Saturday & Sunday.

Proceed to level 3 for trains departing on tracks 11 and 19 for Baden in direction of Graz. To get to the tourist information office from the rail station, use the station under-

Vienna–Baden

DEPART VIENNA (WEIN) SÜDBAHNHOF STATION	TRAIN NUMBER	ARRIVE IN BADEN STATION	NOTES
0740	E1551	0804	(1)
0840	E1535	0904	(1)
0940	E1553	1004	(1)
1240	E1631	1304	(1)

Plus frequent commuter trains. Check schedules for track Nos. 11 and 19 on top (third) level of the Südbahnhof (South Station). Most trains departing for Graz stop at Baden.

DEPART BADEN STATION	TRAIN NUMBER	ARRIVE IN VIENNA (WIEN) SÜDBAHNHOF STATION	NOTES
1456	E1636	1520	(1)
1656	E1730	1720	(1)
1756	E1732	1820	(1)
1856	E1734	1920	(1)
2056	E2718	2120	(1)

Plus frequent commuter trains. Check schedules in Baden railway station.
(1) Daily, including holidays

Distance: 17 miles/27 km

---

pass to the town side of the tracks. Walk directly through the park in front of the station and bear right onto Bahnstrasse (Station Street) at the end of the park. Two blocks farther along, you will see a Fussgangerzone (pedestrian area). Turn right and walk to the town square. Pass the Rathaus (city hall) on its left side and proceed toward the end of the pedestrian area through Gruner Markt (the market place). The tourist office is just behind Gruner Markt.

Baden is situated on the eastern edge of the Vienna woods and surrounded by extensive vineyards and woodlands. Because it also lies on the edge of Europe's great eastern Pannonian plain, it enjoys a moderate climate, much sunshine, and favorable temperatures. In fact, Baden is in the warmest part of Austria and it is well known as a health resort.

Baden sits on 15 ancient thermal water springs—with a regular temperature of 36 degrees Celsius (97 degrees Fahrenheit). The early Romans were always keen on baths and they spent legions of hours soaking in the medicinal, hot sulfur springs of the area they called "Aquae." In the nineteenth century, Baden became the center of social life for Vienna's growing sphere of influence. Today, it is a world-renowned spa and vacation spot, full of charm, flowers, and more swimming pools than one can possibly enter in a single day excursion.

Swimming is a year-round pastime, either outdoors in the thermal and mineral pools or indoors at a thermal pool. The thermal public swimming pool (Thermal Strandbad), with its 5,000-square-meter pool area and extensive sandy beach is an adventure-bath for the whole family.

For those who feel that water is only approached safely in a glass or a wash basin, Baden offers other forms of relaxation ranging from quiet paths leading in and around the eastern edges of the Vienna woods to a lively game of Black Jack in its casino opposite Kurpark.

Baden is ideal for shopping—its entire center is a pedestrian zone filled with small specialty shops. When you tire of bargain hunting, retreat to the city rose garden in Dublhoff Park to watch chess played on a larger-than-life chess board.

Another interesting pastime is visiting the informal wine taverns scattered throughout the town. Since the Middle Ages, every citizen of Baden has had the right in his own house to sell the wine he has produced himself, as well as meat and sausage specialties. These "taverns" are identified by a pole decorated with fir twigs, or you can seek them out by following the tavern signs displayed in prominent places throughout the town. With even more wine taverns in Baden than swimming pools, visitors engaged in "researching" taverns might do well to come to Baden as early as possible and leave only when they have discovered the best vintage—or spend the night in Baden, depending upon how much research they conducted.

Day Excursion to

Melk   Alternative Cruise up the Danube

Depart from Vienna Westbahnhof (West Station)

Distance by Train and Boat: 102 miles (192 km)
Total Time: 7 hours, 40 minutes
Tourist Information Office: Rathaus (town hall)
Tel: 23 07 32
Hours: Daily 0900–1200 and 1500–1800
DDSG ship line: Tel: 20 88

As you emerge from the bahnhof (rail station), walk toward the abbey, which dominates the foreground. The town hall sits at the base of the abbey, three blocks from the station.

The Danube is Europe's grand river, second in length only to the Volga and stretching almost 1,800 miles across eight countries. As plains, hills, and mountains succeed one another along its course, the Danube can be sluggish, swift, or even wild.

The Danube rises in Germany's Black Forest—the length of a football field away from the watershed of the Rhine. By the time its waters reach the German city of Ulm, the Danube becomes navigable by river craft. Between Ulm and Vienna, the Danube takes on an Alpine character. The Danube is unusual among the rivers of the world in that it flows from west to east. At its delta, it empties into the Black Sea.

The Blue Danube Waltz is a musical expression of the attractiveness and charm of Austria along the banks of the Danube. The vast countryside—fringed by the Austrian Alps on the south—offers a vista of natural beauty. Although the waters of the river do not always display, especially in times of flood, the color of which the song sings, the beauty of the countryside through which the Danube flows makes it easy to forget that the waters are actually milky white throughout most of the spring and summer.

We recommend taking the 0833 train to Melk, the point from which the cruise down the Danube begins. It will bring you to Melk in time for unhurried connections with the ship, but Melk itself is steeped in history and warrants your visit. The earlier train will permit you to wander about Melk's ancient streets, still guarded by the watch towers of its town wall, and to visit Melk's Benedictine Abbey, the epitome of Baroque architecture in Austria.

Melk marks the beginning of the Wachau region of the Danube Valley, where ancient castles stand watch over the steep vineyards and orchards that stretch from the castle's walls downward to the banks of the river below. It is the most picturesque section of the Danube. Have lunch and sample the fine quality regional wines in one of Melk's charming "Heurigen" taverns before proceeding to the DDSG pier, known locally as the "Schiff Station." You can walk or taxi to the pier. Check with the information desk on the pier for boarding instructions.

European Cruise Ships of the First Danube Steamship Company (DDSG) (Tel: 43 1 588 800) ply regularly between Melk and Vienna from mid-May through the end of September. The Eurailpass is accepted under certain conditions and becomes your boarding ticket. The trip from Melk to Vienna is downstream in the Danube's swift current. It takes 5½ hours to complete the cruise portion; the train time to Melk from Vienna is about 1 hour.

Carry a map of the Danube and refer to it often, for it's one fine scene after another. The market town of Spitz, on the Danube's left bank, is readily recognizable because it nestles at the base of the Tausendeimer mountain. The name of the mountain (a thousand vessels) doesn't refer to the river traffic—it refers to the fact that the vineyards on its sides, in a good year, can produce a thousand vessels of wine.

Vienna-Melk (Up the Danube)

DEPART REICHSBRUCKE PIER, VIENNA	ABOARD FIRST DANUBE STEAMSHIP	ARRIVE AT KREMS AN DER DONAU	NOTES
0830	(2)	1340	(2)(3)

DEPART KREMS AN DER DONAU		ARRIVE AT MELK PIER	
1555		1850	

DEPART MELK RAIL STATION	TRAIN NUMBER	ARRIVE IN VIENNA WEST-BAHNHOF STATION	NOTES
1910	EC 1709	2018	(1)

Vienna-Melk (Down the Danube)

DEPART VIENNA WEST-BAHNHOF RAIL STATION	TRAIN NUMBER	ARRIVE IN MELK RAIL STATION	NOTES
0833	E1824	0940	(1)
1245	E1620	1355	(1)

DEPART MELK PIER	ABOARD FIRST DANUBE STEAMSHIP	ARRIVE IN KREMS AND ER DONAU	NOTES
1410	(2)	1550	(2)(3)

DEPART KREMS AND ER DONAU		ARRIVE IN REICHSBRUCKE PIER, VIENNA	
1650		2045	

(1) Daily, including holidays
(2) Runs mid-May through mid-September. Check schedules in Vienna before departing
(3) Food service available

Distance: 53 miles/85 km

When the ship calls at Durnstein, with its red roofs, you should recall that it was here that King Richard I, the Lionhearted of England, was captured and held prisoner when he returned from the Third Crusade. (Like world wars, the Crusades had numbers, too.) The next port of call will be Krems, which marks the eastern area of the Wachau. Since olden times, Krems has been the hub of the Wachau wine trade. Here, the Danube becomes dotted with islands as the ship draws nearer to Vienna.

Day Excursion to

Innsbruck

JEWEL OF THE ALPS

Depart from Munich, Germany	From Vienna Westbahnhof
Distance by Train: 107 miles (172 km)	*Distance by Train:* 319 miles (513 km)
Average Train Time: 2 hrs, 10 min.	*Average Train Time:* 5 hrs., 10 min.

City Dialing Code: 512
Tourist Information Office: Burggraben 3, A-6021
Tel: 0 512/5353-36; *Fax:* 0 512/5356-43
Internet: http://tiscover.com/innsbruck
Email: info@innsbruck.tvb.co.at
Hotel Information: Innsbruck Hauptbahnhof
Tel: 0 512/58 37 66; *Fax:* 0 512/58 37 66-67
Hours: Monday–Friday 0800–1600

Leave the main station hall by the exit on the left-hand side and proceed past the "Checked Baggage" area.

Located only 2 hours, 10 minutes away by train, Innsbruck is a convenient excursion to make from Munich. Translated, *Innsbruck* means "bridge over the Inn River." Situated at the junction of the Inn Valley and the Sill Gap, on the road and railroad route running into Italy through the Brenner Pass, the city is the cultural and tourist capital of the Austrian Tyrol.

Innsbruck is surrounded theatrically by its mountains. There is an exhilarating mountain view from nearly every street corner and every window in town. Looking northward from its main street, Maria-Theresien Strasse, you will confront the towering Alps, which seem to encroach upon the city. The scene is breathtaking. (American kids say, "It's awesome!")

This day excursion offers an opportunity to explore the Tyrolean Alps in the comfort of a cable car—plus a visit to one of the most picturesque "old towns" in Austria. To top it off, a circuitous return on the Mittenwald railroad is possible; it takes you on a fantastically scenic rail route straight through the heart of the Austrian and Bavarian Alps en route back to Munich via Garmisch-Partenkirchen.

You are in for an eye-filling day. Even the regular rail line running out of Munich is loaded with Alpine scenery. Take a seat on the right side of your coach outbound from Munich for the best views. Keep your eyes on the edges of the pine forest. We can almost guarantee that you'll see a family of deer that way. The fawns venture farther into the clearing but scamper back faster into the woods as the train passes.

Most of the shops and restaurants in Innsbruck accept German currency. If you want to change money into Austrian schillings, however, the exchange office is located at your far left just as you exit from the trains. Hours are 0730-2000 daily. The Hotel-Information office located in the station is an official exchange, too.

Munich-Innsbruck

DEPART MÜNCHEN HAUPTBAHNHOF	TRAIN NUMBER	ARRIVE AT INNSBRUCK HAUPTBAHNHOF	NOTES
0659	5405/5465	0949	(1)
0729	EC 81	0922	(1)(2)
0800	RE 5407	1059	(1)
0929	EC 85	1122	(1)(3)
0944	EN 483	1140	(1)
1000	RE 5411	1250	(1)
1100	RB 5413	1357	(1)
1129	EC 87	1322	(1)(4)

(1) Daily, including holidays
(2) EC 81 is the Garda
(3) EC 85 is the Michelangelo
(4) EC 87 is the Tiepolo

Vienna-Innsbruck

DEPART VIENNA WESTBAHNHOF STATION	TRAIN NUMBER	ARRIVE AT INNSBRUCK HAUPTBAHNHOF	NOTES
0510	EC 562	1030	(1)
0720	EC 160	1230	(2)
0920	EC 162	1430	(3)

(1) Daily, except December 25 and January 1
(2) EC 160 is the Maria Theresia
(3) EC 162 is the Transalpin

The **Innsbruck Card** provides discounts on admission fees for many sights, museums and other attractions (even a free welcome drink at the casino) and unlimited use of the public transportation network within the city. Valid from March 1 to October 31 for periods of 24, 48, or 72 hours at 200, 280, and 350 schillings, respectively.

Also purchase the large guide map if you plan a walking tour of the city, then head west for a few blocks to Innsbruck's **Arc de Triumph**. From this point, turn north and wend your way slowly through the Altstadt (Old Town), which lines both sides of the street all the way to the **Goldenes Dachl** (Golden Roof) at the end of Herzog-Friedrich Strasse. It may come as a mild disappointment, but the so-called Golden Roof is actually made of heavy, gilded copper. Bus tours of the city are available throughout the year. Biking tours are a great way to see Innsbruck, too.

We suggest you eat lunch in the **Goldener Adler** (Golden Eagle), the oldest inn in the city. It was founded in 1390! It is around the corner on the left and can best be described as a delicious experience. If you go there for dinner, enjoy the Tyrolean music in the cellar restaurant. It will complete a perfect evening.

Day Excursion to

Salzburg   FORTRESS CITY

Depart from Vienna Westbahnhof (West Station)

Distance by Train: 196 miles (315 km)
Average Train Time: 3 hours, 23 minutes
City Dialing Code: 662
Tourist Information Office: Auerspergstrasse 7, A-5024
Internet: http://www.salzburginfo.or.at
Email: tourist@salzburginfo.or.at
Hauptbahnhof: On train platform of station alongside Bahnsteig (track) No. 2a
Tel: 889 87 340
Hours: Daily 0845-2130 (closes 1945, depending on time of the year)
Mozartplatz: Mozartplatz 5; *Tel:* 889 87 330

If Vienna gives you the impression that it is musically inclined, wait until you see and hear Salzburg. It has frequently been described as a music festival that never seems to end. No wonder—Salzburg is the birthplace of Mozart. His home is now a museum, and his music has become the very soul of Salzburg.

Music isn't the only thing that makes Salzburg an interesting city. It has the largest completely preserved fortress in Central Europe—the **Hohensalzburg Fortress** (circa 1077). You can reach the fortress by taking the cable car from Festungsgasse 4 (tel. 84 26 82), located right behind the **Neptune Fountain.** Directly behind the Neptune Fountain, you will find the cable-car station. These conveyances can whisk you to the top of Salzburg and the Hohensalzburg Fortress in a minute. There is a foot path leading to the top, but it takes a lot of huffing and puffing. Conducted tours include the **State rooms, Fortress Museum,** and **Rainer Museum.** The tour takes about 50 minutes. January-March: 1000-1630; April-June: 0930-1700; July-August: 0930-1730; September-October: 0930-1700 and November-December: 1000-1630. Tour costs: adults AS 30; children 6-15, AS 15; Family Pass (2 adults and up to 5 children), AS 90. In summer there is a terrace restaurant on its south side where you may view the mountains surrounding Salzburg as you dine.

The trip to Salzburg aboard the *Mozart Express* is an event in itself. Between

Vienna-Salzburg

DEPART VIENNA WESTBAHNHOF STATION	TRAIN NUMBER	ARRIVE IN SALZBURG STATION	NOTES
0720	EC 160	1028	(1)(2)
0728	IC 640	1050	(1)(2)
0828	IC 844	1150	(1)(2)
0850	EC 64	1155	(1)(2)(3)
0928	IC 540	1250	(1)(2)

DEPART SALZBURG STATION	TRAIN NUMBER	ARRIVE IN VIENNA WESTBAHNHOF STATION	NOTES
1532	EC 163	1845	(1)(2)
1610	IC 941	1935	(1)(2)
1710	IC 547	2035	(1)(2)
1805	EC 65	2118	(1)(2)(3)
1910	IC 647	2235	(1)(2)
1932	EC 161	2245	(1)(2)
2005	EC 17	2315	(1)(2)

(1) Daily, including holidays
(2) Food service available
(3) Mozart Express: Reservations recommended

Distance: 196 miles/315 km

Vienna and Linz the train skirts the fertile Danube Valley. When the train leaves the river at Linz, you are treated to a rolling tableau of farmland followed by a magnificent view of the Alps as you skirt their northern escarpment.

To conduct your own tour, begin in the old section of the city. Board bus No. 1, 5, 6, or 51 at the Autobusbahnhof (bus stop station) in front of the railway station and ride to the Staatsbrucke, the fifth stop. This places you on the perimeter of the Old Town where most of the sightseeing is located. Orient yourself with the **Kapitelplatz** (Capital Place), and you are right in the center of everything.

The music-festival season starts in January and ends in December. In other words, it never ends. Afternoons in Salzburg may be spent in one of its comfortable coffeehouses watching theatergoers and opera buffs flocking to a performance—everyone in formal attire. In Salzburg, elegance is the way of life.

Salzburg has a charming narrow street, Getreidegasse, which is lined with gilt and wrought-iron trade signs, pictorial devices dating back to the time when few people could read. This is one of the best areas in town to find authentic Austrian souvenirs.

House No. 9 on the Getreidegasse is probably the most visited house in Salzburg. It is the birthplace of Mozart and is now a museum covering three floors. The **Mozart House** at Makartplatz 8 is where the Mozart family resided from 1773 to 1787. It was damaged severely during World War II, and all that remains of the original house is the entrance. Mozart died a pauper in Vienna at age thirty-five and his body was dumped into an unmarked grave there. Mozart's life story supports the expression applicable to too many of the world's greatest artists: "To be appreciated, one must first die."

Belgium

Belgium may be small in size—about the size of the State of Maryland in the U.S.—but it is large in its significance to the European Community. Belgium played an important role in creating the European Union, which now comprises fifteen members. The Treaty on the European Union was signed in Maastricht in 1992 in an effort to safeguard peace in Europe and to move toward economic and monetary union with intergovernmental cooperation. Belgium's capital city Brussels is the seat of the European Union, NATO, and many other world trade and finance companies.

In 1830, Belgium gained its independence. No longer a part of the Netherlands, Belgium became a federal state of communities and regions. The three Communities are based on the Dutch, French, and Germanic languages and culture—the Flemish Community, the French Community, and the German-speaking Community. The three regions (Flemish, Brussels Capital, and Walloon) were based on economical concerns.

Belgium has a hereditary constitutional monarchy, but the king does not "govern"; he serves as protector of the country's unity and independence. King Albert II became Belgium's sixth king in 1993.

Perhaps not as well known is Belgium's significant gastronomic role in Western Europe. After all, it was the Flemish Benedictine monks who invented beer, and the beers considered to be "the best" are the ones still brewed traditionally in Belgian monasteries. Restaurants of the Ardennes are well known for their wild game and the coastal restaurants serve some of the finest North Sea fish and shellfish dishes. A not so well known culinary fact about Belgium: The ratio of restaurants to population is equal to that of France.

For more information about Belgium, contact the Belgian Tourist Offices in North America:

New York: 780 Third Avenue, Suite 1501, New York NY 10017. Tel: (212) 758-8130; Fax: (212) 355-7675; Email: belinfo@blythe.org; Internet: http://www.visitbelgium.com

Montreal: P.O. Box 760, Succursale N.D.G., Montreal, Quebec H4A 3S2. Tel: (514) 484-3595; Fax : (514) 489-8965

Banking
- **Currency:** Belgian Franc (BEF)
- **Exchange rate at press time:** 36.75 BEF = $1.00 U.S.

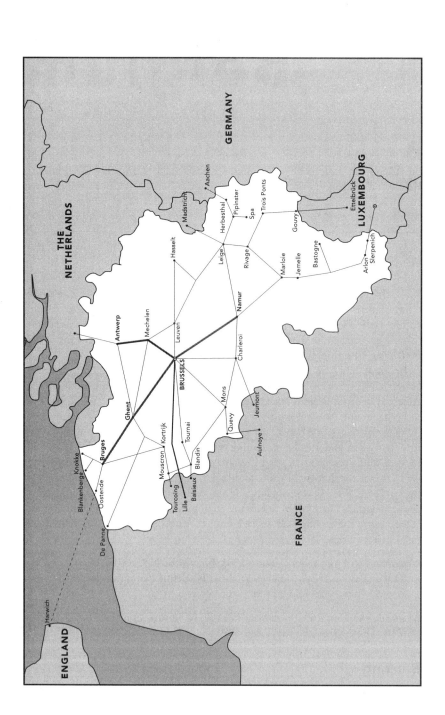

Hours 0900-1530 or 1600 Monday-Friday; closed Saturday, Sunday, and holidays.

Communications

- **Country Code:** 32
  For telephone calls within Belgium, dial a zero (0) preceding area code.
- **Direct dial:** AT&T Direct: 0-800-100-10; MCI: 0-800-100-12; Sprint: 0-800-100-14

Rail Travel in Belgium

The Belgian railways were the first to be constructed on the continent of Europe and Belgian National Railways (SNCB) is said to operate one of the densest rail networks in the world (3,396 kilometers). Brussels serves as an international crossroads. InterCity (IC) trains connect the main towns and regions of Belgium; the Inter-Regional (IR) trains include stops at local stations. Rail service is frequent—usually every hour between most major cities and towns, and with SNCB's integrated schedules, you need not wait long for train connections.

The new TGV Thalys trains link Brussels to Paris in 2 hours and to Amsterdam in the Netherlands in only 3 hours; the high speed Eurostar trains can whisk you from Brussels to London in only 3 hours. Trans-Euro Night Trains (TEN) can take you to from Brussels to as far away as Berlin and beyond.

The Belgian National Railways accepts **Eurailpass**, **Europass** (with the purchase of the Benelux (Belgium/Netherlands/Luxembourg option), and the regional **Benelux Tourrail Pass,** which provides unlimited rail travel for any 5 days within a 1-month period in Belgium, the Netherlands, and Luxembourg. If you are two adults traveling together, purchase the special "Tourrail for Two" pass and save a total of $108 first class or $77 for the second class passes. A complete list of types of rail passes and their costs may be found in the Appendix of this edition. For rail pass information or orders call **Rail Pass Express, Inc.,** at **(800) 722–7151.**

Benelux Tourrail Pass

	1st Class	2nd Class
5 days in 1 month	$217	$155
Youth (age 4-25)	—	104

Saver Special: Benelux Tourrail for Two Pass

2 people traveling together	1st Class	2nd Class
5 days in 1 month	$326	$233

Base City...

Brussels

City Dialing Code: 2

Arriving by Air

Brussels National Airport, B-1930, Zaventem, Tel: 32 2 753 39 13 (0700–2200). Located 14 kilometers from city center.

Airport–City Links: Airport City Express trains every 20 minutes to/from Brussels Gare du Midi (South Station), Gare du Nord (North Station), or Gare Centrale (Central Station). Journey time—about 30 minutes. Fare one-way BEF 135 1st class; BEF 90 2nd class. (Eurailpass/Europass not accepted) Bus station located on ground floor, beneath Arrivals Hall. Take escalators/elevators through the Diamond Area of the terminal.

Taxis about 1,100 BEF, tip included. Available outside Arrivals Hall. Look for yellow and blue logo on taxi. Save 20-50% by phoning for a Brussels taxi instead of using the vehicles waiting at the airport. Avoid using unmetered taxis!

Money Exchange: "GWT" located in Arrivals Hall

Arriving by Train

Brussels has three train stations along its main line: one in the north (Gare du Nord), one in the south (Gare du Midi), and a mid-city underground station (Gare Centrale). EuroCity trains and the major express trains do not stop in the central station. Change at either the north or south station and then transfer to a local train if Gare Centrale is your destination. Those arriving in Brussels on the Eurostar train from London will arrive at Brussels Midi.

North Station (Brussel Nord)

Gateway to Holland, Germany, Switzerland, Italy, and eastern France.

- **Money-exchange:** in a corridor to the left when exiting from the trains into the main station area. Hours: daily, including Sunday, 0800-2000.
- **Hotel reservations:** at the information booth in the departure hall. Hours: 0900-1700 Monday-Friday. Also, American Express can make hotel reservations and advance reservations in other cities.
- **Train information:** in the corridor off the left-hand side of the main station area as you exit from the trains. Hours: 0700-2100 daily, except Sunday.
- **Train reservations:** ticket window No. 3 or No. 4 in the main station area.
- Eurailpass validation is at windows No. 3 or No. 4.

A railway museum is located on the mezzanine of the North Station. Turn right when entering the main station from the train area and walk up the stairs at the end of the concourse. The museum holds an interesting collection of rail-transportation vehicles ranging from the first Belgian steam locomotive to some of the present-day diesel and electric traction units. The museum is well worth the time of your visit. Admission is free.

Central Station (Gare Centrale) links both North and South stations via underground trackage. Many of the express trains do not stop here. You may, however, board any of the local trains as a shuttle to either of the main stations and vice versa. Therefore, it is possible to establish yourself in one of the downtown hotels or pensions quite near Central Station yet be able to make any train connection with a minimum of inconvenience.

- **Money-exchange:** Center hall of the station. As you stand looking at the train information board above the ticket windows, the office is on your right. Hours: daily, 0800-2000.
- **Hotel reservations** cannot be made in Central Station. Hotel accommodations can be obtained by visiting the tourist information center in the town hall facing the Grand'Place. (Refer to the section "Tourist Information/Hotel Reservations")
- **Train information** is displayed in the main station area immediately above the ticket windows. This is hourly information. Regular printed schedules are also displayed.
- **Train reservations:** Available only at North and South (Midi) stations.
- **Rail pass validation** must be completed at either North or Midi station.

South Station (Gare du Midi)

Gateway to Great Britain (via Eurostar trains through the Channel tunnel), France, and Spain. On the main floor you will find all the necessary train and tourist services. The tracks are located on the floor above and each track has its own escalator leading to it. The underground metro station is underneath the rail station.

- **Money-exchange:** left-hand side of the main hall as you enter from the street. Daily hours: 0700-2300.
- **Hotel reservations:** "Information" booth in the center of the main hall. Hours: 0900-1700 Monday-Friday. If this booth is closed, use the Brussels Tourist Information Office (T.I.B.) in the Grand'Place.
- **Train reservations:** local trains, at the ticket counters in the main hall. Reservations for international trains including the Eurostar must be made in the Relations Internationales Office on the far right-hand side of the main hall. Take a number from the ticket machine to wait for your turn.
- **Rail pass validation:** Railtour office (see above). Eurostar has its own terminal.
- **Eurostar Terminal:** Right side of the main hall as you enter from the street. Automatic ticket check-in (a simple insertion of your ticket into a

machine) begins one hour prior to departure. Then enter the main terminal, which consists of a large waiting room, cafes, and duty-free stores. Keep in mind that you will carry your luggage onto the train as there is no baggage check-in. If you did not purchase your Eurostar tickets before departing for Europe, they may be purchased at the Relations Internationales Office.

Tourist Information/Hotel Reservations

Tourist and Information Office of Brussels (T.I.B.): Town Hall, Grand'Place, 1000 Brussels

Tel: 32 2 513 89 40; *Fax:* 32 2 514 45 38

Hours: 0900-1800 Monday-Saturday; Sundays 0900-1800 April 1-September 30 and 1000-1400 October 1-November 30; hotel reservations available.

To reach the Grand'Place from Gare Centrale (Central Station), walk downhill in the direction of the Town Hall's spire until you reach the square. The tourist office is to the right of the spire when you are facing the Town Hall.

The T.I.B. has everything you will need to make your visit to Brussels enjoyable. In addition to tourism information and hotel reservations for Brussels, this office can also provide guides to restaurants, museums, and monuments; tickets to shows; city tours; public transport information; and books and maps.

Tourist Information Office: Rue du Marche aux Herbes/Grasmarkt, 63, 1000 Brussels. Information/hotel reservations for all of Belgium

Tel: 504 03 90; *Fax:* 504 02 70.

Hours: June 1-September 30, daily 0900-1900; November 1-March 30, Monday-Saturday 0900-1800; Sunday 1300-1700; April-May and October, daily 0900-1800.

Located one block north of the Grand'Place

Getting Around in Brussels

Brussels boasts a highly efficient public transport system encompassing metro, tram, and bus (STIB-MIVB). **Transport information:** 32 2 515 20 00. A free map is available from the tourist office. The signs for the metro are blue with a white letter "M"; tram and bus stop signs are red and white. Note that the trams and buses stop "on request." This means you should raise your hand to signal the driver to stop.

Purchase transport tickets at metro stations, STIB-MIVB offices, or newsstands: 1 trip: 50 BEF; 5-Journey Card: 320 BEF.

A **Tourist Ticket** is available (125 BEF) from the Brussels Tourist Office; it provides for travel on any underground, tram, or bus service for one calendar day.

Sights/Attractions/Tours

The city abounds in things to see and do, ranging from its elegant Grand'Place to historic Waterloo. If you visit Brussels during the summer, sign up at the tourist office for what we believe is the best way to browse Brussels— "Summer Routes"—attractive, unique, theme packages and tours incorporating trams, coaches, boats, or bikes, as well as feet. These are not the usual whistle-stop tours; you get off the beaten track and you can choose the theme tour that appeals to you. The T.I.B. also conducts other city tours—in 14 languages!

If you want to conduct your own tour, arm yourself with maps and information from the T.I.B. Then head for the Grand'Place. You can reach it from the Central Station (Gare du Centrale) by walking downhill toward the spire of the Town Hall. When you reach the square, take a minute to drink in the splendor of the ornate medieval guild houses facing the square. You will realize immediately why it is called the most beautiful square in all of Europe. If you are looking for a souvenir or a gift for someone, we can suggest pralines (hand-dipped chocolates), speculoos (brown sugar biscuits), or some fine Brussels lace. All three of these Belgian specialties are available from shops in and around the Grand'Place.

Following your map, proceed down C. Bulstraat (just to the left of the Town Hall as you face it). The name changes to Stoofstraat. At the corner of Eikstraat and Stoofstraat, you can view one of Brussels' most beloved, albeit somewhat irreverant, symbols—Manneken Pis. It's a fountain statue—sometimes costumed—doing just what its name implies.

Want to see Brussels and the rest of the European Community in one day? You can. Ask the tourist information office for details about Mini-Europe (Tel. 478 05 50) in Bruparck (metro stop: Heysel). You'll see Europe in miniature— more than 300 models of famous buildings and monuments of the European members constructed on a scale of 1:25, complete with animation and sound effects. Watch a TGV glide by, an Airbus take off, or Mt. Vesuvius erupt simply by pushing a button. Open April-December; admission 390 BEF (children under 12, 290 BEF).

Bits and Bites of Brussels

Brussels has stood for more than 1,000 years as a signpost of ideals and ideas, a crossroad of people and events. Less than 150 miles from Amsterdam and 200 miles from Paris, Brussels is a bonanza for travelers desiring to see Europe by Eurail. Few people realize how short distances actually are in Belgium, of which Brussels is the capital. Its most opposite points are only 195 miles apart.

Latin and Nordic cultures meet in Brussels, making it a city of contrasts. French is spoken by the Walloon people of French origin, and Flemish is the tongue of its Germanic inhabitants. French, German, and Flemish are official languages in Belgium. Consequently, all signs are bilingual in Brussels. English is spoken in all of the train stations, hotels, and (the majority of) public places.

Brussels is old; it celebrated its millennium in 1979. Brussels is new; it's the headquarters of the European Common Market and the North Atlantic Treaty Organization (NATO). It is amazing that the people of Brussels have been able to preserve the city's quaint atmosphere while immersed into all this international activity.

Brussels' cosmopolitan population knows how to enjoy itself. Eating and drinking well in Brussels is not a problem. Succumbing too easily to gastronomic temptation is the real difficulty. Bruxellois, it is said, is like French cuisine served in German portions—although some lighter touches of the nouvelle cuisine have inched their way into Brussels' menus. For the finest gourmet dining, experience the city's most famous culinary establishment, Comme Chez Soi at 23 Place Rouppe. For reservations, call 512 29 21 (closed Sunday and Monday). It's only a 15-minute walk from the Grand'Place, at the end of rue du Midi.

In Belgium, beer is not just beer; it's an art form, and the local cafes and bistros are as much an attraction as are the brews they dispense. In Brussels, some offer more than one-hundred different labels of Belgian beer alone. Curious? Order a "gueuze," "lambic," or a "krick" (cherry beer?).

For bistro-type dining with a modest price tag, we suggest that you head for the pedestrian-only Rue des Bouchers (Street of the Butchers), a stone's throw from the Grand'Place. For lobster with morels or shrimp served in an art-deco atmosphere, try Aux Armes de Bruxelles at No. 13 (Tel. 511 55 98). Or, if you prefer quaint, rustic decor, try Le Marmiton (Tel. 511 79 10) at No. 43. Don't miss having mussels in Brussels—Chez Leon on Rue des Bouchers serves mussels a myriad of ways, and we love them all. Along with the gastronomy, in the evening the area presents numerous sidewalk displays by local artisans.

If you've never eaten a Brussels waffle, you haven't lived a full and rewarding life. We are not referring to the "Belgian waffle" that you'll find at concession stands in every state fair from Maine to Mexico, nor do we refer to the highly touted desserts served by fancy restaurants using a waffle as a base piled high with candied fruits and buried in whipped cream. These confections are good, mind you, but nothing in the world can surpass the kind of waffle that Brussels offers. There's nothing fancy about a Brussels waffle. The vendor will hand it to you wrapped in a small napkin.

Brussels waffles are a part of the scene—you can buy them from several small waffle shops located in the area around the city's opera house, and you should only buy them from a shop that actually makes the waffles right on the premises. Look for the sign GAUFRES in French or WAFELS in Flemish.

Day Excursions

It is difficult to choose from the numerous day excursions Brussels has to

Train Connections to Other Base Cities from Brussels

TO:	DEPART*	ARRIVE	TRAIN NUMBER	NOTES
Amsterdam★★	0907	1204	2481	(1)
	1407	1704	2486	(1)
Berlin (Zoo)	0747	1651	413/IC 849	(1)(2)
Berne	0715	1512	EC 91	(1)(10)
	1216	2012	EC 97/IC 893	(1)(3)
Copenhagen	1847	1235	233	(1)
Hamburg	0957	1707	417/IC 524	(1)(2)(10)
Luxembourg★★	0821	1115	956	(1)
	1521	1815	963	(1)
Milan	0715	1925	EC 91	(1)(10)
	1911	0710+1	299	(1)
Munich	0947	1816	417/IC 109	(1)(6)
Nice	0904	1839	TGV 9532	(7)
Paris	0707	0905	TGV 9308	(5)
	1207	1405	TGV 9328	(5)
	1707	1905	TGV 9348	(5)
Rome	1911	1225	299/ ES 9409	(1)(8)(10)
Zürich	0715	1500	EC 91/EC 103	(9)
	1216	2000	EC 97	(10)
	1557	0006+1	295	(9)

★ All departures from Gare du Midi. Daily departures unless otherwise noted. Make reservations for all departures (except to/from Amsterdam).
★★ Hourly service

(1) Stops at Brussels Nord
(2) Transfer in Cologne (Köln)
(3) Transfer in Basel to train 893
(4) Transfer in Copenhagen to IN 384/684
(5) Reservations required
(6) Transfer in Köln IC 109, transfer in Mannheim IC 595
(7) Leaves at 1907, Fridays June 7–September 27 and Sundays June 30–August 25
(8) Transfer in Milan to P 9413
(9) Transfer in Basel to EC 103/1797
(10) Supplement payable

offer. With its central location and plentiful trains available, a day excursion to Paris, Amsterdam, Luxembourg, or Cologne is quite feasible. Via the Channel Tunnel and its Eurostar trains, even London becomes a day excursion. We, however, present four day excursions going to various points within Belgium itself. We offer **Antwerp**, city of diamonds and Rubens; **Bruges** and its famous Markt; **Ghent** with its Flower Show; and **Namur**, gateway to the beautiful Ardennes.

Day Excursion to

Antwerp

THE DIAMOND CITY

Depart from Brussels Midi (South) Station

Distance by Train: 35 miles (57 km)
Average Train Time: 40 minutes
City Dialing Code: 3
Tourist Information Office: Grote Markt 15, B-2000 Antwerp
Tel: 3 232 01 03; *Fax:* 3 231 19 37
Email: toerisme@antwerpen.be
Internet: http://www.dma.be
Hours: Monday-Saturday 0900-1745; Sunday 0900-1645

To get there on foot, the walk takes about 15 minutes. Antwerp's metro system also can get you there, but first stop at the metro office in the railway station for fare and routing information. In a hurry? Follow the pictograms to the taxi queue.

If your wife has convinced you that diamonds are a girl's best friend and if the kids are hankering to see one of Europe's finest zoos—take them to Antwerp. Be certain the train you take from Brussels is marked "Antwerp Central." EuroCity and other through trains continuing to Amsterdam stop only at stations on the edge of Antwerp. The central station is right in the city center. If you do end up in one of Antwerp's suburban stations, board an inbound local train.

The city's name is spelled three ways: "Antwerp" is the English version; in French it is "Anvers"; and its Flemish title is "Antwerpen." Call it what you will, this fine city with nearly half a million people is a marvelous place to visit. Its contrasts will amaze you. Antwerp is Belgium's second city, the third largest port in the world, reputed to be the world's diamond center, and a Renaissance treasure house.

Train-departure information for your return trip to Brussels can be found on the many train bulletin boards located throughout the station. A train information office is on the street side of the station, between the two main exits.

Brussels-Antwerp

DEPART BRUSSELS MIDI STATION*	ARRIVE IN ANTWERP CENTRAL STATION	NOTES
0710	0749	(1)
0810	0849	(1)
0910	0949	(1)
1010	1049	(1)

Plus other frequent service throughout the day

DEPART ANTWERP CENTRAL STATION	ARRIVE IN BRUSSELS MIDI STATION*	NOTES
1649	1730	(1)
1749	1830	(1)
1849	1930	(1)
1949	2030	(1)

Plus other frequent service throughout the day

★ Also stops at Brussels Centrale and Nord stations

(1) Daily, including holidays

Distance: 35 miles/57 km

The train information office does not dispense tourist information, but they can assist you in finding the tourist office.

Because Antwerp is one of the world's major seaports, it offers an unusual harbor tour that the entire family can enjoy. During the summer, motor launches depart from the Steenplein on the river. With more than 3,000 acres of docks, seventeen dry docks, and six locks (including the largest in the world), the harbor is a spectacle you should not miss. There are a variety of waterborne tours to select from and a short trip on the river Scheldt takes fifty minutes. The port sightseeing tour that we recommend takes two and a half hours. A combination zoo-harbor ticket is available, too. This will take care of the kids, but we doubt that mom will forget the diamonds.

Antwerp boasts twenty museums, among them the **Plantin–Moretus,** featuring a sixteenth-century printing press. Most of Antwerp's museums are closed on Mondays, but the zoo, which is just to the right as you exit from the railway station, is open daily until sunset.

If you are interested in the **Zoo–Harbor Tour** combo ticket, check with the city tourist information office and pick a time to participate. Most seasoned travelers put **Rubens's House** at the top of their list of sightseeing "musts." Rubens bought a beautiful patrician dwelling where he lived with his family from 1615 until his death in 1640. Works of the great Flemish master also are kept in many of the museums and churches in Antwerp. Rubens is buried in **St. James Church,** where you may view the painting *Madonna with Child and Saints,* which he directed be placed on the altar shortly before his death. Rubens and Antwerp remain inexplicably linked to each other.

Other sightseeing musts are the **Cathedral of Our Lady** (largest Gothic church in Belgium), containing four Rubens masterpieces; the **Grote Markt** (marketplace); and the **Open Market** (known locally as the Birds Market). The **Birds Market** is open on Sunday mornings, when miscellaneous wares are sold. All these city highlights will be on the map you receive at the city tourist office, and all are within reasonable walking distance.

The Flemish term, "De Rubenswandeling," means **The Rubens Walk.** It's all laid out for you in a colorful brochure, its map detailing eleven points of interest associated with Rubens. For a bit of variety, there is a *Stadswandeling/ Rondwandeling*—city round-trip walking tour—prepared in a similar format. Both are available at the tourist office.

According to legend, the site of Antwerp was once inhabited by a giant who extracted tribute from all who navigated the river and cut off a hand of those who refused to pay. He was slain by a Roman soldier, who cut off the giant's hand and threw it into the river. Thus, the city's name: *Ant* (hand) and werpen from the verb "to throw." In support of the legend, the city fathers erected a statue of **Silvius Brabo**, the Roman soldier, in front of the city hall. Those not subscribing to the legend say the name was derived from *Aenwerpen* (higher land). There's always someone who doesn't believe in the tooth fairy.

Day Excursion to

Bruges (Brugge)   OLD LACE AND CHURCH SPIRES

Depart from Brussels Nord (North Station)

Distance by Train: 65 miles (105 km)
Average Train Time: 1 hour, 7 minutes
City Dialing Code: 50
Tourist Information Office: Burg 11, B-8000 Brugge
Tel: 50 44 86 86; *Fax:* 50 44 86 00
Email: toerisme@brugge.be
Internet: http:P//www.brugge.be
Hours: April 1-September 30: 0930-1830 Monday-Friday; 1000-1200 & 1400-1830 Saturday-Sunday; October 1-March 31: 0930-1700 Monday-Friday; 0930-1300 & 1400-1730 Saturday-Sunday

Arriving in Bruges, check schedules posted in the station for your return train to Brussels. Train information office inside the station on the left side as you exit from the train platform (Tel. 50 38 23 82). Tourist information is available outside the station near the Video Palace, or go to the central tourist office in Burg Square.

To get to the tourist office in Burg square, board any bus stopping in front of the railway station that is marked CENTRUM at the entrance side of the bus. The bus will take you to the Markt. It stops in the center of the square in front of the Provincial Palace. To return to the station, board the bus marked O STATION at the library on the square close to the Markt, which can be reached by walking through Kuiperstraat off the Markt.

Bruges has magnetic attractions—many of which date from the Middle Ages and the Renaissance—as well as picturesque canals, art treasures, and antique shops. Probably the most interesting sight is the Burg, where history has been in the making since the ninth century. Surrounding the Burg are museums of all descriptions, spectacular church spires, peaceful canals, and fascinating alleyways. Next to the Burg is the **Markt** (Marketplace) where you will find the **Town Hall** and the **Belfry,** a remarkable building that dominates the Markt with its famous 280-foot-high octagonal tower. If you are up to it, climb up the Belfry for a panoramic view.

Brussels-Bruges

DEPART BRUSSELS NORD STATION*	TRAIN NUMBER	ARRIVE IN BRUGES STATION	NOTES
0747	530	0854	(1)
0847	531	0954	(1)
0947	412	1054	(1)
1047	232	1154	(1)

Plus other frequent service throughout the day

DEPART BRUGES STATION	TRAIN NUMBER	ARRIVE IN BRUSSELS NORD STATION*	NOTES
1650	515	1757	(1)
1725	667	1829	(1)
1850	517	1957	(1)

Plus other frequent service throughout the day

* Also stops at Brussels Midi and Gare Centrale

(1) Daily, including holidays

Distance: 65 miles/105 km

During the thirteenth and fourteenth centuries, Bruges stood at the cross-roads of traffic between the Mediterranean and the Baltic. Rich cargoes piled high on its docks and in its warehouses held treasures of spices, cloth, and other luxuries. Bruges was bursting at the seams during this period. Hundreds of ships dropped anchor in its harbor. In its medieval magnificence, Bruges boasted a population double that of London. There was no equal to the grandeur of its court—and no one seemed alarmed that the estuary linking Bruges with the North Sea was growing narrower and shallower as the silt from the River Zwyn slowly oozed seaward.

Inexorably, the waterway began to close. Deep-draft ships could no longer navigate the estuary. The docks were abandoned and Bruges became a victim of its own progress, a landlocked city. Today, Bruges is a museum of the Middle Ages, with gabled roof lines casting shadows on its cobblestone streets. Despite the loss of its commerce with the sea, Bruges has managed to maintain its former opulence.

Remnants of grand days past, the canals of Bruges weave in and around the city graced by a bevy of swans. Oddly enough, the birds' presence is attributable to a murder. In 1488, the good people of Bruges beheaded a tyrant named Langhals ("Long Neck"). Miffed by this deed, the counts of Flanders decreed that the "long necks," the symbolic swans, would be kept at public expense forever—and they are.

Although walking is the best way to see Bruges, there are other interesting ways of getting around the city, one being by canal boat—board behind the Belfry. The trip lasts thirty-five minutes. Or, if pedal power appeals to you, rent a bicycle at the station. Yet another, and no less pleasant, way of seeing the city is by horse-drawn cab. The cabs wait on the Burg (city square) in front of the tea room directly in front of the Belfry.

In addition to all the sights of historic significance in Bruges, there are many stores selling exquisite, handmade Flemish lace, excellent reproductions of Flemish paintings, and colorful ceramics. In general, prices are slightly lower than in Brussels, and the quality is as high.

Note: The rail route from Brussels to Bruges is the main line to the port of Oostende. Consequently, most of the trains going in that direction stop at all three of the main Brussels stations. Check the departure information in the station you plan to depart from in Brussels.

Day Excursion to

Ghent (Gent) HISTORIC BEAUTY

Depart from Brussels Nord (North Station)*

Distance by Train: 40 miles (64 km)
Average Train Time: 45 minutes
City Dialing Code: 9
Tourist Information Office: Botermarkt 18, B-9000 Ghent
   Inquiry desk in the Crypt of the Town Hall
Tel: 9 266 52 32 and 9 224 15 55
Hours: November–March, 0930-1230 & 1315-1630 daily; April–October, 0930-1830 daily
   To reach the tourist office, take tram No. 1 to the town center at Botermarkt.
Internet: http://www.gent.be

Ghent is one of the true Flemish water towns. Three rivers—the Schelde, the Lys, the Lieve—plus a canal flow through it. This accounts for its more than one hundred bridges and its Celtic name, "Ganda," meaning a place of confluence. In the fourteenth century, Ghent was the second largest city, after Paris, north of the Alps. In 1827, the cutting of the Terneuzen canal made Ghent the second largest seaport in Belgium. In more modern times, Ghent has become world-famous for its flower show and the International Ghent Fair. Both are held in the Flanders Expo, a new trade fair complex a few kilometers from the center of Ghent.

The "All Information for Tourists" brochure can help you plan your own walking tour. The map in the back outlines different walking-tour suggestions. Each is color-coded, and places of interest are indicated. If you didn't bring your walking shoes with you, the tourist office can arrange a taxi tour for you with an English-speaking guide. A bit expensive—but shoes are expensive, too!

Saint Michael's Bridge, in the heart of the city, is a good place to begin your walking tour. The view from here is impressive, with church towers and guild houses rimming the skyline. In the distance you can see the **Castle of the Counts,** one of the most imposing feudal fortresses in Europe today. It played a prominent role in Ghent's history during feudal times. The trades people had united in a number of strong guilds and could offer armed resistance against their feudal lords, the counts, when said gentry came to collect the rent. The town hall and the Belfry, symbols of civic freedom, were also erected during that period. The Castle of the Counts was completely restored in 1887 and is well worth your inspection.

If you visit Ghent on a Sunday, you can join the crowds of townspeople and farm folk as they browse and bargain around the flower market at

Brussels-Ghent

DEPART BRUSSELS NORD STATION*	TRAIN NUMBER	ARRIVE IN GHENT ST. PIETERS STATION	NOTES
0747	530	0830	(1)
0847	531	0930	(1)
0947	412	1030	(1)
1047	232	1130	(1)
1147	534	1230	(1)

Plus other frequent service

DEPART GHENT ST. PIETERS STATION*	TRAIN NUMBER	ARRIVE IN BRUSSELS NORD STATION	NOTES
1548	665	1629	(1)
1648	666	1729	(1)
1748	667	1829	(1)
1848	668	1929	(1)
1948	669	2029	(1)
2048	670	2129	(1)
2314	521	2357	

Plus other frequent service

★ Also stops at Brussels Midi and Centrale stations
(1) Daily, including holidays

Distance: 40 miles/64 km

Vrijdagmarkt. The vegetable and fruit markets are Monday through Saturday at the **Groentenmarkt.** As the commercial activity diminishes, the social activities gain tempo.

In early times Ghent, like many other Flanders towns, was involved in warding off the Norse invaders coming off the beaches of the North Sea to loot and plunder. Later, Ghent was able to turn to more peaceful activities. Growing in opulence, Ghent fostered the emerging artists of Flanders and today is considered the cradle of Flemish Art.

Each September and October, Ghent plays host to the **Flanders Festival of Music.** Some of the world's greatest musicians and the most celebrated Belgian orchestras and choirs perform. Many other annual events take place. International regattas are held every May at the **Georges Nachez Aquatic Stadium.** During the summer season many of the city's historic places, such as the Castle of the Counts, are illuminated at night. The **Ghent Festivities** are staged each year from the third to the fourth Sunday in July. The town is alive with music, all sorts of entertainment, and cultural happenings at every street corner. it's a great time to visit Ghent.

Hungry? With more than 350 restaurants to choose from, something will suit your tastebuds—Italian, Greek, French, Chinese, vegetarian—you name it, you can find it. Opposite the town hall, try the **Hotel Cour St. Georges.** Although Ghent lies inland from the North Sea, it is, in fact, a seaport and offers some exceptional seafood. If you enjoy shellfish, order the Belgian specialty, *moules mariniers* (steamed mussels).

★Most trains from Brussels to Ghent stop in all three of Brussels metropolitan rail stations. Check departure information in your station.

Day Excursion to

Namur
GATEWAY TO THE ARDENNES

Depart from Brussels Midi (South Station)*

Distance by Train: 43 miles (69 km)
Average Train Time: 50 minutes
City Dialing Code: 81
Tourist Information Office: Square de l'Europe Unie B-5000 Namur
Tel: 81 22 28 59 or 24 64 49; *Fax:* 81 24 65 54
Hours: 0930-1800 daily

In the Namur station, leave the train-platform area via an underground ramp. Once on the ramp, walk past sortie 1 to sortie 2 and take the escalator to the street level. Bear right around the "C & A" store and proceed to the park, where the tourist office will be in plain view.

If you would like to revisit the eighteenth century, go to Namur. It is one of the most attractive towns in Belgium. Its tourist office offers several excellent walking tours and theme tours. It can also provide personalized tours upon request. For the footsore and those wanting to range farther afield, book an "All-In-One" ticket that includes boat tours, cable-car ascensions, and a traction-train ride around and through the Citadel of Namur, complete with underground explorations.

On Saturday mornings, don't miss the colorful flower market at the **Fountain of Angels** and the **Leopold Square** shopping center. Probably you will not find such a concentration of museums and monuments anywhere else in Europe.

The dominating landmark of Namur—**the Citadel**—looms on its skyline. It is in the center of the **Parc du Champeau.** The walk there can be delightful, particularly if you ascend via the cable car that departs from the Place Pied-du-Chateau. The tourist bureau will provide full details. You can also reach the Citadel by bus. Board bus No. 3 in the town square, adjacent to the railway sta-

Brussels-Namur

DEPART BRUSSELS MIDI STATION*	TRAIN NUMBER	ARRIVE IN NAMUR STATION	NOTES
0821	956	0920	(1)
0921	957	1020	(1)
1021	958	1120	(1)
1121	959	1220	(1)

DEPART NAMUR STATION	TRAIN NUMBER	ARRIVE IN BRUSSELS MIDI STATION*	NOTES
1622	990	1721	(1)
1722	991	1821	(1)
1822	992	1921	(1)
1922	993	2021	(1)
2022	994	2121	(1)
2122	995	2221	(1)
2222	996	2321	(1)

* Also stops at Gare Centrale and Brussels Nord stations
(1) Daily, including holidays

Distance: 43 miles/69 km.

tion. A tour of the Citadel is included in the "All-In-One" ticket, too.

The Citadel of Namur sits at the confluence of the Meuse and the Sambre. Two thousand years of history are contained within its walls. Originally a Celtic stronghold with primitive fortifications, it was altered into a strongly defensive castle. Underground fortifications were added in the fifteenth century and again expanded century after century until modern weaponry brought a cessation of such defenses in the eighteenth century. Throughout its history, however, the Citadel, as one of the most important strongholds of Europe, faced twenty sieges!

Namur's tourist office has a wide selection of excursions for you to select from. Here are but a few: **The Gardens of Annevoie,** famous for their eighteenth-century style of flowers and fountains, are open 0900–1900; a visit can be made in forty-five minutes. A restaurant and tavern are on the grounds. **Cruises on the River Meuse** are available in a variety of schedules, including a picnic on board or ashore.

Continuing with Namur's excursion offerings, the city is justly proud of its space-telecommunications ground station and offers a tour of the facility that includes guide service plus a documentary film. The visit requires one and a half hours; food and beverage self-service is available.

For aquatic buffs, a kayak or boat trip down the river Lesse is available, with departures daily throughout the season at 1000 and 1400. Looking for something a bit less strenuous? Perhaps a water tour of the **Caves of Neptune** would fill the bill. It's a forty-five-minute tour and includes a twenty-minute boat ride plus a sight and sound show.

Namur is the gateway to the Ardennes, the forests and mountains of Belgium. It has all the amenities of a holiday resort. Should you find yourself with time to spare (a very unlikely thing), take a stroll on the **Boulevard de la Sambre,** an attractive, tree-lined avenue. If, on the other hand, you are looking for exquisite gifts, the **Rue de l'Ange** has excellent shops.

Denmark

Danes are a fun-loving people, and their sparkling humor is unsurpassed. For example, Victor Borge, one of Denmark's leading exponents of such jocularity, explains that his ultra-expensive, concert grand piano is "every bit as good as a Rolls-Royce, except," quips Victor, "it has smaller wheels." This is typical Danish humor, and this fairy-tale land of Denmark abounds in it. No doubt you will find the Danes to be the most happy and humorous of all Europeans. Why are they that way? One of our Danish friends explains it in this manner: "For centuries, we Danes were the most feared of the Vikings, destroying and plundering at will. Now, we've got that all out of our system and have nothing left to do except to be happy!" This happy attitude seems to exist throughout the country.

Legend has it that the ancient Vikings, fierce as they were, never missed the chance to throw a party, and apparently their descendants are just as enthusiastic when it comes to having a good time. In summer, there are festivals throughout Denmark where eating, drinking, singing, and dancing are the orders of the day. In winter, the Danes go inside for their celebrations, where eating, drinking, singing, and dancing are the orders of the day. Oddly enough, this never seems to be monotonous to the Danes—or their visitors.

For more information about Denmark, contact the Danish Tourist Board in North America:

New York: 655 Third Avenue, New York, NY 10017 Tel: (212) 885-9700; Fax: (212) 885-9710; Internet: http://www.deninfo.com

Banking

- **Currency:** krone
- **Exchange rate at time of press:** 6.82 krone = $1.00
- **Hours:** 0930-1600 Monday-Friday; Thursday until 1800

Shopping

- **Hours**: Monday–Thursday, 0900/1000-1730/1800; Friday, 0900/1000-1900/2000; Saturday, 0900/1000-1200/1300/1400 (until 1700 for most shops in Copenhagen)

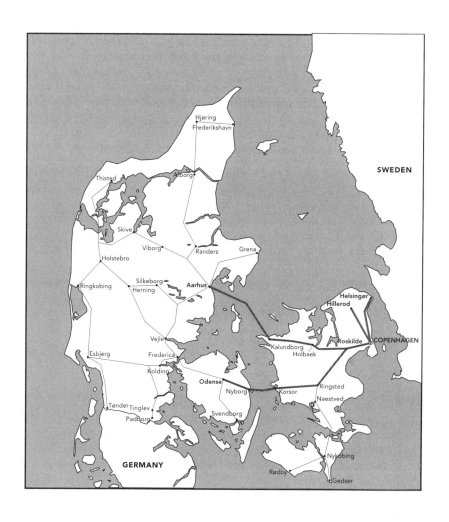

SWEDEN

Hjøring
Frederikshavn

Thisted

Alborg

Skive

Viborg
Randers
Grena

Holstebro

Ringkobing
Silkeborg
Herning
Aarhus

Helsingør
Hillerod

Roskilde
COPENHAGEN

Vejle
Kalundborg
Holbaek

Esbjerg
Frederica

Kolding
Odense
Nyborg
Korsor
Ringsted

Naestved

Tønder Tinglev
Padborg
Svendborg

GERMANY

Nykøbing

Rødby
Gedser

Communications

- **Country Code:** 45
- **No city codes** required for calls within Denmark. Danish phone numbers are usually 8 digits. Direct dial: AT&T Direct: 8001-0010

Denmark has a hefty 25 percent Value Added Tax (VAT). It may be avoided in two different ways. Have your purchases sent home. This way, you pay only the purchase price of the item plus shipping and insurance. Second plan, take the goods home yourself by paying the VAT; save your purchase slips and get the VAT refunded at the Copenhagen Kastrup Airport tax-free shop. In that case, plan to arrive at the airport an hour ahead of your original reporting time.

Rail Travel in Denmark

The dynamic Danish State Railways (DSB) is on the move. In June 1997, the newly opened tunnel and bridge made crossing the Great Belt by train more than an hour faster than going by ferry. The "Lyntog" (high speed diesel) trains now cruise from Copenhagen to Aarhus in only 2½ hours instead of 4. By the year 2000, the 16 km tunnel and bridge complex connecting northeast Denmark and southern Sweden will be completed.

Denmark's InterCity and Lyntog trains feature seats with headphones for listening to music, 220-volt outlets for computers, and play areas for children. In first class, passengers can help themselves to tea, soft drinks, and newspapers. The DSB wants to make your trip fast but comfortable.

The following bonuses apply if you have a **Eurailpass:**

- Ferry crossings operated by Swedish and Danish State Railways—Fynshav-Bojden v.v. and Helsingør-Helsingborg (Sweden)—Free passage
- DFDS Scandinavian Seaways—Aarhus-Kalundborg—Free
- Esbjerg-Harwich (Great Britain) v.v.—20 percent discount
- Esbjerg-Foroyar (Faeroes) v.v.—20 percent discount
- Copenhagen-Oslo (Norway)—20 percent discount
- Stena Line, Frederikshavn-Goteborg (Sweden)—50 percent discount
- Color Line, Hirtshals-Kristiansand (Norway)—30 percent discount
- Hjorring private railway, Hjorring-Hirtshals v.v.—50 percent discount
- Flyvebadene Company hydrofoil service Knudshoved-Halskov v.v.—Free and Copenhagen-Malmo (Sweden)—25 percent discount
- Rodby Faerge-Puttgarden (Germany)—Free

If your European travels are within Scandinavia, consider the **Scanrail Pass** that you can purchase in North America. It provides unlimited rail travel in Denmark, Finland, Norway, and Sweden, plus discounts on certain ferry crossings and private railways. Although you can purchase a Scanrail Pass at train stations in Scandinavia, it is considerably more expensive than if you purchase it in North America.

Scanrail Pass

	1st Class	2nd Class
5 days travel in 15-day period	$222	$176
10 days travel in 1 month	354	284
1 month unlimited travel	515	414

Scanrail Pass 55+

(For persons age 55 and older; purchase only in North America; proof of age may be required):

	1st Class	2nd Class
5 days travel in 15-day period	$198	$157
10 days travel in 1 month	315	253
1 month unlimited travel	459	368

Scanrail Youth Pass (for persons under age 26; purchase only in North America)

	1st Class	2nd Class
5 days travel in 15-day period	$167	$132
10 days travel in 1 month	266	213
1 month unlimited travel	387	311

Scanrail 'n Drive Pass

(purchase only in North America; car rental not available in Finland). Prices are per person. Valid for 5 days of unlimited rail travel and 3 days of car rental to be used within a 15-day period.

	1st Class		2nd Class		Additional
	2 Adults	1 Adult	2 Adults	1 Adult	Car Day
Economy	$298	$378	$248	$328	$55
Compact	318	428	268	378	70
Intermediate	338	458	288	408	80

For our more detailed list of European rail passes, please consult the Appendix.

Base City...

Copenhagen (Kobenhaven)

No city dialing code required.

Arriving by Air

Kastrup Airport. Tel: 32 31 32 31; Fax: 32 31 31 32

Located 12 kilometers southeast of city center. Most international flights to and from Denmark use Kastrup (Copenhagen) Airport. About 60 airlines have regular services to Copenhagen and there are several daily connections to/from all other major European airports.

Airport-City Links: At press time, the new Airport Rail Terminal linking the Airport to Copenhagen city center by train is not completed (scheduled to open mid-1998), but frequent airport-coach, public-bus, and taxi service is available. A shuttle bus operates between Kastrup Airport and City Central Railway Station 0630-2310 (weekends/holidays 0545-1110). Journey time: 20 minutes. Intervals: 10-15 minutes. From Central Railway Station to Kastrup Airport 0542-2145 daily. The ride to the downtown SAS terminal (located at the main railway station) costs 40 kroner. For only 15 kroner, public bus No. 250S will take you from the airport to the Town Hall Square, near Tivoli Gardens, and to the railway station, where your ticket still entitles you to transfer to any other bus within one hour from the time of purchase. Taxi service has a minimum charge of 7.15 kroner per kilometer plus a 20-kroner "start" charge.

The airport has money-exchange facilities, and you may obtain hotel reservations at the service department in the airport's arrival hall. The airport operates a tax-free shop, but only departing or in-transit passengers are permitted to use it. The shopping area is one of the largest and most attractive in Europe, perhaps because the experts from Tivoli influenced its design.

Arriving by Train

There are direct train connections from Copenhagen to the major cities in Europe including Stockholm, Oslo, Hamburg, Berlin, Amsterdam, Brussels, Paris, and Basel.

Copenhagen has four major railway stations, but, unlike the situation in Paris, only the central station, **København Hovedbanegaard**, is of concern to Eurail travelers. Signs in and approaching the station are marked KØBEN-HAVN H. The abbreviation of Hovedbanegaard (Central Station), an "H," reflects the efficiency of this huge train complex right in the heart of the city. The tracks run below street level, and the architecture of the station blends well with the locale. København H. is suggestive of a great Viking hall with two great wooden archways that span its enclosed area.

The station is served by twelve tracks joined by six exits as you ascend from train level to the station's arrival area. *For your orientation, upon arrival you will exit in a northerly direction.* Tivoli Gardens flank the station's east side, and a huge square fronts the station to the north. The arrival hall serves mainly for baggage handling. The lost-and-found office and the politi (police station) are alongside tracks 11 and 12.

Most services are located in the north departure area. Here you will find the SAS coach terminal, a cafeteria, and an excellent restaurant in the northwest corner. Taxi service is available at both the north and the east exit. City bus lines also serve the station, but inquire at the train information office before using one. Train arrival-and-departure information is displayed in bulletin form at both the arrival exits and the east and west entrances. Modern, airport-style digital displays give train-departure information automatically at each departure gate and on the train platforms. Elevator service, as well as stairways, is available between the station and the train platforms. If you are using a baggage cart, be certain to use the elevators to move your baggage.

- **Baggage Storage.** Lockers are available in two sizes—the small one, 20 kroner; the large one is 30 kroner for 24 hours.
- **Money Exchange.** Den Danske Bank is located along the wall opposite the tracks and across from McDonalds. It also has an ATM. The hours of operation are 0700–2100 daily. A similar banking facility may be found in the row of shops across from tracks 3 and 4, and their hours are 0900–2200. There is a 40 kroner charge for cashing traveler's checks, so you may want to utilize the ATM.
- **Train Information.** Tel: 33 14 88 00 or 33 14 17 01. Between the entrances to tracks 3/4 and 5/6 on the departure (north) side of the station. One or more of the windows is open daily 0700–2100. Train information departures (yellow) and arrivals (white) bulletins are displayed. During the times that international trains are arriving or departing, the Danish State Railways personnel wearing "Information" hats will be seen in the station. They speak English and are eager to assist you.
- **Train Reservations.** RejseCenter on the north side of the station, just opposite the departure gates for tracks 1/2 and 3/4. Inside the office, take a number for domestic or international assistance. Hours: 0800–1900 daily. International reservations: Tel. 33 14 30 88; Domestic reservations: Tel. 33 14 88 00.
- **Rail pass validation** is in the same office where international tickets are purchased, 0630–2400 daily.
- **Inter-Rail Center,** in the middle section of the south side of the station between tracks 2 and 4. Enter by showing your rail pass. You can pick up

information on what's going on in the *Copenhagen This Week* pamphlet, and the center personnel can help with reservations for youth hostels. For a few kroner, you can even take a shower.

Through-passengers to the Swedish ferry port of Helsingborg (via Helsingör north of Copenhagen) need only assure that they are in a coach properly marked for the crossing. Frequently (such as is the case at Helsingör), seven or eight coaches arrive at the ferry dock, but only three or four are loaded for the trip. Check before boarding the train and also advise the conductor of your destination. If you do miss the connection, the ferry service is very frequent.

For hydrofoil service between Copenhagen and Malmo, check with the train information office. Connections may be made either by public bus from the central station to the hydrofoil pier or by taxi directly from your hotel. If you are burdened with luggage, the taxi would be the service to use.

For rail service between Oslo or Stockholm and Copenhagen, it's a tossup between using the hydrofoil or taking the ferry crossing between Helsingborg (Sweden) to Helsingör (Denmark). The hydrofoil route is about one hour faster—aside from the time spent getting from the station to the pier. We still prefer the ferry. You don't have to change conveyances, rail passes are accepted, and tax-free shopping is on board.

Copenhagen Tourist information/Hotel Reservations

Kobenhavns Turistinformation, Bernstorffsgade 1, DK-1577 Kobenhavn V, Denmark. Tel: 33 11 13 25; Fax: 33 93 49 69. Hours: May 1-September 15, 0900–2100 daily; September 16-April 30, 0900–1700 Monday-Friday, Saturdays 0900–1400, closed on Sunday.

To reach the tourist office on foot, exit the central station and walk toward the corner on the right side, toward the front of the Tivoli Gardens. Turn right at this point. The office will be on your right and readily identifiable by the familiar ı sign.

Hotel reservations (Tel: 33 12 28 80; Fax: 33 12 97 23) can be made at the tourist office. The personnel are authorized to accept advance payments on behalf of the hotels to ensure reservations.

For convenience and comfort, we can recommend the four-star hotel Plaza at Bernstorffsgade 4, DK-1577 (Tel: 33 14 92 62; Fax: 33 93 93 62). Room rates range from 1550 krone and up for a single; doubles begin at 1750 krone and go up to 2000 krone for a deluxe room.

Getting Around in Copenhagen

In Copenhagen an electrified metropolitan S-train railway network connects the city center with the suburban areas at frequent intervals and when the Metro is completed in 2000, City Line will run every 1.5 minutes during rush hour.

A great convenience is the **Copenhagen Card,** which entitles you to unlimited travel by buses and trains in the entire Metropolitan area as well as the whole of North Zealand, Roskilde, and Köge, plus free entrances to more than 60 museums, attractions, and sights, including Tivoli and Tivoli Museum, Believe it or Not!, Danish Toy Museum, Frederiksborg Castle, and many more. A four-color, 88-page guide booklet accompanies the card and includes a map of the city. And that's not all—you also receive a 25–50 percent discount on four ferry crossings to Sweden and a 20 percent discount on canal tours and the city tour. What a bargain! Cards are issued for 24 hours (140 kroner), 48 hours (230 kroner), or 72 hours (295 kroner).Children age 5-11 pay 70, 115, or 145 kroner.

Copenhagen has invested heavily in providing bicycle paths alongside many of its main streets and the city provides more than 2,000 free bicycles for visitors to use while sightseeing. Look for one of the 110 Citybike parking areas located throughout the city center, deposit a 20-kroner coin, and start pedaling. When you return the bike, you get your money back. Check with the tourist office for more details.

Sights, Attractions, Tours

Tivoli Gardens (Tel: 33 15 10 01; Fax: 33 93 18 81) is open from May through mid-September. It's not the world's largest amusement park, but it is unique. It has been in business since 1843. Each year, people come from all over the world to enjoy its very special blend of attractions old and new. Tree-lined walks, resplendent with flowers and sparkling illuminations, form the backdrop to its theaters and open-air amusement areas. There are more than twenty restaurants to choose from. Four evenings each week, the park closes with a giant display of fireworks.

During its day of entertainment for young and old alike, international artists appear at the Tivoli Concert Hall, Gilbert & Sullivan scenarios are acted out at the Pantomime Theater, and the Tivoli Boys Guard parades frequently to the delight of all. There's also an impressive assembly of quality rides to thrill you, games to play, and seven great restaurants to select from when you get hunger pangs. Tivoli cannot be described adequately in words; it must be experienced.

Amalienborg Palace is a beautiful example of Rococo architecture and has served as the permanent residence of the Danish royal family since 1794. See the changing of the Royal Guard at 1200 every day in the palace square.

Those with more prurient interests may want to visit the **Museum Erotica** at Købmagergade 24, 1150 København K, Tel: 33 12 03 11 to experience the "Love Life of Homo Sapiens." Hours: 1000–2300.

Tour the colorful **Nyhavn canal** area with its quaint restaurants or take the city harbor tour—a comfortable way to see beautiful Copenhagen.

Want more? Tour the city's world-famous breweries, Carlsberg and Tuborg. Get details from the tourist office. Yes, they provide samples of their products.

Contact Carlsberg in advance by calling 33 27 13 14.

Year-round, visit *Den Lille Havfrue* (**The Little Mermaid**), symbol of today's Copenhagen. It is an enchanting, soul-touching statue and next to Queen Margrethe it is probably Denmark's most famous female. A city harbor tour is a perfect way to see beautiful Copenhagen.

Copenhagen Condensed

Shopping? Copenhagen can accommodate you. You'll learn quickly about Stroget (pronounced "stroy-it"). It's not one but actually five different shopping areas, each designated pedestrian-only and lined with shops that might make you want to hide your credit cards. All the well-known Danish specialties are in profusion here. Just north of the Stroget in the Latin Quarter there are some good cafes and restaurants, so you can get anything from a hot dog to a five-course banquet. Try the world famous Danish delicacy, "smorrebrod" which usually consists of rye bread topped with marinated herring or liver pâté and onion rings.

For the best salmon specialties, we enjoyed the Queen's Restaurant & Pub at Vester Voldgade 25. For reservations, telephone 33 12 59 02. For an extraordinary evening, St. Gertruds Kloster at 32 Hauser Plads can provide you with an unforgettable dinner in a fourteenth century atmosphere—in medieval monastery vaults—accompanied by the romantic light of 1,500 candles. For reservations, call 33 14 66 30 or fax 33 93 93 65.

If you have a sweet tooth, please, don't go home before you have tried the Danish waffle–ice cream combination.

Day Excursions

Five delightful day excursions await whenever you can break away from the charm that is distinctly Copenhagen's. Admittedly, this is a difficult thing to do because the Danish capital has so much to offer, what with its Tivoli Gardens, Circus, and pedestrian-only shopping streets; but leave it you must. The entire country is a fairyland. Go out and enjoy it.

Jutland is the Danish mainland, the tip of the European continent that reaches northward toward the Scandinavian peninsula. **Aarhus** is Jutland's cultural center and Denmark's second largest city. Fans of William Shakespeare will, no doubt, make **Helsingör** (Elsinore) their prime day-excursion choice. Castle buffs will head for **Hillerod** and its gracious Frederiksborg Castle. **Odense,** birthplace of Hans Christian Andersen, will delight day excursioners of all ages. **Roskilde** is loaded with Danish folklore and history, including a Viking-ship museum, Museum Island (opening July 1997), and Denmark's most important medieval building—the Roskilde Cathedral—for centuries the final resting place of Denmark's royalty.

Train Connections to Other Base Cities from Copenhagen

TO:	DEPART	ARRIVE	TRAIN NUMBER	NOTES
Amsterdam	2105	0954+1	232/EC 140	(4)
	2205	0948+1	1236	(1)(5)
Berlin (Zoo)	0920	1732	EC 187	(9)
Berne	1905	1210+1	483/EC 101	(2)
Brussels (Midi)	2105	1044	232	
Hamburg	0920	1426	EC 187	(9)
	0730	1223	EC 189	(9)
Munich	1905	0921+1	483	
Oslo	1130	1952	IR 694	
	2145	0707+1	392	(6)
Paris	2105	1329+1	232	
Stockholm	1125	1917	286	(7)
	2315	0753+1	282	
Vienna (Westbf.)	1520	0845+1	EC 183/EN 491	(3)
Zürich	1905	1623+1	483/EC 94	(8)

Daily departures unless otherwise noted. Make reservations for all departures.

(1) Couchettes only
(2) Transfer in Basel
(3) Transfer in Hamburg
(4) Transfer in Duisburg, Germany
(5) June 15 through August 27
(6) Monday through Friday
(7) Runs June 10 through August 18
(8) Transfer in Munich
(9) Supplement payable

Day Excursion to

Aarhus
Jutland's Cultural Center

Depart from Copenhagen Central Station (Kobenhaven H.)

Distance by Train: 139 miles (223 km)
Average Travel Time: 2 hours, 30 minutes
No city code required
Tourist Information Office: Town Hall, DK-8000 Aarhus
Tel: 86 12 16 00; *Fax:* 86 12 95 90
Hours: June 23-September 14, 0930–1900 Monday-Friday, 0930–1700 Saturday, and 0930–1300 Sunday; September 15-April 30, 0930–1630 Monday-Friday, 1000–1300 Saturday; May 1-June 22, 0930-1700 Monday-Friday, 1000-1300 Saturday.

To reach the tourist office, exit the station and cross the street. Turn left, proceed to the first traffic light, and cross the street to the SAS building. From this point, you will see the town hall close by on the left. Entrance is at the fountain. Money-exchange service is available in the tourist office when banks are closed.

The newly opened Great Belt Tunnel decreased the travel time between Copenhagen and Aarhus from 4 hours to 2½ hours. And, travel aboard the Danish Railways (DSB) InterCity trains is comfortable and a pleasant way to see the Danish countryside. When you arrive in Aarhus, disembark and follow the signs to the main rail station, where you mount stairs leading to the station's main concourse. Lift (elevator) service is available should you or a member of your party require it. After turning left, walk to the end of the corridor. The train-information office is to the left at the end of the corridor (open daily 0800-1900).

People have lived in Aarhus ever since the Vikings settled at the mouth of the river, where it meets the bay. There the Norsemen constructed a harbor, built houses, and erected a church. During the 1960s, contractors excavating under a bank in Aarhus came upon the remains of a semicircular rampart that the Vikings of a thousand years ago used to protect their small community. Today, the site is a museum, where you can see the reconstructed ramparts with a typical house of that time, together with tools and other belongings used by the first inhabitants of Aarhus. This museum, and an outdoor collection of more than seventy half-timbered houses known as the "Old Town," are "musts" during your visit. Between the two, you will be able to range through Danish history from the Vikings to the era of Hans Christian Andersen.

Aarhus has many other worthwhile attractions. It's Denmark's second largest city and Jutland's uncontested cultural center.

Between Kalundborg and Aarhus, there is a hydrofoil ferry service which

Copenhagen-Aarhus

DEPART COPENHAGEN STATION	TRAIN NUMBER	ARRIVE IN AARHUS STATION	NOTES
0638	LYN 115	0905	(4)(5)(6)
0652	LYN 119	0957	(1)
0952	IC 129	1313	(1)
1052	IC 133	1413	(1)
1252	IC 141	1613	(3)(6)

Via catamaran or ferry crossing Kalundborg–Aarhus—Transfer to catamaran/ ferry at Kalundborg.

DEPART AARHUS VIA ODENSE	TRAIN NUMBER	ARRIVE IN COPENHAGEN STATION	NOTES
1526	IC 152	1851	(1)(2)(6)
1626	IC 156	1951	(1)(2)(6)
1726	IC 160	2051	(1)(2)(6)
1826	IC 164	2151	(1)(2)(6)

Via Odense and Nyborg–Korsor ferry—Stay aboard train at Nyborg.

DEPART AARHUS STATION	ARRIVE IN COPENHAGEN STATION	NOTES
1630	1942	(7)

Via catamaran crossing Aarhus–Kalundborg—Transfer to train IC 552 at Kalundborg.

(1) Daily, including holidays
(2) Via ferry crossing Nyborg–Korsor (circuitous route)
(3) Monday through Saturday
(4) Via catamaran crossing Kalundborg-Aarhus
(5) Daily except Saturdays
(6) Reservation obligatory

Distance: 139 miles/223 km

takes only 90 minutes. You can return to Copenhagen via this same route, but we recommend the "great circle" tour, which includes stops at the cities of Fredericia and Odense.

The "Old Town" in Aarhus is a part of the city's botanical gardens that has been transformed into a Danish market town typical of the seventeenth century. Its half-timbered houses have been transferred there from every region of the country to re-create an entire landscape complete with narrow streets, shops, public squares—even a millrace. Be certain to visit it. Check with the tourist office for the seasonal hours of operation. To reach it, follow the city map for a ten-minute walk or take the No. 3 bus.

Admission to the Viking Museum is free and it's only three blocks from the tourist office. You may want to visit other attractions by taking the bus. You can purchase a Tourist Ticket (45 kroner), which is valid for an unlimited number of bus rides in the Borough of Aarhus for twenty-four hours. It includes a two-and-one-half-hour guided city-bus tour, which departs daily from the tourist office at 1000 from June 23-August 31. Buy it at most newsstands or at the tourist office. If you plan to stay longer or make Aarhus your base city, you can buy the **Aarhus Passport** for two days (adults, 110 kroner; children under age 16, 55 kroner) or for one week (adults 155 kroner; children, 75 kroner), which gives you unlimited access to public transport as well as free entrance to many of the town's attractions.

South of Aarhus you'll find the Prehistoric Museum at Moesgaard, one of Denmark's top attractions. (Hours: daily 1000-1700 in summer; closed Mondays during winter.) The museum contains collections from the Stone Age, the Bronze Age, the Iron Age, and the Viking period. To get there, take bus No. 6 from the railway station.

Day Excursion to

Helsingør
HAMLET'S HIDEAWAY

Depart from Copenhagen Central Station (Kobenhaven H.)

Distance by Train: 26 miles (44 km)
Average Train Time: 45 minutes
Helsingør Turistbureau: Havnepladsen 3, DK-3000 Helsingør
Tel: 49 21 13 33; *Fax:* 49 21 15 77
Hours: June-August, 0900–1900 Monday-Friday; 1000–1800 Saturday. September-May, 0930–1700 Monday-Friday and 0900–1300 on Saturday.

Located just across the street on the left side of the station. Look for the TURIST AGENCY sign at the end of tracks 1 and 2 for more explicit directions. Words of caution—obey the traffic signals when crossing to the tourist office, and use the designated walkway. A local, private railroad uses the street as a siding, and it could be hazardous to your health

Helsingør is one of Denmark's oldest populated places. Documents dating back to 1231 record its development. In the vaults under Kronborg Castle, there is a statue of Holger Danske, a Viking chieftain, who voyaged to the Holy Land as a crusader about A.D. 800, and there are many buildings of ancient vintage.

For example, nearby No. 27 Strandgade is the oldest half-timbered house in town. It was built in 1577. Other structures date back to the fifteenth century.

It's the lure of Shakespeare's Hamlet that usually brings visitors to Helsingør (Elsinore). The town has many other attractions, however, not the least of which is the world's biggest and best ice cream cone. Read on, MacBeth!

Local train service between Copenhagen and the town of Helsingør (sometimes referred to by its older name, "Elsingore" or "Elsinore") runs every twenty minutes throughout the day and is interspersed with frequent express train service.

The Helsingør railway station is the terminus for the train ferries that ply between Denmark and the town of Helsingborg in Sweden. The distance across the sound between the two countries is less than three miles. This is the reason why Helsingør was founded there and also the reason why it flourished from 1426 through 1857 by the collection of the "sound dues" from all merchant ships that passed.

If you are interested in maritime ferry operations, Helsingør is the place to observe it. Arrivals and departures take place almost endlessly throughout the day and into the night. You will probably note upon arrival in the Helsingør station that rail cars are being loaded or unloaded from the tracks immediately on your right. When you emerge from the station, you will see that this

Copenhagen-Helsingør

From Copenhagen to Helsingør:

Trains depart daily (Monday through Friday) every twenty minutes at 9 and 29 minutes past the hour, from 0509 through 0029. Trains depart every twenty minutes from 0649 through 0029 on Saturdays and Sundays. Journey time is approximately forty-five minutes. Check with the train-information office in the Kobenhavn (H) Terminal.

From Helsingør to Copenhagen:

Trains depart daily every twenty minutes at 39 and 59 minutes past the hour, from 0439 through 2339 (service begins at 0539 on Sunday). Check with the train-information office in the Helsingør train station.

Ferries between Helsingør, Denmark, and Helsingborg, Sweden:

Most Copenhagen–Helsingør trains connect with ferries to Sweden. Eurail pass is accepted for passage. Ferries depart at 10, 30, and 50 minutes past, each beginning at 0610 and running until 2330. Service in either direction takes approximately twenty-five minutes. If desired, you may combine a day excursion to Helsingør, Denmark, with a round trip ferry crossing to Helsingborg, Sweden.

Distance: 46 km

operation also includes passenger cars, trucks, and foot passengers.

One of the tourist office's publications is *Helsingør—Hamlet's Town.* It describes, in great detail, Kronborg Castle, the churches of Saint Olai and Saint Mary, and the Carmelite monastery. These highlights of Helsingør are all nearby.

The Kronborg Castle, the city's most famous landmark, was built by Christian IV between 1574 and 1582. With this formidable fortress came the rapid development of the town under its protective shelter. For several centuries, Helsingør was the second largest city in Denmark. The castle is open May–September, 1030-1700. During April and October, hours are 1100–1600; November–March, 1100–1500 (closed Mondays).

Hamlet's residency in the castle was imaginary, but the play was performed there from 1916 until 1954, when performances were curtailed for financial reasons. It was again performed in 1979, but there are no definite plans for the future. In the castle the King's Chamber, the Queen's Chamber, and the Great Hall must be seen to appreciate the once-great splendor of this fortress. Cannon still stand along the seawall.

While admiring the Great Hall, you'll probably note that there are no fireplaces or other heating devices. Apparently, they were overlooked by the royal architect. This created no problem for the royal occupants, however, when they wanted to lay on a royal mid-winter bash; they merely marched several thousand men of the royal guard into the area and the troops' body heat sent the mercury soaring—along with a few other atmospheric additives, no doubt.

While in Helsingør, make certain that a part of your tour includes a stop at the Raadhus (town hall). In its council chamber, you can see a stained-glass window that depicts the history of the town. Outside of the town hall you will see a narrow street (Brostraede) leading to the sea. Follow it. The ice cream shop is there.

Day Excursion to

Hillerod   PICTURE-BOOK SCENERY

Depart from Copenhagen Central Station (Kobenhaven H.)

Distance by Train: 19 miles (30 km)
Average Train Time: 40 minutes
No city code required
Hillerod Turistbureau: Slotsgade 52, Postboks 5, DK-3400 Hillerod
Tel: 42 26 28 52; *Fax:* 42 26 28 06
Hours: June-August, 1000–1900 Monday-Friday; Saturday, 1000–1800. September-May, 1000-1700 Monday-Friday; Saturday, 1000-1300. Closed Sundays and holidays.

To get there, follow the signs to the castle, starting just outside the station building. The tourist office is next to the castle on the right-hand side of the pedestrian-only street. If you like, you can obtain a brochure in the railway station that contains a city map to help guide your way. Or take bus 701 or 702 and ask the driver to let you off at the tourist information office. You can buy tickets on the bus for 11 kroner. However, your train ticket also includes the bus fare.

Hillerod can become the crowning touch to your visit to Denmark. The town has an atmosphere distinctly its own. A picture-book lake rests in the town's center, faced on one side by the old town and its market square and on another by the majestic Frederiksborg Castle. There are few places in the world where nature and culture blend together so perfectly.

No doubt the Frederiksborg Castle will be the first stopping point on your tour of Hillerod. A tour boat plies between the castle and the marketplace from May through September, and it is a delightful way of seeing both the city and the castle.

The castle actually spans three islands. The first of its structures, erected by Frederik II in 1560, occupied the largest island. The balance of this imposing castle complex was built by Christian IV between 1600 and 1620. Between 1570 and 1840, Danish monarchs were anointed in the castle chapel and it was used for the wedding of Danish Prince Joachim and Alexandra Manley from Hong Kong in 1995.

In 1859, a disastrous fire destroyed the interior of the main building, and irreplaceable treasures were lost forever. The chapel and all of its valuable contents, however, remained relatively undamaged. Among those items was the celebrated chapel organ built by Esaias Compenius in 1610. The chapel organist plays every Thursday between 1330 and 1400. The castle has been restored, at first by royal contributions and public donations, and, more recently, by philanthropic support from J.C. Jacobsen, former owner of the Carlsberg Brewery and the Carlsberg Foundation. The museum is open daily from 1000-1700 May-September; 1000–1600 October; 1100–1500 November-March; and 1000–1600 April (admission: 40 kroner, adults; children, 10) There is an interesting open-air exhibit known as the North Seeland Folk Museum by a small pond in a corner of the castle's gardens.

In 1996, the reconstruction of the French baroque park was finished and inaugurated by Danish Queen Margrethe II, resembling the original park from 1720. In another section of the castle garden, known as the *Indelukket*, you can inspect a charming little country house built in 1562 for the king to conduct informal entertainment.

The shop-'til-you-drop group will enjoy Hillerod's shopping center, the "Slotsarkaderne," with more than forty-seven specialty shops. It, too, is conveniently located on Slotsgade. When coming from the railway station, the glass-covered Slotsarkaderne shopping mall is on the left-hand side of Slotsgade.

There is a museum at No. 38 Slotsgade on your way to the castle. It should

Copenhagen-Hillerod

DEPART COPENHAGEN STATION	TRAIN NUMBER	ARRIVE IN HILLEROD STATION	NOTES
0814	Local	0853	(1)
0914	Local	0953	(1)
1014	Local	1053	(1)
1114	Local	1153	(1)

Additional hourly service at 34 and 54 minutes past the hour through 0034

DEPART HILLEROD STATION	TRAIN NUMBER	ARRIVE IN COPENHAGEN STATION	NOTES
1508	Local	1546	(1)
1608	Local	1646	(1)
1708	Local	1746	(1)
1808	Local	1846	(1)

Additional hourly service at 08, 28, and 48 minutes past the hour through 0028

(1) Daily, including holidays

Distance: 19 miles/30 km

---

attract coin collectors of all ages. It comprises a very fine collection of Danish and foreign coins as well as other means of payment used in ancient times. Illustrations tell the story of political, historical, and cultural aspects of money and coinage.

Just outside Hillerod, you may want to visit an exhibit of dolls in costumes. You can reach it on bus No. 736. The display features seventy dolls with hand-made costumes that present the history of dress as well as the history of man. You'll see everything from Queen Victoria to the bustle that your great grand-mother used to wear.

Day Excursion to

Odense

HOME OF HANS CHRISTIAN ANDERSEN

Depart from Copenhagen Central Station (Kobenhaven H.)

Distance by Train: 103 miles (165 km)
Average Travel Time: 1 hour, 40 minutes
No city code required

Internet: http://www.odenseturist.dk
Odense Turist Bureau: Radhuset (Town Hall), DK-5000 Odense C
Tel: 66 12 75 20; *Fax:* 66 12 75 86
Hours: June 15-August 31, Monday-Saturday 0900–1900; Sunday 1100–1900.
September 1-June 14, Monday-Friday 0930–1630; Saturday 1000-1300.
   When you arrive in the Odense railway station, look for the train information
booth on the second floor. There you can obtain train information and a map of
Odense showing how to get to the Turist Bureau at the Radhuset (Town Hall).
Information booth hours: Monday-Saturday, 0600–2100; and Sunday, 0700–2200.

Hans Christian Andersen, Denmark's famous teller of fairy tales, was born
in a tiny yellow house in Odense on 2 April 1805. One hundred years later,
the city bought the house and turned it into a museum—probably the best
investment that the city ever made. Tourists of all ages still flock to this magic
point to see what his early life was like and to wonder what developed an
imagination that could captivate the entire world.
   Many of Andersen's stories were set in or near Odense. Most of the locations can be seen today. The small, half-timbered house where he was born,
now the nucleus of the Hans Christian Andersen Museum, is set in a cluster
of other small houses from the same period. A visit there is like stepping back
into the nineteenth century.
   The Hans Christian Andersen house (near the tourist office, about a 10-
minute walk from the rail station) is open daily June-August 0900-1800;
September-May, 1000–1600 daily and is well worth a visit. The area surrounding Hans Christian Andersen's home, with its little colored houses and
cobblestone streets, is very attractive.
   If you are visiting the museum area at mealtime, we suggest that you eat in
a charming little restaurant across the lane, Under the Linden Tree. It's but one
of a score of excellent restaurants in Odense. The tourist office has a handy
pocket guide describing many of these eating establishments. You'll find an
interesting selection—including such names as Jensen's Boefhus and Den
Grimme Ælling (Ugly Duckling).
   The house of Hans Christian Andersen is not the only attraction in Odense.
The city is Denmark's third largest. Industrial and vigorous in its life style,
Odense has smart shops, spacious parks, and sparkling residential areas. Situated
in the center of Denmark's second largest island, the Isle of Funen, the city is
the focal point for those wishing to explore the island's rolling countryside.
   The German emperor Otto III officially mentioned Odense for the first
time in a letter dated 18 March 988. Although there were people living there
at the time and a church had been previously erected, the present-day residents
applied the emperor's date as a benchmark and declared 1988 as the "1,000th
Anniversary of Odense."
   A Hans Christian Andersen fairy tale is presented from mid-July through

Copenhagen-Odense

DEPART COPENHAGEN STATION	TRAIN NUMBER	ARRIVE IN ODENSE STATION	NOTES
0652	IC 117	0833	(1)(2)
0752	IC 121	0933	(1)(2)
0852	IC 125	1033	(1)(2)
0952	IC 129	1133	(1)(2)

Via ferry crossing Korsor–Nyborg
Stay aboard train at ferry dock.

DEPART ODENSE STATION	TRAIN NUMBER	ARRIVE IN COPENHAGEN STATION	NOTES
1308	IC 136	1451	
1408	IC 140	1551	(1)(2)
1508	IC 144	1651	(1)(2)
1608	IC 148	1751	(1)(2)
1708	IC 152	1851	(1)(2)
1808	IC 156	1951	(1)(2)
1908	IC 160	2051	(1)(2)
2008	IC 164	2151	(1)(2)
2108	IC 168	2251	(1)(2)

Via ferry crossing Nyborg–Korsor
Stay aboard train at ferry dock.

(1) Daily, including holidays
(2) Seat reservations mandatory

Distance: 103 miles / 165 km

---

the first week in August at the Open Air Theater in Funen Village. The village is one of the largest open-air museums in Denmark, characterized by a coherent layout of landscape and a real village of seventeenth-century houses assembled from the Island of Funen and the surrounding islands. Here you will find farms with animals, a rectory, a school—even a brickyard and a forge. The theater seats 2,000 people.

Odense has a museum for every interest—from art to transportation. The Brands Klaedefabrik Art Gallery (European Museum of the Year, 1988), Danish Museum of Printing, Danish Press Museum, and the Museum of Photographic Art are all located in Brandts Passage. The Danish Railway Museum is next to the railway station at Dannebrogsgade 24 (Tel: 66 13 66 30). Experience 150 years of train and ferry history. It is open daily from 1000–1600.

The Odense Adventure Pass will provide free public transport within the Odense area and either free or reduced-price admission to Odense's many museums, sights, and the zoo. A 24-hour pass costs 50 kroner for adults and 25 for children. To reach the zoo, board one of Odense Aafart's covered cruise boats for a relaxing journey.

Day Excursion to

Roskilde THE VIKING SHIP MUSEUM AND THE CATHEDRAL

Depart from Copenhagen Central Station (Kobenhaven H.)

Distance by Train: 19 miles (31 km)
Average Train Time: 25 minutes
No city code required
Roskilde-Egnens Turistbureau: Gullandsstraede 15, DK-4000 Roskilde
Tel: 46 35 27 00; *Fax:* 46 35 14 74
Hours: July-August, 0900-1800 Monday-Friday; 0900-1500 Saturday; 1000-1400 Sunday. September-June, 0900-1700 Monday-Friday; 0900-1300 Saturday.
 Ten-minute walk from the railway station, or take a taxi for about 50 kroner. If walking, exit the station and proceed downhill to the main street. Turn left at this point to the city square. The tourist office is only about 300 yards off the pedestrian street Gullandsstraede

Since Roskilde is so close to Copenhagen, you might think that it would be so much like Denmark's capital city that a day excursion there would be pointless. On the contrary, Roskilde is as different from Copenhagen as night is from day. Known as the "Town of Viking Ships and Royal Tombs," Roskilde warrants a visit. In fact, it is difficult to see all that you might want to see in Roskilde in just one day.
 We recommend at least three things to do during your day excursion: (1) visit the cathedral, (2) take a guided tour, and (3) visit the Viking Ship Museum.
 Roskilde's twin-spired, brick cathedral dominates the city's skyline. Its construction was begun in 1170 on the same site where King Harald Bluetooth erected a church in A.D. 960. Today it's considered Denmark's most important medieval building. It is an international attraction primarily because it has been the burial place of Danish royalty for centuries. Thirty-eight kings and queens of Denmark are buried there, representing the longest reign of family monarchy in the world.
 The cathedral is one of Denmark's first brick buildings, and it is said that it has as many tales to tell as it has bricks in its walls. Originally, a limestone edifice was erected on the foundation of Harald Bluetooth's church, only to be

Copenhagen-Roskilde

DEPART COPENHAGEN STATION	TRAIN NUMBER	ARRIVE IN ROSKILDE STATION	NOTES
0652	IC 117	0713	(1)(2)
0752	IC 121	0813	(1)(2)
0852	IC 125	0913	(1)(2)
0952	IC 129	1013	(1)(2)
1052	IC 133	1113	(1)(2)

Plus other frequent service

DEPART ROSKILDE STATION	TRAIN NUMBER	ARRIVE IN COPENHAGEN STATION	NOTES
1429	IC 136	1451	(1)(2)
1529	IC 140	1551	(1)(2)
1629	IC 144	1651	(1)(2)
1729	IC 148	1751	(1)(2)
1829	IC 152	1851	(1)(2)

Plus other frequent service

(1) Daily, including holidays
(2) Seat reservations mandatory

Distance: 19 miles/31 km

---

torn down and replaced slowly by the present brick structure, which was completed in the year 1280.

Some less significant, but nevertheless interesting, features of the cathedral are its granite measuring column and a 500-year-old clock. The column was used to measure the height of royal visitors. The tallest, Peter the Great of Russia, checked in at six feet ten inches! The clock features Saint George and the dragon. For nearly 500 years, Saint George mounts his trusty horse each hour and attacks the dragon, which screams in pain before going off to dragon heaven to be refurbished for the next hour's performance. The cathedral is open (except when services are being conducted) April-September, 0900–1645 Monday-Friday; 0900–1200 Saturday and October-March, 1000–1545 Monday-Friday; 1130–1545 Saturday. Sundays and holidays, 1230–1645 May through August and 1230–1545 September through April.

If you visit Roskilde on a Wednesday or a Saturday morning, you will find the city's market in full operation. The market is unique in that it isn't limited to the sale of meats, poultry, fish, and produce—the usual bill of fare that you find throughout Europe. The market activities include a flea market that could rival the best American garage sale ever held. All of this activity takes place in the town square "the Staendertorvet" fronting the Town Hall.

The Viking Ship Museum is an interesting addition to Roskilde's many attractions (open daily April-October, 0900–1700; November-March, 1000–1600). Admission is 40 kroner for adults, 25 for children. Proceed downhill from the cathedral.

Viking ships, circa A.D. 1000 to 1050, have been restored piece by piece in this most modern of maritime museums on the banks of the Roskilde fjord. For centuries legend had it that a barrier at the fjord's narrowest point actually had a Viking vessel beneath it. The legend was only partially correct in that a cofferdam operation in 1962 revealed that not one but five vessels had been sunk there to protect Roskilde's harbor from enemy fleets. The museum area was recently enlarged and a Viking ship harbor created. You can even sail aboard a Viking ship replica.

Just six miles west of Roskilde is the Prehistoric Village-Historical-Archaeological-Experimental Centre at Lejre, representing one of the most profound studies of prehistoric housing. Ask the tourist office about free bus connections from the small station in Lejre to the center.

If you visit during the last week in June, be sure to check out the **Roskide Festival,** the greatest rock-and-jazz fest in northern Europe.

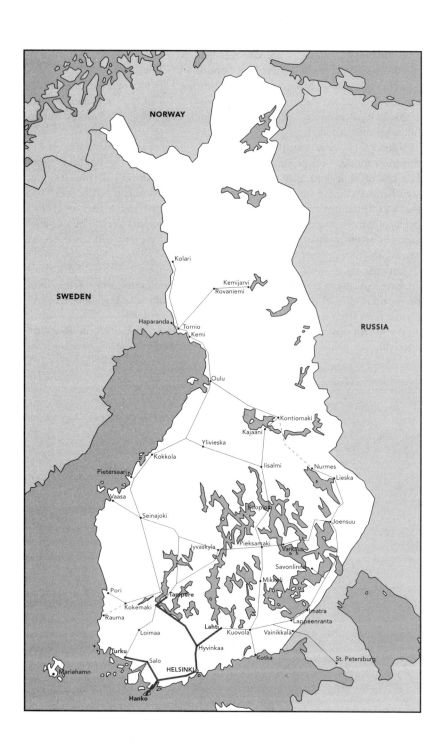

NORWAY

SWEDEN

RUSSIA

Kolari

Kemijarvi
Rovaniemi

Haparanda
Tornio
Kemi

Oulu

Kontiomaki
Kajaani

Ylivieska

Kokkola

Iisalmi
Nurmes
Lieska

Pietersaari

Vaasa

Seinajoki

Kuopio

Joensuu

Jyvaskyla
Pieksamaki
Varkaus

Savonlinna

Mikkeli

Pori

Tampere

Kokemaki
Imatra

Rauma
Lappeenranta

Loimaa
Kuovola
Vainikkala

Turku
Hyvinkaa

Salo
Kotka
St. Petersburg

Mariehamn

HELSINKI

Hanko

Finland

Finland is well known for its unique natural beauty including 188,000 lakes, 179,000 islands, and Europe's biggest archipelago. Known as the "Land of the Midnight Sun" in summer, it is an artistic array of color in autumn, dazzling white in winter, and swashed with green beauty in spring. Finland is a country for all seasons.

Finnish and Swedish are the two languages spoken most frequently. English is a second language for many Finns, particularly for those involved in tourism and transportation.

Since they share a common border, Finland has long been associated with Russia in one way or another. During the Napoleonic Wars, Russia invaded Finland and it became a Russian grand duchy in 1809. Finnish nationalism grew, however, and the Finns proclaimed their independence in 1917. The Finns were again defeated by Soviet troops in the beginning of World War II. In the late 1980s, the Soviet's political demise fostered development of closer relations with Western Europe and in 1995, Finland joined the European Union.

Finland is still considered a gateway between East and West. If you've always wanted to visit Russia, now's your chance. There are daily rail connections from Helsinki to Vyborg, St. Petersburg, and Moscow.

For tourist information, contact the Finnish Tourist Board Offices in North America:

New York: 655 Third Avenue, New York, NY 10017. Tel: (212) 885-9700; Fax: (212) 885-9710; Email: fininfo1@mail.idt.net; Internet: http://www.travelfile.com/get?finninfo

Ontario: P.O. Box 246, Station G, Ontario, CAN M4T 2MI. Tel: 800-FININFO; Fax: (416) 964-1524

Banking

- **Currency:** Markkaa (FIM)
- **Exchange rate at press time:** 5.29 FIM = $1.00 U.S.

• **Hours:** 0900-1600 Monday. Hours may vary regionally. Foreign currency and travelers checks can also be exchanged in the following currency exchange offices: Katajanokka harbor, Helsinki, open daily 0900-1899 and during the arrival and departure of ships and the Helsinki-Vantaa Airport, open daily 0630-2300.

Communications

• **Country Code:** 358
For telephone calls within Finland, dial a zero (0) preceding area code.
Direct dial: AT&T Direct: 98100-100-10

Rail Travel in Finland

The Finnish Railways (VR) operate Finland's mass transportation system. High-speed Pendolino S220 trains and InterCity and express trains provide long distance services and local and commuter trains provide connections for shorter routes. **Eurailpass** is accepted on the national rail network of Finland and the crossing by Finnjet from Helsinki to Travemunde (Germany) is included. The country rail pass, Finnrail Pass, and the regional Scanrailpass are also accepted.

Finnrailpass
Valid for any 3 days unlimited train travel within a 1-month period
First Class $185; Second Class $123; children 6-16 years; children under 6, free

Scanrailpass
Unlimited train travel in Denmark, Finland, Norway and Sweden for a specified number of days. Also includes 20-50 percent discounts on certain ferries and bus connections. The passes range from 5 days of travel within a 15-day period ($222 adult First class) up to 1 full month of travel $516 adult First class); special Senior (age 55 and over), Youth (age 12-25), and Child (age 4-11) rates.
See Appendix for a more detailed list of rail pass types and prices.

Base City...

Helsinki

City Dialing Code: 9

Arriving by Air

Vantaa Airport: Tel: 358-9-82771; Fax: 358-9-8277309
Location: 20 kilometers north of Helsinki, 25 kilometers northeast of Espoo.
Airport-City Links: By Bus—Finnair buses run between the airport, the Air
Terminal, Toolonkatu 21 and the Finnair City Terminal, Asema-aukio three
next to the main railway station two to four times an hour; journey takes 35
minutes. Fare 24 markkaa (FIM) Local bus service: operated by Sirolan
Liikenne Oy, take bus No. 615 between the airport and the station square two
to four times an hour; trip takes 40 minutes. Fare 15 FIM.
By Taxi—Airport to the Central Railway Station takes 20 minutes. Fare
about 100 FIM. Yellow Taxi is a new service; minimum of three passengers
sharing the ride is required.
Passengers should check in at the airport a minimum of forty-five minutes
before departure time for overseas flights. Contact Finnair several hours before
flight time to check weather conditions at the airport.
Duty-free shops in the departure lounge of the Vantaa Airport are loaded
with gifts of Finnish origins.

Arriving by Train

Helsinki is served by a single train terminal, the **Central Terminal**, which is
considered the most important work designed by Eliel Saarinen, the prominent
Finnish-American architect. The terminal lies right in the heart of Helsinki and
is close to everything. The train platforms have a total of fourteen tracks. The
tracks are not covered, so an umbrella or a raincoat will come in handy if you
are arriving in, or departing from, Helsinki during inclement weather.
- **Baggage storage** available on the far right of the mail hall entering from
  the trains. Baggage lockers are scattered throughout the station. A standard
  charge is required for all lockers, regardless of size.
- **Money exchange** is located in the main hall. Hours: 0800-2100 daily.
  Banks are open 0915-1615 Monday through Friday.
- **Hotel reservations** at the hotel booking center in the main hall. Tel. (90)17
  13 33, Fax (90)17 55 24. Reservation fee 10 FIM for either a single- or
  double-room reservation; 15 FIM for three; 18 FIM for four persons. This

is the only hotel-reservations office in Helsinki. Hours: 0900-1900 Monday-Saturday; 1000-1800 Sunday; September 1-May 30, Monday-Friday, 0900-1700.

• **Train information** on the left side of the station's main hall (Tel. 358 9 82 27 66). Train-seat reservations can be made at window Nos. 1-8. Rail pass validation also can be accomplished at these windows. Hours: 0700-2100 daily. The charge for seat reservations on the "Rapido" trains is 9.00 FIM. Reservations on these trains are obligatory.

A large cafeteria on the main level serves fast-food specialties for the hurried traveler. On the floor above, a modern ravintola (restaurant) serves from 0900-0100 daily.

Similar to Munich's Hauptbahnhof, Helsinki's Central Terminal connects with a vast underground system lined with shops and restaurants. This lively underground shopping area is open until 2200 every day, including Sunday. It's a great place when returning late from a day excursion to pick up a loaf of crusty bread, tasty cheese, and a beer—but on the other hand, there's always room service.

Arriving by Ship

The Silja Line ferries arrive at Helsinki's South Harbor. The Viking Line ferries dock at Katajanokka Harbor. Each ferry company maintains spacious passenger facilities complete with food services, lounges, currency exchanges, and connections to public transportation. Shipping activities in the harbor present many photographic opportunities. If you are continuing your Eurail journey back aboard the Silja Line, a money-exchange service is offered aboard by the ship's purser. The rates are governed by the Swedish banks but have basically the same exchange rates as the on-shore facilities in Helsinki.

Tourist Information/Hotel Reservations

• *Helsinki City Tourist Information Office:* Pohjoisesplanadi 19, 00100 Helsinki
• *Tel:* (90) 169 3757; *Fax* (90) 169 3839
• *Internet:* tourist.infor@hel.fi
• *Hours:* Summer, 0900-1900 Monday-Friday; 0900-1500 Saturday and Sunday. October-April, 0900-1700 Monday-Friday; 0900-1500 Saturday; closed Sunday.

Located in the market square area of the harbor. To reach this office, board tram No. 3T immediately in front of the train station. The fare for adults is 9.00 FIM; for children, 4.50 FIM. In about 10 minutes, the tram will pass the Silja Line Terminal. Disembark at the next stop, which is the market square on the harbor. Look for the green "I" sign.

Getting Around in Helsinki

The Helsinki Card is a veritable key to the city. This card not only grants you free travel on buses, trams, trains, and the Metro in the metropolitan area, it also provides free entry to about fifty museums and other places of interest in and around Helsinki and includes a free guided sightseeing tour by bus. Showing the card in department stores brings you a free gift; it will spoil you in many of the city's restaurants, theaters, the opera, and concerts. A ninety-six-page brochure describing the scores of opportunities the Helsinki Card provides may be obtained from the Helsinki City Tourist Office or in the Hotel Booking Centre at the railway station, as well as at some travel agencies, hotels, and department stores. The cards are issued for periods covering 24 hours for 105 FIM, 48 hours for 135 FIM, and 72 hours for 165 FIM. Kids ages 7 to 16 pay reduced rates. It's a value you can't refuse.

Sights/Attractions/Tours

During the summer, Helsinki operates an unusual form of sightseeing—a tram (streetcar) named "3T." It circles the city and takes in most of its important sightseeing points. Board the tram from the rear, where you pay your fare to the driver. Pick up a pamphlet containing a map and descriptions of the sights you'll see on your tour from the city tourist information office. The round trip takes about forty-five minutes. Fare: 9.00 FIM; kids under 12, 4.50 FIM.

Another way to become acquainted with the city is to take a guided bus tour. City tours depart from the Station Square June-August at 1100 and 1300 daily. The fare is 90 FIM (free for Helsinki Card holders), the duration is one and a half hours. The same tours are conducted on a more limited schedule throughout the year. Check with the Helsinki tourist information office for details.

For a more intimate way to get to know Helsinki, ask the tourist office for the brochure "See Helsinki on Foot." Tour No. 5—Market Square-Kaivopuisto-Eira interested us. Just follow the route on the map in the brochure. The sights are numbered and explained. If you begin at Market Square, one of the first sights will be the Havis Amanda (a beautiful mermaid) Fountain by the sculptor Ville Vallgren in 1908. Next, you'll see the first public monument in Helsinki—the Czarina's Stone, designed by C.L. Engel to comemorate the Czarina Alexandra's visit. About mid-way through your tour, you may want to stop at the Ursula Seaside Café (No. 33 on the map).

Other tours originate at the Silja Line or Viking Line terminals in the harbor area. These tours run two and a half hours, and some schedules include lunch. Again, the tourist information office has the details.

Highlights of Helsinki

Helsinki is a city born of the sea, and it is from the sea that it draws its soul and nature. It is the beautiful daughter of the Baltic—a jewel with the blue sea as its setting. Helsinki is a modern city. Here the visitor does not come face to face with the past as he does in many long-standing European capitals. Great fires destroyed the original Helsinki many times, but it was always rebuilt. The only original remains of the trade-and-seafaring town that Swedish King Gustav Vasa founded in 1550 at the mouth of the Vantaa River are the foundations of a church.

Helsinki did not become Finland's capital until 1812. Now it has become very cosmopolitan, the heart of cultural and artistic experiences for the Finns. The city's colorful market square on the harbor is characterized by the glittering sea and an abundance of flowers and fruit, white sea gulls, and busy saleswomen. Helsinki has an ambiance that is all its own, supported by a friendly population and the physical comforts to enable you to enjoy fully its many features.

Helsinki's market square, besides presenting flowers, fish, vegetables, fruits, and souvenirs, also can provide visitors with coffee and delicious sugared buns at the square's tent café. Market hours: 0700-1400 Monday-Saturday. From mid-May through August, the evening market hours are 1530-2000 Monday-Friday. Most shops in Helsinki are open 0900-1800 (or 2000) weekdays and 0900-1400 on Saturdays.

Surrounded as it is by the sea, there is a lot of island hopping you can do while visiting Helsinki. A ride on a ferryboat will take you to Korkeasaari Island, Helsinki's zoo; by ferry you can also reach Suomenlinna, a fortress island started by the Swedes, captured by the Russians, and shelled by the British before being given to Finland, which used it as part of its sea defenses until 1973.

Should you tire of all this activity, you can plan to relax in one of Helsinki's excellent saunas.

Day Excursions

When you have finally broken the fine Finnish spell Helsinki casts over its visitors, you will want to venture forth into the Finnish countryside. We have selected four such adventures for your pleasure. They are **Hanko, Lahti, Tampere,** and **Turku**. Hanko, Finland's southernmost city, is a very popular summer resort with miles of wide beaches, good fishing, sailing, and all types of amusements. Lahti, site of the 1978 World Ski Championships, is about sixty-five miles north of Helsinki and provides an opportunity to ride trains plying between Helsinki and Saint Petersburg. Also north of Helsinki lies Tampere, Finland's second-largest city. Both industrial and recreational,

Tampere has much to offer visitors year-round. Turku, Finland's gateway to the west, was its former capital and an important cultural center before Helsinki was founded. Wherever you go, the friendly Finns will make you feel right at home. Enjoy Finland as the Finns do.

Ferry Connections to Stockholm from Helsinki

TO:	DEPART	ARRIVE	NOTES
Stockholm	1800(2)	0830 (3)	(1)
Stockholm			
via Turku★	0920(4)	2000(3)	(5)
	2145(4)	0730(3)	(5)
	1000(4)	1900(3)	(5)
	2000(4)	0700(3)	(6)

★ For train connections from Helsinki to Turku, see page 99.

Note: Eurailpass holders are entitled to discounted passage on Silja Line ships between Stockholm and Turku or Helsinki.

(1) Daily, including holidays (except December 25 and January 1)
(2) South Harbor, Silja Terminal, Helsinki
(3) Silja Terminal, Stockholm
(4) Silja Terminal, Turku
(5) Daily, June 1–August 10, 1998
(6) Daily, August 11, 1998–May 31, 1999

Day Excursion to

Hanko (Hango)   SOUTHERNMOST CITY

Depart from Helsinki Central Terminal

Distance by Train: 85 miles (137 km)
Average Train Time: 2 hours, 15 minutes
City Dialing Code: 19
Tourist Information Office: 10 Bulevardi, P.O. Box 14, 10901 Hanko
Tel: 2203 411; *Fax:* 2485 821
Hours: 0900-1700 Monday-Friday year round

To get to the Hanko tourist office, depart the station and proceed along the overpass crossing the railroad, which will be on your left as you arrive. Turn left immediately after the overpass onto Berggatan Street to where it interesects with Bulevardi. The tourist office is at the intersection.

Hanko is Finland's southernmost town. It is best known as a summer resort; but as the climate in this part of Finland often is very mild, you can visit Hanko in any season. In September, for example, the seawater is still warm enough for swimming. If you do not want to swim, you can lie on the beach, take a walk in the surrounding area, go for a bicycle tour, hire a horse, or just relax. Hanko in autumn is an unusually peaceful place. No matter when you go there, you will find clean water, lots of fresh air, and lots of things to do.

The peninsula where Hanko lies, known long ago among seafarers, was used for centuries as a harbor where sailing vessels could seek refuge from storms or winter ice packs. With time on their hands, many navigators, merchants, and soldiers kept themselves busy by carving their names or family coats of arms in the rocks along the shoreline of the harbor. More than 600 of these carvings have been found. Due to these inscriptions, the area gained the title "Guest Book of the Archipelago." You can inspect this handiwork during the sightseeing cruises available in the harbor area.

Hanko did not begin as a town until the 1870s. With the introduction of iron ships, winter navigation became possible, and Hanko's peninsula was found to be well suited as a year-round harbor. Both a railway and harbor were constructed, and Hanko was well on its way to becoming an important part of the Finnish economy.

By the end of the nineteenth century, Hanko was a fashionable summer resort, especially among the Russians coming from the St. Petersburg area. The Russian influence is visible in the architecture of many wooden villas in Hanko, most of which are in the Spa Park. The peninsula on which Hanko lies was ceded to the Soviet Union in 1940 but was regained in 1941.

Hanko is inseparably linked to the sea. There are about ninety islands just within its town limits! The town has four small boat harbors, including the

Helsinki-Hanko

DEPART HELSINKI STATION	TRAIN NUMBER	ARRIVE IN HANKO STATION	NOTES
0634	121	0828	(1)(2)(3)
0906	123	1052	(1)(2)(3)(4)
1106	125	1302	(1)(2)(3)

DEPART HANKO STATION	TRAIN NUMBER	ARRIVE IN HELSINKI STATION	NOTES
1312	357	1458	(1)(2)(3)(4)
1612	359	1802	(1)(2)(3)
2120	143	2334	(1)(2)(3)

(1) Daily, including holidays
(2) Light refreshments available from Helsinki to Karjaa
(3) Transfer in Karjaa (train numbers refer to Helsinki-Karjaa trains)
    (Trains between Karjaa and Hanko are second class only.)
(4) Supplement payable

Distance: 85 miles/137 km

---

largest harbor for visiting boats in all of Finland, two commercial harbors, four industrial harbors, and an important rail-ferry loading facility in Finland. None of this activity is detrimental to tourism; in fact, it attracts it. More than 200,000 tourists visit Hanko annually. They come not only for the long sandy beaches and aquatic sports but for the more than 1,000 events that take place every year.

The day excursion to Hanko requires a change of trains at Karjaa, which you reach in just over an hour from Helsinki. In Karjaa, you will transfer to a local train that makes an interesting trip through southern Finland's woods and quaint little rail stations before reaching Hanko. The Hanko station is the last stop on the line, so there's no chance of missing it.

Between the years 1880 and 1930, thousands of emigrants set off from Hanko for the United States, Canada, and Australia. In 1967, a statue commemorating this period was erected near the beach, a short distance from the tourist office. Depicting wild birds in free flight, this "independence monument" is well worth the time to visit. Also worthwhile is a visit to the Fortress Museum in the Eastern Harbor and the City Hall Art Gallery, which features exhibitions from local, Finnish, and foreign artists.

To experience Hanko's spa history, visit the famous "Summer Restaurant

Casino," one of the largest summer restaurants in Finland. To get there, head down Bulivardi toward the sea. Turn left onto Appelgrenintie. As you enter the Spa Park, you will see the beaches on your right. The villas in the park once housed Russian noblemen and their families as guests.

Hanko has several other interesting restaurants, some of which are open year round in the Eastern Harbor area. You can find seafood, Italian-style food, or homemade Finnish foods.

Other tours of Hanko and its surroundings can be arranged through the city tourist office. Brochures, maps, and special information leaflets are available, and guides can be hired. Sea cruises operate every day from mid-June to the end of August. The sea tours start at the Eastern Harbor and last about two hours. Tickets are sold on board. Fishing trips also may be arranged, but before angling off, check with the tourist office and obtain a general fishing permit from the town's post office. Hanko is packed with exciting as well as relaxing things to do.

Day Excursion to

Lahti
SKI, SKATE, SAIL, OR CYCLE

Depart from Helsinki Central Terminal

Distance by Train: 81 miles (130 km)
Average Train Time: 1 hour, 30 minutes
City Dialing Code: 3
Tourist Information Office: Torikatu 3 B, PL/Box 175, SF-15111 Lahti
Tel: 814 4568; *Fax:* 814 4564
Hours: June–August 0800-1700 Monday-Friday; 0900-1400 Saturday. September–May 0800-1600 Monday-Friday

When you arrive in Lahti from Helsinki, exit on the left-hand side of the train. Use the underground exit and walk toward track No. 4 to the station. Exit the terminal and proceed along Rautatienkatu Street to Aleksanterinkkatu Street where you turn left. Walk to Torikatu Street. Following a right turn, the office is at the intersection of Torikatu and Vapaudenkatu streets. (It's easier than it sounds.) Some tourist information is available in the rail station, as well as in the Sports Center and the Passenger Harbour, throughout the summer.

Lahti is the seventh largest city in Finland, with nearly 100,000 inhabitants. It is particularly noted for its timber and wooden furniture, brewers' products, and clothing. It is equally famous as a winter sports center. Sporting events have always played a prominent role in Lahti's life-style. The Salpausselkä Games, as well as the Finlandia and other skiing events, have made Lahti world-famous.

Helsinki-Lahti

DEPART HELSINKI STATION	TRAIN NUMBER	ARRIVE IN LAHTI STATION	NOTES
0802	71	0927	(1)(2)
1026	3	1153	(1)(2)
1122	73	1247	(1)(2)
1324	5	1452	(1)(2)

DEPART LAHTI STATION	TRAIN NUMBER	ARRIVE IN HELSINKI STATION	NOTES
1458	8	1628	(1)(2)
1736	10	1906	(1)(2)
1830	76	1956	(1)(2)
2041	14	2204	(1)(2)
2131	80	2258	(1)(2)

(1) Daily, including holidays
(2) Buffet car

Distance: 81 miles/130 km

Perhaps the most spectacular sight in Lahti is its 115-meter ski jump, located in the Lahti Sports Center. The jump is about a fifteen-minute walk from the tourist information office. It merits everyone's inspection. An observation platform on top of the jump can be reached by elevator and is accessible to visitors daily during summer months, and on weekends during low season. In addition to the 115-meter ski jump, there are smaller ski jumps and practice areas nearby. The ski-jump area actually is a year-round attraction for tourists. In addition to the observation platform, there is an open-air, heated swimming pool at the foot of the ski-jump complex.

The Sports Center is not the sole attraction in Lahti. In the 1920s and 1930s the city had the most powerful broadcasting station in Finland and now stands as a Radio and TV Museum. The museum contains more than a thousand items of great interest in the field of radio technology. The tourist information office has complete details.

In Lahti, general fitness is a feature of everyday life. There are illuminated trails for walking, jogging, and skiing—about forty kilometers of them—as well as non-illuminated trails. Summer weekly events include outdoor theater, concerts, a lively marketplace, and hiking.

The city is unique in that it is one of the few metropolitan areas where you can live in a one-family house in the center of the city on the shore of a lake. (We would like to suggest that the city planners of America go to Lahti to pick up a few pointers.) Much of Lahti's housing is spread over a wide area, along the city's green hillsides and lake shores. Many visitors are surprised to find Lahti so sophisticated and versatile. The infrastructure of quality department stores, good hotels, and good restaurants coupled with civic convention centers capable of handling large numbers of people are the elements of Lahti's success. Lahti is modern yet traditional.

Shopping for excellent Finnish glassware can be a full-time occupation. Numerous Lahti department stores, as well as specialty shops, feature fine Finnish glassware and other high-quality items. The city is well known for its ready-to-wear garments for both men and women. The Finnish furniture industry is centered here, and Lahti bread and beer are known all over Finland for their quality.

In summer, Lahti's cultural life includes performances in the Kariranta open-air theater and the open-air concerts at the Mukkula Tourist Center. Lahti provides an interesting as well as relaxing day-excursion site; it's a year-round attraction you shouldn't miss.

Sights to see while in town include the Historical Museum, the Museum of Military Medicine, the Ski Museum, and the Museum of Art. The City Tourist and Marketing Bureau conducts a two-hour city tour every Wednesday starting at 1700 from mid-June through mid-August.

Lahti has been described as Finland's most American city. Founded in 1905, Lahti is, historically speaking, a young city, but it has grown more rapidly than towns of similar age or older. One reason for its vigorous development is its geographic position in the center of southern Finland, at the junction of major traffic routes. Another, we might add, is its friendly, courteous people.

Day Excursion to

Tampere   CITY OF THEATERS

Depart from Helsinki Central Terminal

Distance by Train: 116 miles (187 km)
Average Train Time: 1 hour, 55 minutes
City Dialing code: 3
Tourist Office Office: Verkatehtaankatu 2, Box 487, FI-33101 Tampere
Tel: 219 6800; *Fax:* 219 6463
Hours: June-August 0830-2000 Monday-Friday; 0830-1800 Saturday; 1100-1800; Sunday. September-May 0830-1700 Monday-Friday.
Internet: http://www.tampere.fi
    To get there, walk from the rail station down Hämeenkatu Street, which lies directly in front of the station. After four blocks, just before the river, turn left to

Hatanpaan valtatie. The city tourist information office, a red brick building beside a small park, will then be in front of you.

Tampere is the youngest of the "triangle towns" of Finland, the others being Helsinki and Turku. The reference to a triangle comes from the fact that all three cities are approximately 93 miles (150 km) apart from each other. The town of Tampere was granted its charter in 1779 by Gustavus III, who was king of both Sweden and Finland at that time. From a modest start, Tampere developed into an industrial and resort center early in the nineteenth century. Today, Tampere is the third largest city in Finland and the biggest inland city in all of Scandinavia with its 180,000 inhabitants.

Tampere is a city of lakes and parks. Its two major lakes are connected by rapids flowing over three waterfalls. Tampere is considered to be a "small" city. The city center is located on a narrow isthmus that is divided by the rapids. The "smallness" actually means that all shops, stores, restaurants, and other places are within easy reach of each other, which makes Tampere an easy city to explore on foot.

Among the noteworthy places to see and visit during your day excursion in Tampere is the city's Sarkanniemi, an amusement area containing a dolphinarium, an amusement park, and a children's zoo which are open daily in summer. An aquarium, a planetarium, an observation tower, and the Sara Hilden Modern Art Museum also are located in the complex. These attractions are open daily throughout the year.

In the Sarkanniemi aquarium, you will find some 2,000 fish of more than 200 species from all over the world. There is a seal tank, too. The seals are fed daily at 1100 and again at 1600. In the planetarium, a veritable sea of 6,000 twinkling bodies will open up before you. Here you will see both past and future movements in space projected on the planetarium's dome ceiling in a thirty-minute space adventure.

The Sarkanniemi also offers a separate amusement park area complete with a roller coaster ride, big and small bumper cars, and many other attractions. The little ones in the family will love getting to know all the fluffy animals in the children's zoo. Art lovers will enjoy the Sara Hilden Art Museum, with its outstanding collection of contemporary art. The paddle-wheel steamboat *Finlandia Queen* starts its one and one-half hour cruises from the Sarkanniemi quay from June through August running daily. Need we say more—except that the Sarkanniemi is the place to be?

Another place of interest in Tampere is the revolving auditorium of the Pyynikki Summer Theater. It is world renowned and was the first of its kind when it opened in 1959. Nearby Pyynikki Park and Pispala Ridge, with their old timbered houses, also are worth visiting.

In Tampere, you can find a good cross section of Finnish architectural history. It ranges from charming wooden houses and art nouveau houses in the

Helsinki-Tampere

DEPART HELSINKI STATION	TRAIN NUMBER	ARRIVE IN TAMPERE STATION	NOTES
0658	49	0856	(1)(2)
0958	51	1157	(1)(2)
1258	53	1457	(1)(3)

DEPART TAMPERE STATION	TRAIN NUMBER	ARRIVE IN HELSINKI STATION	NOTES
1500	52	1702	(1)(3)
1800	54	2002	(1)(3)
1954	180	2154	(1)(2)
2102	58	2302	(1)(2)

(1) Daily, including holidays
(2) Buffet car
(3) Restaurant car

Distance: 116 miles/187 km

center of the city to the most modern designed office buildings and red brick factory buildings at the city's rapids. Tempere's oldest building is the Messukyla stone church, which dates back to the fifteenth century. The city's cathedral with its architecture and frescoes is a good example of Tempere's art nouveau period. A newer place of worship is the Kaleva Church, a strikingly modern construction completed in 1966. Another fine example of modern Finnish architecture is the city's main library. The Moomin-Valley Museum in the same building also is worth a visit. If you are interested in architectural design, Tampere can come up with a good serving of it.

In the center of Tampere, there is the Verkaranta Arts and Crafts Center with Finnish articles of high quality on exhibition. Close by, you can browse about in Tampere's colorful old market hall and the outside markets that surround it. If you happen to be in town during the summer (June-August), there's a concert at 1900 at the Old Library Park in the city center on Thursdays. Folk dance groups perform at 1830 on Wednesdays.

Day Excursion to

Turku

FINLAND'S FIRST CAPITAL

Depart from Helsinki Central Terminal

Distance by Train: 124 miles (200 km)
Average Train Time: 2 hours
City dailing code: 2
Turku Tourist Information: Aurakatu 4, Fin-20100
Tel: 233 6366; *Fax:* 233 6488
Hours: 0830-1800 Monday-Friday and 0900-1600 Saturday and Sunday.

Turku's tourist information office can be reached by proceeding from the rail station down Humalistonkatu (Humlegardsgatan). Turn left at Eerikinkatu and proceed for two blocks, then turn right onto Aurakatu. The tourist information office will be at your right near the city hall. If arriving at the harbor from Stockholm, check with the Silja Line desk for city information and directions to the city.

Turku is a city of contrasts, where past and present meet and blend. Finland's oldest established town, Turku celebrated its 760th anniversary in 1989. Turku was never founded; it seems it was always there. It developed naturally at the crossing of the northern trade routes at the mouth of the Aura River. The present population of approximately 165,000 is hard working, industrious, and friendly.

With a Eurailpass or Scanrailpass, you can choose from two forms of traveling to Turku. You can go by train on a day excursion from Helsinki, or you can take the Silja ferry from Stockholm. Whether you go by train or ferry, Turku deserves an extended examination because it has many interesting sights to offer.

Turku has three rail stations. Arriving from Helsinki, your train will make a brief stop at the Kupittaa suburban station before arriving in the city's main station. Do not detrain at Kupittaa. If you arrive in Turku on a day excursion from Helsinki and your train is scheduled to terminate at the ferry port (the third stop), rather than getting off at the main station (second stop), stay aboard the train and ride to the end of the line. There you can inspect the Silja Line's ferry terminal at the mouth of the Aura River and then, time permitting, visit the nearby Great Castle of Turku, the museum ship *Sigyn,* and the sailing ship *Suomen Joutsen* (the "Swan of Finland"). Return to the town either on foot or by taxi. The taxi fare is approximately 30 FIM; the walk from the port to the station should take about twenty to thirty minutes, and there's a lot to see en route. Bus service also is available. Bus No. 1 plies between the town's marketplace and the port. The bus fare is 8.00 FIM.

Tours depart the Aurakatu tourist office Monday through Saturday from mid-June through August. Check with either of the city's tourist information offices for full details regarding sightseeing opportunities in and around Turku.

The Great Castle of Turku, which is only a brief walk from the Silja Line

Helsinki-Turku

DEPART HELSINKI STATION	TRAIN NUMBER	ARRIVE IN TURKU STATION	NOTES
0634	121	0834(2)	(1)(3)
0906	123	1100	(1)(3)(6)
1106	125	1306	(1)(3)
1306	127	1506	(1)(3)
1602	133	1812	(1)(5)(6)
1734	135	1933	(1)(3)
1838	137	2041	(1)(3)

DEPART TURKU STATION	TRAIN NUMBER	ARRIVE IN HELSINKI STATION	NOTES
0640	124	0830	
0730	126	0930	(1)(3)
0900	128	1102	(1)(3)
1100	130	1302	(1)(3)(6)
1425	134	1630	(1)(3)
1550	136	1802	(1)(3)(7)

(1) Daily, including holidays
(2) Arrives at Turku Harbor 10 to 15 minutes later
(3) Light refreshments available
(4) Departs from Turku Harbor, 23 minutes earlier than from Turku Station
(5) Restaurant car
(6) Reservation obligatory
(7) Daily except Saturdays

Distance: 124 miles/200 km

terminal, was begun in the 1280s. It is the largest castle in Finland and once served as a prison, but now it provides a magnificent banquet hall for state and civic functions. Also of interest to visitors is the historical museum that is housed in the Great Castle. Its collection provides insight regarding 400 years of Finnish history. Hours of operation are 1000-1800 daily from April 16–September 15; 1000-1500 from September 16–April 15 (on Mondays 1400-1900 in winter).

An interesting museum combination is the Aboa Vetus Museum and the Ars Nova Museum. The Aboa Vetus tells of how life in Turku developed since the fourteenth century, while Ars Nova focuses on twentieth century art. Multimedia programs help guide you through the museums. The museums are open daily 0830-1900 May 1-August 31 and 1100-1900 the rest of the year.

The Turku Cathedral, another thirteenth-century structure, is open throughout the year. The Cathedral is open to visitors 0900-2000 daily from April 15-September 15 and 0900-1900 daily from September 16-April 15. Turku Cathedral, the major medieval ecclesiastical building in Finland, is regarded as the national shrine. You will see many interesting neoclassical buildings surrounding the cathedral. Turku boasts two major universities—one Finnish and one Swedish—with a combined student body exceeding 15,000.

During the early hours of the day, the bustling marketplace is full of life. There you will see brisk bargaining amid a brilliant display of flowers, fruit, vegetables, and fresh fish. Fire destroyed a major part of Turku in 1827, but Cloister Hill, a neighborhood of carpenters and stonemasons, escaped damage. Today the area houses the Cloister Hill Handicraft Museum with workshops that reflect the eighteenth and nineteenth centuries.

The word "turku" means "market place." The city, born out of the needs of commerce, is still one of the largest commercial centers in Finland. The Hansa Shopping Center, the country's largest, is adjacent to the city's marketplace and features more than one hundred shops and boutiques—plus a supermarket. Also there are hotels, theaters for movies and live performances, a gym, more than 100 restaurants, and four banks.

If you, too, are a rail travel enthusiast, be certain to stop at The Blue Train Café in the shopping center. Its decor originates from a wooden long-distance Finnish railway car built in 1952 and is typical of the Finnish passenger rail cars of the 1950s.

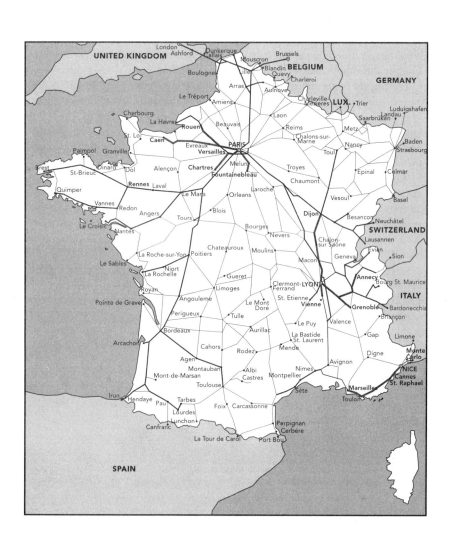

France

*"**H**ow can you be expected to govern a country that has 246 kinds of cheese?"*
—Charles de Gaulle, 1962

Now, France has 340 different kinds of cheese and more than 450 types of wines. France is Western Europe's largest and probably its most diverse country. Each of France's 22 regions has its own culture and scenery, its own style of architecture and art, its own gastronomy and lifestyle and in many cases, its own dialect. It is this delightful diversity that makes travel in France so intriguing.

The primary language is, of course, French, but most tourism officials and rail personnel speak at least *un peu* (a bit) of English. The best way to obtain the most help and cooperation in France is to first of all smile and then ask *in French, "Pardonez moi, parlez-vous Englaise?"* Even if your pronunciation makes the French language unrecognizable, the idea that you at least attempted to ask in French makes a big impression.

Banking

- **Hours:** 0900-1400/1600 Monday-Friday (Some are open Saturday and closed Monday)
- **Currency:** French Franc (FRF). The franc is divided into 100 centimes. Coins: 1, 2, 5, 10 francs; 5, 10, 20 and 50 centimes. Notes of 20, 50, 100, and 500 francs.
- **Exchange rate at press time:** 5.96 franc = $1.00 U.S.

Communications

- **Country Code:** 33
  For telephone calls within France, dial a zero (0) preceding area code.
- **Direct dial: AT&T Direct:** 0800 99 00 11
  Communications services available at post office (PTT or Bureau de Poste). Usual hours: 0800-1200 and 1430-1900 Monday-Friday; 0800-1200 Saturday Phone cards available (40 francs). To place calls from Paris to elsewhere in France, dial 16.

For more information on France contact the French Government Tourist Offices.

North America: http://www/fgtousa.org; Tel. Information: 1-900-990-0040 in the U.S. (charge is 95 cents per minute).

Chicago: 676 N. Michigan Avenue, Suite 3360, Chicago, IL 60611; (312) 751-7800; Fax: (312) 337-6339

Los Angeles: 9454 Wilshire Blvd., Suite 303, Beverly Hills, CA 90212; (310) 271-6665; Fax: (310) 276-2835

New York: 444 Madison Ave., Sixteenth Floor, New York, NY 10011; (212)838-7800; Fax: (212)838-7855

Montreal: 1981 McGill College Avenue, Suite 490, Montreal, Quebec PQ H3A 2W9 Canada; Fax: (514) 845-4868; Email: mfrance@passeport.com

Toronto: 30 St. Patrick Street, Suite 700, Toronto, Ontario M5T 3A3 Canada; Fax: (416) 979-7587

Rail Travel in France

Seemingly, France has more varieties of trains than it has cheeses. The French lead the world in rail technology and their TGV (*Train a grande vitesse*) trains hold the world speed record at 320 mph.

French National Railroads (*Societe Nationale des Chemins de Fer Francais,* or SNCF) operates some 21,100 miles of rail lines, supplemented by SNCF buses in mountainous areas.

French National Railroads accepts Eurailpass, Europass, and their own FrandePass. **Eurailpass bonuses** in France include:
* Calais, France - Dover, England   P&O European Ferries (ship)—30 percent discount
* Cherbourg/Le Havre, France - Portsmouth, England (ship)—30 percent discount
* Paris, France - London, England via Eurostar thru the Chunnel—Special Fare

Europass includes a Special Fare for travel via Eurostar (Paris - London) trains through the Channel tunnel.

The **France Pass** provides any 3 days of unlimited rail travel in France within a 1-month period. Purchase additional travel days (up to a maximum of 6 extra days) for $30 per day. The First Class France Pass is $198; Second Class, $160. Children age 4-11 pay half the adult fare and children under age 4, travel free. The France Pass also provides discounts on the Paris metro and bus pass and discounted fares on the Thalys train supplements.

Base City...

Lyon

City Dialing Code: no code required

Lyon bustles with industry, trade fairs, and business. Its origins, however, go back to Roman times. Founded in A.D. 43, its old town stands on a hillside of volcanic soil containing some of the richest archaeological sites in France and still contains an unspoiled area of fourteenth- and fifteenth-century houses.

Lyon also claims to be gastronomic capital of the world, and it has some impressive credentials to back its claim. The gastronomic tradition comes from its geographic position in the center of such great culinary areas as Bourgogne, Savoy, Beaujolais, and many others. With tongue in cheek, Lyon citizens say that the whole world cannot come from Lyon—there has to be at least a little from elsewhere. With our tongue in cheek, we note that Lyon also has several American-style fast-food establishments. Touché!

Although proud of its history and devoted to preserving its antiquity, Lyon forges ahead toward the twenty-first century with a continuous modernizing, building-and-expansion program that rivals even that of Paris. Part-Dieu, a complete and separate metropolis on the left bank of the Rhône, rises like a modern phoenix above the rest of Lyon, most of which was built during the eighteenth century. Lyon's contrasts are great. By virtue of these contrasts, Lyon is becoming one of the great cities of France and of Europe.

Arriving By Air

Satolas Airport, 15 miles (25 km) to the east of Lyon. International air service between Lyon and New York is provided by Air France. Frequent air service to Paris, Frankfurt, Brussels, and Amsterdam provides additional connections for passengers with North American destinations.

- **Airport-City Links:** Airport bus (Satobus) service to Lyon's Perrache Station. Every 20 minutes 0500-2100 Monday.-Friday.; every 30 minutes Saturday-Sunday. Journey time: about 45 minutes; fare, 46 francs.
- **Limousine** service is also available direct to most of the city's hotels. Journey time: about 45 minutes.
- **Taxis:** about 180 FRF (daytime) and 270 FRF (nighttime).
- Air France office closest to the station: 17 rue Victor Hugo. Tel: 04 72 56 22 20.

Arriving By Train

The new TGV Duplex train (it's a double-decker) service from Paris to Lyon stops at Part-Dieu before going on to terminate at Perrache, and rail service to Switzerland departs from the Part-Dieu station. Otherwise, Perrache handles all major train traffic.

The facilities provided by **Gare de Perrache** have been expanded by the addition of an ultramodern annex appended to the front of the present station building. This annex houses a bus terminal, the terminal for the city's metro system, and a bevy of offices, shops, snack bars, and restaurants. The terminal for the airport bus and local taxi services is also located in the annex.

Access to the annex is gained by escalators immediately in front of the station's main doors. Pedestrian traffic, moving from the station through the annex and into the city, utilizes another escalator system to exit into Lyon's, Place Carnot. The square, with its statues, fountains, and waterfalls, is one of the city's showplaces and an excellent place to spend a few quiet moments.

Gare de Perrache, together with its annex, is a large and sprawling complex. Access to train platforms is through two underground passageways—SORTIE NORD and SORTIE SUD (north and south exits)—and escalators that descend from the ticket office and the waiting-room areas. Use of either passageway will take you to platform No. 1 and, in turn, to exits leading to the street side of the station. Fortunately, there's an abundance of pictographs throughout the station.

If you have baggage, be prepared to carry it. Baggage carts for passenger use are not available, probably due to the platform stairways. The escalators serve only the tracks reserved for express-train service.

There are times in the Perrache station when two trains are scheduled to depart on the same track—one in each direction, of course. Check for the departure position (north or south) of the day-excursion trains; otherwise, you might be standing at the wrong end of the track as your train departs. Train-departure signs are displayed in the underground passageways at the bottom of the platform stairways. The north passageway, however, will not list a south-bound departure, nor the south a northbound one, unless it is a train running through Lyon Perrache and not originating there. All train departures are displayed over the ticket windows in the main station hall.

The **station restaurant,** located on the north end alongside track A, next to the north-passageway staircase, has a convenient feature—a take-out window à la Wendy's. Look for the sign PROVISIONS A EMPORTER.

Money exchange services are available at the Thomas Cook Bureau de Change in the Perrache station. Hours: 0800-2000 daily. From the train information area, follow the pictographs and proceed either by escalator or elevator to the station's TGV departure lounge on the second level.

To reach the **bank,** use the escalator on the side of the station annex facing

Place Carnot, the city square immediately in front of the station. When you reach ground level, walk down the steps alongside the waterfall to the fountain at the bottom. At this point, turn to the right between the fountain and the waterfall, and then proceed across the square. When you approach the first street, you will see the bank across the intersection to your left. This is the only bank in the vicinity of Place Carnot.

Tourist information within the Perrache station: annex on the first floor above ground level. Use the escalator located in the front of the station and follow the conventional "I" signs to the office. Hours: 0900-1300 and 1400-1800 Monday.-Friday; 0900-1700 Saturday

Train Information office is within the main building of the Perrache station. Use the main entrance, turn right once you have entered the hall, and proceed through an archway to the train information office. Hours: 0800–1920 Monday-Saturday; 0900–1200 and 1400–1830 Sunday/holidays.

The French National Railroads produces *Le Fiches Horaires* (mini-timetables) which are free. A selection is normally kept immediately outside the train information office door and inside the office on the left-hand wall. These timetables may eliminate standing in line to make inquiries.

Train reservations may be made in the train information office at any one of the operating windows. We did not find the train information staff too adept at English. Consequently, we recommend submitting your reservation requests in writing.

Rail pass validation is handled at any window in the train information office. Write the starting and ending dates on a piece of paper and obtain concurrence from the attendant before the entry is made on your rail pass.

Transportation between Gare de Perrache and Gare Part-Dieu is facilitated by Lyon's ultramodern metro (subway) system that serves both rail stations.

Tourist Information/Hotel Reservations

Lyon Tourist Information (central office), Pavillon du Tourisme, No. 25 Place Bellecour (two Metro stops from Gare de Perrache).
Tel: 04 72 77 69 69; *Fax:* 78 42 04 32
Hours: 0900-1300 and 1400-1800 Monday-Friday; 0900-1700 Saturday

The city also maintains a tourist information office in the Perrache station and in the old town at Avenue Adolphe Max next to the Metro St. Jean.

Hotel reservations for within the city of Lyon may be made at any of the tourist information offices for a nominal fee. Advance hotel reservations for other parts of France, 30 francs.

Getting Around in Lyon

Lyon has an ultramodern metro (subway) system. One of its main terminals is in Gare de Perrache; there's another in the rail terminal at Part-Dieu. Trains run every three to ten minutes from 0500-2400 daily. A single-ride ticket costs 7.50 francs; a book of 10 tickets, 65 francs; 1-day tourist tickets, 24 francs.

Sightseeing/Attractions/Tours

Lyon Vision operates a 2-hour sightseeing bus tour of Lyon April 1-October 31. The buses are equipped with headsets providing explanations of the tour sights in five languages including English. Fare for adults,110 francs; children under age 16 is 55 francs. Buses depart daily at 0915, 1415, and 1615 from Place Bellecour No. 25. Ask for a folder at the tourist office.

Or, join the Lyon Tourist Office's guided tour, "A Stroll Through Old Lyon," which is conducted on foot over a 2-hour period. Departures are daily throughout the tourist season at a charge of 50 francs. An evening tour also is available. Check with the tourist office for the daily schedule.

Le Vieux Lyon (Old Lyon) is a charming area to visit. For your convenience, use the *funiculaires* (funicular) to gain the summit. Take bus No. 44 from the station annex and ask the driver to let you off at the St. Jean bus stop. The funicular station is located at rue St. Jean and avenue Max, immediately to the left of **Place St. Jean.**

Old Lyon is said to be the most extensive Renaissance area in France. It covers about one mile along the right bank of the Saone River at the foot of **Fourviére Hill.**

While visiting the Fourviére Hill area, check out Lyon's answer to Paris's Eiffel Tower located behind the basilica. The Lyonese claim their tower is five feet higher than the Parisians', and it is—above sea level, that is.

Day Excursions

Contrasts continue in the selection of day excursions from Lyon, the third largest city in France. A scant 25 miles short of Geneva, the town of **Annecy** and its crystal-clear lake wait to charm you. Annecy's old quarter, lying back from the lake, has one of Europe's finest marketplaces.

Dijon vies with Lyon for gastronomic honors. During your visit to Dijon, you will want to shop for its world-renowned product, mustard. But that's not all it has to offer. The history of Burgundy breathes in Dijon, its capital, and you will want to catch its scent.

Grenoble is situated in the midst of a breathtaking panorama of mountains. A ride on its téléphérique will provide an even more remarkable view of the city and the countryside surrounding it. Via TGV from the Part-Dieu station in Lyon, Grenoble is only 70 minutes away!

Vienne, 20 miles to the south, is almost a suburb of Lyon, but it is very different. It has some of the best preserved Roman buildings and amphitheaters in all of Europe and one of the world's finest restaurants, La Pyramide.

Train connections to other base cities from Lyon

TO:	DEPART*	ARRIVE	TRAIN NUMBER	NOTES
Milan	0720	1250	EC 142/IC 503	(1)
	0421	1455	5433/EC 17	(2)(6)
	1851	2350	EC 138	(5)
Nice	0957	1543	5001	(2)
	1206	1742	5003	
Paris	0844	1104	TGV 612	(3)
	1149	1404	TGV 618	
	1549	1804	TGV 624	
	1748	2004	TGV 628	
Rome	0708	1855	EC 142/IC 503	(1)
Zürich	0739	1257	5750/IC721	(4)
	1226	1753	5757/IC 533	(4)
	1721	2253	5760/IC 743	(4)

* All departures from Lyon Part-Dieu station unless otherwise noted.
Daily departures unless otherwise noted. Make reservations for all departures.
(1) Transfer in Torino Porta Nuova and Milano Centrale
(2) From Lyon Perrache Station
(3) Daily, except Sunday
(4) Transfer in Genève
(5) Global fares apply
(6) Transfer in Chambery

Day Excursion to

Annecy ALPINE LAKE

Depart from Lyon Part-Dieu Station

Distance by Train: 99 miles (130 km)
Average Train Time: 2 hours, 25 minutes
City Dialing Code: 450
Annecy Tourist Information, Bonlieu Center, 1 rue Jean Jaurés
Tel: 450 45 00 33; *Fax:* 450 51 87 20.
Internet: http://www.lac-annecy.com
Hours: 0900–1830 daily, 0900–1200 and 1500–1800 on Sundays (from April–November). If closed, go to the bureau of information in the city hall, which is open until 1900 daily, except Sunday and holidays.

Reach the information office via bus No. 1 from in front of the station to Place de la Liberation, where you'll find the office in the Bonlieu Center. On foot, use the underground pedestrian passageway to the left of the station as you exit. Continue to walk a block ahead to rue Vaugelas. Here, you turn left and walk 4 blocks to where rue Vaugelas ends at place de la Liberation (a large open area).

Annecy (pronounced "Ahn-see") still remains largely undiscovered by North Americans, although it has long been a retreat of the French themselves. A crystal-clear lake, a spectacular view of the Alps, foothills that touch the town, an old quarter where quaint canals cross arcaded lanes, an engaging market selling everything from apples to zinnias—these are Annecy.

Annecy is a health spa as well as a popular holiday center. It has innumerable hotels, casinos, and, best of all, the lake. The basin in which the lake lies is so protected against pollution that the latter is almost transparent in its purity. The Thiou River, flowing out of the lake and through the old quarter of Annecy, runs through canals and meanders around islands en route to the Rhône and the Mediterranean.

Tour-boat operators offer a wide variety of tours around the "sea" of Annecy. Rapid tours, lasting just over an hour, have frequent departures. The more vigorous traveler can opt to cycle around it. Either mode will provide a spectacular view of alpine meadows, rivers, waterfalls, and the bountiful natural riches surrounding the lake.

Visit the town hall, **Hôtel de Ville,** just a short walk along **quai Chappuis.** But exercise caution when crossing the street—the locals stage a "Grand Prix" on occasion.

The tourist information office has several brochures describing the city and its lake, including an illustrated booklet, *Through the Old Town.* The office also contains bulletin boards with numerous announcements of cultural events in Annecy.

Lyon—Annecy

DEPART LYON PART-DIEU STATION	TRAIN NUMBER	ARRIVE IN ANNECY STATION	NOTES
0637	5401	0904	(1)
0811	5403	1024	(1)

DEPART ANNECY STATION	TRAIN NUMBER	ARRIVE IN LYON PART-DIEU STATION	NOTES
1554	5424	1812	(1)
1713	5426	1923	(1)
1905	TGV 938	2105	(1)(2)

(1) Daily, including holidays
(2) Transfer in Aix les Bains

Distance: 99 miles/160 km

From the bridge crossing the Thiou River, you will catch your first glimpse of the **Palais de l'Isle** sitting astride the river. As its name suggests, this curious palace was an island stronghold. It remains one of the most arresting monuments of Annecy. Its oldest sections date from the twelfth century. At one time it housed Annecy's municipal offices, the high judges' private apartments, and it also served as a dungeon.

Beyond the Palais de l'Isle lies the enchanting marketplace of Annecy's **Old Quarter.** A network of narrow streets filled with every type of shop imaginable is augmented on market days by hundreds of stands erected in the streets, where only pedestrians are allowed to pass.

Along with the chic boutiques and appliance shops, the marketplace vends every imaginable food product, pastry, flower, and condiment. Lavender, picked in the Alps, and locally manufactured culinary wares are also available.

The picturesque medieval appeal of Annecy stems from both the French and Italian civilizations as a result of having changed sides several times during its 2,000-year existence. The area became a part of the French empire in 1792, although it reverted to the Italian Kingdom of Sardinia in 1815. It was not until 1860 that all of Savoy, where Annecy is situated, was again reunited with France as a reward to the French for helping Italy in her war with Austria.

Annecy slipped quietly into the twentieth century with the introduction of TGV train service directly from Paris. The distance from the Gare de Lyon station in Paris to Annecy is covered in just three and a half hours—a trip that formerly consumed at least eight hours. Currently, there are four trains daily, making the possibility of a day excursion to Annecy from Paris a reality.

Departing Paris on a TGV at 0642, you would arrive in Annecy at 1030; boarding TGV 938 in Annecy at 1921, you would be back in Paris by 2300. It's a full day but a fun-packed one, too.

Day Excursion to

Dijon
CUTTING THE MUSTARD

Depart from Lyon Gare de Perrache or Part Dieu

Distance by Train: 119 miles (190 km)
Average Train Time: 1 hour, 30 minutes
City Dialing Code: 380
Dijon Tourist Information, Place Darcy
Tel: 3 80 44 11 44
Hours: May 1–November 15: 0900–2100 daily; 0900–1300 and 1400–1900 daily the remainder of the year.

Exit through the main doors of the station and bear to the right onto Avenue Maréchal Foch. Average walking time: 5 minutes. Use the Hotel Climat de France as a landmark. Proceed along Avenue Foch for one block. As you approach Place Darcy, you will find the tourist information office on the left-hand side of the street.

Say "Dijon" to any American who likes to eat well and he will respond, "mustard." Mention Dijon to any Frenchman, and his eyes will roll and his hands will fly as he describes the gastronomic wonders of the Burgundian city's pastry shops, restaurants, cassis (black-currant liquor), *and* mustard—but not necessarily in that order. Dijon, the ancient capital city of Burgundy, has something for everyone. It sets a fine table, lives its history, and preserves its art.

Dijon is the gateway to France's most famous wine region. It became important historically in 1015 when Robert I, Duke of Burgundy, made it the capital of his duchy. The city's most brilliant era, however, was from the fourteenth through the eighteenth centuries, when it gained most of its art and beautiful monuments.

Dijon cannot be visited in a hurry. Actually, an entire day can easily be spent visiting its **Palace of Burgundy Dukes** and the **Museum of Fine Arts,** which is housed in the palace. The museum, founded in 1783, is the most important in France after the Louvre in Paris. Don't miss the huge banquet room of the palace. Identified as the Guards Room, the tombs of the dukes are located here. They provide some descriptive background as to how the populace rated the four "Valois" Dukes of Burgundy: Philip the Bold, Jean the

Lyon—Dijon

DEPART LYON PERRACHE STATION	TRAIN NUMBER	ARRIVE IN DIJON STATION	NOTES
0740(2)		0936	(1)(5)
0916(3)	5070	1104	(1)
1224	6634/35	1405	(3)

DEPART DIJON STATION	TRAIN NUMBER	ARRIVE IN LYON PERRACHE STATION	NOTES
1535	6132/33	1707(3)	(3)
1705	5009/6134/35	1845(3)	(1)
1927	5073	2137(3)	(4)
2047	6106	2228(2)	(4)

(1) Daily, including holidays
(2) Perrache Station
(3) Part-Dieu Station
(4) Daily, except Saturday
(5) Arrives 0946 on Saturdays, Sundays, and holidays

Distance: 122 miles/197 km

Fearless, Philip the Good, and Charles the Rash.

Modern art has made an entry in the palace in the form of a department housing an exhibition of impressionist works from the Granville collection. There's also a gallery devoted completely to the works of local artists from the Burgundy area.

The city is particularly proud of its artists, among them François Pompon (1855–1933). Sculptor Pompon began his career as a Burgundy marble cutter. He attended Dijon's school of fine arts before further studies and apprenticeships in Paris. He sculpted 300-plus works, almost all depicting animals. His fresh, clear style has astonishing simplicity.

Engrossing as Dijon's works of art can be, don't forget to break for lunch—another Dijon work of art that can't be hurried. Whatever entree you select, we are certain that you will want to enhance it with a dab or so of Dijon mustard. A word of caution, make that dab a small one and determine first if it suits your palate. Dijon's favorite condiment has some varieties that exceed the fire power of any Mexican pepper.

Dijon's railway station is unique in that its main hall is circular. Train information is available in the area marked "information voyageurs" on the right as you enter the main hall of the station. Hours: 0830–1900 Monday-Friday; 0830–1830 Saturday. A map showing the location of the city's tourist information office in relation to the rail station is displayed prominently in the station's foyer.

The tourist office displays a room-availability list immediately outside the office entrance. This depicts the number of vacancies existing in the various hotels of Dijon and its surrounding areas. Within the tourist office, you will find hotel-reservations facilities and money-exchange services. There is a nominal fee for each call within Dijon to secure hotel reservations.

The **Saint Benigne Cathedral** probably holds the record for being destroyed and rebuilt more times than any other place of worship in France— four times since its origins back in the sixth century! The present church was built between 1281 and 1325.

Also constructed in the thirteenth century, the **Church of Notre Dame** in Dijon fared better over the centuries. Both edifices are typical Burgundian Gothic.

Day Excursion to

Grenoble AND THE BASTILLE CABLEWAY

Depart from Lyon Part-Dieu Station

Distance by Train: 80 miles (129 km)
Average Train Time: 1 hour, 23 minutes (1+10 via TGV)
City Dialing Code: 476
Grenoble Tourist Information, 14, rue de la République Tel: 04 76 42 41 41; Fax: 04 76 51 28 69
Hours: 0900–1230 and 1330–1900 (until 1800 during winter) Monday through Saturday. It is also open on Sundays from 1000–1200.

Located some distance from the railway station in a labyrinth of winding streets. Reach it by either of the tramways in the direction of Grand Place, Universités, or Auguste Delaune. Your stop is Hubert Dubedout/Maison du Tourisme. Maison du tourisme signs are displayed at many intersections.

Grenoble will remind many North Americans of Denver, Colorado. Lodged on a wide plain, butted against the swift waters of the Isere River, and backdropped by the French Alps, it is a breathtaking scene of man and nature in concert.

Known as "The capital of the French Alps," Grenoble lies at the feet of three majestic mountain ranges at the crossroads of a number of large valleys. Its Isere River was first bridged by Roman legion engineers in 43 B.C.; Napoleon

Lyon—Grenoble

DEPART LYON PART-DIEU STATION	TRAIN NUMBER	ARRIVE IN GRENOBLE STATION	NOTES
0710(2)	5453	0831	(4)
0817	5455	0941	(6)
1015	5457	1138	(6)
1227	5459	1350	(1)
1415(2)	5463	1544	(1)
1630(2)	5465	1800	(1)
1720(2)	6304	1838	(1)

DEPART GRENOBLE STATION	TRAIN NUMBER	ARRIVE IN LYON PART-DIEU STATION	NOTES
1600	5466	1726	(1)
1658	5468	1819	(1)
1725	—	9010	(1)
1814	5470	1932(2)	(5)
1915	5472	2045	(1)
2106	—	2259(3)	(1)

(1) Daily, including holidays
(2) Part-Dieu Station
(3) Perrache Station
(4) Monday–Friday only
(5) Daily, except Saturday
(6) Monday through Saturday

Distance: 80 miles/129 km

---

employed the concealment of the area to move his armies into the Italian campaign; and modern mountaineering was born on its towering peaks.

Grenoble unfolds the past as well as the present in its monuments and art. The **Musée de Grenoble** houses one of the finest collections of old and modern masters in France. The classics of Rubens and Watteau, along with those of Utrillo and Picasso, adorn its galleries. The **Cathedral of Grenoble** dates to the twelfth century. Its early **Renaissance Palace of Justice** was built in the sixteenth century.

The **University of Grenoble** was founded in 1339—making it one of the oldest in Europe—and is considered by many academics as one of the best in France. Grenoble's student population exceeds 40,000, more than 8,000 of whom are foreigners from 150 different countries. With university students nearby snow-covered slopes, it was inevitable that winter sports should develop. The 1968 Winter Olympics were hosted by Grenoble, and many other sports gatherings, including the Davis Cup finals, have taken place in the city's magnificent Sports' Hall.

To ride the **téléphérique de la Bastille,** wend your way to the banks of the Isere River and then to the Jardin de Ville (city garden). From practically any point on the river front, you can see the "bubbles" of the cableway flying up and down the hillside in groups of three. A photographic hint: Ride the rear "bubble" up and the front one down for better views of Grenoble and its environs.

The terminal at the top of **Guy Pape Park** provides a spectacular view of the city and its surrounding countryside. Dominating the heights is the **Bastille,** a nineteenth century fortress housing a military museum and a restaurant featuring traditional, regional cuisine. On a suitable day, you may opt to descend on foot through the Guy Pape Park to the **Jardin des Dauphins** (Dauphins' garden) on the banks of the Isere.

TGV service makes a Grenoble day excursion from Paris practical. Departing Paris at 0648 places you in Grenoble at 0944, depart Paris at 0968 and arrive at 1254. There are six TGVs departing from Paris Gare de Lyon Monday-Friday and three TGVs on Saturday and Sunday. The last daily TGV returning to Paris departs Grenoble at 1819 and arrives at Gare de Lyon in Paris at 2127. On Sunday, the latest TGV departs Grenoble at 2030 for arrival at 2337 in Paris.

Day Excursion to

Vienne   OF ROMAN ORIGIN

Depart from Lyon Gare de Perrache on Part-Dieu

Distance by Train: 20 miles (32 km)
Average Train Time: 24 minutes
City Dialing Code: 474
Vienne Tourist Information: No. 3 Cours Brillier Tel: 04 74 85 12 62
Hours: Mid-June-mid-September, 0900–1230 and 1330–1900 Monday-Saturday; 1000–1200 and 1430–1800 Sunday

About a 10-minute walk from the railway station. Depart from the statue in front of the rail station down Cours Brillier to the tourist pavilion on the left-hand side of the street.

Turn a corner in Vienne and you turn a page of history. Roman in origin, this charming city lies on the Rhône River to the south of Lyon but so close (20 miles) that it could be mistaken easily for a Lyon suburb. Such is not the case. Vienne is distinctly different.

Among the remains of this once-great city of the Roman Empire, and dating from the first century B.C. to the end of the third century A.D., stand a temple, an amphitheater, and a pyramid that was once the center of a Roman circus. Roman Vienne spread to both sides of the Rhône River, where ruins of a warehouse and baths have been uncovered.

A statue to the fallen during 1914 and 1940 stands in the square fronting the railway station. Take a moment to pause and reflect here. Note, too, that many of the names have family extensions in North America.

Attendants at the tourist office will assist by marking a suggested walking tour on your map. The majority of the city's sights, concentrated in the old north quarter, allow visitors to move quickly from one attraction to another.

Collections of bronze, ceramics, and jewels are on display at the **Museum of Fine Arts.** Perhaps the most impressive Roman ruin of Vienne is the **Temple of Augustus and Livia,** which is perfectly preserved. One almost expects toga-clad senators to step through its portals and into a local pastry shop. The temple is surrounded by more modern structures in the center of the city. No doubt the close proximity of other buildings has helped shield and preserve the temple through the ages.

The great **amphitheater of Vienne** was cleverly built into the slope of the hillside on which the town now stands. In its original state, it could hold 13,000 spectators. It was covered entirely by soil in the first century, but excavations between 1922 and 1938, when activities were curtailed by World War II, have brought to life some very beautiful remnants of statuary, coins, and jewels from the era.

The amphitheater, modernized with stage lighting, is now the scene of many fine theatrical presentations in Vienne for thousands of spectators throughout the summer season, including the Vienne Jazz Festival. Similar lighting of the Temple of Augustus and Livia makes an evening visit to the city a memorable one.

The pyramid was erected in the center of a Roman circus to guide the racing chariots, but it was never completed. For centuries it was believed to be the tomb of Pontius Pilate, who, according to a twelfth-century legend, had died in Vienne while living there in exile. Little else remains of the circus site, but it stirs your imagination.

The city's famous restaurant, **La Pyramide** (named for its location on Boulevard Fernand-Point at the former Roman circus), has been endorsed by many gourmets as the world's finest. Reservations are recommended at La Pyramide, which is closed every Wednesday and Thursday at noon in season and annually from November through mid-December. Call ahead on 74 53 01 96 or fax 04 74 85 69 73. It's expensive, but you only live once!

When departing from the main part of town, you can reach Vienne's pyramid and the restaurant La Pyramide by taking the main road running to the south, Cours de Verdun (RN 7), to Boulevard Fernand-Point, on your right. When proceeding from the tourist information office at Cours Brillier, head south on Quai Riondet and turn left onto Boulevard Fernand-Point.

Vienne also has its share of medieval buildings. Most of them are still being lived in and look very much as they probably did back in the fifteenth and sixteenth centuries.

Although its industrial history is not as well known, for more than 200 years Vienne was an important center for textiles, especially carded wool and a cloth called "Renaissance." The Musée de la Draperie, housed in the Saint Germain building, is worth a visit. Hours: April 1-September 30, 1430–1830; closed Mondays and May 1. Still a center of a lively wool trade, the town manufactures chemicals and flourishes from other industries, too. The people of Vienne are justly proud of their industrial endeavors set in the midst of a richly wooded countryside.

Lyon–Vienne

DEPART LYON STATION	ARRIVE IN VIENNE STATION	NOTES
0756(2)	0819	(4)
0835(2)	0856	(1)
1221(2)	1240	(1)

DEPART VIENNE STATION	ARRIVE IN LYON STATION	NOTES
1400	1438(2)	(1)
1657	1721(2)	(1)
1750	1808(2)	(6)
1929	1950(3)	(1)
2012	2037(2)	(5)
2200	2222(2)	(1)

(1) Daily, including holidays
(2) Perrache Station
(3) Part-Dieu Station
(4) Daily except Sundays and holidays
(5) Daily except Saturdays
(6) Monday through Friday only

Distance: 20 miles/32 km

Base City...

Nice . . .
and the French Riviera

City Dialing Code: No code required
Internet: http://www/nice-coteazur.org

Nice, "the gateway to southern Europe," has changed more in 50 years than it did over the past two centuries. According to Nice's Convention and Visitors' Bureau, Nice's "history advances, but its past remains."

In the days before World War I, the Riviera was a haven for rich Russian dukes and English lords seeking escape from the rigors of a more northerly winter. When such aristocracy, particularly the Russian version, began to fade from the scene, summer became the popular season, bringing with it hordes of Americans and others seeking the sun and all sorts of fun, including the nocturnal varieties.

The Riviera began to change. Towns and fishing villages that earlier visitors knew have grown together into an almost continuous resort town stretching from Saint-Raphael to the Italian border. Nice, the largest community in the area, lies about halfway between these two points and is our base city for numerous day excursions in either direction. However, because of the relatively short distances between points and excellent rail service, one could select any one of the day excursions (Cannes, Monte Carlo, or Saint-Raphael) as a base city.

Arriving By Air

Nice Côte d'Azur Airport, 4 miles west of the city.

The airport has a convenient *Rendezvous* (meeting place) just beyond the arrival gates and a Bureau des Change (**money exchange**) and **information** desk farther into the international terminal, Terminal 1. Terminal 2 is for flights within France. If you are not certain of your transportation mode to your final destination, make inquiry at the airport's information desk or at one of the airline counters inside.

Airport-City Links: Bus and **limousine** service is available between the airport and the railway station. Bus fare: 21 francs; departs every 30 minutes. It makes three stops between the airport and the station; the limousine goes direct. Journey time: about 30 minutes by bus; 20 minutes by limousine. Connections for both can be made in the front-left section of the airport building as you exit.

Taxis are available at the exit from the airport terminals. Fare between airport and rail station: 120-150 francs. Journey time: about 15 minutes. Taxi service between the airport in Nice and the resorts of Cannes and Monte Carlo is also available.

Several resort hotels offer free or reduced-rate transportation to their locations along the Riviera. Inquire at the airport information desk.

Arriving By Train

Nice Central Station—Gare SNCF Centrale, avenue Thiers Tel: 04 36 35 35 35

Nice is a major rail terminus for the Mediterranean region, with 20 daily connections from France's largest cities and 11 from other countries.

The exterior of the central station in Nice is deceptive. There is a lot more activity, more facilities than those you see. Although it is smaller than most major train terminals in Europe, it seems to function equally as well, with the exception of long ticket lines. Here again, a rail pass will prove to be an invaluable convenience.

Automatic lockers are available (Tel: 06 30 23 30).

If your luggage is lost or stolen, if you missed your train, or if you need help with a handicapped or elderly passenger, don't panic. The railway station provides a helpful service—the **SOS Voyageurs SNCF** (Travelers' SOS Service). Tel: 04 93 16 02 61 Monday-Friday, 0900–1200 and 1500–1800, for assistance.

Money-exchange office is outside the main station and on the right as you exit from the trains. (Tel: 04 93 82 13 00). Hours: June-September, 0700–2300 daily; remainder of the year, 0800–2000 daily.

Train-information, reservations and rail pass validation office is inside the main station on the extreme left side when exiting from the trains. The office is marked RESERVATION INFORMATION—RENSEIGNEMENTS. Hours: 0800–1830 Monday-Saturday; 0800–1130 and 1400–1730 Sunday/holidays (Tel: 08 36 35 35 35).

Remember, when having your pass validated, write out the starting and ending dates on a piece of paper and get the railroad clerk to agree to the correctness of the dates before the validation information is entered onto your rail pass.

Tourist Information and Hotel Reservations

Office du Tourisme et des Congres, Avenue Thiers, B.P. 4079, 06302 Nice Cedex 4, France.

Tel: 04 93 92 82 82; Fax: 06 93 92 82 98.

Hours: June-September: 0800–2000 daily; remainder of the year: Monday-Saturday, 0800–1900; 0800–1200 Sunday. Nominal fee for hotel/pension reservations.

Located outside the station and beyond the train administration office on the left.

- The **Office du Tourisme** (Tourist Bureau) has four offices in the city of Nice, plus one in the international terminal at the airport. The one in the railway station can probably best serve all of your needs. If you need to call ahead to the tourist office in the rail station, the number is 04 93 87 07 07 or 04 94 92 14 48 00, Fax: 04 93 14 48 03.
- **Hotel reservations** are handled by the tourist office on avenue Thiers. Room vacancies in Nice and throughout the Riviera are extremely hard to come by during the months of June, July, and August, as well as during the winter holiday period. If possible, reserve your accommodations well in advance by writing ahead.

  Hotel rates in Nice and the rest of the Riviera vary according to the season of the year, so be specific when requesting reservations. The most expensive time of the year is between late March and the end of October. If you are looking for bargain rates, late October through January is when the rates are lowest.
- **American Express,** 11 Promenade des Anglais(Tel: 04 93 16 53 53) Second bus stop en route from the rail station to the airport. Hours: May–September, 0900–2000 daily; remainder of the year, Monday-Friday. 0900–2000; Saturday, 0900–1800, with a lunch break from 1300–1400. Bank holidays it is open from 1000–1800.

Getting Around in Nice

The best way to get around in Nice is on foot, by bicycle/scooter, or by bus. *Bus Services:*
- Agence Sunbus, 10, avenue Felix Faure
  (Tel: 04 93 16 52 10 (0715-1900 Monday-Friday; 0715-1800 Saturday)
- Auto Nice Transport, 14, rue Francois Guizol
  (Tel: 04 93 56 35 40; Fax 93 56 26 90)
- Glaude Transport Service (GTS)
  (Tel: 04 92 29 50 19; Fax: 04 92 29 50 10)
- Bikes: Arnaud, Town Centre, (Tel: 04 93 87 88 55 (bikes, mopeds, scooters)
- Nicea Location Rent, Town Centre, (Tel:04 93 82 42 71; Fax 04 93 87 76 36)

Sights/Attractions/Tours

Nice boasts more than 300 hotels and 600 restaurants. Most of these facilities are located in the modern section of Nice, west of the Paillon River, which divides the town in two.

The Riviera is noted for its spectacular scenery. Every proper ingredient of sea, shore, cliffs, and mountains is present. Grapes and flowers are the predominant crops of its highly cultivated farmlands. It is one of the great flower-growing areas of Europe and probably the most famous center in the world for perfume production.

The Riviera is also a center for modern art. The works of many twentieth-century artists can be found in its numerous museums and exhibition halls. Picasso spent the last years of his life in a villa overlooking the Mediterranean.

In selecting Nice as the base city for the day excursions in the Riviera area, we considered the variety of features and attractions that the city has to offer, and they are many.

In the maze of its narrow streets, you will discover, in variations of light, shade, and fragrances, the **fish market,** the **Palais Lascaris,** the public squares of the city—each one different in function but all with an air of grace and function—and, in a sudden burst of sunlight, the beaches.

To the east, the old town and port offer many attractions to those who have a feeling for the past. At 300 feet above the **old town,** in a public park where once a fortress stood, the views are unforgettable. Streets and houses in the old town date from the seventeenth and eighteenth centuries.

The **March-aux-Fleurs** (Flower Market), one of the most beautiful and truly native sights in the old town of Nice, is held daily except Monday in the **Cours Saleya,** a block south of the **Prefecture Palace** near the opera. At Cours Saleya, you'll discover what makes Nice so fragrant and colorful. You will also discover what makes the cuisine of the area so appetizing: A fruit-and-vegetable market flourishes right in the midst of the floral beauty. Mondays are a bit different in the Cours Saleya, since that's when the market is reserved for antique dealers. But, here again, is another opportunity to delve into the priceless things that make Nice so nice.

There are ten casinos within 40 miles of Nice and three international ski resorts only 2 hours away. The world-famous **Nice Carnival** takes place every February. Other festive events, however, are to be found in Nice throughout the year. The King Carnival takes place just before Lent and rivals New Orleans' Mardi Gras.

Turn from the sea in Nice and your eyes confront **Mont Alban** and its fortress overhanging the harbor. If you choose to go to the Alpine area behind the city, there's a charming narrow-gauge railroad, **Chemin de Fer de Provence** (Railroad of Provence), that will transport you through rocky gorges and sheer cliffs and Lingostiere, on the invasion route used by Napoleon, to an exceptional panorama of the Alps and the Mediterranean Sea.

For another train ride, this one within the city, board the **Nice "little train"** at its station on the Promenade des Anglais for a scenic ride through the shady, narrow streets of the Old Town to **Castle Hill** for a vista of the *Baie des Anges* (Bay of Angels) and the Port of Nice.

Train Connections to Other Base Cities from Nice

TO:	DEPART	ARRIVE	TRAIN NUMBER	NOTES
Brussels (Midi)	1835	0947	1170	(2)
Lyon (Part-Dieu)	1030	1541	5002	
	1730	2305	5016	
Milan	0711	1345	1142, 1143	(1)
	1004	1450	IC 343	
	1826	2300	347, 348	
Munich	1000	2230	IC 343	(3)
Paris (Lyon)	0647	1321	TGV 842	
	1256	1922	TGV 846	
Rome	0821	1656	6476	(6)
	2035	0648	369	
Zürich	0740	1853	IC 525	(4)
	1146	2153	IC 343	(5)

Daily departures unless otherwise noted. Make reservations for all departures.

(1) June 2 through September 28
(2) Departs 1835 on Saturday and Monday. Train number 1180
(3) Change in Milan to EC 83
(4) Change in Milan to IC 382
(5) Change in Milan to 343
(6) Change in Genova to IC 525

Day Excursions

With Nice as their pivot point, four wonderful day excursions have been selected. **Cannes** was picked for its beaches and bikinis (or something even less); **Marseilles**, melting pot of the Mediterranean, because of its flare for bouillabaisse and its Bogart background; **Monaco (Monte Carlo)** for its coastline and casino; and **Saint-Raphael**—the resort on the Riviera with something for everyone—and at popular prices.

Day Excursion to

Cannes

TOP OF THE RIVIERA

Depart from Nice Central Station

Distance by Train: 19 miles (31 km)
Average Train Time: 25 minutes
City Dialing Code: No code required
Cannes Tourist Information: Cannes Syndicat d'Iniative in the rail station, Officé de Tourisme, Place de la Gare, 06 400
Tel: 93 39 24 53; *Fax:* 93 99 84 23
Hours: 0900-1900 daily
    Reach it by turning left in the main station hall, then take the stairs located immediately outside. Elevator service is also available. Look for the sign that reads, SERVICES DU TOURISME DE LA VILLE DE CANNES, SYNDICAT D'INITIATIVE ACCUEIL DE FRANCE, SYNDICAT DES HOTELIERS.

- **Cannes Syndicat d'Iniative, Palais des Festivals**, blvd. de la Croisette, across from the Majestic Hotel.
  Hours: 1830 Monday-Saturday; during July-August, 0900-1830 Monday-Friday; 0900-2000 Saturday-Sunday
- **American Express,** 3 blvd. de la Croisette 06 400
  Hours: 0900-1800 Monday-Friday.

Cannes has been described as a magnet that attracts the famous, the rich, and the dreamers. It also has a reputation of being impossibly expensive. No doubt this is true of **La Croisette**—the waterfront boulevard of Cannes lined with sandy beaches, extravagant restaurants, and elegant hotels. But this reputation does not apply to all of Cannes.

Cannes is a large resort with an official list of more than 5,000 hotel rooms within its city limits and that many again in its suburbs. A hundred yards or so back from the waterfront, hotels charge a fraction of the rates extracted from the famous, the rich—and the dreamers—who insist on living at the water's edge.

The Cannes railway station is modern and efficient. All services are grouped conveniently in or near its main hall. As you exit from the track area, you can reach the **train information and reservations office** via the escalator to your right. Summer hours: Monday-Saturday 0900–1230 and 1400–1830; winter hours: 0900–1900 Monday-Friday. Coin-operated baggage lockers are available on the main level at either end of the station.

Walking through Cannes is enjoyable and easy. Certainly no one would want to miss a stroll along the Promenade de la Croisette, one of the most beautiful and highly celebrated seaside walks on the Riviera. It borders the Bay

Nice—Cannes

DEPART NICE STATION	TRAIN NUMBER	ARRIVE IN CANNES STATION	NOTES
0703	—	0742	(1)
0805	—	0855	(1)
0901	—	0927	(1)
1026	164	1053	(1)
11451	6638	1210	(1)

Plus other frequent service throughout the day

DEPART CANNES STATION	TRAIN NUMBER	ARRIVE IN NICE STATION	NOTES
1456	—	1535	(1)
1608	—	1648	(1)
1714	TGV 845	1736	(1)
1817	—	1834	(2)
1912	TGV 9532	1952	(1)

Plus other frequent service throughout the day

(1) Daily, including holidays
(2) Mondays to Fridays

Distance: 19 miles/31 km

---

of Cannes for about two miles until you reach its extreme eastern end at the Palm Beach Casino—with its gaming rooms and gala evenings—on place Franklin D. Roosevelt.

Along the way, you will see some of the world's finest yachts berthed close by magnificent rose gardens in the Port Pierre-Canto and the famous **Palais des Festivals et des Congress,** home of the International Film Festival. Walk along boulevard Du Midi to the old part of town called **"Le Suquet"** which overlooks the harbor and offers a marvelous view of the bay.

Except for the brief period in the late fall when the Mistral winds make things a bit uncomfortable, the climate of Cannes is wonderfully mild and temperate. Because of a few canes and reeds growing in the bay, the Romans named the spot "Castrum de Canois," and for centuries Cannes remained a small village inhabited only by fishermen.

History relates that in 1834, the Lord Chancellor of England, Lord Brougham, "whilst" en route to Nice, was prevented in reaching there due to a cholera quarantine and paused briefly in Cannes. Taken by the place, his lordship decided on the spur of the moment to build a house in Cannes and did so, straight away—the transaction in real estate taking a matter of only eight days. For the next 34 years, until the time of his death, Lord Brougham left the winter fogs of London for the sunshine of Cannes.

His lordship's example was quickly followed by other English aristocracy, and Cannes' population began to swell accordingly. Alluding to the eight days required to get Cannes underway, locals point out that God took only seven days to create the universe—so Cannes, necessarily, is a cut above all else in the universe.

The center of Cannes is ideal for strolling and shopping. Locals claim that you get more than what you pay for because the area has a theatrical atmosphere about it, and the show is free. Not so on the Croisette, the waterfront. Here the most elegant of shops extol the virtues of high fashion at equally high prices. Window shopping, however, is free to all.

Excursion-boat services from the main port take you to the islands of **Sainte-Marguerite** and **Saint-Honorat**. Sainte-Marguerite's prison incarcerated the Man in the Iron Mask, and the island named after Saint Honorat has the remains of the monastery the saint started in the fourth century. Boats run daily throughout the year.

Another very delightful boat ride provides an unequaled panorama of the Mediterranean and the Alps each afternoon from June through September. This excursion departs at 1430, cruises the Bay of Cannes and the **Esterel Coast**, and returns at 1730. If you don't happen to be one of the millionaires with a yacht tied up in Port Pierre-Canto, now's your chance to enjoy the same exhilarating view that they enjoy—at a more reasonable price.

Day Excursion to

Marseilles

CITY OF INTRIGUE

Depart from Nice Central Station

Distance by Train: 140 miles (225 km)
Average Train Time: 2 hours, 15 minutes
City Dialing Code: 491
Tourism Office: Maison du Tourisme Marseilles, No. 4 La Canebiere, 13000 Marseill Cedex 01
Tel: 91 13 89 00; *Fax:* 91 13 89 20
Hours: July-September, 0830–2000 daily; October-June, 0900–1900 Monday-Saturday; 1000–1700 Sunday/holidays.

Located adjacent to the municipal docks. You may taxi there just by showing the driver the address. To reach it on foot—about a 15-minute walk—leave the railway station by descending the steps to street level. Directly in front is the boulevard d'Athens (a promenade from the original settlers, no doubt). Follow this street to the third traffic signal, including the one at the foot of the train-station steps. Turn to the right onto the boulevard La Canebiere, and just beyond the second traffic light now in front of you, look for the tourist office in the last building on the left-hand side of the street just before the small boat harbor.

Also, there is a small tourist office in the train station on the track level which is open during summer 0900–1900 and during winter 1000–1800.

Marseilles, the great port of France, is second only to Paris in population and one of the oldest surviving towns in the world. Although French in character, Marseilles is distinctly Mediterranean with an international flare. There is much to compare in the character of Marseilles to the contents of its epicurean delicacy, bouillabaisse, and the three ingredients so essential in its making.

Greeks, fleeing out of Asia Minor from the Persians, founded Massalia (Marseilles) in 600 B.C. Their enterprising nature disturbed the Ligurians, who came from Italy, as well as the Iberians coming from Spain, and a lot of head smashing took place until the Greeks appealed to Rome for help. Romans came by the legions and promptly named the area a Roman province. Hannibal and his elephants created some disturbance, but nothing like that of 360,000 Teutonic warriors in 102 B.C. who were seemingly bent on destroying the civilized world and all that was in it.

Rome, again to the rescue, dispatched Caius Marius to the province; he, in turn, disposed of 100,000 Teutons near Aix-en-Provence, just north of Marseilles, thus saving the day for the province and impacting the future of modern-day France. Even today, the most popular name for men in this region is Marius.

The French national anthem, *The Marseillaise*, was composed in Strasbourg by a young French military officer, Rouget de Lisle. The battle song was published and reached Marseilles just at the time when the city was giving a sendoff banquet to 500 volunteers bound for Paris and the revolution. Someone sang the new song and immediately the banquet room picked it up in chorus.

The song was an immediate success, and the volunteers sang it in unison at every stopping place en route to Paris. By the time they reached Paris they had become somewhat of an accomplished choir, which electrified the Parisians as they marched through the streets of Paris singing the stirring words at the tops of their voices.

All the foregoing was given to set the mood for your arrival in Marseilles. Although the city is not famous as a tourist center, it is a very enjoyable place to visit. Its unusual character and mixture of peoples cannot be found anywhere else in the world.

Not far from the tourist office, you will find the **Vieux-Port** and its fish market, which defies description. This is one of the few places in the world

Nice–Marseilles

DEPART NICE STATION	TRAIN NUMBER	ARRIVE IN MARSEILLES STATION	NOTES
0550	6964	0831	(1)
0815	6676	1047	(1)
0930	TGV 9572	1145	(1)(2)
1026	164	1245	(1)
1141	6638	1408	(1)

DEPART MARSEILLES STATION	TRAIN NUMBER	ARRIVE IN NICE STATION	NOTES
1555	6464	1816	(1)
1650	162	1907	(1)
1737	6172	2004	(1)
1840	6452	2132	(1)
2026	6132	2247	(1)

(1) Daily, including holidays
(2) Seat reservations required

Distance: 140 miles/225 km

where you can obtain those three essential ingredients for bouillabaisse: red gurnet, conger eel, and a Mediterranean fish known locally as *rascasse*. Nearby restaurants serve it to perfection.

Here in the Vieux-Port, from a pier known as the Quai des Belges (Wharf of Belgium), you can take a ferry for the 15-minute crossing to the island of **Chateau d'If,** made famous in *The Count of Monte Cristo* by Alexandre Dumas. The castle is an interesting place to visit, and your guide will dramatically conclude your tour by showing you the opening through which the count was said to have made his escape. The visit to the island takes about 1½–2 hours, including the tour of the dungeons where the Man in the Iron Mask and many other political prisoners were imprisoned.

Day Excursion to

Monte Carlo

ROULETTE AND RELAXATION

Depart from Nice Central Station

Distance By Train: 9 miles (14 km)
Average Train Time: 20 minutes
Tourism Office: Monaco Government Tourist/Convention Bureau in North America:
565 Fifth Avenue, New York, NY 10017
Tel: (800) 753-9696 or (212) 286-3330; *Fax:* (212) 286-9890
Internet: http://www/tourism.org.mt
Monaco Country Dialing Code: 377
City Dialing Code: 92 or 93
Tourism Office: Monte Carlo Tourist Information 2, blvd. des Moulins
Tel: 92.16.61.16
Hours: Monday-Saturday 0900-1900; Sunday 1000-1200
   The bus terminal is a short distance downhill from the railway station. Board bus
No. 4 and ask the driver to let you off at the Office National du Tourisme (the
National Tourist Office). From June 15-September 30, there's a small tourist
information kiosk in the station lobby open daily from 0800-2000.

   The Principality of Monaco lies 4,092 miles east of Philadelphia—two
cities inexorably linked by the memories of their princess, Grace Patricia Kelly,
who died as the result of a tragic accident on 14 September 1982.
   Monaco consists of 0.7 square miles (453 acres) of rocky coastline along the
Riviera. It has been ruled by members of the Grimaldi family for the past ten
centuries. Its famous gambling casino is located in Monte Carlo, one of four
sections that make up the principality. The other three are Monaco-Ville itself
(the capital and site of the palace), La Condamine (a commercial and residential area), and Fontvieille (a residential and light-industries section).
   Monaco operates a highly efficient bus system consisting of five major lines:
No. 1 (Red), No. 2 (Blue), No. 4 (Gold), No. 5 (Brown) and No. 6 (Green),
which serves the Fontvieille-Larvotto (beach) area. These are augmented by
Line No. 3 serving the beach area during the summer.
   French francs are the legal tender in Monaco, so there is no need to change
your currency. Travelers' checks can be cashed at "Credit Lyonnais," a bank
opposite the train station, 0845-1155 and 1330-1600 Monday through Friday.
The American Express office is just to the west of the casino at 2, avenue de
Monte Carlo.
   If cracking casinos is your cup of tea, Monte Carlo's public gambling rooms
open at 1000 daily. You must be twenty-one to enter. Youngsters are not barred,
however, at the National Museum and Collection of Dolls and Automats of
Yesteryear, located at 17, avenue Princesse Grace. Hours: daily April-

Nice–Monte Carlo

DEPART NICE STATION	TRAIN NUMBER	ARRIVE IN MONACO STATION	NOTES
0758	183	0816	(1)
0837	—	0909	(1)
0922	6196	0941	(1)
1004	343	1024	(1)
1122	—	1145	(1)

DEPART MONACO STATION	TRAIN NUMBER	ARRIVE IN NICE STATION	NOTES
1556	—	1618	(1)
1645	—	1707	(1)
1750	—	1813	(1)
1939	345	1956	(1)(2)
2104	—	2125	(1)
2337	1144	2354	(1)

(1) Daily, including holidays
(2) Supplement payable

Distance: 9 miles/14 km

September, 1000-1830; October-March, daily, 1000-1215 and 1430-1830. Admission 26 francs, adults; children age 6-14 and students, 15 francs.

Pomp and ceremony still prevail in Monte Carlo. The changing of the guard takes place daily in front of the **Place du Palais** exactly at 1155. The charge for visiting the Prince's **Palace State Apartments** is 30 francs; children 8-14, 15 francs. Tours are conducted daily June-September, 0930-1830, and during October, 1000-1700. One of Europe's greatest aquariums, the **Musee Oceanographique,** lies near the palace on the seaside. Hours: July–August 0900-2000; reduced hours during the rest of the year. Admission: 60 francs; children, 30 francs.

While at the Place du Palais, you should visit the **Museum of Napoleonic Souvenirs** and **Collections of the Palace Historic Archives**. Hours: 0930-1830 daily June-September; reduced hours during the balance of the year. Admission 20 francs; children 8-14 pay 10 francs.

Other attractions include the **Wax Museum of the Princes of Monaco,** the **Museum of Old Monaco,** and the **Museum of Prehistoric**

Anthropology, the last featuring the **Exotic Gardens** and the **Observatory Cave.** The tourist office publishes a brochure listing all places of interest, opening times, and admission fees. Also available is a map showing the city's "semi-pedestrianized" zone, 12 public lifts, and the bus system.

The grandeur of the Monaco yacht harbor may be viewed from many vantage points. The view from the casino's restaurant **Le Prive** is impressive—expensive, too. Probably the best site (at popular prices) is a canopy-covered table at the **Portofino Restaurant,** which clings to the cliff just above the quai President Kennedy.

Day Excursion to

Saint-Raphael   "In" Place on the Riviera

Depart from Nice Central Station

Distance by Train: 37 miles (59 km)
Average Train Time: 50 minutes
City Dialing Code: 494
Saint-Raphael Tourist Information: Office de Tourisme, rue W. Rousseau, 83 700
Tel: 94 19 52 52; *Fax:* 94 83 85 40
Hours: Sunday from 0830–1200 and Monday through Saturday from 0830–1200 and 1400–1900. From June 15 to September 15 it does not close for lunch.

Located across the street and to the left of the main entrance to the railway station. It is identified by a white "i" sign together with TOURISME in brown letters.

If you arrive late there is also a tourist information stand available on the Veillat Beach, one block away from the main tourist information office. It is open from 0200–2200.

Saint-Raphael is the Riviera resort that has something for everyone—and at popular prices. Its primary asset is its delightful weather, which is mild in the winter and moderate throughout the entire summer. Sportsmen are attracted by its 18-hole golf course, tennis clubs, riding academy, and well-protected bay. Its 16 miles of coastline fringe magnificent pine forests. Nearby mountainous peaks beckon hikers, while sandy beaches and a casino fill the needs of those seeking sun and fun.

Before leaving the railway station, check the departure schedules for trains returning to Nice. There is a train information office in the station on your right as you exit the train platform. Hours: Monday-Saturday 0800–1930. Tel: 36 35 35 35

The fishing-boat dock in Saint-Raphael is not far from the railroad station. The tourist office can point the way. Here you will find some unusually fine

Nice–Saint-Raphael

DEPART NICE STATION	TRAIN NUMBER	ARRIVE IN SAINT-RAPHAEL STATION	NOTES
0703	Local	0818	(1)
0901	5682/83	0950	(1)
0930	TGV 9572	1019	(1)(2)
1035		1150	(1)
1141	6638	1234	(1)

DEPART SAINT-RAPHAEL STATION	TRAIN NUMBER	ARRIVE IN NICE STATION	NOTES
1650	TGV 845	1736	(1)(2)
1727	6464	1816	(1)
1819	162	1907	(1)
1932	TGV 847	2020	(1)(2)
2037	6452	2132	(1)
2159	6132	2247	(1)

(1) Daily, including holidays
(2) Seat reservation required

Distance: 37 miles/59 km

local restaurants where, in the summer, you can dine at tables set under trees close to the boats. It is a relaxing atmosphere.

Saint-Raphael has an interesting history. Its modern origins stem from the era of the Roman Empire, when it was a fashionable suburb of the Roman port of Frejus. Napoleon passed through Saint-Raphael in both victory and defeat. In 1799, the emperor and his generals disembarked there upon returning from Egypt; a pyramid standing in the town still commemorates the event. In 1814, he sailed again from Saint-Raphael, this time for Elba and exile. On April 28, as Napoleon, overcome with emotion, was saying good-bye to the soil of France, the English frigate he was to sail in fired a salute of twenty-one guns.

The site where the present town of Saint-Raphael now stands has played an exciting part in the history of the Mediterranean. Because of its natural harbor, which is deep enough to accommodate even the deepest-draught warships, the Romans developed it first as a holiday center. The town's casino is built over the original foundations of the Roman baths and a fish-holding tank.

Villas of the rich Romans who had come to Saint-Raphael to "take the sea air" were destroyed by Saracen pirates. By the time the pirates were driven from the area in the tenth century, the land lay deserted.

Development was hindered by poor drainage and the diseases that accompanied this impairment. Even by the eighteenth century, when fishermen and peasants began to rehabilitate the area known today in Saint-Raphael as the "old quarter," they were so weakened by marsh fever that they became known in the region as "pale faces." The introduction of drainage and improved sanitation turned it into a pleasant land again.

Much of Saint-Raphael's modern development has been due in great part to the establishment of the cut-flower industry started there in 1880 by Alphonse Karr. Although its biggest revenues today are developed by the tourist industry, Saint-Raphael is still a large and prosperous center for cut flowers.

An excellent excursion-boat service operates from Saint-Raphael. The tourist information office will have to provide you with schedules and fares, as they are too varied to mention here. There are short cruises on the Mediterranean as well as full-day excursions to many ports of call on the Riviera.

Saint-Tropez, summer home of Brigitte Bardot and one of the better "topless" beaches of France, can be reached from Saint-Raphael by bus. Journey time: 1 hour, 25 minutes in each direction, but connections can be made that allow almost 7 hours of visiting and sightseeing in this quaint resort town. For details on bus service between Saint-Raphael and Saint-Tropez, consult the rail information office in Nice or Saint-Raphael, or ask for assistance from the tourist office in Saint-Raphael. There is no rail service between Saint-Raphael and Saint-Tropez.

Base City...

Paris

City Dialing Code: 1 (followed by 9 digits)
Internet: http://www.paris.org

"Every traveler has two cities," wrote Edna St.Vincent Millay, "his own and Paris." Besides being one of the most beautiful and captivating cities in Europe, Paris is the center of one of the most interesting regions of France. Local people call the area around Paris the **Ile de France** (Island of France), for it is here that the nation began in the forested lands stretching out in all directions around Paris. The city is not only the political capital of France, it's the country's industrial and commercial center as well. To understand and appreciate it, follow the suggestion of British poet and novelist, Lawrence Durrell, watch it "quite quietly over a glass of wine in a Paris bistro."

Arriving By Air

Charles de Gaulle Airport, 17 miles north of the city center
- **Airport-City Links: Roissybus** departures every 15 minutes 0600-2300; journey time about 45 minutes. Fare, 40 francs.
- **Taxis** take about 45 minutes; average fare, 180 francs.
- **Tourist information** is available from 0700-2200 (Tel: 48 62 27 29).
- **Currency exchange** is open 0615-2300.
- **SNCF (French Rail) airport office** is open 0730-2015. You can immediately board a train to Lyon, Avignon, or Nice without having to transfer to Paris.

Orly Airport, 10 miles south of Paris
- **Airport-City Links: Orlybus** buses run every 10-15 minutes between 0600-2300, 30 minutes en route. Fare, 30 francs.
- **Taxis:** average 130 francs.
- **Tourist information** is available 0600-2330 (Tel: 49. 75 00 90).
- **Currency exchange hours:** 0630-2300.
- **SNCF (French Rail) office hours:** 0800-2000 Monday-Saturday; 1000-1300 and 1500-1830 Sunday/holidays.

Arriving By Train

Paris has six major railway stations, but arriving there by train from one of the other base cities listed in this edition of *Europe by Eurail* will place you either in Gare du Nord (North), Gare de l'Est (East), Gare de Lyon, or Gare d'Austerlitz. Details of these stations follow.

Transfers between rail stations in Paris may be made by bus, Métro, or taxi. If you have baggage, a taxi is your best bet. There are, however, inter-station buses that provide baggage storage. Rule out the Métro unless you are without baggage. Suggestion: Consult the conductor on your train at least 30 minutes prior to arrival. If you are transferring between stations to continue your journey, the railroad is obliged to assist you.

The Railway Stations

Gare du Nord (**North Station**) 18, rue de Dunkerque, 75015 Paris (Tel: 49 95 10 00)

Gateway to the channel ports of Calais and Boulogne plus Belgium, Germany, The Netherlands, and London via Eurostar.

- **Money-exchange office:** in the station concourse area across from track No. 3. Hours: 0615–2230 daily, except holidays.
- **Train information:** displayed in digital format throughout the station. A rail information office is located across from track 1. Hours: 0600–2300 daily, including holidays.
- **Train reservations,** including TGV and sleeping cars, may be made in the train information office. A layout of the station can be seen on a chart across from track No. 5.
- **Eurostar** has its own terminal, reservations, and waiting room upstairs from the main part of the station. The well-marked signs will direct you to it.
- **Tourist information/hotel reservations:** in the Paris Convention and Visitors Bureau, opposite track 21. Hours: May-October, 0800-2000 Monday-Saturday. This is a branch of the central tourist office located on the Champs Elysées. Charge for hotel reservations varies.

Gare de l'Est (**East Station**), Place du 11 Novembre 1918, 75010 Paris.(Tel: 40 18 20 00)

Gateway to eastern France, Germany, Luxembourg, and Switzerland. Located a short distance from Gare du Nord and can be reached on foot or by the Métro.

- **Money-exchange:** in the main reception hall area opposite tracks 25 and 26. Hours: 0645–2200 daily.
- **Train information:** displayed in digital format throughout the station. A rail information office is located on the left-hand side of the station coming from the trains, between tracks Nos. 6 and 7. Hours: 0845–2000 every day although on Sunday for information only (no reservations).
- **Train reservations:** may be made in the train information office.

- **Tourist information/hotel reservations** available in the branch office of the Paris Convention and Visitors Bureau across from track No. 27. Hours: May-October, 0800–2100 Monday-Saturday; November-April, closes at 2000.

Gare de Lyon (Lyon Station) 20, boulevard Diderot, 75012 Paris (Tel: 40 19 60 00)

Gateway to the Riviera, southeastern France, Italy, and western Switzerland. Located on the right bank of the Seine, some distance south of the north and east terminals.

- **Money-exchange:** on the left side of Sortie (Exit) 1 as you enter the station and proceed toward track A. Hours: 0630–2300 daily.
- **Train information:** in digital format throughout the station. The office for train information, marked INFORMATION AND RESERVATIONS, is in the center of the station, to the left of the *Billets Grandes Lignes* area. Hours: 0800–2200 Monday-Saturday; 0800–1900 Sunday/holidays. **Train reservations** at the same office.
- **Tourist information/hotel reservations:** in the Paris Convention and Visitors Bureau located in the main ticket hall. Hours: May-October, 0800–2100 Monday-Saturday; November-April, closes at 2000.
- **Restaurant le Train Bleu** is located on the mezzanine of Gare de Lyon. Without doubt, it is the most elegant restaurant of any train station in the world. Opened in 1901, it was originally called the *Buffet de la Gare de Lyon.* Quickly, however, it became the fashionable place for well-heeled passengers to partake of a late supper prior to boarding the Train Bleu, the stylish sleeper that traveled between Paris and the French Riviera, and so it was renamed. The food is good, and the decor is France at the turn of the century at its opulent best: crystal chandeliers, shimmering brass, and mahogany.

Gare d'Austerlitz (Austerlitz Station), 55, quai D'Austerlitz, 75013 Paris (Tel: 45 84 14 18)

Gateway to central and southern France as well as eastern Spain. Located on the left bank of the Seine, a short distance from Gare de Lyon, which may be reached on foot or by the Métro.

- **Money exchange** within the main hall of the station, close to the ticket windows. Hours: 0630–2300 daily.
- **Train information** is displayed in digital format throughout the station. A rail information office is located in the foyer of the station just before entering the main hall. It is open 0730–1945 Monday through Saturday.
- **Train reservations** may be made in the train information office.
- **Tourist information/hotel reservations** can be made in the Paris Convention and Visitors Bureau office located in the main hall of the station. Hours: 0800–1500 daily.

Other major railway stations in Paris include **Gare Saint-Lazare** (north and west of France) and **Gare Montparnasse** (west of France). There are four Métro stations (Routes 4, 6, 12, and 14) in or adjacent to the Montparnasse railway station. Consequently, it is easy to reach from other parts of the rail network. Route 4 connects directly with Gare du Nord (North Station) and the Gare de l'Est (East Station). Trains departing Paris for Chartres from Montparnasse also stop in Versailles, but this station is some distance from the Palace of Versailles and should not be used for that day excursion.

In these railway stations, the **reservation offices** are open 0800-2000 daily; **Information offices,** 0800-2030.

Central reservations office (Tel: 45 82 50 50)

Central information office (Tel: 45 65 60 60)

In addition to the six major railway stations of Paris, there are six smaller or suburban-type stations.

- **Gare des Invalides,** another station that begins underground with its trackage until well past the Eiffel Tower, is exclusive for trains running to the Palace of **Versailles.**
- **Gare Bercy** and **Gare Charolais** are two auxiliary stations serving the Gare de Lyon complex on the right bank of the Seine.
- On the Rive Gauche (Left Bank) side, **Gare Tolbiac** serves the Austerlitz station network, and **Gare Vaugirard** performs the same function for the extensive train trackage terminating in the Montparnasse station compound.

A system of buses connects the major Paris stations, Gare St. Lazare, Gare du Nord, Gare de l'Est, Gare de Lyon, Gare Montparnasse, and Gare d'Austerlitz. Operated privately, the system charges a fare slightly higher than that of the Métro, and it is much more convenient for passengers with luggage than the regular city buses.

Tourist Information/Hotel Reservations

Office de Tourisme de Paris, 127, avenue des Champs Elysées.
Tel: 49 52 53 54; fax 49 52 53 00
Hours: 0900-2000 daily
Branch office at Eiffel Tower open May-September 1100-1800 daily
Tel: 45 51 22 15.

A good map of Paris is available for 5 francs. You may also consult the Galeries Lafayette travel agency, 40, boulevard Haussman; hours: Monday-Saturday 0930-1900 (until 2100 on Thursdays). (Tel: 42 85 21 20)

Getting Around in Paris

The mainstay of transportation within Paris is its subway system, the Métro. It has thirteen main lines, several with rubber-tired coaches that sort of sneak up on you in the station. The system covers all of the city and much of its suburbs. You can reach all the railway stations in Paris via the Métro.

Obtain a map of the Metro system from one of the tourist offices and ask for a brief explanation of its operation. Many of the Métro stations have an illuminated map in their entrances, where, by pushing the button of your desired destination, the entire route will light up showing what line to take, in what direction, and, when necessary, where to make transfers.

The French refer to transfers as *correspondances*. Although the lines are numbered, the reference you should remember is the direction, which refers to the last station on the end of the line in the direction in which you are traveling. For example, Line No. 1 has two directions: Grande Arche de la Défense in the west, Château de Vincennes in the east. If you were visiting the Louvre and wanted to see the Place de la Concorde next, look for the direction Grande Arche de la Défense because your destination lies to the west.

At transfer points, watch for the transfer station, then disembark and look for the direction sign for the line you want to transfer to. Proceed to that platform and there determine from the line map how many stops to your destination.

Purchase a **Paris Visite** (tourist pass) valid for 3 or 5 consecutive days, which provides for first-class travel on public transportation in Paris plus discounts on services and attractions. Prices vary according to the number of zones selected.

Paris Visite

ALL ZONES	DAYS	COST
	3 days	230 francs
	5 days	315 francs
There is also a Formule 1 Pass valid for one day.		

If you are staying in Paris for the prescribed number of days and plan to make more than three one-way trips on the Métro or bus systems per day, the pass will definitely save you money, and the convenience is invaluable. These passes may be purchased in all of the main train stations in Paris, at Charles de Gaulle Airport, and at Orly Airport.

American Express
38, avenue de Wagram
Hours: 0900-1730 Monday-Fridayday. and
83, rue des Courcelles; hours: 0900-1730 Monday-Friday; 1000-1200/1400-1700 Saturday

Thomas Cook
8, place de l'Opéra, has Métro stop on both the No. 3 and No. 8 lines.
Hours: Monday-Saturday, 0900–1900; Sunday, 1000–1900.
and
125, Champs Elysees
Hours: Monday-Saturday, 0915–2200; Sunday,1000–2000.
Acquaint yourself with the **Paris RER,** the high-speed, limited-stop rail service that runs *under*—that's right—*under* the regular Paris Métro. If you need to get somewhere in a hurry, the RER's the way to go. For example, we have ridden from Gare de Lyon to the Arc de Triomphe (the Etoile) in less than ten minutes.

The RER (Regional Express) consists of three lines. *Line A* goes west to east from St. Germain-en Laye, La Défense, the Étoile, Auber, Châtelet, Gare de Lyon, and the Marne Valley. *Line B* goes north to south from Roissy-Charles de Gaulle Airport to Gare du Nord, Châtelet, Pont St. Michel, Luxembourg, and the Chevreuse Valley. Finally, Line C runs from Versailles and follows the Seine through Paris to the Orly airport.

Eurailpass and Europass are accepted on parts of the RER, but not all, so inquire at the tourist information office or any one of the major Métro stations for specific information. You may also ask at the train information office alongside platform 1 in the Gare du Nord for details of the RER.
• **Train information** (Tel: 36 35 35 39) and request an English- speaking operator. Available 0800-2000 daily.
• **Bus information** (Tel: 43 46. 14 14)
• **Taxi** (Tel: 47 39 47 39, 45 85 85 85, 49 36 10 10, or 41 27 27 27. To reserve a taxi for the airport, call before 2100 the night before.

Sights/Attractions/Tours and Paris Potpourri

Musts during your stay in Paris include:
• A visit to the **Louvre** to view the *Mona Lisa* and *Venus de Milo.*
• A cable-car ride up to **Montmartre** for a view of the "City of Light" or by elevator up the **Eiffel Tower** to the highest point in Paris.
• Walk the **Champs Elysées** to the **Arc de Triomphe** and look deep into its "flame of remembrance" for the faces of France and its allies who fought and died in the two world wars.
• Lunch at a sidewalk café.
• Ride the **Seine on a** *bateau* (boat).
• Get a gargoyle's point of view from high atop **Notre Dame.**
• Dine at Maxim's (if your waistline and wallet can afford it).
Paris has triumphed once again in the arts—this time in a museum that served the city as a train station for nearly 40 years. **Gare du Quai d'Orsay** was inaugurated on Bastille Day, 1900. Designed by architect Victor Laloux, it

included a 400-room hotel in part to serve the nearby 1900 World's Fair. By 1939, the Gare d'Orsay was obsolete, its platforms too short to accommodate the longer, electrified trains of the day. In 1971, the city of Paris reluctantly scheduled the structure for demolition, creating an uproar from its citizens equal in furor to the march on the Bastille.

The history of the Gare d'Orsay, although short in time, had made impact. Charles de Gaulle made his announcement to return to power from the hotel in 1958; Orson Wells used the station in the filming of *The Trial* (1952). Under pressure, the government reversed itself and saved both the station and the hotel, which became the **Musée (museum) d'Orsay.**

Located at 1, rue de Bellechasse (at entry to Quai d'Orsay RER station and near Solferino Metro stop), Musee d'Orsay boasts a glorious collection of nineteenth- and twentieth-century French painting and sculpture. Hours In summer: the museum is open every day (except Monday), 1000–1800 Tuesday-Sunday (closes 2100 Thurs. and opens 0900 Sunday. Winter hours: 1000–1800 daily. Entry fee, 35 francs. It is usually most crowded on Thursday night and the weekend.

An interesting mix of ancient and modern can be found at the **Musée du Louvre.** Its glass-pyramid entrance designed by I. M. Pei has sparked much controversy, similar to that brought about by Gustave Eiffel and his iron tower. Referred to by the writer Guy de Maupassant as the "disgraceful skeleton," the Eiffel Tower did, of course, become the city's most recognizable landmark. While you ponder Pei's pyramid, visit inside the museum. Hours: 0900–2200 Wednesday, 0900–1800 Thurs.-Monday (Tel: 40 20 53 17). Entrance fee, 35 francs.

To avoid queueing up and having to purchase a separate ticket for each museum and monument, consider purchasing the **Carte Musées et Monuments,** which covers entrance fees to about 65 museums and monuments in Paris and Ile de France.

1-Day pass	70 francs
3-Day pass	140 francs
5-Day pass	200 francs

In France, you can purchase the pass at any of the museums, at more than 100 Métro stations, or at the tourist information office.

The Champs-Elysées is the most famous thoroughfare in Paris, but you should also see Paris from her most beautiful avenue, the River Seine. Aboard a *bateau* (boat), sights such as The Louvre, Notre Dame, and the Eiffel Tower take on a different perspective—particularly at night when the floodlights of the bateaux illuminate the passing scenes. Add a meal served in the tradition of French gastronomy and you will have the best that Paris can offer!

Bateaux Parisiens, Port de la Bourdonnais (at the foot of the Eiffel Tower) Tel: 44 11 33 44 for schedules, rates, and reservations. *Bon voyage!*

Train Connections to Other Base Cities from Paris

TO:	DEPART	ARRIVE	TRAIN NUMBER	NOTES
Amsterdam	0740	1228	TGV 9309	(1)
	1040	1528	TGV 9321	
	1737	2228	TGV 9349	
Barcelona (França)	2015	0815	475	
Berlin (Zoo)	2046	0850	243	
Berne	1548	2022	TGV 429	
Brussels (Midi)	0740	0838	TGV 9309	
	1140	1338	TGV 9325	
	1440	1638	TGV 9337	
Copenhagen	1637	1837	TGV 9345	
Dublin				
via Le Havre	1512	1755+1	3147	(5)(6)
via Cherbourg	1456	1755	3311	(5)(10)
Hamburg	0725	1707	EC 33	
	2131	0708+1	235	
Lisbon	1600	1125	TGV 8543	
Luxembourg	1042	1435	EC 357	3)(6)
	1716	2052	EC 53/1834	(3)
Lyon (Part-Dieu)	0800	1004	TGV 605	(4)
	1000	1204	TGV 607	(4)
	1300	1504	TGV 613	(4)
Madrid (Chamartin)	2000	0848	TAL 409	(2)
Milan	0812	1455	TGV 17	(4)(8)(14)
	1112	1755	TGV 19	(4)(9)14)
Munich	0750	1611	EC 65	(3)
	1348	2211	EC 67	(3)
	2229	0849	261	(3)
Nice	0747	1417	TGV 843	(4)
	1102	1733	TGV 845	(4)
	1350	2017	TGV 847	(4)
Rome (Termini)	1933	1005+1	EN 213	(4)
Vienna (Westbhf.)	0750	2118	EC 65	(3)
	1749	0835	263	(3)
Zürich	0730	1403	EC 113	(3)
	0841	1522	1743/EC 975	(13)
	1140	1803	1745/1783	(13)
	1659	2245	EC 115	
	2238	0643+1	469	

Daily departures unless otherwise noted. Make reservations for all departures.

(1) Departs Paris Gare du Nord
(2) Departs Paris Gare d'Austerlitz
(3) Departs Paris Gare de l'Est
(4) Departs Paris Gare de Lyon
(5) Departs Paris Gare St. Lazare
(6) Mon., Wed., Fri. only (July 15 to Sept. 6)
(7) Transfer in Cologne (Köln) to IC 524
(8) Transfer in Lausanne to CIS 35

(9) Transfer in Lausanne to IC 335
(10) Mon. through Fri. only (check ferry schedule for service dates)
(11) Departs Paris Montparnasse
(12) Transfer in Irun (Spanish border) to train 312
(13) Transfer in Basel
(14) Global fares apply

Day Excursions

Three of the six Paris day excursions have been selected to introduce the traveler to Ile de France: **Chartres, Fontainebleau,** and **Versailles.** These places are every bit as important to what Paris is today as the Louvre, the Place de la Concorde, or the Eiffel Tower. The three remaining day excursions venture farther afield in express trains to visit **Caen and the Normandy Beaches, Rennes,** and **Rouen.**

Day Excursion to

Caen
& THE NORMANDY BEACHES

Depart from Paris St. Lazare

Distance by Train: 148 miles (239 km)
Average Train Time: 2 hours, 20 minutes
City Dialing Code: 231
Caen Tourist Information: Office de Tourisme et accveil de France, Place Saint-Pierre, 1400
Tel: 31 27 14 14; *Fax:* 31 79 14 13
Internet: http://www.normandy-tourism.org
Hours: Monday–Saturday 1000–1300 and 1400–1800; Sundays and bank holidays 1000–1300.

More than five decades have passed since one of the greatest battles in history took place in Normandy. At dawn on June 6, 1944, American, British, and Canadian forces, along with elements of the Free French, assailed the Normandy beaches along a broad spectrum of the coastline at five preselected landing points, Utah, Omaha, Gold, Juno, and Sword. Preceded by the drop of three airborne divisions during the predawn hours, between 0630 and 0730, 120,000 men and about 20,000 vehicles were landed from the sea. The assault upon Adolf Hitler's "Fortress Europe" had begun.

By the night of August 21, seventy-six days later, the **Battle of Normandy** was over. The German 7th Army had been encircled and forced to surrender. It had cost the Germans 640,000 men—killed, wounded, or taken prisoner. Allied losses were tallied at 367,000 dead or wounded. American losses were set at 127,000 casualties—31,000 of that number died in battle.

The town of Caen was the pivot of the battle and paid heavily for its part in the conflict. By the second day of the invasion, the whole of the town center had been flattened by Allied bombing. The German garrison fought fiercely. It wasn't until July 9 that the British and Canadian troops were able to take the town. The Germans, however, retreated to the right bank of the Orne

River, where they continued to direct mortar fire into the ruined town. Caen was not completely liberated until August 9. The Battle of Caen lasted more than two months. Seventy-five percent of the town was destroyed.

For years following the war, Caen was one vast building site in which life was gradually beginning to return to normal. Reconstructed and restored, the town decrees that now is the time for all men of good will to be reconciled. To that purpose, the **Caen Memorial** has been established on the site of one of the bloodiest battles in history to take you on a compelling journey from the dark years of world wars to a vision of peace.

The memorial is unlike any other museum devoted to the theme of warfare. It employs audiovisual presentations to explain the sequence of events that led up to the outbreak of hostilities in 1939, suffering of the people involved, the preparation for the invasion, and the strategies behind it. Peace can never be taken for granted; consequently, the memorial ends its presentation with a powerful and moving film emphasizing the need for vigilance if we are to have peace in our world in our own time and in our children's.

Allow one day for the Caen Memorial and sightseeing in Caen—a typical day excursion. If you want to tour the landing beaches and the various museums mentioned, consider purchasing a rail/drive package (see rail/drive package types and prices in the Appendix).

The **Hertz** office in Caen is directly across from the rail station. Reserve your first car rental on your rail/drive package at least seven days prior to your departure for Europe by calling Hertz at (800) 654–3001.

If you prefer not to drive, check with the Bus Verts office at the side of the Caen Railway station for Bus Verts' programs for visiting the D-Day landing areas.

This day excursion is a pilgrimage that every American should make. Arriving in Caen, you can proceed directly to the memorial on city bus No. 17 going in the direction of the memorial. It departs from the bus station outside the rail station on the right.

The memorial is open daily, 0800–1900 (until 2100 during June, July, and August). Tours are unaccompanied and last at least two hours. Check at the information desk for the starting times of the English language programs. A cafeteria is located on the second floor for refreshments.

Returning from the memorial to the station take bus No. 17 in the direction of **Grace de Dieu**. The bus makes a stop in the center of the town at Tour Leroy near the tourist office (Office du Tourisme). Walk along **Boulevard des Allies** and proceed one block to where it intersects rue Saint-Jean. From this point, the tourist office sign may be seen across the street to the right. The tourist office can advise on accommodations in Caen and the Normandy towns close to the beaches. There is a pass that will give you discounts to the museums in the D-Day Landings and the Battle of Normandy region. The pass, available at the museums, costs 30 Francs.

Tours of the invasion beaches start in Caen and proceed west through the Anglo-Canadian sectors of Sword, Juno, and Gold before arriving in the American sectors of Omaha and Utah. With a Hertz rental car, proceed west from Caen on Route 13 past Bayeux, LaCambe, and Carentan until reaching Ste.-Mere-Eglise, the first town in France to be liberated on D-Day, June 6, 1944. Visit the Airborne Museum with its CG4-A glider and a C-47 airplane and gaze in wonder at the 82nd Airborne paratrooper's predicament when his parachute caught on the church steeple opposite the museum.

Proceed from there to the **Utah Beach Landing Museum** at Ste.-Marie-Du-Mont. An audiovisual presentation explains how Utah beach was used to land about one million men on its shores. Your next stop should be **Pointe-Du-Hoc,** which was captured by the 2nd Ranger Battalion in a spectacular assault on June 6, 1944, scaling 100-foot cliffs to destroy a German battery of coastal guns. The Rangers made it, but they paid a high price for their valor—seventy-seven dead with an overall casualty rate of about 60 percent.

Leaving Pointe-Du-Hoc, head east to **Colleville-St.-Laurent,** where on a summit overlooking Omaha beach you enter the American cemetery. Pay your respects to the 10,000 Americans resting there. To paraphrase Sir Winston Churchill, "This part of a foreign field shall forever be American."

Paris—Caen

DEPART PARIS ST. LAZARE STATION	TRAIN NUMBER	ARRIVE IN CAEN STATION	NOTES
0712	3303	0856	(1)
0840	3337	1045	(1)
0908	3305	1057	(2)
1010	3339	1217	(2)

DEPART CAEN STATION	TRAIN NUMBER	ARRIVE IN PARIS ST. LAZARE STATION	NOTES
1424	3354	1633	(1)
1644	3356	1853	(1)
1651	3358	1901	(2)
1813	3362	2023	(3)
2131	3328	2327	(3)

(1) Monday through Friday only
(2) Saturday, Sunday and holidays
(3) Sunday only

Distance: 148 miles/239 km

En route back to Caen, stop in Bayeux at the **Memorial Museum** that you passed earlier while en route to Ste.-Mere-Eglise—time permitting. Otherwise, plan to return there the following day and plan to visit the Anglo-Canadian sectors as well. Take advantage of your rail/drive package.

Day Excursion to

Chartres   CATHEDRAL COUNTRY

Depart from Paris Montparnesse

Distance By Train: 55 miles (88 Km)
Average Train Time: 50 minutes
City Dialing Code: 237
Tourism Office: Chartres Office de Tourisme (tourist information) Place de la Cathedrale, 28 000, at the far end of Cathedral Square
Tel: 02 37 21 50 00. *Fax:* 37 36 34 18
Hours: Hours vary according to the season, but it is usually open 0930–1830 Monday through Saturday. On Sunday, it is open 1030–1300 and 1430–1730. The office is open on Sunday during the winter 1030– 1300.

Exit the station, cross the street in the direction of the cathedral, and continue straight ahead until you come to a large square. Bear left at the square and follow the cathedral signs that you will begin to see from that point onward. The tourist information office is in a building at the far end of Cathedral Square. Its sign reads, OFFICE DE TOURISME.

Mention Chartres and anyone who has been there recalls the **Cathedral of Notre Dame** but not much more. But, Chartres has many other attractions. To mention a few, we start with the town itself. Beguiling, gabled houses galore line its streets. Make it a point to stroll through the **old quarter** of town along streets with the appealing names of rue du Soleil d'Or (Street of the Golden Sun) or rue des Ecuyers (Street of the Horsemen). The tourist office has a special walking-tour program for the Old Town incorporating the rental of a pre-recorded "walkman" cassette in English. The length of the recording is 60 minutes.

Food is another one of Chartres' attractions, so plan to dine there during your visit. There are many excellent restaurants: the one in the ancient **Inn of the Grand Monarque** at 22, place des Éfpars, for example, or we can highly recommend restaurant **La Truie qui File**, which is located in a fifteenth century house at the Place de la Poissonnerie. Tel: 02 37 21 53 90.

On arrival in the Chartres station, check the train departures for Paris on the posters displayed in the main hall near the ticket windows. The cathedral

Paris–Chartres

DEPART PARIS MONTPARNASSE STATION	TRAIN NUMBER	ARRIVE IN CHARTRES STATION	NOTES
0701	13613	0755	(3)
0856	3859	0954	(2)
0912	—	1015	(1)
1114	—	1225	(1)

DEPART CHARTRES STATION	TRAIN NUMBER	ARRIVE IN PARIS MONTPARNASSE STATION	NOTES
1403	—	1510	(1)
1520	—	1630	(5)
1643	—	1748	(1)
1845	—	1954	(1)
1937	13624	2033	(4)

(1) Daily, including holidays
(2) Daily, June 28–Aug. 31
(3) Daily, except Saturdays
(4) Saturdays, Sundays, and holidays
(5) Monday to Friday

Distance: 55 miles/88 km

---

is illuminated at night, so if you would like to see this, check for a later train departure.

The **Cathedral of Notre Dame** in Chartres is in plain view from the railway station and will draw you like a magnet. It is said to be the most beautiful Gothic cathedral in Europe. To get there, just follow the directions above to the tourist office, which is located in the same area. The cathedral's stained-glass windows, the superb lines of its pillars and vaulting, and its interior are overwhelmingly beautiful. Fire destroyed the original eleventh century building. The present cathedral was rebuilt between 1194 and 1220.

It is interesting to note that the cathedral has two nonmatching spires. The plain one of simple architecture was built first; the elaborate spire in late Gothic followed later. On Sunday afternoons at 1645 during July and August, you can enjoy the organ recitals at the cathedral. Admission to these performances is free.

The district surrounding the cathedral is noted for its medieval houses. Time permitting, you should walk down to the river for a look at the old houses and bridges close to the restored Romanesque **Church of Saint André.**

The Cathedral of Chartres may be the most famous of the city's attractions. There is a lot more to this ancient town, however. In addition to the Church of Saint André, there are others that warrant your inspection. The **Church of Saint Pierre** is a Gothic masterpiece. Its stained-glass windows dating back to the fourteenth century, when added to those of the cathedral, make Chartres the metropolis of stained glass.

The **Episcopal Palace,** now the Museum of Fine Arts, has a lovely seventeenth-century facade in addition to its interesting contents. The exhibit includes a unique collection of harpsichords, painted wood carvings and art from Oceania, and a great deal of French, Flemish, and Italian paintings.

To assist visitors in seeing *all* of the city's attractions, Chartres has introduced *Le petit train de Chartres* (The little train of Chartres). From April through October, the "train" departs daily on the hour from in front of the cathedral on a 35-minute tour of "Old Chartres." The first departure is at 1000; the last departure, at 1800. Adults, 30 francs; children, 18 francs. All aboard!

Day Excursion to

Fountainebleau   PALACE OF KINGS

Depart from Gare de Lyon

Distance By Train: 37 miles (60 km)
Average Train Time: 45 minutes
City Dialing Code: 1
Chartes Tourism Information: Office de Tourisme, 4 rue Royale, 77 300.
Tel: 60 74 99 99; *Fax.:* 60 74 99 98
Hours: 0800-dusk daily, except closed Tuesday; Royal Apartments tours conducted 0930-1700 in June; 09300-1800 July-August; 0930-1230/1400-1700 November-May.

To reach the palace from the railway station in Fontainebleau, take the No. 1 bus marked "Château" from the station to the palace. The ride takes ten minutes. No admission charge to palace grounds; Tour charge, 23 francs.

The **Palace of Fontainebleau** is most famous today as the residence of Napoleon Bonaparte, but the site attracted the presence of the kings of France and other royalty as far back in history as the twelfth century. For many, Fontainebleau signifies the spirit of France more so than does Versailles.

In 1169, Louis VII had the chapel of his manor at Fontainbleau consecrated by Thomas à Becket, the famous English archbishop of Canterbury. The palace that stands today probably owes more to the imagination of Francis I of France than any other of its monarchs. In 1528, he had the remains of prior centuries torn down and rebuilt; he then filled the new structure with sumptuous jewels,

Paris–Fontainbleau

DEPART PARIS GARE DE LYON STATION*	ARRIVE IN FONTAINEBLEAU STATION	NOTES
0827	0905	(1)
1134	1212	(1)
1345	1424	(1)

Plus frequent commuter service
Trains call at Melun twelve minutes before reaching Fontainebleau.

DEPART FONTAINEBLEAU STATION	ARRIVE IN PARIS GARE DE LYON STATION	NOTES
1336	1415	(1)
1458	1543	(2)
1719	1802	(1)(3)
1930	2021	(1)

Plus frequent commuter service
Trains call at Melun twelve minutes after leaving Fontainebleau.

(1) Daily, including holidays
(2) Daily, except Saturday
(3) Saturday only

Distance: 37 miles/60 km

---

weapons, statues, and pictures—among them the *Mona Lisa*—as a suitable reclining palace for his mistress, the Duchess d'Etampes. In 1539, with the place set in order, he received his great rival, Emperor Charles V, in the new diggings.

The fortunes of Fontainebleau slumped under the reign of Louis XIV. He was giving more attention to his new project at Versailles and his dalliances with Madame de Maintenon; but his successors, Louis XV and Louis XVI, were faithful to the palace as an autumn residence. Slowly, Versailles became the "in place" with French courtiers, and only the old retainers showed up to probe the forest surrounding the château for wild game. Fortunately, Fontainebleau survived the French Revolution much better than did Versailles and other royal residences closer to Paris. (Suburban living had its advantages even then.)

Fontainebleau has probably bedded more queens, court favorites, and royal mistresses than all other palaces in France. (Versailles had its headliners, like

Pompadour and Du Barry, but Fontainebleau was more discreet.) Under the new management of Francis I, the Duchess of Etampes was granted a chamber that later became known as the "King's Staircase" when Louis XV needed freer access to her apartments. Madame de Maintenon moved to Fontainebleau under the auspices of Louis XIV in 1686 and into a room that bears her name even today.

Since the beginning of the seventeenth century, every queen of France has slept in the queen's bed chamber within the palace. Marie Antoinette ordered the bed that now graces the chamber, but because of unfortunate developments, she never had the opportunity to lay her head upon its pillows.

When Napoleon Bonaparte became Emperor of France in 1804, he had Fontainebleau refurbished and refurnished to receive Pope Pius VII, who had come to crown him as Emperor of France. From 1812 to 1814, the pope was also in residence in Fontainebleau—only this time he was not an invited guest but Napoleon's prisoner.

Not all of Napoleon's residence at Fontainebleau was surrounded with the fringe benefits befitting an emperor of his stature; he had some bad days, too. He signed his abdication in a room known now as the "Abdication Chamber" (formerly a bathroom) on 6 April 1814. Nineteen days later, he bade farewell to his officers and bodyguard in the Court of the White Horse from the horseshoe-shaped grand staircase that is now the main entrance to the palace.

Fontainebleau, unlike Versailles, possesses the secret of intimacy, no doubt due to the fact that each successive generation of kings or emperors added a wing of his own to the structure. The palace is full of nooks and crannies. There are back staircases and tapestries that pull aside to reveal secret hallways. Living in Fontainebleau, its occupants were surrounded by romance and intrigue. In a sense, it probably was the earliest version of the present "no-tell motel," but it had far more class!

The Germans used Fontainebleau as a military headquarters during World War II. Following the war, it served as a seat of the North Atlantic Treaty Organization (NATO) until 1965, when it became a public museum.

If you take the tour, and you should, your tour guide will lead you first through the Red Room, scene of Napoleon's abdication, then, in turn, through the Council Room, the Throne Room, and the Queen's Bedroom. From there, you pass through the Royal Apartments, then down the King's Staircase to the Oval Court, where the tour ends. It's intriguing.

The gardens and parks surrounding the palace are lovely throughout the year. You are invited to bring your own picnic lunch and spread it out on the royal grass as long as you don't litter the imperial landscape.

Day Excursion to

Rennes

CAPITAL OF BRITTANY

Depart from Paris Montparnasse Station

Distance By Train: 232 miles (374 km)
Average Train Time: 2 hours, 4 minutes
City Dialing Code: 299
Tourism Office: Rennes Tourist Information, in the rail station:
Tel: 02 99 53 23 23; *Fax:* 02 99 53 82 22.
Hours: 0800–1900 Monday through Friday; Saturday and Sunday the office is open 1000–1300 and 1500–1800.
    Located on the station's mezzanine level you will see it immediately after stepping off the escalator coming from the TGV arrival platform.
Rennes Tourist Information, at Pont de Nemours in the center of the city.
Tel. 99 53 82 22; *fax* 99 79 31 38.
Summer hours: 1300-1800 Monday; 0900-1900 Tuesday-Saturday
    From the rail station, take Avenue Janvier to the River Vilaine, where a left turn puts the office in view two blocks farther on.

    There's an expression that has been making the rounds of the travel trade for some time now, "Half the fun is in the going." Rennes fully qualifies as such a day excursion, since you can go there on the TGV Atlantique, the pride of the French rail fleet and holder of the world's rail speed record.
    Once outside of Paris and onto its special right-of-way, the TGV (*train à grande vitesse* or train of great speed) cruises at 186 mph and you will be experiencing the finest rail travel in the world. It's not a "seat belt" ride—it's smooth and totally enjoyable. Outbound in the morning, you can enjoy breakfast as the French countryside flashes by; inbound returning to Paris, you are in for a "Happy Hour" you'll never forget!
    Be certain that you have a seat reservation. You can obtain seat reservations in Gare Montparnasse, the TGV Atlantique's home station in Paris, or at the time you purchase your rail pass in the U.S.
    Rennes is unique in that it doesn't remind you so much of France as it does the area around Cornwall in Britain. As the cultural capital of the French province of Brittany, it has some strong ties to its Celtic origins in its architecture and gastronomy. Rennes stands at the confluence of the Ille and the Vilaine rivers. This junction of waterways came to the attention of Julius Caesar, and in 56 B.C., his legions conquered its original Celtic settlers, the Riedones. After this flurry of activity, however, things settled down for the balance of the Middle Ages.
    At the beginning of the eighteenth century, Rennes still looked as it had for several hundred years—with narrow alleys and houses constructed of lath and

Paris–Rennes

DEPART MONTPARNASSE STATION	TRAIN NUMBER	ARRIVE IN RENNES STATION	NOTES
0710	TGV 8705	0913	(3)(4)
0820	TGV 8609	1035	(1)(4)
0940	TGV 8713	1143	(1)(4)
1220	TGV 8623	1437	(1)(4)
1435	TGV 8739	1638	(1)(4)
1520	TGV 8641	1723	(1)(4)

DEPART RENNES STATION	TRAIN NUMBER	ARRIVE IN PARIS MONTPARNASSE STATION	NOTES
1303	TGV 8632	1515	(1)(4)
1515	TGV 8742	1720	(1)(4)
1600	TGV 8746	1815	(1)(4)
1720	TGV 8654	1925	(2)(4)
1835	TGV 8764	2040	(2)(4)
1935	TGV 8770	2140	(2)(4)

(1) Daily
(2) Daily, except Saturday
(3) Daily, except Sunday
(4) Reservations mandatory

Distance: 232 miles/374 km

---

plaster and no running water for sanitation or fire fighting. History records that in the evening of 22 December 1720, a drunken carpenter set fire to a pile of shavings, which, in turn, set fire to his house and then spread rapidly throughout much of the town, destroying a thousand or more other buildings before it burned itself out.

The part of the town destroyed by that fire was rebuilt in stone along well-ordered lines. Gabriel, architect to the French King Louis XV, then designed a new Town Hall. Thus, Rennes developed its **"New Town"** that stands yet today and awaits your inspection following your arrival in its ultra-modern train station designed specifically for the high-speed TGV Atlantique.

With a population of 200,000, Rennes describes itself as a youthful, well-established, and dynamic city that is striving to uphold the best interests of its citizens and the surrounding area as it moves toward the year 2000. Well equipped with prestigious theater and museum facilities and augmented with a city orchestra and the National Centre for Dramatic Art, the city plays a major role in the cultural activities of the region.

In the first week of July, during the *Tombees de la Nuit* (Summer Festival), Old Rennes is illuminated with spotlights while ballets, songs, plays, or visual arts presentations are performed. Daytime attractions include the contemporary architecture of the Law Courts, *Le Triangle*, and the cultural center. Saturday mornings are always special with the open-air market.

Guided tours depart from the main tourist information office at Pont de Nemous daily at 1030 and (also at 2100 on Tuesday and Thursday only) 1500 July 1–August 31.

Evenings in Rennes are pleasant. The city is home to numerous eating places offering a wide range of local or exotic cuisine—each establishment exhibiting a character all its own. Located close to the Atlantic Ocean as well as the English Channel, Rennes offers a selection of seafood second to none. For fine seafood served in an authentic Fifteenthcentury house, dine at **l'Auberge St. Sauveur,** at 6, rue St. Sauveur (Tel: 02 99 79 32 56). Being a university city, the bars in Rue Saint-Michel and Rue Saint-Malo attract the younger set, and there are plenty of concerts, plays, or films to keep the elders fully occupied, too.

TGV Atlantique service to Rennes opens up another day excursion opportunity, **Mont–Saint–Michel,** one of the great wonders of France. Operated by Les Courriers Breton, a special luxury bus runs between the rail station in Rennes to Mont-Saint-Michel, taking only one hour and ten minutes. The bus runs daily during summer and Friday through Sunday only during the balance of the year. For details, check with the House of Brittany in Paris, the Tourist Information Office in Rennes, or Les Courriers Breton in Saint Malo (Tel: 02 99 56 79 09).

A Day Excursion to

Rouen   Joan of Arc Memorial

Depart Paris St. Lazare

Distance By Train: 87 miles (140 km)
Average Train Time: 1 hour, 15 ,minutes
City Dialing Code: 235
Internet: http://www.mairie-rouen.fr
Rouen Tourist Information: Office de Tourisme et accueil de France, 25 Place de la Cathédrale, 76 000
Tel. 32 08 32 40; *Fax:* 32 08 32 44.
Hours: May-September, 0900-1900 Monday-Saturday; 0930-1230/1430-1800 Sunday; remainder of the year: Monday-Saturday, 0900-1830; Sunday 1000-1300.

The office is 5 minutes away from the station by taxi; 10 minutes on the underground, which stops at the Théâtre des Arts, just 2 blocks away from the office. Walking—and it's downhill all the way—takes about 20 minutes. Follow Rue Jeanne d'Arc from in front of the station, turning left at Rue du Gros Horloge (Big Clock). After walking under the clock, bear right at the Cathedral plaza for a few yards to the tourist office.

Rouen was established by the Romans, who selected the site as the first point from the sea where a bridge could be built across the Seine. Rouen became the capital of Normandy at the beginning of the Christian era, and, despite many thrashings in many wars, it still contains a number of lovely churches, towers, and other reminders of its colorful past, such as half-timbered houses and town clocks. Rouen is steeped in history. During the Hundred Years' War, the city was held by the English from 1419 to 1449. **Joan of Arc** was burned at the stake in Rouen by the English in 1431.

Your train from Paris will arrive in Gare Rive Droite, the rail station in

Paris–Rouen

DEPART PARIS ST. LAZARE STATION	TRAIN NUMBER	ARRIVE IN ROUEN RIVE DROITE STATION	NOTES
0816	13103	0950	(4)
0915	3135	1023	(1)
1048	3193	1204	(3)
1240	3139	13457	(2)

DEPART ROUEN RIVE DROITE STATION	TRAIN NUMBER	ARRIVE IN PARIS ST. LAZARE STATION	NOTES
1644	3192	1825	(3)
1709	3194	1845	(5)
1817	13118	1950	(4)
1959	3196	2125	(3)
2037	3158	2150	(4)
2153	13128	2309	(3)

(1) Daily
(2) Daily, except Sunday
(3) Sundays and holidays only
(4) Monday–Friday
(5) Saturdays, Sundays, and holidays

Distance: 87 miles/140 km

Rouen on the right bank of the Seine. Several hotels, restaurants, and bars are clustered about the station's plaza. The city abounds with eating and drinking establishments—even McDonald's—so finding refreshments in Rouen during your visit will be no problem.

The tourist office has prepared an English-language pamphlet describing a tour itinerary of approximately two hours. It starts at the tourist office and takes the visitor to the principal points of interest within the boundaries of the historical town center. The railway station appears on the map, so you need not worry about finding your way back to the station.

First stop on the tour is the city's cathedral, which stands as one of the most beautiful examples of French Gothic architecture. Construction began in the twelfth century. It was leveled by a devastating fire in 1200, however, and it was not until the fifteenth century that it began to take on is present appearance. The cast-iron spire atop the cathedral's central tower is a nineteenth-century addition. Heavily damaged during the Second World War, restoration work on the cathedral still continues.

In order to rebuild the cathedral, Rouen had to revive the medieval skills of its original creators. The cathedral's structure, was said to have gained its name from the fact that it was built with money paid by the faithful members of the parish for the privilege of consuming butter during Lent.

Following the tour itinerary suggested by the tourist office, the midway point of the tour will be the Palace of Justice. Three short blocks beyond, you will enter Rouen's old market area, with its narrow streets and half-timbered houses. There are more than 700 structures in Rouen illustrating the typical architecture of the city from the Middle Ages to the end of the eighteenth century. The houses were termed "half-timbered" because their external and internal walls were constructed of timber frames and the spaces between the structural members were filled with brick plaster or wattle—woven reeds covered and plastered with clay. You'll note that the upper stories of many half-timbered houses in Rouen project out over the ground level. By doing so, the lower part of the house was protected against inclement weather.

Born a peasant in 1412, Joan of Arc believed she heard celestial voices. In 1429, during the Hundred Years' War when the English were about to capture Orleans, Joan convinced Charles VII (then Dauphine of France) of her divine mission and led the English at Compiegne in 1430. Subsequently, she underwent fourteen months of interrogation by her captors until burned at the stake in the Old Market Square at Rouen on 30 May 1431. The Maid of Orleans, national heroine and patron saint of France, by her valor decisively turned the Hundred Year's War in France's favor.

The place in the old market where Joan of Arc met her fate is marked by a huge cross of concrete and metal. Towering over it is a modern church, completed in 1979, its roof representing the flames of the stake. It blends masterfully into the scene against a background of black-and-white timbered houses. The impact of history can be felt here.

Last stop on the city tour is that huge clock you may have passed under en route to the tourist office. It was positioned at ground level until 1527, when the people of Rouen asked that it be raised so they could see it better. The city council obliged by housing it in the elegant Renaissance structure you see today. The clock is unique in that it has only one hand. The globe at the top, which is no longer functioning, used to indicate the phases of the moon. Although the clock was converted to electricity in 1928, the original mechanism is still in place.

Day Excursion to

Versailles   CELEBRATED SITE OF FRANCE

Depart Paris for Versailles from any station on RER Line C

Distance By Train: 11 miles (18 km)
Average Train Time: 30 minutes
No city code required
Versailles Tourist Information: Office de Tourisme, 7 rue de Reservoirs, 78000
Tel: 39 50 36 22; *Fax:* 39 50 68 07

Paris' RER Line C runs between Orly Airport and Versailles. Suggested stations are Austerlitz, Orsay, Pont St. Michel, or Invalides, the railway station close to the Hotel des Invaldes, which was founded by Louis XIV to serve as a military hospital and home for veterans. Gare Invalides can be reached via Métro line 8 or 13. Get off at the "Invalides" Métro stop.

Trains for Versailles also run from Montparnesse station, but those should not be used. The station in Versailles to which this line connects is a considerable distance from the palace. Trains running from Gare Invalides, however, take you to within easy walking distance. Trains on RER Line C from Gare d'Austerlitz in Paris terminate in Versailles. Therefore, stay on the train until it reaches the end of the line. The main function of this station appears to be assisting visitors coming to Versailles to see **the palace**. Bilingual signs and voice announcements will assist you.

Turn right as you exit the rail station and walk about one-hundred yards to the next main intersection, the one at the traffic light. Turn left at this point and proceed to the palace, which is readily visible from the intersection.

The palace is open May 2-September 30, Tuesday-Sunday, 0900-1800. The hours for the rest for the remainder of the year are Tuesday through Friday 1000-1200 and 1400-1700 on Saturdays and Sundays from 1000-1700. You may take guided tours (25 francs) inside the buildings and around the grounds,

Paris–Versailles

DEPART PARIS SAINT LAZARE STATION*	ARRIVE IN VERSAILLES STATION*	NOTES
0829	0842	(2)
0845	0915	(1)
0945	1015	(1)
1114	1127	(1)

DEPART VERSAILLES STATION	ARRIVE IN PARIS SAINT LAZARE STATION*	NOTES
1453	1507	(1)
1541	1609	(1)
1641	1709	(1)
1746	1759	(1)

(1) Daily, including holidays
(2) Daily, except Sundays

Distance: 11 miles/18 km
References: SNCF Indicature Officiel: Ville á Ville.

Note: An alternate mode of transportation is via the RER (express metro),
Line C, from Paris Austerlitz Station to Versailles Rive Gauche. Trains run
every fifteen to thirty minutes from 0530–0030. Journey time via RER is
thirty-seven minutes.

or you may purchase a small guidebook and conduct your own tour.
Admission, 45 francs; 35 francs for 18-25 year olds and Senior over 60; children under age 18, free.

The only way to understand the powerful influence that was exerted by
France during the centuries of rule by her monarch is to visit Versailles. Here,
only at Versailles, can you come to appreciate the spiritual, artistic, and political renown of France and its lineage of kings.

In 1623, Louis XIII (1601-1643) ordered a hunting lodge built on a hill
named Versailles in place of a windmill that had occupied the site until then. His
orders were followed immediately because there was no arguing with kings in
those days. The lodge was erected in 1624. Liking the spot so well, he then
ordered the lodge replaced by a grand mansion, which was completed in 1634.

His son, Louis XIV (1638-1715), the Sun King, liked the spot, too, hated
the crowds in Paris with equal vigor, and envied his finance minister's fine

home at Vaux le Vicomte to the extent that he came up with an order that put his dad's to shame—"Build a palace at Versailles to surpass all palaces!" Orders being orders, before long 36,000 men aided by 6,000 horses were at work building palace walls, digging lakes with canals to connect them, and transplanting a forest when the king and his gardener decided that God had planted it in the wrong place to begin with. Work continued on **the Palace of Versailles** over a period of fifty years.

The Sun King made certain that nothing from the outside world would be imported for Versailles if it could be created or found in France. The result was an extraordinary showcase of French culture.

Urged on, first by Madame de Pompadour and then by Madame Du Barry, Louis XV (1710-1774) also ordered additions to the palace, including the Petit Trianon, which Louis XVI (1754-1793) gave to his wife, Marie Antoinette, when he came to the throne.

Despite the splendor of this edifice, Marie and her coutiers were drawn to the fantasies of a hamlet erected for her by her loving husband. There, among other rural objects, stood a dairy barn complete with cows, among which Marie and her companions would cavort—much to the consternation of the bovines, who had never observed such carefree antics before among the peasants of the land.

Versailles is an extraordinary complex of marvels where the kings of France stood in insulation against the distant horrors of the Revolution. Its restoration to the original is a marvel in itself—a testament to the inheritors of its tradition.

Even with the crowds of visitors coming to Versailles on a weekend or a national holiday, it is difficult to realize how life on such a grandiose scale could take place. Let your imagination run by visualizing throngs of court favorites, courtiers, teams of prancing horses pulling royal carriages over the cobblestones of the courtyard, chambermaids scurrying about, valets rushing with the linens of the gentry, and butchers carving the roasts for the banquets under the surveillance of the king's hounds—all of this seventeenth-century tumult, cacophony, and frenzy taking place on a scale many times greater than any Cecil B. DeMille production.

It is impossible to see Versailles completely in one visit—three perhaps, but nothing less than that. Consequently, set priorities (and this may sound silly) by going there the first time and just wandering around. Go back the second time and take the tour. Return the third time to see the things you missed or wanted to see again from the times before.

Germany

Germany's reunification, symbolized by the fall of the Berlin Wall in late 1989, had a great impact on the overall German economy and way of life; it also opened new doors to tourism. Unifying public transportation systems of the East and West did, of course, play a major role in the total reunification process.

Germany is a land based on a rich, complex history on track to a vibrant future. In recent years, Germany has seen an influx of refugees and foreigners that has fostered a political culture more tolerant of the customs and traditions of others.

Located in the heart of Europe, Germany makes a convenient starting point for travel, especially by rail, to nearly anywhere in Europe. Major airports for North Americans are Berlin, Duesseldorf, Frankfurt, Hamburg, and Munich, all of which are connected by rapid transit (S-Bahn) to the city's center.

The Germans are famous for brewing some of the tastiest beer in the world, and they love celebrating dozens of national, regional and local holidays, holy or otherwise, with great passion, beer and wine tents, pageants, beer and wine, parades, beer and wine, festivals, beer and wine, markets, and lots of beer and wine.

The most well known festivals include the German Mardi Gras, also known as Fasching, Fastnacht, or Fastnet, which includes masked balls; Munich's Octoberfest, which attracts people from all over the world; the Hamburg Dom, Nuremberg's Christ Child's Market at Christmas, the Passion Plays at Oberammergau, and the Onion Market in Weimar. Oberammergau hosts the Passion Play only every 10 years and is already gearing up for the next performance in the year 2000.

Don't let the guttural German language frighten you, many Germans, particularly tourism and train personnel, are multi-lingual. It's the majority of Americans who are "uni"-lingual.

For more information on delightful Germany, contact the German Tourist Offices in North America: Internet: http://www.germany-tourism.de

Los Angeles: 11766 Wilshire Blvd., Suite 750, Los Angeles, CA 90025 Tel: (310) 575-9799; Fax: (310) 575-1565

New York: 122 E. Fourty-Second Street, Fifty-Second Floor, New York, NY 10168-0072. Tel.: (212) 661-7200; Fax: (212) 661-7174

Toronto: 175 Bloor Street East, North Tower, Suite 604, Toronto, Ontario M4W 3R8, Canada Tel: (416) 968-1570; Fax: (416) 968-1986

Banking

Hours are from 0830-1300 and from 1430-1600 Monday-Friday. Currency exchange offices are found at main line railway stations, airports, and border crosspoints. They are generally open from 0600-2200.

- **Currency:** Deutsche Mark (DM)
- **Exchange rate press time:** 1.77 Deutsche Marks = $1.00 U.S.

Communications

- **Country Dialing Code:** 49
- **Direct Dial:** AT&T Direct: 0130–0010; MCI 0130–0012; Sprint 0130–0013

Rail Travel In Germany

Deutsche Bahn AG (GermanRail) operates more than 25,000 miles of the unified rail networks of the former East and West Germany. The service in the West is still better than in the East and renovation and upgrades of the decrepit rail service in the East is requiring massive investments of money and ingenuity.

Germany's top-of-the-line, high-speed, long-distance **ICE (InterCity Express)** trains are big, bold, and beautiful, with an emphasis on passenger comfort and a wide range of services. ICEs, reaching speeds of up to 175 mph, depart hourly every day for major centers within Germany and into the Swiss cities of **Basle, Bern, Interlaken,** and **Zurich.** The network connects major cities in the north with the south and extends east to **Berlin** and **Dresden**.

Each train has a restaurant car, termed **BordRestaurant,** with two sections—a traditional-style dining car and a self-service bistro. They're big on other amenities, too, such as headphones, private lockers in which to stowe purses, cameras or other valuables while you visit the **BordRestaurant** car, and some have video systems. These trains operate **Berlin-Bremen, Hannover, Koln,** and in peak hours between **Hannover-Mannheim.**

Changing trains in Germany is a snap. Platforms are designed in such a way that the train you need to transfer to will be standing immediately across the platform from the train in which you arrive. Since most GermanRail trains are configured the same—first-class cars in the front, second-class cars

German Rail Pass

		ADULT	CHILD
5 days in 1 month	First Class	$276	$138
	Second Class	$188	$94
10 days in 1 months	First Class	$434	$217
	Second Class	$304	$152
15 days in 1 months	First Class	$562	$281
	Second Class	$410	$205

German Rail Twin Pass

Price is total for 2 people traveling together

5 days in 1 months	First Class	$414
	Second Class	$282
10 days in 1 months	First Class	$650
	Second Class	$456
15 days in 1 months	First Class	$842
	Second Class	$615

German Rail Youthpass

For travelers age 12–26, 2nd Class Rail Travel

5 days in 1 months	$146
10 days in 1 months	$200
15 days in 1 months	$252

in the rear, you merely cross the platform to find the same type of accommodation on the connecting train.

Train platforms are divided into sections A to E. If you are traveling on a long-distance train, consult the train configuration display to easily determine where you will be sitting.

Just when we thought porters went the way of the dinosaur, **porter service** is available in Dresden, Frankfurt am Main, Hamburg, Leipzig, Munich, Stuttgart, and Berlin Zoo stations. The porters wear blue uniforms and red caps. (DM 5.00 for first 2 items of luggage; DM 2.50 for each additional item.) Luggage require a deposit of 1 or 2 DM.

The new ICE2s have even more leg room, electronic destination indicators on the *outside* of the train cars, digital display seat reservation units above the seats, electronic 220V sockets for laptop computers, increased facilities for the disabled, and one car has a family compartment. The third generation ICE (NeiTec, or tilting) trains will be even more high tech and able to "tilt" to round curves at higher speeds.

Germany's **EuroCity (EC), InterCity (IC),** and **InterRegio (IR)** trains round out the mainline service. The **S-Bahn** ("Schnell," or "fast") rapid-transit system provides service to and from the suburban areas of Berlin, Cologne (Koln), Frankfurt, Hamburg, Leipzig, Munich, Nuremberg, and Stuttgart.

Eurailpass, Europass and **GermanRail Pass** are accepted on the above-mentioned trains. **Eurailpass, Europass and German Railpass bonuses** free travel on KD River Steamers on certain Rhine, Main and Moselle River sections and free travel on selected bus lines operated by Deutsche Touring/Europabus.

Base City...

Berlin

City Dialing Code: 30
Internet: http://www.berlin.de

Although eons apart, the modern city of Berlin and the ancient city of
Jericho shared a common occurrence—their walls "came tumblin' down."
The Bible (Joshua 6) is a bit vague concerning the actual date of the occurrence in Jericho; but we do know the Berlin Wall "fell" on November 9, 1989,
28 years after it was built. Berlin is now a whole city; Germany is one country; Berlin is the capital of the new Germany; and communism is on the wane
worldwide.

For Berlin, World War II ended on the afternoon of May 2, 1945. Of the
245,000 buildings in Berlin before the war, 50,000 had been destroyed or ren-
dered beyond repair. There was no electricity, no gas, no water. Before the
war, Berlin had 4.3 million inhabitants; in May 1945, the remaining 2.8 million began the task of clearing away the debris.

In July of that year, Berlin became a four-power city with a joint-Allied
administration composed of Britain, France, Russia, and the United States.
This division into zones turned the former German capital into an island of
occupation surrounded completely by a sea of Soviets. East and West were in
complete agreement about abolishing Nazism, but they had no common or
precise answer as to what would replace it. Moreover, it quickly became evident that the Soviet intention was to gain complete control of the city.

On June 24, 1948, the Soviets sealed off the West's section of the city and,
on the basis of "technical disorders," shut off their supply of electricity. They
were left with a meager thirty-six-day food supply. A disaster appeared immi-
nent, but two days later the largest airlift in history began. From July 1948 to
May 1949, the Western Allies transported, in some 213,000 flights, more than
1.7 million tons of food and other supplies to the beleaguered city. While
operating the airlift, seventy members of the Allied Air Forces lost their lives.
On May 12, 1949, the siege was lifted. Berliners began demonstrating their
political choice by moving en masse to the Western sectors.

By August 1961, faced with mass evacuation of their sector, the Soviets
began erecting the Berlin Wall. In 1989, after twenty-eight years of division,
the wall that Winston Churchill called the "Iron Curtain" was breached in
one night. Before it "fell," more than one hundred people lost their lives while
attempting to cross it. The eastern part of Berlin, including its historic center,
is once again easily accessible to visitors. The infamous Checkpoint Charlie
was dismantled. Its guardhouse is now a museum piece. Except for a small sec-

tion that will stand as a mute reminder, every vestige of the Berlin Wall has been removed.

With the demise of the Wall, Berlin nearly doubled in size. The reunited metropolis is rediscovering its traditional rhythm that made it famous throughout the world. Travelers from around the world are passing the word, "Berlin is worth the trip." Come to Berlin and stand in history.

Once again, Berlin is without boundaries. As it's been explained to us, "Berlin is more than the sum of two halves," and we agree.

Arriving By Air

Tegel (TXL), Tempelhof (THF), and Schönefeld (SXL). All three airports are connected with the city center by buses and trains.

- **Tegel Airport,** 5 miles northwest, is your most likely arrival airport. Exiting from Customs, you'll see an information office between two rows of ticket counters. Go there for transportation information. From that position, look over your right shoulder and you will see the money exchange office across the hall.

  Airport-City Links: Bus line 109, or X9, as well as the Airport Transport, takes you from Tegel Airport to Berlin Zoo rail station in about 20 minutes. If you have baggage, the Airport-Transport system is recommended.

- **Schönefeld** is served by many European airlines; you should check with the airline taking you into Berlin as to its landing airport. Tempelhof, which served as the Allies' airport during the Berlin Airlift (1948–1949), is in the southwest section of the city. Surrounded by a sea of buildings, it is used for regional flights.

  Airport-City Links: Airport-Transport or S-Bahn line S-9. Both connect with the Berlin Zoo rail station.

Arriving By Train

There are three major railway stations in Berlin: Zoo, Hauptbahnhof (Hbf.), and Lichtenberg. If you disembark at the Zoo Station, Berlin's main tourist information office is located nearby. There's ample time to get off the train since it will stand in the station at least five minutes before proceeding on to the Hauptbahnhof. The S-Bahn trains and the city's U-Bahn (subway) connect the three stations.

The day excursions to Dresden and Leipzig depart from the **Berlin Lichtenberg Station.**

- **Rail Information** by phone: Tel. 19419
- **Berlin's Zoo Station** is centrally located in the former "West" sector of Berlin. The majority of the city's hotels, pensions, hostels, restaurants, shopping centers, and entertainment also is in this area.

- **Baggage Storage.** Berlin Zoo is not a baggage cart station, since ramps to the train level are nonexistent and elevators normally are not available for public use. Porters are available by prearrangement, but the best assurance for a no-hassle visit to Germany's capital is to observe the golden rule of rail travelers: Take one medium-size suitcase—nothing else.
- **Money Exchange** is available at the DVB Bank Zoo. Use the Kaiser-Wilhelm Gedachtniskirche exit. Bank hours 0730–2200 Monday through Saturday and 0800–1900 Sunday. There is a 7.50 DM charge for cashing traveler's checks. An ATM is available outside the bank.
- **Train Information, Reservations, and Rail Pass Validation.** Descending from the trains into the main hall of the Berlin Zoo Station, there's a train information office (Reisezentrum) to the far left. Open daily 0530–2230. Facing the Reisezentrum, you'll find lockers on the left-hand side. Train departure and arrival information is posted on boards above the stairway.

Lichtenberg Station
- The **train information** office (Reisezentrum) is located on the far left side of the station as you come up from the trains. Hours: 0530–2230 daily. The Deutsche Bundesbahn (DB), or German Rail service counter is open 7 days a week, 24 hours a day for schedules.
- There is a Deutsche Bank across the street with an ATM. Hours: Monday and Wednesday, 0900–1300 and 1400–1530; Tuesday and Thursday, 0900–1300 and 1430–1800; Friday 0900–1230.

Berlin Hauptbahnhof
Deutsche Bundesbahn (DB) or German rail) service counter is located in the center of the main hall. The personnel can give schedule information 24 hours a day, 7 days a week, but don't count on them speaking English.
- For detailed information and to make reservations, go to the **Reisezentrum (train information office),** located along the back wall of the station, opposite the street exit. Hours: 0530–2230 daily. Lockers are to the right of the Reisezentrum as you face it.
- **Money exchange** facilities can be found by ascending either flight of stairs and walking toward the back hall. Hours: Monday-Friday, 0700–2200; Saturday 0700–1800; Sunday 0800-1600. There's also an ATM behind the DB service center.

Tourist Information/Hotel Reservations

For written information in advance, write to *Berlin Tourismus, Marketing GmbH*, am Karlsbad II, D-10785 Berlin.

Tel: (030) 25 00 25, *Fax:* (030) 25 00 24 24
Hours: Monday-Saturday, 0800–2200; Sunday, 0900–2100

The city's main tourist information office is within easy walking distance. To reach it, leave the Berlin Zoo Station via the Kaiser-Wilhelm-Gedachtinskirche (Kaiser Wilhelm Memorial Church) exit and walk toward the ruins of the church. Its jagged steeple is a stark reminder of war's destructive power. You see the **Europa Center** and its globe fountain, which Berliners affectionately refer to as "the wet dumpling." Stay on the left side of the Europa Center. The tourist information office is on the street side of the center, just before the Palace Hotel.

Another tourist information office is located at Brandenburg Gate and offers the same services as the one in the Europa Center. Hours: 0930–1800 daily. Both tourist offices can make hotel reservations (charge, 5 DM).

Getting Around in Berlin

One of the first things visitors should do on arrival in Berlin is to acquaint themselves with the city's phenomenal fast-train system—the S-Bahn ("S" is for *schnell*—fast) and the U-Bahn (underground train or subway). During rush hours, trains run every 3-5 minutes and approximately every 5-10 minutes at other times. The S- and U-Bahn systems are augmented by trams and buses. You can purchase an excellent city map for 1 DM and the map of the S-Bahn and U-Bahn system is free of charge

Standard tickets (*Einzelfahrschein*) for all forms of Berlin transportation cost 3.90 deutsche marks (DM), 16 DM for a 24-hour Welcome Card, or 29 DM for the 72-hour **Berlin and Potsdam Welcome Card** at any Berlin Transport Authority office (at Tegel Airport, look for the sign BVG in the airport's main hall) or tourist information office.

The city even operates an all-night bus system of buses and trams to "gather the barflies and the birds of paradise from the disco scene on the Kurfürstendamm."

Sightseeing/Attractions/Tours

The Top Tour is an innovative tourist bus system that makes 20 stops within the unified city, ranging from the Zoological Gardens in the west to Alexanderplatz in the east. You are free to hop off the red double-decker bus whenever you fancy and hop back on another bus when you want. The operator, Berlin's public transport company (BVG), will provide you with a free street map and information describing the stops. In effect, you become your own tour guide. Purchase a ticket at the tourist office for 35 DM.

Berlin is a fascinating city. Don't miss walking on the **Kurfürstendamm** and **Friedrichstrasse,** its shopping and entertainment streets. The **Berlin Zoo** is one of the finest in Europe, and there's no better place to relax than in the attractive **English Gardens**, dedicated by Sir Anthony Eden. Berliners call it the "Garden of Eden." The Berlin Welcome Card includes vouchers for many discounts or free admission to numerous museums, sightseeing tours, theaters, and other attractions in addition to the public transport tickets. Make use of it.

The **Friedrichstadtpalast** is Europe's largest light entertainment theatre and the 1998 program features gala performances, artistic displays, dancers and solo singers, and a live orchestra.

The **Berlin Teddy Museum** has a collection of some 3,000 teddy bears on display. It's located at No. 147 Kurfurstendamm. Hours: Wednesday-Friday, 1500-1800; donations welcome. Tel: 30 893 39 65.

Berliners claim they have more museums than they have rainy days. There are 168 museums housing collections of art, original artifacts, and other intriguing creations. Following Germany's reunification, the State Museums are being restored, extended and new buildings are being built to create an outstanding cultural center.

The **Old National Gallery** is closed as of summer 1998 for extensive restoration. A selection of its works, however, is on exhibition at the **Old Museum.**

Best of all, stand at the **Brandenburg Gate**—on either side—and feel democracy in action.

Day Excursions from Berlin

Three day excursions have been selected. All of them—**Dresden, Leipzig,** and **Potsdam**—are typical German cities in their own right. Since the end of World War II, and until the "Fall of The Wall," they had been a part of the German Democratic Republic, more often referred to as "East Germany." Consequently, tourist facilities are more limited and travel is a little slower than that which you may have experienced in the western part of Germany.

Dresden is an important city in the historic German state of Saxony, and probably best known for its product, Dresden china. **Leipzig** is also a part of Saxony and owes much of its prestige to its cultural accomplishments. **Potsdam** owes its appeal to Frederick the Great, who took the concept of *sans souci* (without care or worry) and transformed it into the reality of the delightful Sanssouci Palace. It was also the scene of the Potsdam Conference in 1945, where Harry (Truman) met "Old Joe" (Stalin) and got to like him— at least for a little while.

Train Connections to other Base Cities from Berlin

TO:	DEPART	ARRIVE	TRAIN NUMBER	NOTES
Amsterdam	0750	1448	IR 2344	(5)
	1150	1848	IR 2342	
Brussels (Midi)	0913	1803	IC 621	(8)
	2100	0655 + 1	242	
Hamburg	0927	1152	IC 876	(7)
	1227	1440	IC 808	(7)
	1627	1847	IC 804	(7)
Copenhagen	1227	2000	IC 808	(1)(8)
	0627	1420	EC 182	(6)(8)
Munich	0940	1706	IC 813	(2)
	1140	1906	IC 803	(2)
Oslo	1227	0707	IC 808/EC 186/+392	(1)(4)
Paris (Nord)	1113	2235	EC 32	(3)
	2100	0908 + 1	242	25
Prague	0646	1139	EC 171	
	1046	1539	EC 175	
	1646	2130	EC 179	
	1246	1730	EC 177	
Stockholm	2314	1353 + 1	318/530	(2)(4)(8)

All departures from Berlin Zoo Station unless otherwise noted. Daily departures unless otherwise noted. Make seat reservations for all departures.

(1) Departs from Berlin Lichtenberg
(2) Departs from Berlin Hauptbahnhof
(3) Transfer in Köln to 238, transfer in Brussels to TGV 9344
(4) Transfer in Malmo
(5) June 2 starts from Hanover
(6) Transfer in Hamburg to EC 188
(7) Hamburg Altona
(8) Supplement payable

Day Excursion to

Dresden   China, Carillons, and Culture

Depart from Berlin Lichtenberg Station

City Dialing Code: 351
Distance By Train: 117 miles (189 km)
Average Train Time: 2 hours, 30 minute
Dresden Tourist Information Office: Dresden Tourist Board, Goetheallee 18, D-01309
Tel: 49 19 20 *Fax:* 310 52 47
Internet: www.dresden-info.fhg.de
Hours: 0900–2000, Monday-Friday; 0900–1600 Saturday; and 0900–1400 Sunday from April-October.

In the winter, the center is open on weekdays, but for fewer hours. Five-minute walk on Prager Strasse across the street from the rail station will take you there.

Dresden's name is derived from *Drezdzane,* the old Slavic word for "forest people," who were the early settlers in the area. Dresden is situated in the wide, gentle valley of the Elbe River, about 19 miles (30 kilometers) from the northwest border of the Czech Republic. Although the city's fame comes mainly from its past cultural achievements, Dresden also is economically important and is best known for its Dresden china.

Dresden has always enjoyed the delightful harmony of the river and nature in which to develop from its beginnings as a small Slavonic fishing village. As it grew, its scenic beauty was enhanced in the seventeenth and nineteenth centuries by builders who erected fine examples of baroque and rococo architecture. This, in turn, attracted a great number of artists and writers as Dresden grew into a modern, confident city of a half-million citizens. With its architectural landmarks and its art treasures of Dutch, Flemish, and Italian collections, Dresden gained the well-deserved title, "Florence of the Elbe."

On February 13, 1945, more than a half-million bombs rained down on Dresden from Anglo-American aircraft. Thirty-five thousand citizens died and more than fifteen square miles of the inner city were reduced to rubble. The air raid devastated nearly all of the city's cultural monuments. Dresden was declared dead.

But Dresden is rising like a Phoenix. Dust from the air raid scarcely settled before restoration began on the **Semper Opera House**. Forty years to the day, February 13, 1985, Dresden's population celebrated the reopening of this world-famous theater and many other cultural and historic edifices have been rebuilt.

Dresden's *Altmarkt* (old market) is the historic center of the city. Between 1953 and 1956 it was rebuilt. The city's botanical gardens, completely destroyed in 1945, were rebuilt in 1950. Only nine zoo animals survived the

Berlin—Dresden

DEPART BERLIN LICHTENBERG	ARRIVE IN DRESDEN HAUPTBAHNHOF	TRAIN NUMBER	NOTES
0646	0848	EC 171	(1)(2)
0846	1037	EC 173	(1)(2)
0932	1137	IR 2373	(1)(3)
1046	1237	EC 175	(1)(2)
1246	1437	EC 177	(1)(2)
1447	1637	IC 871	(1)(2)

DEPART DRESDEN HAUPTBAHNHOF	ARRIVE IN BERLIN LICHTENBERG	TRAIN NUMBER	NOTES
1517	1710	EC 176	(1)(2)
1717	1910	EC 174	(1)(2)
1917	2110	EC 172	(1)(2)
2117	2310	EC 170	(1)(2)

(1) Daily, including holidays
(2) Restaurant car
(3) Light refreshment

Distance: 117 Miles/189 km

---

air attack, but in 1961 the zoo reopened with a stock of more than 2,000 animals representing nearly 500 species.

With typical Dresden determination, on February 13, 1992, the city announced that the **Frauenkirche** (Church of Our Lady)—decried by the communists to stand in ruin forever—would be rebuilt. Dresden has returned!

Obtain the *"Tourist City Guide"* from the tourist office. It contains a city map, places of interest, sightseeing tours, and just about everything you might ever want to know about Dresden. The **Old Town** is on the left bank of the Elbe and the **New Town** is across the river on its right bank. If you are an average sightseer, as we are, you can reach the Old Town area on foot from the city center in no more than 15 minutes.

Ask about the **Dresden Card**, which provides for free public transportation, free entrance to many museums, and discounts on city tours and boat tours on the Elbe for a 48-hour period. In typical German fashion, the city's *Rathaus* (town hall) has a *Ratskeller* (restaurant) in its cellar where you may enjoy a cold draft and a sample of Saxon food before setting out to see the town.

One of the many magnificent edifices vying for your attention during your Dresden visit is the **Zwinger**. It is known as the most important late baroque building in Germany. The name "Zwinger" is a term used in the construction of fortresses and defines the space between the outer and inner ramparts. Heavily damaged in 1945, the reconstruction of the Zwinger was said to have begun "instantaneously" despite communist objections. It was restored to its present condition by 1963.

If you cross the Elbe, be sure to use Dresden's famous **Loschwitzer-Blasewitzer Bridge.** Opened in 1893, it was the only bridge to remain intact by 1945. The SS had the bridge set for destruction, but two Dresdeners, each unaware of the other's action, cut the wire to the explosives. The grateful populace of Dresden now refer to the bridge as the "Blue Miracle."

Make it a point to visit the **Old Masters Picture Gallery** in the Zwinger Semperbau and examine the famous views of the court painter, Bernardo Bellotto. They show the city at the peak of its splendor.

The dome of the **Frauenkirche** (Church of Our Lady) dominates the scene. The Frauenkirche is the largest German Baroque and Protestant church and also the world's largest centrally planned Protestant church. It is undergoing archaeological reconstruction, i.e., incorporating the remaining fragments in the reconstruction. Another feature is **Raffael's** *Sistine Madonna.*

The church's reconstruction site is near the **Albertinum Museum** at Brühlsche Terrace. The Albertinum houses the New Masters Picture Gallery, the "Green Vault," treasure chamber, and numismatic and sculpture collections. Hours: 1000–1800 daily, except Thursday.

Day Excursion to

Leipzig

Bach and Mendelssohn Memories

Depart from Berlin Zoo or Lichtenberg Stations

City Dialing Code: 341
Distance By Train: 113 miles (182 km)
Average Train Time: 2 hours, 15 minutes
Leipzig Tourist Information, Richard-Wagner-Strasse 1, D-04109
Tel: 7 10 43 32; *Fax:* 7 10 43 41
Internet: http:www.uni-leipzig.de/leipzig/Its
Hours: 0900–1900 Monday-Friday; Saturday-Sunday. 0930–1400
      Located directly opposite the rail station—5-minute walk

Like many cities and towns in Europe, Leipzig has an old and a new section. Leipzig's old town is located between three rivers, the Parthe, the Elster, and the Pleisse. No doubt the site selection had much to do with safety, and the proximity to three navigable rivers also indicates an early interest in trade. Leipzig has been known for its great trade fairs that date back to the Middle

Berlin–Leipzig

DEPART FROM BERLIN (ZOO) HAUPTBAHNHOF	TRAIN NUMBER	ARRIVE IN LEIPZIG STATION	NOTES
0743	IC 703	0934	(1)(2)
0943	IC 813	1134	(1)(2)
1143	IC 803	1334	(1)(2)

DEPART FROM LEIPZIG STATION	TRAIN NUMBER	ARRIVE IN BERLIN (ZOO) HAUPTBAHNHOF	NOTES
1422	IC 804	1615	(1)(2)
1622	IC 812	1815	(1)(2)
1822	IC 802	2015	(1)(2)
2022	IC 702	2215	(1)(2)

(1) Daily, including holidays
(2) Restaurant car

Distance: 113 miles/182 km

Ages and still attract business people from all over the world.

The city's name is derived from *Lipsk*, the original Slav settlement named for the lime trees (*lipa*) growing there. Built as a walled city in the eleventh century, the walls surrounding the old town were replaced in the eighteenth century by a ring of parks and promenades. Subsequently, Leipzig expanded in all directions by gradually incorporating the suburbs that were growing up around it—a tactic followed by many American cities.

Newly reconstructed in 1997, Leipzig's main rail terminal *(Hauptbahnhof)* has 23 platforms (plus 4 outside platforms) and is the largest rail terminal in Europe. The three-level station houses restaurants, shops, cafes, meeting rooms, travel agencies, money exchange, and other tourist facilities. More than 800 trains move through the terminus daily, carrying an estimated 75,000 passengers. There's no need to worry about its size, since the Hauptbahnhof comes well equipped with pictographs.

The **Leipzig Card** provides transport on trams and buses and on the city railway to the New Trade-Fair Centre. There are also reductions on city tours, museums, and concerts. 1-Day Card, 9.90 DM; 1-Day Party Card (2 adults and up to 3 children under age 14), 3-Day Card, 21 DM; 3-Day Party Card, 34 DM. Purchase at the tourist office, rail station, and many hotels.

The main attraction on the old town's market square is the **Old Town Hall.** It was built in the record time of nine months in 1556 by Hieronymus

Lotter. The building is one of the oldest Renaissance town halls still standing on German soil. Although severely damaged by fire during the Allied air raid on December 4, 1943, the building's facade remains almost unchanged from the sixteenth century. The city was governed from here until 1905, when a new town hall was erected in a more spacious area. Since 1909 the building has been the **Museum of History of the City of Leipzig**. Its attractions include the Old Council Chambers, the Mendelssohn Room, and special exhibits.

The **new town hall,** built between 1899 and 1905 on the foundations of earlier buildings, also will attract your attention with its 115-meter tower. It houses both the mayor and the city council.

Within the rim of the old town, the spires of the **Church of Saint Nicholas** and the **Church of Saint Thomas** stand as sentinels over the scene. The first mention of Saint Nicholas was made in 1017; Saint Thomas was erected between 1212 and 1222 as the collegiate church of the Augustinian Choir. Its late-Gothic hall was added at the end of the fifteenth century.

The stained-glass windows of Saint Thomas, dating from the end of the nineteenth century, depict three historical personalities closely associated with Leipzig: Johann Sebastian Bach, Martin Luther, and King Gustav Adolf II of Sweden. Saint Thomas became world famous from its association with Johann Sebastian Bach. The great composer served as cantor of the church from 1723 to 1750. Since 1950, the remains of the great composer have lain in the church.

The Church of Saint Nicholas, although containing some of the oldest building remains in Leipzig, recently played an important part in the reunification of Germany. From 1982, the prayers for peace held every Monday under the sheltering roof of the church "transmitted" loud and clear signals to the Leipzig demonstrators—impulses that, during the days of October and November 1989, brought about the "gentle revolutions" that led to the downfall of the communist dictatorship.

Outside Leipzig's old town you can visit the **Leipzig Zoo,** which was founded in 1878. The city information center will tell you it's "only a 15-minute walk," but perhaps a taxi would be better. The zoo is noted for its lions and tigers, including the breeding of some 2,500 purebred Berber lions. An unusual feature of the zoo is its "shop-window" whereby spectators are separated from the animals only by a moat—a *deep* moat.

Like Munich, at the end of World War II, the city constructed a stadium seating 100,000 spectators from the rubble left by the war. The stadium was the first major building project in Leipzig following the war. Three million cubic meters of rubble were used for the 23-meter-high terraces.

Day Excursion to

Potsdam
WHERE HARRY MET JOE

Depart from Berlin Zoo or Wannsee Station

City Dialing Code: 331
Distance By Train: 22 miles (36 km)
Average Train Time: 26 minutes
Potsdam Tourist Information: 5, Friedrich-Ebert-Strasse
Tel: 0331/275580 or 0331/291100; *Fax:* 0331/293012
Hours: April-October, 0900-2000 Monday-Friday; 1000-1800 Saturday; 1000-1600 Sunday.
November-March, 1000-1800 Monday-Friday; 1000-1400 Saturday-Sunday.

Located in the old market, a 10-minute walk from the railway station. Turn right out of the station and walk across the Lange Brucke (Long Bridge) and up the Friedrich-Ebert-Strasse to the center, which is located on the right side of the street. Ask for the illustrated pamphlet, *Info—Stadtplan Potsdam.*

Originally a small settlement of Slavs, Potsdam first appeared in German chronicles under the name *Poztupimi* (Under the Oak Trees) in a Deed of Gift dated July 3, 993. There are virtually no oak trees left in present-day Potsdam, but you will find a large number of handsome mansions and palaces from days gone by surrounded by beautiful parks.

After a period of almost total insignificance during the Middle Ages, Potsdam eventually entered the sphere of German history in the seventeenth century when Frederick William, the Elector of Brandenburg, decided to make Potsdam his place of residence.

In the eighteenth century, during the reigns of King Frederick William I and his son Frederick II, known as Frederick the Great, Potsdam grew to be a prestigious royal seat and garrison town. Frederick William I established a military orphanage where the boys "learned to work" in nearby factories and also drilled in "square bashing," which came in handy whenever the impoverished peasants could no longer stand their plight and chose to demonstrate in the town square.

Unlike many towns emerging from the Middle Ages, Potsdam was not surrounded by a wall until the eighteenth century. Oddly enough, the wall served not so much as a military protection as it did to prevent soldiers from deserting and dishonest folks from smuggling. Whether the wall contributed to the growth of the town is not known, but Potsdam did flourish under the Fredericks. The Alten Markt (old market), the Hollandisches Viertel (Dutch quarters), the **Brandenburger Strasse,** and the **Sans Souci Park and Palace** date to the era of their reign.

Frederick II was growing a bit "long-in-the-tooth" and decided he want-

Berlin–Potsdam

DEPART BERLIN (ZOO)	TRAIN NUMBER	ARRIVE IN POTSDAM STADT	NOTES
0750	IR 2344	0807	(1)(2)
1150	IR 2342	1207	(1)(2)

Plus frequent S-Bahn service between Berlin Zoo and Potsdam Stadt

DEPART POTSDAM STADT	TRAIN NUMBER	ARRIVE IN BERLIN (ZOO) STATION	NOTES
1622	RE 3509	1639	(1)(2)
2022	RE 3513	2039	(1)(2)

Plus frequent S-Bahn service between Potsdam Stadt and Berlin Zoo

(1) Daily, including holidays
(2) Light refreshment

Distance: 22 miles/36 km

---

ed to live "without cares" (*sans souce*). So, beginning in 1744 and during the following three decades, "Old Fritz" supervised the building of the palace and several other buildings, including his own tomb as a last resting place beside the palace.

The rococo Sans Souci Palace was built from sketches by the king himself, together with designs by his architect, Knobelsdorff. With a large number of further additions during the nineteenth century, Sans Souci stands today on a 717-acre complex as one of the largest and most significant parks in Europe.

But "Old Fritz" would not rest. After the Seven Years' War, in which he lost all the battles but won the war, he celebrated his "victory" by building another palace—the **Neues Palais** (new palace).

The Potsdam Information Center conducts two bus tours. The first, a city tour that includes a stop at the **Cecilienhof Palace,** the scene of the Potsdam Conference, begins at 1215. Cost: 27 DM. The second tour, which includes a tour of the **Sans Souci Palace** and its gardens, leaves the center at 1245 (3-hours). Cost: 35 DM. Open year round and closed Mondays.

If you like palaces, you've come to the right place. **Charlottenhof Palace,** a part of the Sans Souci complex, comes complete with Roman baths. The baths, by the way, were not intended for the purpose of hygiene but formed a part of a museum-like dream world reflecting the romantic yearnings of Crown Prince Frederick William (Fat William).

The **Marble Palace** and the **New Garden**—called "new" in contrast with the "old" gardens at Sans Souci—were ordered built by "Fat William" when he was crowned in 1786. At press time, the Marble Palace is still closed for restoration but scheduled to reopen in mid-1998.

Potsdam's **old town** is a great place to browse. Right in the center of it you feel as though you've been transferred to Holland. To attract Dutch crafts-men to Potsdam, more than one hundred middle-class Dutch baroque-style houses were built between 1734 and 1742. The project failed in that it did not attract Dutchmen in the number expected, but the houses were inhabited, in turn, by Potsdam's craftsmen, artists, and military. Sometimes things just don't work out the way you want them to. Perhaps that is Potsdam's penchant—read on.

The son of Kaiser Wilhelm, Crown Prince William, built a second palace at the New Garden from 1913 to 1915. He named it **Cecilienhof** after his Crown Princess. Unlike his father, who never returned from his Dutch exile, the ex-Crown Prince did move back into Cecilienhof Palace in 1923 and stayed there until 1945, bringing a number of interesting guests.

From July 17 until August 2, 1945, Cecilienhof played host to the Potsdam Conference, the third and final meeting of Churchill, Stalin, and Truman. One of the conference aims was the unity of Germany, though what followed was actually its division. Harry Truman returned from the conference stating that he "liked old Joe." But just like the time when Harry met Sally, things didn't quite work out the way they wanted them to.

Base City...

Hamburg

City Dialing Code: 40
Internet: http://www.hamburg.de

The Free and Hanseatic City of Hamburg is an impressive title—for an equally impressive city. Its 1.7 million residents are intensely proud of their city and are most anxious to show it. Hamburg is the largest in a league of "Hansa" cities in Germany that medieval merchants organized to secure greater safety and privileges in trading. For a long time, nobility was barred from entering this affluent city that sits poised between the Elbe River and Alster Lake.

Hamburg is full of surprises. It has more bridges than the combined total of Amsterdam and Venice. The city's harbor is one of the leading ports in Europe and ranks as one of the top twelve container ports in the world—notwithstanding the fact that it is 68 miles inland from the North Sea!

Chartered in 1189, Hamburg occupies a 288-square-mile area, 20 percent of which is covered by water. To the delight of residents and visitors alike, about 10 percent of the city's total area has been landscaped into public parks. Many of these areas date back to the eighteenth century, when landscaping was fostered by the city's wealthy residents as one of the arts.

Hamburgians have their port to thank for the development of their city to its present stature—an expansive metropolis of international business and culture. During the first weekend of May, the Hamburgians begin a three-day celebration to commemorate the year 1189 when Emperor Frederick Bararossa granted Hamburg its "free port" status. The term, "free port" means that transit cargo is exempt from all custom duties. All goods may be stored, transported, inspected, sampled, or processed for special storage without formalities or restrictions. For example, coffee, tea, and tobacco are refined in a free port so as to make them immediately consumable when they are forwarded to their final destination, where customs duties are then levied for the first time.

Not all of the harbor area is classified as a "free port." In 1881, Chancellor Otto von Bismark rescinded Hamburg's "free port city" status and restricted it to only have a free port zone. Fortunately, it had little effect. In fact, port trade flourished as never before and Hamburg quickly rose to the rank of the third largest port in the world.

Arriving By Air

Fuhlsbüttel International Airport, 8 miles north of the city center. Although it has four terminals, all international arrivals and departures utilize Terminal 4.

- **Airport-City Links:** Express bus service between the airport and a nearby S-Bahn station where frequent train service into Hamburg is available. If you are burdened with baggage, use the Airport-City bus; departures every 20 minutes, 0530–2300, for Hamburg"s Hauptbahnhof (main rail station). Journey time: 25-30 minutes. Fare, 8 deutsche marks (DM); round trip, 12 DM. From city center to airport, service 0540-2120. For taxis, follow the pictographs. Average taxi fare to the city center, 25 DM.
- **Tourist information** is opposite the airport information desk in Terminal 4 on the arrivals level. Hours: 0800–2300 daily.
- **Money exchange:** Deutsche Bank in the arrivals hall of Terminal 4, hours 0630-2030 daily. Icelandair and Lufthansa operate transatlantic services to and from Hamburg.

Arriving By Train

The Hamburg **Hauptbahnhof** (rail station) appears as though it was constructed to handle the dirigible *Hindenburg*. Its immensity is impressive. There are 14 gleise (tracks). Gleise 1 to 4 serve the S-Bahn, the suburban rail service; gleise 5 through 14 are for regular train service.

Hamburg is the northern terminus of the InterCity Express (ICE). These sleek trains glide in and out of the Hauptbahnhof on gleise 13 and 14.

For a full service restaurant, visit the InterCity Restaurant, accessible by elevator, on the station's second floor front. The Gourmet Station on the main floor features national and international dishes. It's informal. Opposite the Gourmet Station are various boutiques in the "Wandelhalle."

- **Baggage storage** carts are scarce. The baggage room is the best source for a cart or a porter.
- **Money exchange** hours, 0730-2200 daily.
- **Post office** hours, Monday-Friday, 0700-2100; Saturday-Sunday, 0800-2000.
- **International telephones** are on the second floor of the post office.
- **Train information** is in the *Reisezentrum* (central ticket office). Hours: 0530-2300 daily.
- **Rail passes** can be validated at window 20 or any window marked AUS-LAND. Information windows are 21 to 24. If the attendant does not speak English, you will be referred to one who does.
- **Tourist office** in the main rail station open daily, 0700-2300 (Tel: 300 51 201 or 202).

Tourist Information/Hotel Reservations

The Hamburg Tourist Board has two information offices—one at St. Pauli Landungsbrücken (landing pier) facing the harbor and one in the main rail station.

For advance planning, contact

Hamburg Tourist Board
Post Office Box 10 22 49
20015 Hamburg, Germany
Tel: 40 300510; Fax: 40 30051333

Hotline for **hotel reservations**: 40 30051300

In addition to general information, the board's information service can provide accommodation bookings; bookings for port tours and Alster cruises; arrangements for guides; and tips on sightseeing, dining, and shopping.

Visitors of Germanic origins will be interested in the **Historic Emigration Office** (Tel: 40-30051-282) of the Hamburg Tourist Board. It is Germany's only historic emigration office, based on the register of German emigrants kept by the municipal authorities from 1850 to 1934. The register has five million names of people who set sail via the Port of Hamburg for a new life overseas. Family-tree hunters need the emigrant's name and year of emigration. There is a charge of $30 for the search and a passenger list print-out.

Getting Around in Hamburg

Purchase a **Hamburg-CARD** at tourist information offices, metro (in-city) station vending machines, and at most hotels. The CARD is a real bargain. It entitles you to travel free on the city's bus and train systems, subways, and port ferries at any time within the card's period of validity. It also provides free admission to 11 museums and includes reductions up to 30 percent for such activities as the Alster tour, the Port tour, and many others.

The **Hamburg-CARD** is available as a daily card or a multiple-day card. The tourist information office will provide you with a brochure, *City Map and Tips from A to Z*, which explains the card's features.

Sightseeing/Attractions/Tours — Hamburg Highlights

A **tour of the harbor** by launch is available year-round. (The launches are heated in winter.) In summer, the tour operates every half hour from 0900-1800; for winter tours contact the tourist information office. The launches sail from St. Pauli pier. From the Hauptbahnhof, take either the metro line U2, or S-Bahn lines S1, S2, or S3 to the Landungsbrücken station. Tickets: 15 DM adults; 7.50 DM children. Hamburg-CARD holders pay 11 DM and 6.50 DM, respectively. The tour takes about one hour. Ask for a launch with an English-speaking captain.

From April through October, leisure cruise boats depart from the quay at Jungfernstieg—Hamburg's elegant shopping street—to **cruise on Lake Alster**. Actually, the Alster is not really a lake. It is a tributary of the Elbe River that has been widened into a lake just before it flows into the Elbe River. This 460-acre lake, an area larger than the entire principality of Monaco, was created when the Alster was dammed in the early thirteenth century.

There is a wide selection of tours available on the Alster ferries, including a one-hour trip along its shoreline, a tour of the city's canal system, a bridge tour where you'll see a sampling of the city's 2,400 bridges, and a twilight tour. A guided tour of the **Inner and Outer Alster** operates every half hour, 1000-1800; tour duration, about 50 minutes. Adults:14 DM; children, 7 DM; Hamburg-CARD holders receive a discount. To inquire, visit the **Alster-Touristik office** on the quay where the boats depart. (Tel: 3574240). Brochures also are available in all of the Hamburg tourist offices.

Take a ride on the **Hamburger Hummelbahn.** Hamburg-CARD holders get a substantial discount. Hummel is German for "bumble bee," and this amazing form of transportation literally "buzzes" all over town. The train does not run on tracks. Its open platforms are ideal for photographing. It's a fun trip.

If you are in Hamburg on a Sunday, reserve a good part of the day for a visit to the **Fischmarkt** (fish market). Dating from about 1703, it is the oldest licensed market in Hamburg where just about everything that is movable is sold or traded. Fish? Well, fish have become incidental to the market's activities; freshly caught fish, however, are still sold any day of the week from fishing boats at the city's pier.

On Sunday mornings, the pubs scattered around the fish market area draw crowds of early-risers and late-night-revelers alike. Take in the Sunday morning auction activities held in the **Fischauktionshalle** (fish auction hall). The auction hall opens promptly at 0500 (0700 in winter), and lasts only until 1000, so hurry. Following the auction, treat yourself to a jazz breakfast right in the Fischauktionshalle.

Shopping is an international pastime and Hamburg is a wonderful place to pursue such interests. No city on the Continent has so many covered shopping arcades. As a jumping-off place, start at the **Jungfernstieg** where the white ferries depart for water tours of the Alster Lake. Here, you will find covered arcades where shoppers may stroll regardless of the weather. For big department store shopping, head for **Monckebergstrasse** directly east from the **Rathaus,** Hamburg's city hall. Or, get off to a flying start right after arriving by train in Hamburg at the Wandelhalle, the covered mall above the train platforms in the Hauptbahnhof.

Hamburg abounds in museums catering to all interests. As a port city, Hamburg maintains two museum ships, the **Rickmer Rickmers,** a reminder of bygone days when sailing ships ruled the waves, and the **Cap San Diego,** the "White Swan of the South Atlantic." Both museum ships offer discounts to Hamburg-CARD holders and are open daily starting at 1000.

Those interested in erotic art will not want to miss Hamburg's **Erotic Art Museum** located in the very heart of St. Pauli, between the Reeperbahn and the Hafenstrasse. Hours: 1000-2400 daily.

As the night lengthens, **St. Pauli,** the entertainment district, springs into action with numerous pubs, restaurants, and discos along the (in)famous **Reeperbahn, Hans-Albers-Platz,** and the **Grosse Freiheit.** Hamburg has no inhibitions and no curfew. See for yourself—there's a 4-hour bus tour, "Hamburg at Night," that starts from the Hauptbahnhof at 2000 every evening except Sunday and Monday. The cost is 99 DM and includes admission to selected bars.

Day Excursions

Hamburg is situated in the center of a vast railway network. Consequently, the availability of day-excursion opportunities is virtually limitless.

Bremen, another great Hanseatic city of Germany, is in contrast to Hamburg, although jointly the two provide the largest operation of seaports within Germany today.

To the south of Hamburg, in the midst of the Weser Hills, stands the fascinating town of **Hameln,** where the tale of the legendary Pied Piper is reenacted every Sunday.

Ride the pride of the German fleet—the German ICE (InterCity Express)—to **Hannover** for a rewarding day of sightseeing amid the city's beautiful parks and gardens.

Lübeck is Germany's largest Hanseatic port on the Baltic and one of the oldest and most beautiful towns in Germany today. Go early and enjoy!

Train Connections to Other Base Cities from Hamburg

TO:	DEPART	ARRIVE	TRAIN NUMBER	NOTES
Amsterdam	0953	1448	IC 729	(1)
	1353	1848	IC 625	(2)
	1753	2248	IC 829	(3)
Berlin (Zoo)	0903	1132	IC 803	
	1103	1332	IC 805	
	1303	1532	IC 807	
	1703	1932	IC 705	
Brussels (Midi)	0753	1455	EC 29/422	(4)
	1053	1801	IC 621/EC 46	(4)
	1153	1855	IC 823/430	(4)
Copenhagen	0730	1159	EC 180	
	0912	1420	EC 182	
	1512	2031	EC 186	
Munich	0853	1441	ICE 585	
	1053	1641	ICE 587	
	1453	2043	ICE 681	
Oslo	1512	0707	IC 521	(5)
Paris	0853	1805	ICE 621/EC 38	(4)(9)
	1253	2235	ICE 523/EC 32	(4)
Stockholm	1827	0753+1	EC 188/282	(6)
Vienna	2038	0845+1	EN 491	
Zürich	0636	1403	ICE 79/IC 775	(7)(8)
	1036	1803	ICE 71/EC 3	(7)
	1236	2003	ICE 77	(7)
	1436	2213	ICE 775	(7)

Daily departures from Hamburg Hauptbahnhof unless otherwise noted. Make reservations for all departures.

(1) Transfer in Osnabrück to train 2344
(2) Transfer in Osnabrück to train 2342
(3) Transfer in Osnabrück to train 2340
(4) Transfer in Cologne (Köln), supplement payable
(5) Transfer in Copenhagen
(6) Transfer in Copenhagen
(7) Transfer in Basel
(8) Monday through Saturday only
(9) Transfer in Brussels

Day Excursion to

Bremen

AND THE TOWN MUSICIANS

Depart from Hamburg Hauptbahnhof

City Dialing Code: 421
Distance By Train: 76 miles (120 km)
Average Train Time: 55 minutes
Bremen Tourist Information: Hillmannplatz 6, D-28195. Opposite the Hauptbahnhof (main rail station) or on Liebfrauenkirchhof Square
Tel: 308400–5051; *Fax:* 30 814-30
Hours: 0930-1830 Monday-Friday (until 2000 on Thursday and Friday), 0930-1600 Saturday-Sunday.

Bremen is Germany's oldest maritime city. Bremen got its start as a port city in the tenth century when Emperor Otto I approved the construction of its docks.

It lies on the Weser River, 44 miles upstream from the mouth. Bremen is the second largest port in Germany. With so much to see and do in Bremen, we recommend that rail travelers visiting Bremen for the first time confine their sightseeing to the area in and around the city's market square, then follow up on a second visit with an inspection of the city's extensive harbor facilities. Certainly the charm of the market and its immediate surroundings will beckon the traveler to return again.

Finding your way from the Bremen railway station to the **market square** is an easy task. Attendants there can give you a considerable amount of information regarding Bremen. Particularly informative is a brochure entitled "Bremen, Cosmopolitan and Historic" (free). The brochure contains background information on all aspects of Bremen.

The most direct route to the market square is down **Bahnhofstrasse,** which begins in front of the station. Proceed to where it intersects with Sogestrasse and crosses a former moat. A landmark at this point is a large windmill, seen in the distance on the right when crossing the bridge. Proceeding two blocks straight ahead on Sogestrasse brings you to the threshold of the old city center. A short walk through a shopping area and you are in the market square, where the **cathedral,** the *Rathaus* (city hall), and the **Liebfrauenkirche** are all clustered.

Bremen's oldest resident, the statue of **Roland** which was erected in 1404, is the center of attraction in the market square. Roland is a symbol of justice and freedom. Legend has it that Bremen will not pass away as long as the stone giant is still standing in the marketplace. Legend also has it that the city fathers have a replacement ready—just in case.

No one is quite certain as to Roland's origins. City history first mentions

Hamburg–Bremen

DEPART HAMBURG HAUPTBAHNHOF	TRAIN NUMBER	ARRIVE IN BREMEN STATION	NOTES
0753	EC 29	0847	(1)(2)
0853	IC 521	0947	(1)(2)
0953	IC 729	1047	(1)(2)
1053	IC 621	1147	(1)(2)
1153	IC 823	1247	(1)(2)
1253	IC 523	1347	(1)(2)

DEPART BREMEN STATION	TRAIN NUMBER	ARRIVE IN HAMBURG HAUPTBAHNHOF	NOTES
1615	IC 524	1707	(1)(2)
1715	IC 728	1807	(1)(2)
1815	IC 620	1907	(1)(2)
1915	IC 522	2007	(1)(2)
2015	IC 520	2107	(1)(2)
2215	IC 724	2307	(1)(2)

(1) Daily, including holidays
(2) Food service available

Distance: 115 miles/183 km

---

the existence of the knightly statue in the marketplace in 1366, but it was made of wood and went up in flames. So did its wooden replacement. The stone statue has fared better.

The seventeenth-century facade of the Rathaus makes it one of the most photographed public buildings in the world. Rising above the town hall are the twin towers of the eleventh-century **Saint Peter's Cathedral,** site of an ancient sand dune where the earliest Bremeners sought refuge from the surging tides of the Weser River.

Seek out the cellar of the town hall. It is said that the people of Bremen are most at their ease in a cellar—and this cellar is one of the best. It's a *Ratskeller* with more than 600 varieties of German wines to sample. Chances are if you find it, it may be a while before you see the light of day again.

The bronze statue of Bremen's **"Four Musicians"** (the donkey, dog, cat, and rooster) is stashed away in a cranny between the Rathaus and the Liebfrauenkirche, the Church of Our Blessed Lady. Be certain you find and photograph it, or your kids will never forgive you. The "Four Musicians" is one of several statues erected in Bremen honoring the Brothers Grimm fairy tales. If you delve into the true origins of the odd assortment of these domestic animals, apparently they are symbolic of a peasants' revolt against aristocracy rather than the Grimms' version of frightening off robbers—but don't tell the kids.

The **Bottcherstrasse,** a narrow street leading off the market square, was redeveloped as a center for arts and crafts, with shops, workshops, art collections, and fine restaurants—even a casino. At the end of the street you will come to the Martini Church on the banks of the Weser. Boat tours of the Bremen harbor depart from the pier immediately in front of the church.

Another area that you can reach on foot by walking upstream along the banks of the Weser is the **Schnoor.** The oldest surviving residential area within the city of Bremen, it boasts quaint little houses, inns, and workshops dating back to the sixteenth, seventeenth and eighteenth centuries.

City sightseeing tours depart daily from the bus station in front of the main railway station at 1030. Tickets must be obtained beforehand at the tourist information office. Trips around the harbor depart the Martini Church jetty daily at frequent intervals from March through October. The trip lasts one and a quarter hours.

Anywhere in Bremen, the marketplace, the Bottcherstrasse, and the Schnoor included, you may come upon a chimney sweep garbed in his traditional swallow-tailed coat and high, black hat. Reach out and touch him, for it is said that it brings good luck. Everyone does, and it's quite an exciting time when one passes through a crowd. Legends old and new abound in Bremen. Enjoy your visit.

Day Excursion to

Hameln
WHERE THE PIED PIPER PLAYED

Depart from Hamburg Hauptbahnhof

City Dialing Code: 5151
Distance By Train: 145 miles (218 km)
Average Train Time: 2 hours, 30 minutes
Hameln Tourist Information: Verkehrsverein Hameln, Deisterallee 3, D-31785 Hameln
Tel: 20 23 48; *Fax:* 20 25 00
Hours: May-September, 0900-1300/1400-1800 Monday-Friday; 0930-1230/1500-1700 Saturday; 0930-1230 Sunday. October-April, 0900-1300/1400-1700 Monday-Friday

A short walk from the Hameln railway station. Walk through the square in front of the station, turning right onto Bahnhofstrasse. At the first traffic light, turn left onto Deisterstrasse. When you note a tree-lined shopping plaza on the right of the main street, look for the tourist information office near the next main intersection on the right.

Hameln's Old Town will hold you spellbound with its cobblestone walks, ancient facades, and cozy eating places. If a time machine is ever invented, its first journey might well be to Hameln to confirm—or dispel—the *Legend of the Pied Piper.*

Fact or fable, the town's archives reflect that on June 26, 1284, an itinerant *Rattenfanger* (rat catcher) attired in a multicolored costume trilled his flute, and 130 children followed him out of town to an unknown fate. Only three children survived—one boy had returned for his coat and was left behind, a little blind lad lost his way, and a mute youngster returned but was unable to tell the story.

This most famous kidnapping supposedly happened in retribution for the town's elders' not paying the Pied Piper for his previous performance, when he trilled the town's burgeoning rat population to the Weser River, where they drowned. Moral of the story: you have to "pay the Piper."

The story of **Hameln's Pied Piper** is the most well known of all German folklore. It appeared in Grimm's German Legends and has been translated into at least thirty languages. There are probably as many theories as to what actually happened as there are children who disappeared—maybe more. The most probable explanation relates to the colonization of an area in the Czech Republic to which many citizens of Hameln migrated after being recruited by wealthy noblemen during the same time in history. Peasants were referred to frequently as the children of towns, so it is quite possible that the tales became tangled. The present citizens, however, appear to be happy that it worked out the way the Brothers Grimm recorded it.

Every Sunday from mid-May through mid-September, a live reenactment of the event is staged in the town square. The colorful Piper, plus fifty or so of the town's children (attired in charming "rat" costumes) and another twenty adults representing the town mayor and citizens of Hameln, begin their performance promptly at noon.

You will have about 20 minutes to change trains in Hannover. You will realize you are approaching Hameln when you see the silhouette of the famous Piper on the railroad control tower.

If you plan to arrive in Hameln on the 1135 train for the performance at noon on Sunday, go directly to the town square. There is a tourist information office next to the stage in the town square that is open from 1000–1400 during summer.

Adjacent to the main tourist office at Deisterallee on the right is a beautiful park, the **Burgergarten**. The park is readily identified by its pleasant green gate with the silhouette of the Pied Piper. The tourist information

Hamburg–Hameln

DEPART HAMBURG HAUPTBAHNHOF	ARRIVE IN HANNOVER	DEPART HANNOVER	ARRIVE IN HAMELN	NOTES
0708	0825	0850	0939	(1)
0900	1025	1050	1139	(1)
1108	1225	1250	1339	(1)

DEPART HAMELN	ARRIVE IN HANNOVER	DEPART HANNOVER	ARRIVE IN HAMBURG HAUPTBAHNHOF	NOTES
1421	1508	1533	1652	(1)
1621	1708	1733	1852	(1)
1821	1908	1933	2052	(1)
2021	2108	2133	2252	(1)

(1) Daily, including holidays

Distance: 130 miles/214 km

---

office conducts 1-hour guided walking tours every day from May through September at 1000 and 1500 (cost 3.5 DM per person). You can even arrange for a tour with the Piper himself!

If you're making your own walking tour, turn right when leaving the tourist information office and take the pedestrian underground route. Follow the signs reading ALTSTADT (Old City). When you leave the underground passageway, you will be on Osterstrasse. The **Gaststatte Rattenfangerhaus** (Pied Piper House), which is a charming café, will be to your immediate left. Either pause for refreshments here or proceed on Osterstrasse to the town hall, situated at the end of the street by the marketplace. En route, you will find several other attractive restaurants and cafés.

The Pied Piper isn't Hameln's only attraction—sightseeing in the *Altstadt* alone could fill your entire day. During the summer, it is possible to take a steamboat trip on the Weser River or stroll through the extensive woods surrounding Hameln. Visit **Museum Hameln** on Osterstrasse. Hours: 1000-1630 Tuesday-Sunday. It contains an extensive collection of civic art and culture dating back to the origins of Hameln, including the Pied Piper Legend.

You can observe the 2000-year-old craft of glass-blowing and engraving in the historical **Pulverturm** (glassworks). The old and the new have been blended successfully in Hameln.

Day Excursion to

Hannover

FOLLOW THE RED THREAD

Depart from Hamburg Hauptbahnhof

City Dialing Code: 511
Distance By Train: 111 miles (178 km)
Average Train Time: 1 hour, 30 minutes
Hannover Tourist Information: Theodor-Heuss-Platz 1-3, D-30175
Telephone: 30 14 22; *Fax:* 30 14 14
Hours: 090830–19800 Monday-Friday; 0930–15400 Saturday

Exit the station and turn to the right. The tourist office is on the right in the Hauptpost (main post office) building. Watch for the "Red Thread," a painted red line that runs directly to the information office.

Hannover is known throughout the world for its trade fair and will serve as the site for **EXPO 2000.** Known as the "green metropolis" on the southern edge of the North German Plain, one of the many highlights in this city of parks and gardens is the famous **Royal Gardens of Herrenhausen.** In its 300-year-old landscaping, you will find the only example in Germany of early baroque gardens that have survived in their original form.

The history of Hannover is interesting in that it produced the lineage of Britain's present royal family. George I of England was born in Hannover, as was his son and successor, George II. Thoroughly German in tastes and habits, both monarchs made frequent trips back to Hannover, where they also ruled under the title of "Elector." George III, who presided over the loss of Britain's American colonies, was the grandson of George II and the first English King George to be born on British soil.

Hannover's rail station, constructed initially between 1876 and 1879, has had numerous improvements, although it has retained its original nineteenth century facade. Fourteen tracks serve passenger traffic from an elevated platform. A concourse at ground level connects all the tracks with the main station area. Running under the main station area and extending under the station's plaza and into the city is a shopping mall.

The **"Red Thread"** (the painted red line on the ground) is actually an unusual walking tour of the city. Follow the red line that runs through the city's sightseeing points, but do it with a Red Thread booklet that you can pick up at the tourist office for 3 DM. The booklet fits easily in your hand— or it's small enough to slip into your pocket if you want to avoid looking like a tourist. It contains a map outlining the 2-hour walking tour and describes 36 points of interest you will pass while following the Red Thread. Take a camera with a wide-angle lens. Each point of interest has been numbered and the number placed so that if you stand on the number while photographing

Hamburg–Hannover

DEPART HAMBURG HAUPTBAHNHOF	TRAIN NUMBER	ARRIVE IN HANNOVER	NOTES
0708	ICE 583	0825	(1)
0803	ICE 793	0920	(1)
0900	ICE 585	1025	(1)
1008	ICE 787	1125	(1)
1108	ICE 587	1225	(1)

DEPART HANNOVER	TRAIN NUMBER	ARRIVE IN HAMBURG HAUPTBAHNHOF	NOTES
1610	ICE 872	1722	(1)(2)
1733	ICE 586	1852	(1)(2)
1833	ICE 784	1952	(1)(2)
1933	ICE 584	2052	(1)(2)
2038	ICE 792	2157	(1)
2238	ICE 790	2357	(1)

(1) Daily, including holidays
(2) Arrives 20 minutes later on Saturdays and Sundays August 31–September 22

Distance: 111 miles/178 km

---

the scene, you'll have the best shot possible.

Highlights of the Red Thread walking tour include the **Passerelle,** a pedestrian shopping area, the city's **1852 Opera House,** the old city wall, and the new city hall. Hannover's oldest half-timbered building, dating from 1566, is also seen on the tour, which ends "under the stallion's tail"—unless you have succumbed on the tour route to the charm of the local *frauleins* or *bierstubes*.

Bus tours are conducted daily (except Sundays and holidays) May–September and twice weekly on Wednesday and Saturday the remainder of the year. The tour, which is described in English, takes two and one half hours; ticket, 20 DM for adults and 10 DM for children and college students.

Purchase a one-day **HannoverCard** at the tourist information office for 14 DM (single) and receive a 50 percent reduction on the tour. Other benefits include free travel on all GVH buses and trams in fare zones 1 and 2 and a myriad of other sightseeing reduced fares, including a cruise on Hannover's downtown lake, Maschsee.

Hannover's **Zoo** is less than five minutes from the central station by U-Bahn Line 6/16. The stop is called **"Kropcke."** As one of its features, the zoo has the world's largest antelope collection. All of the zoo's animals are exhibited in modern, fenceless enclosures.

The **Great Herrenhausen Garden and Garden Theater** is one of Europe's greatest tourist attractions (3 DM entrance fee for people 14 years and older). Herrenhausen Avenue, facing the gardens, is lined with 1,219 lime trees set in four rows; they link Hannover's inner city with the gardens of the former summer residence of the Royal House of Hannover in Herrenhausen. Many sections of the garden have remained unaltered through the centuries.

The garden is open 0800-1630 in winter and until 2000 in summer. Throughout the summer, the ornamental fountains of the garden operate from 1100-1200 and 1400-1600 daily. Either U-Bahn No. 4 or No. 5 will take you to the Herrenhausen Garden, or you will be able to see a portion of the gardens during a stop on the city bus tour.

Hannover has six major museums spanning 6,000 years of history. Entry to all is free, except the **Busch Museum** in the **Georgengarten,** a natural park developed in the eighteenth century. In sharp contrast to the baroque world of the Herrenhausen Garden, the Georgengarten is a mature example of English landscape gardening.

Many of Hannover's residents believe that a day in their city should have 48 hours. The refurbished city center alone—an ambler's paradise (reserved entirely for pedestrians) with shops, cascading fountains, and cafés—can captivate you. With the frequent train service between Hamburg and Hannover, you can easily extend your stay into evening.

Day Excursion to

Lübeck
RENAISSANCE AND ROTSPON

Depart from Hamburg Hauptbahnhof

City Dialing Code: 451
Distance By Train: 39 miles (63 km)
Average Train Time: 38 minutes
Lübeck Tourist Information: Hanseatic City of Lübeck, Beckergrube 95, D-23539.
Tel: 22 81 08; *Fax:* 12 28 190
Hours: 0900-1300 and 1500-1800 Monday-Saturday
In the train station opposite track No. 1

The Hanseatic City of Lübeck extends its hospitality in a phrase, "Welcome, to yesterday, today, and tomorrow." The city's origins go back to the year 1000 when "Liübice" was established as a royal seat, artisan settle-

Hamburg–Lübeck

DEPART HAMBURG HAUPTBAHNHOF	TRAIN NUMBER	ARRIVE IN LÜBECK	NOTES
0715	RE 3008	0754	(1)
0815	RE 3014	0854	(1)
0916	RE 3018	0955	(1)
0912	EC 182	0950	(1)
1115	RE 3028	1154	(1)
1315	RE 3040	1354	(1)

DEPART LÜBECK	ARRIVE IN TRAIN NUMBER	HAMBURG HAUPTBAHNHOF	NOTES
1603	RE 3053	1645	(1)
1803	RE 3067	1845	(1)
1948	EC 183	2026	(1)
2003	RE 3079	2045	(1)
2139	EC 181	2215	(1)

(1) Daily, including holidays

Distance: 38 miles/63 km

ment, and a trading center on the banks of the Trave River near the Baltic Sea. Today, parts of the old town of Lübeck have become a UNESCO World Heritage Site, and tomorrow is well in the hands of its energetic citizens who number more than 210,000.

Destroyed by fire in 1157, the present city dates from 1159 when it was rebuilt. In 1358, it was chosen as the administrative headquarters for the Hanseatic League. Between 1806 and 1813, Napoleon I held Lübeck as a part of his empire. Until the turn of the twentieth century, when it began to build its own industries, Lübeck was known only as a Baltic port. Its industrial strengths and strategic maritime location, however, brought destruction to Lübeck during World War II when most of Lübeck's industrial complex and some one-fifth of its Old Town were destroyed by Allied aerial bombardment. In 1949, the reconstruction of Lübeck, including the historic Old Town, began. As Germany's largest Baltic port, this proud city has once again become a center of economic, cultural, and commercial interests.

Lübeck is noted for two culinary specialties that you should sample during your visit—marzipan and rotspon. **Marzipan,** as a sweet specialty, is produced in a countless variety of forms. Try a piece of marzipan cake. The origins of marzipan are hidden in history. Lübeck's version is that during the famine of 1407, bakers produced a bread made from the stocks of almonds since wheat flour was unavailable. Others believe that marzipan originated in Venice, and the recipe came to Lübeck through trade links.

In the early days, when salt was used to preserve fish, ships sailing from Lübeck began carrying salt mined in the Lübeck area to fishing ports along the French coast of Biscay. Rather than return empty, the ships brought back casks of French wine to mature in Lübeck prior to bottling. A combination of sea climate and storage in Lübeck's wine cellars brought about an amazing improvement in the quality of the wine. This was first discovered in 1806 during Napoleon's occupation, when French officers found that the Bordeaux wine from Lübeck's wine cellars tasted considerably better than at home. Try a glass of *Lübeck er rotspon* and judge for yourself.

Lübeck's architecture ranges from Gothic to neoclassical and you can find typical examples of these as well as Renaissance, baroque, and rococo in almost every part of the town's old section. Frequently, the various styles can be seen side by side. For example, starting with the College of Music at the head of Grosse Petersgrube you can see all five styles mixing in harmonic unity within one small block of the town.

With Lübeck 's illustrated brochure in hand you can become your own tour guide, or you might want to opt for one of the town's regular guided walks that start from the tourist office in the marketplace. The guided walks take about two hours to complete. The tourist office in the train station can give you directions for finding the marketplace.

After you leave the train station, your point of reference will be the **Holstentor,** an imposing structure perched prominently at the head of the harbor just before the bridge leading over the Trave River into Old Town. Built between 1464 and 1478, more as a prestige symbol for the town than to protect its harbor, the unique design of its twin towers has become the symbol of Lübeck . The museum of city history housed in the Holstentor is very interesting and features a model of Lübeck in 1650.

After crossing the river, follow **Holsten Strasse,** which leads directly to Lübeck's *Rathaus* (town hall) in the marketplace. It is one of the oldest town halls built in Germany between the thirteenth and sixteenth centuries and certainly one of the most beautiful. The **Ratskeller Restaurant** in the basement of the Rathaus is a delightful place to pause for lunch or to sample a glass of *rotspon*. We can also recommend the **Schiffergesellschaft Restaurant** at No. 2 Breite Strasse, site of a meeting house built in 1535 for shipmasters and brimming with treasures from the world of shipping. Credit cards are not accepted. Bring money—lots of it—the ambiance and food are worth it. (Closed on Mondays.)

For an aerial view of Lübeck , cross Holsten Strasse from the marketplace to *Petrikirche* (St. Peter's Church). Destroyed in the war, the church no longer has its own parish since its restoration, but it serves as a popular center for meetings, concerts, and exhibitions. Here you can ride the elevator to a viewing platform 162 feet (50 meters) above the city.

Base City...

Munich (München)

City Dialing Code: 89
Internet: http://www.muenchen-tourist.de

Munich, the capital and heart of Bavaria, is situated in the center of a vast plain washed by the Isar River. The immaculate and astonishing beauty of its countryside is visible in any direction. Rimmed by the Alps to the south and dark green pine forests in all other quadrants, Munich becomes the gateway to day excursions galore. With a population of well over a million, Munich is Germany's third largest city, but it still retains its unmatched roisterous elegance.

Munich's mood is always festive, but twice a year the tempo soars even higher as the city observes Fasching and Oktoberfest. Fasching celebrations are held during January and February. The festivities could be compared to Mardi Gras, only Muncheners get a head start on everyone by cranking up just after New Year's Eve and never letting up until the sun sets on Ash Wednesday!

During this period of Fasching revelry, thousands of masked balls and parties are staged. Many are in fancy dress, and sometimes masks are worn because individuals don't wish to reveal their identities to their partners—who are seldom the ones they came in with. If they are, it's a complete surprise when the inevitable unmasking takes place.

The coming of Lent doesn't dampen Munich's spirits one drop, for it marks the beginning of the strong beer season. Munich's monks, limited to one meal a day throughout Lent (but with no limit on their drinking), started this ancient custom that still prevails today. They asked the brew masters if, during Lent, they could increase the regular alcoholic content of their product; the brew masters agreed—and everyone apparently has lived happily ever after. There are six major breweries in Munich.

Oktoberfest, instituted by a Bavarian King in 1810 on the occasion of the marriage between Princess Therese von Sachsen-Hildburghausen and Prince Ludwig (later King Ludwig I), actually takes place during the latter part of September and ends the first weekend in October. About 660,000 gallons of beer are produced by the city's breweries and dispensed directly from huge, chilled barrels in enormous tents serving as beer halls. Bands play throughout the day and long into the night while drinkers wash down sausages, roast chicken, and oxen with five to six million liter-size drafts of the world's finest brews.

Colorful road signs on just about every highway entering Bavaria declare it to be "Freistaat Bayern," the Free State of Bavaria. Insurrection? Not really. It is the manifestation of the free and roisterous spirit of its citizens, who love their homeland and feel that there is no place quite like it anywhere else in the world.

Arriving By Air

Munich's International Airport is located 28 kilometers northeast of the city center. Tel: 975 21313

The airport features a system of passenger modules connected by a system of walkways, referred to as PTS (Passenger Transport System), that run the entire length of the terminal on level 03. The PTS also connects with the central area, where there is a 24-hour information area staffed by multilingual personnel.

- **Airport-City Links:** Munich's rapid transit **rail** system, **S-Bahn No. 8** line, which stops at the Marienplatz (city center) and the Hauptbahnhof (main rail station). From the central area, descend to level 02. Trains depart every 20 minutes from 0355-2455. Fare: 13 deutsche marks (DM) for a one-way ticket, which you can purchase from machines at the airport (near the escalators leading to the S-Bahn).
- **Lufthansa Airport Bus** departs every 20 minutes for Munich Hauptbahnhof from 0750–2050 daily. From Munich Hauptbahnhof to airport, buses depart every 20 minutes, 0650-1950. Tickets: 15 DM; round trip, 25 DM. Travel time, about 45 minutes
- **Taxi stands** in front of modules A, B, C, D, and E. Due to traffic congestion, the time it takes to travel between the airport and the city by road can exceed one hour and can cost 100–120 DM. Check at the taxi information desk in the central area of the airport. For advance taxi arrangements and information, Tel: 2 6101 in Munich or Fax: 7470260.
- Tourist information located in the central area of the airport. Tel. 975 92815

Arriving By Train

Munich has several suburban stations, but most international trains stop only at the Hauptbahnhof.

Munich's Railway Station—The Hauptbahnhof is actually a city within a city. It even has its own hotel. In addition to the regular rail-station services, all you need do is descend one level on any one of the station's many escalators to discover a veritable city of shops, ranging from bakeries, beer stubes, fruit stands, and supermarkets, as well as the subway entrances to many of Munich's department stores. This shopping colossus extends from the

Hauptbahnhof all the way to Karlsplatz-Stachus—more than one quarter of a mile. Most shops in the immediate Hauptbahnhof area are open late during the week as well as on weekends and holidays.

Money exchange (Geldwechsel-Exchange-Cambio): located in the far left corner of the main station hall next to the main entrance. Hours: 0600-2300 daily. This facility is operated by the Deutsche Verkehrs-Kredit-Bank (DVB) and offers a service not usually found in other exchanges. It will accept foreign coins (except coins from Eastern Europe). Most exchanges will only accept notes. If you have collected a variety of coins moving from country to country, here's your chance to unload if you're willing to accept 30 percent less than the total value.

An ATM (automated teller machine) is located on the left-hand side as you face the bank. A walkup currency exchange office operated by DVB may be found by turning right when exiting the trains, directly across from the tourist information office by track 11 at the street exit. Hours 0730–1900 daily. There also is an ATM just before the Bayrerstrasse exit.

Make the **EurAide office** one of your first stops upon arrival and pick up their free newsletter. EurAide is located in Room 3 next to track 11 in the Hauptbahnhof. It is open primarily during the summer months: 0730–1200 and 1300–1630 daily in May; 0730–1200 and 1300–1800 daily from June 1-end of September.

EurAide is operated by the German railroads (DB). They specialize in answering Eurail-related questions. They can make room reservations; they have information on tours with English-speaking guides and tours utilizing the city's public transportation systems. Those intending to exchange money in the Munich Hauptbahnhof should note that by showing the yellow EurAide *Inside Track* newsletter the standard 7.50 DM service fee is halved when cashing travelers checks at the station's DVB (bank) locations.

Tourist Information/Hotel Reservations may be made in the same office. To reach it, exit through the Bahnhof Platz exit, and turn right. It is the second office on the right, next to the ABR Reisebüro. It is within the station complex, but can only be reached from the outside. A nominal charge is made for reservations. The attendants are very helpful in finding local reservations. Hours: 0900–2100 Monday-Saturday; 1100–1900 Sunday.

The **InterCity Hotel** is located conveniently in the train station. As you are exiting from the train-platform area (by passing through the first set of doors on your way to the main concourse of the station), turn to the right just before the main concourse hall and walk to the street entrance. The hotel will be on the left just before the doors leading to the street. It's convenient, but get reservations early—it's also popular. Tel: (89) 545560; Fax: (89) 54556610.

Train reservations for EuroCity, InterCity, ICE, and express-train services can be made in the "ABR office (*Amtliches Bayerisches Reiseburo*) located in the extreme front end of the station on the right-hand side, directly opposite the money-exchange office. Hours: 0900–1800 Monday-Friday; 0900–1200 Saturday It can be very crowded, particularly on weekends and during the summer tourist season. You must make train reservations at least one day in advance. They can also be made at counters with signs RESERVIERUNGENS.

Rail pass validation and train information can be obtained in the rail travel center marked REISEZENTRUM located in the center of the station in front of tracks 21 and 22. Use windows 19, 20, or 47 for rail pass validation. For train schedules only (international or domestic), use windows 2 or 3 or the service counter in the middle of the station across from tracks 18 and 19. The sign reads DB SERVICE.

Prior to entering the train information office, prepare a list or an itinerary of the rail trips you intend to make. Too many people enter the office without a thought of where they want to go or when they want to arrive. This office can tell you what train to take and the time that it leaves the Munich Hauptbahnhof. They are not a travel agency, however, and you should not ask for suggestions of things to do.

Food services are available in several parts of the station. The most famous is the stand-up wiener-and-beer stube immediately to the right of the entrance into the main station concourse. Behind it, there are three full-service restaurants with posted prices and menus.

Luggage lockers are available in four areas of the station. Look for signs reading SCHLIESSFÄCHER. There is also a check luggage office on the main floor under the Burger King.

Another tourist information office is located in the New Town Hall in Marienplatz (same building as the Glockenspiel). Hours are Monday –Thursday 0830–1600; Friday 0830–1400; they are closed Sundays. This office also will make hotel reservations.

Getting Around in Munich

Munich's fine S-Bahn (rapid train) system is operated by the German Federal Railways. Eurailpass, Europass, Eurail Flexipass, and German Rail Pass are accepted for travel throughout the entire S-Bahn system. The aforementioned rail passes are *not* accepted on the U-Bahn (underground or subway system) nor on the trams (*Strassenbahnen).*

The S-Bahn has eight main operating lines, S-1 through S-8. All of these lines converge on the Marienplatz and Hauptbahnhof. You can obtain maps and fare information at the tourist information office. A chart of the S-Bahn and the U-Bahn systems appears on the following page.

A U-Bahn (subway) station is located directly under the plaza in front of the railway station. The Munich Hauptbahnhof is the center of train, tram,

Train Connections to Other Base Cities From Munich

TO:	DEPART	ARRIVE	TRAIN NUMBER	NOTES
Amsterdam	0741	1552	ICE 598	(1)
	1241	2052	ICE 794	2)
	2249	0940	214	
Berlin (Hbf.)	0752	1501	ICE 882	(8)
	1117	1801	ICE 588	
	1352	2101	ICE 784	
Berne	0815	1346	EC 92	(3)
	1402	1946	EC 166	
Brussels (Midi)	0641	1455	ICE 894	(4)
	0838	1655	ICE 798	(5)
	0983	1801	ICE 596	(6)(7)
Budapest (Keleti)	0925	1745	EC 63	(7)
	2319	0728	D269	
Copenhagen	1928	0930+1	D482	
Hamburg	0914	1330	ICE 680	
	1317	1852	ICE 586	
Milan	0729	1450	EC 81	
	1329	2050	EC 13	
	2340	0830+1	289	
Paris (Est)	0746	1625	EC 66	
	1346	2222	EC 64	
	2100	0707+1	260	
Prague (Praha)	0657	1123	IR 2063	
	1408	1826	EC 167	
	2306	0632+1	1580	
Rome	0924	1950	EC 85	
	2030	0815+1	D287	
Vienna (Westbhf.)	0925	1418	EC 63	(7)
	1825	2315	EC 17	
Zürich	0815	1226	EC 92	(7)
	1215	1626	EC 94	(7)
	1402	1826	EC 166	(7)
	1815	2223	EC 98	(7)

Daily departures unless otherwise noted. Make reservations for all departures.

(1) Transfer in Mannheim to IC 502 and transfer in Cologne (Köln) to EC 148
(2) Transfer in Mannheim to EC 104
(3) Transfer in Zürich to IC 924
(4) Transfer in Mannheim to IC 604 and transfer in Cologne (Köln) to 422
(5) Transfer in Mannheim to IC 500 and transfer in Cologne (Köln) to 426
(6) Transfer in Mannheim to IC 602 and transfer in Cologne (Köln) to EC 46
(7) Supplement payable
(8) Transfer to Gottengen

bus, suburban train, and subway services for the entire city.

A great value is the MVV-Single (valid for one person) or Partner (valid for two adults) Tageskarte (Day Tickets). The Day Ticket provides unlimited travel on the S-bahn (rapid transit line), U-Bahn (subway), streetcars, and buses on the date of validation until 0600 the following day. A Single Day Ticket for Munich's entire transport network costs 16 DM; Partner Day Ticket, 24 DM.

All of Munich's public transportation operates on the honor system. You must have a ticket for any conveyance you board, but you may not be asked to show it—then, again, you may. If you are apprehended without a valid ticket, you will be fined 60 DM on the spot.

Sights/Attractions/Tours

Munich's heart pulsates at the Marienplatz, the city's central square. From the tower of the new town hall in the center of the Marienplatz, a glocken-spiel chimes every morning at 1100 (again in summer at 1200 and 1700) and is followed by a performance of mechanical figures including knights on horseback and a crowing rooster. You will have to see it to believe it.

Dallmayr's delicatessen is nearby. Facing the glockenspiel, walk around the right side of the town hall to the smaller square in the rear. Dallmayr's store will then be in plain view immediately across the street to your right at 14 Dienerstrasse. You really don't have to buy a thing—the sights and the aromas are wonderful.

Munich has a great variety of things to see and do. There are approximately 100 historic buildings, 2 castles, 200 churches, 53 art collections and muse-ums, and 69 performing theaters—all within the city limits and most of them within reasonable walking distance from the Marienplatz. An excellent illus-trated folder containing a city map showing the exact location of each of the above points of interest is published by the Munich tourist information office.

There are 14 additional places of interest, including the 1972 **Olympic Park,** identified by color-coded circles. For admirers of the brew master's art, the map also pinpoints twelve of Munich's most famous beer gardens. The **Hofbrauhaus** (the state-owned beer hall) is a short walk from the Marienplatz via Dallmayr's delicatessen. (It would be un–American not to stop!)

The Hofbrauhaus dates back to the year 1591. It is no longer operated as a brewery but beer is drayed in to be consumed daily from one-liter (one-and-three-quarter-pint) mugs while bands play lively tunes, often accompa-nied by the singing of the drinkers. There's a full-service restaurant on the sec-ond floor, where decorum is a bit more in evidence. **The Platzl,** directly across the street from the Hofbrauhaus, is another place to go for oom-pa-pa music, yodeling, and food.

If you tire of city dining, take a southbound S-1 train on the S-Bahn from the main transfer station under the Marienplatz and get off in the **Village of Aying**—about a 40-minute ride. Walk four blocks toward the church steeple to the Aying Hotel, where you'll find the best Bavarian food, beer, and atmosphere.

Those visiting Munich for the first time probably will want to take a guided tour by bus. A 4-hour leisurely paced bicycle tour is also available for 28 DM. For information call Mike's Bike Tours, Tel: 651–4275.

Munich also has the finest delicatessen in the world—it's **Dallmayr's** at 14-15 Dienerstrasse (Tel:. 21 35 100) Hours: 0900-1830 (1600 in winter) Monday-Friday; 0900-1400 Sat; closed Sunday. Extravagant beyond description, it demands to be seen. If for no other reason, go to Munich to savor the sights and scents of Dallmayr's! There's a restaurant specializing in seafood and a unique gift shop on the second floor. Not your usual "deli," you'll find rich German chocolates, caviar, lobster, fine wines—order a gourmet lunch "to go." Gift shop.

Day Excursions

South to the Alps and **Garmisch**. Into the Alps to **Berchtesgaden**. Through the Alps to Austria and its beautiful cities of **Innsbruck** and **Salzburg**. North to **Nuremberg, Ulm,** or **Rothenburg** and the **Romantic Road**. For a special adventure, up the peak of Germany's highest mountain, the **Zugspitze.** Take your choice—and at your leisure.

Day Excursion to

Berchtesgaden   ALPS, LAKES, AND SALT MINES

Depart from Munich Hauptbahnhof

City Dialing Code: 4
Distance By Train: 112 miles (180 km)
Average Train Time: 3 hours
Berchtesgaden Tourist Information (Kurdirektion), Berchtesgadener Land, Konigsseer Strasse 2, D-83471. Opposite the railway station.
Tel: 8652/967–150; *Fax:* 8652/63300.
Hours: June 15-October 15: Monday-Friday, 0800-1800; Saturday, 0900-1700; Sunday, 0900-1500; October 16-June 14: Monday-Friday, 0800-1700; Saturday 0800-1200; closed Sunday.

To reach the tourist-information office, cross the street in front of the station at the traffic light, incline to the left, following the KOENIGSSEE sign. The office is located in a large cream-colored building on the right-hand side.

Don't let the train time to Berchtesgaden deter you from making this day excursion. The train follows a route that passes through some of the most beautiful countryside in the world, and the tours waiting for your arrival in Berchtesgaden are simply out of this world.

After Adolf Hitler seized power in 1934, he ordered the expansion of the facilities in **Obersalzberg,** an appendage to Berchtesgaden, with the intent of making it the equivalent of a summer White House. Der Führer's dream was destroyed, however, when the greater part of Obersalzberg was demolished by an air attack on 25 April 1945.

If possible, take the early train out of Munich so as to arrive in ample time to select a tour and still have time for a relaxing lunch in one of Berchtesgaden's charming inns. Current schedules are always posted in the main hall of the Berchtesgaden railway station.

Berchtesgaden Mini-Bus Tours (located in the tourist office) specializes in English-speaking historical tours of Berchtesgaden's sights, including the Obersalzberg and **Eagle's Nest.**

The village of Berchtesgaden has many attractions. Among them is the Folk Museum housed in the **Adelsheim Castle** (Schloss Adelsheim) where you will find displays of wood carvings and the famous Berchtesgaden wood-shaving boxes.

For one of the most spectacular scenic views in the world, take the Jennerbahn two-person cable cars to the top of Mount Jenner above **Lake Köenigssee** (literally translated "Royal Lake"). Start from the valley station at Lake Köenigssee. Your breathtaking 20-minute ascension to 1,834 meters (6,017 feet) unveils vistas of mountain summits stretching as far as the eye can see. This wondrous landscape once caused Bavarian writer Ludwig Ganghofer to cry out: "Lord, if you love anyone, then set them down in this land!"

In addition to sightseeing in Berchtesgaden and its immediate surroundings, there are many interesting guided tours that can be taken outside of the village. The most popular ones for North Americans are visits to Obersalzberg, the Salt Mines, the Köenigssee, the Sound of Music/Salzburg Tour, and the Eagle's Nest. All tours are available year-round with the exception of the Eagle's Nest, which is open from mid-May to mid-October.

The **Obersalzberg tour** features a visit to the former location of the Berghof, Adolf Hitler's official home and the site of many pre-World War II conferences. Included on the tour is a trip through its air-raid shelters and bunkers, which provided protection to the conferees in the event that the Allied air forces wanted to disrupt the proceedings.

The **Salt Mines** are located a few miles outside the town of Berchtesgaden. The tour is a thrilling experience. In miner's protective clothing, you ride a mine train, slide down chutes, and cross over subterranean lakes. The kids love it, but a word of caution—it's not for older folks or the faint of heart.

Munich–Berchtesgaden

DEPART MUNICH STATION	TRAIN NUMBER	ARRIVE IN BERCHTESGADEN STATION	NOTES
0725	IC 191	1017	(1)
0749	IR 2095	1114	(1)
0938	IR 2191	1314	(1)
1033	RE 3513	1338	(1)

DEPART BERCHTESGADEN STATION	TRAIN NUMBER	ARRIVE IN MUNICH STATION	NOTES
1549	RE 3540	1928	(1)
1641	IR 2096	2020	(1)
1749	EC 62	2036	(1)
1949	IR 90	2234	(1)

(1) Daily, including holidays; transfer in Salzburg

Distance: 112 miles/180 km

The **Köenigssee** is considered the pearl of Berchtesgaden and provides some of the most romantic scenery in Upper Bavaria. In order to preserve the quietness of the lake and the clearness of its waters, electric boats have been the only crafts permitted to navigate there since 1909. A tour aboard an electric boat runs daily whenever the lake is ice-free. Midpoint in the cruise, the captain shuts down the motor and, in the silence of the lake, lets go with a blast on a trumpet that resounds and resounds for as many as seven times off the alpine palisades surrounding the lake.

The **Eagle's Nest** tour begins in May and is conducted daily until winter snows block its access. A bus conveys you to a height of 5,600 feet, where an elevator lifts you the final 400 feet to a never-to-be-forgotten experience. Despite the publicity gained by the Eagle's Nest's connection with Adolf Hitler, Der Führer only visited there about five times. The road running to the elevator that takes you to the summit is beyond doubt a uniquely daring feat of road building. It's a white-knuckle ride all the way. The tour itself is far less strenuous than that of the Salt Mines, but the weather is all important.

Despite its ancient facade, Berchtesgaden is actually very modern in its tourist and recreational facilities. Should its charm overcome you—as it does many—consider an overnight stay. The Berchtesgadener Land tourist information office, opposite the rail station, can assist you in finding accommodations.

For lunchtime, try the **Gasthof Neuhaus,** opposite the fountain in the town square. Its selection of *Schmankerl* (Bavarian specialties) is a treat, and their ice cream specialties will make you forget all about Baskin-Robbins—at least for a while.

Day excursion to

Garmisch-Partenkirchen   Bavaria at its Best

Depart from Munich Hauptbahnhof

Distance By Train: 63 miles (101 km)
Average Train Time: 1 hour, 30 minutes
City Dialing Code: 8821
Garmisch-Partenkirchen Tourist Information, Schnit-Schulstrasse 19, D82467
Tel: (08821) 1806; *Fax:* (08821) 180–55
Internet: Http://www.Garmisch-Partenkirchen.De
Hours: 0800-1800 Monday-Saturday and 1000–1200 Sunday
      Reach it by turning left outside the station and walking downhill about 300 yards to Bahnhof Strasse. Turn left and walk about 150 yards to Richard Strauss Platz and the Kongresshaus (Congress Hall).

Bavaria's eccentric King Ludwig II spent lavishly, admired Wagner, and went mad—though not necessarily in that order. Two of his famous castles, **Neuschwanstein** and **Linderhof,** can be visited on tours from Garmisch-Partenkirchen, as well as the village of **Oberammergau** (home of the Passion Play) and the **Zugspitze,** Germany's highest mountain.

Tourism started in the area with the building of a railroad between Munich and Garmisch-Partenkirchen in 1889. Prior to that time, the area waned or prospered according to who was in town. The Romans occupied the area as far back as the first century B.C. At the beginning of the eighteenth century, the area was suppressed by the Spanish and then, by the Austrians and the French. It wasn't until 1802 that the area was finally made a part of Bavaria. Because of its interest in winter sports, in 1966 the twin-city of Garmisch-Partenkirchen became the sister city of Aspen, Colorado, ski capital of the United States.

The U.S. Armed Forces maintain a recreation center in Garmisch and also conduct tours in the area. Tour participation, however, is limited to U.S. military personnel, their dependents, and retirees. Payment for these tours must be in U.S. dollars. If you qualify, to reach the recreation center follow the ZUGSPITZBAHN signs to the cog railway station, where the U.S. facilities will be in plain view and just ahead. Follow the signs.

Munich–Garmisch-Partenkirchen

DEPART MUNICH HBF. STATION	TRAIN NUMBER	ARRIVE IN GARMISCH STATION	NOTES
0800	RE 5407	0916	(1)
0900	RE 5409	1025	(1)
1000	RE 5411	1116	(1)
1100	RE 5413	1223	(1)
1200	RE 5415	1316	(1)

Zugspitze trains depart Garmisch thirty-five minutes past the hour from 0835 to 1435.

DEPART GARMISCH STATION	TRAIN NUMBER	ARRIVE IN MUNICH HBF. STATION	NOTES
1534	RE 2424	1653	(1)
1627	RE 5426	1754	(1)
1733	RE 5428	1854	(1)
1833	RE 5430	1955	(1)
1934	RE 5432	2052	(1)
2028	RE 3434	2153	(1)

Zugspitze trains arrive at Garmisch hourly from 1000 to 1600.
Depart Garmisch hourly 0835 to 1435 (80-minute journey; last train back at 1600).

(1) Daily, including holidays

Distance: 63 miles/101 km

ABR, a German tour agency, offers a wide selection of tours in the Garmisch-Partenkirchen area, including King Ludwig's **Neuschwanstein Castle** and his **Linderhof Castle.** The ABR agency is immediately adjacent to the Garmisch-Partenkirchen rail station.

Proceed to track No. 1 by turning to the left at the bottom of the stairs leading from the arriving train platform. ABR is visible from the rail station lobby. Most tours are conducted daily.

Garmisch-Partenkirchen (actually two villages that united in 1935) hosted the 1936 Winter Olympics and the World Alpine-Ski Championship in 1978. Just visiting the Olympic facilities can consume an entire day. A downtown shopping spree can do the same, but with more injury to pocketbooks. In wintertime, the Winter Olympics ski jump provides spills and chills, and the Olympic Ice Stadium is open year-round.

The alpine ski runs extend sixty-eight miles in length, and there are ninety-three miles of tracks for the growing sport of cross-country skiing. Two of the most popular alpine cable-car runs in summer are the **Eibsee-Zugspitze** system (9,678 feet) and the **Wank Bahn,** which takes you to the promontory of the Wank Alp (5,874 feet). There are others as well. One that is particularly convenient starts at the Olympic Ski Stadium on the fringe of Garmisch-Partenkirchen and scales the Eckbauer Alp to a height of 4,127 feet. From any of these points on a clear day, the view is extraordinary.

The Zugspitze is the highest mountain in Germany—9,718 feet to be exact. A cog railway was completed in 1931 to the Zugspitzplatt, along with a cable car that scaled the last 2,000 feet to the top. Another cable car running from Eibsee, a station stop on the cog railway at the 3,500-foot level, was placed in operation during 1963. This system lifts passengers directly to the peak in a spectacular ten-minute ride.

These two systems make a circuitous routing possible—up one way and down another. The round-trip fare from Garmisch is 72 DM (only 52 DM for rail pass holders). The ticket entitles you to ride on any part of the total system. When you arrive in the Garmisch-Partenkirchen station, walk about a   hundred yards to your right to the cog-railway station. The cog railway stops in Eibsee about 30 minutes after departing Garmisch. Transfer at this point to the Eibsee cable car.

The cable-car trip from Eibsee to the top of the Zugspitze takes about 10 breathtaking minutes. If you are in a hurry to return to Garmisch, you could retrace your trip by returning to Eibsee on the cable car, but we recommend that you proceed to the **Sonn Alpine Glacier Restaurant** via the "Gipfelbahn" cable car. At the Sonn Alpine, you join up with the cog railway, which terminates there in a huge vaulted hall blasted out of solid rock. Trains depart on the hour, and the trip back to Garmisch takes one hour and ten minutes.

Day Excursion to

Innsbruck   JEWEL OF THE ALPS

Depart from Munichen Hauptbahnhof or München Ost

Austria Dialing Code: 43
City Dialing Code: 512
Distance By Train: 107 miles (172 km)
Average Train Time: 2 hours, 10 minutes
Innsbruck Tourist Information: Burggraben 3, A-6021
Tel: 0 512/5353-36; *Fax:* 0 512/5356-43

Internet: http://tiscover.com/innsbruck
Email: info @innsbruck.tvb.co.at
Hours: Monday–Friday, 0800–1800; Saturday 0800–1200
  Tourist information is available in the rail station at the "Hotel Information Office," which you can find by leaving the main station hall by the exit on the left-hand side and proceeding past the "Checked Baggage" area.

Theatrically surrounded by its mountains, Innsbruck is the cultural and tourist capital of the Austrian Tyrol. There is an exhilarating mountain view from nearly every street corner and every window in town. Looking north-ward from its main street, **Maria-Theresien Strasse,** you will confront the towering Alps, which seem to encroach upon the city. The scene is breath-taking. (American kids say it's "awesome!")

This day excursion from Munich to Innsbruck offers an opportunity to explore the **Tyrolean Alps** in the comfort of a cable car—plus a visit to one of the most picturesque "old towns" in Austria. To top it off, a circuitous return on the Mittenwald railroad is possible; it takes you on a fantastically scenic rail route straight through the heart of the Austrian and Bavarian Alps en route back to Munich via Garmisch-Partenkirchen.

You are in for an eye-filling day. Even the regular rail line running out of Munich is loaded with Alpine scenery. Take a seat on the right side of your coach outbound from Munich for the best views.

When you arrive in Innsbruck, you will note that train information is posted throughout the main station, and a train information office is immediately to the right of the exit from the trains.

Most of the shops and restaurants in Innsbruck accept German currency. If you want to change money into Austrian schillings, however, you may do so at a change booth located at your far left just as you exit from the trains. The **exchange office** hours are 0730–2000 daily. The local tourist-office branch office, also located in the station, is an official exchange, too.

Purchase a large guide map at the tourist office if you plan a walking tour of the city. Bus tours of the city are available throughout the year. Biking tours are a great way to see Innsbruck, too.

If you decide to become your own tour guide, check the map, then head west for a few blocks to Innsbruck's Arc de Triumph. From this point, turn north and wend your way slowly through the **Altstadt** (Old Town), which lines both sides of the street all the way to the **Goldenes Dachl** (Golden Roof) at the end of Herzog-Friedrich Strasse. It may come as a mild disappointment, but the so-called Golden Roof is actually made of heavy, gilded copper.

Eat lunch in the **Goldener Adler** (Golden Eagle), the oldest inn in the city. It was founded in 1390! It is around the corner on the left and can best be described as a delicious experience. If you go there for dinner, enjoy the

Munich–Innsbruck

DEPART MUNICH HBF. STATION	TRAIN NUMBER	ARRIVE IN INNSBRUCK STATION	NOTES
0729	EC 81	0922	(1)
0929	EC 85	1122	(1)(2)
1129	EC 87	1322	(1)
1329	EC 13	1522	(1)

DEPART INNSBRUCK STATION	TRAIN NUMBER	ARRIVE IN MUNICH HBF. STATION	NOTES
1637	EC 3630	1830	(1)
1710	D 482	1915	(1)
1837	EC 86	2030	(1)
2037	EC 80	2230	(1)

(1) Daily, including holidays
(2) Scenic route via Mittenwald/Garmisch; see Thomas Cook Table 785

Distance: 107 miles/172 km

Note: Train numbers refer to the German Train Number

Tyrolean music in the cellar restaurant. It will complete a perfect evening.

Mountain scaling via cable car? Rail pass holders get a 20-percent reduction on the following private lines: Seegrube, Hafelekar, Patscherkofel, and Mutterer Alm. The Seegrube (6,287 feet) and the Hafelekar (7,700 feet) await your conquest, and scaling them by cable car makes mountaineering a sport for all ages.

Ready for that fantastic train trip back to Munich? Board the Express 5430, which *usually* departs from track 12-B in the Innsbruck Station at 1705 and returns to Munich via Mittenwald and Garmisch daily at 1954. (Check in the station for the proper departure platform.)

You start by crossing the Inn River, then the train begins climbing the steep valley walls that skirt the Inn. Approaching the Alpine station of **Hochzirl,** you will have a sheer, 1,500-foot vertical view of the river and the green valley through which it runs. Select train seats on the left-hand side for the best opportunity of seeing these sights.

Later, the train will stop in **Seefeld,** a delightful Alpine community, before continuing on to **Mittenwald** and Garmisch, where the Express 5430 cars are switched to another Munich train.

Day Excursion to

Nuremberg BEER, GINGERBREAD, AND TOYS

Depart from München Hauptbahnhof or Müchen Pasing

City Dialing Code: 911
Distance By Train: 125 Miles (201 Km)
Average Train Time: 1 Hour, 36 Minutes
Nuremberg Tourist Information: Frauentorgraben 3, D-90443. In the main hall of the rail station, one level below the train platforms.
Tel: 233 61 17; *Fax:* 233 61 66
Internet: http://www.nurnberg.de
Hours: Summer hours: 0900–1800 Monday-Saturday; 1000–1300/1400–1600 Sunday. Winter hours: 0900–1900 Monday-Saturday; closed Sunday from October-April (except during Christmas Market).

Nuremberg must have originated the "Day Excursion"! On 7 December 1835, the first German train chugged its way from Nuremberg to Furth, a neighboring city, with honored guests *and* two barrels of beer.

On this day excursion the ICE trains average 76 miles per hour between Munich and Nuremberg—considerably faster than in 1835—and Nuremberg's brew is every bit the match for Munich's, for Nuremberg is a part of Bavaria, too. Get ready for an enjoyable day excursion.

When you arrive in Nuremberg, you will find the tourist office in the main station hall, one level below the train platforms. Another tourist information office is in the city hall.

Conducted tours of the city from May to October depart daily at 1400. Individual tours of the city may be arranged at any time; one of the Tourist Board's experienced city guides will serve as escort Tel: 0911/2336123.

The train information office is in the arcade on the left of the main exit. Train schedules, posted in several prominent locations in the station, will confirm the departure time and track location of your return train to Munich.

One of the main gates of the old walled city of Nuremberg, the **Kingsgate**, is directly across from the railway station. Picking up Köenigstrasse (King Street) at this point, you can follow it to the heart of the old walled area known as the Hauptmarkt (Central Market). Plan to be there at noon, a mechanical clock will entertain you at the stroke of twelve with its seven electors paying homage to the emperor.

Connoisseurs of the brewers' art won't want to miss a visit to Nuremberg's **Museum Brewery** and **Medieval Cellars**. The museum is really the Altstadthof brewery, who's motto, "Beer like our Forefathers," is observed today by the use of only the finest materials and brewing methods, which date from the nineteenth century. The cellars, going down eighty-five feet through

Munich–Nuremberg

DEPART MUNICH HBF. STATION	TRAIN NUMBER	ARRIVE IN NUREMBERG STATION	NOTES
0752	ICE 882	0932	(1)
0849	IC 804	1032	(1)
0952	ICE 788	1132	(1)
1052	IC 812	1232	(1)

DEPART NUREMBERG STATION	TRAIN NUMBER	ARRIVE IN MUNICH HBF. STATION	NOTES
1526	IC 813	1706	(1)
1626	ICE 789	1806	(1)
1726	IC 803	1906	(1)
1826	ICE 881	2006	(1)
1926	IC 805	2115	(1)
2026	ICE 883	2206	(1)

(1) Daily, including holidays

Distance: 125 miles/201 km

solid rock, form a labyrinth of tunnels dug in the fourteenth century for the storage of beer. A guided tour is available.

Nuremberg offers not only beer, but gingerbread and toys as well. The aroma of Nuremberg's special gingerbread, **Lebkuchen,** fills the Hauptmarkt every Christmas. At other times, the same aroma may be savored—and tasted—in the many pastry shops throughout the city. The traditional recipes of the original gingerbread are kept secret by the bakeries that produce it. Two such companies invite visitors to sample their products. Arrangements may be made by either of the tourist offices.

Toy shops are in profusion, and the **Toy Museum on Karl Street,** two blocks from the Hauptmarkt via Augustinerstrasse, has a splendid display of dolls, puppets, and tin soldiers. The museum also houses an interesting model-railway layout, featuring—of all things—the train station in Omaha, Nebraska. Real toy fans will want to be in Nuremberg around the first of February for the International Toy Fair. From the Hauptbahnhof, take the U-Bahn (underground) to Spielwarenmesse.

Nuremberg's most famous citizen was Albrecht Dürer, a man who towered above his time. The stately home in which he lived, from 1509 until his death in 1529, is located two blocks north of the Toy Museum, past the Wine Market, on Albrecht Dürer Strasse. The house holds a collection of the famed artist's works, and the area surrounding it is probably the most interesting section within the walled city. Unfortunately, Dürer's most famous work, *The Four Apostles*, now rests in Munich, but a number of his paintings are exhibited.

If you have any doubt about that first day excursion by train originating in Nuremberg, check in at the **Verkehrsmuseum (Transport Museum)**, three blocks to the right of the train station as you face it. The museum is open 1000–1700 Tuesday-Sunday. There you will find the *Adler* (Eagle), the first German locomotive, complete with the two beer barrels mounted on its tender.

If you are a model-railroad fan, you will be pleased to note that, in addition to the Toy Museum, two of Germany's largest manufacturers of HO-and N-gauge equipment, **Arnold and Fleischmann,** are located in Nuremberg. **E.P. Lehmann,** the manufacturer of G-scale equipment for the increasingly popular outdoor garden railways, is located at Sagnerstrasse 1–5 (Tel: 0911/834021). They have operating layouts, and visitors are welcome. The operating hours are seasonal, so check with one of the tourist information offices if you would like to visit.

Day excursion to
The Romantic Road DELIGHTFULLY MEDIEVAL

Depart from München Hauptbahnhof

City Dailing Code: 9861
Distance By Train: 345 miles (554 km)
Average Train Time: 12 hours, 36 minutes
Rothenberg Tourist Information: Rothenburg o.d.t. Tourist Office, Markplatz 2, D-91541
Tel: 40492; *Fax:* 8 68 07
The Romantic Road, Deutsche Touring GmbH, Am Romerhof 17, 60486 Frankfurt/Main
Tel: 69/7903256; *Fax:* 69/7903219

Too long and too far? Not in the least. **The Romantic Road**, packed with superb scenery and delightful medieval villages, is worth every minute. The Deutsche Bundesbahn (German Railroad) bus that takes you from Munich to **Wurzburg** makes two stops en route: one in **Dinkelsbuhl** for lunch and one in **Rothenburg** for sightseeing. After these pleasant interludes, plus a return trip to Munich on one of Germany's lightning-fast InterCity trains, you will wonder where the day has gone.

The Romantic Road bus is unique in that it carries an English-speaking

Munich–The Romantic Road

	DEPARTS	ARRIVES	NOTES
	Munich Hbf.	Dinkelsbuhl	
Bus	0900	1245	(3)★
	Dinkelsbuhl	Rothenburg	
Bus	1400	1440	(3)★★
	Rothenburg	Würzburg	
Bus	1615	1835	(3)

Return to Munich

VIA TRAIN	WÜRZBURG	MUNICH HBF.	
ICE 883	1927	2206	(1)(2)
ICE 683	2024	2244	(2)(4)
ICE 885	2127	0006	(1)(2)

★   Stops for lunch
★★ Stops for sightseeing
(1) Daily, including holidays
(2) Food service available
(3) Daily, April 1–October 31
(4) Daily, except Saturday

Distance: 172 miles/276 km by bus plus 173 miles/278 km by train

guide. This trip has become so popular that seat reservations are recommended. Reservations can be made at the Europabus office in the Munich railway station opposite track Nos. 33 and 34. The office is open 0800–1900 Monday-Friday 0830–1900 Saturday Tel: 91824. Seat reservations are free of charge, and the Eurailpass, Europass and GermanRail Pass are accepted.

The Romantic Road bus has no special markings. Ask for its departure position (which is usually No. 23) when you make reservations. Your reservation assures you of a seat on the bus, but not a specified seat. Be at the bus station at about 0830, therefore, to ensure getting a window seat.

Rothenburg is one of the most frequently visited places in Germany. Every year thousands of visitors from all parts of the world come to this ancient walled city. You will see why Rothenburg is picturesque and photogenic. Be sure to take a camera. Probably more photographs have been taken of its **Kobolzeller Gate** and **Siebers Tower** than of any other scene in Germany.

The town is a museum piece of medieval character. Most of its 12,500 citizens living within or just outside the city's walls work to serve the tourist in some manner. This town has survived, even in the twentieth century, as the "Jewel of the Middle Ages."

Enjoy your visit in Rothenburg but keep your eye on the town clock, for the Romantic Road bus continues on its journey to Würzburg and its final destination, **Frankfurt,** promptly at 1615. If, for some reason, you do miss the 1615 bus departure, the German railroad also operates another bus line between Rothenburg and Steinach, where you can connect with train service back to Munich.

Arriving in Würzburg at 1835, you have the early opportunity of returning to Munich at 1922 aboard ICE 883; or, you might want to have dinner and linger as late as 2041, when the IR 2187 speeds back to Munich. The later departure would allow you to stay in Würzburg for several hours. But remember that the IR 2887 is the last regular train for Munich in the evening. There are several restaurants immediately across from the park fronting the east side of the Würzburg rail station where you could enjoy dinner. The IR 2887 serves limited food selections only.

Rothenburg is loaded with living legends. One concerns the salvation of the town from certain destruction by its wine-drinking mayor. In 1631, during the Thirty Years' War, the town was captured by imperial troops under the command of General Tilly. While the general toyed with the idea of destroying the town and executing its councilors, he was handed a tankard holding more than three quarts of heavy franconian wine to aid his meditation.

The general promised mercy to Rothenburg if one of its councilors could drain the "bumper" in one mighty draft. Mayor Nusch did and thus saved the town. Although he slept for three days and nights following the mighty quaff, apparently he suffered no other effects, for he lived another 37 years and died at the age of 80—with a smile on his face. The historic deed is re-enacted daily by a glockenspiel installed in the gable of the Councilors' Tavern at 1100, 1200, 1300, 1400, 1500, 2000, 2100, and 2200. Be there!

Day Excursion to

Ulm
WORLD'S TALLEST CATHEDRAL

Depart from München Hauptbahnhof

City Dialing Code: 731
Distance By Train: 92 miles (148 km)
Average Train Time: 1 hour, 13 minutes
Ulm Tourist Information: Ulm/Nell-Ulm Touristik GMBH, Neustrasse 45, D-89073. In the Stadthaus at Münsterplatz.
Tel: 0731161283; *Fax:* 1611646
Internet: http://www.ulm.de; *Email:* unt@exteru.uni-ulm.de
Hours: 0900–1800 Monday-Friday; 0900–1200 Saturday
    There is a display of tourist information in the railway station to your left when entering the station from the train platforms.

The Gothic spire of the Ulm Cathedral, silhouetted against a blue Bavarian sky, is a scene you are not likely to forget. Poised on the banks of the swift-moving Danube, Ulm is a picturesque representation of a typical Swabian city. Birthplace of Albert Einstein, Ulm has withstood the onslaughts of many conflicts, including Napoleonic campaigns, with great dignity. It is considered a miracle that its cathedral escaped damage throughout World War II, although serious damage was inflicted in the town by Allied bombing. All of Ulm's original facades have now been repaired or replaced.

The spire of the cathedral, with its skyward thrust of 528 feet, is the tallest in the world. Although the foundation stone of the cathedral was laid in 1377, the two towers and the spire were not completed until 1890. When the central nave was completed in 1471, it could hold 20,000 people—twice as many as the town's population at that time. Truly, this was an ambitious undertaking right from the start.

The clear vertical lines and the lightness of the cathedral's architecture are beautiful. The interior is open 0900–1700 daily, except when services are being conducted. There is no entrance fee but a small admission charge to ascend the spire.

Speaking of the spire, a breathtaking panorama of Ulm, the Danube, and the surrounding area rewards those who climb its 768 steps. A word of caution—the climb is rigorous and should not be attempted unless you have good physical stamina. Back on the Münster square in front of the cathedral you will notice the remarkable contrast of the old gothic style and the contemporary architecture of the **Stadthaus** (Town House), built by Richard Meier in 1993. It is worthwhile visiting this modern building with its varying activities (exhibitions, concerts, conferences) and views of the cathedral.

You will get a brief view of the Danube and the cathedral when crossing

Munich–Ulm

DEPART MUNICH HBF. STATION	TRAIN NUMBER	ARRIVE IN ULM STATION	NOTES
0738	ICE 598	0849	(1)(2)(3)
0746	EC 66	0903	(1)(2)(3)
0838	ICE 798	0949	(1)(2)(3)
0938	ICE 596	1049	(1)(2)(3)
1041	ICE 796	1149	(1)(2)(3)
1141	ICE 594	1249	(1)(2)(3)

DEPART ULM STATION	TRAIN NUMBER	ARRIVE IN MUNICH HBF. STATION	NOTES
1508	ICE 593	1618	(1)(2)(3)
1608	ICE 795	1718	(1)(2)(3)
1708	ICE 595	1818	(1)(2)(3)
1808	ICE 797	1921	(1)(2)(3)
1908	ICE 597	2021	(1)(2)(3)
2108	ICE 599	2221	(1)(2)(3)

(1) Daily, including holidays
(2) Food service available
(3) Reservations mandatory

Distance: 92 miles/148 km

---

the railroad bridge entering Ulm. Watch on the right-hand side of the train immediately after passing the Neu Ulm (New Ulm) suburban station. The railroad bridge has a pedestrian crossing, so you may want to return to that vantage point again for a more prolonged observation. The bridge can be reached after leaving the station by walking to the right to an intersection where the trolleys swing farther right down an underpass. Continue straight ahead, not turning with the trolleys, on the promenade to the river's edge and the approach to the bridge.

Another route to the Danube is through the **Fischerviertel** (Fisherman's Quarters), which lies to the south of the cathedral. En route, you will pass the picturesque **Schiefes Haus** (Crooked House), which has settled over a canal. If you walk downstream on the Danube's left bank, the river promenade will bring you to the **Metzgerturm** (Butcher's Tower), another Ulm landmark. Have a walk on the ancient city wall and see the old traditional Ulm river boat—the so-called "***Ulmer Schachtel***"—on the other bank of the Danube. Walking to the city centre from the Mezgerturm you'll reach the **Rathaus** (Town Hall) from 1370, famous for its opulent frescoes and ornamental carved figures. On the east gable, beautiful astronomer's clock (1520). Visit the **Ulm Museum,** where you will find displays of art and culture ranging from the Middle Ages to modern times. Notable features are the collections of modern graphics and important examples of late Gothic. There are also exhibits concerning some of Ulm's famous citizens, such as the physicist Albert Einstein and Albrecht Berblinger, the "tailor of Ulm," who in 1811 made man's first serious attempt to fly. A short visit merits the funny Einstein Fountain in front of the former Imperial city's arsenal ("Zeughaus") at the east of the old city centre.

Although the cathedral dominates the scene, a stroll through Ulm will reveal its other aspects—exclusive shops, boutiques, and department stores. And for refreshment in between times, you will find traditional old taverns, pleasant restaurants, comfortable inns, and good hotels where you may enjoy Swabian specialty dishes accompanied by drafts of good Ulm beer.

Unique in the field of museums is Ulm's **German Bread Museum,** situated in the beautifully restored salt warehouse from 1592. It presents an impressive display of that major ingredient of our daily diet. Not only does the museum effectively tell the story of breadmaking, it makes you aware of how serious hunger can be.

Very remarkable and to be noticed everywhere in Ulm and Neu-Ulm are the buildings and installations of the former Federal Fortification Ulm ("Bundesfestung"). Important landmarks of Europe's largest remaining nineteenth-century fortifications are the **Citadel Wilhelmsburg** on the "Michelsberg"—from where you have a splendid view of the city—Blaubeuren Gate or the "Glacis" bastion, now Neu-Ulm's municipal park.

Ulm University offers a unique Path of Art. More than 60 large works by artists of repute such as Niki de Saint-Phalle or Max Bill are presented along a 1.5-km tour around the university and Science Park Ulm. To get there take bus line 3 or 5 from the central station to James-Franck-Ring.

Wiblingen Monastery with its Baroque basilica and splendid Rococo library is only 5 km away (bus line 5 from Rathaus [town hall] to Pranger). The famous library is open from 1000–1200 and 1400–1700 except Monday (April till October). Church visit is free, but there is an admission charge for the library.

Greece

M̶ost famous for its archeological finds and its significance in antiquity, many visitors to Greece are astounded to learn that this scenic, sun-drenched country also includes about 1,400 islands and more than 7,500 caves, many of which contain subterranean rivers, lakes, and waterfalls. Complementing this varied geographical wonder are the mountain ranges such as the Pindus and, of course, the waters of the Mediterranean, the Aegean and the Saronic Gulf linking Attica (Athens area and its port Piraeus) to the Peloponnese.

CHAT Tours, a leading tour operator in Greece for more than 44 years offers many delightful sightseeing tours and cruises to the Greek islands. They are located at 4, Stadiou Street, Athens, Greece (Tel. 323 0827, 322 2886, or 322 3137; Fax: 323 5270 or 323 1200).

For tourist information, contact the Greek National Tourist Organization in North America:

Chicago: 168 North Michigan Avenue, Suite 600, Chicago, IL 60601. Tel: (312) 782-1084; Fax: (312) 782-1091

Los Angeles: 611 West Sixth Street, Suite 2198, Los Angeles, CA 90017. Tel: (213) 626-6696; Fax: (213) 489-9744

New York: 645 Fifth Avenue, Olympia Tower, 5th Floor, New York, NY 10022. Tel: (212) 421-5777; Fax: (212) 826-6940

Montreal: 1233 rue de la Montagne, Suite 101, Quebec H3G 1Z2. Tel: (514) 871-1535; Fax: (514) 871-1498

Toronto: Upper Level, 1300 Bay Street, Toronto, Ontario M5R 3K8. Tel: (416) 968-2220; Fax: (416) 968-6533

Email: gnto@aurora.eexi.gr

Banking

- **Currency:** Drachma
- **Exchange rate at press time:** 281.35 drachma = $1.00 U.S.
- **Hours:** 0800-1400 Monday-Friday

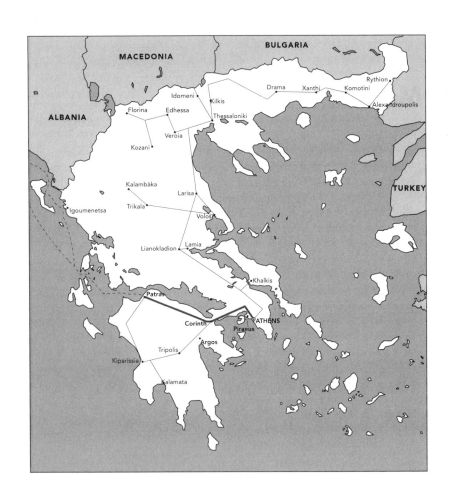

Communications

- **Country Code:** 30
Direct dial: AT&T: 00-800-1311; MCI: 00-800-1211; Sprint: 00-800-1411.
Phone Cards may be purchased at most kiosks and Greek Telecommunications offices. 1,000 drachmas for 100 units; also available for 500 and 1,000 units. All calls charged by units.
   Public red phones operated with a 10-drachma coin and gray phones at kiosks are metered for long distance calls. Pay the kiosk owner for number of units charged.

Rail Travel in Greece

   The rail system of Greece is limited and it presents a challenge to rail travelers. The trains can be too few and too slow. With a little perseverance, however, traveling by train in Greece can be charming, especially on overnight trains in first class sleepers.
   The line from Athens to Thessaloniki in the north has been modernized, but it still takes 5 hours, 40 minutes on the Greek Railways Organization (OSE) standard-gauge InterCity train *Hermes Express*. Narrow-gauge lines serve the Peloponnesus, the southernmost part of Greece. Both networks serve Athens.
   The OSE accepts a variety of multi-country rail passes including **Eurailpass, Europass** (with purchase of the Greece add-on), the **Balkan Flexipass,** and the singular-country rail pass—the **Greek Flexipass,** for travel solely within Greece. (See the Appendix for prices and types of multi-country rail passes.) The Greek Flexipass provides unlimited first class rail travel for any 3 or any 5 days within a 1-month period:

	ADULT	CHILD (AGE 6-12)
3 days in 1 month	$86	$58
5 days in 1 month	120	85

Greece to Italy via Eurail – Crossing the Mediterranean

   The Eurailpass and Europass (with purchase of the Greece option) provide free deck passage on either **Hellenic Mediterranean Lines** (Greece) or **Adriatica Lines** (Italy) ferry crossing between Brindisi, Italy, and Patras, Greece. Some ships also stop at Corfu and Igoumenitsa—check with the Hellenic Mediterranean Lines office in the U.S., Italy, or in Greece.

Hellenic Mediterranean Lines
1 Hallideie Plaza
San Francisco, CA 94102, USA
Tel: (415) 989–7434
Fax: (415) 986–4037

8, Corso Garibaldi
72100 Brindisi, Italy
Tel: 831 521 531

28 Amalias Avenue
10555 Athens, Greece
Tel: 32 36 333
Fax: 32 36 412

Adriatica Lines
AND Adriatica di Navigazione
Zattere 1411-Venezia (Italy)
Tel: 41 781 861
Fax: 41 781 864

Having either type of rail pass is quite a bargain considering that deck space for the crossing is about $110 U.S. first class, $90 second, plus there is a high-season surcharge (even for rail pass holders) from June 1-September 30 of $15. Cabins or reclining-type chairs cost extra.

The following prices are applicable at press time but subject to change for Eurail or Europass holders:

Deluxe 2-berth cabin (with Shower & toilet)	$145
2-berth cabin	91★
3-4 berth cabin	47
Couchettes Pullman	31

★50-percent supplement for single occupancy

Advance reservations are recommended ($3.00 U.S. each), especially during June through September, and they can be made through Hellenic Mediterranean Lines' agent in the U.S. (above). If you have access to Internet, book online at **http://www.hml.it/indexen.htm.**

Patras-Brindisi-Patras Ferry Service

DEPART PATRAS	ARRIVE BRINDISI	DEPART BRINDISI	ARRIVE PATRAS	NOTES
2200	1700 next day	2230	1700 next day	(1)
1800	1000 next day	2000	1400 next day	(2)
1900	0900 next day	2000	1100 next day	(3)

(1) Both Adriatica and Hellenic
(2) Summer only, Hellenic
(3) Summer only, Adriatica

Arrivals and departures are shown in local times and are subject to cancellation or alteration without notice. Days of operation vary. Check with the Adriatica and Hellenic offices mentioned previously for other services between Corfu or Igoumenitsa and Brindisi.

To reach the **Patras Ferry Terminal** (Tel: 42 95 20 or 42 16 14) from the Patras rail station, turn left as you exit the station. Walk along the street side of the quay about 300 yards to the office marked "Central Agency." Summer hours are 0900-2200 daily. Winter hours are 0900-1300 and 1700-2200. You report to the terminal on the day of embarkation only. No baggage checking is available. From June 19 to September 8, bus transportation is available between Patras and Athens or vice versa for about $15 (US).

Base City...

Athens (Athinai)

City Dialing Code: 1

Arriving by Air

Athens Hellinikon Airport, East Terminal, Tel. 969 4111; West Terminal (or Olympic Terminal), Tel: 966 6666. Located 9 km from Athens.

Airport-City Links: Express yellow buses run between the airport and Syntagma (Constitution) Square at a fare of 160 drachmas and a journey time of about thirty minutes. Express Bus No. 90 runs to/from Syntagma and Omonia Squares to/from the West Terminal and Bus No. 91 runs to/from the East Terminal to/from Omonia Square. Yellow, metered taxis are available opposite the arrivals exit at the East Terminal and outside the international arrivals exit at the West Terminal. Taxi journey time, about 20 minutes and cost 2,000-2,500 drachmas.

Money exchange: Branches of the National Bank of Greece, the Commercial Bank of Greece, and the Agricultural Bank in both terminals remain open until late in the evening every day.

Tourist information: in the arrivals hall of the East Terminal, Tel: 969 4500.

If you are departing Athens by air, the airport's tax-free shopping area offers a wide selection of Greek wearing apparel, liquors, and delicacies. Unlike many tax-free shopping facilities, the one in Athens's airport has some reasonable values, but you can't bargain with the sales people—leave that for shopping in the city.

Arriving by Train

Arrivals from Eastern European countries and points in northern Greece terminate in Athens's Larissa Station, a standard-gauge facility. If you are traveling with a Eurailpass via the Adriatica Lines or Hellenic Mediterranean Lines ferries to the port of Patras, the Peloponnesus Station (narrow gauge) will be your arrival point. The two stations lie parallel to each other, with a connecting, overhead footbridge. Each has a train-information booth with a limited amount of city information available.

Both stations have taxi stands and bus service, but we recommend that new arrivals use the taxi. The taxi fare from the station area to the tourist office on Syntagma (Constitution) Square is inexpensive, about 525 drachmas plus baggage charges, and well worth it.

Larissa Station serves the standard-gauge rail lines to the north.

Money-exchange at the north end of the train platform. The sign reads "Bank." Hours: 0800-1830 Monday-Friday; 0900-1400 Saturday; 0900-1300 Sunday.

Train information is in a booth to your immediate left when entering the station from the train platform area. Open daily, 0600-2330. Tel. 823-7741.

Baggage storage in "Left Baggage Office" located to the left as you enter the station from the track-side of the station (open 0630-2300).

Train reservations are best obtained at the Greek Railways office at No. 1-3 Karolou Street or No. 6 Sina Street. Get taxi instructions from the tourist office on Syntagma Square.

Rail pass validation is also available at the Greek Railways' main office. Eurailpasses also can be validated at ticket windows in the stations, but only on your departure day.

Athens's Peloponnesus Station serves the narrow-gauge lines to the south.

Money exchange is not available. Use the footbridge to cross to the Larissa Station Bank, or use the exchange services in the tourist information office on Syntagma Square.

Train information is in a booth to your immediate left when entering the station. Open 0730-1900 daily throughout the summer. The hours are split, 0730-1230 and 1630-1900, the rest of the year. Tel. 513-1601.

Train reservations are best obtained at the **Hellenic Railways'** office at No. 1-3 Karolou Street or No. 6 Sina Street. Get taxi or bus instructions from the tourist office on Syntagma Square.

Rail pass validation is available at ticket windows in the stations, or go to the aforementioned Hellenic Railways' office.

Tourist Information/Hotel Reservations

Greek National Tourist Organization: No. 2 Amerikis Street, Syntagma, Athens *Tel:* 322-3111; *Fax:* 322 4148

Hotel reservations: Hellenic Chamber of Hotels, hours: 08300-1400 Monday-Saturday

Money exchange hours: 0800-1830 daily.

Tourist information hours: 0900-1830 daily

Located in the vicinity of Syntagma Square. When facing the Parliament Building from the bottom of the square in the café area, the tourist information office is just across the street on the left. The tourist office offers complete services for the tourist, including hotel and pension accommodations, money exchange, and tour information about Athens.

Getting Around in Athens

Transportation in Athens is inexpensive—75 drachmas for a ticket covering one or two sections of Athens' subway system, the Athens-Piraeus Electric Railway (ISAP), and 100 drachmas includes all three sections with 22 stations along the 14-mile route. Purchase tickets at ticket machines and ticket booths in the stations and validate them prior to boarding. ISAP now numbers 195 rail cars and carries more than 80 million passengers annually.

Sights/Attractions/Tours

Most of the tours being offered are bus tours that include some walking. Consequently, you should inquire as to the tour's duration and terrain before signing up, and don't forget to wear comfortable walking shoes. To avoid the daytime heat, select an evening tour when available. Most of the tourist attractions are illuminated.

The city tourist office is an excellent source for information concerning other areas of the country. Be certain to inform the attendant you speak with that you hold a Eurailpass. Otherwise you might find yourself signing up for a bus tour when a rail trip would suffice for the transportation to the site you want to see.

Although there is more to Athens than **the Acropolis,** it should be the first place to visit during your stay in the city. If you use the ISAP electric railway, detrain at Thission for the Acropolis. All else in and around Athens becomes secondary to this symbol of classic perfection that has stood majestically above Athens for about 2,500 years. Don't rush your visit or you will regret it. Plan to spend an entire day, and if you go there during the summer months, go prepared with some sun screen, sun hats, bottled water, and comfortable walking shoes.

The Parthenon is the focal point of the Acropolis, but there is much more to see. Study the Propylaea, the impressive entrance to the sanctuary, along with the Temple of Athena-Niki and the elegant row of maidens along the facade of the Erechtheion. You can peer down on the Theater of Dionysius from the rim of the Acropolis, but go there later to feel its "presence."

During the tourist season, a light-and-sound show of the Acropolis is presented in several languages. Don't miss it. The program in English starts at 2100. The tourist office can provide you with more details. You view the show from an opposite hillside and it can cool down considerably. You may want to take a light sweater or pullover.

The Romans made their presence known in Athens, too. A group of ruins dating back to the days of Julius Caesar clusters about the Roman Forum at the beginning of Aeolou Street. There are so many other sights to be seen that we recommend a guided tour as the only means of possibly scratching the surface of this wonderful city where Western civilization began.

With an extensive history like Athens, expect to find a full retinue of museums. You won't be disappointed. Be aware that you may be required to check any bags, including purses, and that most museums charge a fee for videotaping within the museum. If your stay in the city is limited, visit the **Benaki Museum,** located on the corner of Vassilissis Sofias Avenue and Koumbari Street (telephone 361-16178). In its twenty-eight chambers, you will see exhibits ranging from the Bronze Age to the beginning of the twentieth century. As you pass through the centuries of statuary development, take note of the style by which the sculptors slowly developed the technique of depicting fingers and toes.

The modern city of Athens also holds much interest for visitors. You must visit the **Tomb of the Unknown Warrior,** with its colorful guards. Go to a café on **Syntagma Square** for coffee and pastry. Climb the time-worn steps leading through the **Plaka Quarter,** which hugs the base of the Acropolis. Take the ISAP electric railway to Faliro Station and sample the fruits of the sea at one of Mikrolimano's charming seafood restaurants.

Despite being one of the easternmost cities in Europe, Athens has a distinct Western appearance. Modern Athens surrounds the splendor of its ancient Acropolis, which has a nobility that survives time and change. That first glimpse of the Parthenon from the window of the plane or train that brought you to Athens remains a once-in-a-lifetime experience.

Addendum to Athens

Select one of Athens's "tavernas" and enjoy its food, music, and dancing. To experience a popular form of Greek entertainment, visit a Bouzouki nightclub. Bouzouki music is similar to American blues in that the music reflects the pain and pathos often present in love and friendships. Before you participate in the traditional plate breaking, check with the management as to the cost per dozen. You could end up spending a lot of drachmas.

Tourists are targets for ploys and pranks throughout the world. Athens is no exception. A waiter may suggest that you consume bottled water with your meal. After all, you may have been warned not to drink the regular water. Bottled water is a good idea, but insist that the waiter open the bottle at your table. Otherwise, you might receive an opened bottle of water that was just recently filled from the water tap in the kitchen. Or order a bottle of carbonated water. That's hard to bootleg!

Day Excursions

Riding a narrow-gauge train through areas steeped in the history of Western civilization is sufficiently stimulating to make the traveler overlook the lack of

air conditioning, posh dining cars, and other amenities. Our day excursion to
Argos, the oldest continuously inhabited town in Greece, is one such adventure. **Corinth,** both modern and ancient, is rich in Greek history, from
Alexander the Great down through Roman rule. **Patras,** port city and scene
of the most spectacular carnival in Greece, is still another place to see on the
Peloponnesus. **Piraeus,** main port of Athens, provides culinary delights from
the surrounding sea.

An InterCity train between Athens and Larissa provides an opportunity to
spend several hours in Larissa during a day excursion out of Athens. Depart
Athens at 0800, arrive in Larissa at 1203 and depart at 1810 to arrive back in
Athens by 2214. Or, depart Larissa at 1910 for arrival in Athens at 2314.
Although the IC 60 does not haul a restaurant car, there are beverages and
some food available. Also you will find an abundance of cafés and patisseries on
the town square. Larissa, the "citadel," is the capital of Thessaly, and, for a time,
it was the home of Hippocrates, the Father of Medicine.

Train/Ferry Connections to Other Base Cities from Athens

Routing: Depart Peloponnesus Station by train to Patras. Depart Patras by ferry
to Brindisi, Italy. Depart Brindisi, for selected base city.

DEPART ATHENS	TRAIN NUMBER	ARRIVE PATRAS	DEPART PATRAS	ARRIVE BRINDISI	NOTES
1208	IC 10	1553	1900	1130	(1)
1528	304	1957	2200	1530+1	(2)
			2100	1530+1	(3)

TO:	DEPART BRINDISI	ARRIVE MILAN	TRAIN NUMBER	NOTES
Milan	1213	2155	IC 586	(4)
	2121	835+1	E 928	(4)

	DEPART BRINDISI	ARRIVE ROME	TRAIN NUMBER	NOTES
Rome	0708	1255	ES 9334	(4)(5)
	2156	0630+1	E 952	(4)

(1) Train daily, ferry summer only (ferry departs alternate days June 19–September 7)
(2) Train daily; ferry schedule varies April 3–July 8; September 10–October 4 (alternate days)
(3) Ferry schedule—alternate days July 10-September 8
(4) Daily
(5) Pendolino supplement payable

Day Excursion to...

Argos (Arghos)   OLDEST GREEK TOWN

Depart from Athens Peloponnesus Station

Distance by train: 89 miles (144 km)
Average train time: 2 hours, 30 minutes
City Dialing Code: 751

Argos does not have a tourist information office. Neither does it have a tourist police office such as one finds in many of the smaller towns throughout Greece. But these absences present no great hardship, for most of its sights are within the city limits. The area must be the birthplace of all Greeks who have ever worked in the United States as waiters. We met two of them by just standing on a corner and looking perplexed.

The railway station is about a kilometer from the town square in Argos. To reach the town square on foot, walk straight out of the station to the main road, where a road sign points to the right in the direction of town. Taxis are available for a nominal fare.

For sightseeing, orient yourself with the church in the town square. From its front door, you can reach the Argos museum by crossing the street, turning left, and proceeding to the first cross street, where you then turn right. The museum is half a block farther on the left-hand side of the street. It is open daily, except Tuesdays. Admission is charged. It has an excellent collection of archaeological exhibits.

The ancient theater and Roman ruins lie on the outskirts of town, in the direction of the hillsides. They are a five-minute taxi ride or a fifteen-minute walk from the museum. On foot, turn left at the next street beyond the museum and walk until you reach the next main intersection. Turn right, and walk straight ahead to the site. If there is the slightest tinge of archaeology in your blood, you'll love this spot. It is relatively unchanged and a perfect place to probe and peer for priceless treasures.

The theater has ninety tiers, which were cut into the hillside on rather a steep angle, making it possible for a perfect, uninterrupted view of the stage area from any seat in the house. Oddly enough, the 20,000 seating capacity of this amphitheater is more than adequate for the present 19,000 population of Argos.

History comes out to meet you on this day excursion. Argos lies in the plain of Argolis on the Peloponnesus peninsula, land of myth and magic. Your mind can run rampant as you journey there. The Iliad, the Odyssey, and the beautiful Helen hover over all travelers who enter.

Modern history appears first as the train crosses the Isthmus of Corinth. Below the railroad bridge lies the canal connecting the Aegean and Ionian seas.

Athens-Argos

DEPART ATHENS STATION	TRAIN NUMBER	ARRIVE IN ARGOS STATION	NOTES
0724	1430	1017	(1)(2)
1010	422	1326	(1)

DEPART ARGOS STATION	TRAIN NUMBER	ARRIVE IN ATHENS STATION	NOTES
1511	423	1758	(1)
1852	1433	2142	(1)(2)
2003	425	2248	(1)

(1) Daily, including holidays
(2) Second class only

Distance: 89 miles/144 km

Alexander the Great, Caesar, and Nero all failed in their attempts to construct the waterway through four miles of solid rock. A French engineering firm finally succeeded in 1893. Watch for it about an hour and twenty minutes after leaving Athens. The best view is from the right side of the train. The railroad bridge is only 108 feet long; so if you intend taking pictures, have everything poised and ready to go, for it passes quickly.

Medieval history is next in line as you approach Argos, where the hillsides northwest of the city reveal at their highest point a Venetian fortress, which dominates the White Chapel of the Prophet Elias and Our Lady of the Rocks Convent lying below.

Ancient history unfolds in Argos itself, with the 20,000-seat theater, and five miles east of the town with the Argive Heraeon and the scattered remains of Greece's oldest recognizable temple (800 B.C.). Tiryns, legendary birthplace of Hercules, is also in the area. These last two sights are not on the rail line and are best visited by taxi from Argos.

Argos is the oldest continuously inhabited town in Greece. Many archaeologists suspect that it may be the oldest in all of Europe. Legends, many of them the basic stuff from which most of Greek mythology sprang, have their origins in Argos and the area surrounding it. In the legendary time of Danaus, story tellers relate how his fifty daughters slew their husbands on their wedding night and then tried to make amends with the devil by trying to fill a bottomless cask with water carried in sieves from the river Stykes. If this would happen in our times, no doubt Congress would investigate—taking equal time to determine the outcome.

The legend does, however, have a happy ending. One of Danaus's daughters, realizing that it could ruin her honeymoon, thought it over once or twice and then let her spouse escape the murderous nuptial-night activities. For this, she was rewarded by becoming the ancestral matriarch of a long line of mythological heroes.

The modern town of Argos was built up over ancient ruins from previous centuries of conflict. The last ethnic group to participate in that form of urban renewal was the Turks, who ravaged the town in 1397. As a result, Argos has scant visible remains of its ancient origins except the theater and the Roman baths.

Day Excursion to...

Corinth (Korinthos) And the Isthmian Canal

Depart from Athens Peloponnesus Station

Distance by Train: 57 miles (91 km)
Average Train Time: 1 hour, 32 minutes
City Dialing Code: 741

This day excursion runs from modern Greece back through the millennia to the Bronze Age. You have the opportunity to see modern Corinth, a typical "new" Greek city, and its port on the Peloponnesus. You may delve as well into the hillside of ancient Corinth, where Saint Paul established a church, Nero fiddled around with a canal, and Julius Caesar implemented an earlier version of the Marshall Plan.

En route to Corinth, the railroad skirts the Aegean Sea and crosses the Isthmian Canal. Watch for the canal when the train is about one hour and twenty minutes out of Athens. The center of the canal runs 285 feet deep through solid rock. The railroad bridge passes 200 feet above the level of the water for a spectacular view.

Greek and Roman rulers (the infamous Nero included) periodically attempted to breach the Isthmus with a canal, but until a French company using modern methods succeeded in the years 1882–93, all had failed. The ancients hauled their small ships across the Isthmus on rollers. Vestiges of the portage road are still visible just after the train crosses the bridge. Watch on the right side of the train for the best view. Have your camera poised and ready— the train traverses the area quickly.

The present "new" city of Corinth, moved to its site in 1858 after an earthquake destroyed "old" Corinth, was leveled by an equally devastating earthquake in 1928. The site has had its share of earth tremors; ancient scribes record devastation in A.D. 522 and 551. Termed an "undistinguished town," new Corinth is interesting in that it represents a community rebuilt on antiseismic principles of low buildings that, paradoxically, give it an air of impermanence.

In fear of pirates, old Corinth was built well back from the sea. This strategic position served the city well. It prospered and became one of the three great city-states of Greece, along with Athens and Sparta. Things went reasonably well until Corinth led the Achaean League against the Romans in 146 B.C. The Romans won the ball game and, a la Carthage (as was the custom in those days), laid waste to Corinth. After the city withstood a hundred years of total desolation, Julius Caesar decided to rebuild Corinth, and it blossomed into one of the great trading cities of the Roman Empire.

During his eighteen-month sojourn in Corinth, Saint Paul became alarmed about the sinful ways of the Corinthians and frequently "read the riot act" to the city fathers. Because of his violent condemnation of moral laxity, he was charged with inciting a riot. Instead of dispensing punishment, the city fathers issued Saint Paul a reprimand—and the suggestion that he leave town as soon as possible, which he did.

Historians estimate that at one time the ancient city of Corinth had a population of more than 460,000; today, its citizens number about 21,000. Although termed a citadel, the old city was attacked repeatedly and conquered down through the ages. During their sweep through Greece, the Turks took over the city in 1458 and again in 1715. In 1458, the Turkish conquest ended when they retreated hastily in ships. The siege of the city in 1715 was described in prose by Lord Byron. There is little Turkish architecture visible in the Corinthian area, due mainly to the short time they were on the premises.

There is excellent bus service between the city and the archaeological site. Departures are daily on the hour from 0615 to 2100. The one-way fare is 160 drachmas. Round-trip cab fare, including a reasonable wait, runs about 1,000 drachmas. The bus terminal is on the south side of the city park. The sign over the terminal reads "apxaia." A taxi will take you there from the railway station for a nominal fare.

To reach the bus station on foot, turn left after leaving the station and then right onto Damaskinou Street and right again onto Ermou Street, just before the Hotel Belle Vue. Turn left at this point and, three blocks later, you'll arrive at the bus terminal on the far left-hand corner of the city park. For further information, check with the "**Tourist Police.**" Walk through the park past another bus terminal to a pharmacy on the right-hand side. Turn right and find the police station half a block farther on the left-hand side.

Excavations have been in progress on the site of old Corinth for many years.

Athens-Corinth

DEPART ATHENS STATION	TRAIN NUMBER	ARRIVE IN CORINTH STATION	NOTES
0850	IC 20	1022	(1)(2)
0937	302	1135	(1)
1035	422	1226	(1)
1208	IC 10	1339	(1)(2)

DEPART CORINTH STATION	TRAIN NUMBER	ARRIVE IN ATHENS STATION	NOTES
1611	423	1758	(1)
1657	303	1856	(1)
1829	IC 11	2000	(1)(2)
1954	1433	2142	(1)(3)
2033	IC 25	2203	(1)(2)

(1) Daily, including holidays
(2) Supplement payable
(3) Second class only

Distance: 57 miles/91 km

Literature describing the excavations and the contents of the museum is available as you enter the site. Between 1925 and 1929, extensive excavations were made. Among the findings, an inscription was found that recorded the story of Androcles and the lion. According to Roman history, Androcles removed a thorn from a lion's paw. Later, when he was sentenced to death and thrown to the lions, the lion remembered Androcles' kindness and let him off without a scratch.

In ancient Corinth, you must pay for admission to the grounds and an additional fee to enter the museum. Hours: Monday-Friday, 0730-2100 (or sunset); Sundays, 1000-1300 and 1500-1900. Plan to spend a minimum of four hours at the site. There is a lot of walking. Several canteens serve refreshments outside the main entrance.

Day Excursion to...

Patras PORT CITY

Depart from Athens Peloponnesus Station

Distance by Train: 138 miles (222 km)
Average Train Time: 3 hours, 49 minutes
City Dialing Code: 61
Peloponnese and Western Greece Tourism Bureau Office: 110 Iroon Politehniou, Glifada, P.C.
262 23 Patras
Tel: 65358-61; *Fax:* 423866
Hours: Daily, 0900–1400

      Ask at the rail station or the ferry terminal for directions. Otherwise, turn right at the quay and walk well beyond the ferry terminal and look for the signs leading to the office. There also is an information office at the entrance of the port of Patras (at Glyfada).

      The railway station in Patras lies on the quay, but it's about 500 yards from the pier where ferries depart for Brindisi. You'll spot the pier to the right as the train slows for its stop in the Patras station. A tourist information booth is located at the entrance to the ferry terminal. For complete information regarding Patras and its surroundings, visit the Peloponnese and Western Greece Tourism Bureau at the address listed above.

      Patras is the fourth largest city in Greece. It is also the country's western gateway. Located at the entrance to the Gulf of Corinth, Patras has been a Greek seaport since the beginning of recorded history. Ships large and small are constantly arriving in, and departing from, its harbor. The ferry services of the Adriatica and Hellenic Mediterranean lines ply between Patras and Brindisi, Italy. If you are a Eurail traveler, no doubt you will either enter or leave Greece through the Port of Patras.

      Patras is the port where the majority of Greek emigrants sailed for the United States. It is interesting to note that in 1922, refugees fleeing Asia Minor arrived at the pier in Patras penniless. Many of them paid for their passage to America by selling their oriental carpets, which they had carried from their homelands. Since the early 1960s, Patras has developed into a major Adriatic ferry port.

      Eurailpass and Europass (if Greece option was purchased) holders are cautioned to use either the Adriatica or the Hellenic Mediterranean Line if they intend paying for their deck passage with the rail pass. Although other ferry companies operate between Greece and Italy, these lines are the only ones honoring the Eurailpass and Europass.

      Spreading below its Venetian castle, Patras is where Saint Andrew taught Christianity and was crucified. The saint's head rests in a shrine following its return from Saint Peter's, Rome, in 1964. It was here in Patras in 1809 that

Athens-Patras

DEPART ATHENS STATION	TRAIN NUMBER	ARRIVE IN PATRAS STATION	NOTES
0634	300	1044	(1)
0850	IC 20	1215	(1)(2)
0937	302	1420	(1)
1208	IC 10	1533	(1)(2)

DEPART PATRAS STATION	TRAIN NUMBER	ARRIVE IN ATHENS STATION	NOTES
1351	303	1856	(1)
1635	IC 11	2000	(1)(2)
1838	IC 25	2203	(1)(2)

(1) Daily, including holidays
(2) Supplement payable

Distance: 143 miles/230 km

Lord Byron first set foot on Greek soil.

The quay is an interesting part of Patras. The long mole, with its benches for resting, extends into the harbor and is a favorite place from which to watch the activity in the harbor. From it you can photograph the arrival of the ferryboats running between the ports of Patras and Brindisi. Patras is not just a busy harbor, however. Its eucalyptus-soaked shorelines, topaz waters, and vast sandy beach at Kilini have made it well known since antiquity for its spas.

Patras has two noteworthy celebrations: the stately procession of Saint Andrew on November 30 and a spectacular carnival during the last ten days before Lent. The city also conducts a classic-theater season during the summer. We suggest a walking tour of Patras starting at the Trion Symmahon Square across from the station and on the right. The long arcaded avenue leading off the park in the direction of the city's heights is studded with stores, restaurants, and specialty shops.

Continue walking on this avenue (Ayiou Nikolaou) to the foot of a broad flight of steps, which will bring you to the site of the ancient Patras Acropolis. Enjoy a wonderful view of the city, its harbor, and the surrounding hills and mountains from this point. Return to the base of the steps and proceed to the left on Yeoryiou Street, which will lead you to the Odeum, a characteristic Roman theater. It was discovered in 1889, but enterprising building contractors subsequently removed much of its marble, requiring the theater to be restored extensively in 1960.

Visitors seeking Saint Andrews Church should begin their quest at the Trion

Symmahon Square and walk southwest along Andreou Avenue to the church, which stands by the sea at the avenue's end. A park dedicated to Andrew, the patron saint of Scotland, is across from the church.

To reach the city's museum, turn left at the Trion Fountain in Trion Symmahon Square and walk for two blocks, then turn right and walk for two more. The museum has an extensive collection of classic Greek and Roman statues plus a collection of prehistoric pottery. There is an admission charge. The area surrounding Patras is steeped in history. Use Patras as a "base city" when visiting Olympia, original site of the Olympic Games. In Olympia, you can visit the site of the Olympic flame, which is carried by runners to any point in the world where the games are to be held. Also of interest is the arch commemorating Nero's "victory" in a chariot race staged in A.D. 67. The emperor's chariot was pulled by ten horses, while all other competitors had to make do with four—needless to say, Nero won.

Another interesting side trip can be made to the Achaia Clauss Winery, five miles outside Patras, to view the wine-making process and sample a bit of the product. If interested in either excursion, obtain information at the tourist office.

Culinary delights abound in Patras. A sea-bass dish, *tsipoures*, is a specialty of the area. This and other Greek dishes are available in the tavernas scattered throughout the upper part of town. An American-style restaurant lies just before the Hellenic Lines office on the quay. Customers may stow their suitcases and backpacks there free of charge while waiting for the ferry.

Day Excursion to…

Piraeus

SEAFOOD BY THE SEASIDE

Depart from Athens Peloponnesus Station

Distance by train: 5 miles (8 km)
Average train time: 20 minutes
City Dialing Code: 1

Piraeus, main port of Greece, basks in the warm embrace of the Saronic Gulf just a few miles and minutes outside the heart of Athens. Piraeus today is one of the principal ports of the Mediterranean. It serves both commercial shipping and pleasure craft. Most tourists go to Piraeus not to view its remains of antiquity but, rather, to enjoy the picturesque atmosphere of its port and to indulge in some of the wonderful seafood served in its restaurants.

Throughout the centuries, Piraeus has had its successes and its failures. In 86

B.C., the Roman General Sulla destroyed the city and its docks, and for centuries Piraeus was considered an unimportant village. Its reconstruction began only in 1834, when Athens became the capital of Greece. Resettled by islanders, Piraeus grew rapidly throughout the nineteenth century and played a large part in the revival of Athens.

Between 1854 and 1859, Piraeus was occupied by an Anglo-French fleet to prevent Greek nationalists' forays against Turkey, an Allied power in the Crimean War. In World War II, the port was put out of action in April 1941 by a German air attack. The ammunition ship *Clan Fraser*, carrying 200 tons of TNT, together with two other ships loaded with ammunition exploded and destroyed the port.

You won't need your rail pass for this day excursion. You'll be traveling on Athens's privately owned electric line—ISAP. The line is the "subway" for the city. A major portion of the rails running to Piraeus, however, are above ground.

Begin your journey from Omonia Square in the city. It connects with Syntagma (Constitution) Square via Stadhiou Street, which starts right outside the entrance to the tourist information office. The entrances to the underground terminal are clearly marked. Be certain to purchase and validate your tickets before boarding. The station uses a center platform for all trains, so check the directional signs for Piraeus before boarding.

Travel at off-peak hours to avoid the crowds. Service is frequent throughout the day. Train etiquette in Greece dictates that men relinquish their seats to ladies and that the young do the same for elders. When in Greece, do as the Greeks do.

Leave the electric train at the end of the line in Piraeus. The terminal lies right at the harbor. To stroll along the quay, exit the station straight ahead, turning left at the side along the sea. Commercial ships and ferries to hundreds of island points occupy the piers along the waterfront of the main harbor. The railway station serving the Athens-Peloponnesus Line is to the right of the subway terminal. Trains for Patras, Corinth, and Argos originate from there, but passengers are not accepted for the short ride between Piraeus and Athens.

In addition to its main harbor, Piraeus has two small-craft harbors, Zea and Mikrolimano. Zea shelters pleasure craft, and Mikrolimano features fishing craft and seafood restaurants, the latter rimming its waterfront like pickets of a fence. Bus No. 20 will take you to either of the smaller ports. Board it from the bus terminal on the left side of the train station. Bus No. 20 stands in the far line, facing away from the sea.

After skirting the main harbor, the bus passes through a built-up area before it again sides with the sea at Zea. If Mikrolimano is your destination, ride four stops beyond Zea and dismount. The Castella Hotel is on the left side at the bus stop. From there, walk down to the harbor. If you're going for lunch, try to arrive before 1230, when the area is invaded by a horde of tour buses packed with hungry tourists. At night the tables in the restaurants overlooking the sea groan under their loads of fresh fish, luscious lobsters, and opulent oysters. Top off your evening by climbing the hill behind Mikrolimano for a magnificent view of the Mediterranean's Saronic Gulf.

Many restaurants employ solicitors to influence your selection of eating places. You can ignore them. We have found that the better places lie to the right of the harbor. "Kanaris 2" is one of the more expensive restaurants, but it is well worth it. While on the subject of price, a word of caution: Check menu prices carefully before ordering. Many menu prices are given for one kilo (2.2 pounds) of fish—a price that the government requires the restaurants to list. Certainly, your platter won't hold that much, but some places will try to charge you on that basis. *Caveat emptor*—let the buyer beware.

During the summer, Piraeus is considerably cooler than Athens. Should the temperatures soar during your stay in the Greek capital, take a quick trip on the Athens subway to the seaside at Piraeus. In the evening, the tavernas and night clubs there provide a resort-type life style. The city's night spots feature popular singers.

Athens-Piraeus

PIRAEUS

Electric subway trains run every few minutes between Omonia Square Station in Athens and the port rail terminal in Piraeus. Journey time: 20 minutes. Caution: board Piraeus-bound (south) trains; trains to Kifissia (northern suburbs of Athens) depart from the same platform.

Lacking museums, Piraeus's archaeological discoveries are displayed in the Athens National Museum. Of particular interest is a collection of statuary stored and forgotten by General Sulla in 86 B.C. Perhaps the general lost his claim check.

Hungary

Hungary, the seventeenth member country to join the Eurailpass system, is a unique addition in that it is the first Eastern European nation to do so. Of the country's 10.7 million inhabitants, 2.1 million live in its capital city of Budapest.

Present-day Hungarians descended from the Magyars, a nomadic, horse-riding people who conquered the land in the ninth century. The Magyars spoke a language unlike any other language of Europe, except Finnish, and even today other Europeans have difficulty understanding it. English and/or German, however, are spoken by many Hungarians in the tourism industry, particularly in hotels and restaurants.

During World War II, the Hungarian government sided with the Axis powers. In April 1945 the country fell to Russian troops. Encouraged by the Polish defiance of the Soviet Union, Hungarians staged an uprising in 1956 that was quickly suppressed by Soviet troops and tanks. Hungary was under the "Iron Curtain" until 1989. The last Soviet troops left the country June 1991. The Hungarian People's Republic became the Republic of Hungary with a newly elected democratic government—a coalition of six parties.

For more information on Hungary, contact the Hungarian National Tourist Office in North America:

New York: 150 East Fifty-Eighth Street, Thirty-third Floor, New York, NY 10155-3398. Tel: (212) 355-0240; Fax: (212) 207-4103; Email: huntour@idt.net

Banking

- **Currency:** Hungarian Forint
- **Exchange rate at press time:** 192.83 Forints = $1.00 U.S.

Communications

- **Country Code:** 36
  For telephone calls within Hungary, dial a zero (0) preceding area code.
- **Direct dial:** first dial 00 and wait for second dial tone, then dial-AT&T: 800-01111; MCI: 800-01411; Sprint: 800-01877

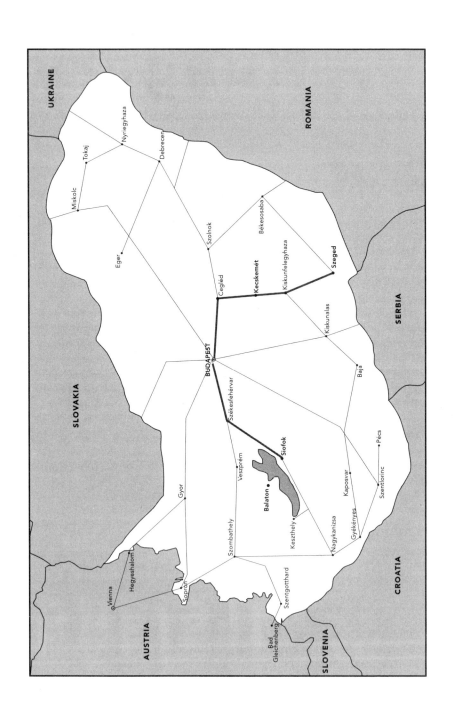

Rail Travel in Hungary

The Hungarian State Railways (Magyar Allamvasutak, or MAV) includes more than 4,844 miles (7,750 km) of rail lines with 1,423 miles (2,277 km) electrified. Fifty-four international trains per day arrive in Budapest, including Euronight (EN) service from Zürich and Bucharest. All international trains have dining and sleeping facilities; however, many of the Hungarian intercity and express trains still do not afford all of the same amenities that can be found on the trains of western Europe.

The **Hungarian State Railways** accepts **Eurailpass, Europass** (with purchase of the **Austria/Hungary add-on), the European East Pass,** and its own national pass—the **Hungarian Flexipass.**

Hungarian Flexipass

5 days travel within 15-day period	$61.00 (U.S.)
10 days travel within a 1-month period	$76.00 (U.S.)

Children ages 5-14, half the adult fare; children under 5 are free.

For more detailed information on types and prices of other rail passes, please see Rail Pass Express' European Rail Passes listing in the Appendix.

Base City...

Budapest

City Dialing Code: 1

Budapest's tree-lined boulevards and spacious public squares bordered by magnificent buildings make it one of the most attractive and beautiful capitals of Europe. Hungary welcomes more than 24 million visitors annually, the majority of whom pass through Budapest, pausing to enjoy its special charm and atmosphere.

The city is a combination of two ancient towns, Buda on the west bank of the Danube and the community of Pest on the east bank. Buda stands on a terraced plateau and contains relics of a Turkish occupation; Pest rises from a plain and is the site of the Houses of Parliament, the Palace of Justice, the Museum of Fine Arts, and the National Museum. Buda and Pest are linked by six bridges over the Danube, including the beautiful Stone Chain Bridge.

Budapest's origins date back to about 10 B.C. when the Romans established the colony of Aquincum on what is now Buda. The Vandals took it over from the Romans in A.D. 376 and, in turn, management changed hands frequently during invasions by the Tartars and the Turks until armies under Austrian leadership liberated what was left of the towns in 1686. Some Roman ruins withstood the assaults and may be seen even today.

Arriving by Air

Budapest's international airport, **Ferihegy,** consists of two terminals. Ferihegy 1 is about 20 km southeast of the city center and Ferihegy 2 is 24 km.

Terminal One

Flight information (arrival, departure)	157-7155
Luggage location service	157-7690

Terminal Two

Flight information	
Departures	157-7000
Arrivals	157-8000
Luggage location service	157-8108
Customs information	157-8306

Airport–City Links: Bus Service departs from either Terminal No. 1 or Terminal No. 2. The bus stop at the airport is located immediately to the right of the main exit.

Airport Minibus (fixed-route taxis), (Tel: 157-855), operate between the two terminals and any address in Budapest. Fare: 1,000 forints.

Budapest Transport Enterprise (BKV) services, bus No. 93 between Terminals 1 and 2 and terminus of M3 metro line Kobanya-Kispest.

The airport **taxi** stand is further to the right, about 200 feet beyond the bus stop. Taxi service is available twenty-four hours a day. All taxis in Hungary must have yellow license plates and meters that print out receipts. To reserve a taxi telephone: Fotaxi, Tel: 222-2222; City Taxi, Tel: 211-1111; Palotaxi, Tel: 272-0616; Radiotaxi, Tel: 177-6766; or Tele 5 Taxi, Tel: 155-5555.

Tourist information: Terminal 1 at the airport. You will find it on your right as you approach the main exit. Hours: daily 0800-2300.

Customs control uses the red-green corridor system just like the western European countries. If you have nothing to declare, you should use the green corridor.

Arriving by Train

Keleti (East) Station, (*Tel:* 113-6835), is the terminus for most international express trains, with exception of the *Adriatica*, *Agram*, *Lehar* EuroCity, *Maestral*, and *Graz* trains which terminate in Budapest Deli (South) Station. Although it has undergone extensive improvements and restoration since its original construction in 1884, the old charm is still evident. Statues of George Stephenson, the inventor of the locomotive, and James Watt, creator of the steam engine, grace its entrance. The modern touch is found in the digital departure boards displayed at the platform entrances.

Stairs at the front of the station take you to the city's Metro, a modern three-line subway system, but arrivals burdened with luggage should opt for the taxi queue immediately outside the station on the right. A word of caution: Be sure that the taxi you hail has a meter—and uses it. The best taxi service is City Taxi and most drivers speak English. Call them at 211–1111 and tell the English-speaking operator the telephone number you called from and a taxi will arrive in just a few minutes. Any "no-name" taxi is almost certainly a rip-off.

Keleti Station has all of the usual tourist services. For rail reservations, proceed to the sign FOREIGN RAILWAY TICKETS—SEAT RESERVATIONS on your right when exiting from the trains. Note that window 2 is for currency exchange, window 3 for hotels, and window 6 is where you request tickets and seat reservations. Pay for all services in cash (U.S. dollars, forints not accepted).

Deli (South), (*Tel:* 175-6293), a modern concrete edifice on the Buda side of the Danube, features a huge supermarket on the ground level. Trains arrive overhead on uncovered platforms that lead to a covered concourse, with an enclosed waiting room and ticket office just beyond. The designation of Deli as Budapest's "south" station is a bit confusing in that it actually lies to the

west of the city. A visit to the supermarket is a must. The products and produce selections offered may be fewer than those offered by even your local
Seven-Eleven store, but it's a great place to pick up the local flavor and mix
with the citizens.

The Metro line Z (or Red) terminates at the Deli Station, with direct connections to the other two rail stations, Keleti and Nyugati. To access, follow
the "M" pictographs leading from the train level; same for taxis.

Nyugati (**West**), (*Tel:* 149-0115), stands at the head of Teréz Boulevard just
before Nyugati Square. Nyugati Station has a TOURINFORM office as well
as the usual amenities found at Keleti and Deli.

Budapest Tourist Information/Hotel Reservations

Tourism information office: TOURINFORM, Main Hall, Nyugati (West) Rail
   Station
Tel/Fax: 132-0597.

The National Tourism Information Service has 754 travel offices in
Hungary and offers information about tourism office hours and their services
for visitors, including money exchange, hotel reservations, travel reservations
(including rail and air), tour bookings, and general tourist information (*Tel:*
117-9800).

If you are interested in organized tours, TOURINFORM offers quite a
selection of sightseeing and tour activities. The "City Tour" is a three-hour
sightseeing adventure by bus to Budapest's famous spots, including Castle Hill
for a panoramic view. You may also want to take a two-hour sightseeing cruise
on the Danube.

For a night on the town, you have the option of a Goulash Party with wine
and a show, or you can pull out all the stops with the "Budapest By Night"
tour, which offers dinner, a floor show, dancing, and wine tasting accompanied by Gypsy music. If you can work it in, the full-day Danube Bend bus
tour on the right bank of the Danube to the towns of **Esztergom,**
Visegrad, and **Szentendre** is well worth it. The area is not accessible by
train, and the vistas along the river are captivating.

Train Connections to other Base Cities from Budapest

TO:	DEPART	ARRIVE	TRAIN NUMBER	NOTES
Munich	1242	2046	EC 62	(1)
Paris	1705	1024(4)	262	(1)
Prague (Praha)	0625	1418	EC 174	
	1025	1818	EC 174	
	1445	2245	IC 1110	
	1855	0341	378	
Rome	1227	0930+1	EC 62/235	(1)(2)
Vienna	0912	1207(2)	EC 24	(1)
	1242	1530(2)	EC 62	(1)
	1525	1830(2)	344	(1)
	1857	2122	EC 40	(1)(3)

Daily departures unless otherwise noted. Make reservations for all departures.
All departures from Keleti (East) Station.

(1) Food service available
(2) Transfer from Vienna Westbahnhof to Südbahnhof
(3) Transfer in Györ to train 344

Day Excursions

Four day excursions have been selected for your Hungarian explorations. Two excursions explore **Balaton** and **Siofok,** resort towns along the shores of Lake Balaton, a large, long lake lying to the southwest of Budapest. The other two take you south through Hungary's Great Plain to the historic cities of **Kecskemet,** and **Szeged.**

Day Excursion to Balaton–Szentgyorgy

Distance by Train: 112 miles (180 km)
Average Train Time: 2 hours, 46 minutes

DEPART BUDAPEST DELI (SOUTH) STATION	TRAIN NUMBER	ARRIVE IN BALATON	NOTES
0710	862	0956	(1)
0810	8502	1111	(1)

DEPART BUDAPEST KELETI (EAST) STATION	TRAIN NUMBER	ARRIVE IN BALATON	NOTES
1000	202/864	1301	(1)

DEPART BALATON	TRAIN NUMBER	ARRIVE IN BUDAPEST	NOTES
1737	851	203 Deli	(1)
1438	863	1733 Keleti	(1)
2017	243	2248(6)	(3)

Day Excursion to Kecskemet

Distance by Train: 66 miles (106 km)
Average Train Time: 1 hour, 27 minutes

DEPART BUDAPEST NYUGATI (WEST) STATION	TRAIN NUMBER	ARRIVE KECSKERMET	NOTES
0720 (4)	IC 702	0832	(1)(2)(3)
1030 (4)	712	1155	(1)(2)(7)

DEPART KECSKEMET	TRAIN NUMBER	ARRIVE BUDAPEST	NOTES
1632	753	1758	(1)(4)
1832	711	1954	(1)(4)

Day Excursion to Siofok

Distance by Train: 72 miles (115 km)
Average Train Time: 1 hour, 39 minutes

DEPART BUDAPEST DELI (SOUTH) STATION	TRAIN NUMBER	ARRIVE SIOFOK	NOTES
0710	862	0849	(1)
0810	8502	0954	(1)

DEPART BUDAPEST KELETI (EAST) STATION	TRAIN NUMBER	ARRIVE BUDAPEST	NOTES
1000	202	1151	(1)

DEPART SIOFOK	TRAIN NUMBER	ARRIVE BUDAPEST	NOTES
1554	863, 314	1733	(1)(6)
1744	203	1933	(1)(6)
1855	861, 851	2033	(1)(5)
2113	243	2248	(1)(3)(6)

Day Excursion to Szeged

Distance by Train: 119 miles (191 km)
Average Train Time: 2 hours, 7 minutes

DEPART BUDAPEST NYUGATI (WEST) STATION	TRAIN NUMBER	ARRIVE SZEGED	NOTES
0720	IC 702	0927	(1)(2)(3)
0820	752	1101	(1)
1030	712	1256	(1)

DEPART SZEGED	TRAIN NUMBER	ARRIVE BUDAPEST	NOTES
1530	753	1758	(1)
1730	711	1954	(1)
1835	IC 701	2045	(1)(2)(3)

Notes for Balaton, Kecskemet, Siofok, and Szeged
    (1) Daily, including holidays
    (2) Reservations obligatory
    (3) Food service available
    (4) Nyugati (West) Station
    (5) Deli (South) Station
    (6) Keleti (East) Station
    (7) Daily, except Sunday and holidays

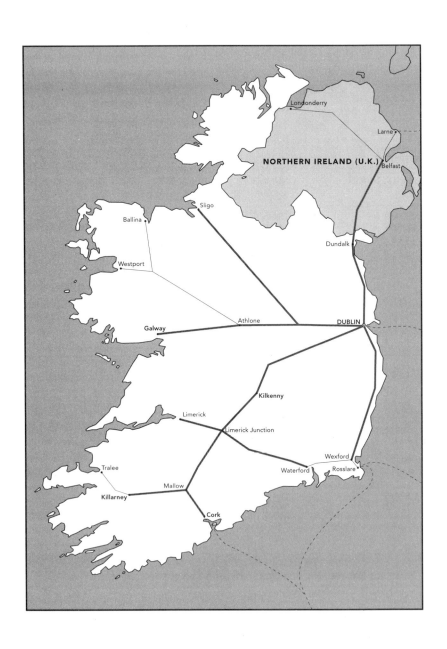

Londonderry

Larne

NORTHERN IRELAND (U.K.)

Belfast

Sligo

Ballina

Dundalk

Westport

Athlone

DUBLIN

Galway

Kilkenny

Limerick

Limerick Junction

Wexford

Tralee

Waterford

Rosslare

Mallow

Killarney

Cork

Ireland

Known as "the Emerald Isle," there is no doubt that Ireland is the greenest country of Europe. According to legend, a true Irishman can recognize at least forty shades of green. The breeze that blows across the seas to Ireland drops its moisture from the time it touches the Irish shoreline on the Atlantic Ocean until it's well out into the Irish Sea. A raincoat or an umbrella—or both—is essential equipment for your visit. But the sun also shines a bountiful bit of the time, and most of the time, showers disappear as quickly as they come.

Today's tourists to Ireland are discovering a new Ireland. Tourism is growing rapidly, with more than a 20 percent increase last year alone. To accommodate these increases, Ireland has expanded all forms of its public transportation. Even Ireland's five international airports—Dublin, Shannon, Cork, Knock, and Belfast (in Northern Ireland) are undergoing major expansions, reflecting an increase of air traffic from all parts of the world.

With all of the enhancements in Ireland, some things remain unchanged—Irish friendliness. Its citizens still seem to have the time to be genuinely interested in you and wondrously literate when discussing almost any subject. Even if scurrying for a bus, the Irish will stop to chat when they spy a friend—after all, there's always another bus. In Gaelic, *céad mile fáilte* means "one hundred thousand welcomes!" You'll hear it frequently.

For more information about Ireland, contact the Irish Tourist Board offices in North America:

U.S.: 345 Park Avenue, New York, NY 10154; Tel: (212) 245-6470; Fax: (212) 371-9052

Canada: 160 Bloor Street East, Suite 1150, Toronto, Ontario M4W 1B9; Tel: (416) 929-6783; Internet: http://www.ireland.travel.ie

Northern Ireland Tourist Board

U.S.: 551 Fifth Avenue, Suite 701, New York NY 10176; Tel: (800) 326-0036 or (212) 922-0101; Fax: (212) 922-0099

Canada: 111 Avenue Road, Suite 450, Toronto, Ontario M5T 3JB; Tel: (416) 925-6368; Fax: (416) 961-2175; Internet: http://www.northernireland.com.

Republic of Ireland

- **Currency:** Irish pounds, £ (punts)
- **Exchange rate at press time:** 0-6856 Irish pounds = $1.00 U.S.

Communications

- **Country Code:** 353
- **Direct dial:** AT&T: 1-800-550-000; MCI: 1-800-551-001; Sprint: 1-800-552-001

Rail/Bus Travel in Ireland

Because the country is only about the size of the State of Pennsylvania in the U.S., travelers can easily discover Ireland by using the rail and bus systems. **Irish Rail**—a division of Coras Iompair Éireann (CIE), Ireland's transport company—is upgrading its railroads and rail facilities as an essential part of Ireland's development plan, with the goal of reliable, convenient, and fast passenger travel throughout the country. Much of the equipment compares favorably with the EuroCity trains operated on the Continent.

In North America, contact **CIE Tours International,** 100 Hanover Avenue, Cedar Knolls NJ 07927-0501 (800-243-7687).

Ireland's new high-speed trains are modeled after the futuristic TGV-style Eurostar trains and aptly dubbed "the trains of the future." *The Enterprise* is one of the new high-tech trains which connects Dublin with Belfast in Northern Ireland. The air-conditioned carriages include digital displays and satellite route maps.

First class is referred to as "super-standard," and second class is known as "standard." First-class rail pass holders are entitled to travel in super-standard coaches without payment of supplements. First class coaches are equipped with reclining seats and headphones with a choice of listening to radio, cassette tape, or CD unit. A facsimile service is provided, as is "Silver Service" meals served at the seats.

Standard-class coaches include a "family room" at one end of the car for those with children. Light meals are available from the mobile food service cart and the buffet (pronounced "buffey" in Ireland) area of the coach.

Some trains operate with standard-class (second class) coaches only. Standard class seats are not reservable for individuals, only groups (no seat reservations on bank holidays or weekends). You are required to show your ticket (or rail pass) when entering the train platforms in Irish rail stations, so have it handy.

Food and beverages are served by CIE's own catering service. The service varies according to the type of train. Full-service restaurant cars are hauled on main-line routes operating between Dublin–Cork, Dublin–Galway, Dublin–Limerick, Dublin–Tralee, and Dublin–Belfast, and then only on a few express trains. Most catering consists of buffet cars or snack-bar service. Food carts are used on some routes. When traveling on a train hauling a restaurant car, in-seat catering is provided for super-standard passengers. In buffet cars, you can obtain hot food, but trains equipped with snack-bar service offer only sandwiches and other prepared food. You may take your own food and beverages aboard. Take some candy treats with you—it's a good way to get acquainted with other passengers.

Service to the cities in the Republic slated for faster, more efficient service include: Galway, Sligo, Westport and Tralee.

Eurailpasses are accepted for rail travel in the Republic of Ireland, but not in Northern Ireland. Eurailpass bonuses include passage on the **Irish Ferries** between Ireland (Rosslare or Cork) and France v.v. (Cherbourg or Le Havre), and a reduced rate, about £25, for the **Bus Eireann "Rover Ticket,"** valid for 3 days of travel within an 8-day period on the following bus services: Bus Eireann Expressway, provincial buses, and city buses in Cork, Limerick, Galway, and Waterford. The **BritRail Plus Ireland Pass** is accepted in both the Republic of Ireland and Northern Ireland, as well as in England, Scotland and Wales, and covers a round-trip connection on your choice of three **Stena Line** ferry routes: between Dun Laoghaire and Holyhead, Rosslare and Fishguard, or Belfast and Stranraer.

For more detailed information on travel in Britain, please read our guide-book, ***Britain by Britrail**–How to Tour Britain by Train*, published by The Globe Pequot Press.

The **Irish Rover Passes** cover the Republic of Ireland only; the **Emerald Cards** cover both the Republic and Northern Ireland.

A variety of rail passes and rail/bus combination tickets are available to help in exploring the Emerald Isle.

The **Irish Rover Pass** (Republic of Ireland and Northern Ireland) offers 5 days of unlimited rail travel to be used within 15 consecutive days (IR£75, Adult; IR£37, Child) on Irish Rail, DART, Intercity, Suburban Rail, and Northern Ireland Rail.

The **Emerald Card** offer rail service throughout the Republic of Ireland and Northern Ireland combined with bus services in Belfast, Cork, Dublin, Galway, Limerick, and Waterford.

Emerald Card

	Adult	Child
8 Day Ticket 15 consecutive Days	IR£105	IR£53

15 Day Ticket
30 Consecutive Days   IR£180   IR£45

The **Irish Explorer,** offers travelers two pass options of either 8 days of unlimited rail/bus transport or 5 days of purely rail travel. Both are valid only in the Republic of Ireland.

Irish Explorer

	Adult	Child
Rail Only		
5 Day Ticket		
15 consecutive Days	IR£60	IR£30
Rail/Bus		
8 Day Ticket		
30 Consecutive Days	IR£90	IR£45

See the Appendix for a detailed list of multiple-country passes and the chapter, **"Ferry Crossings"** for detailed information on sailing from Ireland to France and Britain.

Base City...

Dublin

City Dialing Code: 1

About one-third of the Republic of Ireland's population lives in or near Dublin. The city is as intoxicating as its national brew—Guinness—also lovingly referred to as Dublin's "water supply."

O'Connell Street is Dublin's "Main Street," the pulsating heart of the city, and Ireland's broadest boulevard. A grand statue of the Irish patriot Daniel O'Connell, "The Liberator," stands at the foot of O'Connell Street, where O'Connell Bridge crosses the River Liffey. Statues of other national heroes are posed along the way to the Garden of Remembrance at Parnell Square.

Art galleries, museums, shopping areas such as the Powerscourt Townhouse Center and Grafton Street, famous cathedrals, and elegant cafes are within walking distance of O'Connell Street. The best preserved examples of eighteenth century houses are also found nearby. **St. Stephen's Green** at the top of Grafton Street is ringed with magnificently restored, stately Georgian residences with solid-colored enameled doors and sparkling brass fixtures.

Arriving by Air

Ireland has two main gateways for air travelers: **Shannon International Airport,** on the west side of the Republic, and Dublin Airport, six miles northeast of the city's center. Aer Lingus and Delta service both Shannon and Dublin. Other air carriers stop only in Shannon, which has a world-famous, duty-free shopping area featuring items produced in Ireland. Shannon's major renovations are scheduled for completion by the year 2000.

Airport-City Links: Shannon connects with the rail station in Limerick by airport bus service. Journey time: 45 minutes; fare, £3.50 (£4.60 round trip).

Dublin Airport is more than half-way through its substantial (£95 million) redevelopment plan to increase its terminal building capacity to 15 million passengers per year.

Airport-City Links: bus to Dublin's central bus station. Journey time: 25 minutes; £2.50.

Arriving by Train

- **Connolly Station and DART,** 35 Lower Abbot St., (*Tel:* 01 366 222) Connolly station is the terminal in Dublin for trains arriving from

Northern Ireland. and for boat trains connecting with the Irish Ferries that sail from the port of Rosslare, south of Dublin, to the French ports of Cherbourg and Le Havre.

Coming from London by train requires a transfer to either a Stena Line or Irish Ferries ferry at Holyhead. The Stena Line ferries serve the port of Dun Laoghaire, a suburb of Dublin, where passengers can transfer to the center of the city by the local rapid transit train service, DART.

The northwestern coastal city of Sligo is also reached by train service departing from the Connolly station, as are the towns of Wicklow and Wexford, located south of Dublin in the direction of Rosslare.

• **Heuston Station:** west of City Center on the River Liffey, (*Tel*: 01 703 2132)

Heuston Station serves as the departure point for *Europe by Eurail* day excursions to Cork, Galway, Kilkenny, and Killarney.

City buses depart from the head of track No. 5 in Heuston Station and take passengers near the O'Connell Bridge. There is also a taxi stand on the opposite side of the station immediately beyond track No. 1 and outside the ticket-office entrance.

Heuston Station has eight main tracks. Ticket offices are located on the side of the station serving track Nos. 1 and 2. Train information and rail pass validation are available at any of the ticket windows.

Advance seat reservations may be obtained from CIE (Irish Rail) ticket office at Connolly and Heuston stations and at the CIE Travel Centre at 35 Lower Abbey Street. Reservations are made up to 1700 on the preceding day. Without seat reservations, we suggest arriving in the station about a half hour before your train's scheduled departure time just in case the travel is heavy on the day you have selected for your excursion.

Shopping for Waterford crystal? Depart Heuston station via Kilkenny to the town where it's made—and take money, lots of it!

Tourist Information/Hotel Reservations

Tourist Information Office: 14 Upper O'Connell St.
Tel: 112233–24-hour service; *Fax:* 2844968

Dublin is well equipped to offer a wide range of accommodations to visitors. Two exceptions, however, come during the Dublin Horse Show in early August and St. Patrick's Day in March. The principal sporting and social event of the year in Ireland, the horse show attracts thousands of visitors from all parts of the world. Don't plan to be in Dublin during the horse show unless you have confirmed reservations. The city is filled to overflowing at that time. If you are planning a visit to Dublin on St. Patrick's Day or during the summer months, it would be wise to check in advance with the Irish Tourist Board in New York.

Travelers looking for home-like accommodations, can purchase the Irish Tourist Offices' new "**Self Catering**" **services guide** describing apartments or houses for short-term rent (for a few days, a weekend, or a week). For reservations, Tel: 051 852444 or Fax: 051 877388.

Bed-and-Breakfast establishments are also a viable alternative to large, expensive hotels. Again, the Irish Tourist Offices maintain current descriptions. Mary and Brian Bennett's extraordinary bed-and-breakfast **Number 31** at Leeson Close, Dublin 2, (*Tel:* 1-676 5011), is the former home of Sam Stephenson, one of Dublin's renowned architects.

Getting Around In and Outside Dublin

* **DART,** 35 Lower Abbot Street, *Tel:* 01 836 6222
* **Bus Eireann,** Store Street, *Tel:* 01 836 6111

DART, or Dublin Area Rapid Transit, is the electric commuter service running around Dublin Bay and provides the fastest way of getting around Dublin as well as convenient access to the many resorts and other attractions outside of Dublin.

Much of the route is coastal and gives many different vies of the bay. It's excellent for short excursions to places such as the carming fishing village of Howth at its northern end or to Dun Laoghaire, the busy harbor for the Stena Line ferry service to England via Holyhead. DART accepts Eurailpass, as well as the various Irish Rail and/or Bus combination passes.

Dublin's DART has expanded to include new stations at Clontarf Road, Kilcock and Drumcondra. They also have improved their public address system, electronic information displays, signs and lighting, and provided easier accessibility for the handicapped.

Service to the cities in the Rupublic stlated for faster, more efficient service include: Galway, Sligo, Westport, and Tralee.

Sights/Attractions/Tours — Discovering Dublin

Dublin, with a population of about one-million people in its greater metropolitan area, offers the excitement of a vital city yet the ambiance of an old-world town.

Sightseeing on foot is easy. During your visit to the Dublin tourist information office, purchase the walking tour guide booklets that are of interest to you: **Heritage Trails,** or the **Rock 'n Stroll Trail** (significant sites in Dublin's music history), which is popular among the younger set. The success of bands like U2 and singers like Sinead O'Connor, who began her career by singing traditional Irish songs, have made Dublin a rock music capital.

Each of these brochures describes specially selected, sign-posted walking tours through the center of Dublin and include many points of interest. The tours are so designed that you can pick up the trails anywhere within the downtown area. The routes cover much of what is of interest historically and culturally to visitors and take about three hours.

If you plan to visit the **Dublin Writers Museum**, the **Joyce Tower, Shaw's Birthplace**, the **Viking Adventure**, Malahide Castle, **Newbridge House** and the **Fry Model Railway Museum,** purchase the **Dublin Super Saver Card** at the tourist office and save 25 percent off the total admission charges (£15 adults; £12 seniors and students; £8 children).

One of Dublin's sights to see is **O'Connell Street,** where, from the Liffey River Bridge, you can look at the pulsating heart of the city. A block away on the river's south bank stands **Parliament House** (now the Bank of Ireland), which faces the entrance to Trinity College, founded in 1591. The **Book of Kells,** considered its greatest treasure, is housed in the Collonades. Tourist trails lead from that point to **St. Stephen's Green** at the top of Grafton Street, where its twenty-two acres are surrounded delightfully by splendid Georgian houses.

For an insight into Irish life, **visit a Dublin pub**. In general, the Irish treat their pubs as a second home. The French seem to spend a relatively short time in a café before heading off for lunch, dinner, or whatever. The English go to a pub for a chat with friends and the barmaid and perhaps a game of darts before heading homeward. But the Irish, when they have the time (and they generally seem to), are in the pub for the entire evening.

The main pub activities are drinking and talking, although many serve appetizing meals and snacks and provide entertainment in the form of traditional music and song. You are free to sit and watch or join in. To take the latter option, merely turn to your neighbor and mention the weather. With that, the ball's in play. What is revealed then is fascinating. You'll find that everyone has positive but sensible opinions about a myriad of subjects. Make certain that what you say about a topic is relevant, for unlike most bar conversationalists, the Irish listen when you speak. Listening is an art that can be developed to a fine degree in a Dublin pub. Unless you are a Scot, try not to match the Dubliners' drinking ability or verbal athletics.

Suburban Dublin Day Excursions

Travelers can stay in Dublin, their "Base City," and easily make day excursions to visit other areas outside of Dublin. Or, they can use the "flip side" of the Base City-Day Excursion concept by taking advantage of less-expensive accommodations outside the city and making day excursions into Dublin.

Some Dublin suburban-area day excursions include:

Dun Laoghaire—a charming, lovely port on the Irish Sea which can be reached in only 15-minutes by DART from Dublin's Connolly Station. The new ferry terminal and new DART station are much more convenient for travelers than the former underground facility. The Stena Line's HSS (High-speed Seacat Service) catamaran provides inexpensive passage to and from Great Britain in less than 2 hours. A variety of hotels, bed and breakfast establishments, hostels, and the new "self-catering" apartments and houses are available in Dun Laoghaire for those who prefer to stay just outside of Dublin.

For a high-standard hostel on a low-cost budget, consider **The Old Schoolhouse,** Eblana Avenue, Dun Laoghaire, (Tel: 1-280 8777; Fax: 1-284-2266). It's a former Christian Brothers school that was renovated to create a modern, comfortable hostel that includes a laundry, television room, and use of fully equipped kitchen facillities.

Other Dublin suburban areas within easy reach via DART, Suburban Rail and the Arrow lines include:

Bray, 30 minutes from Dublin, is where writer James Joyce and artist Neil Jordan once lived and where Rock star Bono of U2 makes his home. Connecting buses can take you to the quaint little village of **Enniskerry,** with its delightful cafes, coffee shops, and comfortable bed and breakfast facilities.

Howth, only 25 minutes from Connolly Station via DART, is a charming fishing village on the northern side of Dublin Bay.

Naas, southwest of Dublin, can be reached by the Arrow train line departing from Heuston Station. Naas is famous as a center for horse breeding and race horse owners from all over the world attend the October yearling sales held nearby.

Kildare, also famous with the equestrian set as a center for horse breeding and home of the Irish National Stud, is only 48 kilometers away and the last stop on the Arrow line trains departing from Dublin's Heuston Station. For luxurious resort-type accommodations (at resort-type prices, of course) the Kildare Hotel and Country Club is top notch. Opening in 1991, the transformation of the former fifth-century Straffan mansion into a luxury hotel took more than 2 years to complete. The clubhouse and 18-hole golf course designed by Arnold Palmer were completed in 1995.

Waterford, a twelfth century Norman fortress positioned on the banks of the Suir has been a significant port since the sixteenth century. The Dominican Blackfriars and ruins of the French Church are reminders of medieval times, as is the twelfth century Reginald's Tower, where the city's museum is located. In 1170 Strongbow was married to Princess Aoife, daughter of the King of Leinster in Christ Church Cathedral where today an audio video presentation using the excellent acoustics of the nave recreates an one-thousand-year-old history of the area. Hook Tower, one of the oldest light-houses in Europe stands proudly at Hook Head at the beginning of the estuary in Waterford Bay. Waterford is home to Waterford Crystal, the largest crystal factory in the world. From April through October, the **Waterford Crystal Visitor Centre** is open seven days a week from 0830-1800. Tours and audiovisual presentations are available, and the gallery features some of the most unique and valuable crystal pieces ever created.

Waterford Castle (*Tel:* 051 878203; in the U.S.A.; *Tel:* 800-221-1074) located on an island, began as a monastic settlement in the sixth century. It ultimately became one of the estates of the Fitzgeralds, who were the Kings of Ireland during the fifteenth and sixteenth centuries. Purchased by Eddie Kearns in 1987, it was developed into a luxurious Hotel and Country Club. The castle's guest rooms are comfortable and bright, with beautiful views of the estate. Conference facilities are available and special arrangements are made for business entertaining. The main dining room seats 65 guests and often hosts a resident pianist. Hunting and polo are available as is deep sea and freshwater fishing. Croquet is played on the Castle lawns. An excellent country club and championship golf course and luxurious leisure center also grace the island.

More Day Excursions

Other day excursions made conveniently with Irish Rail/Bus are **Cork, Galway, Killarney,** and **Kilkenny.** Cork provides a double treat when you tread its fascinating quays and kiss the renowned stone at nearby Blarney Castle. Galway, the western capital of Ireland, has all the charm of an ancient city, plus the vitality of expanding industries and popular holiday-resort attractions. The combination of Kilkenny Town and Kilkenny Castle offers a delightful variety of attractions from cats and choir lofts to castle tours and witches' tales.

Train Connections to and from Port of Rosslare for Ferry Connections to Cherbourg and Le Havre, France

Dublin to Rosslare		Rosslare to Dublin	
DEPART CONNOLLY	ARRIVE ROSSLARE	DEPART ROSSLARE	ARRIVE CONNOLLY
(Daily except Sunday)		(Daily except Sunday)	
0845	1150	0725	1020
1333	1630	1455	1755
1830	2125	1800	2050
(Sunday)		(Sunday)	
1000	1255	0900	1155
1830	2125	1800	2050

Note: For more information, telephone (1)8366222
Standard class only on all trains

Distance: 95 miles/168 km

Day Excursion to

Cork

Depart from Dublin Heuston Station

Distance by Train: 165 miles (266 km)
Average Train Time: 2 hours, 20 minutes
City Dialing Code: 21
Cork Tourist Information: Tourist House, Grand Parade
Tel: (021) 273251;Fax: (021)273504
Hours: Monday-Saturday 0900–1900. In winter, 0915–1730 Monday-Saturday (closed for lunch 1300–1415). Guided tours of the city depart daily at 1100 and 1430. *Tel:* (021) 293822 to reserve your place on the tour.

Cork, Ireland's second largest city (about 200,000 residents) and commercial and passenger port, is easily accessible from both Dublin or Shannon (via train from Limerick). From Dublin a special executive car called "City Gold" is available, with special amenities for doing business, including facsimile and telephone.

Cork City, *Corcach* in Irish meaning marshy place, was actually built upon the marshes and wetlands of the River Lee. **Saint Finbarr's Cathedral** is located where Cork's first settlement and monastery was founded by the missionary in the seventh century. The **Guinness International Jazz Festival,** held in October, attracts world-famous musicians, including famous American stars.

The village of **Blarney** is a short 25-minute bus ride north of the city, where the "touristy" thing to do is visit **Blarney Castle** and kiss the legendary **Blarney Stone,** which promises the gift of eloquence to anyone believing enough to be lowered backwards from the battlements on the roof of the castle to achieve it. You will, of course, be following thousands of other tourists' lip prints who have attempted the same thing.

Board the bus marked "Blarney" in the city's bus terminal at Parnell Place. It's only a ten-minute walk down Glanmire Road to the river and the bus station. On Sunday buses depart Cork on the hour 0900–2300 and return at 35 minutes past the hour. During the week, buses run about every 15 minutes.

There are many legends regarding the origins of the Blarney Stone. According to one, it was brought to Ireland from the Holy Land during one of the crusades. Another theorizes a MacCarthy professing to be a Baron of Blarney and true to Queen Elizabeth never fulfilled any promise or condition he made to her highness. His "fair words in soft speech" caused the queen to term them as "just blarney."

The moist, temperate climate of Cork makes for splendid gardens and wonderful parks. And shopping the maze of streets between Patrick St. and

South Mall provides a plethora of fashions and fashionable cafes. Clifford's, 18 Dyke Parade; The Oyster Tavern, in Market Lane; and Michael's Bistro, Mardyke St. are eateries offering finely-prepared foods at various prices.

Dublin—Cork

DEPAR HEUSTON STATION	ARRIVE CORK STATION	NOTES
0730	1005	(1)(3)
1035	1305	(2)(3)
1125	1402	(1)(3)
1320	1615	(1)(3)
1525	1750	(1)(3)

DEPART CORK STATION	ARRIVE HEUSTON STATION	NOTES
1445	1735	(1)(3)
1730	1950	(1)(3)
1845	2125	(2)(3)(4)
1900	2200	(1)(3)

(1) Daily, except Sundays and holidays
(2) Sundays only
(3) Food service available
(4) Second-class only

Distance: 165 miles/266 km

Day Excursion to

Galway
ROUNDSTONE

Depart from Dublin Heuston Station

Distance by Train: 129 miles (208 km)
Average Train Time: 2 hours, 40 minutes
Tourist Information Center: Victoria Place, Eyre Square,
Tel: 091 563081; *Fax:* 091 565201
Hours: daily 0900-1945 July-August

　　Emerging from the railway station, you'll see Eyre Square with the Kennedy Park in its center. Turn left and left again at Victoria Place. The traditional green "ı"" signs will lead you to the tourist office. Fronting the square is the Great Southern Hotel, a hostelry combining the charm of both old and new and an ideal place to halt for a libation or a luncheon.

Dublin–Galway

DEPART HEUSTON STATION	ARRIVE GALWAY STATION	NOTES
0720	1000	(1)(4)
1100	1350	(2)(3)(4)
1425	1705	(1)(3)(4)

DEPART GALWAY STATION	ARRIVE HEUSTON STATION	NOTES
1525	1813	(1)(3)(4)
1805	2152	(3)(4)
1810	2050	(1)(2)(4)

(1) Daily, except Sundays and holidays
(2) Sundays only
(3) Standard class only
(4) Light refreshments available

Distance: 129 miles/208 km

Like some other Irish cities, Galway was established initially by foreigners. Since medieval times, it has been a significant port dominated by an oligarchy of fourteen Norman and Welsh merchant families. As a thriving trade with Spain developed, the **Spanish Arch** was erected in 1594 created to protect the Spanish ships as they unloaded their cargo. It still remains below the Claddagh Bridge and has a museum adjacent. The avenue leading from the arch known as the "Long Walk" is where Spanish merchants supposedly strolled into Galway City. From the tourist office, walk four blocks south on Merchants Road. The area is still resplendent with Spanish architecture.

Galway has become Ireland's fastest growing city. A university town since the fourteenth century, Galway still has a huge student population and is a still a cultural center writers and scholars. In October, March, and July, Galway (as in Dublin and Cork) hosts an **international film festival** to showcase new cinema.

Eyre Square, given to the city by Edward Eyre in 1710, is the heart of Galway city activity and where the John F. Kennedy Memorial Park is located. Fronting the square is the **Great Southern Hotel,** a hostelry combining the charm of both old and new and an ideal place to halt for a libation or a luncheon. The shopping center west of the square is also where the last section of the old wall has been preserved, along with the Penrice and Shoemaker towers.

At 19 Eyre Square, the Bank of Ireland displays the priceless **Silver Sword** and Great Mace, the finest examples of Irish silver work remaining in the Republic.

Galway is a ferry port for the Aran Islands which lie 30 miles offshore, as are Spiddal, Doolin 5 and Rosaveal. Air service is available via Connemara airport. The islands are a tribute to traditional Irish life and culture, and, as in Galway and Connemara where Gaelic is still proudly spoken among the natives.

The new **Galway Bay Conference and Leisure Centre** (Tel: 091 520520) is a prime example of Galway City's growth. The new deluxe facility is located on Galway's promenade, just 5 minutes from Eyre Square and the City Center. It includes a fitness center with swimming pool, sauna, and steam room. Restaurant, bar, and lounge each have panoramic views of Galway Bay. With its proximity to **Leisureland,** the hotel is one of the most extensive conference and leisure centers in the country.

Supposedly, the word "lynching" entered the English language through an act of Galway's chief magistrate, James Lynch-FitzStephen, elected to his post in 1493. According to a popular but dubious legend, his son, Walter, murdered a Spanish visitor and then confessed to the crime. He was condemned by his own father, but no one could be found to carry out the execution. So Judge Lynch, no doubt a firm believer in "spare the rod and spoil the child," hanged his own son and afterwards retired into seclusion. **Lynch's Castle** stands today on Shop Street, and the Lynch Memorial attesting to this stern and unbending justice lies nearby, close to the **Church of St. Nicholas,** erected in 1320. Legend has it that Columbus worshipped in the church before setting out on his voyage of discovery to America.

An unusual feature of Galway is its downtown salmon weir, where shoals of salmon swim in the clear river en route to spawning grounds. This unique sight may be viewed from the **Salmon Weir Bridge** crossing the Corrib River by the city's cathedral.

Roundstone is a picturesque fishing village on the southern shores of Connemara. Already well known for superb seafood and quaint bed & breakfast style hotels, Roundstone is also "the home of the bodhran"—a one-sided framed drum made from goatskin—Ireland's oldest product made famous more recently when played by Christy Moore in *Riverdance*. A bus leaves daily from Foster Street in Galway City for Roundstone and Clifden.

If you have never seen *Riverdance* nor heard the haunting tones of the bodhrans, you've missed one of the most exciting music and dance shows in the last 1,000 years. Visit Master bodhran maker **Malachy Kearns'** (known locally as Malachy Bodhran) quaint craft and music shop. Malachy and artist/wife Anne are the only full-time bodhran makers in the world and they've been making them for 22 years.

You can purchase the hand-made bodhrans with Celtic designs, family crests, or names. The shop is open daily 0900-1900. Malachy Kearns mixes the goat skins with secret ingredients and soaks them for 7-10 days before stretching them over a beech wood frame. Mr. Kearns attributes the bodhran's haunting tones to the goat skins; we think his secret ingredients have something to do with achieving such extraordinary sound. It is truly fascinating!

    Roundstone Music, Roundstone, Connemara, Co. Galway
    Tel: 095 35875; Fax: 095 35890
    Email: bodhran@iol.ie
    Internet: http://www.musweb.com/kearns.htm

Day Excursion to

Kilkenny

GHOSTS AND GIFTS GALORE

Depart from Dublin Heuston Station

Distance by Train: 81 miles (130 km)
Average Train Time: 1 hour, 49 minutes
Kilkenny Tourist Information: Rose Inn Street, Kilkenny
Tel: 056 217555
Hours: May-July, Monday-Saturday 0900-1800, Sunday 1100-1700

    To reach it, turn left onto John Street after leaving the station and walk to the bridge crossing the river. Cross the bridge and John Street then becomes Rose Inn Street. Continue walking up Rose Inn Street and you will find the office in the Shee Alms House on the right.

Kilkenny may be Ireland's smallest city, but it is one of the most popular destinations from Dublin. **Kilkenny Castle,** a twelfth century grand stone fortress on the River Nore, dominates the scene and sets the theme. It was the chief residence of the Butler family from 1391 until 1935—almost 550 years. Recently restored to the majesty of the 1820's, it is now home to the National Furniture collection and the modern Butler Gallery. The castle is impressive and reminiscent of the great bastions along the Rhine River.

    Other sites include the thirteenth century **St. Canice's Cathedral,** reputed to be one of the most beautiful in Ireland; **Rothe House,** home of the Kilkenny Archeological Society and **Shee Alms House,** a restored sixteenth-century building which houses the Tourist Information Office and the "City Scope Exhibition," an exciting re-creation of the medieval city.

    Though small, Kilkenny is cosmopolitan, with a pub and club life that draws visitors from major cities. In fact, the new **Paris Texas Bar & Restaurant** has to close its doors by 2100 because of the crowds. **Langtons,** a four-year winner of the National Pub of the Year award, is a traditional pub

Dublin–Kilkenny

DEPART HEUSTON STATION	ARRIVE IN KILKENNY STATION	NOTES
0740	0926	(1)(4)
0950	1133	(2)(3)
1140	1322	(1)(4)

DEPART KILKENNY STATION	ARRIVE IN HEUSTON STATION	NOTES
1542	1723	(1)(4)
1848	2037	(2)(3)
1912	2058	(1)(4)

(1) Daily, except Sundays and holidays
(2) Sundays only
(3) Standard class only
(4) Light refreshments available

Distance: 81 miles/130 km

and restaurant in grand surroundings with a disco club that stays open to the wee hours of the morning. (A new "five-star" hotel facility is adjacent to the disco *Tel:* 056-65133).

Another interesting landmark is **Kytler's Inn,** which has the distinction of being the oldest residence in the city and, by tradition, the house of the witch Dame Alice Kytler, born there in 1280. Dame Alice seems to have been a very nice lady except that she acquired and disposed of husbands—four in all—in rapid succession. This aroused the curiosity of the local folks, and in 1324 she was charged by Bishop de Ledrede with witchcraft, heresy, and criminal assaults upon her husbands. Brought to trial and condemned to burn at the stake as a witch, Dame Alice eluded her accusers and escaped across the Irish Sea to England. Her maid, Petronilla, was not as fortunate; the bishop had her burned at the stake as a suitable substitute. Locals claim that Petronilla's ghost still haunts the cellar of what is now the Kytler Inn on St. Kieran Street—possibly asking for back wages?

Day Excursion to

Killarney

LAKES AND JAUNTING CARS

Depart from Dublin Heuston Station

Distance by Train: 185 miles, 298 km
Average Train Time: 3 hours, 30 minutes
Killarney Tourist Information: Town Hall,
Tel: 064 31440
Hours: July-Aug., Monday-Saturday 0900-1000, Sunday 1000-1300/1400-1800; June and September, Monday-Saturday 0900-1900; October-May, Monday-Saturday 0930-1830

 To reach the tourist information office, turn left on Railway Road just after passing the Great Southern Hotel on your left as you leave the railway station. Railway Road crosses Muckross Road a short distance from the station and almost immediately ends as it runs into Main Street. The jaunting-car stand will be on your left at this point. The tourist information office is housed in the Town Hall just ahead on your left.

Killarney is the number one tourist attraction in the Republic of Ireland. Horse-drawn carriages known as jaunting cars take tourists to feature sights including: **Muckross Abbey**, the ruins of a fifteenth century Franciscan monastery; **Ross Castle,** on the banks of Lough Leane; and **Muckross House,** a nineteenth century manor with a museum depicting local folk life, and housing various craft shops with blacksmiths, weavers, and potters. Jaunting-car rates are usually based on four passengers. If your party is fewer than four, the tourist office may be just the place to find other passengers willing to share the cost. The central jaunting-car stand in Killarney is a stone's throw from the tourist office; so you won't have to return to the railway station.

Killarney's **St. Mary's Cathedral** is an impressive neo-Gothic structure worthy of a visit. The **Great Southern Hotel,** opposite the railway station, is a fashionable hostelry of great beauty and its amicable Punchbowl Bar is a good place to pause for a libation and friendly conversation.

There are many eating places to choose from. We found the food at the **Flesk Restaurant** to be tasty and satisfying. It's on Main Street, a few doors past the tourist office on the left-hand side. One of the favorite spots of the locals, too, the Flesk is known for its daily fresh fish specials, such as wild salmon, and its live Dingle Bay lobsters. Four-course menus range from £8 to £12.

A classic Killarney countryside excursion is by bus to **Kate Kearney's Cottage,** a coaching inn, where you are fortified with Irish coffee. Then, setting out by pony through the **Gap of Dunloe,** you are refreshed again at **Lord Brandon's Cottage** before returning by boat to Lough Leane and to Killarney by jaunting car. You can obtain information on prices from the tourist office.

Dublin–Killarney

DEPART HEUSTON STATION	ARRIVE IN KILLARNEY STATION	NOTES
0830	1142	(2)(3)(4)
0855	1228	(1)(4)

DEPART KILLARNEY STATION	ARRIVE IN HEUSTON STATION	NOTES
1446	1825	(1)(4)
1757	2100	(2)(3)(4)

(1) Daily, except Sundays and holidays
(2) Sundays
(3) Standard class only
(4) Food available

Distance: 185 miles/298 km

Italy

Why do we find Italy so inviting? Just ask any Italian—it can be summed up in three little words: *La dolce vita*, the sweet life. Italy is pasta, Pavarotti, and popes; it's fashion, Ferrari, and films; it's *vino* (wine), Venus, and villas—it's all of our favorite things which culminate in *La dolce vita*.

Perennially a tourist favorite, Italy's allure continues with the advent of the Holy Year, or Jubilee 2000. The Holy Year, founded in 1300 by Pope Boniface VIII, is a spiritual pilgrimage that is celebrated only every 25 years. At press time, the Italian Government Tourist Board (ENIT) is establishing a special office to assist those who plan to visit Italy during the Holy Year.

Most visitors are aware of Italy's predominantly Catholic heritage, but not many are aware that Italy also has a rich Jewish heritage dating as early as 140 B.C. Most Italian Jews are descendants of the group Sephardim, who were expelled from Spain and Portugal in the fifteenth and sixteenth centuries. Many outstanding synagogues and other Jewish sites are most evident in Florence, Rome, and Venice.

For more information about Italy, contact the Italian Government Tourist Boards (ENIT) in North America:

Chicago: 401 North Michigan Avenue, Suite 3030, Chicago, IL 60611. Tel: (312) 644-9448; Fax: (312) 644-3019

New York: 630 Fifth Avenue, Suite 1565, New York, NY 10111. Tel: (212) 245-4822; Fax: (212) 586-9249

Los Angeles: 12400 Wilshire Boulevard, Suite 550, Los Angeles, CA 90025. Tel: (310) 820-009; Fax: (310) 820-6357

Montreal: 1 Place Ville Marie, Suite 1914, Montreal, Quebec, H3B 3M9. Tel: (514) 866-7667; Fax: (514) 392-1429

Banking

- **Currency:** Lira
  Coins are in 50, 100, 200, and 500 Lire. Banknotes are in 1,000, 2,000, 5,000, 10,000, 50,000, and 100,000 Lire.
- **Exchange rate at press time:** 1,761 Italian Lire = $1.00 U.S.

Communications

- **Country Code:** 39
  For telephone calls within Italy, dial a zero (0) preceding area code. Direct dial: AT&T: 172-1011; MCI: 172-1022; Sprint: 172-1877 in Bologna, Brindisi, Catania, Cozena, Florence, Formia, Genoa, Latina, Milan, Naples, Olbia, Padua, Palermo, Perugia, Pescara, Pisa, Pordenone, Trieste, Turin, and Venice.
  Buy telephone cards at any tobacco or newsstand for 2,000, 5,000 or 10,000 lire. Within the city, it costs 200 lire for the first 9 minutes. It's also possible to use 200 or 500 lire coins for calls. Public phones are available in rail stations, post offices, and most bars and restaurants.

Rail Travel in Italy

The **Italian State Railways** (*Ente Ferrovie Italiane dello Stato, or FS*) provides excellent and frequent train services linking all of Italy, including Sicily and Sardinia via train ferries, with Austria, France, and Switzerland. All main lines and many minor lines are electrified. Italy's principal express trains, the Eurostar services (not to be confused with the cross-Channel Eurostar trains) such as the ETR Pendolino and ETR 500, are among the best in Europe.

Keep in mind that Italian trains are not just for tourists; the Italians are heavily dependent upon their rail system and 2nd class rail cars are often crowded. We recommend traveling in 1st Class when in Italy.

The Italian State Railways accepts **Eurailpass, Europass, Italy RailCard, Italy Flexi RailCard,** and the **Italian Kilometric Pass.** The Eurailpass and Europass bonus includes the ferries operated by FS between Civitavecchia and Golfo Aranci (Sardinia) and between Villa S. Giovanni and Messina (Sicily). Ferries operated by Adriatica Lines and Hellenic Mediterranean Lines between Brindisi, Italy, and Corfu/Igoumenitsa/Patras, Greece, are also included (high-season surcharge of $15 U.S. applicable).

The Italy RailCard provides for unlimited rail travel for the specified number of days consecutively, or for more flexibility, choose the Flexi RailCard for traveling the specified number of days within a 1-month period.

Italy RailCard

1997 RATES	VALIDITY	2ND CLASS	1ST CLASS
RailCard			
	8 Days	$187	$269
	15 Days	$228	$335
	21 Days	$263	$386
	30 Days	$312	$462

Italy Flexi RailCard

4 Days within 1 Month	$150	$214
8 Days within 1 Month	$204	$306
12 Days within 1 Month	$259	$380

Italy RailCard and Flexi RailCard are valid for unlimited travel on the entire Italian State Railways network including InterCity, EuroCity and Rapido trains with no surcharge. **Supplement required for Eurostar ETR 450-(Pendalino) trains.** Children under 12 years of age, pay half adult fare. under 4 years of age, free.

The Italian Kilometric Pass (1st Class $264; 2nd Class $156 U.S.) provides up to 3,000 kilometers (1,875 miles) of rail travel within a 2-month period, with a maximum of 20 single train trips. The pass may be used by as many as 5 persons, but each trip is calculated by multiplying the distance by the number of persons traveling. It also requires a supplement for traveling on *all* high-speed trains (and Italy has a lot of them), such as InterCity, EuroCity, Rapido, and ETR 450s. A "single trip" means boarding a single train by a single person. This pass is inconvenient in that it deviates from the general concept of a rail pass because travelers must show the pass at ticket windows before each train trip.

Base City…

Milan (Milano)

City Dialing Code: 2

Milan is fashionable and futuristic—as evidenced by the growing number of high-rise structures and the accelerating pace of its population. At the same time, Milan is ancient and respectful of its glorious past. For instance, the **Duomo** (cathedral) is the second largest church in Italy, a beautiful example of Gothic stonework begun in 1386. *The Last Supper*, Leonardo da Vinci's famous painting, may be seen in the refectory of the **Santa Maria delle Grazie** convent. It was painted between 1495 and 1498.

Like a typical Milanese, Leonardo was concerned with the future, and his drawings of machines in flight, together with some of his futuristic inventions, are exhibited in the **Leonardo da Vinci National Museum of Science and Technology.**

To promote its future, Milan created one of the most extensive fairgrounds in Europe; each year, thousands of businesses display or investigate products there. Milan does not live up to the stereotype of the Italian town. Lunches tend to be shorter, conversations seem more direct and to the point, and the Milanese appear to be in a bit of a hurry.

Unlike many Italian cities, transportation is abundant and unusually dependable. Several decades ago, the five o'clock train never left Milano Centrale on time; today, the five o'clock train leaves at five o'clock. Milan has an excellent underground transportation system (Metropolitan). A ticket costs 1,500 Lire and is valid for 75 minutes on buses and trams, or for one underground (metro) trip. There is also a day ticket available for 5,000 Lire and a two-day ticket for 9,000 Lire. Hotel services rival the finest in Europe; shops are sophisticated, efficient. In a word, Milan "works."

There is one crucial thing about Milan. It is virtually impossible to get a hotel room in the city during those periods when the major fairs and fashion shows are in progress—September, October, and early March. Forget about August. That's when the Milanese go on vacation and the majority of the hotels are closed.

Arriving by Air

Milan has two airports serving international travelers. Milan's main international airport, **Malpensa,** is thirty miles northwest of the city, and fifty to sixty minutes is required to reach the downtown air terminal. Closer in, Milan's

Linate Airport is located slightly more than six miles to the east of Milan; transit time is twenty to forty minutes. Check with your airline regarding which airport will be used for your flight.

Airport-City Links: Malpensa Airport Bus service connects Malpensa Airport with Linate Airport (travel time of 50 minutes) and Malpensa Airport with the Central Station (travel time of 75 minutes). Fare: 13,000 Lire. For schedules or information for both bus services (*Tel:* 02/66984509).

Buses run every 20 minutes between Linate Airport and the bus terminal at the side of Central Station at Piazza Luigi d' Svoia from 0700–2100. Purchase tickets on board the bus (4,500 Lire).

Bus, limousine, and taxi services are available at both air terminals. The taxi services are quite expensive. We recommend the airport bus services.

Arriving by Train

Milan has seven railway stations, but luckily, readers need be concerned with only one, the Milan Central Station (**Milano Centrale**). Milan's central station is enormous.

Money exchange offices can be reached by going through the archway leading off *binari* (tracks) Nos. 10–15. Once through the archway and into the main hall of the station, you will see several exchange offices, two of which have hours daily from 0700–2300. Avoid the so-called "money changers" who frequent this area. Like the gypsies in the Paris Metro, their main purpose is to relieve you of your money. The gypsies do it by picking your pocket; the "money changers" are much more gentle in their approach—they just short-change you. You will find the best rates inside the official exchange office at the counter.

Tourist information is across from the exact change office in the main hall. Maps and tour information are available. This office is not equipped to assist in locating hotel accommodations but they can give you directions to the central tourist office at Piazzo del Duomo. Hours: 0800–2000 daily; Sunday and holidays, 0900–1230 and 1430–1800 (*Tel:* 02 669–0532). A hallway on the left side of the tourist office will lead you to a public telephone.

Train information office is marked with a black "I" sign, located at the extreme right end of the station as you come from the trains. Illuminated flags indicate what language is spoken at the windows. The British flag means English is spoken. Hours: 0700–2100.

Train reservations for ETR 450 Pendolino, EuroCity, InterCity, and Rapido express-train services are made in an office separate from the one dispensing train information. To reach it, go through the main station hall and descend to the station foyer on the lower (street) level. Turn left and look for a huge door marked BIGLIETTERIA EST (ticket office east). Go through the door, and take a number from the ticket machine to wait your turn. You will see counter Nos. 49–53, labeled PRENOTAZIONI (Reservations). Hours: 0800–2200 Monday through Friday and 0800–1300 on Saturday and Sunday. **Rail pass validation** requires that you descend to the street level via the escalator in the middle of the station, make a right turn, and look for a sign, *biglietteria ovest*. Then proceed to windows 20 or 22 marked INTERNATIONAL TICKETS.

Food services range from trackside vendors to a full-service restaurant. The restaurant, with a large and efficient self-service cafeteria next to it, is located on the far left side of the main hall as you exit from the trains. A snack bar is also there. Downstairs near the BIGLIETTERIA OVEST sign you will find an excellent cafeteria that serves traditional Italian hot entrees and sandwiches. Just behind the cafeteria there is a supermarket.

In this snack bar, as in the various smaller ones scattered throughout the main hall and track area, you need to purchase tickets for the particular food or beverage you desire from a cashier, then give the tickets to a counter attendant. The system works, but now you know how the Italian immigrant felt when he ordered his first American hamburger and was asked if he wanted it with mustard, catsup, lettuce, tomato, pickles—and "was that to go?"

If this is your first rail trip into Italy, this will probably be your first acquaintance with the trackside vendors. Similar to the pushcarts that grace many of the streets in New York City, they offer a convenient variety of refreshments—and the price is right.

Baggage-checking facilities may be reached by taking the exit at the end of tracks 6 and 7. Across the main hall and to the right, you'll see a sign in red letters, DEPOSITO BAGAGLI. Rates vary according to what you store. The facility is open all the time. To store one bag costs 5,000 Lire per 12 hours.

The main baggage room, located on the street level of the station, can be reached either from the plaza facing the Michelangelo Hotel or from the bottom of the main escalator, between the street level and the train concourse. Hours: 0700–2230 daily. Through experience, we have learned that you should check items to be forwarded at least one day in advance, and then only to other major points in Italy. We would not advise forwarding anything to France or Switzerland.

There is a checkroom in the restaurant-and-cafeteria entrance that is convenient and safe to use for temporarily storing suitcases and wearing apparel while you are eating or searching for a place to stay. If you check your baggage here, it is most important that you find out when the attendant plans to leave. Otherwise, you could return to collect your duds only to learn they have been moved to a safe area until the operation starts again in the morning. The hours of operation are posted as "0700–2400," but it appears to be an individual enterprise rather than one under the supervision of management.

Station miscellany. Milan's railway station has many other services. There is a large and rather comfortable first-class lounge leading off the street side of the main hall. Its entrance is just to the left of the tourist information office. Inside the lounge you will find a computer that can give you train information.

Milano Centrale is a multilevel station, but elevator service from the train level to the street level is available. The entrance on the train level is inside the first-class lounge. If you have a first class rail pass, you have full access to the passenger lounge and elevator service.

Taxi service is available at both side entrances and the front, and **bus service** is in the Piazza Duca d'Aosta in front of the station. Pictographs of the station's facilities are located conveniently at the end of many tracks.

Double-check your departing train number and platform location. For example, when departing Milan for Munich aboard EuroCity 11/12 *Leonardo Da Vinci*, you will note that signs in the station indicate the train's destination as MONACO. In Italian, this means "Monk," and Munich (in German) is the "City of Monks." So, you are on the right train and you are not bound for Monaco, which, in French, means Monte Carlo. InterCity 341/2 *Ligure* is the proper train to board if you are, in fact, going to Monaco and Monte Carlo via Genoa.

Emerging from the train platforms, if you detect the aroma of an American-style hamburger, it's coming from Wendy's. To get there, turn right in the station hall and take the escalator at the far end to the street level. Skirt the tram terminal to the left then look for the Wendy's sign.

Tourist Information/Hotel Reservations

Tourist Information Office: Piazza del Duomo
Hours: 0830-2000 Monday-Friday; 0900-1300/1400-1900 Saturday; until 1700 on Sunday. To reach the central tourist information office, take bus No. 65 in front of the station to Piazza del Duomo, site of Milan's cathedral. You can also take line 3 of the metro to the Duomo stop. Attendants in the railway station information office will direct you.

There are times when the Milan reaches the visitor saturation point and no-vacancy signs go up all over town. Should you arrive in Milan without hotel reservations and this is the situation you encounter, you have two alternatives to consider.

If there is no housing in Milan, you can leave town. A EuroCity train can have you in Como in 32 minutes, where hotel rooms probably will be more plentiful. In fact, you may be taken with the idea of residing in this lovely lake location throughout your stay in the area. There is express-train service back to Milan every morning.

Another alternative is a fast but systematic search of the concentrated hotel area adjacent to the railway station. There is a covey of luxury and first-class hotels to the left of it. Dominating the scene is the 17-story Michelangelo, with the Bristol, the Anderson, the Andreola, and the Splendido close by.

For lower cost but comfortable lodgings, walk two blocks on Via Roberto Lepetit, beginning at the Michelangelo, to Piazza San Camillo. Within this distance, you pass the Florida, the Colombia, and the Boston hotels. No luck? Turn right at the Plaza onto Via Napo Torriani. Between this point and Piazza Duca d'Aosta three short blocks ahead (where you can again see the station), you pass on your right the hotels Berna, Atlantic, and San Carlo; on your left, the Canova, Garda, Flora, Bernina, and Augustus.

If you have not found a room by this time, head back to Milano Centrale and one of the EuroCities. By this time, you'll be sure to fall in love with Lake Como.

The main tourist office charges a nominal fee for making accommodations reservations, but they are not authorized to accept deposits to guarantee that your reservation will be honored on your arrival at the hotel or pension. If you have made a room reservation through the tourist office, proceed immediately to your hotel to confirm your reservation in person. Many Italian hoteliers operate on a "first-come, first-housed" basis, and even though you have a reservation, someone else may end up with your room.

Day Excursions

A total of four day excursions have been selected from Milan. The first two take you south of Milan into the Italian peninsula to Italy's gastronomic capital, **Bologna,** and the birthplace of Christopher Columbus, **Genoa.** Another day excursion will take you to where Switzerland meets Italy, **Lake Lugano,** the Swiss city with an Italian flair. The remaining day excursion will take you east to "the Queen of the Adriatic," **Venice,** and the romance of its gondoliers and grand canals. You'll enjoy each of them.

Train Connections to Other Base Cities from Milan

TO:	DEPART	ARRIVE	TRAIN NUMBER	NOTES
Amsterdam	2125	1152	200	(6)
Barcelona				
(Franca)	200	0930	EN 372	(1)
Berne	0815	1202	IC 332	
	1025	1440	EC 90	
	1115	1426	IC 334	
	1525	1934	EC 60	
	1715	2026	CIS 36	
Brussels (Midi)	1025	2237	EC 90	(5)
	2135	0930+1	298	
Luxembourg	1025	1956	EC 90	
Munich	0910	1630	EC 15	(5)
	1510	2230	EC 83	(5)
Nice	0710	1146	IC 341	(5)
	1510	1956	IC 345	
	1815	2351	1144	(4)
Paris (Lyon)	0900	1628	IC 330	(2)
(sleeper)	1320	0837+1	EN 216	
Rome	0800	1225	ES 9409	(5)
	1320	1855	IC 559	(5)
	1520	2055	IC 521	(5)
Vienna (Sudbhf.)	2015	0842+1	2113	(3)
Zürich	0825	1253	EC 386	(5)
	1025	1453	388	
	1225	1653	380	
	1425	1853	IC 382	
	1625	2053	IC 354	
	1815	2153	CIS 152	
	1925	2334	IC 356	

Daily departures unless otherwise noted. Make reservations for all departures.

(1) Salvador Dali, special fares apply
(2) Transfer in Lausanne to TGV/EC 24
(3) Arrive 0853 Sunday through Wednesday
(4) July and August only
(5) Supplement payable
(6) Transfer at Basel

Day Excursion to

Bologna
ITALY'S GASTRONOMIC CAPITAL

Depart Milan's Central Station

Distance by Train: 136 miles (219 km)
Average Train Time: 1 hour, 45 minutes
City Dialing Code: 51
Tourist Information Office: Piazza Medaglie d'Oro,
Tel: 246541; *Fax:* 251947
Hours: Monday-Saturday 0900-1230 and 1430-1900
> Piazza Medaglie d'Oro lies directly in front of the station. To reach the tourist office in the station you must first exit the main entrance of the station. Incline to the right and enter the station hallway at that exit.

Tourist Information Office: No. 6, west side of Piazza Maggiore
Tel: 239660; *Fax:* 231454
Hours: Sunday 0900-1300; Monday-Saturday 0900-1900.
> To reach it, turn left when exiting the rail station and walk two blocks to Via Dell'Independenza, one of Bologna's main avenues. Turn right onto the avenue, and a delightful fifteen-minute walk will bring you to Neptune's Fountain. Then, continue your walk in the same direction a short distance into Piazza Maggiore.

Bologna specializes in two areas—thinking and eating. When you think about it, you'll probably conclude, as we did, that it is not too bad a life style to follow.

Bologna's university, the oldest in Europe, was founded in 1088. By the 13th century, its student body numbered 10,000. One of its more recent students, Guglielmo Marconi (1874–1937), studied wireless telegraphy there. The university was noted for employing women professors. One professor, Novella d'Andrea, was said to be so beautiful in face and body that she had to give her lectures from behind a screen to avoid distracting her students.

Bologna is the capital of **Emilia-Romagna,** a northwest-to-southeast slice of the Italian peninsula just below its juncture with the European Continent. An economically strong region, with the nation's highest employment rate, Emilia-Romagna holds the uncontested title of the "richest gastronomic region in Italy." Endless strings of sausages and thousands of cheese varieties adorn the windows of its delicatessen shops. Restaurants line the city's arcaded streets, filled with people devouring delicacies to the accompaniment of fine wines. Many of them are in the luxury class, but you can also dine very well in the less expensive restaurants. Many maintain an "open kitchen," which you're welcome to inspect and where you may chat with the cooks.

The famous prosciutto of Parma is absolutely unlike any American prosciutto—and, like most Italian meat products, it cannot be sold in the United States.

Milan–Bologna

DEPART MILAN CENTRAL STATION	TRAIN NUMBER	ARRIVE IN BOLOGNA STATION	NOTES
0700	ES 9407	0843	(1)(2)
0800	ES 9409	0933	(1)(2)
0900	ES 9411	1043	(1)(2)
1000	ES 9413	1143	(1)(2)
1100	ES 9415	1243	(1)(2)

Plus other frequent service throughout the day

DEPART BOLOGNA STATION	TRAIN NUMBER	ARRIVE IN MILAN CENTRAL STATION	NOTES
1610	ES 9416	1800	(1)(2)
1710	ES 9418	1900	(1)(2)
1810	ES 9420	2000	(1)(2)
1910	ES 9422	2100	(1)(2)
2010	ES 9424	2215	(1)(2)
2216	ES 9428	2359	(1)(2)

Plus other frequent service throughout the day

(1) Daily, including holidays
(2) Reservations required (Pendolino and ES trains)

Distance: 136 miles/219 km

Bologna is an ideal base for exploring the Emilia-Romagna area. Among the towns to visit are: **Faenza,** for its ceramics; **Ferrara,** for its fortress; **Ravenna,** for its early Christian art; **Rimini,** for its Adriatic beach; and, of course, **Parma,** for its ham and Parmesan cheese. All are about one hour or less by rail from Bologna. All of these cities may be visited out of Milan, too. Consult the schedules in Milan's Central Station.

Bologna also has much to offer architecturally. An ensemble of rare Italian beauty is concentrated in its two enjoining squares, the **Piazza Maggiore** and the **Piazza del Nettuno.** Combined with the **Piazza di Porta Ravegnana,** the heart of Bologna even today reflects its Renaissance greatness.

Neptune's Fountain (Fontana del Nettuno) is the focal point of its piazza. Completed in 1566, it aptly depicts Bologna's vigorous nature. Saint Petronius Basilica, facing the Piazza Maggiore, was begun in 1390, but remains unfinished even today.

The Piazza Ravegnana contains not just one leaning tower, but two. The taller, built by the Asinelli family between 1109 and 1119, stands 330 feet with a tilt exceeding seven and a half feet. The other, the Garisenda Tower, is only

165 feet high, but it leans out ten feet over its foundation. If you're in good physical condition and feel like climbing 498 steps, there's a fine view from the top of the Asinelli Tower.

Day Excursion to

Genoa (Genova)   Great Port of Italy

Depart Milan's Central Station

Distance by Train: 93 miles (150 km)
Average Train Time: 1 hour, 25 minutes
City Dialing Code: 10
Internet: http://www.apt.genova.it
Tourist Information Office: on the right-hand side of the station foyer after the second escalator coming from the trains.
Tel: 2462633
Hours: 0800–2000 Monday-Saturday
Tourist Information Office: Porto Antico-Palazzina Santa Maria (old harbour-aquarium area).
Tel: 39 102487; *Fax:* 2467658
Hours: 0800–1830 daily

Ride the InterCity *Ligure* out of Milan to Genoa in the morning. Enjoy a leisurely walk along Genoa's avenues. Lunch in full view of the city's great harbor—largest in all of Italy. Board an InterCity late in the afternoon and be back in Milan for dinner that same day. Or, fall in love with Genoa by lunchtime and return to Milan on InterCity *Ligure* on its return run to Milan just before midnight. The relatively short time en route between these cities makes a "set your own pace" schedule ideal.

Be mindful that Genoa has two major railway stations, **Porta Principe** and **Brignole**. If you come from Milan, Porta Principe is the first stop after the train emerges from a tunnel. Digital schedule boards in both stations advise what time the next connecting train departs for the other station. To be certain, board your returning train to Milan from Porta Principe because many through-trains do not call at Brignole. You can, however, ride any shuttle train from Brignole north to the next stop, which is Porta Principe.

A boat tour of the city's harbor is an excellent way for visitors to acquaint themselves with Genoa. To reach the quay, turn right leaving the station, then make another right turn as you pass the bank on the corner. Walk downhill to the pedestrian crossing. Cross, and continue to walk downhill until the harbor

Milan–Genoa

DEPART MILAN CENTRAL STATION	TRAIN NUMBER	ARRIVE IN GENOA P.P. STATION	NOTES
0710	IC 341	0852	(1)
0815	IR 2183/2184	1020	(1)
1110	IC 660	1252	(1)

DEPART GENOVA P.P. STATION	TRAIN NUMBER	ARRIVE IN MILAN CENTRAL STATION	NOTES
1540	IR 2164	1745	(1)
1709	IC 667	1850	(1)
1836	IR 2168	2040	(1)
1940	IR 2172	2145	(1)
2119	IC 348	2300	(1)
2140	IR 2176	2345	(1)

Note: Genoa has two main railway stations—Porta Principe (P.P.) and Brignole. Porta Principe is the first station when arriving from Milan.

(1) Daily, including holidays

Distance: 93 miles/150 km

---

is sighted to the left. After turning left and passing through Piazza Principe, you'll arrive at the Maritime Building. The tour boats are berthed on its right side. The tour runs every hour starting at 1000 and   ending at 1900 when a minimum of 15 persons is present. Another tour by boat leaves from the aquarium, in the old port area, daily at 1515.

Most visitors link Genoa with Christopher Columbus (1451–1505). This association begins as you leave the Porta Principe Station fronted by **Piazza Acquaverde,** where a statue stands in honor of Columbus. A part of the city bus tour takes you to the Church of San Stefano, where Columbus was baptized, and into the Piazza della Vittoria—a vast expanse of lawns where the three ships of his fleet, the *Niña, Pinta,* and *Santa Maria,* are depicted in grass and flowers.

Plan a walking tour of Genoa. Depart Genova Porta Principe Station and follow Via Balbi to Via Cairoli, which connects with "the street of Kings"—Via Garibaldi. At the end of Via Garibaldi, turn right (south) and proceed to the city's center, Piazza de Ferrari. From this point, you can continue along Via XX Settembre to the park in front of the Brignole Station or return on foot to the Porta Principe Station by turning south and walking along the harbor. Both tourist information offices have maps to assist you in the walking tour. Be certain to include Genoa's great aquarium.

The city of Genoa lies beside a fine natural harbor at the foot of a pass in the Italian Apennines. It rivals Marseilles as the leading European port on the Mediterranean. Genoa's harbor facilities, which were damaged heavily during World War II, have been expanded and modernized. Shipbuilding is the leading industry of Genoa.

Ever since its birth, Genoa's calling has been the sea. Genoese ships transported Crusaders to the Middle East and returned laden with booty. Genoese merchants, profiting from the newly created demand in Europe for goods from the Middle East, expanded their operations throughout the Christian world. Genoese forts and trading posts soon spread throughout the Mediterranean and Aegean seas, creating a rivalry between Genoese and Venetians.

Genoa is proud of its Lanterna, the lighthouse that has become the international symbol of the city. Built on the site of an ancient tower in the first half of the 16th century, it has guided mariners to its safe harbor for more than four centuries.

In the time of Christopher Columbus, another son of Genoa, Andrea Doria (1468–1560), did much to promote the development of the city's maritime power. Serving as captain-general of Genoa's navy until defeated by Spanish forces in 1522, he served the French briefly before restoring the republic of Genoa as an ally of the Holy Roman Emperor, Charles V. Andrea Doria's birthplace can be seen during the city tour.

Day Excursion to

Lake Lugano   THE SWISS RIVIERA

Depart Milan's Central Station

Distance by Train: 48 miles (77 km)
Average Train Time: 1 hour, 15 minutes
Switzerland Dialing Code: 41
City Dialing Code: 91

Holders of Eurailpass or Europass need not purchase separate rail tickets to make excursions from Milan into Switzerland since both Italy and Switzerland are included on these passes.

Lake Lugano, known as the Swiss Riviera, is sheltered from the north by the Lepontine Alps. It is favored with a climate that is exceptionally mild, and purportedly the sunniest of all central European resorts. Considered a year-round resort, the city of Lugano sponsors a multitude of events to attract visitors.

Milan–Lake Lugano

DEPART MILAN CENTRAL STATION	TRAIN NUMBER	ARRIVE IN LUGANO STATION	NOTES
0735	1188	0904	(1)(2)(3)
0825	386	0954	(1)(2)(3)
0925	EC 8	1054	(1)(2)
1025	388	1154	(1)(2)(3)
1125(3)	EC 4	1254	(1)(2)

DEPART LUGANO STATION	TRAIN NUMBER	ARRIVE IN MILAN CENTRAL STATION	NOTES
1606	385	1735	(1)(2)(3)
1706(3)	EC 5	1835	(1)(2)
1806	387	1935	(1)(2)(3)
1906	EC 9	2035	(1)(2)
2006	IC 381	2135	(1)(2)(3)
2106	IC 257	2235	(1)(2)
2148	CIS 157	2345	(1)(2)(3)

(1) Daily, including holidays
(2) Food service available
(3) Supplement payable in Italy

Distance: 48 miles/77 km

Although Lugano is a very short distance from Milan, you will be crossing the Swiss border on this day excursion. Don't forget your passport. There is a currency-exchange desk in the railway station (open daily, 0515–2230), and the town abounds in banks and cambio (exchange) offices that offer official rates.

There is a **hotel-reservations-and-information office** to your immediate right as you leave the station. Train information may be obtained in the office bearing the "I" sign to the left of the main exit.

To reach it, ride the *funicolare* (cable railway) to Piazza Cioccaro and proceed on foot downhill to the center of Lugano, Piazza Riforma. As you continue downhill toward the lake, stop at the town hall where the tourist office is located.

When the lake beckons, there is a choice of nine round trips by boat, each offering an opportunity for a special vista. If the mountains attract you, ascent is possible by cableways and funiculars in many different directions. Two funiculars, one at each end of Lugano, carry you swiftly up 3,000 feet to breathtaking views of either Monte Bre or Monte San Salvatore.

The list of things to do and see doesn't stop there. Take a motorcoach to either **Sonvico** or **Tesserete**—typical Swiss mountain villages— even a journey to the world-renowned resort of **St. Moritz** is possible. In fact, anything's possible—just ask at the Lugano tourist information office.

For a relaxing day on the lake, select the cruise to the **Swiss Miniature Village,** a unique exhibition of towns, hamlets, castles, mountains, and railways—all on a scale of 1:25. It's an all-day outing, but it has wooed millions of other visitors—why not you?

The tourist information office will gladly mark out a walking tour of the city and its interesting areas, or opt for a free guided walking tour every Thursday morning from April until October.

For lunch in Lugano, you can make it a stand-up affair by selecting from a vendor's cart at lakeside or perhaps aboard a lake steamer. For an enjoyable sit-down meal, we recommend these quality restaurants: **Bianchi** (famous and expensive), **Galleria, Gambrinus, Orologio,** and **Da Armando.** All of these are in the center of Lugano.

Shopping in Lugano is a pleasant experience. The place to do this is concentrated in the market area stretching from the bottom of the funicolare to the city square fronting the lake. Mouth-watering food vies for your attention along with a wide selection of Swiss products and crafts. We have yet to see a visitor enter the market area around lunchtime and not emerge a few minutes later with a sandwich in hand rivaling anything that Dagwood could concoct.

Shopping in this market area is, for the most part, in the shelter of overhead arcades. If you have been looking for specialty items of the **Ticino** area of Switzerland, you will find them here. Although firmly Swiss, the market in Lugano does have that piquant touch of Italy.

For a special treat, be certain to visit our "secret hang-out" **Gandria,** a small cliff-side village that clings precariously to the mountains descending from the east into Lake Lugano. Gandria has no streets, but there is a bus stop on the mountainside above. The best, and more romantic, access is by lake steamer. If you want to share in our secret, inquire at any steamer pier regarding schedules to Gandria. You will want to take the Lugano-Porlezza line and plan to have an early dinner at one of Gandria's restaurants. It's superb!

Day Excursion to

Venice
GRAND CANALS AND GONDOLAS

Depart Milan's Central Station

Distance by Train: 166 miles (267 km)
Average Train Time: 2 hours, 45 minutes
City Dialing Code: 41
Tourist Information Office: in Santa Lucia rail station.

Proceed to the head of the train platform. Enter the main hall of the station. The train information office is on the immediate left. No tourist information is available at this office. Beyond that, you'll see a sign directing you to a self-service buffet. Digital train information is prominently displayed above the buffet sign. Telephones, ticket windows, newspaper stands, and specialty shops are on the right-hand side of the station hall. Just prior to exiting the station, you'll see tourist information.

Upon arrival in Venice, the American humorist Robert Benchley telegraphed his publisher, "Streets are flooded, please advise." Things have changed little since. Venice is situated on 120 islands surrounded by 177 canals in a lagoon between the Po and Piave rivers at the northern extremity of the Adriatic Sea. The islands on which the city is built are connected by 400 or so bridges. Not only by its site, but also by its architecture and history, Venice is known as "the Queen of the Adriatic."

Venice was founded in A.D. 452 when the inhabitants of several northern Italian cities sought refuge there from the Teutonic tribes invading Italy during the 5th century. The Venetians improved their fortifications and erected bulwarks of masonry to protect their growing city from the sea and from their enemies.

During the Crusades, Venice developed trade with the Orient and quickly became the center for commerce with the East. Venice became the leading wartime power of the Christian world by the end of the 15th century. In 1797, Napoleon Bonaparte conquered Venice and turned its government over to Austria. Through subsequent political maneuvers, Venice became part of the newly established kingdom of Italy in 1866.

Be sure to obtain full details regarding the canal transportation system. Water taxis are extremely expensive; the public water buses are far more affordable. Also, ask for a map of Venice. The canal navigation services (*Linee di Navigazione Lagunare*) are described in full detail on the reverse side of the map. If in Venice on a day excursion, purchase a one-way rather than a round-trip water-bus ticket from the rail station to **San Marco** on Line 1 and return to the station on foot.

Ticket in hand, board Line 1-Accelerata at Station 2 in front of the rail station. The dock and vessels are marked PIAZZALE ROMA-FERROVIA-LIDO, and the

Milan–Venice

DEPART MILAN CENTRAL STATION	TRAIN NUMBER	ARRIVE IN VENICE SANTA LUCIA STATION	NOTES
0705	IC 605	0955	(1)
0805	EC 9437	1055	(1)
0905	IC 609	1155	(1)
1105	IC 615	1355	(1)(2)

DEPART VENICE SANTA LUCIA STATION	TRAIN NUMBER	ARRIVE IN MILAN CENTRAL STATION	NOTES
1558	IC 632	1855	(1)(2)
1705	IR 2110	2045	(1)(2)
1758	IC 644	2055	(1)
1858	IC 646	2155	(1)
1958	IC 650	2255	(1)(2)

(1) Daily, including holidays
(2) Light refreshments

Distance: 166 miles/267 km

boat should be moving to your left as you come from the station. Boats proceeding to the right terminate at Station 1, Piazzale Roma, where you're required to disembark and purchase another ticket to get back on course!

Line 1 moves along the Grand Canal until emerging into open water from the canal at **Piazza San Marco** (St. Mark's), the center and most frequented part of Venice. The **Grand Canal** is Venice's principal traffic artery. It is lined with churches, museums, palaces—even a fish market—so keep your guidebook open so you can recognize these landmarks as you glide by.

Go ashore at St. Mark's and revel in the staggering sights before you. St. Mark's Bell Tower dominates the scene, but it won't be long before you'll find yourself standing in front of the Cathedral. If time permits, take the elevator to the top of the Bell Tower for a spectacular view of vibrant Venice.

With so much to see, be mindful of the time or you will miss the train back to Milan. You can't hail a taxi at the last minute since there are none, so allow at least forty-five minutes for the return trip from St. Mark's to Santa Lucia Station by water bus. Or start ambling through Venice by following the signs, ALLA FERROVIA (to the rail station). They are posted everywhere and easy to follow. Allow two hours to reach the station on foot, although a reasonable pace should get you there about 30 minutes sooner.

En route, you will cross the **Rialto Bridge**—the best place to view the Grand Canal and a good place to shop, too. There are 24 shops right on the bridge and a variety of vendors selling their wares along both sides of the canal. Further on, you will cross the **Ponte Degli Scalzi (Station Bridge)** and arrive at the rail station where you started.

We're sure you will return to Venice, but heed the plight of tourists burdened with too many bags on the water buses—come back with minimum luggage or stow it in the lockers at the Venice Mestre Station.

Base City...

Rome

City Dialing Code: 6

Italians refer lovingly to Rome as the "Eternal City." In the days of the Caesars, all roads led to Rome. Today, the same may be said of Italian State Railways.

No one knows exactly when people first started living along the Tiber River where Rome developed. Archaeologists continue to find evidence of still earlier civilizations than that of the Romans buried under those remains that they have already identified. Etruscans ruled the area long before the Romans. Remains of that earlier Mediterranean civilization continue to be discovered in and around Rome.

According to legend, Rome was founded by Romulus and Remus, who, in their infancy, were nursed by a wolf. Apparently there is some truth to the tale, because some Roman males still behave in a wolflike manner, particularly in the presence of a pretty foreign woman.

Rome has already had two periods of greatness in the civilized world, each of which has had a significant impact. Two thousand years ago, Rome ruled a good part of Europe and the Middle East. Rome contributed roads, architecture, art, law, literature, and political experience to the entire area.

Conquered by barbarians during the fifth century A.D., the city managed to remain the home of the popes, and through them and their armies, political power was regained. During the Renaissance, Rome again became a great center of art and learning. Since 1870, when Italian troops captured the city from Pope Pius IX, Rome has been the capital of Italy.

Readers considering "open jaw" (arrive in one European city, depart from another) air transportation to and from Europe should give serious consideration to Rome as either their entry or exit point. For example, in the spring, enter Europe through Rome and wend your way northward as the weather improves. Leave from Amsterdam. In autumn, reverse the procedure. Follow those lingering fall days southward from Amsterdam to Rome. By planning a Eurail vacation itinerary in this manner, you can assure yourself of having more moderate weather.

As a matter of fact, the average daily temperatures of Amsterdam and Rome vary by ten to twelve degrees Fahrenheit—Rome's, of course, being the higher. So, when in Rome, do as the Romans do—move north as the mercury soars in the summer, south again when it begins to sink.

Arriving By Air

Rome has two airports but because Ciampino Airport is small and deals mainly with charter flights, we focus on the main **airport Leonardo da Vinci,** also called **Fiumincino. Fiumincino Airport** is twenty-two miles southwest of Rome.

Airport-City Links: Direct **train** service from Fiumincino Airport to Rome's Stazione Termini (Central Station) in Rome runs from 0700-2205. Journey time: 30 minutes; fare: 13,000 lire. It leaves and arrives at track No. 22 in Roma Termini.

There is also another train service from Fiumincino Airport to Tiburtina Station (total travel time, 45 minutes) with stops at local stations **Trastevere** and **Ostiense.** The train runs every 20 minutes from 0615-0015; fare, 7,000 lire. If you arrive at night there is the 42 night bus service between Fiumincino Airport and Tiburtina Station. A taxi from Fiumincino Airport to the center runs about 70,000 lire (or at least $40) but we caution against using taxis unless your airline representative arranges it and dtermines the fare beforehand.

Arriving by Train

When you arrive at the railway station in Rome, beware of the many willing "helpers" eager to carry your luggage and find you a cab. If you need a taxi, carry your own bag and get in the regular taxi line.

Roma Termini. Rome has several suburban stations, but the InterCity and express trains stop only in the main station—Roma Termini. It is like a city within a city. In its main concourse, the section separating the train platforms from the main hall, you will find a bar and restaurant. On the lower level of the station you will find services you normally associate only with the most modern airports—barbershops, hairdressers, showers, and lounges.

Money-exchange facilities are located throughout the railway station. In the main concourse, there is an office just to the left of *binari* (track)12, between gateways 2 and 3. Hours: daily, 0830–1930, and 0830–1400 and 1400–1930 on holidays. In the main hall, another currency exchange, including an ATM, is operated by the Bank of Rome. Turn left when entering the hall from the concourse and walk past all the ticket windows to the bank. Hours: Monday-Friday 0825–1335 and 1440–1600; holidays, 0825–1155; Saturday 0830–1130.

Hotel reservations. Hotel reservations in Rome and other Italian cities can be made directly across from track No. 10. It is open Monday through Sunday 0700–2200. You are required to leave a deposit and arrive at the hotel within one hour. We found that the line was always very long. If this is the case, telephone Rome's free hotel reservation service 0700-2200 Sunday-Monday, (Tel: 06 699–1000).

Train information may be obtained from three free-standing computer touch-tone screens from which you can gather schedule information for your destinations. The computers are located across from the tracks in the center and sides of the station, across from tracks Nos. 1, 9, and 22.

Train reservations can be made at ticket windows 30 through 45. There are 45 ticket windows with their services indicated in Italian. Windows Nos. 7–29, labeled BIGLIETTI ORDINARI E RIDOTTI, sells tickets. At windows Nos. 30–38, labeled PRENOTAZIONI POSTI-WL-CUCCETTE-PENDOLINO you can make reservations, including couchette and sleeper reservations. Finally, at windows Nos. 42–45 labeled PRENOTAZIONI, PENDOLINO, *partenza in giornata* you can make reservations for trains leaving today. The cost of the reservation varies depending on destination. To assure that you receive the proper reservation, determine the day and date of your travel, the number and departure time of your train, and its arrival time at your destination. This information can be taken from any of the train schedules posted throughout the station.

Print this information on a plain piece of paper, starting with the date, the train number, and the departure time. Draw a short arrow, then add the arrival time of the train and, finally, the name of the destination. Indicate the number of reservations required, then present the information to the attendant together with the rail pass you will use for the trip. Submission of this information may draw a small grin from the attendant making the reservations, but it will save time and lessen the possibilities of errors in completing your train reservations..

Rail pass validation may be made at a window labeled in English located in the center of the train station near the main entrance facing the bus station. It is rather hidden away and there are not any signs directing you. Just follow the signs for taxi and bus service, and right before you exit the station behind several tobacco shops you will see several windows, including the Eurail window and other windows that can provide you with information.

If you plan an early morning departure on the first day you use your rail pass, either allow an extra hour at the station that morning or inquire at one of the validating windows mid-evening the night before about the possibility of predating the validation.

Tourist Information/Hotel Reservations

- **Ente Provinciale Per Turismo-Rome**, 5 Via Parigi,
  Tel: (06) 48899253 or 48899255, Fax: 48899228.
  Hours: 0815-1915 Monday-Saturday; closed Sundays/holidays.
  To visit this office, exit the main entrance of Roma Termini, skirt the left side of the city square in front of the station, and proceed past Museo Nazionale Romano (the National Roman Museum) to Via Parigi. Turn

right at that point, then look for the office on the left-hand side of the street.

- **"Enjoy Rome,"** a very helpful tourist office especially designed for English speakers, very close to the station at 39 Via Varese.

  To get there, cross Via Marsala adjacent to the station on the right as you exit the train terminal. After two more blocks, turn right onto Via Varese. Number 39 is at the end of this one-way street.

- **National Tourist Office, ENIT,** at 2 Via Marghera, one block east of the railway station (Tel: 4971282).

- For tours in Rome and vicinity, the Sesante office in the main hall of the railway station will be happy to oblige.

Rome abounds with tourist facilities. Every citizen seems to know the exact location of everything and seems to be eager to direct you. But Rome has more than three million citizens, and each has a different opinion regarding the best way to get there—even if it's only around the corner.

Consequently, depend on the official tourist office staff, hotel staff, or city policemen, not the man on the street, for reasonably correct information. Above all, watch out for the "cab-and-coin" man. He'd be more than glad to take you where you want to go but probably at three times the   regular rate. The legitimate taxicab service in Rome is moderate in price and equipped with meters. Ask your hotel personnel to hail one for you or telephone. Telephone numbers to call in Rome for radio-dispatched cabs are: 3570, 4994, or 6645.

American Express has a convenient location in Rome near the Spanish Steps at 38 Piazza de Spagna (Tel: 67641). American Express can assist in   making train or hotel reservations in Rome or any other of the base cities. They also conduct excellent tours, in English, of Rome and its surroundings.

Sights/Attractions/Tours

Rome is a great walking city. First, get a map from your hotel or the tourist office, then find your way to the **Spanish Steps** and walk down Via Condotti—with detours down some of the side streets—to the Tiber. Sightseeing musts during an initial visit include the **Pantheon,** the **Coliseum,** and, close by, the **Forum.** Set aside at least a few hours for a visit to the **Sistine Chapel** and **St. Peter's.**

Roaming around Rome is like moving through history. Columns that looked down on the mighty Caesars, walls that saw Saint Peter and Saint Paul passing, statues sculpted by Michelangelo—these are Rome, where present-day life flourishes in the midst of monuments from past civilizations. Throw a coin in the **Trevi Fountain** as a down payment on your return trip because you certainly will want to return.

When walking in Rome, keep pocketbooks, camera bags, etc. away from the curb side of the street and on a short leash. Motor-scooter thieves find them easy targets.

So vast is the city that it is essential to take some of the organized tours in order to see all of it. We recommend the tours conducted by the CIT (Compagnia Italiano Turismo). It is the general passenger agent for the Italian State Railways, and its tours can be booked through most hotels and pensions.

To dine differently, try **Da Meo Patacca** at 30 Piazza Mercanti (Tel: 58161198)—excellent food and entertainment. For that once-in-a-lifetime splurge, dine in the rooftop restaurant of the **Hassler Hotel,** Rome's finest hostelry; it overlooks the Spanish Steps. The view of the city from there on a summer's evening is unmatched. (Tel: 679-2651 for reservations.) Ignore the cost. You only live once!

Day Excursions

Four interesting day excursions from Rome await your visit: **Anzio,** scene of an Allied beachhead during World War II; **Florence,** one of the most prominent art centers of the world; **Naples,** with its world-renowned **Isle of Capri,** and **Pisa,** where the tower really tilts

Train Connections to Other Base Cities from Rome

TO:	DEPART	ARRIVE	TRAIN NUMBER	NOTES
Amsterdam	1635	1133	ES 9422/2000	(3)
Berne	1035	1934	ES 9410/EC 60	(1)
Brussels (Midi)	1545	1050	1294	(4)
Luxembourg	1545	0804+1	1294	(4)
Milan	0805	1305	EC 52	
	0935	1400	ES 9408	
	1135	1600	ES 9412	
	1335	1800	ES 9416	
	1535	2000	ES 9420	
	1835	2300	ES 9426	
Munich	0815	1830	EC 84	
	2045	0830+1	286	
Nice	1305	2200	IC 526	
	2315	0950	368	
Paris (Lyon)	1915	0950+1	EN 212	
Vienna (Süd)	0710	2032	EC 30	
	1910	0853+1	234	
Zürich	0805	1753	EC 52	(6)
	0935	1853	ES 9408	(7)(8)
	1135	2053	ES 9412	
	1435	2334	ES 9472	(7)

Daily departures unless otherwise noted. Make reservations for all departures. Depart from Rome Termini unless otherwise noted.

(1) Transfer in Milan to IC 836
(2) Transfer in Torino Porta Nuova to train 418
(3) Transfer in Cologne (Köln)
(4) June 27 through September 5
(5) Transfer in Vienna (from Vienna Süd to Vienna West) to train 345, arrive in Budapest 1318+1
(6) Transfer in Arth Goldan
(7) Transfer in Milan
(8) Reservation required

Day Excursion to

Anzio
HISTORIC BEACHHEAD

Depart Rome Termini Station

Distance by Train: 35 miles (57 km)
Average Train Time: 1 hour
City Dialing Code: 06
Tourist Information Office: No. 19 Pia Square, Anzio
Hours: June-September 0830–130230 and 16700–2000 daily. Off-season hours 0830–130230 and 15030–19800 Monday-Saturday. If the office is closed, directions will be posted on how to reach another office in Anzio where information is available.

To get to the tourist office on Pia Square: When leaving the Anzio railway station, walk downhill along the palm-lined avenue to Cesare Battisti Square. Then continuing on via dei Fabbri, you will be in the main square of Anzio, Pia Square, where you will find the city's tourist information office to the left, just near the church.

"Nothing more beautiful, nothing more agreeable, nothing more peaceful," wrote Cicero about Anzio. The Roman emperor Nero was born in Anzio. The villa where he spent his childhood and studied music still stands. Anzio's sandy beach attracted many important leaders over the centuries, which made it a VIP sanctuary, so to speak. Roman emperors such as Tiberius, Hadrian, Antoninus, and Commodus found escape from Rome and their affairs of state in Anzio.

American and British forces stormed ashore at Anzio and nearby Nettuno on 22 January 1944 to establish a beachhead, which they held until the taking of Rome on 4 June 1944. The devastated town that endured both the crossfire of the Germans and the bombardment of the Allied fleet offshore during that time has been restored completely, but row upon row of white crosses mark the graves in nearby military cemeteries, where lie 7,862 American and more than 6,000 British troops killed between Sicily and Rome. Those missing in action, 3,194 of them, "sleep in unknown graves." A visit to these cemeteries is a sobering event.

If you, like the Roman emperors, want to escape the rigors of Rome or, on the other hand, wish to pay tribute to fallen comrades, Anzio extends a warm and pleasant welcome to all.

Because of the city's proximity to Rome and frequent train connections, rail travelers might consider accommodations in the area during their visit. Anzio, together with the neighboring sea resorts stretching southward to it from **Lida dei Pini,** can offer a wide selection of housing amenities and accommodations. If interested, telephone Anzio's tourist information office at (06) 9845–147 or 9846–119 (Fax 9848–135) for details and rates. For a longer stay, villas and apartments are available for rent at moderate rates.

Rome–Anzio

DEPART ROME TERMINI STATION	TRAIN NUMBER	ARRIVE IN ANZIO STATION	NOTES
0755	Local	0905	(2)
0825	Local	0930	(1)
1125	Local	1230	(1)
1225	Local	1330	(2)

DEPART ANZIO STATION	TRAIN NUMBER	ARRIVE IN ROME TERMINI STATION	NOTES
1505	Local	1610	(2)
1550	Local	1655	(1)
1745	Local	1850	(1)
1945	Local	2050	(1)
2150	Local	2255	(1)

(1) Daily, including holidays
(2) Daily except Sundays and holidays
Note: all trains second class only

Distance: 35 miles/57 km

Commuter trains depart the Roma Termini frequently for Anzio. For complete information regarding train service, check the *Partenze* (departure) information board in the main hall of Roma Termini.

Anzio is listed in the **Roma-Nettuno** section. It is one stop before Nettuno and the end of the line. Nettuno is where the American beachhead was established in World War II. We suggest that you inform the train conductor regarding your destination. He will be glad to alert you.

Upon arrival in Anzio, you will find directions for reaching Nettuno and the American Military Cemetery posted inside the train station; but before proceeding, check with the Anzio tourist office and obtain the details on the bus service running between Anzio and Nettuno.

Places to visit in Anzio are, of course, the beach area and the harbor, where the Allied forces landed. The beach is now lined with cabanas and the sand is excellent and the surf, usually moderate. Be certain to visit the beachhead museum on **Via di Villa Adele** near the rail station.

The harbor holds many interesting places to investigate. Watercraft of all types are moored there, and the waterfront is lined with seafood restaurants to which fishermen sell their catch right from the dock. Deciding where to have lunch can be difficult—they all look inviting. On the street side of the harbor you will find a number of smart shops with eye-catching selections of nautical clothing.

Aside from the beach and the port area, places of particular interest are **Nero's Grottoes,** those ancient warehouses of the port located at the northern end of the Riviera Mallozzi. Beyond Anzio's western harbor wall lie the remains and mosaics of Nero's villa, which runs from the beach up to the level of Via Fanciulla d'Anzio. It's an impressive sight.

At the foot of the **Innocenzio wharf** in Anzio you can examine the remains of an eighteenth-century fort, and from the wharf itself, there is a view of the gulf with the Astura Tower and Circeo visible in the distance. The monument commemorating the Allied landings in 1944 is situated nearby on the western shore.

Nettuno, a seaside town of Saracen origins, is less that three miles distant. The American Military Cemetery is located there. The two British cemeteries are in Anzio. En route to Nettuno, you'll pass the Villa Colonna on the right and the **Villa Borghese,** with its magnificent gardens, on the left.

Anzio's involvement with the sea is reflected in its festivals. One such festival, the "Festa del Mare" (Feast of the Sea) is held in June in honor of Saint Antony of Padua, patron saint of the town.

Day Excursion to
Florence (Firenze)   CITY OF BEAUTY

Depart Rome Termini Station

Distance by Train: 197 miles (317 km)
Average Train Time: 2 hours
City Dialing Code: 55
Tourist Information Office: 1R, Via Cavour
Tel: (055) 290832; *Fax:* 2760383.
Hours: Summer: 0800-1915 Monday-Saturday; 0800-1330 Sunday; Winter: 0800-1330 daily
Take a taxi there or board bus 1, 6, or 17. Tourist Information also available in the rail station concourse at the end of track 16 (in front of the pharmacy).

Florence as a day excursion is suggested for the traveler on a time-compressed itinerary. It is impossible to see all the beauty of Florence in one day. A week—or even a lifetime—could easily be devoted to such a pursuit. No other city in the world pays more homage to the genius of man and his ability to create and, in turn, appreciate beauty than does Florence.

Although a part of Italian history since 200 B.C., it wasn't until the turn of the eleventh century that Florence began to develop power and influence. Coincident with this growth came the development of the city's powerful guilds.

Rome–Florence

DEPART ROME TERMINI STATION	TRAIN NUMBER	ARRIVE IN FLORENCE STATION	NOTES
0710	EC 30	0928	(1)
0805	EC 52	0957	(1)
0905	IC 706	1058	(1)
1005	IC 554	1220	(1)
1145	ES 9442	1320	(1)
1205	IC 556	1425	(1)

DEPART FLORENCE STATION	TRAIN NUMBER	ARRIVE IN ROME TERMINI STATION	NOTES
1630	IC 559	1855	(1)
1649	ES 9421	1825	(1)
1749	ES 9423	19525	(1)
1908	ES 31	2105	(1)
2004	EC 53	2155	(1)
2054	ES 9429	2230	(1)

(1) Daily, including holidays

Distance: 197 miles/317 km

Florence was established on those banks of the Arno River spanned by the bridge of the Roman road Via Flaminia and where the Ponte Vecchio (old bridge) still stands today. With the single exception of Ponte Vecchio, all of the city's bridges were destroyed in 1944 during World War II. In 1966, a major flood damaged numerous art treasures in Florence, but many have been restored in succeeding years by the use of sophisticated techniques.

Hotel reservations can also be arranged at the tourist office in the rail station or the one at Via Cavour. Maps are available at the tourist offices, the CIT office (the Gray Line office) outside the station, or purchase the illustrated book **Florence, Pisa** and **Siena** at the newsstand inside the main hall of the station. An excellent map of Florence is contained in this informative book.

A **train-reservations** office (hours 0700-2000 daily) and **money exchange** (open 0820-1920 Monday-Saturday) are located inside the main station hall.

You can see most of the city's highlights by walking and, when needed, by taxi. Start by walking or taking a taxi to **Il Duomo** (the cathedral) in the center of Florence. Here you can examine the three huge bronze doors of the **Battistero** (baptistery), enjoy the view from the top of the cathedral's cupola, and enter the **Museo dell'Opera del Duomo** (cathedral museum), where you will find the priceless Altar of Saint John the Baptist displayed. The **Galleria dell'Accademia** (Academy Gallery) is next. Hours: Closed Mondays; open 0900-1900 Tuesday-Saturday; 0900-1400 Sunday. Admission: 12,000 lire. Walk three blocks on Via Ricasoli, off Piazza Duomo's north side, to Piazza St. Marco. *David* by Michelangelo is displayed there. This alone may be worth your entire trip to Europe.

Taxi from here to **Piazza della Signoria,** which lies on the opposite side of the cathedral near the Arno River. (A brisk walk and some expert map reading will get you there in about twenty minutes.) This is the former center of Florence. The concentration of art treasures here is immense. The building with the tower is Palazzo della Signoria (Palace of the Lords), also known as **Palazzo Vecchio** (the Old Palace). Among its wealth of treasures is the little chapel of Eleonora of Toledo, with its magnificent frescoes by Bronzino (1503–1572). Closed Thursdays; open other weekdays 0900–1900 and 0800-1300 Sunday. Admission: 10,000 lire.

On the south side of the square, you will see the **Loggia dei Lanzi,** which picked up a few other names, such as "Loggia dei Priori" and "Loggia della Signoria," since it was built in 1376. Statuary such as *Hercules and the Centaur* (1599) and *Rape of the Sabine Women* (1583), both by Giambologna, surround Cellini's *Perseus* (1545).

The **Galleria degli Uffizi** (Office Gallery) is, in fact, a converted office containing the priceless works of art acquired by the Medici family. Located on the right flank of Palazzo della Signoria, it has forty-five exhibit rooms. Its vast collection includes the ancient sculpture *Medici Venus* from 300 B.C., Leonardo da Vinci's *Adoration of the Magi*, and Michelangelo's *Holy Family*, plus an entire roomful of Rembrandts. Closed Mondays; open other weekdays 0900–1900, and 0900–1400 on Sunday. Admission: 12,000 lire.

This concludes your "quick" tour of the world famous "City of Art, Florence," and it's time to taxi back to the rail station for the train back to Rome—unless, of course, you have succumbed to Florence's charms. It's a difficult decision to make. If you are still ambulatory, the walk back to the station will take about 20 minutes.

Aside from its buildings, art galleries, museums, and parks, Florence has had an interesting and rather hectic development as a municipality and seat of government. It was ruled by the Medici family until 1737, when the family died out and its leadership was assumed by Grand Duke Ferdinand III (1769–1824). Driven out by the French in 1799, the duke made several abortive attempts to resume power. He wasn't successful, however, until 1814.

Ferdinand's successor, Leopold II (1797–1870), held on until he was expelled in 1849. Florence was the capital of Italy under King Victor Emmanuel from 1865 to 1871, when the seat of government became Rome.

Day Excursion to

Naples (Napoli)   CITY BY THE BAY

Depart Rome Termini Station

Distance by Train: 134 miles (216 km)
Average Train Time: 2 hours
City Dialing Code: 81
Tourist Information Office: Main Hall of Napoli Centrale Rail Station (English-speaking staff)
Tel: 268779 or 206666; *Fax:* 401961
Hours: 0815-2000 Monday-Saturday; 0900-1400 Sunday.

Naples is a world apart. There is no other place in Italy quite like it. In fact, there's no place that we have visited in the rest of the world quite like Naples. When you go there, you don't really see Naples—you feel it, hear it, and taste it. After you've been to Naples, you come away either loving it—or hating it. You alone must be the judge.

Naples itself is a coalescing of gaiety and sadness. Its inhabitants, the Neapolitans, are expressive, noisy, and vivacious. They are imaginative, superstitious, and (about a third of them) unemployed, either by choice or by circumstance—it's difficult to determine which. But as a consequence, crime is rampant, so watch your wallets, pocketbooks, cameras, and other valuables.

But don't go to Naples in fear of your life; just be cautious. The Neapolitans don't want to harm you; they are only interested in your valuables. They want you to enjoy yourself and come back again—with more valuables. Deal only with official agencies. If you plan to take a city tour or sign up for a trip to **Vesuvius** and **Pompeii,** do it in an office, not on the street. Ignore the uniformed people who approach you on the street or in the rail station wearing badges proclaiming they are "official guides." There are several small shops on the square facing the station where you can buy one of those badges yourself.

Now for the fun part. Spaghetti was invented in Naples, as well as Neapolitan-style ice cream. Pizza first saw the light of day in Naples. If you can, enjoy a pizza in one of the pizzerias located in the old quarter of Naples. If you do, you'll probably not patronize your local pizza parlor for at least thirty days following your return home. The Neapolitan version of a Cajun fish-fry, *frittura di pesci,* is also well worth sampling. So much for tasting Naples.

You can't avoid hearing Naples. The musical style of Bel Canto is exclusively that of the Neapolitans. *Santa Lucia, Funiculi-Funicula,* and *O Sole Mio*! are but part of the repertory you will hear being played by hurdy-gurdies, all of it mixed in with the constant background noise of the crowded streets. Dray animals such as mules wear bells so that their presence can be acknowledged in the crowd.

Rome–Naples

DEPART ROME TERMINI STATION	TRAIN NUMBER	ARRIVE IN NAPLES STATION	NOTES
0715	D 2385	0954	(4)(5)
0815	D 2387	1054	(2)(4)
0910	IR 2417	1115	(4)

DEPART NAPLES STATION	TRAIN NUMBER	ARRIVE IN ROME TERMINI STATION	NOTES
1400	IC 526	1555	(4)
1433	IR 2420	1650	(2)(4)
1606	D 2402	1845	(2)(4)
1706	D 2404	1945	(4)
2000(3)	IC 732	2150	(2)(4)

(1) Piazza Garibaldi Station
(2) Food service available
(3) Centrale Station
(4) Daily, including holidays
(5) Reservations obligatory

Distance: 134 miles/216 km

If you haven't developed a feel for Naples after exposure to some or all of the above, you should take an early train back to Rome.

You will find the **Napoli Centrale** and **Napoli Piazza Garibaldi** terminals side by side in the city center and flanked by the two narrow-gauge railway stations serving the **Circumvesuviana Line** from Naples to **Pompeii** and **Sorrento**.

Money-exchange, train information, and food services are all housed within the Napoli Centrale terminal. A train-information-and-reservations office is located to the side of the main hall (open daily, 0700–2115).

Naples, a city with a population well over one million, is just large enough so that unguided sightseeing can become difficult. Several reputable tour operators provide excellent service. The **Tourcar Travel Agency.** Tel: (081) 552 0429. The American Express Office located at Piazza Municipio 5/6 also provides tours under its travel agency. Tel: (081) 5518564, Fax (081) 722242.

Local trains leave the Napoli Circumvesuviana railway station for **Pompeii** and **Sorrento**. To reach this station, walk in the direction of the Garibaldi statue in the center of Piazza Garibaldi. Just before reaching the statue, turn left on Corso Garibaldi and proceed to the station, which is close by. The train time from Naples to Pompeii averages about 25 minutes. To Sorrento, the average time is 60 minutes. Pompeii is fifteen miles from Naples; Sorrento is twenty-eight. Check at the rail station for complete schedules. Eurail and Europasses are not accepted on this line.

Day Excursion to

Pisa   NEW SLANT ON AN OLD SCENE

Depart Rome Termini Station

Distance by Train: 208 miles (335 km)
Average Train Time: 3 hours
City Dialing Code: 50
Tourist Information office: in the station plaza
Tel: 42291
 -or-
Tourist Information Office: Piazza del Duomo
Tel: 560464.
    Take Bus No.1 from rail station plaza to Piazza del Duomo.

Many consider Pisa to be the most beautiful city in Italy. Pisa possesses one of the loveliest architectural groupings in Europe. Known either as **Piazza dei Miracoli** (Square of the Miracles) or **Piazza del Duomo** (Cathedral Square), it contains, in addition to the famous **Leaning Tower** and the cathedral, the **Baptistery** and the **Campo Santo** (burial ground), each in its own stead a masterpiece of sculpture and architecture.

If you have never been to Pisa and actually stood and looked at the Leaning Tower—you are in for a surprise. Forget any photograph, painting, or motion picture you may have seen of the tower prior to your personal encounter. It is not an optical illusion—it *really* leans.

Ride bus No. 1 from Pisa's station plaza to Piazza dei Miracoli. Dismount from the bus on the southern end of the square—the direction in which the tower is leaning. You will have no doubt whatsoever that: (1) the tower leans; (2) it's leaning in your direction; and (3) you had better get out of its way before it topples on you. No other work of art provokes the instinct of self-preservation like this one. You can spend hours gazing at it, but there is never a moment when you are not consciously aware of the trajectory it will take if it topples.

Bonanno Pisano began the construction of the tower in 1174, but the project was not completed until 1350. The primary reason for the delay in its completion was that the tower began to tilt when it reached its fourth level. With an annual increase of about one millimeter per year, the tower was closed to public access in 1990.

By using sonar soundings of the ground, the foundation of an ancient village was discovered under the north side of the Leaning Tower. This explains why the north side has remained relatively stable, while the south side has sunk almost three-quarters of a meter. Various plans have been proposed to stabilize the tower. One plan is to use sonic waves to break up the ancient foundation under the north side so that it will sink at the same rate as the south. Another proposal requires a ring of steel to be inserted into the base of the landmark. Perhaps the Italian Public Works Ministry should expedite its plans. Studies reveal that the tower is nearly 17 feet off plumb.

For a spectacular meal, visit the **Ristorante Antonietta,** a delightful Tuscan-Italian restaurant at 179 Via Santa Maria, immediately south of the square. It serves excellent food, and the location can't be beat. According to our best high-school geometry, if the tower topples, it will fall some thirty feet short of the first table at Antonietta's.

When at last you can turn your attention away from the tower, you will realize that Piazza dei Miracoli holds some other fantastic sights that warrant your inspection. Among them is the cathedral, on which construction was initiated in 1063. The first work of art to catch your eye is the splendid bronze doors of its entrance. Inside the cathedral and opposite the pulpit, Lorenzi (according to legend) hung a bronze lamp on a chain so long that Galileo figured that it must be the first pendulum and proceeded to work out the theory of isochronism—one of the better "isms" existing today.

The astronomer and physicist Galileo (1564-1642) lived in Pisa and used the buildings of the **Piazza del Duomo** to conduct studies concerning the laws of gravity, the acceleration of falling bodies, and the movement of the pendulum. He used the Leaning Tower to work out his theories on gravity and acceleration and the cathedral for the accurate measurement of time. Galileo was said to have quarreled with his scholars over his theory of the rotation of the universe. During the Inquisition, when compelled to renounce his theory that the world turned, not the universe—because the Pope thought otherwise—in despair he whispered, "Nevertheless it does turn."

Last of the edifices within the confines of the Piazza dei Miracoli is the building known as the **Compo Santo** (cemetery). It began when fifty-three shiploads of earth were transported from Calvary in the Holy Lands to the site and then surrounded by the building, which, after completion in 1283 by Giovanni Pisano, was frescoed by local Tuscan artists. The structure suffered damage during World War II bombings, but repairs have all but removed those scars.

During its days of prominence, Pisa was in close touch with the Orient. As a result, you'll note an eastern flavor in its architecture. In the 9th century, the city was a naval power of considerable proportion. Pisa and its ally, Genoa, drove the Saracens out of Sardinia and Corsica in the eleventh century. Pisa's

Rome–Pisa

DEPART ROME TERMINI STATION	TRAIN NUMBER	ARRIVE IN PISA STATION	NOTES
0705	IR 2336	1045	(1)
0810	IC 518	1113	(1)
1010	IC 520	1313	(1)
1110	IR 2338	1445	(1)

DEPART PISA STATION	TRAIN NUMBER	ARRIVE IN ROME TERMINI STATION	NOTES
1449	IC 527	1750	(1)
1515	IR 2343	1850	(1)
1649	IC 529	1950	(1)
1849	IC 533	2150	(1)
1915	IR 2347	2250	(1)

(1) Daily, including holidays

Distance: 208 miles/335 km

powers, however, then went on the wane. No longer allied with Genoa, the city was taken by Florence in 1406, proving that, as is so often the case, your allies are not there when you really need them.

Luxembourg

The Grand Duchy of Luxembourg is one of Europe's small countries—51 miles (84 km) long and 32 miles (52 km) wide, encompassing 999 square miles (2,586 km)—a little smaller than the state of Rhode Island. It is a constitutional monarchy with a population of about 400,000. Germany borders it to the east, France to the south, and Belgium adjoins it on the north and west. Luxembourg vies with Switzerland in the field of international banking. A substantial number of corporations doing business in the European community maintain accounts there.

The Grand Duchy once dominated an area nearly 300 times its present size. In more recent times, as well as in the past, Luxembourg's fate and fortunes have been linked with those of Belgium. The forces of French King Louis XIV conquered the city of Luxembourg in the mid-seventeenth century. Subsequent fortifications built by the French and succeeding conquerors earned the city the title "Gibraltar of the North."

Luxembourg was overrun by the Germans during World War I, but its independence was restored by the Treaty of Versailles. It was occupied again by German forces during World War II. During the Battle of the Bulge in December 1944, the tides of war surged around Luxembourg. Liberated earlier by U.S. Forces, the city was recaptured by the Germans, who executed many members of the Belgian and Luxembourgese underground before Luxembourg was again taken by the Allied Forces.

Luxembourg's monetary unit, the franc, has the same value as the Belgian franc. Belgian money is circulated freely throughout the Grand Duchy, but Luxembourg francs are not accepted in Belgium. If you cash a traveler's check in Luxembourg and plan to leave immediately, insist that you receive Belgian francs or the currency of the country where you are going.

For more information on Luxembourg, contact the Luxembourg National Tourist office in North America:

New York: 17 Beekman Place, New York, NY 10022; Tel: (212) 935-8888; Fax: (212)935-5896; Email: luxnto@aol.com

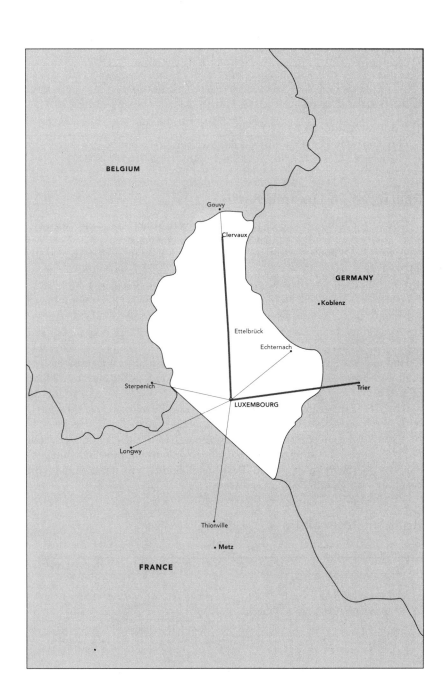

BELGIUM

Gouvy

Clervaux

GERMANY

Koblenz

Ettelbrück

Echternach

Sterpenich

Trier

LUXEMBOURG

Longwy

Thionville

Metz

FRANCE

Banking

- **Currency:** Luxembourg Franc
- **Exchange rate at press time:** 37.11 francs = $1.00 U.S.

Communications:

- **Country Code:** 352
- City codes are not used when dialing within Luxembourg.
- Direct dial: AT&T: 0-800-0111; MCI: 0800-0112; Sprint: 0800-0115

Rail Travel in Luxembourg

The information service of **CFL, the Luxembourg national railways** (also giving country bus information), can be contacted by (+ 352) 4990-5572 or (+ 352) 4990-5572 (every day GMT: 0500-1900) and by Fax: (+352) 49 35 32.

From the capital, Luxembourg City, you are no more than 1 hour away from anywhere within the Grand Duchy of Luxembourg. The **"Oeko–Pass"** is available at rail stations throughout the country, and at Findel airport. It covers unlimited travel on all forms of public transport (city buses, trains and country coaches) for one day (which is considered to last until 0800 the following morning) throughout the Grand Duchy. It is not valid on sight-seeing buses, however. You can purchase a single ticket for 160 LUF or a block of 5 tickets for 540 LUF.

The CFL also accepts the multi-country passes **Eurailpass** and **Europass,** with purchase of the Benelux—Belgium, Netherlands, Luxembourg—add-on. (See the Appendix for a detailed list of multiple-country and regional rail passes and prices.) If your travels are confined only to the Benelux countries, consider the **Benelux Tourrail Pass** for unlimited rail travel throughout Belgium, Netherlands, and Luxembourg:

Benelux Tourrail Pass

	1ST CLASS	2ND CLASS
5 days in 1 month	$ 217	$155
Youth 5 days in 1 month	—	$ 104

Saver Special: Benelux Tourrail for Two Pass

2 PEOPLE TRAVELING TOGETHER	1ST CLASS	2ND CLASS
5 days in 1 month	$326	$233

Day Excursions

Four day excursions have been selected for the Grand Duchy and its surrounding countries. Each is distinctly different in its points of interest. The day excursion to **Clervaux** takes you through the rugged north country of the Grand Duchy, where the Ardennes campaign was contested bitterly in 1944. The day excursion to **Koblenz** is saturated with scenic views along the Moselle and Rhine rivers and the charm of Koblenz, one of the oldest cities in Germany. **Metz** measures up to a most interesting day excursion into France. The German city of **Trier,** founded by Augustus Caesar, provides an exciting opportunity to explore many Roman ruins and to titillate your taste buds with the most delectable Moselle wines.

Base City…

Luxembourg

Internet: http://www.luxembourg-city.lu/touristinfo

Arriving by Air

Findel International Airport, about 4 miles (6 km) from city center. Luxembourg, because of its central European location and convenient rail connections, attracts an increasing number of visitors from North America. Regularly scheduled flights to Luxembourg from New York's J.F. Kennedy, Orlando, Ft. Lauderdale, and Washington-Baltimore airports are provided by Icelandair.

Airport-City Links: Bus service from the airport terminates at the Luxembourg rail station and Luxair downtown air terminal. Municipal buses (Bus No. 9) depart every half-hour throughout the day and evening from a platform about 50 feet outside the air terminal. Journey time: 25 minutes; fare 40 LUF, plus 35 LUF for each suitcase. Presently, there is no underground or train service link, but there are very interesting plans proposed to improve on the existing link from the airport to the railway station via a direct connection.

Luxair Coach to the rail station: 120 LUF with no charge for luggage.

Taxis: from 600-700 LUF (supplements for nights, Sundays and extra luggage). All taxis are equipped with meters. No tips are expected.

Tourist information at Findel Airport: (Tel: 40 08 08. Hours: 1000-1430 and 1600-1900 Monday-Friday; 1000-1345 Saturday; 1000-1430 and 1530-1830 Sunday.

Arriving by Train

The City of Luxembourg is served by a single railway station located conveniently in the city center. Connections can be made directly to Belgium, France, Germany, Italy, the Netherlands, and Switzerland from the station. The city tourist information office, the downtown air terminal, and the city bus terminals are all clustered conveniently about the railway station, which, like the airport, has been modernized to handle an increasing number of passengers.

Luxembourg Central Station is actually located in what historians call the "new city." From 1855 to 1866, when the first rails were laid, the gorge of the Alzette River remained too wide to be bridged. Consequently, the rail station was established on the far side of the gorge opposite the city as it existed then, and the new section of the city began to develop around it.

The station has three platforms (quais) serving five tracks. Track 1 is served by platform 1, which is directly connected to the station with level access to the platform. Trains arriving on the other tracks, however, require passengers to utilize an underground tunnel to reach the main station hall.

A system of elevators serves the outer train platforms. To access them, take the hallway off to the right of the main hall until you arrive at the entrance to the elevator service tunnel just beyond the last ticket window and before reaching the baggage room.

The entrances to the elevators serving the train platforms are marked clearly, although it seems a bit confusing when you first use them. You descend from the train platform to a tunnel. There, you walk a short distance to another elevator, which you ascend to the station level; you then take another short tunnel into the main hallway.

Money exchange on the right side of the main station hall as you enter from the train-platform area. Hours: 0900-2100 daily. An additional exchange facility is located in the nearby air terminus, which also houses the Luxembourg tourist information office. Hours: 0830-1200 and 1330-1600 Monday-Friday.

Train information is to your immediate left when exiting from the train platform area. Hours: 0700-2000 daily. A free mini-timetable describing the best train connections between Luxembourg and other major European cities is available.

Train seat reservations for EuroCity, InterCity, and regular express trains can be made in the train information office. Sleeper reservations and rail pass validation may also be made here.

Luxembourg Tourist Information/Hotel Reservations

Office National du Tourisme, Luxembourg Air Terminal, Place de la Gare. Tel: 48 11 99. Hours: July-mid-September: 0900-1900 Monday-Saturday and Sunday 0900-1200/1400-1830 (closed Sundays November-March).

Stands in the air terminal to the right of the railway station as you leave the main exit. It is easily identified by its air terminus sign and the usual "ı." Tourist information on your left. In addition to making hotel reservations, they can also provide information on youth hostels, camping grounds, and holiday flats and chalets available to tourists.

Luxembourg City Tourist Office, Place d'Armes, PO Box 181; *Tel:* 22 28 09; *Fax:* 47 48 18
Internet: http://www.luxembourg-city.lu/touristinfo
Email: touristinfo@luxembourg-city.lu
Hours: April-October: 0900-1900 Monday-Saturday; 1000-1800 Sunday; January-March and November-December 0900-1800 Monday-Saturday and 1000-1800 Sunday.
Hotel reservations can be made by the tourist information offices. Also, there are numerous hotels on the side streets near the station in addition to some charming smaller hotels within reasonable taxi or city-bus distances. The four-star **Hotel International** is across the street from the rail station. For those who prefer an American-style hotel with all the amenities, the **Sheraton Aerogolf** is located near the Findel Airport.

Our choice is a small, quaint hotel with European-style charm and service—**Hôtel Italia** (20 rooms). Located at 15-17 rue d'Anvers, Hôtel Italia is near the rail station and features an excellent Italian restaurant. Tel: 48 66 26/27or Fax: 48 08 07. Rates range from 2,500-3,100 LUF and major credit cards are accepted.

Getting Around in Luxembourg City

The city center is condensed and most sights are accessible on foot, despite the cliffs and ramparts which characterize this fortress city. For longer distances, utilize Luxembourg's efficient network of buses (single fare, 40 LUF). Taxis are metered.

Sights/Attractions/Tours

Luxembourg City Tourist Office offers a basic sightseeing tour by bus which departs from Platform 5 at the downtown bus terminal every Tuesday, Thursday, and Saturday (June-September) at 1030 and lasts about two hours. The tour includes the Old Town, the rail station district, the fortress ruins, the Casemates (underground fortifications), European Center, the relief miniature model of the fortress and Luxembourg's "Wall Street"—the banking district. Guided visits are also available of the European Court of Justice.

The **Casemates** (Tel: 352 4796 2709 or Fax: 352 47 48 18) are a unique network of underground rooms, one of the most interesting being the archeological crypt. This room presents an audiovisual show relating the history of the Casemates (open March 1-October 31, 1000-1700). Admission: 70 LUF adults; 40 LUF children.

From April-October, you can rent a tape tour "City Walk" and a walkman for 190 LUF (between the hours of 1000 and 1500 daily).

The **"City Promenade"** is a guided tour on foot and encompasses Place d'Armes, Place de la Constitution, the Government District, the Plateau du St. Esprit, the Corniche, the Monument of the Millenium, the Old Town, Place Guillaume, and the exterior of the Grand Ducal Palace.

The **"Wenzel Walk"** is an interesting historical and cultural tour that can either be done on your own or as a guided tour by making reservations through the Luxembourg City Tourist Office. Touted as "1000 Years in 100 Minutes," this tour takes you through the oldest quarters of the city.

There are other tours by bus which take you through the Ardennes and the Moselle Valley; or opt to see much of the area on your own during day excursions to Clervaux, Metz, and Trier.

"The soldier, above all other people," said Douglas MacArthur, "prays for peace, for he must suffer and bear the deepest wounds and scars of war." Such is the drama of 5,100 grave sites in **The American Military Cemetery** near the village of Hamm, three miles outside the city of Luxembourg. Among the crosses standing row upon row, you will see one marked "George S. Patton, Jr., General, Third Army, California, December 21, 1945." Solemn in its simplicity, beautiful in the manner whereby it attests to the American spirit, this cemetery must be seen. It is a moving, memorable moment. Guided bus tours from Luxembourg City will take you there as a part of their tour program, or you can taxi there for about the same price as the airport-to-rail-station fare. Telephone for a return taxi.

Luxembourg's low value added tax (VAT) of 13 percent makes it a bargain base city in comparison to some other European cities. Even residents of Luxembourg's neighboring countries make purchases of tobacco, alcohol, and fuel in the Grand Duchy because the taxes are lower.

Although hotel rates and restaurant prices are lower than those of most other European cities, the quality is not. Some Luxembourgers actually believe "the way to a man's heart is through his stomach," and they've made believers out of us. Try the smoked pork with broad beans or the delicate Ardennes ham cut paper-thin. For a real treat, try trout from the Moselle accompanied by a fine Luxembourg wine—all at popular prices. Luxembourg abounds in international cuisine. One of our favorites is the **L'Hotel-Restaurant Italia** at 15-17 rue d'Anvers, (Tel: 48 66 26/27, which offers excellent Italian specialties. Phone ahead for reservations—it's popular with the local folks, too.

Train Connections to Other Base Cities

TO:	DEPART	ARRIVE	TRAIN NUMBER	NOTES
Amsterdam	0827	1404	984	(1)★
	1127	1704	987	(2)★
Berne	1001	1512	EC 91	
	1459	2012	EC 97	(3)
Brussels (Midi)	0827	1121	984	
	1210	1440	296	
	1659	1928	EC 96	
Milan	1001	1925	EC 91	
Munich	1033	1812	IR 2431	(6)
Paris (Est)	0723	1103	351	(4)
	0802	1141	353	(5)
	1308	1711	EC 54/1835	
Prague (Praha)	1433	0812+1	IR 2433	(8)
Zürich	1001	1500	EC 91/EC 103	(7)
	1459	1945	EC 97	
	1901	0006	295/1797	(7)

Daily departures unless otherwise noted. Make reservations for all departures.
★ Similar service hourly
(1) Transfer in Brussels Nord to train 2483
(2) Transfer in Brussels Nord to train 2486
(3) Transfer in Basel to IC 893
(4) Sundays only
(5) Daily, except Sundays
(6) Transfer in Koblenz to IC 613
(7) Transfer in Basel
(8) Transfer to 353 in Cologne

Day Excursion to

Clervaux   GRAND DUCHY'S MEDIEVAL CHARM

Depart from Luxembourg City Central Station

Distance by Train: 38 miles (61 km)
Average Train Time: 54 minutes
Clervaux Tourist Information Office, Clervaux Castle, L-9712 Grand Duchy of Luxembourg
Tel: 92 00 72; *Fax:* 92 93 12
Hours: April-June, 1400-1700; July-September, 0945-1145/1400-1800; September-October, 1300-1700 Monday-Saturday. (Also open Sundays July 1-August 28.)

Start at the station by walking along the main street in the direction the train came from. When you reach the town square, turn right and follow the paths and steps leading up to Clervaux Castle. The Clervaux tourist information office is located at the entrance to the castle in a tower-like structure on the right-hand side as you face the castle.

Clervaux is a medieval town nestled in the valley of the Clerf River deep in the Ardennes of northern Luxembourg, through which runs the scenic rail route from Luxembourg through Liege in Belgium to Amsterdam in the Netherlands.

The scenic beauty of the train ride begins the moment you leave the Luxembourg station and the train crosses a viaduct high above the Alzette River. Take a seat on the left side of the carriage to enjoy best a spectacular view of the city of Luxembourg from the viaduct. Have your camera ready and start shooting a moment after the train clears a short tunnel just beyond the rail station. The morning departure is best for photographing the ramparts of Luxembourg because the sun will be shining directly upon them at a rather low level at that time. You will pass the same scene on later departures; however, the sun will be at a higher angle and the shadows will be less dramatic.

Clervaux is the fourth express-train stop en route after stops at **Mersch, Ettelbruck,** and **Kautenbach.** Beyond Ettelbruck, you enter the hilly and heavily wooded Ardennes, where the Battle of the Bulge was fought during World War II in December 1944. Some of the buildings along the right of way still bear the scars of this engagement. Don't be alarmed if you should spot a German or an American tank at a road intersection en route. The locals have intentionally placed it there.

The Clervaux railway station is a fifteen-minute walk from the town's main square. It's a delightful stroll along the river and easy to do with the aid of several maps posted along the way with "you are here" arrows to assist you.

Clervaux is packed with points of interest. Three of the most prominent ones are the **DeLannoi Castle,** the **Benedictine Abbey of St. Maurice**

Luxembourg–Clervaux

DEPART FROM LUXEMBOURG STATION	TRAIN NUMBER	ARRIVE IN CLERVAUX STATION	NOTES
0810	110	0900	(1)
1010	112	1100	(1)
1210	114	1300	(1)
1410	116	1500	(1)

DEPART FROM CLERVAUX STATION	TRAIN NUMBER	ARRIVE IN LUXEMBOURG STATION	NOTES
1451	117	1539	(1)
1751	119	1839	(1)
1936	121	2024	(1)
2051	123	2139	(1)

(1) Daily, including holidays

Distance: 38 miles/61 km

---

and St. Maur, and the **parish church.** All three tower over the town and its surrounding countryside.

The DeLannoi family are some of Franklin Delano Roosevelt's maternal ancestors. The DeLannoi Castle has so much to offer that we recommend you concentrate on it first and see the rest of Clervaux's sites in the time remaining at the end of your visit. The castle was heavily damaged during the Ardennes offensive in 1944, but it is being restored. It now houses the "Battle of the Bulge" museum, an exhibition of ancient Luxembourg castle models, and the world famous **"Family of Man"** photo exhibition of Edward Steichen, an American citizen born in Luxembourg.

No one is quite certain about the castle's origins. There are several hypotheses; some historians believe that it was built on top of an ancient Roman citadel, while others speak of Celtic origins. In any event, it has been established that the oldest part of the castle dates back to the twelfth century.

There's an immediate impact upon entering the castle's outer courtyard. One of General Patton's tanks is parked there, along with its chief antagonist, a German Army 88-mm cannon. History buffs of all ages will enjoy climbing aboard the tank to inspect its armor and speculate as to the role it played during the liberation of Clervaux and the Battle of the Bulge. Bear in mind that by December 1944, the castle you see now was reduced to a burned-out hulk. The authentic restoration that has been accomplished by the townspeople of

Clervaux and the Duchy of Luxembourg is laudatory.

The "Family of Man" exhibit and the castle model exhibit are immediately inside the first gate leading off the courtyard (open 1000-1800 daily except Monday; closed January-February). The "Bulge" museum is located farther along toward the center of the castle off an inner courtyard.

Steichen considered the Clervaux castle an ideal location for his exhibition. The collection was given to the Grand Duchy of Luxembourg by the U.S. government in 1975, three years after Steichen's death.

Enjoy lunch in the castle. The **Café du Vieux Chateau,** dating from 1671, is a part of the castle's outer courtyard. During the summer, the café provides tables and chairs in the courtyard. You will find the café just inside the tower gate and on the left. It was constructed originally as a dwelling for the guardian of the castle. Today, it would be a good place to launch hang gliders.

Day Excursion to...

Koblenz

HEART OF THE RHINELAND

Depart from Luxembourg City Central Station

Distance by Train: 101 miles (163 km)
Average Train Time: 1 hour, 14 minutes
Germany Dialing Code: 49
City Dialing Code: 261
Koblenz Tourist Information, opposite the rail station
Hours: June 15-October 14, 0830-2015 Monday-Saturday; 1400-1900 Sunday. (Hours shorter and vary remainder of the year)

To reach the tourist office, use the pedestrian crossing in front of the rail station. (If you need to convert from Belgian or Luxembourgese francs to German marks, stop by Exchange-Geldwechsel-Cambio on your left as you exit track area.) The tourist office is just opposite the rail station.

The Koblenz railway station is just far enough away from the meeting of the Moselle and Rhine rivers and the city's major tourist attractions to cause a "walk or ride" decision soon after arrival. If you decide to ride into the city center, the tourist office can help you hail a cab or provide you with the city's bus schedule and fare information. If you are planning to stay in Koblenz, they can make hotel reservations for a nominal fee.

Just as there is a subtle difference between Rhine and Moselle wines, so is there a difference between the scenic beauty of the two great rivers from which the wines take their names. At the rivers' confluence in Koblenz, how-

Luxembourg–Koblenz

DEPART LUXEMBOURG STATION	TRAIN NUMBER	ARRIVE IN KOBLENZ STATION	NOTES
0940	D 1272	1148	(1)
1033	IR 2431	1237	(1)
1433	IR 2433	1637	(1)

DEPART KOBLENZ STATION	TRAIN NUMBER	ARRIVE IN LUXEMBOURG STATION	NOTES
1655	D 1273	1904	(1)
1719	IR 2430	1923	(1)

Note: Returning from Koblenz at 1519 via Trier (see below) provides two hours to become acquainted with Germany's oldest town.

DEPART KOBLENZ STATION	TRAIN NUMBER	ARRIVE IN TRIER STATION	NOTES
1519	IR 2336	1638	(1)(2)

DEPART TRIER STATION	TRAIN NUMBER	ARRIVE IN LUXEMBOURG STATION	NOTES
1838	IR 2430	1923	(1)

(1) Daily, including holidays
(2) Transfer at Trier

Distance: 101 miles/163 km

---

ever, you will be able to enjoy both. Koblenz claims that it can offer 2,000 years of history to its visitors—and all within the span of a few hours. The historical background of this city in the very center of Germany's Rhineland makes this no idle boast.

The area around Koblenz was settled originally by the Celts. Julius Caesar, dividing and conquering as he went, arrived with his legions and established domain along the Rhine's western banks. Roman tranquillity thrived until the fifth century, when Rome's power weakened and the Franks took over.

Napoleon's "memorable campaign against the Russians" was inscribed on the St. Castor's fountain in the city during 1812. In 1814, the tables were turned when the Russians captured the town and added a postscript, "seen and approved" beneath the original inscription. At the Deutsches Eck, a monument erected at the confluence of the Rhine and the Moselle in 1897, the statue of the German emperor Wilhelm I was toppled into the Rhine by the U.S. Army's Corps of Engineers in 1945. The base of the monument was made as a memorial to German unity in 1953 by President Theodor Heuss. Since September 1993, Wilhelm I is back— in minimodel form on top of the monument.

If you choose to see Koblenz under your own foot power guided by the city map, a ten-minute walk down the Markenbildchenweg brings you to the Rhine, and a left turn at that point sends you in the direction of the Deutsches Eck, where the Rhine meets the Moselle. The riverside gardens along the Rhine join up with those on the Moselle to provide a delightful five-mile promenade along their banks.

If you plan to whiz around the city on wheels, Bus No. 1, marked RHINE (DEUTSCHES ECK) will deposit you on the promenade at a point opposite the Rheinkran, an antique building that once housed the harbor crane. The bus route takes you through the narrow streets of the old city along the Moselle and past the Deutsches Eck before reaching its final stop on the Rhine. Returning to the train station, the bus follows a more direct (and less interesting) route through the town's shopping areas. If your "walk or ride" decision is still up for grabs, we suggest you compromise by taking the bus outbound and returning on foot. From the river to the station, the bus is bannered HAUPTBAHNHOF. The bus ride takes about fifteen minutes. Allow a little more time if you're walking.

Make the **Koblenz Weindorf** (Wine Village) a must stop during your visit. It consists of four taverns clustered around a village square that, in turn, is enclosed within a real vineyard along the Rhine. The taverns are actual copies of half-timbered houses found in the notable German wine areas. Six hundred or more guests can be accommodated in the taverns and more than 1,000 outside when the weather is good—as it usually is.

The wine village was built on the occasion of the 1925 German Wine Exhibition. Since then, it has achieved fame for its products and romantic atmosphere. The village offers an excellent menu and wine list daily from 1100 to midnight. From November through March, an advance booking is required.

Day Excursion to

Metz   MOSELLE STRONGHOLD

Departs from Luxembourg Station

Distance by train: 39 miles (63 km)
Average train time: 53 minutes
France Dialing Code: 33; *City Dialing Code:* 87
Internet: http://www.mairie-metz.fr:8080
Metz Tourist Information: Office de Tourisme, Place d'Armes, BP 67002, 57030 Metz, France
Tel: 87 55 53 76/78; *Fax:* 87 36 59 43
Hours: Mid-July–September, Monday-Saturday 0900-2100, Sunday 1000-1300/1400-1700; remainder of the year Monday-Saturday 0900-1900; Sunday 1000-1300/1500-1700.

To get there, turn right leaving the arrival gate and walk the length of the station hall to the departure gate (served by the northern underground passageway). The station's north end houses the train information office and faces the General de Gaulle Square. Money can be changed in the Post Office, the huge red building in front of the station. Board either minibus line A or B at the bus terminal directly in front of the rail station. Get off Hotel de Ville (town hall) stop in front of the cathedral. The tourist office will be on the right in Place d'Armes.

Throughout its 3,000-year history, Metz has been a great Roman city, a religious center of the Carolingian Empire, an independent republic, a part of Germany, and a bastion of France. Throughout the ages, various cultures have left their marks in the form of various architectural styles throughout the city.

Poised at the confluence of the Moselle and Seille rivers, Metz claims one of the oldest churches in France, the fourth-century **St. Pierre-aux-Nonnains.** The center of attraction, however, is its gothic Cathedral of **Saint Etienne** (thirteenth-sixteenth centuries). The cathedral has been described as the "apotheosis of light" due to the luminescent quality of its stained-glass windows—two of the largest surface stained-glass windows in the world. Its 300-foot-high nave is among the highest France.

Metz further claims the largest railway station in eastern France. Due to its size, visitors arriving by rail may find the facilities somewhat confusing. When arriving from Luxembourg in the north, take the southern stairway rather than the northern one when transiting from the arrival platform to the main station hall via the underground passageway.

Obtain a map of Metz and a copy of Transports Par Minibus describing the two minibus lines from the tourist office. The two lines cover the city's major sights and shopping areas and terminate at the main railway station. The minibus stops throughout the city are marked with devices very similar in appearance to barber poles, to which are attached maps showing the course

Luxembourg–Metz

DEPART LUXEMBOURG STATION	TRAIN NUMBER	ARRIVE IN METZ STATION	NOTES
1001	EC 91	1043	(1)
1308	EC 54	1355	(1)(2)
1459	EC 97	1544	(1)

DEPART METZ STATION	TRAIN NUMBER	ARRIVE IN LUXEMBOURG STATION	NOTES
1602	EC 96	1649	(1)
1911	EC 90	1956	(1)

(1) Daily, including holidays
(2) Supplement payable

Distance: 39 miles/63 km

of the bus making that particular stop. Each pole is marked with the name of the stop, and inside the bus is a circular chart showing all of the stops that the bus makes. By noting first the name on the pole stop and then relating it to the map inside the bus, you can easily identify your position. Both minibus lines operate 0730–1930 daily except Sundays and holidays. A bus leaves the main railway station approximately every six minutes. Tickets are available in the bus.

Metz has many other interesting sights, such as the fourteenth-century St. Louis market square with its Italian influence. Its majestic buildings are constructed of yellow limestone, which seems to give them an aspect of light. The city's eighteenth-century theater, Place de la Comédie, is another typical example of this "brightness."

From the end of August and into early September, Metz goes "plum crazy." The golden mirabelle plum is celebrated in various deliciously edible forms—perhaps on a tasty tart or in a luscious, languid liqueur. Other gastonomic specialties include frog-legs pie, freshwater fish, and traditional stews, as well as not-so-traditional stews—snail stew.

Want to try a different type of city tour? Take a tour via Metz's "Petit (little) Tourist Train" (Tel: 87 73 03 08). It has departures at 1030, 1145, 1330, 1445, 1600, 1715, and 1830. Fare, 35 French francs; children, 20 francs.

The Metz tourist office proposes an audio-guided walking tour that covers the highlights of the city with an English narration. If you are sightseeing on your own in Metz, you should include the city's museum with it's Gallo-Roman collections and impressive display of seventeenth-century paintings by Dutch masters and artists of the French School. Top off your visit with a stroll along the city's Esplanade on the banks of the Moselle River.

Day Excursion to

Trier

GERMANY'S OLDEST TOWN

Depart from Luxembourg Central Station

Distance by Train: 32 miles (51 km)
Average Train Time: 41 minutes
Germany Dialing Code: 49; *City Dialing Code:* 651
Trier Tourist Information:
Tel: 651 978080; *Fax* 651 44759
Hours: 0900–1830 Monday-Saturday; 0900–1530 Sunday, with shorter hours in the winter months. If closed, use the coin-operated machine that dispenses a hotel list and city map. Operating instructions are in English.

Money exchange available in rail station. The tourist office is about a ten-minute walk from the rail station or there is a taxi stand at the right-hand front of the station. On foot, proceed down Bahnhofstrasse, which runs from the station into Theodor-Heuss-Allee leading to the Porta Nigra. Located immediately in back of the Porta Nigra monument. Walking tip: Avoid the din of traffic by using the park pathways on the left of the main thoroughfare for a relaxing stroll.

"Before Rome, there was Trier." Although this is legend, it is also a historical fact. Evidence of human settlements as early as the third century B.C. have been discovered in and around the city of Trier. Further legend attributes the founding of Trier in 2000 B.C. to the Assyrians. But history more soberly attributes its roots to the Emperor Augustus, who founded (or refounded) Trier in 16 B.C., thereby beginning Trier's part in Roman history.

In A.D. 293, Trier became the capital of Rome's province of Belgica Prima and the seat of the emperor's court. History records that no less than six Roman emperors held court here. The city's population swelled to about 80,000 citizens, and its cultural growth kept pace with its expanding population. Many magnificent edifices and archaeological finds attest to this growth today.

Trier came to be known as the second Rome. By the end of the third century A.D., it had become a capital of the western part of the Roman Empire. Its many monuments from that time attest to its greatness. The fourth-century Roman cathedral has among its treasures the "Holy Robe," said to have belonged to Christ. In ancient Roman records, Trier was among the first places north of the Alps to bear the name of "city."

Trier's pride is the Roman gateway building, the Porta Nigra (Black Gate), standing on the town's northern edge. Known as the "northern gate of the Roman Empire," it takes its name from the dark patina that formed over its sandstone facade. It was transformed into a church during the eleventh century, but Napoleon restored the building to its original appearance in 1804. Other Roman ruins still remaining are the Barbara Baths (A.D. 150), the Imperial Baths (A.D. 300), the Forum Baths (A.D. 100), the core of the

Luxembourg–Trier

DEPART LUXEMBOURG STATION	TRAIN NUMBER	ARRIVE IN TRIER STATION	NOTES
0730	IR 2433	0810	
0830		0910	(1)
0930		1010	(1)
1033	IR 2431	1115	(1)
1433		1515	(1)

DEPART TRIER STATION	TRAIN NUMBER	ARRIVE IN LUXEMBOURG STATION	NOTES
1644		1732	(1)
1742		1826	(1)
1840	IR 2430	1923	(1)

(1) Daily, including holidays

Distance: 32 miles/51 km

Cathedral (A.D. 330/380), an amphitheater (A.D. 100), and a bridge crossing the Moselle River.

Trier fell to the Franks in the fifth century, but the city's life did not end. During the thousand years that followed, churches, monasteries, convents, and mansions were built literally on top of, and around, its ancient structures. A cross, erected in 958 to signify Trier's right to conduct a market, marks the Hauptmarkt (central market) of today's city. On the other side of the coin, in 1818 a man was born in Trier whose ideas were in opposition to the free market concept; his name was Karl Marx.

Trier is an appealing city. It probably can attribute much of this appeal to the fact that it has been an imperial residence since the days of the Caesars. Strolling through Trier and you will see examples of Renaissance, baroque, and rococo architecture standing side by side. More recently, during the nineteenth century, several impressive citizens' houses of outstanding architectural beauty were built.

Not all of Trier's attributes are readily visible, for beneath the city in the storage cellars of its wineries there are vats and casks capable of holding more than three million gallons of the Moselle, Saar, and Ruwer wines produced annually in the area surrounding the city.

A small street to the side of the great cathedral in Trier is named Sieh um Dich (Look Around You)—an expression that depicts the city's greatness, for you can see two thousand years of history in just about as many steps. In fact, one of the tours conducted by the city bears the title, "Trier— 2,000 steps— 2,000 years."

The Netherlands

Traditionally, when we think of Holland, windmills, wooden shoes, and wondrous flowers come to mind. While these things probably will always be a part of Dutch traditions and landscape, there is another not-as-well known facet to the Netherlands and its people—its important and enviable economic position in Europe.

Dutch innovation and know-how are responsible for making the computer software Windows accessible for blind users through the use of a cordless mouse which utilizes sound instead of visual images.

Developments in agribusiness include cattle comfort (how about bovine water beds?) Developed by the Dutch Dunlop-Enerka company, the water bed for cattle is more hygenic and safer than customary straw beds.

The Dutch seem to have an idea or an answer for just about everything. One Dutch company has an answer to automobile congestion and pollution problems by developing a new concept in public transport—People Movers—a combination of ski-lift design and the already existing airport-style people movers.

Another Dutch firm, Spectrum Buoca, has targeted another type of pollution—the acrid urine odor that plagues public facilities (particularly during hot weather). Biological Urine Odour Control Agent (Buoca) is a mixture of natural enzymes and bacteria which "eats" the smelly problem.

It doesn't take too long to discover that the Netherlanders are not only multi-talented, they're also multilingual. The Dutch laughingly refer to their own language as "more of a throat condition than anything else" and readily join you in *your* native tongue. English is the primary second language spoken in the Netherlands, but French, Spanish, German, and many others are heard daily.

Although the Dutch are seemingly inventing the future, they are not forgetting their traditions. There are still about a thousand working **windmills** which are functioning the same way they did more than a hundred years ago. A group of 19 windmills may be found at **Kinderdijk** in the province of South Holland, some of which you may tour inside. It's amazing—mills that were built in 1740 are still running.

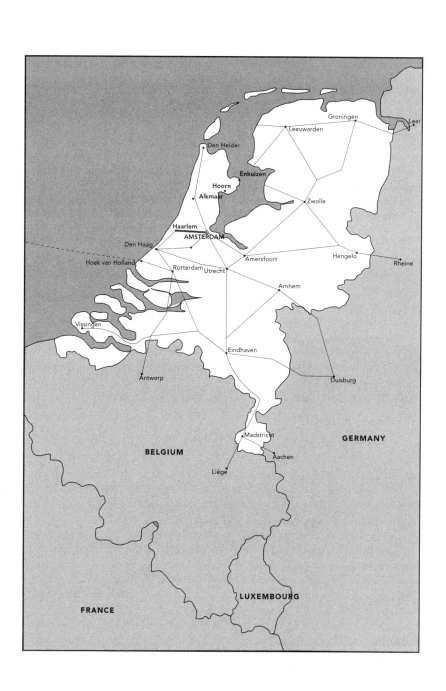

Groningen
Leer
Leeuwarden
Den Helder
Enkuizen
Hoorn
Alkmaar
Zwolle
Haarlem
AMSTERDAM
Den Haag
Amersfoort
Hengelo
Rheine
Hoek van Holland
Rotterdam
Utrecht
Arnhem
Vissingen
Eindhaven
Duisburg
Antwerp
Madstricht
GERMANY
BELGIUM
Aachen
Liége
LUXEMBOURG
FRANCE

Wooden shoes may not be worn very often anymore, but thanks to tourists, their production has continued. Now, almost any Dutch souvenir shops sells them and a few farmers in some rural areas still don their wooden clogs when they work in the fields or stalls.

Wondrous flowers are, of course, still in generous supply in Holland. Spanning about 70 acres, the **Keukenhof in Lisse** (accessible from Haarlem via the *Tulip Train*); (Tel: 252-465555, Fax: 252-465565) is the most famous and biggest bulb show in the world. It is open to the public from 0800-1930 daily in the spring from March through the end of May, welcoming more than 800,000 visitors to gaze upon some six million bulbs. Admission: 17 guilders, adults; 8.50 children age 4-12; 15 guilders age 65 and over.

For more information on the Netherlands, contact The Netherlands Board of Tourism in North America:

Chicago: 225 North Michigan Avenue, Suite 1854, Chicago, IL 60601. Tel: (888) GO HOLLAND; Fax: (312) 819-1740; Internet: http://www. Nbt.nl/holland; Email: go2holland@aol.com

Banking

- **Currency:** Netherlands Guilder (NLG)
- **Exchange rate at press time:** 2.02 NLG = $1.00 U.S.

Communications

- **Country Code:** 31
  For telephone calls within the Netherlands, dial a zero (0) preceding area code.
  Direct dial: AT&T: 0800-022-9111; MCI: 0800-022-9122; Sprint: 0800-022-9119

Rail Travel in the Netherlands

The Netherlands Railways (Nederlandse Spoorwegen, or NS) has many of its own day excursions. Because Holland is a very compact country, it is possible to take any one of the day excursions from any railway station within the country and return to your point of departure the same day (a strategy similar to that outlined in *Europe by Eurail.*

Frequent trains run to every part of Holland and most of the stations are linked with bus services and train taxis. The new Dutch **Rail Idee** program offers the day excursionist the convenience of a one-stop shop before hitting the rails. Travelers may purchase day passes directly from the rail station which include, not only their transportation (train, bus, taxi, even bicycle rental), but also their admission to a variety of sightseeing attractions in the Netherlands. Rail Idee ticket packages range in price according to destination and offers a choice of more than 200 attractions. On average, one can save around 20% compared to separately buying transportation and admission tickets. The day pass also offers bonus discounts at various shops and restaurants.

To find out more about these day excursions, ask at the train information office in the Amsterdam Central Station. Or, contact The Netherlands Board of Tourism for the brochures **"Holland by Rail '98"** and **"50 Excursions in & Around Amsterdam."**

Many Dutch cities, such as **The Hague, Rotterdam,** and **Utrecht,** are less than an hour away from Amsterdam. In just two hours, you could be in Antwerp, Belgium, shopping for diamonds. Add another thirty minutes and you could hop on the fast Thalys train and have lunch in Brussels before shopping for lace. Continue your shopping spree—the quaint town of **Delft,** where the world-renowned Delft blue pottery is made, is only fifty minutes' train time from Amsterdam.

The Netherlands Railways accepts **Eurailpass, Europass,** the **Benelux Tourrail Card,** and the **Holland Rail Pass.** A bonus for Eurailpass and Europass holders is a 30 percent discount on Stena Line ferries crossing from Hoek van Holland to Harwich, Great Britain.

Holland Rail Passes* are available for 3, 5, or 10 days of unlimited rail travel within Holland during a 1-month period:

3-DAY			5-DAY	
1ST CLASS	2ND CLASS		1ST CLASS	2ND CLASS
$88	$68	Adult	$140	$104
n/a	56	Junior	n/a	73
44	34	Child	70	52

10-DAY		
1ST CLASS	2ND CLASS	
$260	$184	Adult
n/a	130	Junior
130	92	Child

*1997 prices in U.S. dollars applicable at press time. Visit www.eurail.com on the Internet or call toll-free (800) 722-7151 for up-to-date prices.

For a more detailed list of European rail pass types and prices, please consult the Appendix of this edition.

Base City...

Amsterdam

City Dialing Code: 20

One of the most unusual cities in Europe, Amsterdam is a "fun city"—fun to see, fun to be in. It is a pleasant, human city where handsome houses stand on quiet canals, shoppers walk uninterrupted on streets without vehicles, and street organs play in the parks (even on rainy afternoons). It is the kind of city that, when you are lost, sends a smiling old gentleman on his bicycle or a bevy of flaxen-haired schoolgirls to your rescue. Amsterdam is a patient city whose people listen as you attempt to read Dutch expressions from a phrase book—then respond in perfect English. Amsterdam is a city to fall in love with.

Though picturesque, by European standards Amsterdam is not an ancient city. In the thirteenth century it was a small fishing village tucked behind a protecting dam on the Zuider Zee. It wasn't until the 17th century that it emerged as northern Europe's most prosperous port. Dutch influence declined at the end of the 17th century, but Amsterdam survived in style, having been built on 90 islands linked by more than 1,000 bridges arching 160 canals. Although their interiors have been altered many times, the fronts of seventeenth-century houses along the canals remain unaltered.

In keeping with the Dutch liberal attitude, the Netherlands Board of Tourism is the North American representative for the Foundation of Gay & Lesbian Games Amsterdam 1998. Amsterdam expects to host more than 50,000 visitors per day when the Gay Games are held August 1-8, 1998.

As the Netherlands Board of Tourism states: "Amsterdam is to Holland what New York is to the United States. It is the cuckoo in the Dutch nest, the strange bird with the big mouth, New York with a more easygoing nature. But that shouldn't be surprising. After all, New York was founded by Amsterdammers. Now you are invited to discover our Amsterdam."

Arriving by Air

Schiphol Airport, PO Box 7501, 1118 ZG Schiphol Airport, The Netherlands; Tel: 20-601 9111; Fax: 20-604 1475; Internet: http://www.schiphol.nl

Amsterdam's **Schiphol Airport,** which ranks fourth in Europe after London, Paris, and Frankfurt, is one of the most modern and efficient air terminals in the world. Schiphol handles over 25.4 million passengers per year and has some of the best tax-free shopping in Europe. It was built to be convenient. At last count, the airport provides flights to more than 200 destinations in 85 countries by more than 80 international airlines. After you have cleared customs, proceed to Schiphol Plaza to the **Holland Tourist Information** (**HTI**) center (open daily 0700–2200). There you can get all the information you may need for getting into downtown Amsterdam.

Airport-City Links: Rail service between the airport and Amsterdam's Central Station takes about 20 minutes and costs 10.50 guilders for a round trip. Trains run approximately every 15 minutes. If your destination is in the southern part of the city, you can board a train for the Zuid (South) Station as well. In fact, direct train service from Schiphol Airport to many other points in the Netherlands, such as The Hague, Rotterdam, and Delft, is available. Within Holland (Tel: 0900–9292) for bus, tram, subway, and rail connections (75 cents per minute), or for international train information, (Tel: 0–0900–9296, 75 cents per minute).

KLM Road Transport operates a shuttle-bus service between Schiphol Airport and the major hotels of Amsterdam. The bus stops at the Luchthaven Schiphol, Hilton Amsterdam, Barbizon Centre, Hotel Pulitzer, Krasnapolsky, Holiday Inn, Renaissance, and Barbizon Palace hotels. The one-way fare is 17.50 guilders, and tickets may be purchased on the bus. If your hotel is not listed above, ask at the HTI desk for the listed hotel nearest to yours and get off there—first checking that your hotel is only a short distance away.

Otherwise, a **taxi** may better serve your needs. A taxi takes about forty-five minutes and costs about 55-60 guilders. Again, the HTI desk will be helpful.

Money-exchange machine is available in the South Lounge. It changes 17 different currencies into guilders. The West Lounge has an ATM (bank cards only).

Duty-Free Shopping. Amsterdam's Schiphol Airport Shopping Centre is actually three centers, totaling 47 shops with more than 120,000 different items. The shops are open from first to last flight departure. Duty-free shopping is available only to passengers departing Schiphol to destinations outside The Netherlands.

Schiphol Plaza shopping is available to everyone, but normal VAT is payable. Hours: 0700-2200 daily.

Arriving by Rail

The **Amsterdam Central Station** is the focal point of all rail, tram (trolley), bus, and Metro (subway) traffic within the city. All train service for the listed day excursions depart from, and arrive in, this station. Trams, buses, and the Metro (entrance) are available immediately in front of the station, the hub of Amsterdam's city-transportation network; practically everything in Amsterdam begins and ends here.

The schedules appearing at the end of this section list train services—most of which are direct—between Amsterdam and other base cities: Barcelona, Berlin, Berne, Brussels, Copenhagen, Hamburg, Luxembourg, Milan, Munich, Nice, Paris, Vienna, and Zürich.

Amsterdam's Central Station has managed to preserve its old-world charm, but it is not a sparkling example of chrome and polished marble, as many rail terminals in Europe have become. The Central Station's facade is unchanged. Its ability to handle incoming and outgoing passengers alike, however, has improved.

Although it abounds in digital train-information displays, the station still provides the standard train-departure posters with their yellow background giving train-departure information by separate directions. Rail service throughout the Netherlands is so dense—departures approximately every half-hour—that these sectional timetables to Rotterdam, Utrecht, and other cities are most helpful.

Amsterdam's Central Station is virtually a city within a city, with many restaurants and shops operating over extended hours—a good place to stock up for a trip. A word of caution regarding the station: It's an originating point for long-distance express trains, including the Thalys train connections to Brussels and Eurostar to London, as well as the EuroCity network. This means lots of tourists—and tourists attract pickpockets. Watch when boarding the trains, particularly for people who are apparently traveling without luggage and are following you closely with only an empty shopping bag in hand. Chances are that they are "shopping" for your wallet and they plan to leave the train before it departs.

Money-exchange office "GWK" is on the street side of the station foyer. It is open daily, twenty-four hours per day. Money exchange is also possible at the VVV Amsterdam offices.

Tourist information for all of Holland, including Amsterdam, is available from the VVV Amsterdam Tourist Office located in the train information office on the far right of the main station hall as you exit from the trains or at the office in front of the rail station.

Train information may be obtained in the office of the Netherlands Railways (information for trains within Holland (Tel: 0900–9292), located on the far right of the main station hall as you exit from the trains. This office has the familiar "i" sign. Open daily 0630–2230. Take a number as you enter.

Seat reservations as well as **rail pass validation** may be made in this office. Complete information regarding the Netherlands Railways day-excursion program is also available. Remember, when having your pass validated, write out the starting and ending dates on a piece of paper and have the railroad representative agree to the correctness of the dates before the information is entered on your pass.

Amsterdam Tourist Information/Hotel Reservations

VVV Amsterdam Tourist Office: P.O. Box 3901, 1001 AS, Amsterdam
Tel: 06 340 340 66
Fax: 20 625 28 69
Hours: 0900-1700 daily
    Located immediately in front and slightly to the left as you exit Amsterdam's Central Station, in the Noord-Zuidhollands (NZH) Koffiehuis.

This office can provide complete city and national information for all of The Netherlands. Hotel, hostel, camping, and apartment bookings can be made here. Maps of Amsterdam are available at a vending machine for 3.50 guilders. You can also call 0900–4004040 ($1 U.S. per minute), Monday–Friday, 0900–1700 for information. Three other VVV offices are located at Leidseplein and Stadionplein and in the Central Station.
    Hotel reservations can be made at the Holland Tourist Information (HTI) office at Schiphol Airport, at the VVV Amsterdam Tourist Office (above) in the Noord-Zuidhollands Koffiehuis (NZH coffee house), in the VVV office in the CentralStation, or at the Leidseplein and Stadionplein VVV offices.
    For convenience, comfort, and cuisine all in one place, we selected the **Victoria Hotel,** one of the Park Plaza Hotels Benelux.

- Convenience—centrally located in Amsterdam and across the street from Amsterdam Central Station. The hotel will even send someone to help with your luggage.
- Comfort—the stately Victoria Hotel, built in 1890, offers all of the modern "creature comforts" such as deluxe rooms, indoor heated swimming pool, Turkish steam baths, beauty salon, and fitness room—even a free 1st class train ticket to and from Schiphol Airport.
- Cuisine—fine French and international dinners in the Seasons Garden Restaurant.

Park Plaza Hotels Benelux are located either opposite, next to, or very close to the central rail stations in Amsterdam, Utrecht, and Eindhoven in the Netherlands, as well as in Antwerp, Belgium. In addition, they **offer** *Europe by Eurail* **readers a 20 percent discount** off their normal rack rates.
    Just mention *Europe by Eurail* when you make your reservation and present the coupon on the following page upon check-in to receive your 20 percent discount. For reservations, call 31 20 62 71 166; fax: 31 20 62 74 259.

r--¬

Europe by Eurail Special Offer
from
The Park Plaza Hotels Benelux

Discount: 20% off rack rates!
Offer valid in the following hotels:
- **Victoria Hotel Amsterdam,** opposite central rail station
- **Park Plaza Utrecht,** next to the central rail station
- **Mandarin Park Plaza** in **Eindhoven,** near the central rail station
- **Astrid Park Plaza** in **Antwerp,** Belgium, opposite the central rail station

Offer valid until December 31, 1998, upon rate availability and only by using this discount coupon.

L--┘

Getting Around in Amsterdam

GVB: located on square opposite Central Station
Tel: 06 9292
Hours: Monday-Friday 0700-1900; Saturday-Sunday 0800-1900

Amsterdam's public transportation system encompasses trams, buses, the Underground, Light Rail, ferries, and canal boats. The transport office, GVB (Gemeentevervoerbedrijf) is located in front and slightly to the left as you exit Amsterdam's Central Station. Check with this office for up-to-date information, public transportation maps, and to purchase transport tickets.

There are a variety of one-day or multiple-day transportation passes that have to be stamped only with the first use; strip tickets also are available but they require stamping with each use. The tourist transportation tickets are accepted on all trams, express trams, buses, and subway. For transportation information, Tel: 0900–9292.

Circle Tram 20 provides flexible access to sights and attractions, museums, hotels, and restaurants—30 different stops—in Amsterdam. Hop on and off when and where you please. Circle Tram 20 operates 0900-1900 daily and departs every 10 minutes in two directions. Purchase 1, 2, 3, or 4-day tickets at the VVV Information offices, the GVB transport offices, from the conductor at the back of the tram, or from tobacco shops and large hotels. The tickets are valid on all public transport everywhere in Amsterdam. With Circle Tram 20, a helpful conductor is on-board. If you have an Amsterdam Paspoort, you can purchase a 2-day Circle Tram 20 ticket for the price of a 1-day ticket.

The "**Amsterdam Paspoort**" costs NLG 33.60. It offers substantial discounts or free entry for various museums, including the Rijksmuseum, the Stedelijk, and the new Metropolis museum with its focus on science, technology, and art. The Pass also includes discounts on other attractions, excursions, a welcome drink, and guided tour at one of the five exclusive diamond houses, a two-day public transportation ticket for the price of a one-day ticket, a 25 percent discount on Holland International's romantic Candlelight and Wine Cruise, reduced costs in typical restaurants—even a free canal boat cruise and discounts on the Museum Boat and the Canal Bus.

Sights/Attractions/Tours

If you'd like to see Amsterdam on foot, the VVV's color-coded signboards and map will guide you along six walking routes. More than thirty attractions are incorporated into the walking routes.

A boat trip on Amsterdam's canals and other waterways is, undoubtedly, the most relaxing way to see the city. Canal-boat terminals line the city's pier-studded canals, many of which may be found immediately outside the station. The closest of these is the **Holland International** pier (Tel: 6227788). It is just across the bridge on the right. A canal tour costs 15 guilders for adults and 7.50 guilders for children age 4-12 and senior citizens over age 65. Other tour-boat terminals are scattered throughout Amsterdam.

There are several canal cruise companies to choose from—all are excellent. During summer evenings, when the buildings along the canals are illuminated and the canal bridges are outlined by tiny lights, Holland International offers a "Candlelight and Wine" cruise (approximately 48 guilders)—the perfect way to end your day. (Receive a 25 percent discount if you've purchased an Amsterdam Paspoort.)

Amsterdam's old "inner city" is famous for its compactness. Most museums, markets, monuments, shopping streets, and other attractions are all within walking distance—or a short tram ride—from your hotel. Several of the city-center shops are open on Sundays—somewhat unusual when compared to the rest of Europe. Amsterdam boasts the largest historical inner city in Europe, with more than 6,800 National Trust buildings.

The city has more than 60 museums, including the famous **Rijksmuseum** (open daily 1000–1700), where you can view Rembrandt's renowned *Night Watch*, along with an extensive collection of his other dazzling works. The South Wing (opened April 1996) is devoted to a wide-ranging overview of eighteenth- and nineteenth-century Dutch impressionist art. All the paintings now have explanations in English, and for 7.50 guilders you can rent a CD-ROM player that describes in English, German, or French the 200 most significant paintings in the collection.

While the **Van Gogh Museum** is undergoing a 30-million NLG ($15.5 million U.S.) renovation and construction of a new wing, part of its permanent collection is on display in the South Wing of the Rijksmuseum. The refurbished Van Gogh Museum is scheduled to reopen in 1999.

Newest (opened June 1997) of Amsterdam's museums and appropriately named **"newMetropolis" Museum**, it is an interesting attraction due to its location on top of one of the major tunnels leading into and out of Amsterdam. Designed by Italian architect Renzo Piano, its roof offers a spectacular view of the city. The building appears to arise from the water of the Oosterdok as a bow of a ship. A twenty-first century public center for science and technology, this new museum fits with our earlier statement, "The Dutch are inventing the future," by using up-to-date hands-on techniques.

"Diamonds are a girl's best friend," and Amsterdam is a good place to see how a glassy little piece of stone can become the most beautiful, desirable gemstone in the world. Take a tour of the **Amsterdam Diamond Center,** located at Rokin 1-5 (Tel: 624 5787; Fax: 625 1220). Hours: 0930-1730 Monday-Saturday, 1030-1730 Sunday. Although free samples are not available, a diamond sure makes a great souvenir!

Dining in Amsterdam is an exercise in international cuisine. The expression "You can eat there in any language" is no exaggeration. First decide what type of food you want—Hungarian, German, Yugoslavian, Greek, Scandinavian, Japanese, or Indonesian—then select from among the many restaurants offering such dishes. Our favorite for Indonesian food is **Restaurant Indonesia**, at 18 Korte Leidsedwarsstraat (Tel: 4203300). Take tram 1, 2, or 5 from the Central Station to the Leidseplein area, about a twelve-minute ride. Their specialty is an eighteen-dish rijstafel (ricetable). Go there hungry—we guarantee you won't go home that way.

For more traditional Dutch bill-of-fare, try another favorite—**Haesje Claes** at Spuistraat 275 (Tel: 20-624 9998; Fax: 20-627 4817). Named after Lady Haesje Claes, this restaurant's slogan is "From canapes to caviar." The eel and salmon with lobster is excellent. Born in 1520 into a prosperous merchant family, Lady Haesje Claes was the founder and patron of the Public Orphanage, now the Amsterdam Historical Museum. Have a typical Dutch lunch or dinner in one of the eight chambers, each with its own special atmosphere.

Visitors from the United States who are hankerin' for a good U.S. steak, should not miss the **Three Sisters restaurant.** The beef is USDA Prime. A porterhouse steak for two is 59.75 guilders. There's quite a story about how the restaurant got its name. Ask the waiter for the menu with the complete version of the story of the three sisters and their New York connections.

Day Excursions

The *Europe by Eurail* day excursions described in this chapter are to **Alkmaar,** home of the world-famous cheese market; **Enkhuizen,** for its open-air Zuider Zee Museum, which depicts what Dutch life was like before the Zuider Zee was sealed off from the North Sea; **Haarlem,** for the Frans Hals Museum and more aspects of life in the Netherlands; and **Hoorn,** for browsing in a medieval market. These day excursions present a cross section of the Netherlands, from its rural to its sophisticated side.

Train Connections to Other Base Cities from Amsterdam

TO:	DEPART	ARRIVE	TRAIN NUMBER	NOTES
Barcelona	1419	913+1	Thalys 9348	(5)
Berlin (Zoo)	0914	1612	2343	
	1314	2012	2345	
Berne	1000	1912	EC 105	
Brussels (Midi)	0919	1157	Thalys 9328	(6)
Copenhagen	2014	0730+1	1237	
Hamburg	0914	1407	2343/IC 826	(2)
Luxembourg	0919	1449	EC 82/EC 97	(3)
Milan	1725	0745+1	201	
Munich	0800	1618	EC 3	(4)
Nice	1530	039+1	2465/1176	(3)
Paris (Nord)	0919	1405	Thalys 9328	(1)
Vienna	1925	0943+1	EN 215	
Zürich	0800	1700	EC 3	
	2005	0815+1	203 EN 471	(7)

Daily departures unless otherwise noted. Make reservations for all departures.

(1) Reservations required
(2) Transfer in Osnabrück
(3) Transfer in Brussels Midi. 12:16 Brus–Lux
(4) Transfer in Mannheim to ICE 593
(5) Transfer in Paris to Train 477, special fares apply. Reservations required.
(6) Reservations required
(7) Transfer in Basel R Basel–Zurich

Day Excursion to

Alkmaar
WORLD FAMOUS CHEESE MARKET

Depart From Amsterdam Central Station

Distance by Train: 24 miles (39 km)
Average Train Time: 30 minutes
City Dialing Code: 72
Tourist Information Office: Waagplein 2-3, 1811 SP Alkmaar
Tel: 72 511 42 84
Fax: 72 511 75 13
Hours: 0900–1730 Monday-Wednesday, 0900–1800 Thursday-Friday, and 0900–1700 Saturday

An easy route to the town square is to follow the street, Geesterweg, running perpendicular to the front of the station and the VVV signs leading you across a bridge toward a large church (Church of St. Laurens). Pass the church on its left side and pick up Lange Straat, still walking in the same direction. Pass the Town Hall, which will be on your right; four blocks farther, at a canal, turn left to the Weigh House, where the cheese market is held. The VVV office is located in the front of the Weigh House.

There is a cheese market in Alkmaar every Friday from mid-April to mid-September. But Alkmaar is such a picturesque town that it deserves a visit any day of the week at any time of the year. Trains run between Amsterdam and Alkmaar about every fifteen minutes.

Alkmaar is famous not only for its cheese; it is steeped in Dutch history as well. It was at Alkmaar in 1573 that the Spanish were first compelled to retreat their occupying forces; hence, the Dutch expression "victory begins at Alkmaar." A festival is held annually on October 8th to commemorate the breaking of the Spanish siege.

Ask at the tourist office about seeing Alkmaar by canal, a popular way to see the town. Boats depart from Mient (near Waaggebouw). Adult fare, 7 guilders; children under age 12; 4.50 guilders. During the cheese market on Fridays, boats sail every 20 minutes from 0930. During May, June, July, and August, they depart daily on the hour from 1100. In April, September, and October, they sail Monday-Saturday, every hour on the hour, from 1100, depending on the weather. The canal trip takes about 45 minutes (Tel: 5117750).

The cheese auction is *the* thing to see in Alkmaar. The square explodes into a frenzy of color and activity as cheese porters trot across the square wearing red, blue, green, or yellow hats according to the group they represent. This auction has continued for more than 375 years and attracts thousands of tourists. It is not, however, merely a tourist attraction. It is a genuine auction, at which cheese merchants sample the product, bargain for the best price, and conclude

Amsterdam–Alkmaar

DEPART AMSTERDAM CENTRAL STATION	ARRIVE IN ALKMAAR STATION	NOTES
0822	0853	(1)
0852	0923	(1)
0922	0953	(1)
0952	1023	(1)
1022	1053	(1)
1052	1123	(1)

Other departures every thirty minutes throughout the day

DEPART ALKMAAR STATION	ARRIVE IN AMSTERDAM CENTRAL STATION	NOTES
1638	1711	(1)
1708	1741	(1)
1738	1811	(1)
1808	1841	(1)
1838	1911	(1)
1908	1941	(1)

Other departures every thirty minutes throughout the day

(1) Daily, including holidays

Distance: 24 miles/39 km

---

the sale "on hand clap." From there the porters move the cheese to the Weigh House, where the weigh master checks the weight and calls it out in a loud voice; then the porters take the cheese from there to the buyers' warehouses.

Alkmaar's cheese makers founded their guild in 1622, only two years after the Pilgrims landed on Plymouth Rock. Unique in the curatorial world, Alkmaar's **Cheese Museum** attracts visitors from far and wide (open April-October, Monday-Saturday 1000-1600, opens at 0900 on Fridays). Entrance fee, 3 guilders, but a **Dutch Museumpass** will get you in for free.

Another unique museum is dedicated to the history of beer production. Featuring the fine skills of brew masters and covering 5,000 years of beer-making history, the city's **National Beer Museum De Boom** deals with all aspects down through the ages that have determined the various characteristics of beer, including the current Dutch favorite, pale lager. It is interesting to note that despite the complicated brewing equipment utilized today, the art of brewing has remained a natural process relatively unchanged from earlier times.

Both the Cheese Museum and the Beer Museum (April–September, open 1000–1600 Tuesday–Friday; 1300–1700 Saturday–Sunday; November–March, 1300–1600 Tuesday–Sunday) are but a few steps from the city square, where the cheese auction takes place.

Alkmaar is a charming town. It is crisscrossed by canals that, in turn, are spanned by humped stone bridges. The shining red roofs of its old houses are guarded by the towering vaults of the aged **St. Laurens Church,** constructed in 1520. Four blocks south of St. Laurens stands **Molen van Piet,** a windmill built in 1769.

There are an amazing number of things to do and see: among them, a visit to the Municipal Museum, the Dutch Stove Museum, and the Hans Brinker Museum; on a Friday, take a look at the stately wooden gabled house complete with an embedded cannonball as a memoir of a war now past. Sample the famous Edam cheese at either lunch or dinner. Time moves slower in Alkmaar.

Day Excursion to

Enkhuizen ZUIDER ZEE MUSEUM

Depart from Amsterdam Central Station

Distance by Train: 37 miles (60 km)
Average Train Time: 1 hour
City Dialing Code: 228
Tourist Information Office: Westfriesland, Veemarkt 4, 1621 JC Hoom
Tel: 31 229 218 344
Fax: 31 229 215 023
Hours: April–mid-September, daily 0900–1700; mid-September–March, Tuesday–Saturday 1000–1700.

After disembarking from the train, bear left approaching the railway station. As you round the station, you will see the VVV tourist office. The route is well marked; just follow the signs.

This day excursion from Amsterdam was made possible by the opening of the **Zuider Zee Open Air Museum** in Enkhuizen, east of Hoorn. Purchase museum tickets at the VVV tourist office or at the museum's ticket office at the pier. Admission: adults, 15 guilders; children age 4–12, 10 guilders; adults age 65 and over, 12 guilders; children under 4 are admitted free. A visit to the Zuider Zee Museum begins with a 15-minute boat ride. After stopping at the VVV tourist office, walk along the right side of the boat yard in front of the rail station to its far end and board the launch at the pier.

The museum was opened formally by Queen Beatrix on 6 May 1983 after

Amsterdam–Enkhuizen

DEPART AMSTERDAM CENTRAL STATION	ARRIVE IN ENKHUIZEN STATION	NOTES
0819	0923	(1)
0849	0953	(1)
0919	1023	(1)
0949	1053	(1)
1019	1123	(1)
1049	1153	(1)

Other departures at nineteen and forty-nine minutes past the hour throughout the day until 2319

DEPART ENKHUIZEN STATION	ARRIVE IN AMSTERDAM CENTRAL STATION
1608	1714
1638	1744
1708	1814
1738	1844
1808	1914
1838	1944

Other departures at eight and thirty-eight minutes past the hour throughout the day until 2108, then 2208 and 2308.

(1) Daily, including holidays

Distance: 37 miles/60 km

---

18 years of construction. It consists of 135 houses and workshops to depict the Zuider Zee culture before it was closed off from the North Sea in 1932 by the Afsluitdijk barrier dam. You will see a foundry, a steam laundry, a sail loft, and a smokehouse, to name but just a few items. There's a fishing village on the quay and a town center complete with a church and a general store, where postcards and wooden shoes and other souvenirs are for sale.

Snacks and various Dutch food specialties are also available, as are tours led by English-speaking guides. Check at the museum office for information. You will pass it just after the foundry. The open-air museum is open mid-April to mid-October, 1000–1700 daily. The indoor portion, known as the **Binnen Museum,** is open throughout the year (except December 25, 26, and January 1). Reduced entrance fees when the outdoor museum is closed.

Enkhuizen has succeeded in preserving its seventeenth-century character. The old center of the city contains a picturesque fisherman's quarter and a corresponding essential from those days (a farmer's corner. Within the old sea wall which was constructed to protect the city from storms on the Zuider Zee, you will find a shopping center, sidewalk cafes, and restaurants.

Ever wonder how artisans build those beautifully detailed ship models inside glass bottles? A visit to the **Bottle Ship Museum** will reveal the secrets of this ancient sailors' handicraft. The world's largest collection of ships-in-a-bottle is housed in an early 17th-century building—the "Spuihuisje"—within easy walking distance of the Zuider Zee Museum. More than 500 models are contained in bottles ranging in size from small perfume bottles to a 30-litre wine flagon. Tickets may be purchased at the VVV office (adults, 5 guilders; children four to twelve, 3.50 guilders).

For the small fry, Enkhuizen offers **Sprookjeswonderland (Fairyland).** Situated in a park setting, it contains a children's zoo with a deer park, a farm, and a "hugging" barn. (Open daily, mid-April to mid-October, Monday–Saturday 1000–1730; Sunday 1000–1730.)

The town of Enkhuizen is a living museum in itself. The Zuiderkerk church, with its spiraling tower and copper-clad roof, dominates the skyline of the city, assisted by the wooden bell tower of Enkhuizen's other church, the "Wester." Together with the ramparts and fortress walls, Enkhuizen assures its future by preserving its rich past.

Day Excursion to

Haarlem   AND THE FRANS HALS MUSEUM

Depart from Amsterdam Central Station

Distance by Train: 12 miles (19 km)
Average Train Time: 15 minutes
City Dialing Code: 23

Haarlem is close to Amsterdam, and this trip has the shortest travel time of any day excursion described in this edition of *Europe by Eurail.* It is also one of the most interesting.

The **VVV tourist information office** is situated on the south right-hand corner of the railway station as you exit. (The train bringing you to Haarlem is headed in a westerly direction as it enters the station.) The office is marked with an ample sign reading VVV HAARLEM and cannot be missed. Attendants will be happy to help you in the planning of your day excursion. The office is open Monday through Friday 0900–1730 and Saturdays 0900–1600.

Haarlem remained relatively undamaged by both world wars. What you find

Amsterdam–Haarlem

DEPART AMSTERDAM CENTRAL STATION	ARRIVE IN HAARLEM STATION	NOTES
0841	0858	(1)
0911	0928	(1)
0941	0958	(1)
1011	1028	(1)
1041	1058	(1)
1111	1128	(1)
1141	1158	(1)

Other departures every thirty minutes throughout the day until 2341

DEPART HAARLEM STATION	ARRIVE IN AMSTERDAM CENTRAL STATION	NOTES
1535	1551	(1)
1605	1621	(1)
1635	1651	(1)
1705	1721	(1)
1735	1751	(1)
1805	1821	(1)
1835	1851	(1)

Other departures every thirty minutes throughout the day until 2305

(1) Daily, including holidays

Distance: 12 miles/19 km

---

there in the **Grote Markt** (Great Market), the old center of the town, has authentic origins dating from the thirteenth century. Haarlem was put to the sword in July 1573, when it fell to its Spanish besiegers and its citizens were butchered. Its devastation, however, was not on the scale that modern weapons could perpetrate.

With the release in 1976 of the motion picture *The Hiding Place*, the attention of the world was drawn to a quaint little watchmaker's shop established in 1837 at 19 Barteljorisstraat in the heart of Haarlem. It was here in the shop and home of a Christian, Opa ten Boom, and his family that Jewish refugees fleeing the wrath of Nazi Germany were hidden for a time during World War II. A hiding place was built in a bedroom where the refugees could go in case the Germans made a surprise inspection. The ten Boom family operated the refuge for more than eighteen months, until they were betrayed on 28 February 1944.

At the time of the betrayal, six persons were concealed in the hiding place. They escaped while the Gestapo was still in the house. The ten Boom family, however, was imprisoned in a concentration camp for their acts of mercy. The ten Boom house is now a museum. It is open for visits from 1100 to 1600 Tuesday through Saturday from April 1 through October 31. It closes one hour earlier the rest of the year. Entrance is free, but a donation is always appreciated. Check with the VVV for directions and details.

The old center of Haarlem is not so large as to require transportation to its points of interest, but the city bus system is available to assist if necessary. You will want to visit the Great Market and see the town hall and the **Church of Saint Bavo,** then proceed to the world-famous **Frans Hals Museum** and from there to the **Teylers Museum** before returning to the railway station.

The Great Market is actually the central square of Haarlem, in which the noblemen of Holland staged their tournaments during the Middle Ages. Today, it is traditionally the social gathering place of the townspeople. A part of the town hall was once a hunting club. The Church of Saint Bavo houses a pipe organ that was once played by the eleven-year-old Mozart.

On foot, head south from the station, crossing the Nieuwe Gracht (New Canal), and proceed to the city's central square, using the tower of the great church as your point of destination. As you enter the square, the church stands on your left, the town hall on your right. This square has been termed the most beautiful in Holland. A pause here in one of the many restaurants, outdoor cafés, or ice cream shops is recommended.

Time permitting, before leaving the Great Market, you may wish to visit the **Meat Hall** and the **Fish Hall.** No longer functioning by their descriptive names, both structures are now employed in the exhibition of modern visual art. The seventeenth-century architect Lieven de Key designed the Meat Hall, which is said to be one of the finest examples of Renaissance architecture in the Netherlands.

From the western end of the church, follow the street running south from the square to the Frans Hals Museum, just before the canal. This street has several names—Warmoesstraat, Schagchelstraat, and Groot Heiligland—appearing in that order as you move to the museum through some of the most heady seventeenth-century atmosphere to be found anywhere in Europe.

The Frans Hals Museum is a moving experience. It's open Monday through Saturday, 1100–1700, and Sunday, 1300–1700. Perhaps nowhere else can you find such a perfect combination of setting and display. The building is a gorgeous sight—its inner courtyard a magnificent example of seventeenth-century architecture. The versatility of the museum's collections is unusual. In one section, the peak achievements of Haarlem's seventeenth-century painters may be viewed; in another wing of the museum, visitors may view an exhibition of modern Dutch art. Admission for adults is 6.5 guilders from October through March and 7.5 guilders from April through September.

A left turn at the canal below the museum takes you to the **Turf Markt** on the Spaarne River, where another left turn takes you winding along the river to Holland's oldest museum, the Teylers Museum, just beyond Damstraat (Dam Street). Here you will be treated to a rich collection of drawings and paintings by Michelangelo, Raphael, Titian, and Rembrandt. The Coin and Medal Room displays Dutch coins and medals from the sixteenth to the twentieth century. The museum also includes a collection of fossils and minerals.

Day Excursion to

Hoorn   OLD DUTCH MARKET

Depart from Amsterdam Central Station

Distance by Train: 26 miles (42 km)
Average Train Time: 40 minutes
City Dialing Code: 299
Tourist Information Office: Veemarkt 4
Tel: 06–34031055
Hours: In summer, 1300-1800 Monday; 0930-1800 Tuesday-Friday (until 2100 Thursday); 0930-1700 Saturday
   Cross the main street in front of the railway station, bear right to the first street, then turn left to the next intersection. Here, you turn left, then take the second street on your right. Green signposts scattered along this route indicate the location.

Ever since its harbor slowly silted in the eighteenth century, the city of Hoorn has taken to relaxing—except on Wednesdays from July to August, when it awakens with colorful markets and fun events.

In stalls grouped around the statue of Admiral Jan Pieterszoon Coen (founder of the East India Company) in the square the town calls Rode Steen, Hoorn's seventeenth-century crafts of clog making, net mending, basket weaving, and many others come to life while groups of folk dancers perform with musical ensembles. If you are not particularly fond of mingling with the crowd, this colorful spectacle may be viewed from the comfort of the **Old Dutch Tavern** on Rode Steen Square.

Although the Zuiderzee has been landlocked since the strait to the North Sea was sealed off in May 1932, Hoorn has managed to maintain its status of a port by establishing four harbor areas with more than 1,100 moorings for commercial and recreational watercraft. The pursuit of water sports, including wind surfing and water skiing, may be observed—or participated in—throughout the season in Hoorn.

Steam-engine buffs will find interest in Hoorn, too. You can travel on a genuine steam train from Hoorn to Medemblik and back in old-fashioned coaches. The Netherlands Railways operates a day excursion, "Historical Triangle," during spring, summer, and fall. Starting either in Hoorn or Enkhuizen, a steam train plies between Hoorn and Medemblik and a boat between Medemblik and Enkhuizen. The VVV office in Amsterdam or the train information office in Amsterdam's Central Station can provide details for this triangle trip. Information for finding Rode Steen Square, as well as the departure point and tickets for the steam train to Medemblik, is also available in the Hoorn railway station.

On Wednesdays, you'll find the market area merely by following the crowd. At other times, follow the directions to the VVV tourist office (above).

Day excursions by train to Hoorn are popular trips out of Amsterdam in the summer. Local trains bear special markings (on Wednesday) from July through August, when the market is staged. Take these trains for a festive mood; but regular train service between Amsterdam and Hoorn runs about every half-hour throughout the day, so you have the option of going and returning whenever you feel like it.

The steam train operates every day but Monday from April through the end of October; so Hoorn stages this market plus many other attractions on days other than Wednesday. In fact, the steam train continues to operate through September and October from Tuesday through Sunday. (For more complete details, check the Netherlands Railways day-excursion brochure.)

Wednesdays during the summer are, of course, the times of high activity in Hoorn, but you may go there at any time throughout the year and spend an enjoyable day in this ancient town on the **Ysselmeer,** a freshwater lake that was once part of the Zuiderzee. It is one of Holland's loveliest cities. As an important fourteenth-century fishing harbor, it grew in stature until the seventeenth-century East Indies trade made it rich. The warehouses and mansions of the East India merchants that still line its streets make exploring the town on foot a sheer delight. You can obtain a street map with a recommended walking tour from either the VVV office or the ticket office in the railway station.

At Rode Steen Square you may inspect the seventeenth century **Weigh House** and the **Westfries Museum,** which houses a collection of antiques, paintings, and objects associated with the city and its surroundings. The museum is crammed with beautiful paintings of Hoorn's citizen soldiers and other memories of Hoorn's "golden age" during the seventeenth century.

Stop at the fifteenth century calligrapher's workshop. Here is where Hoorn's wealthy merchants had their contracts and correspondence penned prior to the invention of the printing press later in the century.

Take time to smell the flowers. It took Hoorn many centuries to become what it is today. Relax and enjoy it.

Amsterdam–Hoorn

DEPART AMSTERDAM CENTRAL STATION	ARRIVE IN HOORN STATION	NOTES
0819	0900	(1)
0849	0930	(1)
0919	1000	(1)
0949	1030	(1)
1019	1100	(1)
1049	1130	(1)

Other departures at nineteen and forty-nine minutes past the hour throughout the day until 2319

DEPART HOORN STATION	ARRIVE IN AMSTERDAM CENTRAL STATION	NOTES
1634	1714	(1)
1704	1744	(1)
1734	1814	(1)
1804	1844	(1)
1834	1914	(1)
1904	1944	(1)

Other departures at four and thirty-four minutes past the hour throughout the day until 2134, then 2234, 2324

(1) Daily, including holidays

Distance: 26 miles/42 km

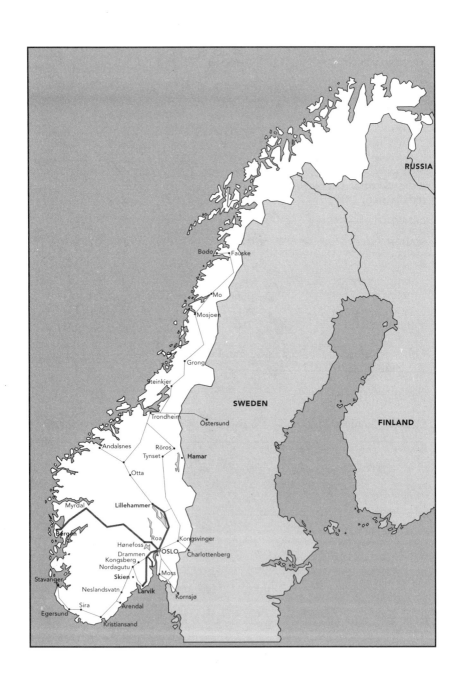

RUSSIA

Bodø • Fauske

Mo

Mosjoen

Grong

Steinkjer

SWEDEN

Trondheim • Östersund

Andalsnes

Röros

FINLAND

Tynset • Hamar

Otta

Myrdal

Lillehammer

Bergen

Roa • Kongsvinger

Hønefoss

Drammen

Kongsberg

OSLO • Charlottenberg

Nordagutu

Stavanger

Skien • Moss

Neslandsvatn

Larvik

Sira

Kornsjø

Egersund

Arendal

Kristiansand

Norway

"*See, darling, how the departing day*
On a scarlet pillow is laid away;
How the sun has set
In clouds of gold and violet."
From the poem "Beautiful Clouds" (1839) by Henrik Wergeland

Norway—Land of the Midnight Sun. In the upper reaches of Norway during the summer, the sun never fully sets, generating extraordinary hues of scarlet, gold, and violet in the northern skies. The Norwegian Tourist Board succinctly describes a visit to Norway as "A nature so incredibly beautiful one can't help but feel spiritual. Overall, a vacation in Norway feels like a spa treatment."

More than 30 percent of Norway's 155,000 square miles is covered by forests, rivers, and lakes, creating majestic landscapes and mystic fjords. Norwegian beauty and charm is not confined to its landscapes—it is reflected in its people.

Norwegian is the official language, but most Norwegians speak English and some also speak French or German. Norwegians are friendly and fun and anxious to make visitors feel welcome.

Norway is a constitutional monarchy with a Parliament, known as "Stortinget," and has been a member of NATO (North Atlantic Treaty Organization) since 1949. Oil and gas are the cornerstone of its economy and its people have one of the world's highest per capita incomes.

From art, beauty, and culture to hiking, skiing, and whale watching, Norway has something for everyone.

For more information on Norway, contact the Norwegian Tourist Board in North America:

New York: P.O. Box 4649, Grand Central Station, New York, New York 10163-4649. Tel: (212) 949-2333; Fax: (212)983-5260; Internet: http://www. travelfile.com/get?NORTRA; Email: gonorway@interport.net

Banking

- **Currency:** Norway Kroner (NOK)
- **Exchange rate at press time:** 7.29 Kroner = $1.00 U.S.
- **Hours:** 0815–1500 (1530 in winter) Monday-Friday, closing at 1800 on Thursday. Some banks are open longer than regular hours in larger cities. Most shorten hours during summer.

Communications

- **Country Code:** 47
  City codes are not used when dialing within Norway
  Direct dial: AT&T: 800-19-011; MCI: 800-19-912; Sprint: 800-19-877

Rail Travel in Norway

The **Norwegian State Railways (NSB)** successfully combines a comprehensive system (4,044 kilometers) of express and local rail service with bus and boat services.

The **NSB** cleverly designed **"Norway in a Nutshell,"** package tours that incorporate various transportation modes to create a great way to see Norway. These packages include hotel, breakfast, and a Norway Rail Pass. Tel: (800) 722-7151, Tel: (614) 793-7650, Fax (614) 764-0711, or Email questions@eurail.com for a free "Norway in a Nutshell" brochure.

Norway's trains traverse difficult geography; consequently, train speeds are limited to a maximum speed of 160 km/h. The new rail connection between Gardermoen Airport and Oslo, however, is built for 200 km/h. Norwegian trains are known for cleanliness and comfort.

On the night trains, sleeper cars contain 1, 2, or 3 beds per compartment and couchettes and/or reclining seats are available on some trains.

NSB accepts the 17-country **Eurailpass, ScanRail Pass** (for rail travel in Denmark, Finland, Norway, and Sweden), and the **Norway Railpass.** Eurailpass holders receive a 30 percent discount on the Color Line steamship fare between Kristiansand and Hirtshals.

Seat reservations are compulsory (20 kroner) on InterCity (ICE) trains and most other express trains. Supplement is charged for use of the ICE's "Bureau car," and for the "Saloon car," which includes a meal.

Norway Railpass

	2ND CLASS	1ST CLASS
7 days (May–September)	$250	$190
(October–April)	200	150
14 days (May–September)	330	255
(October–April)	265	205
Flexipass		
3 days in 1 month (May–September)	$190	$135
(October–April)	170	120

Children age 4–16 pay half fare. Up to 2 children under age 4 travel free with 1 adult. Since few trains in Norway offer First Class, a Second Class Norway Railpass is the better bargain.

Base City…

Oslo

Oslo, known as "the Viking Capital," is unique. If you love to bask in the sun, go to Oslo sometime between May and October, for that is when more sunbeams fall on Oslo than on any other capital city in Europe north of the Alps. About half a million of Norway's 4 million people live in Oslo, and soaking up the sun is *the* thing to do in town during the summer. Sauna baths, of course, become the rage for the balance of the year.

Oslo is also Norway's business, cultural, and fun capital. Frequently referred to as the "Nightclub of the North," Oslo is Scandinavia's center for entertainment and night life. Artists and performers entertain into the wee hours of the morning.

Arriving by Air

Oslo is served by two airports, **Fornebu,** 29 miles northeast of Oslo, and **Gardermoen,** 5 miles southeast. Gardermoen Airport is scheduled to be Oslo's international and main airport as of October 1998. Fornebu Airport will then be closed.

Airport-City Links: Rail connections to Oslo are not available from either airport at present, but express rail connections (NSB) will be available from Gardermoen when it opens in October 1998.

Airport Coach Fornebu—Oslo: Journey time 15-20 minutes; fare, 35 kroner.

Airport Coach Gardermoen—Oslo. Journey time 40-60 minutes; fare, 70 kroner.

Public Bus No. 31 provides transportation from the Fornebu Airport to the city's National Theater, a point about two blocks from the city hall (18 kroner).

Taxi fares from close-in Fornebu Airport are about 120 kroner, but vary according to route and destination. From the Gardermoen Airport, taxi fares should be negotiated with the taxi driver. Expect to pay around 600 kroner. All taxis are equipped with meters and accept all major credit cards. **OsloTaxi service:** Tel. 22 38 80 70; Fax: 22 38 85 92.

Until the new rail line connecting Gardermoen Airport with Oslo city center is officially opened, airport coaches are probably the best value transportation. They offer facilities for storing suitcases and packages. The coach driver may drop you at your hotel if it's en route. The public bus is economical but lacks luggage racks.

Money exchange. Banks at Fornebu Airport operate Monday-Friday. 0630-2000; Saturday 0630-1800; Sunday 0700-2000.

Arriving By Train

Oslo has several suburban rail stations, but all international trains stop only at the **Oslo Sentralstasjon (Oslo Central Station).** You will see the station name frequently abbreviated as "Oslo S," or shortened to "Oslo Sentral."

Within the station, rail travelers can take advantage of a mini-market area amid a variety of kiosks (small shops) selling everything from apples to zircons. The nostalgic market area stands on what was once known as the East Station. The East Station was devoted to steel rails, nail-spiked wooden platforms, and tiles bearing the patina of wear from countless passengers' feet as they hurried to and from the steam-hauled trains.

Oslo Sentral Station is a model of efficiency. Access from the train platforms to the station's main hall is by ramps.

Baggage carts are available for a 10-kroner coin. The coin is refunded if you return it to a rack when you are finished. Although the carts may be used on the ramps, they cannot be used on the station's escalators. You can, however, use the large passenger elevators located at either end of the main hall when moving from one level to another. The elevators are marked *heis,* which comes close to the word "hoist" in English.

Follow the pictographs and you will find every service you might need.

Baggage storage lockers are located on a balcony to the right of the station's main exit. Access to the locker area is open 0700-2300 daily.

Money exchange facilities are located on the mezzanine level of the station, directly across from the ticket windows. Follow the currency exchange pictographs. Hours: June-September, Monday-Friday 0700-1800; Saturday 9000-1500. When the money exchange is closed, you can change money in the Post Office or at the tourist information office in the Norway Information Centre at Vestbaneplassen 1.

Ticket offices are on the left-hand side of the station. Domestic tickets are available 0600-2300 Monday-Saturday; 0630-2330 Sunday. The international ticket office is located next to the domestic ticket windows (open daily 0630-2300).

Tourist Information office: 0800-2000 daily. Located next to the money exchange office. Provides tourist information covering Oslo, hotel reservations, guest house and private accommodations, sales of the Oslo Card and sightseeing tours. To request information/accommodations in advance, write to Tourist Information, Oslo Sentralstasjon, Jernbanetorget 1, N-0154 Oslo.

Train information is located in Oslo Sentral's main concourse area on the left-hand side just prior to the moving walkways. Hours: Monday–Saturday 0700–2300; Sunday 0700–2330. If possible, get the information you need from the regular arrival and departure digital bulletin boards installed throughout the station. Departures carry the heading AVGAENDE TOG, and arrivals are labeled ANKOMMENDE TOG.

Train reservations and rail pass validation are handled at window No. 4 in the ticket office of the main lobby. The ticket windows are marked BILLETTER, and any of the other windows can assist you if No. 4 is closed. This office also can make sleeping-car reservations.

Tourist Information/Hotel Reservations

Tourist information Office: Vestbaneplassen 1, N0250 Oslo
Tel: 22 83 00 50; *Fax:* 22 83 81 50
Information by telephone: 820 60100 (6.56 kroner per minute)
Guide Service: Tel. 22 83 83 80
Hours: 0900–1800 daily
Located opposite Oslo's City Hall in the Norway Information Centre.

The center offers an overview of Norway, such as general information on all aspects of Norwegian life and tips on where to go and what to see. The attitude of the personnel at the center is, "If we can't tell you what you need to know, we can tell you who does and where to go to get it."

You'll find an interesting exhibition of Norwegian design and culture at the Norway Information Centre. A gallery and gift shop, a newspaper kiosk, and a restaurant serving "Norway's best food in a contemporary setting at an attractive price" are also available.

Hotel reservations can be made in the tourist information office in the Norway Information Centre or in the one next door to the money-exchange office in Oslo Sentral Station. This service is operated by Oslo Promotion. It will make reservations for you in hotels, pensions, and private homes (20 kroner fee per booking). Oslo Promotion has an exceptional track record. Few, if any, are ever turned away though the entire town is "fully booked." Oslo is one of the few European cities where you can arrive without an advance reservation and still be reasonably certain of lodgings that night.

Ask for the **Oslo Package** brochure. This package combines your hotel (choose from thirty selected hotels) and the Oslo Card. Prices start from 350 kroner per person, per night, double occupancy.

Tourist information and hotel bookings for Oslo are also available from the tourist information office in the Sentral Station.

Be certain to ask for *The Official Guide for Oslo* since it will aid you in seeing the various attractions in and around Oslo.

USE IT–Youth Information: Mollergata 3
Tel: 22 41 51 32

Internet: http//www.unginfo.oslo.no
Opening hours: Monday-Friday. 1100-1700

Getting Around in Oslo

Both tourist offices sell the **"Oslo Card,"** which provides unlimited use of city transportation by bus, train, tram, suburban railway, and ferry within Oslo's boundaries as well as up to four fare-stages within **Akershus.** It includes free admission to most museums, various sightseeing discounts, a free sightseeing tour by boat (May-mid-August), discounts at Restaurant Dan Turell and Tryvannstua and a surprise on the menu at Holmenkollen Restaurant and Brasserie 45.

The Oslo Card can be valid for 24, 48, or 72 hours and may be purchased at the following Norwegian kroner rates: 24 hours, 130; 48 hours, 200; 72 hours, 240. Children's cards are 50, 80, and 110 kroner.

Sightseeing/Attractions/Tours

Visitors desiring personal-guide services can inquire at the tourist information office or Tel. 22-427020 for reservations and tariffs. Students, taxi drivers, and couriers are not permitted to arrange paid guided tours in Oslo and the museums.

A variety of tours in and around the city are available. For details, call at the tourist information office or consult your hotel. You may book the standard sightseeing bus tours, which normally take 3 hours to complete, or you may want to opt for one of the more specialized tours combining bus and boat transportation. You will find them listed in *What's On in Oslo,* and *The Official Guide for Oslo and Surrounding Area.*

With so much good weather on hand, it is only natural that the majority of Oslo's sightseeing services concentrate their schedules into the summer months. In the period beginning with April and ending with October, a myriad of sightseeing opportunities are available to visitors. Fjord cruises from 50 minutes' duration to several hours are available. Likewise, there are land-and-water combinations to select from that include (among other attractions) a visit to the Kon-Tiki Raft Museum, a cruise on the Oslofjord, and a view from the top of the famous Holmenkollen ski jump.

The usual type of city bus tours are also available, along with a wide selection of things to be seen. There's an old adage that when the weather is nice, you will never find anyone home in Oslo. That is true. Chances are, you will find that many of the passengers on your tour bus or boat are townspeople enjoying the view along with you.

Information describing **Bygdoy** and many other attractions in Oslo is available at the tourist information office at the Oslo Sentral Station or from the Norway Information Centre.

Visit Oslo's famous **Vigeland Park** while you are in town. Among the 193 granite and bronze statues by sculptor Gustav Vigeland, you will be able to examine *The Monolith*, the world's largest granite sculpture.

All members of the family will enjoy a visit to **Akershus,** a medieval castle built in the 12th century and reconstructed as a fortress during the 17th century. Standing at the front of Oslo's City Hall, you can see the fort off to your left. Arkershus's military atmosphere is aided by the presence of two military museums. The **Norwegian Resistance Museum** chronicles Norway's struggle against the Nazis, and the **Norwegian Armed Forces Museum** traces the country's military history from the Vikings to World War II.

The fort maintains a garrison of armed sentries who patrol the grounds in dress uniform and plumed headdress. These troops also have a cannon that they fire every day (except Sunday) promptly at 1200. Don't tell anyone else in your group about this—at least not until 1205. Then, regain the confidence you may have lost by taking everyone to McDonald's for lunch. Oslo has several fast-food eateries. Such is the price of progress.

During your stay in Scandinavia's oldest capital—Oslo was established in 1050 by Harald Hardrade—you should plan to visit the world-famous *Kon-Tiki* raft, the polar vessel *Fram,* and the collection of viking ships on exhibition at Bygdoy, across the harbor from the city hall. Each vessel bears a proud history in nautical accomplishments.

Day Excursions

When you consider that Norway is larger than the British Isles, you can readily appreciate why we deviate from our usual "Base City—Day Excursion" format for Oslo. An "out-and-back" excursion between Oslo and **Bergen** offers an almost limitless variety of travel modes and a visit to the fjord at **Flam.**

Within our usual "Base City-Day Excursion" concept, we selected a variety of daytime trips that will permit you to see the beautiful fjords, lakes, and mountains without daily packing and unpacking.

A day excursion to the towns of **Larvik** and **Skien** takes you into Norway's seacoast towns for a look at some breathtaking scenery as well as a close look at the country's ports.

Hamar lies to the north of Oslo. Its day excursion affords inspection of the countryside surrounding the town and its extensive railroad museum.

The northernmost day excursion takes you to **Lillehammer,** site of the 1994 Winter Olympics and one of Norway's best known summer-and-winter resorts.

Train Connections to Other Base Cities from Oslo

TO:	DEPART	ARRIVE	TRAIN NUMBER	NOTES
Berlin Zoo	2243	1732	393	(2)(4)
Copenhagen	2137	0700+1	IN381	
	2243	0742+1	393	
Hamburg	2243	1426	393	(3)
Helsinki	0903	0830+1	IN55	(1)
Stockholm	0903	1523	55	
	2250	0611+1	397	(5)

Daily departures unless otherwise noted. Make reservations for all departures.

(1) Arrives in Stockholm at 1541. Transfer to Silja Line terminal for sailing at 1800.
(2) Transfer in Malmö to train 317
(3) Transfer in Copenhagen to EC189
(4) June 12–August 27
(5) Daily except Saturdays

Day Excursion to

Bergen
AND THE FJORD AT FLAM

Depart From Oslo Sentral Station

Distance by Train: 293 miles (471 km)
Average Train Time: 6 hours, 40 minutes
City Dialing Code: No dialing code required.
Tourist Information Office: Bryggen 7
Tel: 55 321480
Hours: June-August, 0830-2100 daily; May and September, 0830-2100 Monday-Saturday; 1000-1900 Sunday
  Located by the harbor. There is a map in the station that will point the way. There is also a tourist information office at the rail station during June, July, and August, 0715-2300, which can provide the same services.

Bergen is Norway's second largest city. It is beautifully framed by seven mountains. Two cable cars terminate at mountaintop restaurants overlooking the city. Bergen has a fish market that also has live fish, a sixteenth-century town hall, and a twelfth-century cathedral. It's the home of Edvard Grieg (1843-1907), the most distinguished Norwegian composer of the nineteenth century. The city has a 300-year-old wooden village (**"Old Bergen"**), a symphony orchestra founded in 1765, and the oldest performing theater in

Norway. Inseparable from the sea, Bergen also has the largest aquarium in northern Europe.

Founded about 1070 by King Olaf Kyrre, Bergen grew quickly as a commercial center, and during the twelfth and thirteenth centuries, it was the capital of Norway. Built mainly of wood, the buildings were highly susceptible to fire, and the city suffered severe fires in 1702, 1855, and 1916. Bergen was badly damaged during World War II, when it was occupied by the Germans.

This excursion has more route options than a cat has lives. The variations are such that we can only list a few. The daily train service between Oslo and Bergen has three daytime trains and one overnight train in each direction. During summer, a fourth train operates daily except Saturday. The overnight trains haul sleeping cars between Oslo and Bergen.

Express boats cruise between Bergen and Flam from mid-May to mid-September. As a result, many options are available both in time and mode. Before examining some of the options, let's look at the destinations and some of the reasons for going.

Flam is the terminus of a spectacular railway—the Flamsbanen. It climbs 2,845 feet from Flam in only 12.4 miles, and between May 15 and September 30, it stops for you to take pictures. A supplemental fee is payable for travel on the Flam line during summer (even for rail pass holders).

Option 1 Oslo-Bergen:	January 1 - December 30
Train from Oslo	0742★
To Myrdal	1225
Train from Myrdal	1230
To Flam	1330
Boat from Flam	1430
To Gudvangen	1630
Bus from Gudvangen	1715
To Voss	1830
Train from Voss	1900
To Bergen	2018
Option 2 Oslo-Bergen:	**January 1 - December 12**
ICE train from Oslo	0742★
To Myrdal	1228
From Myrdal	1232
To Flam	1330
From Flam	1440
To Gudvangen	1640
From Gudvangen	1715
To Voss	1830
From Voss	1900
To Bergen	2018

Option 3 Bergen-Oslo:	**June 8–**	**September 22–**
	September 21	**December 30**
Train from Bergen	0830	0830
To Voss	0943	0943
Bus from Voss	1005	1050
To Gudvangen	1125	1150
Boat from Gudvangen	1130	1155
To Flam	1330	1355
Train from Flam	1535	1535
To Myrdal	1616	1616
Train from Myrdal	1733	1733★
To Oslo	2221	2221

★ $10 (U.S.) seat reservation required per person.

Notes on Oslo-Bergen railway "*New Express*": About 30 minutes after stopping at Drammen, the railway travels above the timberline. When you reach Finse, you'll see the looming Hardanger glacier. Further west, you enter the Finse tunnel, the highest point on your way to Myrdal. As you descend toward Bergen, you pass through the longest tunnel on this route—the 5-mile Ulriken tunnel.

To see **"Norway in a Nutshell"** with the Norwegian State Railways' Combination Tours, Tel: (800) 722-7151 or (614) 793-7650, Fax (614) 764-0711, Email: questions@eurail.com, Rail Pass Express, Inc., for a comprehensive brochure.

Day Excursion to

Hamar

HEART OF NORWAY'S LAKE COUNTRY

Depart From Oslo Sentral Station

Distance By Train: 78 miles (126 km)
Average Train Time: 1 hour, 45 minutes
City Dialing Code: No dialing code required.
Tourist Information Office: Parkgata.2, 2300 Hamar
Tel: 62 52 12 17; *Fax:* 62 53 35 65
Hours: June 16-July 29, weekdays 0800-1800; Saturday 1000-1800; Sunday 1200-1800; June 30-August 3, weekdays 0800-2000; Saturday-Sunday 1000-1800; August 4–10, weekdays 0800-1800; Saturday 1000-1800; Sunday 1200-1800; and for the rest of the year, weekdays 0900-1500.
Located to the left just outside the railway station

On 17 September 1976, en route to Hamar for the first time, we wrote "This train passes through some of God's most beautiful countryside along one of His most beautiful lakes." That has not changed.

The countryside is the rich farmland of **Hedemarken,** and the lake is Norway's largest, **Lake Mjosa.** The lake is 75 miles long, and every foot of it is beautiful. Hamar is situated on the eastern slope of Lake Mjosa at its widest point. The train from Oslo traverses the river Vorma from Eidsvoll to Mirucsund and then continues along the eastern shore of Lake Mjosa to Hamar.

Watch for the bridge that the train crosses about an hour and ten minutes out of Oslo. Station yourself on the right side of the coach for a spectacular view down the lake from the vantage point of the bridge as the train crosses.

It seems that you have hardly settled in your seat when the train glides to a stop in Hamar. Time will pass even more quickly here, for there is much to see and do in this most pleasant city. Two of its feature attractions are the **Hedmark Museum** and the **Norwegian State Railways Museum.** These are not stuffy old buildings crowded with relics. Both are spacious, outdoor areas with fascinating displays of what rural and railroad life was like in Norway's earlier times.

Check with the tourist office regarding transportation to the museums. Both can be reached by public bus. If you prefer a taxi, you will find a taxi stand on your right when leaving the station. Fares by taxi to either museum are about 40-50 kroner one way for a maximum of four persons.

Within the Hedmark Museum boundaries are the remains of a medieval cathedral built in 1152. The ruins of the cathedral reveal that, in its day, it was one of the most magnificent churches in Scandinavia. History reveals that the town of Hamar suffered along with the demise of the stately church. Years of civil strife and the Reformation practically wiped out what was once a thriving city.

It was not until 1849 that Hamar once again enjoyed the status and charter of a town. Marking this return to status, the present Hamar Cathedral, replacing its medieval predecessor, was built in 1886.

The museum area also includes Norway's only holography museum and forty buildings from the County of Hedmark. Most of them date back to the eighteenth and nineteenth centuries. One unusual building, the house of a Norwegian emigrant, was built in North Dakota in 1871 and moved to the museum in 1973.

The **Odden Restaurant** on the museum grounds is open for business from mid-May to mid-September each year. From mid-June through mid-August, the museum is open from 1000 to 1800 daily. During the balance of the year, it is open for groups by appointment only.

The Railway Museum rivals anything the Disney folks have come up with to date. If you are a railroad buff, you'll go bananas over it. Included in its col-

Oslo–Hamar

DEPART OSLO SENTRAL STATION	TRAIN NUMBER	ARRIVE IN HAMAR STATION	NOTES
0805	ET 41	0939	(1)(2)(4)
0900	IC 313	1045	(1)(3)(4)
1035	I401	1223	(1)(2)(3)

DEPART HAMAR STATION	TRAIN NUMBER	ARRIVE IN OSLO SENTRAL STATION	NOTES
1511	IC 318	1656	(1)(2)(3)(4)
1703	IC 320	1855	(1)(2)(3)(4)
2051	ET 44	2225	(1)(2)(4)

(1) Daily, including holidays
(2) Seat reservations mandatory
(3) Second class only
(4) Food service available

Distance: 78 miles/126 km

Special Attraction. See Lake Mjosa on an ancient paddle steamer. The *Skibladner* is the oldest paddle steamer in the world still operating. It was built in 1856. Ask the tourist office for excursion timetables and fares.

---

lection of rolling stock are the old royal train, several "stage coach" types, and even an old fourth-class (or shall we say, no-class) wagon—without seats.

Norway's first railway station is among the many buildings found on the seven-and-a-half-acre tract covered by the museum. It is open daily from mid-May through mid-September, 1000-1600 and during July from 1000-1800. From October through April, it's closed on Sundays and holidays but in operation on weekdays with the same schedule.

When the Norwegian government closed the Aurskog-Hoeland railway in 1960, two steam locomotives and a selection of rolling stock from the narrow-gauge line were given to the railway museum together with many structures from this private railway that began operation in 1896. In addition to the two locomotives from the Aurskog-Hoeland line, the museum now has eleven standard-gauge and four narrow-gauge engines—all in operating condition.

Hamar's railway museum is the oldest in Scandinavia, and it is also the oldest technical museum in Norway. No doubt it will still be in full operation during the Norwegian Railway Bicentennial in 2054.

Hamar is also a sporting town, and its Olympic halls can attest to that. Visit Hamar's **Olympia Hall,** the "Viking Ship," and the **Hamar Olympic**

Amphi Hall, or, the "Northern Lights Hall." The Viking Ship is one of the largest sports halls in the world and the architectural symbol of the 1994 Winter Olympics. The Northern Lights Hall is the world's largest wooden building. Check with the tourist office for opening times.

Day Excursion to

Larvik and Skien
FJORD COUNTRY

Depart From Oslo Sentral Station

Distance By Train: 120 miles (193 km)
Average Train Time: 2 hours, 30 minutes
City Dialing Code: No dialing code requried.
Tourist Information Office: Larvik: Larvick OgOfoten Reiseliv AS, Post Boks 318, 8501.
   Tel: 76 94 60 33; *Fax:* 76 94 7405
   Skien: Skien Turist Kontor, Nedre Hjellegat 18, 3724 Skien. *Tel:* 35 581 910; *Fax:* 35 52 26 61.
Hours: Monday–Friday, 0900–1700

If there's a fjord in your future, you'll probably find it on this day excursion. The greater part of that huge seaway known as the Oslofjord unfolds its grandeur as the train wends its way to Larvik and Skien. The sight of huge tankers and ocean liners miles from the ocean, plying between tree-covered mountains, is a breathtaking sight. You are certain to enjoy this outing.

As the train leaves Larvik en route to Skien, you also leave the fjords but begin to travel in an area of beautiful lakes connected by streams running through a wooded countryside. This, too, is fascinating and well worth the trip.

Because a train departs the Oslo Sentral station on the Oslo-Drammen-Larvik-Skien line every two hours throughout the day, you might consider leaving the train at any point that catches your interest and returning to board the train that follows to continue your journey. It's a nice option to take.

There is a need to seek out the local tourist information office in some of the places you elect to stop, and the train gives you an excellent preview of what each town has to offer as you approach. Basically, the route through Larvik takes you to typical Norwegian seafaring towns, and each seems to offer a different type of land- and seascape. In a sense, you'll be window shopping, so be prepared to leave the train on impulse.

A summary of the cities the train passes follows. Be sure to take along a copy of the Norwegian State Railways schedule for this line in order to plan the follow-on portion of your trip as you go.

Drammen (40 km from Oslo): Important center of Norway's timber and paper industries. There are many attractive buildings in town dating back to the seventeenth century. Have your camera handy—the city covers the headwaters of the Drammensfjorden, where it joins the river, and the docks teem with seafaring activities.

Tonsberg (103 km from Oslo): The oldest town in Norway and the seat for centuries of its Viking kings. The Oseberg Viking ship now resting in the Oslo Viking Museum was found in a nearby burial mound. The ruins of a Viking castle overlook the town.

Sandefjord (127 km from Oslo): Home of the Norwegian whaling fleet. Regardless of your opinions about this industry, there's a whaling museum in town, and there's a spectacular whaling monument in the center of the town square. The coastline around Sandefjord is spotted with many islands and inlets, making it very photogenic.

Larvik (146 km from Oslo): The city has its own fjord, which connects to the Lagen River. The beautiful lake country we mentioned begins immediately beyond its city limits. An interesting museum is housed in Herregarden, a seventeenth-century manor house built for the counts of Larvik. The building is one of Norway's best preserved wooden structures. A world-famous mineral water, Farris, originates here. Many of the small fishing harbors along the coast are accessible by bus. For ferry service from Larvik to Frederikshavn and Skagen, Denmark, call (625) 810 00 811.

The Larvik District has published an interesting booklet describing the tourist attractions of the area. If you are interested in obtaining a copy prior to your visit to the area, you may write to:

The Tourist Office
Storgata, 48
Box 200, 3251 Larvik
Norway

Otherwise, when in Larvik call at the tourist office at Storgata. 48, across from the rail station.

Skien (193 km from Oslo): Situated where the Skien River and Lake Hjelle meet, this city has been an active trading center since 900 A.D. Sawmills were an important part of its industry. The first began here in the sixteenth century. Skien is the birthplace of Henrik Ibsen (1828-1906), famous Norwegian playwright. Ibsen's well-constructed plays dealing realistically with psychological and social problems won him recognition as the father of modern drama.

Brekke Park, which looks out over the river and town of Skien, warrants a visit. There you will find the Museum of Telemark and Grenland. (Skien is the administrative center for the District of Telemark.) In the park there are a number of old houses from different parts of the district, including a reconstruction of Ibsen's childhood home in Oslo with his study, drawing room, and

A Day Excursion from Oslo (Senter Station)

DEPART OSLO SENTRAL STATION	TRAIN NUMBER	ARRIVE IN LARVIK STATION	NOTES
0909	IC 807	1118	(1)(2)(3)
1109	IC 811	1318	(1)(2)(3)

DEPART OSLO SENTRAL STATION	TRAIN NUMBER	ARRIVE IN SKIEN STATION	NOTES
0909	IC 807	1206	(1)(2)(3)
1109	IC 811	1404	(1)(2)(3)

DEPART SKIEN STATION	TRAIN NUMBER	ARRIVE IN OSLO SENTRAL STATION	NOTES
1540	IC 828	1851	(1)(2)(3)
1748	IC 832	2051	(1)(2)(3)
1953	IC 838	2250	(1)(2)(3)

DEPART LARVIK STATION	TRAIN NUMBER	ARRIVE IN OSLO SENTRAL STATION	NOTES
1628	IC 828	1851	(1)(2)(3)
1840	IC 832	2051	(1)(2)(3)
2042	IC 838	2250	(1)(2)(3)

TO OSLO VIA NORDAGUTU (CIRCUITOUS ROUTE):
Train number IC 815 departs Larvik 1522, arrives Skien 1612. Train number 584 departs Skien 1833, arrives Nordagutu 1906. Train number 702 departs Nordagutu 1934, arrives Oslo Sentral 2139.

(1) Daily, including holidays   (3) Light refreshments
(2) One class only

Distance: 120 miles/193 km (to Skien)

---

bedroom. Vensdöp is also worth visiting.

Rather than return to Oslo by retracing your route back through Larvik and the other coastal towns, you might want to return to Oslo via the main rail line running from Stavanger on the North Sea. Board train 582 that departs from Skien at 1638 to Nordagutu, where you'll arrive at 1633. Look around Nordagutu, then board the train at 1934 bound for Oslo. You will arrive in the Oslo Sentral Station promptly at 2139.

A Day Excursion to

Lillehammer   NORWAY'S VACATION CENTER

Depart From Oslo Sentral Station

Distance By Train: 114 miles (184 km)
Average Train Time: 2 hours, 35 minutes
City Dialing Code: No dialing code required.
Tourist Information Office: 19 Elvegata,
Tel: 61 25 92. 99; *Fax* 61 25 65 85.
Hours: Summer: 0900-1900 Monday-Saturday; 1100-1600 Sunday. The office remains
open a few extra hours during late June, July, and early August. The remainder of the
year, the office is open 0900-1700 Monday-Friday; 1000-1400 Saturday.
  The office is only about a five-minute walk from the rail station. Just follow the
signs.

This day excursion is one of the most northerly of any appearing in *Europe
by Eurail.* In Lillehammer you will have a sense of really entering the northern reaches of Europe.

Despite its northern latitude, Lillehammer is a famous summer resort.
Thanks to its latitude, it is an important winter-sports center as well. Snow
conditions for skiing are good from December until April, and the long summer evenings are perfect for enjoying the town's beautiful parks and recreation
areas.

If you have succumbed to the charm of Hamar, then you have already been
introduced to the beauty of its Lake Mjosa. The train ride to Lillehammer will
permit you to see the balance of the lake because Lillehammer lies 35 miles to
the north of Hamar. Here, Lake Mjosa narrows to the Lagen River and, in
doing so, provides a scenic blend of green forestlands and the special green
color of the river. If you have ever wondered what most of the world was like
before pollution, here is your answer.

Lillehammer served as the site for the 1994 Olympic Winter Games. The ski
jumps tower, with a view of the entire town, is open 1000-2000 in the summer.

Among the city's attractions, the **Museum of Historical Vehicles** opens
at 1000 daily. Just north of Lillehammer you may visit **Lilleputhammer,** a
scale model town of 62 miniature houses, where kids can romp at
Hunderfossen Family Park. Ask the tourist office for details.

The city's stellar attraction is a one-hundred-acre open-air museum known
as **Maihaugen.** It is within easy walking distance of the tourist information
office. The office can provide you with a city map as well as several brochures
describing the Maihaugen Museum. The museum area is divided into three
sections. Each depicts a different mode of Norwegian life. Its origins spring

from the private collection of a dentist, Dr. Anders Sandvig. As a young dentist just out of school, Dr. Sandvig came to Lillehammer in 1885. He soon learned that many of his patients preferred to pay him in kind. Sometimes it was a farm implement or a piece of furniture. Dr. Sandvig's practice grew, and so did his collection. Eventually, he laid out the museum area and began filling it with old buildings, which he acquired and transported to Lillehammer. Apparently, the museum business was more rewarding than dentistry, for Dr. Sandvig retired from the profession to run the museum personally, which he did until 1946 when he died at the age of eighty-four.

The museum was founded in 1887. There are more than one hundred old buildings in the museum. In the handicrafts section are sixty workshops demonstrating skills of the local craftsmen. The museum is open daily 1100–1600, remaining open an extra hour in May and September. From June–August, the peak season, it is open 0900-1900. One of the most interesting objects of Norway's past on exhibit in the museum is the **Garmo Stave Church,** which was built in the Ottadal Valley area in the 11th century and reassembled at the museum in 1920. Another interesting exhibit is "Slowly We Conquered Our Country," Norwegian history from the Ice Age until tomorrow.

In the dock area of the city from mid-June to mid-August, you can see the *Skibladner*, a paddle-wheel steamer launched in 1856 and still in service today. Its nickname is "White Swan." True to tradition, salmon and strawberries are served on board. It is really difficult to accept the fact that the vessel is now more than 130 years old. It is in as good a condition now as the day it was launched. Some things do get better with age!

After visiting Lillehammer, if you would like to return to Oslo via a different route, board the bus to **Gjovik** in front of the railway station at 1550. You arrive in Gjovik at 1650. Board the train for Oslo that departs at 1934. This train returns to Oslo by a different route and arrives in the Oslo Sentral station at 2127. The train service is one-class only, but it's always clean and neat.

The bus fare from Lillehammer to Gjovik is 73 kroner. You will have time to do some fast sightseeing in this charming little town on the west shore of Lake Mjosa before departing on the 1934 train to Oslo.

Oslo–Lillehammer

DEPART OLSO SENTRAL STATION	TRAIN NUMBER	ARRIVE IN LILLEHAMMER STATION	NOTES
0805	ET 41	1021	(1)(2)(4)
0900	IC 313	1135	(1)(3)(4)
1035	401	1313	(1)(2)(3)

DEPART LILLEHAMMER STATION	TRAIN NUMBER	ARRIVE IN OSLO SENTRAL STATION	NOTES
1419	IC 318	1656	(1)(2)(3)(4)
1620	IC 320	1855	(1)(3)(4)
1821	404	2056	(1)(3)(4)
2011	ET 44	2225	(1)(2)(4)

(1) Daily, including holidays
(2) Seat reservations mandatory
(3) Second class only
(4) Food service available

Distance: 114 miles/184 km

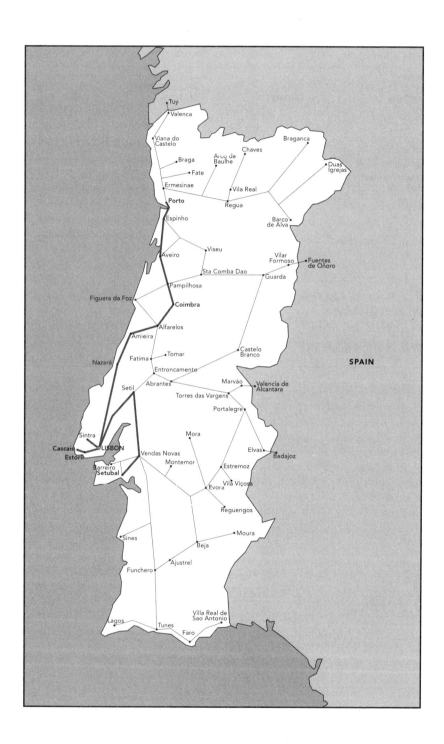

SPAIN

Tuy
Valenca
Viana do
Castelo
Braga
Fate
Ermesinae
Porto
Espinho
Arco de
Baulhe
Chaves
Braganca
Duas
Igrejas
Vila Real
Regua
Barco
de Alva
Aveiro
Viseu
Vilar
Formoso
Fuentes
de Oñoro
Sta Comba Dao
Guarda
Pampilhosa
Figuera da Foz
Coimbra
Alfarelos
Amieira
Nazaré
Fatima
Tomar
Castelo
Branco
Entroncamento
Setil
Abrantes
Marváo
Valencia de
Alcantara
Torres das Vargens
Portalegre
Mora
Sintra
Cascais
Estoril
LISBON
Vendas Novas
Montemor
Elvas
Badajoz
Barreiro
Setubal
Estremoz
Evora
Vila Viçosa
Reguengos
Sines
Moura
Beja
Funchero
Ajustrel
Lagos
Tunes
Faro
Villa Real de
Sao Antonio

Portugal

Portugal is gearing up for hosting the last World Exposition of this century—Expo '98—in Lisbon from May 22 to September 30, 1998, and some 15 million visitors are expected. The theme, "The Oceans and the Seas," serves the dual purposes of being educational yet entertaining. Old castles and monasteries are being renovated and the government has opened additional historic pousadas (inns). In line with the Portuguese Manor House Program, owners of elegant old mansions are also opening up their homes to visitors.

Visitors to Portugal will find the old world traditions, charm, and culture well preserved. Each province retains its own heritage and individual characteristics and its history can be traced through its medieval cities and ancient palaces, castles, and cathedrals.

Being an independent kingdom since 1143, Portugal is one of the oldest nations in Europe. In fact, 10,000-year-old cave paintings have been uncovered in the northern reaches of Portugal and are said to be Europe's greatest outdoor gallery of Stone Age art. Portuguese museums contain some of the finest collections in the world, reflecting the Portuguese exposure to rich cultures explored by courageous Portuguese navigators of the fifteenth and sixteenth centuries.

But Portugal is more than antiquity. Its geography is diverse, making it a popular holiday destination for travelers from all over the world. You will find wonderful white-sand beaches, crystal clear mountain streams, and some of the finest golf courses in all of Europe. You'll even find fun and games at glamorous casinos and discos.

Portuguese is the national language, with English and French being the second languages. Though some words are similar to the Spanish language, Portuguese is its own language, and not a Spanish dialect. According to the Portuguese National Tourist Office, Portugal is "a vision for the future." For more information about Portugal, contact the Portuguese National Tourist Office of North America:

New York: 590 Fifth Avenue, 4th Floor, New York, NY 10036. Tel: (212) 354-4403 or (212)354-4704; Fax: (212)764-6137

Montreal: 500 Sherbrooke Street West, Suite 940, Montreal QC H3A 3C6; Tel: (514) 282-1264; Fax: (514) 499-1450

Toronto: 60 Bloor Street, Suite 1005, Toronto, Ontario M4W 3B8. Tel: (416) 921-7376; Fax: (416) 921-1353

Internet: http://www.portugal.org

Currency

The escudo (abbreviated Esc. or PTE) and centavos are the divisions of Portuguese currency. '$' is used as a decimal point (2$50 means 2 escudos and 50 centavos)
* 1000 Esc is usually referred to as 1 conto
* Coins available are: 1, 1$50, 5, 20, 50, 100, 250 Esc
* Banknotes: 500, 1,000, 2,000, 5,000, 10,000 PTEEsc

Banking

Commercial banks and their branches are available throughout the country and hours are generally from 0830-1500. Banks are also at airports. Exchange facilities are also at airports, hotels, and camping grounds.
Charge: 600 PTE
Automatic Teller Machines with displays in English are available throughout the country. The fee is about 300 Esc.
Exchange rate at press time: 181.04 escudos = $1.00 U.S.

Communications

* **Country Code:** 351
Portugal Telecom operates the public telephones, including pay, Credifone and TLP Card telephones. 10, 20, 50, or 100 Esc are used in pay telephones.
Use 00 before the country code to dial internationally from Portugal.

Rail Travel In Portugal

Portugal's rail system, **Caminhos de Ferro Portugueses** (CP) offers rail information by telephone. CP Information: (Tel: 01 888 4025), available 0800-2300 For Alfa and Intercity Lines: (Tel: 01 888-5092), available 0800-2300 or (Tel: 01 790 1004), 24 hours
The CP accepts **Eurailpass, Europass** and the **Portuguese Rail Pass.**
The **Portuguese Rail Pass** is available for First Class only and valid for any

4 days of rail travel within a 15-day period. It is not, however, valid for travel on the *Luis de Cameos* train. Adults: $99; children ages 4–11 are half fare.

Interregional trains commute through the various regions of Portugal, while CP's **Intercity** service links about 60 Portuguese cities to Lisbon or Porto. The express **Alfa** service connects Lisbon, Porto and Braga with four trains in each direction conveying both first and second class service.

Two other international train connections are available between Porto and Vigo (Spain) and between Lisbon and Badajoz (Spain).

Base City...

Lisbon (Lisboa)
City Dialing Code: 1

Lisbon, Portugal's largest city, is the capital and primary gateway for visitors from North America. It's also the center of the country's rail network and the major industrial and commercial area.

Host of the last World Exposition of the twentieth century, Lisbon is expecting an influx of tourist during the summer of 1998. EXPO'98, themed, "The Oceans, a Heritage for the Future," also marks the 500th anniversary of Portuguese explorer Vasco da Gama's pioneering voyage to India at the end of the fifteenth century. For more information about EXPO'98, visit the website http://www.expo.98.pt.

Built on the terraced sides of the hills overlooking the harbor, lanquid Lisbon is an excellent gateway to the Iberian peninsula and base for rail travel thought Portugal.

Arriving by Air

Lisbon International Airport, Portella, 5 miles north of Lisbon. (Tel: 8416990).

Airport-City Links: Passengers connect to Lisbon's Cais Sodre railway station via the shuttle Aerobus 91. Fare 430 escudos (1-day ticket).

Taxi fare from the airport to the city center averages about 1,200-2,000 escudos, depending on your destination and how much luggage you have. Taxis are metered; a tip is appreciated.

Tourist information at the airport, Tel: 849 43 23; Fax: 848 59 74.

Arriving by Train

Lisbon has four stations and a ferry boat terminal and is the main gateway to other cities in Portugal. **Santa Apolonia** station is Lisbon's international link and the western terminus of most European rail traffic. However, you can also arrive in Lisbon at the "Terreiro do Paço" south railway station, with the train departing from Vila Real St. Antónia to Barreiro (and then the ferry connection) if you come from Seville (Spain).

• **Money exchange:** left side as you exit from the trains, beyond Porta (Gate) 47.

- **Rail Information (CP) and Tourist Information:** Turn to the right as you exit from the trains and walk past ticket window No. 1. Hours: 0900-2200.
- **Rail Pass Validation:** Porta (Gate) 47. Hours 1000-1800 daily. Buses No. 9, 39, and 46 run from Santa Apolónia Station to the **Rossio** Station in downtown Lisbon. The fare may be minimal, but buses frequently are crowded, making it rather difficult for you and your suitcase to board the same bus at the same time. Because taxi fares are reasonable and metered, leave your forays on Lisbon's public transportation system for when your luggage is safely stowed in your hotel room.
- **Rossio Station,** at Praca do Rossio (Rossio Square), is located in the heart of Lisbon in a lovely nineteenth century neo-Gothic building. It is on the immediate left of the Teatro Nacional D. Maria II (National Theater). Rossio station serves as the commuter station to locations west of Lisbon (from Cacem Station to Figueira da Foz). Trains depart for Sintra on tracks number 4 & 5 every 16 minutes.
- **Campolide Station,** the first station past Rossio, is the stop for the Alcantara commuter to Cascais; or for travel to Azambuja.
- **Cais do Sodre Station** is where trains from Estoril and Cascais terminate.
- **Terreiro do Paco Station** is the ferryboat terminal for crossings to Barreiro Station on the east bank of the Tagus River. From Barreiro trains depart for cities in the Algarve.

Lisbon Tourist Information/Hotel Reservations

Available in rail stations, at Praca dos Restauradores in the Palacio Foz building. (Tel: 3466307; Hours: 0900-2000 daily; or at the Lisbon Card office, Rua Jardim do Regedor, 50. (Tel: 3433672; Hours: 0900-1800)

To reach it, take a taxi or bus No. 9, 46, or 39 to Praca dos Restauradores. It is opposite the post office, near Rossio Station. The building, Palacio Fox (Foz Palace) has three main doors. Enter the one on the left marked TURISMO.

Hotel reservations can be made at the rail stations' combined train and tourist information offices.

Getting Around in Lisbon

Electric, cable-car-like trams provide inexpensive and enjoyable transport to many parts of the city. Historic Belem, for instance, can be reached via Tram #15—an alternative to taking the train from Cais do Sodre station

Of super value is the **Lisboa Card,** which provides unlimited travel on the public transportation system (CARRIS) including buses, trams, and the metro (underground) system (except for trams No. 15 and 28 and the Santa Justa lift); free entry to 26 museums, monuments, and other attractions which normally charge admission; and discounts at certain shops.

The Lisboa Card is available at the Central Office, Rua Jardim do Regedor, 50; at Jeronimos Monastery, Praca do Imperio; and at the National Museum of Ancient Art, Rua das Janelas Verdes.

1-Day Lisboa Card, 1,500 escudos; 2-Day, 2,500 escudos; 3-Day, 3,250 escudos; children ages 5-11 pay 600, 900 and 1,250 escudos, respectively.

Sightseeing/Attractions/Tours

Tourist offices or your hotel can arrange for a sightseeing tour of Lisbon. Highlights of any tour will include the sixteenth century **Jerónimos Monastery** and the **Tower of Belém** in the Belém district. Lisbon's more modern side can be seen by visiting the **Discoveries Monument** (Centro Cultural das Descobertas), inaugurated in 1960. Another symbol of Lisbon is the **25 de April bridge** spanning the Tagus River, which is equal to the Golden Gate Bridge of San Fransisco in its structural beauty.

Planned for completion in time for Expo '98, Lisbon's **Vasco da Gama bridge** is a massive engineering feat. The bridge is 18 kilometers long—making it the longest bridge in Europe—one kilometer longer than the one under construction between Sweden and Denmark. Besides providing another modern symbol of Lisbon, it will also provide much needed relief of traffic congestion crossing the Tagus River, especially during the summers.

Lisbon has three distinct districts—the shopping areas clustered around Rossio, **Baixa and Chiado;** the more ancient areas such as the Moorish quarter **Alfama and Castelo;** and the "new Lisbon" with post-modern high-rise structures, **Amoreiras,** stretching out to the airport and to the north. A day can easily be spent in any one of its districts.

Of particular interest to western visitors is the Alfama district, which suffered the least damage during the earthquake and has thereby been able to preserve much of its old facade and narrow, winding cobblestone streets. **St. George's Castle** offers a splendid view of the city. The tourist office has several excellent illustrated brochures describing Lisbon, one of which lists walking tours "From the Castle to Alfama via Mouraria," where examples of Moorish and medieval architecture prevail. A city map is also available.

Spend at least one evening in Lisbon's famous nightlife district—**Bairro Alto.** It can be reached via the Elevador da Gloria, which operates from the west side of the Praca dos Restauradores at Calcada da Gloria. Dine in a typical Portuguese restaurant/music bar called "Fado houses" and listen to **"Fado"** (meaning "fate")—the plaintive, nostalgic, dramatic music of the fadista (Fado singer) that is unique to the Portuguese. Lisbon has its own type of Fado, which is considered to be more emotional than that performed elsewhere.

Such Fado establishments are abundant in Lisbon, particularly in the Alfama and Bairro Alto districts. One of our favorites is **Farcado Restaurant** at Rua da Rosa, No. 219. Phone ahead for reservations: (Tel: 3468579)

Day Excursions

Cascais and **Estoril,** resort towns along the beautiful beaches of Costa do Estoril, are frequented by celebrities, royalty, and just plain folk. **Coimbra** reveals Portugal's academic nature. This fine old university town was at one time the capital of Portugal. **Setubal** is a city of beautiful beaches, hillside castles, and excellent seafood. Castle buffs and romantics will enjoy **Sintra,** with its ancient castles and nearby Cape Roca, the westernmost point of Europe.

Train Connections to Other Base Cities from Lisbon

TO:	DEPART	ARRIVE	TRAIN NUMBER	NOTES
Madrid				
(sleeper)	2200	0835+1	335	(1)(2)
Paris★				
(couchettes)	1703	1500+1	311/310	(1)(2)(3)

★ No day trains. Distance is 1,173 miles/1,887 km

(1) Daily, including holidays
(2) Seat reservations mandatory
(3) Transfer in Hendaye (French border) to TGV 8530 (departs Hendaye 0937)

Day Excursion to

Cascais and Estroil   Lisbon's Riviera

Depart from Lisbon Cais do Sodre Station

Distance by Train: 16 miles (26 km)
Average Train Time: 30 minutes
Costa do Estoril Tourist Information Office, Arcadas do Parque, 2765 Estoril
Hours: 0900-2000
Tel: 466 38 13; *Fax* 467 22 80
> Tourist office is near the rail station. Use the underpass from the ocean side (the trains run on the left) to the city side.

Portugal boasts miles and miles of sun-drenched, white-sand beaches. Probably the most famous stretch lies just to the west of Lisbon along the Costa do Estoril. Here the two resort towns of Cascais and Estoril offer a wide variety of scenes to suit everyone's tastes.

We recommend you make **Estoril** your first stop on your visit to this coastal area because Estoril is two stops before Cascais, which is the end of the rail line. Estoril has long been famous as a chic resort for royalty and a playground for the rich and famous. Besides the beautiful white-sand beach with its excellent facilities, the beautifully landscaped **Casino complex** of gaming rooms, restaurants, bars and movie theater is a major attraction. But, new, moderately priced hotels now make Estoril a major attraction for everyone.

Those who are sports minded can enjoy championship 18-hole golf courses which offer temporary memberships. **The Estoril Golf Course,** with its splendid seascape, has been home to the Portuguese Open. Tennis, horse-back riding, and sailing are also available.

Cascais, which is only 4 minutes beyond Estoril, maintains a slightly lower key atmosphere than its chic neighbor. Its beaches are smaller, but more intimate. Reflecting the traditions of its fishing village past, Cascais's Wednesday morning market is well worth the trip from Lisbon. Locals in their traditional garb hawk everything imaginable. Farmers' wives, suspicious of supermarket packaging, can be seen scrutinizing their chickens while they are still alive and squawking loudly.

To reach the marketplace, bear to the right around the plaza in front of the rail station and continue to the right onto Avenue 25 de April. Two short blocks farther and you will see the market—probably hear it, too. Bring your own market basket.

On Sundays during the summer, locals and visitors alike flock to the **Monumental de Cascais,** the bull ring. Bullfights in Portugal are different from those in Spain in that the bull is not killed but take by the horns (literally) and forced to a standstill. The proceedings often end more on a comic note rather than the tragic end of a Spanish bullfight.

Some Eurail travelers base themselves in a local resort hotel in or near Cascais or Estoril, and then make day excursions into Lisbon for sightseeing or for continuing on with other day excursions. The fast and frequent rail service and the abundance of hotels to fit any budget, makes this concept a feasible one.

Trains depart every 20 minutes from Lisbon's Cais do Sodre Station, and trains run to Estoril in twenty-nine mintutes. Cascais is three minutes beyond Estoril. All trains are one class only.

Distance: 16 miles/26 km

Day Excursion to
Coimbra   University Town

Depart from Lisbon Santa Apolonia Station

Distance by Train: 135 miles (218 km)
Average Train Time: 2 hours
Coimbra Tourist Information Office, Largo da Portagem
Tel: 39 33019 or 33028; *Fax:* 39 25576
Hours: Monday-Friday 0900-1900; Saturday-Sunday 1400-1730
    Trains from Lisbon stop at the Coimbra B. Station, a short distance north of the city center. Either take a taxi to Largo da Portagem or take a shuttle train into the main station. The tourist board is at the approach to the great bridge spanning the Mondego River. If you take the shuttle to the main station, walk four blocks away from the station, upstream along the river, until you come to the bridge approach.

Coimbra is one of Portugal's most charming cities, uniquely blending the old and the new. Site of the oldest university in Portugal, its ancient buildings seem to blend perfectly with the modern spirit of its students. Founded in 1290 in Lisbon, the university was transferred to its present site in 1537 to compensate for moving Portugal's capital from Coimbra to Lisbon.

Coimbra University sits on a hilltop overlooking the river. In keeping with tradition, many students wear black suits and capes, marked with ribbons in tones that denote their scholarship.

There is an air of antiquity surrounding Coimbra. It is the scene of the largest Roman archaeological site in Portugal. Coimbra's cathedral is said to be the finest Romanesque building in Portugal. Gothic tombs and art collec-

Lisbon–Combria

DEPART SANTA APOLONIA* STATION	TRAIN NUMBER	ARRIVE IN COIMBRA B. STATION	NOTES
0722	IC 531	0942	(1)(2)(3)
0800	IC 531	1007	(1)(2)(3)
0806	IR 811	1027	(1)(3)(4)
0905	IR 823	1141	(1)(3)(4)
1100	IC 521	1307	(1)(2)(3)
1205	IR 825	1441	(1)(3)

DEPART COIMBRA B. STATION	TRAIN NUMBER	ARRIVE IN SANTA APOLONIA* STATION	NOTES
1526	Alfa 122	1730	(1)(2)(3)
1706	IC 512	1925	(1)(2)(3)
1826	Alfa 124	2030	(1)(2)(3)
1855	IR 810	2130	(1)(3)(4)
2125	IC 532	2330	(1)(2)(3)

* Take shuttle train to main station.

(1) Daily, including holidays
(2) Seat reservations required
(3) Food service available
(4) Seat reservations recommended

Distance: 135 miles/218 km

---

tion are housed in this twelfth century monument.

An unusual attraction for "children" of all ages is the **Portugal dos Pequeninos** (Portugal of the Little Ones), in which you will find a miniaturized version of architectural styles of continental Portugal, Coimbra, Portuguese monuments, insular Portugal, and its overseas territories. .

In the city center, you can visit the **monastery of the Holy Cross, Santa Cruz,** constructed in the twelfth century. Later additions include a charming Renaissance sacristy and a magnificently carved facade. A pictorial record of the explorer Vasco da Gama's voyages adorns the choir loft.

Day Excursion to

Setubal

SEASIDE AND CASTLES

Depart from Lisbon Terreiro do Paco ferry terminal & Barreiro Station

Distance by Train: 18 miles (29 km)
Average Train Time: 35 minutes
Tourist Information Offices: Regiao de Turismo de Setubal, Travessa Frei Gaspar, 10, 2900 Setubal. *Tel:* 65 524 284; 65 552 70 33 or 65 529 789; *Fax:* 65 36745
Hours: 0900-1230/1400-1900 Monday & Saturday; 0900-1900 Tuesday-Friday; 0900-1230 Sunday.
Town Hall Tourist Information, Praca do Bocage, (534 222)
Hours: 0900-1230/1400-1730 Monday-Friday.

Take a taxi from the station to the regional tourist office (Regiao de Turismo de Setubal) or to the tourist office in the Town Hall, located across from the park, Praca do Quebedo.

A day excursion to **Setubal** begins at Lisbon's Terreiro do Paco ferry terminal and a 25-minute ferryboat ride across the Tagus River to Barreiro Station where you board a southbound train to Setubal. At press time, plans are for trains to cross the Tagus River on the "25 de April" bridge after Lisbon's new **Vasco da Gama bridge** opens for Expo '98 (in May 1998).

Although Setubal is Portugal's third largest city, its location on the estuary of the Sado River provides a more restful, rural-type atmosphere. It can best be enjoyed from **Saint Philip's Castle** which overlooks Setubal from its highest point. The sixteenth century castle was converted into a pousada (inn, or resting place) and it commands an impressive view of both land and sea. A local taxi can take you there. It's a perfect spot for a lunch in its fine restaurant or an overnight stay.

Setubal has a remarkable assemblage of monuments and fine old buildings. The **Church of Jesus** is said to be one of the most beautiful small churches ever built. Next door, the Town Museum displays a priceless collection of old masters. There is also a Maritime Museum and the Bocage Monument, which honors the city's great poet.

About 5 or 6 miles from Setubal at the nearby seaport Sesimbra, the **Pousada do Castelo de Palmela** (Palmela Castle) offers a fantastic view of the surrounding countryside from high atop a hillside. Again, the best way to get there is via taxi.

Lisbon–Setubal

DEPART LISBON TERREIRO DO PACO FERRY TERMINAL	ABOARD	ARRIVE IN BARREIRO STATION	NOTES
0725	Ferry	0755	(1)
0755	Ferry	0825	(1)

DEPAR BARREIRO STATION	ABOARD	ARRIVE IN SETUBAL STATION	NOTES
0835	IR 871	0903	(1)(2)
1635	3801	1707	(1)(2)

DEPART SETUBAL STATION	ABOARD	ARRIVE IN BARREIRO STATION	NOTES
2123	IR 872	2245	(1)(2)
2206	IC 570	2229	(1)(2)

DEPART BARREIRO STATION	ABOARD	ARRIVE IN LISBON TERREIRO DO PACO FERRY STATION	NOTES
1748	IC 582	1830	(1)
2153	IR 872	2245	(1)
2229	IC 570	2315	(1)

(1) Daily, including holidays
(2) Second class only

Distance: 18 miles/29 km (from Barreiro)

Day Excursion to
Sintra
MOUNTAIN PEAKS AND PALACES

Depart from Lisbon Rossio Station

Distance by Train: 17 miles (28 km)
Average Train Time: 45 minutes
Tourist Information Office, Praca da Republica
Tel: 923 11 57 or 924 17 0
Hours: open daily (except Easter and Christmas) 0900-1900; June–September 0900-2000.

The main tourist office is about 1 kilometer from the rail station. Reach it by taxi or by boarding the bus marked S. PEDRO, which leaves from near the station (at Correnteza). The bus stops a short distance from the National Palace of Sintra and the main tourist office. On foot, it is an interesting 15-minute walk.

Sintra is the former home of Portuguese kings with its ancient castles and palaces towering above the countryside. It is surrounded by mountains and close by **Cape Roca,** the westernmost point of continental Europe "where the land ends and the sea begins." This is the place Lord Byron termed, "a glorious Eden," and it's all only 45 minutes from Lisbon by train.

There is no public transportation to most of the places of tourist interest. Taxis and horse-drawn carriages take you there. Since the taxis do not have meters, the fare usually includes up to four passengers plus a fixed amount of time for you to complete your sightseeing. You should also ask the tourist office about the half-day tour, which includes **Pena Palace,** the **Convent of Capuchos** (the Cork Convent), **Cape Roca,** and the **Gardens of Monserrate.**

Of all the sights in the area, you'll probably want to visit the exquisite **National Palace of Sintra** (Palacio Real) first. It is closed on Wednesdays and there are no guides. There is a nominal admission charge to the palace grounds.

Pena Palace's commanding position from the highest peak in the area makes it well worth the visit. It is closed on Mondays.

The **Queluz Palace** captures the style of Versailles, but on a smaller scale. It houses a gourmet restaurant in its former kitchen area. This palace is closed on Tuesdays.

Lisbon–Sintra

Frequent suburban trains run between Lisbon's Rossio Station and Sintra. The journey takes forty-five minutes.

All trains are one class only. Trains for Sintra depart approximately every fifteen minutes. Ride the train to the end of the line.

Distance: 17 miles / 28 km

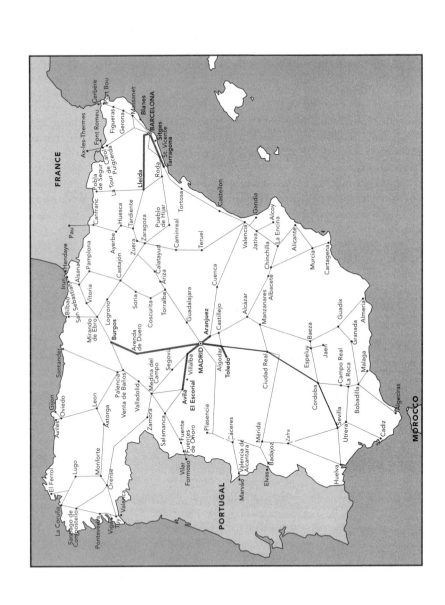

Spain

Spain is a delightful dichotomy—futuristic in many ways yet respectful of its rich history and tradition.

From the *delicato* music of Flamenco to swashbuckling matadors, Spain's culture and tradition is as widely varied as its geography. Flamenco is a genuine Southern Spanish art form influenced by diverse cultures throughout Spain's history, including the Gypsies, the legendary Tartessos, and the Muslims.

Spain shares the Iberian Peninsula with its neighbor to the west, Portugal. France and the tiny country of Andorra lie to the north. The Castilian Spanish is spoken throughout Spain, but Catalan, Valencian, Basque, and Galician Spanish are still spoken in their respective autonomous regions.

One social custom that visitors will notice immediately is that Spaniards get up later in the morning and usually stay out later at night than other Europeans. If you want to dance until dawn, you're visiting the right country. The night life in Spain is intensely zealous with bars and discotheques remaining open until the wee hours of the morning, especially in the larger more cosmopolitan cities of Barcelona and Madrid.

Arriving from North America, our Base City Madrid is the primary gateway with Barcelona being second. During summer, however, there are some direct flights to Malaga on the Mediterranean Sea.

For more information about Spain, contact the Tourist Offices of Spain in North America:

Toll-free Tel: (888) OK SPAIN.

Internet: http://www.okspain.org

Chicago: 845 North Michigan Avenue, Suite 915 East, Water Tower Place, Chicago, IL 60611. Tel: (312) 642-1992; Fax: (312) 642-9817

Los Angeles: San Vicente Plaza Building, 8383 Wilshire Boulevard, Suite 960, Beverly Hills, CA 90211. Tel: (213) 658-7188; Fax: (213) 658-1061

New York: 666 Fifth Avenue, 35th Floor, New York, NY 10103. Tel: (212) 265-8822; Fax: (212)265-8864

Toronto: 2 Bloor Street West, 34th Floor, Toronto, Ontario M4W 3E2. Tel: (416) 961-3131; Fax: (416) 961-1992

Miami: 1221 Brickell Avenue, Miami, FL 33131 Tel: (315) 358-1992; Fax: (315) 358-8223.

Banking

- **Currency:** Spanish Pesetas
- **Exchange rate at press time:** 158 pesetas = $1.00 U.S.
- **Hours:** Open Monday-Friday 0900-1400, with some open Saturday 0900-1430.

Credit and ATM transfers at machines are the best exchange rate, since no commission is charged.

Communications

- **Country Code: 34**
- **Direct Dial:** AT&T: 900 99 00 11; MCI: 900 99 00 14; Sprint: 900 99 00 1

Public telephones are available most everywhere in Spain; they offer instructions in English and may be used to call most parts of the world. Use primarily 25 and 100 peseta coins. Some phones are equipped to take credit cards. Since calling from Spain to America is about 10 times more expensive than calling from America to Spain, it is advisable to access your American Calling Card Connection.

When in Spain, dial 07 to telephone outside of Spain. When calling Spain from abroad, include Spain's country code. It is then necessary to dial the provincial codes for each province. If calling within Spain, you must dial 9 before the provincial code.

Some provincial codes are: Alicante: 6; Avila 18; Barcelona 3; Burgos 47; Cordoba 57; Madrid 1; Malaga 5; Seville 5; Toledo 25; and Valencia 6.

Rail Travel in Spain

With **RENFE** (Red Nacional de los Ferrocarriles Espanoles, or Spanish National Railways), the trains in Spain run mainly on time—98 percent on time. RENFE accepts **Eurailpass, Europass,** and **Spain Flexipass,** but it deviates from the basic rail pass concept in that certain trains such as Trens Hotel, AVE ("Alta Velocidad Espanola," or Spanish High Speed) trains, and Talgos operating on high-speed lines are *not* included, but rail pass holders do receive substantial discounts. (Please see the Appendix for Eurail and Europass types and costs.) Special sightseeing/tour trains such as *Al Andalus* and the narrow-gauge *FEVE* are not included on the rail passes either, but may be purchased separately.

The Eurailpass bonus for Spain includes a 20 percent discount on the Transmediterranea Line ships between Barcelona—Palma de Mallorca and Valencia —Palma de Mallorca.

The Spain Flexipass may be purchased for a minimum of 3 days of unlimited rail travel in Spain within a one-month period.

Spain Flexipass

	1ST CLASS	2ND CLASS
3 Days in 1 Month	$ 180	$ 144
Additional Days	$ 40	$ 32
Children ages 4-11 travel half price.		

Not to be outdone by French high-speed TGVs and Germany's ICEs, RENFE's sleek **AVEs** are derivations of the French TGV ("*Train a Grand Vitesse*," or Train of Great Speed) *Atlantique*. Dynamic RENFE has been "on the move" since the first AVEs cruised into service as the main rail link between Madrid and Seville due to the opening of the International Exposition of Seville—Expo 1992. Via AVE, the Madrid-Seville trip can be done in just under 3 hours.

Reservations for AVE trains are required. Choose Turista, Preferente, or Club class. All three classes include television sets with individual ear phones and four music channels, family areas with games for kids, facilities for the disabled, telephones, cafeteria, and a beverage machine. Club and Preferente classes also include access to AVE club lounges, newspapers, and magazines. In-seat food/beverage service is provided only in Club Class.

For AVE telephone information in
  Madrid: Tel: (91) 534 05 05
  Córdoba: Tel: (957) 49 02 02
  Ciudad Real: Tel: (926) 22 02 02
  Puertollano: Tel: (926) 41 02 02
  Seville: Tel: (95) 454 02 02

Ultra modern Talgo 200 trains link Madrid and Malaga in a little more than 4 hours. These gauge-changing high speed trains also have significantly reduced the travel time between Madrid and Cadiz/Huelva.

The attractive blue and white **Euromed** (*Velocidad Alta Mediterranea* or Mediterranean High Speed) trains debuted June 1997 and provide services to **Alicante, Valencia, Castellon, Tarragona,** and **Barcelona** with a cruising speed of 200 km/hour. These trains offer two classes of service—"Preferente" and "Turista."

Base City...

Barcelona

City Dialing Code: 3

Barcelona as it is formed today, the **New Barcelona,** was created only in 1874 by joining 27 separate municipalities. It has become Spain's most prosperous port and has developed a thriving industrial complex as well. The center of this new metropolitan area is the **Placa de Catalunya,** a square rimmed with trees and highlighted by sculptures and fountains—and an abundance of pigeons. This square is where the old and the new Barcelona meet.

Founded in ancient times by the Phoenicians and occupied by the Romans, **Old Barcelona** is composed of three sections: Barcelona Antigua or Barrio Gotico (the Gothic Quarter), Ribera, and El Raval. A visit to the History Museum in Placa del Rei square provides insight to Barcelona's rich and ancient past .

Arriving by Air

Barcelona has one of the most modern international airports in Europe, having been improved immensely for the 1992 Olympic games. About eight miles from the city, transportation to and from is easily available and inexpensive.

Airport-City Links: Cercanias/Rodalie local Line #1 **trains** connect travelers to Barcelona Sants Station in 18 minutes, and depart every half-hour from the airport between 0612-2242. Trains depart from Track No. 3 in Sants Station every half-hour to the airport, 0542-2212.

Buses connect to the airport from the Placa de Cataluna every 15 minutes Monday.-Friday 0530-2205.; every 30 minutes Saturday, Sunday & holidays 0600-2220. Time en route is 15-20 minutes.

There are 3- and 5-day packages which include round trip airport bus service and unlimited travel on the buses and subway system.

Approximate **taxi** fare from the airport to city center is 2,000–3,000 pesetas.

Arriving by Train

The central Barcelona station **Estacio de Sants,** known as the Sants, at Placa Paisos Catalans, offers tourist information, currency exchange and storage lockers. Information: (Tel: 490 02 02); Station: (Tel: 322 41 42).

The Sants Station is the center of Barcelona's transportation system, including rail, metro (subway), air terminal, and bus service in one location. The entrance to the Barcelona metro system is to the right of the station's arrival-departure board, leading down from the station's ground level and marked with a capital M inside a diamond.

Seat reservations are mandatory on all express trains in Spain. Reservations may be made in Barcelona Sants at the ticket desk in the access area to tracks 9 through 12. If you are making reservations in advance, report to the reservation desk section marked "Venta Anticipada." For same-day departures, report to the section marked "Venta Immediata." This section handles reservations only for the current date. Since reservations may be made up to two months in advance of the departure date, it is sensible to make all of your reservations with one visit to the "Anticipada" section when possible. Waiting until the day of departure to get a seat reservation can be very time consuming.

Barcelona Sants has 12 track platforms running beneath the station's ground level that are accessible by escalators or elevators. Be certain to check the platform and track number on the departure board before descending to the train level.

- **Baggage storage:** Near track No. 12, open 0530-2300.
- **Hotel reservations** adjoin the Hertz facilities. Hours: Monday-Friday 0800–2200 and Sundays 0800–1400/1600–2200. Reservations can be made at this counter for a small fee.
- **Money-exchange** located in the center of the station at ground level. Hours: 0800–2200 daily. Official bank rates. ATM services across from track No. 11.
- **Sala Club Intercity,** RENFE's version of an airline-style passengers' lounge, is located in the center island between elevators for tracks 10 and 11. First-class tickets or rail passes are required for entrance. Free juice, coffee, soft drinks. Magazines and television are also available.
- **Train and Tourist Information/Hotel Reservations:** A combination facility in the southeast section of the station between the escalators for tracks 9–10 and 11–12. (Tel: 490 91); Hours: 0800–2000 Monday-Friday; 0800–1400 Saturdays and Sundays.
- The renovated **Estacion de Francia,** also called **Estacio Temino** is near the port at Avendida Marques de l'Argentera, and provides nearly all transport to and from France.
- Local RENFE (Spanish National Railroads) Information: (Tel:490 11 22)
- Regional RENFE Information: (Tel: 490 56 37)
- Catalan State Railways (FFCC), commuter trains information: (Tel: 205 15 15)

Barcelona Tourist Information/Hotel Reservations

Barcelona City Tourist Office, 99 La Rambla Tel: 301 77 75.
Office of Tourism for Catalunya, 658 Gran Via

Also, the Cassaques Vermelles, tourism officials in red coats, patrol the Rambles and Barri Gotic areas, providing maps and information to tourists in the summer.

Getting Around in Barcelona

The Barcelona Metro has four separate lines and runs Monday-Friday 0500-1300; Saturday-Sunday 0500-100. Stations are marked by signs with red diamonds, and tickets cost 125 pesetas.

Sights/Attractions/Tours

Ramble along La Rambla, one of Europe's most delightful areas originally engineered by nature. It began as an ancient path carved out by mountain streams rushing to the sea and is the best way of getting to know Barcelona. The plural form "Las Ramblas" is often used since this tree-lined boulevard is actually a collection of five different ramblas and two squares. It stretches 2 kilometers between the Placa de Catalunya and the port. It is the very pulse of Barcelona.

Rambla de Canalete, with its refreshing fountain, is a picturesque square surrounded by eating establishments and alive with people.

Rambla dels Estudis derives its name from the fact that it was at one time the site of a university and it is the present location of the Academia de Ciencies (Science Academy). It is also referred to as *Rambla dells Ocells* (birds) because of its animal market offering a variety of birds, fish, dogs, and other animals for sale. Here, you will also find the Poliorama Theatre, Capitol Cinema, Gothic and Baroque architecture, and the recently-restored **Moya Palace** which hosts visiting art collections.

Rambla de Sant Josep is the site of the busiest and probably the finest market in all of Barcelona—**La Boqueria** market located in the arcaded Placa Real with its huge iron and glass roof. Also known as Rambla de les Flors, the flower market and stalls selling vegetables, meats and fish produce aromatic scents and colorful sights, making this Rambla one of the most pleasant. **Placa de la Boqueria** is the square that once was the center of the city and contains an area paving designed by the famous painter Joan Miro.

The **Rambla de Caputxins** or **del Centre** is lined with stylish cafes and streetside bars such as La Opera or Los Italianos. It is also the location of **El Liceau,** Barcelona's opera house, a large impressive building which hosts

Train Connections to Other Base Cities from Barcelona

TO:	DEPART	ARRIVE	TRAIN NUMBER	NOTES
Berne	2015	0751+1	EN 273	(1)(2)
Madrid	0830(3)	1455	TAL 41	(2)
	1200(3)	1905	TAL 377	
	1500(2)	2205	TAL 379	(2)
	2300(3)	0800+1	875	(3)(4)
Milan	1920	1345+1	1142	(3)(5)(6)
	2015	0903+1	EN 371	(1)(2)
Paris (Austerlitz)	2100	0815+1	475	(2)
Rome	1920	1805+1	366	(3)(5)(6)
Zürich	2015	0915+1	EN 272	(7)

Daily departures unless otherwise noted. Make reservations for all departures. Reservations are mandatory in Spain.

(1) Talgo train, *Salvador Dali,* Gran Classe sleeper, supplement payable, Eurailpass or Europass *not* accepted
(2) Departs Barcelona França station
(3) Departs Barcelona Sants station
(4) For days of running check local schedule
(5) Couchettes only
(6) Transfer in Cerbère
(7) EuroNight Train—Special supplement for sleeping accommodations

---

concerts, ballet, plays and carnival festivities.

A convent once stood at the 150-year old **Placa Reial.** Today, it is home to many local artists, bars and pubs, shops, and the Herbolario del Rei (The Kings Herbalist), where "Los Tarantos" flamenco dancing is performed.

Placa del Teatre, the small square separating the Rambla del Centre and Rambla de Santa Monica, is the beginning of the "red light" districts of Barrio Chino and Escudellers and site of the Principal Theatre

Rambla de Santa Monica is typified by flea markets, souvenir shops, jazz clubs and the site of Santa Monica Church. Beyond this Rambla is the Port of Barcelona.

Other interesting sites include: The **Olympic Stadium,** the **Museum of Catalonian Art,** the **Miro Foundation,** and the **Picasso Museum.**

Barcelona conforms to the Spanish tradition of late dinners. In theory, restaurants begin serving the evening meal at 2030. If you arrive earlier than 2130, however, you will probably have the restaurant all to yourself. Don't be alarmed by the increase in traffic at this hour. Barcelona's citizens are not evacuating the city—they're just going out for dinner.

At the city's quay in the harbor, the **statue of Columbus** serenely surveys the scene, which includes a replica of his flagship, the *Santa Maria.* Aboard, there is hardly room for a good-size flag, let alone a ship's crew. You wonder how he made it.

Day Excursions from Barcelona

A visit to **Blanes,** north of Barcelona, along the **Costa Brava (Wild Coast),** provides the breathtaking beauty of the Mediterranean coast and an opportunity to sample culinary delights from the sea. The citadel city of **Lerida,** stormed by Caesar's legions and conquered by the Moors, carries visitors far back into Spanish history. South of Barcelona along the beaches of Spain's Coasta Dorada (Gold Coast), picturesque **Sitges** attracts sun worshippers, gourmets, and wine connoisseurs alike. Farther south, the ancient city of **Tarragona's** first century Roman ruins stir the imagination.

Day Excursion to

Blanes
BEACHES, BOATS, AND BIKINIS

Depart from Barcelona Sants (suburban section) Station

Distance by Train: 38 miles (61 km)
Average Train Time: 1 hour, 10 minutes
Oficina de Turismo, Placa de Cataluna, (Tel: 9 72 330 348)
Hours: Open June-September, Monday-Saturday 0900-2000; July & August Sundays 1000-1400; May-October. Monday-Friday 0900-1500/1600-1900. Winter, Monday-Saturday 0900-1400.

To get there from the rail station, board buses marked "Estacion-Blanes." They will take you into town to the bus terminal at Placa de Cataluna. The tourist office is just a few steps from the bus terminal.

The **Costa Brava** is a breathtaking, 90-mile stretch of rugged coastline blessed with fantastic beaches and hidden coves. And it all begins at Blanes. **Blanes** is best described as a typical Spanish coastal, village, which fishing is still the primary industry. Blanes curves around the Mediterranean much like Cannes on the French Riviera, but it is not a "resort" in the usual, more commercialized sense. Like most Spanish fishing villages, the pace is slow and the people friendly.

The rail station serving Blanes is perched on a hill about a half mile from the center of the village and the sea. Buses marked ESTACION-BLANES will take you into town to the bus terminal at Placa de Cataluna near the sea.

A stroll along the beach is a delightful experience. It is fronted by fishermen's houses and dotted with boats lying at anchor in the curve of the bay. There is an auction of the day's catch each weekday evening at about 1700 at the breakwater. Blanes has plenty of fun-in-the-sun beaches, too.

Other diversions include a delightful botanical garden located near the breakwater where the fish auctions are held. Founded in 1924 by Karl Faust, the garden exhibits more than 4,000 species of regional and international flora. Hours: 0900-1800 daily April–mid-October (reduced hours in winter).

From Blanes, other ports along this rugged and beautiful coast can be accessed by local buses, cars or cruise boats. The Crucerus Line, which identifies its vessels with a blue whale at each bow, operates from June-September. Boats sail north from Blanes to call at places like **Lloret de Mar,** famous for its new hotels and exciting night life, Tossa, and San Feliu de Guixols. Obtain details and schedules from the tourist office.

Barcelona–Blanes

Transport depart Barcelona Sants daily, including holidays, from 0610, 0642, and every thirty minutes until 2042 and then at 2118, 2148, and 2218.

Trains depart Blanes to Barcelona Sants daily every thirty mintues until 2139.

(Second class only).

Distance: 38 miles/61 km

Day Excursion to

Lerida (Lleida)   FROM THE COAST TO THE MOUNTAINS

Depart Barcelona Sants Station

Distance by Train: 114 miles (184 km)
Average Train Time: 3 hours
Oficina de Turismo, 36 Madrid Ave., 25002 Lleida
Tel: 973 27 09 97; *Fax:* 973 27 09 49
Hours: Open June-September, Monday-Friday 0900-2000; Saturday 0900-1400/1600-2000; Sunday 0900-1400.

It's about a 15-minute walk from the rail station to the tourist information office. Exit the station and walk along Rambla de Ferran and Blondel Avenue to Madrice Avenue. The tourist office is in front of the University Bridge. A taxi can get you there in about 5 minutes.

A fast-moving ELT (electrotren) diesel train takes passengers in comfort through the spectacular scenery of the rugged, steep slopes of Sierra de Montserrat in the Pyrenees to the Roman fortress city **Lerida.** The train ride alone is worth the experience.

Be certain to make seat reservations well in advance of your day excursion date since the train's early morning departure does not allow sufficient time to make same-day reservations.

Your train stops briefly in Manresa, after which the scenery becomes more mountainous. Watch from the left side of the train as it approaches Lerida. The sight is unforgettable. Lerida's brooding Seo Antiqua cathedral stands as a sentinel atop a hill on the banks of the segre River.

Lerida served as an important Roman military outpost where Ceasar's legions gathered to pursue their conquests. The Moors left a more lasting impression which is reflected in the discernibly Mediterranean flavor of the city's marketplaces. Lerida's stormy history continued with Napoleon's attempts to annex it to France and artillery fire during the Spanish Civil War.

Constructed in the thirteenth century on the former site of a mosque, **Seo Antiqua** was converted from a church to a military fortress in 1707 by Philip V and then burned and pillaged in the wars that followed. It was restored and reconsecrated in 1950. If you are up to it, scale the tower of Seo Antiqua for a panoramic view of the plain surrounding Lerida.

Lerida's picturesque "Old Quarter" teems with interesting pedestrian streets of shops with colorful awnings and generally lower prices than you'll find in Barcelona.

Barcelona–Lerida

DEPART BARCELONA SANTS*	TRAIN NUMBER	ARRIVE IN LERIDA STATION	NOTES
0730	623	0926	(1)(2)
0830	TAL 41	1016	(1)(2)
1200	TAL 377	1407	(1)(2)

DEPART LERIDA STATION	TRAIN NUMBER	ARRIVE IN BARCELONA SANTS	NOTES
1539	TAL 374	1800	(1)(2)
1839	TAL 42	2035	(1)(2)
2036	TAL 378	2235	(1)(2)

(1) Daily, including holidays. Food service available
(2) Reservations mandatory

Distance: 114 miles/ 184 km

Day Excursion to

Sitges

SPARKLING SEA RESORT

Depart from Barcelona Sants Station

Distance by Train: 25 miles (36 km)
Average Train Time: 25 minutes
Patronat Municpal de Turisme, Pg de Vilafranca.
Tel: 902 10 34 28; *Fax:* 938 94 43 05
Hours: 0900-2100 daily in summer; remainder of the year: Monday-Friday 0930-1400/1600-1830; Saturday 1000-1300.

Only 25 miles south of Barcelona, **Sitges** can be accessed by train from several stations in Barcelona, but Sants and Passeig de Gracia stations are the most centralized. It is one of the most cosmopolitan seaside resorts in Europe and a pleasant escape from Barcelona's summer heat.

Although primarily known for its golden beaches, Sitges is also an important wine exporter for the Penedes region, Spain's largest producer of "Cava" champagne. Ask the tourist office about visiting the wine cellars of the bodegas in Penedes for wine tasting and *tapas.*

Annually, Sitges hosts the national carnation show in June when the town is awash with the brilliantly colored flowers. It coincides with the procession of Corpus Christi, when the city streets are covered with spectacular carpets of flowers.

Fresh seafood is Sitges' specialty, but there are excellent meat and chicken dishes available as well at a multitude of fine restaurants. Typical Sitges dishes include *xato*, a salad of endive, tuna fish, salt-cod, anchovies and olives, dressed with *nyora* peppers, roasted almonds, chilis, garlic, olive oil, more anchovies and salt and vinegar. Or, try *arros a la sitgetana*—rice with a delicious mixture of shellfish, sausage, pork, peas and peppers, seasoned with saffron and almonds. Follow it all with a glass of Sitges' renowned dessert wine, *Malvasia de Sitges*.

Corpus Christi is one of the most renowned festivals in Spain and in Sitges it coincides with the Los Claveles (carnations) celebration in early June. Streets are adorned with splendid carpets of the national flower at this famous event where bands perform and processions glide along narrow streets.

The February carnival, **June International Theater,** and the **October Film Festival** attract a varied mixture of participants and spectators, including international celebrities.

Other Sitges attractions include: **Museo de Casa Llopis,** an outstanding exhibit of antique dolls housed in a refurbished eighteenth-century mansion; **Cau Ferrat,** the magnificent home of twentieth-century artist Santiago Rusinol, which displays Rusinol's best work as well as art by El Greco, Casas, and Picasso; and the **Maricel del Mar Museum.**

Barcelona–Sitges

DEPART BARCELONA SANTS STATION	ARRIVE IN SITGES STATION	NOTES
0706	0736	(1)(2)
0906	0936	(1)(2)
1006	1036	(1)(2)
1206	1236	(1)(2)
1306	1336	(1)(2)

Other local trains are available between the Passeig de Gracia and Sants stations to Sitges.

DEPART SITGES STATION	ARRIVE IN BARCELONA SANTS STATION*	NOTES
1426	1456	(1)(2)
1926	1956	(1)(2)
2101	2130	(1)(2)
2226	2300	(1)(2)

Other local trains are available from Sitges to the Passeig de Gracia and Sants stations in Barcelona.

(1) Daily, including holidays
(2) Seat reservations mandatory

Distance: 25 miles/36 km

Day Excursion to

Tarragona
CITY OF ROMAN SPAIN

Depart from Barcelona Sants Station

Distance by Train: 55 miles (89 km)
Average Train Time: 1 hour
Oficina de Turismo, 39 Carrer Major, (Tel: 245 203). Open Monday-Friday 1000-2000.
To reach it, board a No. 2 bus across from the rail station. Get off at the Roman
Wall where you will see signs directing you to the tourist information office.

Tarragona can be reached via Barcelona's single-class suburban train system
or by the more stylish and comfortable "Rapido" trains which require seat
reservations.

Tarragona is rich in antiquity. It was once considered a jewel in the crown
of the Roman Empire, with more than one-quarter of a million inhabitants
(more than twice the present population) enjoying all the privileges of Rome.
Tarragona's enormous stone walls were constructed in the first century B.C.
Similar to the great pyramids of Egypt, modern engineers still wonder how
the ancient Iberians could position such massive blocks of stone. Its attractive
seascape of azure blue water, gold-colored beaches, and flower-laden cliffs has
attracted visitors for centuries.

St. Paul supposedly preached at the site of Tarragona's twelfth-century
cathedral where a Roman temple to Jupiter once stood. Illustrations of his life
are exhibited in the altar area.

A visit to the **Archeological Museum** is a journey into Tarragona's
rich past, from Roman remains and reflecting the peoples who followed,
including Visigoths, Moors, and Catalans. The penetrating stare of Medusa's
eyes, cornices from the **Temple of Jupiter** (where the cathedral now stands),
and age-old ceramics are on view. The museum operates on seasonal hours.
Check with the tourist information office.

Hungry? While you're in the tourist office, ask for directions to the **Bufet
el Tiberi Restaurant** at 5, Marti d'Ardenya. It features a buffet of local
specialties. **Restaurant el Celler** and **Restaurant el Trull** also feature local
specialties.

Barcelona–Tarragona

DEPART BARCELONA SANTS STATION	TRAIN NUMBER	ARRIVE IN TARRAGONA STATION	NOTES
0700	IC 161	0748	(2)(3)
0800	697	0857	(1)(2)
0900	163	0948	(1)(2)
0930	IC 693	1029	(1)(2)
1103	IC 185	1203	(1)(2)
1230	TAL 463	1324	(1)(2)

DEPART TARRAGONA STATION	TRAIN NUMBER	ARRIVE IN BARCELONA SANTS STATION	NOTES
1600	EM 66	1703	(1)(2)
1800	EM 262	1903	(1)(2)
1955	IC 264	2100	(1)(2)
2100	EM 268	2203	(1)(2)
2224	EM 266	2317	(2)(4)

(1) Daily, including holidays
(2) Seat reservations mandatory
(3) Daily except Sundays and holidays
(4) Daily except Saturdays

Distance: 57 miles/92 km

Base City...

Madrid

City Dialing Code: 1

Madrid's central location in the very heart of Spain makes it a convenient Base City and a major point of entry for Spain. Madrid, the capital of Spain, at first glance appears typical of any other modern capital that serves as a center for government and finance. But it is atypical of a busy metropolis in that the Spanish seem to move at a slower pace. They make time for friends and conversation and as one Spanish writer noted, "Madrid is a city where no one is a stranger."

The Madrilenos are apparently connoisseurs of a variety of night life activities, including a flair for Flamenco—the sensual, gypsy-influenced form of singing and dancing. There are numerous specialized Flamenco clubs in Madrid, including the Corral de la Moreria, Los Canasteros, and Torres Bermejas. It would appear that the Madrilenos never sleep!

According to the Spanish National Tourist Office, "Madrid has turned into the fable of Europe. It is called the capital of joy and of contentment. Describing our city in such terms means that it is welcoming, cordial, free, peaceful and universal."

Arriving by Air

Madrid's Barajas International Airport, about 9 miles (12 kilometers) northeast of the city.
- **Airport Information:** Tel: (91) 305 83 43; 305 83 44; 305 83 45, and 305 83 46; Fax: (91) 393 62 00
- **Flight Reservations:** Tel: (91) 401 99 00
- **INFORIBERIA:** Tel: (91) 329 57 67

At press time, the airport is under reconstruction and improvements are being implemented to handle a burgeoning influx of tourists, including Americans.

Airport-City Links: Airport Bus, (Tel: 431 61 92), a yellow bus service, runs to and from Barajas Airport and Serrano in La Plaza de Colon (Columbus Square) every 10 minutes daily until 0200. Journey time: about 40 minutes; fare, 350 pesetas.

The Atocha metro line is a link to metro-Madrid; and numerous buses carry travelers to and from many locations in the city.

Taxi fare from the airport to city center is about 1,800-2,200 pesetas.

Arriving by Train

RENFE (Spanish National Railways)—For information on fares, schedules and destinations: (Tel: 328 90 20)

Madrid's two main railway stations, **Chamartin** and **Atocha,** are connected by underground trackage via Madrid's Metro system and by "Apeadero Cercanias" (local) trains or any through-trains scheduled to stop at both stations. The Metro stop for Atocha Station is marked **"Atocha RENFE."** Apeadero Cercanias stations also include **Nuevos Ministerios** in the government buildings area and **Recoletos** at the main post office. Rail passes are accepted on Apeadero Cercanias trains, but not on Madrid's Metro.

Chamartin Station, San Agustin de Foxa St., is Madrid's international station connecting with most European capitals, as well as the north, northeast, and south of Spain. The station is near the Chamartin metro stop and buses No. 5 and No. 80 connect from the city and this railway station. High-speed AVE trains shuttle passengers quickly to and from **Seville** (2½ hours), with stops at **Cordoba** and **Ciudad Real.** Other fast trains depart to and arrive from various southern and southeastern Spanish destinations and from Portugal. There are 21 tracks.

- **Money exchange:** opposite tracks 17 and 18. The sign reads CAJA ESPANA. Hours: 0830-1400 Monday-Friday. Banco Bilbao Vizcaya, across from track 12. Hours: 0800-2200 daily (closed for lunch 1415-1500). ATM located next door.
- **Hotel reservations,** opposite tracks 7 and 8. Hours: 0730-2300 daily. Nominal reservation fee. Be certain to ask for accommodations near one of the rail stations or close to public transportation. The check-in counter for Hotel Chamartin is near the luggage locker area.
- **Luggage lockers** available 0730-2330 daily. Follow the sign CONSIGNA AUTOMATICA.
- **Sala Club Intercity:** First-class lounge between entrances to tracks 13 and 14.
- **Tourist information:** opposite track No. 19, (Tel: 315 99 76). Hours: 0800-2000 Monday-Friday; 0900-1300 Saturday.
- **Train information, seat reservations,** and **rail pass validation**: in the center of the station between tracks 11 and 12. Hours: 0830-2000. Take a number from the machine labeled RECOJA SU TURNO to reserve a place in line. Make certain the date (*fecha*) and departure time (*hora salida*) are correct on your reservation. **Seat reservations are mandatory on all express and international trains**.

Puerta de Atocha Station—High-speed AVE and Talgo 200 trains connect Madrid with Andalusia from this station. A pleasant tropical garden and café provide a respite from the heat and noise. The local/suburban Cercanias trains depart from the lower level and connect with Chamartin Station.

Sala Club Intercity: First-class lounge on the mezzanine level.

Principe Pio or Norte, near the Royal Palace on the west side of the city, links Madrid to cities in the north and northeast of Spain via the Cercanias, or suburban, trains. Other stations where you can board the suburban-type Cercanias trains include **Nuevos Ministerios** and **Recoletos.** Eurailpass, Europass, and the national Spain rail passes are accepted on these trains. Although considered "local" trains, they do extend to the surrounding countryside to our day excursions **Aranjuez** (Line C-3) and **El Escorial** (Line C-8a).

Madrid Tourist Information/Hotel Reservations: Offinas de Informacion de Turismo (Tourist Information Centers): Opposite track No. 19 operated by the Madrid province and can provide information about Madrid or nearby cities. Brochures describing all of the day-excursion points are unusual available in English. Monday through Friday from 0800-2000 and Saturday from 0900-1300. Tel: 315 99 76. When closed, the hotel office opposite the track Nos. 6 and 7 will assist you.

Hotel reservations can be made for a nominal charge under the INFORMATCIO Y RESERVA HOTELERA sign opposite track Nos. 6 and 7. The office is open 0730–2300 daily. Madrid is a large city, so be certain that you ask for lodging near one of the rail terminals or close to public transportation.

Getting Around in Madrid

Madrid has an excellent Metro and bus system. Purchase reduced-fare 10-trip tickets called "Bonobus," at newspaper stands, tobacco stores, and at all main bus stops. The tickets are magnetically encoded.

Although Madrid has no Spanish National Tourist offices, the following Provincial and Municipal offices provide general information about Spain. Although most of the tourist and rail personnel speak English, it's always polite to ask: *"¿Habla Ingles, por favor?"* (Do you speak English, please?).

- **Chamartin Railway Station,** (Tel: 315 99 76). Hours: Monday-Friday 0900-1900; Saturday 930-1330.
- **Barajas Airport:** (Tel: 305 86 56) (International arrivals). Hours: Monday-Friday 0800-2000; Saturday 0800-1300.
- **Torre de Madrid in Plaza de Espana,** (Tel: 541 23 25)
- **Metro station: Plaza de Espana,** Duque de Medinaceli
- **Outside the Palace Hotel,** (Tel: 429 49 51). Hours: Monday-Friday 0900-1900; Saturday 0930-1330.
- **Metro station: Banco de Espana.** Hours: Monday-Friday. 1000-1400/1600-1900; Saturday 1000-1330.
- **Metro station: Sol,** below Puerta del Sol
- **Travelers' Hotline,** (Tel: 902 20 22 02) provides tourists with the latest

information about accommodations. A wide variety of accommodations are available in Madrid, including the Palace Hotel, across the square from the Prado Museum. As the name implies, the hotel is on the site of a former palace, (360 80 00. The Hotel Chamartin at Chamartin Station is convenient for those business persons and tourists traveling by train, Tel: 32 3 30 87; Fax: 733 02 14.

Sights/Attractions/Tours

A convenient way to see the sights is on **Madrid Visions Touristic Bus.** For 1,800 pesetas, you can jump on and off the bus at more than 14 various sights, museums, and churches.

Some "don't-miss" sights include **Puerta del Sol** (Gate of the Sun), the center of the old town and the terminus for the city's metro lines and many of the buses. Six of Spain's national freeways radiate from Kilometer Zero, a stone slab buried in the pavement from which all distances are measured in Spain. The **el Oso y el Madrono,** the bush and the bear statue, is Madrid's emblem.

Proceed southwest along **Calle Mayor** to **Plaza de la Villa,** with two stunning buildings dating from the fifteenth century—the **Casa** (house) and the **Torre (tower) de los Lujanes.** Continuing to the right of Calle Mayor and beyond the Plaza de la Villa, turn into the alleyway leading to **San Nicolas de los Servitas,** to visit Madrid's oldest church

Going north along the **Calle del Arenal,** one can view a famous El Greco at the Church of San Gines or visit Joy Enslava, the city's trendy disco. Farther on are the Royal Palace and the Opera House.

Other significant landmarks include the **Palacio Real** (Tel: 541 08 76; hours 0900-1800 Monday-Saturday; 1000-1430 Sunday.)—one of the best conserved palaces in Europe. It's filled with paintings, frescos, clocks, furniture, and porcelain. **Plaza Mayor** behind Calle Mayor is an exquisite seventeenth-century arcaded square

A **Museum Pass,** which costs 1,050 pesetas, is a bargain for visiting Madrid's fine museums. The incomparable **Prado Museum** at Paseo del Prado (Tel: 330 2800; hours 0900-1900 Tuesday-Saturday; 0900-1400 Sunday.) houses more than 3,000 of the world's most precious works of art, including fine collections of the Spanish masters—Goya, Velazquez, El Greco, Murillo, and Zurbaran.

The **Thyssen-Bornemisza Museum** (Tel: 369 01 51; hours 1000-1900 Tuesday-Sunday.), in the Villahermosa Palace, features one of the world's most extensive private art collections now open to the public. The **Reina Sofia National Art Museum** has a fantastic collection of twentieth-century Spanish art and the **National Chalcography Institute** includes 221 original copper and brass engraved plates by Goya.

If you plan to attend a bullfight in Madrid, remember what Ernest Hemingway wrote: "It is a tragedy; the death of the bull, which is played, more or less well by the bull and the man involved and in which there is danger for the man but certain death for the bull."

For people watching, visit several of Madrid's *chiringuitos*, a combination German-style beer garden and discotheque, and cafes that line the **Paseo de la Castellana** (which becomes Paseo del Prado as it nears the Prado Museum).

In the cuisine category, Madrid has some very old and very famous restaurants. The **Casa Botin** (Tel: 366 42 17) is in the *Guinness Book of Records* as the oldest continuously-operated restaurant and Hemingway's favorite for suckling pig and baby lamb. The Zalacain at Alvarez de Baena 4 (Tel: 561 59 35) features Basque seafood and game.

Train Connections to Other Base Cities from Madrid

TO:	DEPART*	ARRIVE	TRAIN NUMBER	NOTES
Barcelona	1100	1800	TAL 374	
(Sants)	1600	2235	TAL 378	(4)
	2300	0800+1	874	(4)
Lisbon	2235	0840+1	TAL 332	(5)
Paris	1000	2305	IC 203	(2)(3)
	1925	0830+1	EC 407	(1)

★ All departures from Madrid's Chamartin Station, unless otherwise noted. Seat or sleeper reservations are mandatory in Spain, except on local trains.

(1) Arrives at Paris Gare d'Austerlitz
(2) Transfer in Hendaye to TGV 8596, daily except Sundays
(3) Arrives in Paris Gare Montparnasse
(4) Daily, except Saturday
(5) Supplement payable
(6) Second class only, transfer in Badojoz

Day Excursions

Aranjuez, Avila, El Escorial, and Toledo are four very different Spanish destinations easily accessed by train from Madrid.

Aranjuez and **El Escorial** are particularly picturesque. Aranjuez, on the fertile banks of the Tagus River, is set in a forested valley less than 1 hour's train journey south of Madrid. El Escorial is a village at the base of the Sierra de Guadarrama, 1 hour north of Madrid. Favorites of the royalty for centuries, they are now popular retreats for Madrilenos.

Avila and **Toledo** are cities with such different styles that they exemplify the diversity of this ancient land. Both are worth more than a day's visit to more thoroughly explore and enjoy.

Burgos, home of El Cid, is about 3 hours journey time from Madrid.

Day Excursion to

Aranjuez   SPANISH ROYAL RETREAT

Depart from Madrid Atocha Station

Distance by Train: 30 miles (49 km)
Average Train Time: 50 minutes
Oficina de Turismo: No. 9, Plaza de San Antonio, (Tel: 891 04 27)
    We recommend taking a taxi from the station to the tourist office, located near Palacio Real.

In the eighteenth and nineteenth centuries, **Aranjuez** was a favorite hangout for Spanish royalty. Now, it's a popular place for "regular" Madrilenos to gather on weekends. You may want to make this day excursion during the week to avoid the weekend crowds.

Aranjuez has often been described as the "Oasis of Castille," due in part because it nestles on the banks of the Tagus River that nurses dense groves of poplars and rich vegetation. Apparently, the jade green waters of the river favorably foster the growth of trees, as evidenced by the city's Circus of the Twelve Streets, a square from which twelve beautifully shaded avenues radiate.

The **Palacio Real** (Royal Palace) is a lavish palace that would vie with Versailles in extravagance. Its 18 magnificent rooms include the Porcelain Salon, the Throne Room, and The Museum of Royal Robes, which displays the court dress of sovereigns up to the nineteenth century. Another highlight is the grand staircase built during the reign of Philip V. During spring and summer, the palace is open 1000–1830 Tuesday-Sunday. It closes one hour earlier in autumn and winter.

Madrid–Aranjuez

DEPART MADRID CHAMARTIN	DEPART FROM MADRID ATOCHA	TRAIN NUMBER	ARRIVE IN ARANJUEZ STATION	NOTES
0905	0920	TAL 228	0948	(1)(2)
1030	1045	TAL 222	1114	(3)
1335	1350	Local	1421	(1)

DEPART ARANJUEZ STATION	TRAIN NUMBER	ARRIVE IN MADRID ATOCHA	ARRIVE IN MADRID CHAMARTIN	NOTES
1724	TAL 23	1754	1808	(1)
1917	Local	1951	2004	(1)
2201	Local	2236	2249	(1)(4)

Note: Seat reservations required on non-local trains

(1) Daily, including holidays
(2) Saturday only
(3) Daily except Saturday
(4) Second class only

Distance: 30 miles/49 km

The Farmer's Cottage with its resplendent furnishings can be reached through the Prince's Garden. The Casa de Marinos, the sailor's house which holds the royal vessels, displays Spain's dominant maritime history. And among the gardens, the Parterre Garden and the Jardinde la Isla (Island Garden) are most memorable.

You can purchase a combination ticket which includes a guided tour of the Royal Palace. The tours operate from 1000-1815 April through August; 1000-1715 September through March. Note that all of the museums are closed on Mondays.

Trains to Aranjuez depart every 30 minutes from Madrid's Attocha station.

Day Excursion to

Avila

WALLED CITY

Depart from Madrid Chamartin Station or Principe Pio

Distance by Train: 70 miles (112 km)
Average Train Time: 1 hour, 15 minutes
Oficina de Turismo: No.4 Plaza de la Catedral
Tel: 920 21 13 87; *Fax:* 920 25 37 17
Hours: Monday-Friday 1000-1400/1700-2000; Saturday 0930-1430/1600-1900;
Sunday 0930-1400/1600-1830.
RENFE at Avila Railway Station: Tel. 22 01 88
        Taxis to the far right of the rail station as you exit. Rail station is about 1 mile
from city center.

Avila is the capital of the province of Avila, and at 1,127 meters it is the
highest provincial capital in Spain and the best preserved walled city in the
world. The city is completely enclosed by 2½ kilometers of century walls aver-
aging 33 feet high and 10 feet thick, with 90 towers and 9 gateways. The
enormity of this project becomes apparent when you realize it was constructed in 1085.

Viewed from **Los Cuatro Postes,** an observation post on the Salamanca
Road outside the city, Avila is a breathtaking sight nestled on the Adaja River
against the mountains. From here, the walled city appears to be a fascinating
giant stage all set for a medieval drama.

Avila is most remembered for Saint Teresa. Her presence is most evident
in the the convent **Nuestra Senora de Gracia** built at the site of her par-
ent's home; and the Monastery de la Encarnacion which depicts her lifestyle;
and "las Madres" (monastery de San Jose) her first foundation.

Across the street from the tourist office is the Gran Hotel Palacio
Valderrabonos. This former nobleman's residence is an excellent place to have
lunch. Its door dates from the fifteenth century.

Other sights in Avila include the Cathedral, which forms a part of the great
wall, thus giving it the distinctive look of a fortress rather than a church. Its
somewhat austere exterior is in contrast to its interior, which has many beautiful details. In the Cathedral's museum, you may view a portrait painted by
El Greco and a colossal silver monstrance, weighing nearly 200 pounds, made
by Juan de Arfe in 1571.

The Cathedral was begun in the twelfth century in Romanesque style and
finished in the fifteenthcentury with a facade of Gothic Towers; the Palacio
de Polention; the Mansion de los Deanes; Mansion de Davila—all magnificent with art and architecture.

The cuisine of this area is fit for a king's palate. Trout from the Tormes

Madrid–Avila

DEPART FROM MADRID CHAMARTIN STATION	TRAIN NUMBER	ARRIVE IN AVILA STATION	NOTES
0800	IC 131	0925	(1)
1130	2	1253	(1)

DEPART FROM AVILA STATION	TRAIN NUMBER	ARRIVE IN MADRID CHAMARTIN STATION	NOTES
1326	IC 202	1456	(2)
1615	TAL 78	1740	(1)
1935	TAL 60	2110	(1)
2045	1430	2220	(1)

(1) Daily, including holidays
(2) Daily, except Saturday

Distance: 70 miles/112 km

River is renowned for its distinctive flavor; the roast suckling pig, lamb, or veal dishes are equally excellent and served with a hearty accompaniment of vegetables, followed by "yemas de Santa Teresa," small sweets made of egg yolks.

Nearby Paradors offer unique accommodations for those who prefer to "base" themselves here. Paradors are historic buildings and palaces that the Spanish government has converted into hotels.

Day Excursion to

Burgos   HOME OF EL CID

Depart from Madrid Chamartin Station

Distance by Train: 211 miles (340 km)
Average Train Time: 3 hours
Oficina de Turismo: 7, Plaza Alonso Martinez Sq.,
Tel: 33 11 50/31 00 50
Hours: 0900-1400/1700-1900 Monday-Friday; 1100-1400/1630-2030 Saturday-Sunday.

To reach the office on foot (about 15-min. walk), exit the station and go straight ahead until you cross the Arlanzon River. Turn right and proceed along General Franco Avenue to the arch where the walkway Paseo del Espolon begins. Or, take a taxi.

Burgos is north of Madrid, approaching France, and on the crossroads to Portugal. Birthplace of the warrior El Cid, Burgos is the capital of Burgos province, one of the nine provinces of Castile and Leon.

El Cid and his wife Ximena are entombed in the **thirteenth century cathedral,** one of the world's outstanding examples of Gothic architecture. Its twin spires rise to greet you long before your Talgo train comes to a halt in the Burgos Station.

The nave of the cathedral and the ambulatory and portals of El Sarmental and Coroneria date from its beginnings in 1221. The latest additions, dating from the sixteenth century include: Diego de Siloe's Golden Stairs; the chapels of La Consolation, Santiago and Navidad; and Juan de Vallejo's exquisite lantern.

Burgos was the site where the Castilians initiated their campaigns against the Muslims to reclaim Madrid in 1083 and Toledo in 1085. In this century, Generalissimo Franco used Burgos as his headquarters during the Spanish Civil War, and here declared the cease-fire in 1939.

The **Casa del Cordon,** a fifteenth century house so named from the huge cord of rope carved in stone fronting its entrance, forms the backdrop for **El Cid's statue.** It was here that Christopher Columbus was received in formal audience by the Spanish monarchs on his return from his second voyage to the Americas.

For lunch, we suggest the Ojeda Restaurant at Calle Vitoria No. 5. It is quite pleasant to have a light snack or even a full meal at its outdoor tables in the summer.

Madrid–Burgos

DEPART MADRID CHAMARTIN STATION	TRAIN NUMBER	ARRIVE IN BURGOS STATION	NOTES
0920	343	1230	(1)(3)
1000	203	1326	(1)
1330	Local	1726	(1)

DEPART BURGOS STATION	TRAIN NUMBER	ARRIVE IN MADRID CHAMARTIN STATION	NOTES
1718	340	2050	(1)
1903	Tal 200	2205	(2)
1920	—	2321	(1)

(1) Daily, including holidays
(2) Daily, except Saturday
(3) Standard class only

Distance: 211 miles/340 km

Day Excursion to

El Escorial

World's Eighth Wonder

Depart from Madrid Atocha or Charmartin Stations

Distance by Train: 32 miles (52 km)
Average Train Time: 60 minutes
Oficina de Turismo, No.10 Calle Floridablanca,
Tel: 91 890 15 54
Hours: daily 1000-1400/1500-1700 Monday-Friday; 1000-1400 Saturday.
    The rail station is about–mile from town. Taxis are to the left of the station exit. To the town square or the tourist office costs about 350 pesetas. Buses are also available that will take you to the town square.

El Escorial names the village and the immense palace-monastery, both havens of Phillip II, who personally supervised construction of the monumental structure to commemorate his victory over France at St. Quentin in 1557. Part monastery, part palace, part cathedral—El Escorial reflects its builder's vanity. The monastery and palace are open 1000-1800 in summer, until 1700 in winter, and closed on Mondays.

El Escorial encompasses 8 acres, 9 towers, 16 courtyards, 86 staircases, 1,200 doors, and 2,673 leaded-glass windows. A force of 1,500 workmen labored 21 years to complete it. Wear your best pair of walking shoes—you'll need them.

The **Hall of Battles** epitomizes Spain's aggressive history in paintings by Italian artists Castello, Grenello, and Tavorone. Priceless art works by Borsch, Rembrandt, Tintoretto, and Titian are also displayed throughout the palace. Tapestries of Spanish country life woven over sketches drawn by Goya also hang on the walls.

Prior to mounting the Armada against England, King Phillip tried to bring England into the Spanish Empire by marrying Mary Tudor, known as "Bloody Mary" for her overzealous persecution of English Protestants. Forty years later, just before his death, Phillip had become a religious fanatic. He returned to the palace to live as though in poverty in a sparse second-floor apartment, which provides stark contrast to its surroundings—one of the grandest palaces in Europe.

Two other attractions of interest are the **Casita del Principe** (the Prince's Cottage) which you pass en route to the station, and **Casita de Arriba,** a hunting lodge 2 miles farther on. Both are open 1000-1800 (1700 in winter); closed Mondays. Both were constructed by Charles III (1759-1788). His friendship with France and hostility towards Great Britain led to the alliance in support of the American Revolution.

Madrid–El Escorial

DEPART MADRID ATOCHA	DEPART MADRID CHARMARTIN	ARRIVE IN EL ESCORIAL	NOTES
0703	0717	0808	(1)(2)
0833	0847	0938	(1)(2)
1032	1046	1137	(1)(2)
1232	1246	1337	(1)(2)

DEPART EL ESCORIAL	ARRIVE IN MADRID CHARMARTIN	ARRIVE IN MADRID ATOCHA	NOTES
1617	1708	1721	(1)(2)
1817	1908	1921	(1)(2)
2017	2108	2121	(1)(2)
2217	2308	2321	(1)(2)

(1) Daily, including holidays
(2) Seat reservations required

Distance: 32 miles/52 km

Day Excursion to

Toledo

CITY OF HISTORY

Depart from Madrid Atocha Station

Distance by Train: 57 miles (91 km)
Average Train Time: 1 hour, 15 minutes
Oficina de Turismo: Puerta Nueva de Bisagra,
Tel: 925 22 08 43
Hours: 0900-1400/1600-1800 Monday-Friday; 0900-1500/1600-1900 Saturday; 0900-1500 Sunday.

Public bus service from rail station into town. Buses depart every 15 minutes. Bus stops first at the tourist information office at Puerta de la Bisagra before terminating in the main square, Plaza de Zocodover (Marketplace) Also, there is an information kiosk in Plaza de Zocodover open Monday-Saturday 1000-1800; Sunday 1000-1500.

Toledo is (as is Avila) capital of a province with the same name. Toledo province is defined by mountain ranges, rivers, and rich rolling valleys: it abounds with game, aromatic plants, and delicate white-leafed rock roses—all of which distinguishes Toledo from the other provinces of La Mancha with their monotonous, flat expanses.

Divided by the River Tagus, Toledo has the rich and varied history of most river towns, and in Europe's south that means conquests by Romans, Visigoths, Moors, and ultimately Christians who declared it Spain's Imperial City. It was ruled by the legendary El Cid. The impact of such a diverse history earned Toledo the UNESCO "Heritage of Mankind" status, defining it as one of the richest historically, culturally, and monumentally endowed cities in Spain.

A Cretan named Domenico Teotocopulo arrived in Toledo in 1577. His arrival might have gone unnoticed, except that Senor Teotocopulo, better known as El Greco, happened to be a painter of some renown. El Greco painted and bequeathed his best to Toledo. The **Museum of Santa Cruz** and the **El Greco House** honor the achievements of one of Spain's most creative artists.

Although Toledo's history may be complicated, its charm is definitely not. Wander the city's narrow, cobblestone streets, visit its friendly cafes which remain open late into the night, and taste fresh fruits from the open market in the morning.

Madrid–Toledo

DEPART MADRID ATOCHA STATION	ARRIVE IN TOLEDO STATION	NOTES
0705	0817	(2)(3)(4)
0825	0937	(1)(2)(3)
1025	1137	(1)(2)(3)
1225	1343	(1)(2)(3)
DEPART TOLEDO STATION	**ARRIVE IN MADRID ATOCHA STATION**	**NOTES**
1430	1548	(1)(2)(3)
1630	1748	(1)(2)(3)
1830	1948	(1)(2)(3)
2100	2218	(1)(2)(3)

(1) Daily, including holidays
(2) Seat reservations required
(3) Second class only
(4) Monday through Friday

Distance: 57 miles/91 km

In 1226, King Ferdinand III laid the first stone in the **Cathedral of Toledo,** and today it is renowned for its art and architecture. The thirteenth century fortress **Alcazar** was in the third century a Roman Pretorian Palace. Toledo also is well known for its craftsmen who work steel into some of the finest blades for knives and swords. The distinctive black-on-gold designs embellishing the handles of blades have been carried over to jewelry and other accessories available in shops throughout the city.

Although there are numerous eateries, most visitors seem to gather in the main square, **Plaza de Zocodover** (Marketplace). Here, you will find cafes and bars to sample local sandwiches and *tapas* (appetizers).

The **Parador Conde Orgaz** or the **Hotel Alfonso VI** are exceptional accommodations in Toledo, if you choose to stay.

Sweden

In size, Sweden is about the same size as the state of California or the country of Spain. It is half covered by forests, dotted with nearly 100,000 lakes, and thousands of islands line its coastline. It is one of the most prosperous countries in Europe and supports a large and efficient industrial complex. Its citizens enjoy a superb quality of life and one of the highest standards of living in the world.

Although Swedish, a Germanic language, is the language of the majority, Finland was a part of Sweden until 1809 and Finnish-speaking natives still occupy the northeastern area along with another minority group, the Sami (Lapp). Fortunately for English-speaking tourists, English is spoken by most Swedes who are involved in tourism, transportation, and international business.

It is difficult to realize that only about a century ago, Sweden was one of the most backward countries in Europe. Today, Sweden is forward thinking—spending a large percentage of national output on industrial research and development. Since 1995, Sweden has played an important role as a member of the European Union. Sweden's strategic geographic location between the North Atlantic and Russia has impacted its foreign policies and security strategies for all of Europe.

For more information about Sweden, contact the Swedish Tourist Board of North America:

New York: P.O. Box 4649, Grand Central Station, New York, New York 10163-4649. Tel: (212)949-2333; Fax: (212)983-5260; Internet: http://www.travelfile.com/get?swetvl

Banking

- **Currency:** Swedish Krona (SEK)
- **Exchange Rate at Press Time:** 7.66 SEK = $1.00 U.S.
- **Hours:** 0900-1700 Mon.-Fri. Close at 1500 on the day before a holiday, which the Swedes refer to as a *halvdag* (half day).

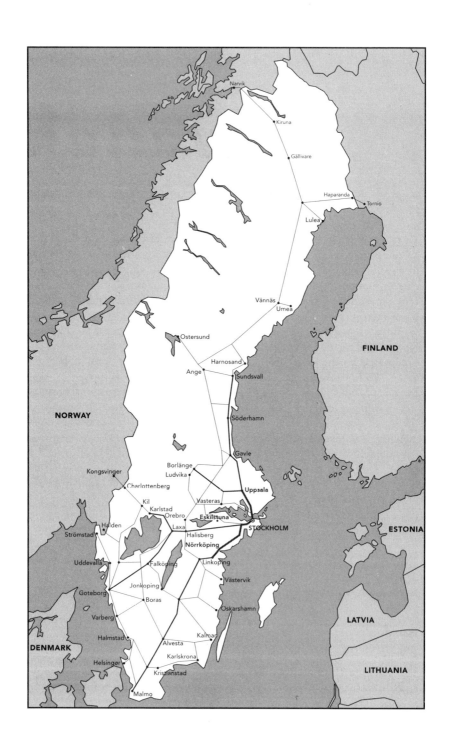

Communications

- **Country Dialing Code:** 46
  For telephone calls within Sweden, dial zero (0) preceding area code.
  Direct dial: AT&T: 020-795-611; MCI: 020-795-922; Sprint: 020-799-011

Rail Travel in Sweden

Swedish State Railways: Central Station, S-105 50 Stockholm
Tel: (8) 696 75 09; Fax: (8) 696 75 35 domestic rail services; (8) 762 26 32
international rail services; Internet site: http://www.sj.se

Swedish State Railways (SJ) operates about 7,000 miles of rail lines. Its
X2000 trains are Sweden's modern high-speed "tilting" trains which operate
at 125 miles per hour between Stockholm, Gothenburg, and Malmo. In first
class, meals are served at travelers' seats. There is also a bistro car which serves
hot and cold meals.

InterCity trains operate between all of Sweden's major cities and between
Stockholm and Oslo. These trains have a restaurant car and a "family car" with
play areas available for children. **InterRegio** trains operate between regions.
These trains have radio sockets at all seats and refreshments available. Train
platforms are referred to in Sweden as "spoors." On most trains operated by
the Scandinavian countries, drinking water is supplied at no charge. Train
reservations are mandatory for trips, more than 90 miles. In addition, SJ
operates a bus network linking the railways to smaller cities and villages.

SJ accepts **Eurailpass, ScanRail Pass,** and the **Sweden Rail Pass,** which
are purchased in North America (see list of European Rail Passes in the
Appendix for prices and ordering information for the multi-country passes,
Eurailpass and ScanRail Pass). Pass prices do not include reservation fees, but a
point-to-point ticket does. Eurailpass holders do not pay a supplement to ride
X2000 trains, but seat reservations are mandatory (about $4.50 US). ScanRail
Pass and Sweden Rail Pass holders pay a supplement of about $45 (which
includes the seat reservation fee) to ride X2000 trains.

Sweden Rail Pass

Unlimited travel on all routes operated by the Swedish Railways. Up to 2
children under age 4 travel free. Children 4-16 pay 50 percent. Prices do *not*
include reservation fees or supplement fees for X2000 trains, sleepers, or
couchettes.

	1ST CLASS	2ND CLASS
Valid for 7 days	$250	$190
Valid for 14 days	$330	$255

Base City…

Stockholm

City Dialing Code: 8
Internet: http://www.kultur98.stockholm.se

Cities are identified with the feminine gender. This makes Stockholm *very* feminine, for she is a city with a will of her own and a whimsy of changing her mind. Stockholm declares her intentions of retaining the old, then in the same breath states her love of progress and things modern. Voted the Cultural Capital of Europe in 1998 by the European Union, Stockholm provides her visitors with the opportunity to experience Sweden's modern culture and to celebrate her ancient traditions.

Stockholm's **Gamla Stan** (Old Town) is located on a small island in the city center. Its narrow cobblestone streets wind their crooked ways over paths unchanged since the Middle Ages past houses bearing the same facades they had when they were built. But behind these old facades you find the most modern of business establishments and apartments whose decors rival those of similar dwellings anywhere in the world. With the delicate touch of a female, Stockholm has made this dualism work in every way.

Another example is **Sergels Torg,** Stockholm's space-age city center. It exists comfortably surrounded by other structures centuries older. Call it what you will, but most people call Stockholm beautiful.

Arriving By Air

Arlanda Airport lies 24 miles (40 km) northwest of the city.

Airport-City Links: Airport coach. Departures every 10 minutes; Time en route, 35-45 minutes. Coach terminates in Stockholm at the World Trade Centre next to the Central Station. Fare for a single trip is 60 kronor for adults; reduced rates for children. For information, (Tel: 600 10 00; Fax: 686 13 62).

SAS Limousine service (Tel: 797 37 00; Fax: 797 41 98)is available 24 hours per day (about $75 US/car) to Stockholm Central Station.

Taxis are available 24 hours daily. The taxi stand is located just outside the arrivals hall of the airport. Taxi fare is 350–400 kronor.

Arriving By Train

Stockholm has several suburban stations, but international trains stop only at the main rail station in the center of the city, Stockholm Central. All of the

day excursions out of Stockholm depart from Stockholm Central Station.
Stockholm's Central Station is modern, well organized, and easy to move about in. International trains usually arrive on track 17 or 18. Luggage carts. Insert a 5-kronor coin in the lock. It's refunded when you return the cart to a rack.

The Central Station is close to several major hotels and directly connected to the Stockholm subway (the Tunnelbanan). The main taxi stand is across the street from the railway station.

The station does an excellent job of moving its passengers to and from the trains. It also provides a full complement of services for the traveler. An arcade of shops, on the lower station level in the proximity of the exits from tracks 17 and 18, provides all types of foodstuffs, beverages, tobacco, newspapers, and so forth.

The *Konsum*—Sweden's answer to the American supermarket—is a good place to restock your larder. It is located in the same area within the station. There are also shops in the main station-concourse area where you may purchase food and soft drinks.

The station's food-service facilities range from a cafeteria to a restaurant with its own gambling casino. The cafeteria is located on the main level of the station to the far right as you stand looking into the station from the train exit. It can be identified by its sign, CAFE OASEN. Cafeteria service is continuous Monday through Saturday 0630–2330 and Sunday 0700–2330; it is a good place to have breakfast, lunch, or dinner.

The Centralens Restaurang (restaurant) Orientexpressen has the previously mentioned casino. You'll see its sign on the right side of the station as you exit from the track area. In addition to the casino, the complex includes a pub and a restaurant with good food at reasonable prices. The "all you can eat" breakfast in the restaurant section is a real bargain. The restaurant has an expansive but relatively inexpensive luncheon-and-dinner menu featuring many Swedish specialties (closed during July).

Across the street from Central Station, along the street Vasagatan, you can find a number of excellent food facilities ranging from fast to fancy.

Train information is displayed on bulletins following the usual format. Departures are printed on yellow paper; arrivals appear on white. Train information is readily available throughout the station, including key positions just inside the main entrance and again in the corridors leading to the track areas. The office is in the main concourse to the left of the main exit. Hours: 0600-2300 Monday-Saturday; 0700-2300 Sunday.

Local train information, usually for commuter trains, is displayed by a bank of large-screen, closed-circuit television sets.

Train reservations can be made in a large ticket office located in the main hall to the right as you proceed from the track area. A sign, FARDBILJETTER PLATSBILJETTER, identifies it. Take a queue number for seat reservations and sleeping-car accommodations. Hours: Monday-Friday 0545-2100; Saturday 0545–1900; Sunday 0800–2100.

Rail pass validation should be completed before making your first train trip. Operating personnel aboard the trains can validate the pass, but they are required to charge for the service. Validation is free in any regular railway station. In Stockholm's Central Station, use the window marked INTERNATIONAL TICKETS to the right of the main exit.

Money exchange is located in the main station concourse and to the right of the main exit as you proceed from the track area. The office displays the regular pictograph sign plus one reading FOREX (exchange office). Hours: daily 0700-2100.

Hotel reservations at Stockholm Information Service, located in the main station concourse next to the post office. Look for the sign HOTELLCENTRAL TURISTINFORMATION. Hours: June-August 0700–2100 daily; September-May, 0800–1900 daily. Small charges are made for obtaining hotel rooms and space in youth hostels. Advance payment is accepted to assure that the hotel or pension will hold your room until your arrival. If your accommodations are located some distance from the train station, this can be a welcomed service.

Tourist information is available in the rail station at the same office, HOTELLCENTRAL TURISTINFORMATION, or in the main tourist center at Sweden House.

Tourist Information/Hotel Reservations

Stockholm Tourist Information Center: Sweden House; Kungsträdgården; Tel. (08) 789–24–90

Hours: May: 0900–1800 Monday-Friday; 0900–1500 Saturday-Sunday; June-August: 0800–1800 Monday-Friday; 0900–1700 Saturday-Sunday; September: 0900–1800 Monday-Friday; 0900–1500 Saturday-Sunday.

Inquiries about the "Sweden At Home" plan of meeting Swedes with similar interests should be made at this information office. An excellent publication is the *Stockholm Guide.*

Getting Around in Stockholm

The city has excellent transportation facilities for sightseeing in Stockholm. The extensive network of bus and subway systems makes it easy to reach practically any point in the city from any other point.

Your key to the use of these city transportation facilities is **The Stockholm Card,** which provides free admission to 70 of the city's museums and sights, as well as free sightseeing and transportation throughout the Stockholm area. Prices are 185 kronor for 24 hours, 350 for 48 hours, and 470 for 72 hours.

One adult and two children (under age 18) can use the same card. Children ages 6-17 pay half price. The card is on sale at the tourist center in Sweden House and at the central station. It is sold undated and is stamped with the date and hour the first time you use it. With the card, you will be given a folder explaining its use.

Stockholm Sights/Attractions/Tours

Gamla Stan—The Old Town dates back to 1290 and is Stockholm's oldest and most enchanting area. Besides containing many historical sights such as the world's oldest existing bank (since 1656), the Royal Palace, and Parliament, you'll also find unusual shops, art galleries, antique stores, and more than 30 restaurants.

With The Stockholm Card in your pocket, you can expand your day-excursion itinerary to include places of interest in and near Stockholm. For example, you can make a day excursion to **Norrtalje,** with its quaint port, and have lunch aboard a vintage steamer permanently moored there. You can also ride one of the Stockholm Transit Authority (SL) buses to **Furusund,** a narrow passage for ships entering and leaving the city's harbor. You can have lunch in a quaint Inn at Furusund or stay aboard and ride on two ferries to **Blido** in the outer archipelago.

Yet another alternative use for the card would be to take a bus ride to historic **Vaxholm** for a great Swedish lunch at the waterfront hotel overlooking the old fortress and then to explore the shops there at leisure. Stockholm has many museums to explore, so it is difficult to single out but a few recommendations. There is one, however, that we are sure you won't want to miss: the *Vasa* **Museum.**

In 1628, Sweden proudly launched what was then the world's largest warship and pride of the nation, the *Vasa*. She carried the name of the royal family, along with sixty-four cannon, and was presumed to be unconquerable. But the nation's joy was short-lived. The *Vasa* capsized in the harbor during her maiden voyage. She was raised in 1961, painstakingly restored, and now rests in a museum especially constructed for her preservation. The warship is enthroned in the middle of a great hall, displaying the *Vasa* in all her grandeur. The cobblestone ground floor suggests a quay, and the restored warship can be viewed from various perspectives from four levels.

Vasa is unique since it is the oldest fully preserved warship in the world. Films of the raising and the restoration of the *Vasa* are shown hourly in the museum, and guided tours following the film are conducted during the summer.

Day Excursions

We have selected a group of day excursions that will give you an excellent cross section of life in Sweden. **Eskilstuna** is often referred to as "Sweden's Sheffield," although it bears little resemblance to its English counterpart. Next, a trip southward through Ostergotland, where the city of **Norrkoping** will unfold its industrial life styles.

Uppsala brings another contrast, that of a university town. Admittedly, planning day excursions in Sweden is made difficult by the distances involved between the centers of population, but all of these are within reasonable travel times and well worth the visit.

Train Connections to Other Base Cities from Stockholm

TO:	DEPART	ARRIVE	TRAIN NUMBER	NOTES
Berlin Hbf.	1418	0634+1	IC 537/319	(2)
Budapest (Keleti)	1206	1512+1	533/1111	(3)(6)
Copenhagen	1036	1823	287	(5)
	2230	0700+1	283	
Helsinki	1800(1)	0830+1	Ferry	
Oslo	0718	1325	51	
	2342	0732+1	399	(4)

Daily departures unless otherwise noted. Make reservations for all departures.

(1) Depart from Silja Line terminal. No sailings on December 25 or January 1.
(2) Transfer in Malmö to train 319
(3) Transfer in Malmö to train 1011
(4) Daily, except Saturdays (daily in summer)
(5) Runs June 10–August 18
(6) Supplement payable

Day Excursion to

Eskilstuna

SWEDEN'S STEEL CENTER

Depart from Stockholm Central Station

Distance By Train: 73 miles (117 km)
Average Train Time: 1 hour
City Dialing Code: 16
Tourist Information Office: Företagens Hus at Munktellstorget
Tel: (016) 107000; *Fax:* (016) 514575
Hours: June–August 0900–1800 Monday-Friday; 1000–1600 Saturday-Sunday; September-May 0900–1700 Monday-Friday.
    Exit by the front of the station and follow Drottninggatan Street all the way down to Hamngatan. Turn left onto Hamngatan and walk two blocks to Tullgatan. Turn right and cross two small bridges.

Eskilstuna is unique in that it has preserved its industrial birthplace in the midst of a great industrial expansion. In a quiet section in the center of Sweden's "steel town," the well-preserved **Rademacher Forges** stand today just as they have for the last 300 years. Be certain to include a visit to this area during your day excursion.

The Rademacher Forges are the scene of many entertainment programs for visitors to Eskilstuna. In spring and late summer, the "Eskilstuna Guards" present concerts there. Folk dancing and theater performances may be seen in this locale throughout July. Descendants of the "smiths" are still at work forming gold, copper, and iron into colorful trinkets for sale.

The forges were erected in 1658 under the supervision of Reinhold Rademacher. Originally twenty in number, six have been preserved as a tribute to the heritage of modern Eskilstuna. The entire area surrounding the forges was restored in 1959 to commemorate the city's tricentennial. The **Faktorimuseet** is a museum of technology and industrial and cultural history situated in the old Musket Factory.

To expedite your arrival and orientation in the Eskilstuna station, look for a RESTAURANG sign in red with white letters and a VANTSAL sign in blue with white letters. Enter the station at this point. Inside the station, look for an UPPLYSNING sign on the left just beyond the ticket windows. Ask here for a map of the city and instructions for reaching the tourist office at Munktellstorget (Företagens Hus).

Eskilstuna is situated in the most populous part of Sweden. Named after the eleventh-century English missionary Saint Eskil, Eskilstuna is the center of the Swedish steel industry. Its parks and squares, combined with its sparkling charm, do seem, however, to make it unlike any steel town visited previously.

A statue of Saint Eskil stands in the churchyard of the **Fors Kyrka.** Both

Stockholm–Eskilstuna

DEPART STOCKHOLM STATION	ARRIVE IN ESKILSTUNA STATION	NOTES
0810	1025	(1)
1010	1220	(1)
1210	1415	(1)

DEPART ESKILSTUNA STATION	ARRIVE IN STOCKHOLM STATION	NOTES
1530	1745	(1)
1730	1945	(1)
1830	2030	(2)
1930	2140	(1)

(1) Daily
(2) Monday through Friday

Distance: 73 miles/117 km

the statue and the church are worthy of a visit. The church and statue are marked as No. 6 on the Eskilstuna map. It can be one of your stops when you are en route back to the railway station, which is No. 24 on the map.

Eskilstuna's town charter dates from 1659. In 1971, five surrounding rural communities, together with the town of Torshälla, merged with Eskilstuna. Torshälla is more than 650 years old. Its name was derived from the Nordic god, Thor, who was worshipped by offertory gatherings of the barbarians occupying Torshälla.

Some 50 prehistoric monuments are in the immediate area surrounding Eskilstuna, the best known being the **Sigurd Rock** carving—Scandinavia's first "strip cartoon." The tourist information office can help in finding transportation to the carvings.

The **Park Zoo** (Parken Zoo) in Eskilstuna ranks as one of Scandinavia's most visited tourist attractions. Open May–September at 1000 daily. In addition to the zoological gardens, there are an amusement park known as the Tivoli, a heated swimming pool with water slides, and Phantom Land, a popular play area for children. For the younger set, the zoological gardens offers its famous Flamingo Valley and a petting zoo in its animal park. The zoo is noted for its collection of animals that are unique and rare to Sweden, including a dwarf panda, walruses, and a family of white tigers. In the wild, the white tiger is thought to be extinct. To our knowledge, Eskilstuna's Park Zoo and the Mirage Hotel in Las Vegas, Nevada, are the only places in the world where one can still see these animals in any number.

The city is well endowed with works of art. The art museum (open daily, except Monday, 1200-1600) is particularly proud of its collection of Swedish art from the seventeenth century to the present. Exhibitions of contemporary art succeed each other at intervals of between three and four weeks throughout the year.

Eskilstuna's **Djurgård open-air museum** of cultural history is centered around **Sörmlandsgården,** a typical nineteenth-century farm commune, and Herrgärden, a manor house from the same period. The farm is complete with a hay barn, stables, a storage shed, and a curious apparatus used for shoeing oxen. The manor house includes a number of rooms furnished in different periods of history.

Eight miles outside Eskilstuna by public bus lines is **Sundbyholm Castle.** Built by an illegitimate son of a Swedish king, it has been restored to its original splendor, and a restaurant has been added.

Day Excursion to

Norrkoping THE NORTHERN CACTUS CENTER

Depart from Stockholm Central Station

Distance By Train: 101 miles (163 km)
Average Train Time: 2 hours
City Dialing Code: 11
Tourist Information Office: Tradgardsgatan & Drottninggatan
Tel: (46) 11-151500
Hours: 0900–1900 Monday-Friday; 0900–1500 Saturday-Sunday in summer. September-May, 1000–1700 daily.

Norrkoping's tourist information office is located conveniently near the railway station. You will find it on the corner of Tradgardsgatan and Drottninggatan, 200 meters from the station.

Believe it or not, Ripley's *Believe It or Not* featured Norrkoping many years ago. People would not believe that 25,000 cactus plants were growing in Sweden. It's true. They are growing there even today. The cactus plantation is in **Karl Johans Park** in front of and at the opposite end from the railway station. Approximately 25,000 cactus plants are rearranged annually according to a new theme by the city's gardeners. The motifs vary from year to year, reflecting important events within the community.

The **Karl Johans Park** must be the best kept park of its kind in the world. Its appearance can only be described as "manicured." From its fountain to its

Stockholm—Norrkoping

DEPART STOCKHOLM STATION	TRAIN NUMBER	ARRIVE IN NORRKOPING STATION	NOTES
0730	IC 23	0917	(2)(3)(4)
1036	287	1212	(1)(2)(3)
1516	IC 39	1705	(1)(2)(3)

DEPART NORRKOPING STATION	TRAIN NUMBER	ARRIVE IN STOCKHOLM STATION	NOTES
1653	IC 40	1847	(1)(2)(3)
1740	286	1917	(1)(2)(3)
2135	IC 50	2325	(1)(2)(3)

(1) Daily, including holidays
(2) Seat reservations mandatory
(3) Food service available
(4) Monday through Saturday only

Distance: 101 miles/163 km

floral arrangements, it reflects a quiet blending of nature's most beautiful assets into an atmosphere of contentment and relaxation. Its tranquillity is broken pleasantly at intervals by the chattering of countless parakeets housed in an aviary near the fountain. Perhaps a primary reason for the high quality of the cactus and floral displays is the presence of Sweden's National School of Gardening and the Flower School.

If roses are your favorites, go to the **Himmelstalundsparken** (Himmelstalund Park) and visit its rose gardens. You can combine this visit with an inspection of the 3,000-year-old Bronze Age rock carvings, also a part of this park, that are to the right of the railway station

The city is one of Sweden's most important industrial cities. Take a walk in the old industrial section. You'll find industrial buildings dating from the nineteenth century.

The town hall has a carillon that is prized by its citizens. It helps create the ambiance of the town that has been referred to often by visitors as the Paris of the North. The time to hear the carillon is at 0955, 1155, 1455, or 1655. Following the carillon performance, it might be a good time to stroll along the banks of the nearby Motala Ström River in the old city center. You can follow the river down to the old Dyer's House to see how wool was made and dyed in the old days. There's also a café where you can relax and have a snack.

While at the tourist information office, inquire about the **Kolmarden-Norrkoping Card**. It's a special ticket that gives you a multitude of visitor admissions and discounts. To mention just a few: sightseeing by boat; entrance to the **Lofstad Castle**; a complimentary ride on the **old Number 1 tram,** restored from circa 1902; and free admission to the animal and nature park, **Kolmarden.**

The ruins of the **Johannisborg Fort** lie on the left of the rail station. All that remain of the Johannisborg Fort now are the gate tower and its ramparts, but these are enough to convey a mental image of how this magnificent construction (started in 1613) must have looked.

Other sights near the railway station are the **Gamla Torget** (Old Square), the Concert and Congress Hall **Louis de Geer**, the **Radhus** (town hall), and the **Hedvigs Kyrka** (German Church). All are clustered in the city's center.

Twenty-five kilometers north of Norrkoping is the largest animal and nature park in Europe—the **Kolmarden Zoo.** There are no bars or cages, and the animals thrive in large outdoor pens. Check with the tourist office for transportation details.

Day Excursion to

Uppsala

UNIVERSITY CITY

Depart from Stockholm Central Station

Distance By Train: 40 miles (66 km)
Average Train Time: 43 minutes
City Dialing Code: 18
Tourist Information Office: 8 Fyristorg
Tel: 27 4800
Hours: July–August: 1000–1800 Monday-Friday; 1000–1500 Saturday; 1200–1600 Sunday. September-June: 1000–1800 Monday-Friday; 1000–1500 Saturday.
    Five-minute walk from the railway station. Exit the station and walk diagonally through the small park in front to the main street, Kungsgatan. Turn right, then turn left on Vaksalagatan (the next crossing). Walk until you reach the square (Stora Torget) where all the city buses meet. Follow the street Drottninggatan from the square and cross the small river Fyrisan. Turn right immediately after the bridge, and the tourist office is identified by the traditional "i" sign.

No other town in Sweden has such a long recorded history as Uppsala. This is where Sweden began. As far back as the sixth century, it was the political and religious center of the expanding Swedish kingdom. According to the ancient legends, pagans from all reaches of the kingdom came to Uppsala every ninth year to feast and offer up sacrifices until the eleventh century, when Christianity began to take over. Legend has it that one of the kings of the period, King Aun, got all wrapped up in the nine-year cycle by sacrificing one of

Stockholm–Uppsala

DEPART STOCKHOLM STATION	TRAIN NUMBER	ARRIVE IN UPPSALA STATION	NOTES
0823	IC 958	0904	(1)(2)(3)
1023	IC 880	1104	(1)(2)(3)

DEPART UPPSALA STATION	TRAIN NUMBER	ARRIVE IN STOCKHOLM STATION	NOTES
1502	IC 883	1553	(2)(3)(4)
1702	IC 963	1745	(1)(2)(3)
2032	IC 965	1843	(1)(2)(3)
2102	IC 885	2043	(1)(2)(3)

(1) Daily, including holidays
(2) Seat reservations mandatory
(3) Food service available
(4) Daily, except Saturdays

Distance: 40 miles/66 km

---

his sons each cycle. His tenth and last son put an end to old dad—and to the cycle, too! Sort of the start of Swedish scams, don't you think?

Modern Uppsala won't remind you of Oxford or Heidelberg—or Bryn Mawr, for that matter. Uppsala is a university town but with an academic environment distinctly its own. The city and the area surrounding it enshrine a great deal of Swedish history encompassing religion (pagan and Christian alike), academe, and politics. This composite results in a city of multifaceted interests, architecture, and customs.

Gamla Uppsala (Old Uppsala) lies three miles north of the present city center. Here, the graves of the sixth-century Ynglinga Dynasty kings are found. The pagan religion of the Vikings persisted here well into the eleventh century. A twelfth-century church, heralding the advent of Christianity, then replaced the pagan temple. The area now is an open-air museum, accessible to visitors daily during June, July, and August.

Uppsala Castle stands on a hill overlooking the city. Begun in the 1540s by King Gustav Vasa as a symbol of his power over the church, it was completed during the reign of Queen Christina. The king had cannon mounted on the castle pointing at the church. They still point that way today. Partially destroyed by fire in 1702, the castle has been restored. After the extensive renovation in 1994, you can now visit new parts of the castle on a forty-five-minute guided tour conducted in English at 1115 and 1415 from June 22 through August 11. You'll see the Hall of State and the castle church's uncovered altar wall.

The great **Hall of State** is frequently the scene of historic events. Both the coronation banquet for Gustavus Adolphus and Queen Christina's abdication took place within the castle's walls. The castle is open 1100–1600 daily from mid-May to mid-September. A more restricted schedule is followed during the remainder of the year.

Three-quarters of Uppsala was destroyed by fire in 1702. It was in the subsequent period of reconstruction that the character of the city changed. The university and its scholars began to dominate, and the reputation of the university spread throughout the civilized world. The present university building was opened in 1887.

The university library houses a collection of more than two million bound volumes and 30,000 manuscripts. The library is open to the public. Weekday access is permitted only during university holidays and vacation periods, but anyone may enter on any Saturday throughout the year from 0900-1700.

In Uppsala, Saint Erik, Saint Olof, and Saint Lars's church is usually referred to as **The Cathedral**. Two of its patron saints, Erik and Olof, were Christian kings in Scandinavia during the eleventh and twelfth centuries, when the Christians finally had the pagans on the run. Lars died a martyr's death in Rome in A.D. 258. Building of the cathedral started in the late thirteenth century, and it took a century and a half to complete. It has been ravaged by fires, and its towers collapsed, but with Swedish determination it was restored. English-language tours of the Uppsala Cathedral are conducted during the summer months.

Switzerland

Switzerland is a year-round wonderland of astonishing beauty and one of the most multilingual countries in Europe. You can experience several different cultures encompassing four national languages—all within one neat little country. The German-speaking Swiss make up 65 percent of the population; French, 18 percent; Italian, 10 percent; and Romansch, 1 percent and 70 plus dialects lend a special charisma to tiny villages and hamlets. And many Swiss can speak all four languages and English, too.

The diversity doesn't end there—from majestic snow-capped mountains to languid palm-fringed lakes, from cowbells and yodeling to craftsmanship and incredible feats of railroad engineering—Switzerland is surprising.

For more information about Switzerland, contact the Switzerland Tourism Offices of North America:

Internet: http://www.switzerlandtourism.com; Email: stnewyork@switzerlandtourism.com

Chicago: 150 North Michigan Avenue, Suite 2930, Chicago. IL 60601. Tel: (312)630-5840

Los Angeles: 222 North Sepulveda Boulevard, Suite 1570, El Segundo, CA 90245. Tel: (310) 335-5980; Fax: (310) 335-5982

New York: 608 Fifth Avenue, New York, NY 10020. Tel: (212) 262-2090; Fax: (212) 262-6116

Toronto: 926 The East Mall, Etobicoke, Ontario M9B 6K1. Tel: (416)695-2090; Fax: (416) 695-2774

Banking

- **Hours:** 0830-1630 Monday-Friday
- **Currency:** Swiss Franc (SFr.)
- **Exchange rate at time of press:** 1.45 Swiss francs = $1.00 US

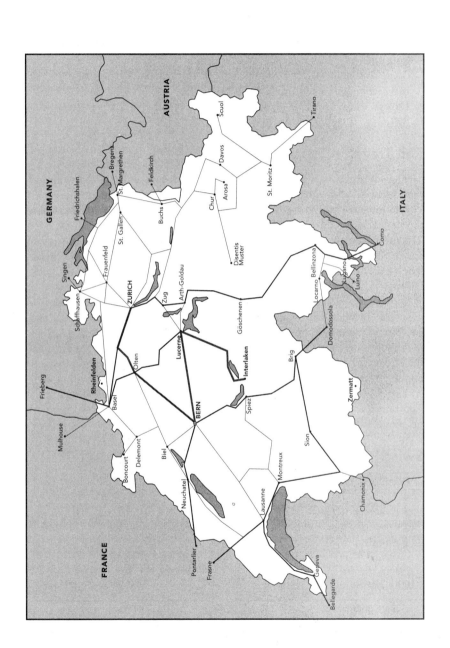

Communications

- **Country Dialing Code:** 41
  For telephone calls within Switzerland, dial zero (0) preceding area code. You can buy a Calling Card for calls within Switzerland at any Swiss post office. International calls can be placed from public phones at the post office and some major railway stations.
- **Direct dial:** AT&T: 0-800-890011; MCI: 0-800-890222; Sprint: 0-800-899777

Rail Travel in Switzerland

The Swiss are well known for their excellence in clock production and they know how to run a railroad with the same finesse—on time.

According to the Swiss, only the "Man in the Moon" knows how dense the network of railroads in Switzerland *really* is. Although Switzerland is only 216 miles from north to south and 137 miles from east to west, more than 3,000 miles of rail lines run through it. Even mountains don't stop the Swiss. They either tunnel through them or scale their heights with funiculars or cog railways.

Switzerland has one of the longest railroad tunnels, the highest railroad, plus more bridges, tunnels, and other engineering works per square mile than any other country in the world.

The Swiss Federal Railways (CFF/SBB) accepted the following rail passes which can be purchased in advance of your departure for Europe: the 17-country **Eurailpass,** the 5-country **Europass, Swiss Pass,** and **Swiss Card.**

The **Swiss Pass** provides unlimited travel on Swiss Federal Railways, private railways, lake steamers, and city and bus lines. Children age 6-15 are 50 percent adult fare; children under age 6 travel free.

Swiss Pass ($US)

CONSECUTIVE DAYS	1ST CLASS	2ND CLASS
4 days	$ 264	$176
8 days	316	220
15 days	368	256
1 month	508	350

Flexipass

3 days of travel within a 15-day period	$264	$176

The **Swiss Card** is a good buy for skiers—it provides one round trip rail journey within a 1-month period for $142 (U.S.) First Class or $116, Second Class. Children age 6-15 pay half adult fare in Second Class and 60 percent of the adult fare in First Class.

The **Swiss Family Card** provides for children under age 16 to travel free when traveling with an adult. This card is *free* when you purchase any Swiss Pass.

Swiss Federal Railways provide the following bonuses to holders of a **Eurailpass or Europass:**
- Alpnachstad-Mont Pilatus (see Lucerne section)—cable railway 35 percent discount
- Biel-Solothurn (on the Aare River)—ship free
- Burgenstock cable railway—50 percent discount
- Jungfrau Region Railways—25 percent discount
- Kriems-Mont Pilatus—cable railway—35 percent discount
- Lake Constance (Bodensee)
- Romanshorn-Friedrichhafen (Germany)—ship 50 percent discount
- Rorschach-Lindau (Germany)—ship 50 percent discount
- Rorschach-Romanshorn (Germany)—ship 35 percent discount
- Schaffhausen-Kreuzlingen (on the Rhine River)—ship Free
- Steamer services on lakes from Biel, Brienz, Geneva, Lucerne, Murten, Neuchatel, Thun, and Zurich—free
- Transportation Museum in Lucerne—35 percent off entrance fee
- Vitznau-Rigi Railways—25 discount

Some of Switzerland's most scenic railroads (below) also accept Eurailpass or Europass; most private railroads, however, do not, although some offer discounts (above). Reservations are mandatory and cost extra.
- Bernina Express—Chur—St. Moritz—Bernina Pass—Poschiavo—Tirano—Valtellina (Italy)—Lugano
- Centovalli Railway—Locarno—S. Maria Maggiore—Domodossola
- Glacier Express—St. Moritz/Davos—Zermatt
  Eurailpass/Europass valid only between Davos/St. Moritz and Disentis. You must purchase an additional point-to-point ticket for the portion from Disentis to Zermatt.
- Golden Pass—Lucerne—*Brunig Panoramic Express*—Interlaken—Zweisimmen—*Crystal Panoramic Express*—Montreux
- William Tell Express—Lucerne—Fluelen—St. Gotthard—Locarno/Lugano
  Reservations compulsory and includes seats on the boat, train, lunch on the boat, journey documentation, and a souvenir.

Base City...

Berne (Bern)

City Dialing Code: 31

Berne has the unique distinction of being the only city in Europe joined by all three of Europe's high-speed trains—the TGV from Paris, the ICE from Berlin, and the Cisalpino from Milan.

Berne, the federal capital of Switzerland, was built between the twelfth and eighteenth centuries. According to legend, it was named after the first animal caught in the area, a bear, and bears have played a part in its history ever since. The city's bear pits, where the animals are raised and displayed, are a "must" stop on any tour.

The most striking thing about Berne is its medieval appearance. Some of the buildings in the city's old town date from the thirteenth and fourteenth centuries. The low silhouette of its roof lines appears to be different from most of Europe's other cities with origins in the same era—and indeed it is, for there is a medieval ordinance still in effect today that mandates each roof line be at a different level from adjoining structures. This ancient architectural asset is most visible when you view the city from the Nydeggbrück Bridge crossing the Aare en route to the bear pits. If you miss it, you'll have another opportunity when you view the city from the location of its rose gardens on the high bluff of the Aare's right bank.

Berne is a medieval city, yet it is a new city as well. Over the centuries, Berne's citizens have developed a remarkable means of combining modern living with the centuries-old facades of their surroundings. It is cosmopolitan, with a wide selection of restaurants, hotels, museums, and concert halls. Modern Berne has grown well beyond the curve of the Aare and into the surrounding foothills. The main commercial, cultural, and political activities of the city, however, still take place in its old sector.

The Aare River embraces Berne in a great natural bend. Like the river, you too will embrace this ancient Swiss city, once you have trod its cobblestone streets.

In summer, Berne leads you to believe it is the geranium capital of the world as well as being the federal capital of Switzerland. These flowers bloom everywhere in an eye-dazzling display of color. Berne was once voted Europe's most beautiful city of flowers. You will be bewitched by Berne, beguiled by its bears, and satisfied with its sights.

Arriving By Air

Switzerland's international airports, Zurich and Geneva, connect incoming flights with trains to Berne. Berne is only one hour and thirty minutes away from Zurich's airport and two hours from Geneva's by comfortable passenger trains that depart daily from the airports every thirty minutes. In Zurich, the rail station lies immediately beneath the airport's terminal. In Geneva, the rail station and the airport terminal are connected by a plaza. At the Bern-Belp Airport (9 km south of the City Centre), direct connections can be made to and from many European cities.

Arriving by Train

Berne's modern rail station is a small city within a city, with an impressive array of facilities including a spacious underground arcade that connects at its surface entrances with the city's fabled, arcaded shopping walkways. Direct rail transport from Berne to such destinations as Amsterdam, Berlin, Brussels, Luxembourg, Milan, Munich, Paris, and Venice is available.

Forty-seven trains a day depart Berne for Zurich at 53 minutes past the hour; the majority of these trains also stop at the Zurich airport following the city stop. Fifteen trains a day depart Berne for Geneva at sixteen minutes past the hour. Upon arrival in Geneva, stay aboard, and nine minutes later you will be at the Geneva airport.

Berne's Railway Station. Berne's railway station is a model of efficiency and functionalism. Trains are reached from its ground level via ramps, thus making the use of baggage carts practical.

With your baggage stacked in one of the station's baggage carts, leave the train platform by descending the ramp, then turn in the direction of track 1 and walk to the end of the passageway, where you will emerge into the station's underground arcade, with its myriad of shops and services. You'll see the escalators directly ahead.

Escalators take you to the other levels of the station. Elevator service is also available. If you have your luggage on a cart, use the elevators. At street level you will find the **train information** and **Bern Tourismus** information offices, plus additional facilities such as shops and restaurants. Snack bars and fruit stands prevail on the ground level; more extensive food-service facilities are on the upper levels, ending at the top of the escalators with a full-service restaurant.

Baggage storage. Visitors burdened with baggage may want to use the coin lockers on the ground (train) level or the HANDGEPACK SERVICE (baggage room) immediately opposite the coin lockers. Taxi service is available from the street level—follow the pictographs—but check with Bern Tourismus before attempting to use the public-bus and streetcar services. Their access ramps, fares, ticket machines, and so forth can be confusing.

A suburban train station is located on the underground arcade level. To reach it, continue past the escalators that run to the street level and watch for its entrance on the left side of the passageway. This system is operated by a private Swiss railroad. Swiss Passes are accepted and Eurailpasses and Europasses are accepted by *some* private Swiss railroads such as RBS. Check prior to boarding the train.

The Berne station, like most of the major rail terminals in Switzerland, will accept your baggage and check it through the Zurich or Geneva airports directly to your U.S. port of entry. Trains for both airports depart the Berne station every 30 minutes throughout the day. Place your baggage on a train an hour or so in advance of your departure for the airport.

- **Money-exchange** facilities, two of them, are located on the ground level of the station. Both may be reached by turning right, just before the elevators, as you come out of the passageway leading from the trains. Both will be on your right as you proceed into the station's arcade. The first office, marked CHANGE SBB, is operated by the Swiss railroads. Opening hours: June-October 15, 0615–2145 daily; October 16-May 31, 0615-2045. There is also an ATM.

   The second facility is a full-service bank, the **Credit Suisse.** It is a few more steps away in the arcade. Hours: 0800–1630 Monday, Tuesday, Wednesday, Friday; 0800–1800 Thursdy. There are several banks in the plaza surrounding the station. The rates of exchange are standard throughout the city each day, however, and the rail-station money-exchange facilities are the most convenient. There is also a money exchange machine available 24 hours a day near the station at Schwanengasse 4.

- **Train information, reservations, and rail pass validations** can be obtained from the rail-reservations center immediately across the passageway from the tourist information office. Look for blue "i" sign. Hours: 0800–1900 Monday–Friday; 0800–1700 Saturday. It dispenses rail information, reservations, and other services, including validation of rail passes. Keep in mind that your Eurailpass is accepted on all of the Swiss federal railways and lake steamers; on the other hand, it is accepted only on a few of the private railroads, the *Golden Pass* being one of them. To be certain, check your day excursions plans with the train information office. For example, if you plan to ascend the **Jungfrau**, a Eurail or Europass will take you to **Interlaken**, where you must purchase a ticket for the private railroads leading out of **Interlaken** to **Grindelwald** or **Lauterbrunnen** and **Wengen** en route to the **Jungfrau.**

- **Tourist information** and **hotel reservations** are available at **Bern Tourismus,** one of the most complete information centers in Europe. Turn left coming off the escalator from the ground level, then right at the passageway leading to the street. The office will be a few steps farther on your right. It is identified by a green "i" sign. Hours during summer

(June–September): 0900–2030 daily; remainder of the year, 0900–1830 Monday-Saturday; 1000–1700 Sunday. Hotel booking fee: 3 Sfr.

Ask here for the booklets *Berne Informations* and *Berne Excursions*, an informative publication listing more day excursions from Berne by rail, lake steamer, and postal buses.

- **Hotel Reservations** can also be made by using an automatic telephone system located beside Bern Tourismus. The automatic telephone system makes finding and booking a hotel an easy task. There is a lighted board showing the locations of the hotels along with pictures of the hotels and their room rates. Press the button for your choice, and you'll be immediately connected with the hotel by telephone to discuss vacancies.

Sights/Attractions/Tours

There are two excellent means of sightseeing in Berne: on foot or by comfortable motor coach escorted by a multilingual guide. From May through October the bus departs from in front of the railway station at 1000 and 1400 daily; November through March, at 1400 on Saturday; and in April at 1400 Monday through Saturday. The bus tour takes two hours.

If interested in the walking tour, ask at the tourist office for the *Short City Sightseeing Map.* It leads you right through the heart of Berne's ancient walled city to its famed **bear pits** (open daily 0800–1800 April-September and 0900–1600 October-March). From there you return to your point of departure by a different route. According to the map, the entire route can be covered in approximately one hour, but without any stops en route. Plan for a minimum of two hours and consider yourself lucky if you make it in three. (According to the tourist office, no one has ever returned within the hour.)

Be certain to see the *Zeitglockenturm,* the city's famous clock tower. It first began ticking in the year 1250, and it is still the city's official timepiece today. The clock's glockenspiel starts promptly at four minutes before the hour as accompaniment to a parade of armed bear figures following a rooster. It's quite a show. What makes it tick? Take the fascinating 45-minute guided tour *inside* the clock tower. Purchase your ticket (6 sfr.) at Bern Tourismus from the tour guide, or at your hotel.

Another unusual feature of Berne is its **shopping arcades**—nearly four miles of them. They line the route of the walking tour suggested by Bern Tourismus and offer one of the finest selections of wares and food to be found anywhere in the world. The shopping arcades are completely covered, so they are weatherproof as well as traffic-free and totally delightful. On Tuesday and Saturday mornings, there are markets where Swiss farmers sell their meat and produce. Shop the city's arcades Monday-Friday 0900–1830 (until 2100 on Thursday), and 0815–1600 Saturday.

Or, if museums appeal to you, Berne has plenty to choose from, including the **Swiss Alpine Museum, Museum of Communication,** and the **Einstein House**—even a **Museum of Psychiatry.**

For a view of Berne from an unusual perspective, take the **city tour by raft** on the river Aare (tickets cost 35 Sfr). The two-hour rafting tour departs at 1730 from Schwellenmätteli (indicated on the city map) and includes a ten-passenger raft, life jackets, paddles and, of course, a guide.

Day Excursions

Berne is an ideal base for day excursions to almost any point in Switzerland. Geneva is one hour and forty train minutes to the west; you can reach Zurich to the east by rail in only one hour and ten minutes. Travel north and, in sixty-eight minutes, your train will set you down in Basel on the banks of the Rhine.

The five day excursions that we have selected for this edition reveal the natural grandeur of the country. The **Golden Pass** adventure takes you through Alpine surroundings, in the comfort of a vista-dome rail car, to Lake Geneva and a cruise on the lake before returning to Berne. The outing to Interlaken unfolds a panorama of towering peaks along the shore of the Lake of Thun, where again you have the opportunity of a lake cruise to conclude a memorable day.

Picture-postcard perfect, **Lucerne** will charm you with its scenery, cuisine, and ambiance. Promenade along its ancient walkways, scale nearby Mount Pilatus, or cruise the Lake of Lucerne during your visit.

For a peek at a Disney-type setting that has been going strong since the eleventh century, journey to **Rheinfelden,** where the mighty Rhine River swirls past a medieval setting that stirs the imagination. Or travel to Brig to catch the **Glacier Express** to **Zermatt** to view the magnificent Matterhorn.

Train Connections to other Base Cities from Berne

TO:	DEPART	ARRIVE	TRAIN NUMBER	NOTES
Barcelona	2122	0913	EN 274	(1)
(França)	1916	0903	378/1472/3	(2)
Berlin	1753	0735+1	1857	(7)(8)
Brussels (Midi)	1448	2237	EC 90	(8)
Luxembourg	0648	1200	IC 952/296	(3)
	1148	1956	EC 90	
Lyon (Part-Dieu)	0840	1224	TGV 868	(1)
	1040	1447	5768	(1)
	1416	1818	5770	(1)
Milan	0850	1245	IC 863	
	1258	1645	IC 333	
	1526	1925	EC 91	
Munich	0814	1357	IC 711/8067	
	1214	1748	EC 95/ IC 721	(5)
Nice	0811	1813	1023/2407	(1)
Paris (Lyon)	0656	1132	TGV 422	
Rome	0850	1755	IC 863/ES 9419	(4)
Zürich	0653	0831	2709	(6)

Daily departures unless otherwise noted. Make reservations for all departures.

(1) Transfer in Geneva
(2) Transfer in Geneva to sleeper train EN 274, *Pablo Casals,* Gran Classe sleeper, supplement payable, Eurailpass and Europass *not* accepted.
(3) Transfer in Basel
(4) Transfer in Milan
(5) Transfer in Zurich to EC 95
(6) Hourly service at 53 minutes past each hour until 2053; most trains continue on to airport
(7) Supplement payable
(8) Transfer in Zürich to EN 359

EURAIL TRAVEL NOTE: A timetable bookshop is operated by the Swiss Federal Railways in St. Gallen, Switzerland, where you may purchase the current official timetables of many European countries, as well as a wide range of rail travel literature and rail maps. St. Gallen is one hour by train from Zurich in the direction of Austria and Germany. Call at Room 224 in the St. Gallen rail station or telephone ahead on 071–222–1021, extension 208, for details.

Day Excursion to

The Golden Pass

THE ALPS Á LA TRAIN

Depart from Berne

Distance By Train: 65 miles (104 km) to Montreux
City Dialing Code: 21
Average Train Time: 10 hours, 25 minutes
Montreux Tourist Information: Place du Debarcadere, 1820
Tel: 962 8484; *Fax:* 963 7895
Internet: http://www.montreux.ch
Hours: October 1–March 1 open Monday–Friday, 090–1800. April 1–September 30
open Monday–Saturday. 0900–1800; Sunday 0900–1200.

Dollar for dollar, or franc for franc, this day excursion is one of the best
Eurail train-travel values in Europe. The Lucerne-Interlaken-Montreux rail
route provides an exciting variety of landscapes and cultures. The Montreux-
Bernese-Oberland Railroad (MOB) operates the **Crystal Panoramic Express,**
the **Golden Panoramic Express,** and the **Panoramic Express.** These trains offer
an unobstructed view of the breathtaking scenery between Zweisimmen and
Montreux.

Before departure, check with Bern Tourism. Inform them you are going
on the *Golden Pass* trip and pick up the booklet *Berne Excursions.* (The booklet is usually available in the train information office as well.) Trains run
through the Golden Pass rather frequently, and you may want to follow a different schedule. We selected the **Crystal Panoramic Express,** a luxury first-
class train with panoramic-view windows and bar car on the portion of the
route from Zweisimmen to Montreux and vice versa.

There is ample time for a leisurely lunch in Montreux before boarding a
lake steamer to Chillon. Disembark and go ashore to visit its famous castle.
Chateau de Chillon is a beautifully restored eleventh century castle which
was made famous by Lord Byron in his poetic story of the imprisonment of
Francois de Bonivard. After touring the castle, board another lake steamer
back to Montreux. Then, ride the funicular adjacent to the steamer dock to
the **Lausanne** train station, and board your train back to Berne. Whew! It's a
day loaded with extras.

Check the weather report the night before embarking on this day excursion. The clearer the day, the better. You will be viewing some of the Alps'
most spectacular scenery, and if it's shrouded in clouds, it just might spoil your
day. To get the weather report in English, dial 162 on any Swiss telephone.

InterCity trains usually depart from the Berne railway station on track 6,
but double-check just to be sure. The destination of this train is **Brig,** and it
makes a stop at **Thun** (pronounced "tune") before it arrives at **Spiez.** At

Thun, the beautiful Lake of Thun comes into view. As you approach Spiez, you'll see Mount Niesen (7,750 feet) towering over this quiet town on the southwestern shore of the lake.

In Spiez you have eleven minutes to cross a platform to board the next train—time enough to enjoy the breathtaking view. **Zweisimmen,** the next stop and transfer point, lies almost halfway between Spiez and Montreux. When you depart Spiez, you will enter the Golden Pass.

The transfer at Zweisimmen places you aboard MOB's *Crystal Panoramic Express* on a narrow-gauge railroad, with Montreux as its destination. The best instruction here is to "follow the crowd" as you move between the standard- and narrow-gauge trains. The *Panoramic Express* narrow-gauge train will make two stops before reaching Montreux (three from mid-December through March, when it calls at **Saanenmose**r during the skiing season).

The first regular stop is **Gstaad,** which, you may recall, is the alpine-resort retreat of many famous movie stars including Elizabeth Taylor and Roger Moore. During his lifetime, Richard Burton frequented the area, and the late David Niven maintained a chalet there on a mountainside for many years.

Berne–The Golden Pass

TRAIN NUMBER	DEPART		ARRIVE			NOTES
IC 865	Berne	0926	Spiez	0956	Transfer	(1)
2346	Spiez	1002	Zweisimmen	1039	Transfer	(1)
2	Zweisimmen	1044	Montreux	1228	Lunch★	(1)
Lake steamer	Montreux		Chillon		Visit castle	(2)
Lake steamer	Chillon	1545	Montreux	1705	Stay aboard	(2)
Lake steamer	Montreux	1545	Lausanne	1705	Transfer★★	(2)
2128	Montreux	1710	Lausanne	1727	Transfer	(1)
2739	Lausanne	1725	Berne	1839	Terminate	(1)(3)
IC 739	Lausanne	1802	Berne	1911	Alternate	(1)(3)
IC 745	Lausanne	2102	Berne	2211	Last train	(1)(4)

★ Majestic Hotel, between rail station and city pier, recommended. Have your Berne hotel concierge call to make reservations: telephone 021/9635181.

★★ From Lausanne pier, cross city park diagonally to rack railroad. Second stop en route is Lausanne Gare Centrale (central station). Eurailpass accepted.

(1) Daily, including holidays

(2) Seasonal, June–September; check at pier

(3) Dining car

(4) Food service

Chateau d'Oex (pronounced "day") is an alpine resort, too, but more at the family level, frequented by the Genevese when they grow tired of viewing beautiful Lake Geneva—possibly because it's flat.

Our "wood pile theory" can be tested—at least two-thirds of it—because you will be passing from a German-speaking area into one of French habitation. Based on research we have made during several decades of European rail travel, the theory is: Germans pile wood with precision, Italians pile it artistically, and the French stack theirs with an air of independence. The two regular stops are Gstaad and Chateau d'Oex. Watch what happens to the wood piles between these two points. Gstaad, as the name may imply, is German; Chateau d'Oex lies in the French-speaking district.

Approaching Montreux, the train descends 2,000 feet to Lake Geneva in much the same manner as a jet airliner does when entering a landing pattern. It whirls through a series of hairpin curves for almost a half hour before coming to rest beside the main Montreux railway station. Have your camera handy, for you are going to see some sensational scenery during the descent.

You have several options while visiting Montreux. You can extend your shopping and sightseeing in the city for one hour and fifty minutes if you forgo Chillon and yet board the same steamer for Lausanne and not miss any of your friends who may have elected to see the castle made famous by Lord Byron. If it's stormy on Lake Geneva, you can still keep to the schedule by proceeding to Lausanne by rail.

Chillon-bound passengers should scurry to the castle as quickly as possible after the lake steamer docks to ensure maximum use of the time ashore. The steamer proceeds on to the French port of St. Gingolph and then returns to Chillon. Check at the Chillon dock for its return time. Should you miss the boat, you still have another option. Hail a cab back to Montreux, then entrain for Lausanne to join your friends in the dining car en route back to Berne.

Day Excursion to

Interlaken

LAKE OF THUN CRUISE

Depart From Berne

Distance By Train: 37 miles (59 km)
Average Train Time: 50 minutes
City Dialing Code: 36
Tourism Office: Interlaken Tourism office is on the left side of the Höheweg, about a five-minute walk from the station During
Tel: 33–8222121; *Fax:* 33–8225221
Internet: http://www.interlakentourism.ch

Email: Mail@Interlakentourism.Ch
Hours: July-August, 0800–1830 Monday-Friday; 0800–1700 Saturday; 1700–1900 Sunday. Hours are shorter the rest of the year, and the office is closed Sunday.

Interlaken can best be described as the cultural and social focal point of Switzerland's Alpine areas. The English poet Lord Byron is said to have exclaimed, "It's a dream!" at his first sighting of Interlaken and its surroundings. Nestled between the **Lake of Thun** and the **Lake of Brienz,** Interlaken (Latin for "between the lakes") began in the twelfth century as a small cluster of buildings surrounding a monastery, traces of which can still be seen today.

The town's main thoroughfare, **Höheweg,** is lined with great hotels, shops, and even a grand casino that is set back from the main promenade and banked with such beautiful flowers that one might think it is a retirement home.

For Interlaken, the Höheweg plays the same part as does the Champs-Elysées for Paris or the Via Veneto for Rome—it is *the boulevard*, with the ambiance for which the Swiss are famous. Just as in its larger counterparts, you'll find strollers on foot or aboard horse-drawn carriages taking in the sights along with those relaxing over coffee and pastries at the sidewalk cafés. Towering over this entire scene is the **Jungfrau,** a massive mountain that tops out at 13,642 feet above sea level, a mere 11 miles south of Interlaken. On a clear day the view is dazzling.

Believe it or not, the Jungfrau can be scaled by train. Beginning in Interlaken at its the east (Ost) rail station, a private cog railroad terminates at the Jungfraujoch station, at 11,333 feet, the highest rail terminal in the world. The round trip takes the better half of a day and it should be made only in ideal weather. Furthermore, the round-trip fare is just as steep as the ascent, 163.60 Swiss francs per person first class and 153.20 francs for second class. Eurailpass or Europass does, however, provide a 25 precent discount. Plan your "assault" on the Jungfrau for a separate day after you have checked the weather—and your wallet.

If you *must* scale a mountain while in Interlaken, take the funicular running up to **Harderkulm,** which overlooks Interlaken to the south from 4,333 feet above sea level. On a clear day you can see both lakes surrounding Interlaken, as well as the Jungfrau. This can be done in about an hour for only 20 Swiss francs per person. The Harderulm station is only a short walk from Interlaken's Ost (east) station. Ask for directions at the tourist office.

Interlaken has two railway stations, west and east. Coming from Berne, you arrive first in the west station. Disembark here rather than riding another five minutes to the east station. Remember, however, if you are closer to the east station as your visit draws to a close, you can catch the same train from that point, too—but five minutes ahead of the west-station schedule.

Berne–Interlaken

DEPART BERNE STATION	TRAIN NUMBER	ARRIVE IN INTERLAKEN WEST STATION*
0822	IC 961	0912
0922	IC 910	1012
1022	IC 969	1112
1122	916	1215

DEPART INTERLAKEN WEST STATION**	TRAIN NUMBER	ARRIVE IN BERNE STATION
1450	IC 924	1538
1650	IC 935	1734
1750	IC 939	1838
1850	IC 941	1938
1950	IC 943	2038
2147	2448	2238

* Arrives Interlaken Ost (East) Station five minutes later. All train departures are daily.

** Departs Interlaken Ost (East) Station five minutes prior to departing Interlaken West Station. All train departures are daily.

Distance: 37 miles/59 km

Lake of Thun Cruise

(Operates mid-April through mid-October)
Sailing #14 and #18

DEPART PIER INTERLAKEN*	ARRIVE THUN	DEPART THUN	TRAIN NUMBER	ARRIVE BERNE
1455	1659	1714	IC 837	1734
1655	1907	1914	IC 888	1934

* Steamer pier adjacent to Interlaken West Station. Other lake-steamer departures available. Check schedules.

The Höheweg starts at the west station, and the grand promenade extends to the east station. With a city map in hand, courtesy of the tourist office, you are all set to tour the town. If walking isn't your forte, you may prefer to see the sights from a surrey. These horse-drawn vehicles are available just outside the west station. Rates vary and must be arranged with the driver.

There are more than one hundred restaurants in Interlaken. We do have a favorite, although it's a bit off the beaten path—the **Hotel Roessli,** No. 45 on the city map. It is run by a friendly gentleman who worked in New York City restaurants for many years before he moved to the German district of Switzerland. The result is German-Swiss food served with a French flair and an American accent—rather unusual.

Interlaken is a good base for explorations of the entire **Jungfrau Region.** We suggest that you devote one day to Interlaken and its immediate area and check with the tourist office regarding other day-excursion possibilities. In addition to the rail ascent to the Jungfrau, you can reach the **Schilthorn** and lunch in the restaurant **Piz Gloria** (at 9,744 feet), where James Bond escaped the murderous intents of the opposition by skiing down the world's longest ski slope in the film *On Her Majesty's Secret Service.*

Wearers of pacemakers should be wary of the higher altitudes, but there's no reason to miss out on the fun around Interlaken. The **Swiss Open-Air Museum** at nearby **Ballenberg** is an ideal alternative and easy to reach by either train or lake steamer departing from the city's east station. Ask for details at the tourist information office.

If the weather is agreeable, a cruise on the Lake of Thun before returning from Interlaken is a must. The ships depart from a pier that can be reached from either the west station by tunnel or the Bahnhofstrasse, where it intersects with the Höheweg alongside the station. There are additional sailings throughout the day, but either of the two shown on the schedule below will take you to the town of Thun at the upper reaches of the lake in late afternoon.

Day Excursion to

Lucerne (Luzern)   AND MOUNT PILATUS

Depart from Berne

Distance By Train: 59 miles (95 km)
Average Train Time: 1 hour, 20 minutes
City Dialing Code: 41
Lucerne Tourist Information: Frankestrasse 1
Tele: 41 410 717; *Fax:* 41 410 7334
Internet: httpp://www.luzern. org
Email: Luzern@Luzern.Org
Hours: April-mid-May, 0830–1800 Monday-Friday; 0900-1700 Saturday.

Mid-May-October: 0830-1800 Monday-Friday; 0900-1700 Saturday; 0900-1300 Sunday. November-March, 0830–1200 and 1400–1800 Monday-Friday; Saturday, 0900–1300.
Located immediately outside and to the left of the railway station. Look for the "I" sign just under the HOTEL WALDSTATTERHOF sign or—better still—look for it directly across from McDonald's golden arches.

This day excursion is weatherproof. Rain or shine, Lucerne has much to offer. So much, in fact, that you may want to return again and again until you have seen it all—an impossible but challenging task.

Lucerne is in its glory on a bright, sunny day, when the city and its surroundings sparkle with a brilliance that defies description. At the northwestern end of Lake Lucerne, where the Reuss River resumes its swift quest for the Rhine, Lucerne's lakefront, rimmed by the mighty Alps, is an unforgettable sight. But a rainy day in Lucerne (and that sort of thing does happen occasionally) won't dampen your spirits one bit, for there are many things to see that are under cover.

The *Kapellbrücke* covered bridge is one example. A symbol of Lucerne, the bridge was built at the beginning of the fourteenth century together with the *Wasserturm* (water tower) at its side. During the seventeenth century, artists painted a total of 112 pictures under its eaves depicting Swiss history, particularly that of Lucerne and its patron saints. The bridge was destroyed by fire in 1993, but the bridge and the artwork were recreated and reopened to the public in April 1994.

The **Swiss Museum of Transport and Communications** in Lucerne is open daily April-October, 0900–1800; November-March, 1000–1700 daily. It is the largest and most modern museum in Europe—also one of the most visited. The museum is reached easily from the center of Lucerne by bus No. 2, which departs from the rail station every 6 minutes for the 10-minute trip, or by lake steamer to the Lido dock (Eurailpass, Europass, and Swiss Pass accepted).

Its special attraction is the **Longines Planetarium,** and the museum also traces vividly the development of Swiss transportation, including rail, road, aeronautical, and water navigation. Tourism since the nineteenth century is also highlighted. Kids from 7 to 77 will be fascinated by the operating scale model of the Gotthard tunnel railroad, and everyone will end up breathless following a visit to the museum's spectacular Swissorama and IMAX Filmtheater. With three restaurants to choose from, you can really plan to spend an entire day.

If you don't mind mixing fondue with frivolity, by all means eat at the **Stadtkeller Restaurant,** just two blocks north of the *Kapellbrücke's* right-bank entrance. It may be a bit "touristy," but if you like yodeling, alphorn blowing, cowbell ringing, beer drinking, and flag throwing, this is the place.

Berne–Lucerne

DEPART BERNE	ARRIVE LUCERNE	NOTES	DEPART LUCERNE	ARRIVE BERNE	NOTES
IR 2807	0847	(1)(2)	1313	1430	(1)(2)
IR 2813	1047	(1)(2)	1713	1830	(1)(2)
IR 2817	1247	(1)(2)	1913	2030	(1)
			2102	2220	(1)
IR 2823	1447	(1)(2)	2204	2326	(1)

(1) Daily, including holidays
(2) Food service

Distance: 59 miles/95 km

DEPART LUCERNE	TRAIN NUMBER	ARRIVE ALPNACHSTAD	DEPART ALPNACHSTAD*	ARRIVE PILATUS
1005	65	1153	1050	1125
1120	71	1305	1310	1345
1400	77	1545	1430	1505

DEPART PILATUS*	ARRIVE ALPNACHSTAD	DEPART ALPNACHSTAD	TRAIN NUMBER	ARRIVE LUCERNE
1425	1505		50	
1505	1545	1550		1718
1545	1625	1635		1825
1625	1705	1710	82	1184

* Via Pilatus cogwheel railway May to end of October. One class only.
Eurailpasses only give a discount on Pilatus railway. Pilatus is 7,000 feet
(2,132 meters) above sea level.

Distance: 3 miles/5 km, Pilatus cogwheel railway

At lunchtime, you should be there no later than 1130. It's a tour-bus lunch stop and fills up rapidly. Reservations can be made at the Tourist Information office. You can watch those poor, tired bus passengers try to determine what country they are seeing today.

For a sobering experience, follow up lunch with a visit to *The Dying Lion of Lucerne.* It is one of the world's most famous monuments. It was hewn from natural rock in commemoration of the heroic, fatal defense by Swiss guards of Louis XVI at the Tuileries in Paris at the beginning of the French Revolution in 1792. Mark Twain described the Lion of Lucerne as "the saddest and most poignant piece of rock in the world."

Next door, you will find Lucerne's **Glacier Garden Museum,** which contains remnants of Lucerne's prehistoric past that were discovered in 1872. Twenty million years ago, Lucerne was a subtropical palm beach on the ocean; twenty thousand years ago, Lucerne was covered by more than a mile of glacier ice. Don't miss it.

On your way to the Lion Monument and the Glacier Garden Museum, you will pass one of Switzerland's most outstanding and attractive restaurants, the **Old Swiss House**. Built in 1859, the restaurant contains an antique collection of rare beauty. The oil paintings are all originals. The food's superb, too! Call ahead for reservations: Tel: 410 61 71, because the Old Swiss House is frequented by the locals.

Visit **Mount Pilatus** as a side adventure during your Lucerne day excursion. Be certain to go on a clear day, for there is nothing more disappointing than a fog-shrouded peak. The world famous Pilatus electric railway, with its maximum gradient of 48 percent, is the steepest cog railway in the world. Discounts available for Eurailpass and Europass holders. It's best to purchase tickets at the Tourist Information office at Frankenstrasse 1. If you have a lot of time, you can take a lake steamer to **Alpnachstad.** For a breathtaking view and a beautiful way to end your day in Lucerne, descend Mount Pilatus in a cable car to **Kriens** and catch the bus to Lucerne. Check with the tourist information office for details and discounts available to rail-pass holders.

Day Excursion to

Rheinfelden   WALLED CITY ON THE RHINE

Depart From Berne

Distance By Train: 76 miles (122 km)
Average Train Time: 1 hour, 30 minutes
City Dialing Code: 61
Rheinfelden Tourist Information, 61 Marktgasse
Telephone: 831 55 20; *Fax:* 831 55 70
Hours: 0800–1200 and 1330–1730 Monday-Friday

To reach the tourist information office, proceed downhill on Bahnhofstrasse (Station Street) to the bottom of the hill, where it meets Marktgasse, the pedestrian shopping area. Turn left and walk a short block to the office at 61 Marktgasse, near the Swiss Customs station at the bridge leading to Germany. Look for the sign identifying the office: *Tourismus Rheinfelden* (Official Tourist Bureau).

A medieval jewel set on the banks of the swift-moving Rhine River just above Basel, Rheinfelden stirs the imagination. Much of its wall and many of its watch towers are still standing, and they were erected back in the eleventh century. An island on the Swiss side of the river's channel forms an important part of a bridge linking Switzerland to Germany. In the thirteenth century, it was the site of the famed "Emperor's Palace" described by Schiller in the tale of William Tell. The castle is gone now, and the island serves mainly as a city park; but the swirls and eddies of the mighty Rhine continue to stimulate one's sense of the centuries of history that have unfolded there.

During World War II, the bridge over the Rhine was the center of intrigue and mystery. Many downed but uncaptured American and British aviators seeking the sanctuary of Switzerland attempted to flee Nazi Germany from there. Some made it; some were apprehended. We have talked with residents who still remember those days and the risks that were taken. One person recalled for us her perilous escape across the Rhine's waters in a rowboat.

Be certain to pick up a city map during your stop at the tourist office. Armed with the map, you can easily wind your way through the labyrinth-like streets to any point of interest and still find your way back to the train station in time for your return to Berne.

Check out the shops lining the Rhine. Here you can find bargains in jewelry, clothing, and sporting equipment. Most shops and restaurants are closed on Monday.

When your stomach (or your watch) tells you it's lunchtime, you have several excellent eating places to choose from in Rheinfelden. Our favorites are the **Hotel Schiff** and the **Café Rheineck** close to the river.

Rheinfelden is home for two of Switzerland's largest breweries, **Cardinal** and **Feldschlösschen.** Tours are available on an irregular basis. Excellent restaurants and beer stubes are located at each brewery.

Clustered about the bridge entrance are several eating places offering menus ranging from light snacks to full-course meals. Want to picnic by the Rhine? Pick up some cheese, bread, and wine at one of the market stalls and have your repast on the island as the Rhine provides the background accompaniment.

Saline deposits were discovered under the town in 1844, and Rheinfelden quickly developed into an international spa. Its natural brine, which is one of the strongest in Europe, is piped from a depth of more than 600 feet to several bathing facilities in town, including the **largest saltwater swimming pool** in Switzerland. The tourist office can provide full details. The structures housing the pumps that bring the brine to the surface from the deep wells bear a striking resemblance to the original oil fields of western Pennsylvania, where oil refining first began in North America.

There is an unusual inside-outside saltwater swimming pool that you should see. You can reach it on foot by walking along the Rhine in an upstream direction. The brine-well structures may be seen nearby.

River steamers ply between Rheinfelden and **Basel.** Returning to Berne via Basel and a boat trip on the Rhine becomes an attractive option between May and September, when the service is in operation. Schedules are posted at

Berne–Basel–Rheinfelden

DEPART BERNE STATION	IN BASEL NUMBER	ARRIVE BASEL STATION	DEPART FELDEN STATION	ARRIVE IN RHEINBERNE STATION
0648	IC 952	0749	0815	0831
0748	IC 854	0857	0915	0931
0848	IC 864	0957	1015	1031
0948	ICE 72	1057	1115	1131
1048	EC 108	1157	1215	1231

DEPART RHEIN-FELDEN	ARRIVE IN BASEL	DEPART BASEL	TRAIN NUMBER	ARRIVE IN BERNE
1608	1724	1703	EC 109	1812
1708	1824	1803	EC 105	1912
1808	1924	1903	IC 936	2012
1908	2024	2153	2549	2312

Distance: 76 miles/122 km

the *Schifflande* (boat landing) opposite the island. Information on the steamer service to Basel, as well as cruises on the Rhine, is also available in the Rheinfelden tourist information office. Rhine steamers, unlike the lake steamers, do not accept Eurailpass or Europass, but the rates to Basel are nominal.

Day Excursion to

Zermatt

VIA THE GLACIER EXPRESS

Depart from Berne

How about a cheese fondue luncheon in Zermatt while viewing the **Matterhorn?** It can be done very easily as a day excursion during your stay in Berne. Board the 0720 or 0820 express from Berne to Brig. There, you connect with the *Glacier Express* private railroad to Zermatt. The earlier train from Berne will have you in Zermatt at 1042; the later one will still get you there in time for that luncheon at 1142. In fact, you could stay in Zermatt for an early dinner, too. Leaving there on the express at 2015 and changing in Brig, you would still be back in Berne at the respectful hour of 2325—all in the same day!

Eurail and Europass holders can travel to Brig, but from there, a round-trip ticket must be purchased to Zermatt. Swiss Pass holders can ride the entire route at no additional charge. Interested? Check with Bern Tourismus for Zermatt information and the rail information office across the hallway.

Advance reservations can be made through
    Rail Pass Express, Inc.
    2737 Sawbury Blvd.
    Columbus OH 43235
Tel: (614) 793-7650 or (817) 545-0265
Fax: (614) 764-0711; email: questions@eurail.com

Base City...

ZÜRICH

City Dialing Code: 1
Internet: http://www.eurospider.ch/zt.html

Some describe it as a garden city by a lake. Others picture it as one of the most elegant cities in Europe. Statisticians term it the largest in Switzerland, and anyone engaged in international business knows it is a world center for industry and commerce. Bankers seem content in knowing that it all begins and ends right there. Zürich can be all things to all people.

Zürich is packed with surprising contrasts. A tree-shaded avenue named Bahnhofstrasse runs charmingly from the railway station to Lake Zurich, yet houses the headquarters of the great world banks and some of the most elegant shops to be found in Europe. A few short blocks away, the scene yields to the Middle Ages around St. Peter's Church near the Limmat River, and the bridge that crosses the river leads into Niederdorfstrasse, the city's roistering nightclub area.

Zürich is a hub for rail transportation. Trains between Milan in the south, Munich in the east, and the great trunk line crossing Switzerland glide in and out of its Hauptbahnhof (Central Train Station) in a never-ending procession

Arriving By Air

Zürich's Kloten International Airport lies 10 miles northeast of the city. Airport-City Links: direct rail connections at the airport for Zurich, Berne, and Geneva. Shuttle train service to the main station in Zürich takes 10 minutes and runs every 15 minutes 0526-2339 from Zürich and 0611-2341 from the airport.

• Limousine service between the city and the airport is also available.
• Taxi queues are found by heading straight out of the international arrivals baggage claim area. Journey time 25-35 minutes. Approx 45 SFr.
• Train information, rail pass validation, and money exchange can be obtained on the main shopping level before descending to the train platforms located beneath the air terminal.

Arriving By Train

The **Hauptbahnhof** is Zürich's central railway station. All EuroCity, InterCity, and express trains stop only in this station even though there are three suburban terminals within the city. Train departures are displayed by electrically operated digital bulletin boards.

• **Money exchange** office (open 0630-2245) is located in a logical spot—on the left side of the main arrival hall as you exit from the trains, just in front of tracks 16 and 17. If you don't have Swiss francs in your possession on arrival, stock up on them. Not only is Zürich expensive, but the Swiss prefer their francs.

• **Hotel bookings** may be made through an automatic telephone system located in the center of the station forecourt or through the city tourist office. The automatic system operates like clockwork—Swiss, that is. There is a lighted board showing the locations of the hotels (and pensions), together with pictures of the establishments and a list of their room charges. Press the button for the one of your choice, and you'll be connected with the hotel by telephone to discuss vacancies. The only disadvantage of this system is that your reservation cannot be confirmed until you arrive at the hotel to register, whereas the tourist office will ensure that the reservation is held or will refund its service charge. Be sure to obtain directions to the hotel when connected with the reservation staff.

• **Train information** can be obtained from the office located in the center of the side hall just to the right of the automatic hotel booking system in the center of the station. You will find one of the attendants there fluent in English.

In addition to train information, this office (open daily 0700-2045) can assist you in obtaining **seat reservations** and the validation of your **rail pass** if you are starting your European rail trip from Zürich.

Tourist information/Hotel Reservations

Zürich Tourist Information: Hauptbahnhof 8023
Tel: 215 400; *Fax:* 212 01 41
Hours: April-October: 0830-2130 Monday-Friday; 0830-2030 Saturday-Sunday. November-March: 0830-1930 Monday-Friday; 0830-1830 Saturday-Sunday.

To reach the Zürich tourist office, exit from the trains, turning right at the end of the tracks, and proceed directly to the street. At the station exit, turn left, then walk past the post office on your left and the cab stand on your right for a short distance to the office entrance immediately beyond the post office.

The tourist office can also make hotel reservations (5 SFr fee). Reservations are held for one hour. A city map and a brochure describing the Zürich public transportation system is available.

Getting Around in Zürich

The *Ride With Us* brochure is particularly helpful because it explains how to use the self-service facilities of the city's transportation system, including rail (S-Bahn), trams, buses, and finiculars. The Swiss Pass includes travel on the city network, but Eurailpass or Europass is accepted only on the S-Bahn network. If you have a Eurailpass or Europass we recommend that you purchase a one-day or multiple-day pass to cover the remaining public transport network in Zurich.

Sights/Attractions/Tours

Obtain a copy of the brochure "Zürich Excursions" from the tourist office. This brochure describes city sightseeing, and excursions by motor coach or by trolley, cruises on the Limmat River as well as those on Lake Zürich, ascension of Mount Uetliberg for a panoramic view of the city and Alps, and how to see Zürich by night.

Escorted and unescorted tours are available at various times throughout the week during certain seasons of the year; so be sure to check with the train-information office or the tourist office. Some of these excursions will require Eurailpass or Europass holders to pay supplemental charges. This is the office where payment of these charges, along with reservations for the excursions, can be made. Reservations are accepted from 0730-1945. Make them at least 24 hours in advance.

Lake steamers at the far end of the Bahnhofstrasse at the Schiffstation (boat station) offer several interesting cruises, including one to the eastern end of the lake to an interesting old Swiss town, **Rapperswil.**

Zürich has its share of cathedrals. The **Grossmunster Cathedral** stands brooding on the east bank of the Limmat River. The cathedral has a statue of Charlemagne, who is said to have built the original church. Almost opposite on the other side of the river stands the **Fraumunster Cathedral,** reached by crossing the Munsterbrucke (Cathedral Bridge). Alongside the central station is the **Swiss National Museum**. On exhibition are authentic rooms of the sixteenth and seventeenth centuries, removed from their original sites and rebuilt within the museum. Zürich is not totally old in face. Its **Kunsthaus** (Fine Arts Museum) is an attractive modern building with a magnificent collection of modern art.

Day Excursions

Zürich provides an alternative Base City to Berne for those arriving via the Zürich Kloten International Airport. The city's proximity to Lucerne and

Rheinfelden decreases travel time for these day excursions when compared to Berne, but this time savings comes at a price. Zürich maintains a reputation for being one of Europe's most expensive cities. Budget-minded travelers may do well to use Berne as their Base City and save Zürich for a day excursion and as a gateway city.

Train Connections to other Base Cities from Zürich

TO	DEPART	TRAIN ARRIVE	NUMBER	NOTES
Amsterdam	1157	2052	ICE 70	(1)
	1300	2152	EC 2	
	2200	0834+1	1794	(1)
Barcelona	1953	09130+1	EN 274	(2)
Berne	0834	0946	IC 714	(3)
Brussels	0700	1440	IC 296	(4)
	1200	1928	EC 96	
Luxembourg	0700	1200	296	(4)
	1200	1649	EC 96	(8)
Lyon	0704	1213	EC 708/5766	(5)
	1606	2124	IC 532/5772	(5)
Milan	0704	1045	IC 15151	(6)
Munich	0733	1152	EC 99	(8)
	0933	1357	EC 167	(7)(8)
	1333	1748	EC 95	(8)
	1733	2154	EC 93	(8)
Paris	0715	1313	EC 114	
	1500	2136	IR 1780	(4)
	2300	0646+1	468	
Prague (Praha)	0933	2012	EC 167	
	1913	0812+1	382/353	(9)
Rome	0833	1725	IC 357	
	1207	2025	2971/EC 53	(7)
	2207	0923	EN 303	(2)
Vienna	0933	1845	EC 163	
	1333	2245	EC 161	
	2233	0805	EN 467	(2)

All trains depart from Zürich Hauptbahnhof.

(1) Transfer in Basel to EC 104
(2) Special supplements apply to EuroNight trains
(3) Hourly departures at 3 and 30 minutes past each hour
(4) Transfer in Basel
(5) Transfer in Geneva
(6) Trains depart every other hour at 7 minutes past the hour
(7) Transfer in Milan to IC 555
(8) Supplement payable
(9) Transfer in Stuttgart

Appendix

RAIL–TOUR ITINERARIES

Three sample rail-tour itineraries are presented in response to readers' requests for sample itineraries combining several base cities and day excursions into a rail-tour package. These itineraries are similar to those used in previous tour programs and are considered "route-tested."

All of the base cities and day excursions in the following rail-tour itineraries are described elsewhere in this edition. Each itinerary can be completed with a 15-day Eurailpass, Flexipass, or Saverpass.

Gateway cities are an important pre-trip consideration. Discuss them with your travel agent before buying air tickets. When suggested gateways are cities other than the rail-tour base cities, we have included rail schedules to assist in your planning. But as stated previously in this edition, our rail schedules are for planning purposes only. Europe by Eurail and its publisher cannot be held responsible for the consequences of either changes which occur after press time or inadvertent inaccuracies.

The following rail-tour schedules have been compiled on the basis of what we consider to be the best trains running at the best times; but in almost every case, there are several other trains departing at other times which may be more convenient for your purposes. For this reason, you may want to contact the Rail Information Department at Rail Pass Express (Phone: 614-793-7650 or fax 614-764-0711, Columbus, Ohio; 817-545-0265 Dallas, Texas; or e-mail: questions@eurail.com).

Hotels suggested for the itineraries have been selected for their convenient locations near the railways stations and/or close to public transportation. Hotel price ranges are quoted in local currencies for planning purposes only and are subject to change without prior notice. To convert the rates to U.S. dollars, consult the Foreign Exchange listing in the financial section of your home-town newspaper. Confirm hotel rates either through your travel agent or directly with the hotel. Most of the hotels listed have U.S. representatives through whom your travel agent can make reservations at no extra cost to you. Hotel ratings are based on government standards.

EUROPE Á LA CARTE

A rail tour using *Europe by Eurail* base cities, Munich, Berne, and Paris in an adventure through the heart of Europe.

Base Cities

Munich: Germany's fun capital. Plan ample time for shopping and sightseeing before beginning your exciting Eurail adventure. Allow for jet-lag, too.

Berne: Medieval elegance in the heart of Switzerland. An all-weather shopping center. Save the sunny days for Berne's eye-filling day excursions.

Paris: Everyone's "second" city and the only one of its kind. Mix Paris's pleasures with its unusual array of action-packed day excursions.

Gateways

Open Jaw: Munich inbound, Paris outbound. Discuss with your travel agent for professional advice.

Frankfurt: ICE 797 to Munich departs 1547 and arrives 1921 or ICE 799 departs 1747 and arrives 2121. Return to Frankfurt on ICE 990 departing 0635 and arriving 0950 or ICE 796, 0941-1411.

Amsterdam: EC 3 to Munich, 0800-1323 (Mannheim), change to ICE 593 departing 1329 and arriving Munich 1618. Return to Amsterdam on ICE 794 to Mannheim, 1241-1531, change to EC 104 Mannheim to Amsterdam, 1536-2052.

Paris: EC 65 Mozart to Munich, 0750-1611. Return to Paris on EC 66 Maurice Ravel, 0746-1623.

Base-City Hotels

Munich: The InterCity Hotel, located in the station, is first choice. Quiet, good restaurant, but usually booked up months in advance. Drei Lowen, one block from the station, is convenient. Balance of those hotels listed are clustered nearby. Hilton and Sheraton properties in suburbs have easy tram connections to city center.

Berne: Schweizerhof, on the station plaza, is tops in location, restaurant—and price. Hotel Baeren and Hotel Bristol are more economical and three minutes walk to station. Other hotels listed are also within a short walk of station and maintain highest Swiss standards.

Paris: For economy and excellent location, choose Rèsidence Elyssées Maubourg, one block from Maubourg Metro stop. Hotel Lyon-Palace-Paris, one short block away from Gare de Lyon's rail, Métro, and RER connections, has excellent neighborhood-restaurant section.

Europe á la Carte 15-Day Rail Itinerary

Day 1   Munich-Salzburg: Visit Mozart's birthplace and listen to Salzburg's sound of music.

Day 2   Munich-Garmisch-Partenkirchen: Host city to Winter Olympics and gateway to ascent of the mighty Zugspitze.

Day 3	Munich-Berchtesgaden: Explore salt mines, then soar to Hitler's ill-famed Eagle's Nest.
Day 4	Munich-Innsbruck: World famous for winter Olympics with year-round exhilarating scenery.
Day 5	Munich-Nuremberg: Germany's leading toy producers spice activities with fresh gingerbread.
Day 6	Munich-Berne: Base-city transfer via Zurich.
Day 7	Berne-Interlaken: A day in Alpine splendor, return to Berne by Lake of Thun steamer.
Day 8	Berne-Lucerne: A rain-or-shine outing with Mount Pilatus and Swiss cheese fondue.
Day 9	Berne-Milan: A change of pace, a change of place to Italy's bustling northern capital.
Day 10	Berne-Paris: Base-city transfer via Geneva.
Day 11	Paris-Rouen: Visit historic site of France's Joan of Arc.
Day 12	Paris-Rennes: Half-timbered houses and a ride on the TGV Atlantique.
Day 13	Paris-Fontainebleau: Visit the scene where Napoleon ruled and later was vanquished.
Day 14	Lyon-Annecy: Breathtaking scenery, sparkling water, and a charming medieval marketplace.
Day 15	Paris-Lyon: City of contrast visited after exciting journey aboard TGV, one of the world's fastest trains.

Tour Tips: Make seat reservations immediately on arrival in Munich. At minimum, reserve all base-city legs. Reservations are obligatory on TGV and many EuroCity trains. Don't overlook the Romantic Road and the Golden Pass day excursions.

TOURING EUROPE BY EURAIL... EUROPE À LA CARTE BASE-CITY TRANSFER SCHEDULE

FROM	TO	DEPART	ARRIVE	NOTES
Munich	Berne	0815	1346	(1)(3)(F)
Berne	Paris	0656	1132(2)	(1)(F)(R)

EUROPE À LA CARTE DAY-EXCURSION SUGGESTIONS*

BASE CITY	EXCURSION	DEPART	ARRIVE	RETURN	ARRIVE	NOTES
Munich	Berchtesgaden	0751	1031	1641	1909	(1)(4)
	Garmisch-P.	0900	1026	1833	1955	(1)
	Innsbruck	0729	0922	2037	2230	(1)(F
	Nuremberg	0752	0932	1826	2006	(1)(F)
	Salzburg	0749	0929	1905	2036	(1)(F)
Berne	Interlaken	0822	0915	1945	2038	(1)(F)
	Lucerne	0730	0847	1912	2030	(1)(F)
	Milan	0850	1245	1715	2026	(1)(F)
Paris	Annecy	0642	1030	1921	2300	(1)(F)(R)
	Rennes	0820	1035	1815	2020	(1)(R)
	Fontainebleau	0827	0905	1719	1802	(1)
	Lyon	0700	0904	1849	2104	(1)(F)(R)(7)
	Rouen	0915	1023	1904	2017	(8)

★ See appropriate base-city chapters for additional day-excursion suggestions.

(1) Daily, including holidays
(2) Gare de Lyon, Paris
(3) Change to IC 924 in Zurich
(4) Transfer in Freilassing
(5) Gare du Montparnasse, Paris
(6) Gare St. Lazare, Paris
(7) Lyon Perrache
(8) Monday through Friday

(F) Food service available
(R) Reservations obligatory

EUROPEAN ESCAPADE

A more than passing acquaintance with some of Europe's most fascinating sights and cities. From gateway Luxembourg, you travel to Berne, Amsterdam, and Paris, with shopping in Brussels.

Base Cities

Luxembourg: Fortress city, steeped in European and American history. Virtually a tax-free city; save some of your dollars for Luxembourg shops.

Berne: Medieval settings in the heart of the Swiss Alps. Berne's arcaded walkways make shopping and sightseeing easy no matter what the weather may be.

Amsterdam: Canals, cheese shops, diamond cutters, and Rembrandt's finest masterpieces await you.

Paris: City of Light. Mix Paris's pleasures with an array of action-packed day excursions.

Gateways

Discuss all gateway possibilities with your travel agent, because the tour's circular itinerary provides a wide selection, including all of the base cities plus Brussels. Depart Brussels for Luxembourg at 1219 for a two-hour-thirty-minute EuroCity trip; same service returns you to Brussels at end of tour.

Base City Hotels

Luxembourg: Pick a price. Most of the hotels listed are near the station. Book well in advance, particularly in summer tour season.

Berne: Schweizerhof for luxury, but the other listed hotels offer only a shade less at varying prices. All are within walking distance of the station.

Amsterdam: Victoria Park Plaza Hotel, a scant block from the station, is most convenient and highly recommended. Grand Hotel Krasnapolsky is just another stone's throw away but posh, with prices to match.

Paris: Best bargain and good location is Rèsidence Elysées Maubourg on the Left Bank. Same for independent Lyon-Palace-Paris Hotel, close to Gare de Lyon.

European Escapade 15-Day Rail Itinerary

Day 1 Luxembourg-Clervaux: An opportunity to visit site of World War II Battle of the Bulge.

Day 2 Luxembourg-Koblenz: A rail excursion along the Mosel to the Rhine in German wine country.

Day 3 Luxembourg-Berne: Base-city transfer via France.

Day 4 Berne-Interlaken: View of mighty Jungfrau and cruise on Lake of Thun highlight exciting rail tour.

Day 5 Berne-Lucerne: Sparkling highlights of Switzerland's lake city plus Mount Pilatus ascent.

Day 6 Berne-Milan: Cross into Italy for a delightful day of sightseeing in fascinating Milan.

TOURING EUROPE BY EURAIL . . . EUROPEAN ESCAPADE BASE-CITY TRANSFER SCHEDULE

FROM	TO	DEPART	NUMBER	ARRIVE	NOTES
Luxembourg	Berne	1001	EC 91	1512	(1)(F)
Berne	Amsterdam	1148	EC 104	2052	(1)(F)
Amsterdam	Paris	0719	TGV 9320	1205	(1)(F)(R)
Paris	Luxembourg	1042	EC 357	1435	(1)(F)

EUROPEAN ESCAPADE DAY-EXCURSION SUGGESTIONS*

BASE CITY	EXCURSION	DEPART	ARRIVE	RETURN	ARRIVE	NOTES
Luxembourg	Clervaux	0818	0900	1436	2024	(1)
	Koblenz	0940	1148	1719	1923	(1)(F)
Berne	Interlaken	0822	1945	2045	2138	(1)(F)
	Lucerne	0730	0847	2056	2318	(1)(F)
	Milan	0734	1045	1715	2026	(1)(F)
Amsterdam	Alkmaar	0752	0823	2008	2041	(1)
	Enkhuizen	0849	0953	1849	1930	(1)
	Hoorn	0819	0900	1949	2030	(1)
Paris	Annecy	0649	1030	1921	2300	(1)(F)(R)
	Rennes	0710	0913	1835	2040	(1)(R)
	Chartres	0701(3)	0755	1845	1954	(1)
	Fontainebleau	0827	0905	1930	2021	(1)
	Lyon	0730(4)	0940	1800	2004	(1)(F)(R)

* See appropriate base-city chapters for additional day excursions.

(1) Daily, including holidays   (F) Food service available
(2) Daily, except Sunday   (R) Reservations obligatory
(3) Daily, except some Saturdays (check local schedules)
(4) Gare de Lyon, Paris
(5) Lyon Perrache

Day 7   Berne-Amsterdam: Base-city transfer via Rhine.
Day 8   Amsterdam-Enkhuizen: Visit the Zuider Zee museum depicting the Dutch battle with the sea.
Day 9   Amsterdam-Hoorn: Steam-engine ride from Hoorn to Medemblik; the old Dutch Market on Wednesdays.
Day 10 Amsterdam-Alkmaar: World-famous cheese market and site of Dutch revolt against Spanish rule.
Day 11 Amsterdam-Paris: Base-city transfer via Brussels.
Day 12 Paris-Chartres: Palaces and castles abound along with Gothic Cathedral of Notre Dame.
Day 13 Paris-Rennes: Experience TGV Atlantique at 186 miles per hour.
Day 14 Paris-Fontainebleau: Visit palace where Napoleon relaxed with Josephine—and a few others.
Day 15 Paris-Lyon: "Newest" city of France, with Roman history, visited aboard one of the world's fastest trains, a TGV.

Tour Tips: Book all seat reservations when you arrive in Luxembourg. Depart Luxembourg (Day 2) at 0940, arriving Koblenz at 1148 (transfer in Trier required during winter months). Transfer to EC-3 at 1156 for Mainz, arriving there at 1239. You'll get a great view of the Rhine from the train. Lunch in the Mainz station restaurant and depart at 1253 in the direction of Koblenz, but get off in Bingen at 1309. Board the KD Line steamer from the Bingen pier at 1415 (Eurailpass with purchase of Beneleux add-on). Then relax on the Rhine until reaching Koblenz at 1800. Service operates April-October. Have dinner at the Weindorf. Catch the 2017 back to Luxembourg (transfer in Trier).

En route to Amsterdam from Berne (Day 7), after departing Mainz, watch on the right-hand side of the train for spectacular Rhine scenery to Koblenz.

For great dining aboard, book a restaurant seat on TGV departing Brussels (Day 11) for Paris at 1707.

SCANDINAVIAN SPLENDOR

Tour Scandinavian capitals of Copenhagen, Helsinki, Oslo, and Stockholm and board the Silja Line's finest cruise ship for adventure on the Baltic.

Base Cities

Copenhagen: Jovial, entertaining, the fun capital of Scandinavia. Save it for the grand finale.

Helsinki: Daughter of the Baltic. A glittering gem set in a picture-book harbor. Make the best of your "shore leave" by enjoying every moment.

Oslo: Friendly, pleasant, and compact. Take the Bergen-Flam excursion option if time permits.

Stockholm: Striking harbor skyline, a city of islands and waterways.

TOURING EUROPE BY EURAIL . . . SCANDINAVIAN SPLENDOR BASE-CITY TRANSFER SCHEDULE

FROM	TO	DEPART	NUMBER	ARRIVE	NOTES
Copenhagen (by sleeper)	**Oslo**	1001	394	1952	(1)(F)(R)
		2145	382	0707	(1)(R)
Oslo	**Stockholm**	0935	55/58	1523	(1)(F)(R)(5)
Stockholm	**Helsinki**	1800	Silja ferry	0900	(1)(F)(R)
Helsinki	**Stockholm**	1800	Silja ferry	0900	(1)(F)(R
Stockholm (by sleeper)	**Copenhagen**	1036	IN 29/287	1823	(1)(F)(R)(4)
		2315	IN 282	0753	(1)(R)

SCANDINAVIAN SPLENDOR DAY-EXCURSION SUGGESTIONS*

BASE CITY	EXCURSION	DEPART	ARRIVE	RETURN	ARRIVE	NOTES
Copenhagen	Aarhus	0619	0905	1736	2028	(3)(F)(R)
	Helsingor	0829	0854	1620	1764	(1)
	Odense	0822	0944	1811	1938	(1)(F)(R)
	Roskilde	0752	0803	1847	1913	(1)(F)(R)
Oslo	Hamar	0900	1045	1913	2056	(1)(F)(R)
	Larvik	0909	1118	1840	2051	(1)
	Lillehammer	0900	1135	2011	2225	(1)(F)(R)
Stockholm	Eskilstuna	0805	1030	1734	1950	(2)
	Norrkoping	0730	0917	1820	1941	(1)(F)(R)
	Uppsala	0823	0904	1802	1843	(1)(F)(R)

* See appropriate base-city chapters for additional day-excursion suggestions.

(1) Daily, including holidays
(2) Monday through Friday
(3) Via ferry crossing Kalundborg–Aarhus (Monday through Saturday)
(4) June 12–Aug 13: Train number IN 33 departs 1212 and arrives 2058
(5) Transfer at Karlstad

(F) Food service available
(R) Reservations obligatory

Sightseeing must include a visit to Old Town, where it all began centuries ago.

Gateways

All the base cities have direct U.S. air service, even Helsinki. The circular nature of the tour's itinerary makes it possible to select any one of the above base cities as both the inbound and outbound gateway. Our choice would be Copenhagen, which is yours?

Base-City Hotels

Copenhagen: Palace Hotel gets the tourists' nod for convenient location, mid-range rates, and so on. The Plaza, facing the station, is great but difficult to book in high season.

Helsinki: No listing, because we recommend using the Silja Line's accommodations for this tour's out-and-back day excursion, but we can recommend the Presidenti if you elect to extend your stay in Helsinki.

Oslo: The Grand Hotel features Old World elegance with modern conveniences—with the exception of price. The Hotel Nobel, with a wider rate range, is near the Grand Hotel.

Stockholm: Take your pick. All three hotels listed face Central Station. Price is probably the deciding factor. All have acceptable restaurants and are clean and well managed.

Scandinavian Splendor 15-Day Rail Itinerary

If Copenhagen is selected as the in-out gateway, spend jet-lag adjustment time there before validating your Eurailpass or Scanrailpass and leaving for Oslo.

Day 1   Copenhagen-Oslo: Scenic base-city transfer.

Day 2   Oslo-Larvik: Put a fjord in your future with an excursion to Larvik and on to Skien.

Day 3   Oslo-Hamar: Drink in the beauty of Lake Mjosa before exploring the rail museum in Hamar.

Day 4   Oslo-Lillehammer: Lillehammer can provide an insight into Norway's culture.

Day 5   Oslo-Stockholm: Colorful base-city transfer.

Day 6   Stockholm-Uppsala: Spend an interesting day in a city that dates from pagan times.

Day 7   Stockholm-Eskilstuna: See Sweden's "steel city" and visit 300-year-old Rademacher Forges.

Day 8   Stockholm-Norrkoping: Surprises such as cacti growing in Sweden await your arrival here.

Day 9   Stockholm-Silja Line cruise to Helsinki: Cruise the Baltic in luxury to Finland.

Day 10   Helsinki-Stockholm: Set sail again for Sweden after an exciting day ashore in Helsinki.

Day 11   Stockholm-Copenhagen: Arrive in Denmark's capital after overland rail through Sweden.

Day 12   Copenhagen-Aarhus: Ferry and rail transportation join to make an exciting day excursion.

Day 13   Copenhagen-Helsingør (Elsinore): A rail visit to north Zealand to inspect Hamlet's castle.

Day 14   Copenhagen-Odense : A rail visit to the birthplace of Hans Christian Andersen.

Day 15   Copenhagen-Roskilde: Five Viking ships await your inspection in Roskilde's museum.

Tour Tips: Make the Silja Line cruise to Helsinki and back a highlight of your tour. Book a round-trip cabin and spend a carefree day ashore in Helsinki sans luggage. In Helsinki, ride tram 3T for a quick view of this remarkable city. The Silja Line can also arrange extended shore leave in Helsinki if desired.

BASE CITY HOTELS AND INFORMATION

All hotel rates, given in local currencies applicable at press time, are subject to change. Rates range from the price of a single to double occupancy. Rates include breakfast on the Continental Plan, taxes, and service charges. The hotels listed are close to the railway stations and/or public transport facilities. The hotel's street location is next to the hotel name. *Tel:* is the telephone number; *Fax:* is the Fax number.

Amsterdam Hotels (rates in Dutch guilders)

Victoria Park Plaza ★★★★	Damrak 1-5 325-425	Tel: (20)6234255 Fax:(20) 6252997 Zip: 1012 LG
Grand Hotel Krasnapolsky ★★★★	Dam 9 350-575	Tel: (20)5549111 Fax: (20)6228607 Zip: 1012 JS
Damrak ★★★★	Damrak 49 135-305	Tel: (20)6262498 Fax: (20)6250997 Zip: 1012 LL
Tulip Inn Dam Square ★★★	Gravenstr. 14-16 200-220	Tel: (20)6233716 Fax: (20)6381156 Zip: 1012NM

To telephone or fax the Amsterdam hotels listed above from the United States, dial 011-31, then the number listed above.

When writing, the mailing address should include the zip code and country name; for example, 1012 JS Amsterdam, The Netherlands.

Berne Hotels (rates in Swiss francs)

Gauer Schweizerhof ★★★★★	Bahnhofplatz 11 240-410	Tel: (31)3114501 Fax: (31)3122119 Zip: CH-3001
Berne-Hotel ★★★★	Zeughausg. 9 175-275	Tel:(31)3121021 Fax: (31) 3121147 Zip: CH-3011
Best Western Bristol ★★★★	Schauplatzg. 10 165++270	Tel: (31)311101 Fax: (31)1311479 Zip: CH-3011
City Am Bahnhof ★★★	Bahnhofplatz 105-175	Tel: (31)3115377 Fax: (31)3110636 Zip: CH-3011
Metropole ★★★	Zeughausg. 26-28 130-220	Tel: (31)3115021 Fax: (31)3121153 Zip: CH-3011

To telephone or fax the Berne hotels from the United States, dial 011-41, then the number listed.

When writing, the mailing address should include zip code and country: for example, CH-3001, Berne, Switzerland.

Copenhagen Hotels (rates in Danish kroner)

Best Western Webers Hotel ★★★★	Vesterbrogade 11 850-1,250	Tel: (31)311432 Fax: (31)311441 Zip: DK-1620
Best Western Mayfair ★★★★	Helgolandsgade 3 650-825	Tel: (31)314801 Fax: (31)239686 Zip: DK-1653
Palace Hotel ★★★★	Raadhuspladsen 57 1,047-1,363	Tel: (33)144050 Fax: (33)145279 Zip: DK-1550
Plaza ★★★★	Bernstorffsgade 4 1,450-2,050	Tel: (33)149262 Fax: (33)939362 Zip: DK-1577

To telephone or fax hotels in Copenhagen from the United States, dial 011-45 then the number as listed.

When writing, the mailing address should include zip code and country name: for example, DK-1620 Copenhagen, Denmark.

Luxembourg Hotels (rates in Belgian francs)

Central Molitor	28 Ave. de la Liberte 3,400-4,400	Tel: 489911 Fax: 483382 Zip: 1930

| Nobilis Hotel | 47 Ave. de la Gare
3,000-6,000 | Tel: 494971
Fax: 403101
Zip: 1611 |
| President | 32 Pl. de la Gare
4,600-6,400 | Tel: 486161
Fax: 486180
Zip: 1024 |

Note: Government of Luxembourg does not rate hotels.

To telephone or fax Luxembourg hotels from the United States, dial 011-352, then the numbers as listed.

When writing, the mailing address should include zip code: for example, 1930 Luxembourg Ville, Luxembourg.

Munich Hotels (rates in Deutsche marks)

InterCity ★★★★	Bayerstr.10 195-400	Tel: (89)545560 Fax: (89)5456610
Located in Munich Hauptbahnhof (rail station)		Zip: D-8000
Drei Lowen ★★★★	Schillerstr. 8 182-250	Tel: (89)551040 Fax: (89)55104905 Zip: D-8000
Germania ★★★★	Schwanthalerstr. 28 120-260	Tel: (89)51680 Fax: (89)598491 Zip: D-80336
Atrium ★★★★	Landwehrstr. 59 219-239	Tel: (89)514190 Fax: (89)535066 Zip: D-80336
Cristal ★★★★	Schwanthalerstrasse.36 140-230	Tel: (89)551110 Fax: (89)55111992 Zip: D-80336

To telephone or fax Munich hotels from the United States, dial 011-49, then the numbers as listed.

When writing, the mailing address should include zip code and country: for example, D-8000 Munich, Germany.

Oslo Hotels (rates in Norwegian kroner)

Grand ★★★★	Karl Johansgt. 31 1,450-3,050	Tel:(22)429390 Fax: (22)421225 Zip: N-0101
Bondeheimen ★★★	Rosenkrantzgt. 8 560-990	Tel:(22)429530 Fax: (22)419437 Zip: 0159
Best Western Hotel Nobel ★★★★	Karl Johansgt. 33 990-1,125	Tel:(22)427480 Fax: (22)420519 Zip: N-0162

To telephone or fax Oslo hotels from the United States, dial 011-47, then the numbers as listed.

When writing, the mailing address should include the postal code and country name: Oslo 1, Norway.

Paris Hotels (rates in French francs)

Hotel Ambassador ★★★	16, blvd Haussmann 1,210–1,710	Tel: (1)42469263 Fax: (1)40220874 Zip: F-75009
Concorde St. Lazare ★★★	108, rue St. Lazare 1,160–1,460	Tel: (1)40084444 Fax: (1)42930120 Zip: F-75008
Plaza Haussmann ★★★	177, blvd Hausmann 620–790	Tel: (1)45639383 Fax: (1)45611430 Zip: F-75008
Best Western Anjou-Lafayette ★★★	4, rue Riboutte 540–700	Tel: (1)42468344; Fax: (1)48000897 Zip: F-75009
Lyon–Palace–Paris ★★★	11, rue de Lyon 525–545	Tel: (1)43072949 Fax: (1)46289155 Zip: F-75012
Maine Atlantique ★★★	55, rue des Plaisance 450–570	Tel: (1)45428143 Fax: (1)45429787 Zip: F-75014

To telephone or fax the above-listed Paris hotels from the United States, dial 011-33, then the numbers as listed.

When writing, the mailing address should include zip code and country: for example, F-75009 Paris, France.

Stockholm Hotels (rates in Swedish kronor)

Sheraton ★★★★	Tegelbacken 6, Box 289 1,400–2,300	Tel: (8)142600 Fax: (8)217026 Zip: S-10123
Scandic Hotel Continental ★★★	Vasagatan/Vattugrand 4 1,175–1,725	Tel: (8)244020 Fax: (8)4113695 Zip: S-10122
Best Western Terminus ★★★★	Vasagatan 20 540–750	Tel: (8)222640 Fax: (8)248295 Zip: S-10125

To telephone or fax the above-listed Stockholm hotels from the United States, dial 011-46, then the numbers as listed.

When writing, the mailing address should include zip code and country: for example, S-10121 Stockholm, Sweden.

FERRY CROSSINGS

In addition to unlimited rail travel and other conveniences, a Eurailpass, Eurail Flexipass, or Eurail Youthpass provides holders with passage on ferries conveying train passengers within the Eurailpass countries. In some instances, passengers must detrain and board the ferries; but on most major rail lines, the passenger coaches are loaded directly onto the ferry. In either case, the ferries are equipped with amenities such as restaurants, bars, boutiques, and, when traveling between countries, money exchanges and tax-free shops.

Three major international ferry connections exist between Italy and Greece, Finland and Sweden, and Ireland and France. The distances are considerable and usually involve overnight travel. Details, including schedules and services available, appear on the following pages.

Other ferry crossings of international importance to Eurail travelers include the lines between Ireland to Britain, the major rail route which lies between Germany (Puttgarden) and Denmark (Rodby); plus several crossings connecting the Scandinavian countries.

Italy–Greece Via Eurail

Eurail covers travel via ferry facilities operated by the Hellenic Mediterranean Lines and the Adriatica Line between Brindisi, Italy, and Patras, Greece. Departing either Greece or Italy, you must present your Eurailpass to the shipping-company office in the port and have a ticket and a boarding pass issued before boarding.

Eurailpass holders are granted free deck passage, but the reservation fee, meals, reclining chairs, or sleeping accommodations are not included. (Reclining chairs, by the way, are similar to those found in commercial airlines and are a great bargain for the budget-minded traveler.) Reclining seats and cabin rates are shown on the opposite page.

Reservations for departure dates and cabin accommodations may be reserved in advance by contacting:

Rail Pass Express, Inc. (agent for Hellenic Mediterranean Lines)
2737 Sawbury Boulevard
Columbus, OH 43235 USA
Telephone: (614) 889-9100
Fax: (614) 764-0711

Patras Ferry Terminal: To reach the office from the railway station, turn left as you exit the station. Walk along the street side of the quay approximately 300 yards to the office marked "Central Agency." Summer hours are 0900–2200 daily. Winter hours are 0900–1300 and 1700–2200. Report on day of embarkation only. No baggage checking is available. Useful telephone numbers for information: 429520 or 421614.

Brindisi Ferry Terminal: A 15-minute walk downhill to the Seno di Levante pier at the foot of Corso (Umberto), Corso Garibaldi, and Via del Mera, the streets leading to the waterfront. The terminal is on the right, just before the pier. It opens daily two hours prior to departure times. With stet peton (a telephone token) and a lot of patience, call ahead to the pier on 22861.

Attenzione (That's "attention" in Italian): From the time you arrive in Brindisi until you are safely aboard the ferry, beware of "entrepreneurs" approaching you with offers to help. Many are garbed in official-looking uniforms or are wearing "Official Guide" headgear. They bear alarming messages such as, "I have bad news. All of the deck space for tonight's sailing has been sold out." Then he relates the good news: "You are fortunate in meeting me, for I can take you to an agency where a few cabins are still available." With that, he'll reach for your baggage unless, by now, you have interrupted his presentation with a firm, "No, thank you." If he insists, *Polizia* is another good word to inject into the conversation.

MEDITERRANEAN (Italy-Greece) FERRY CROSSING

Between Brindisi, Italy and Patras, Greece
Ferry Service Provided by Hellenic Mediterranean Lines

DEPART	ARRIVE	DEPART	ARRIVE
Brindisi	**Patras**	**Patras**	**Brindisi**
2230	1700+1	2200	1700
2000	1400	1800	1000
2000	1100	1900	0900

Reservation Fee: U.S. $5.00 (all year). Advanced reservations recommended during July and August. During high season (June through September), a surcharge (U.S. $15.00) must be paid.

Before boarding, all passengers must check in at the pier office of the ferry line issuing the reservation.

Deck passage is free for Eurailpass holders (but a reservation fee is payable). Meals and port charges are not included. "Deck passage" allows you to board the ferry. Aboard, you are limited to the public areas and facilities of the vessel unless you book accommodations.

Rates*

Reclining Seats and Cabin Rates (Based on Eurailpass or Europass Credit)
Reclining Seats: $40

* Prices quoted at press time are per person, subject to change without notification.

Authors' suggestion: The port cities of Brindisi and Patras are interesting, charming, and steeped in history. Why not take a day to see them at a leisurely pace? Plan to arrive a day before your scheduled ferry departure. Ask your concierge to call ahead for a hotel reservation. Also ask him to check on your ferry reservation. The address and telephone numbers of the city tourist information offices are posted in the arrival halls of the rail stations.

Note: Schedules and prices provided by Hellenic Mediterranean Lines are subject to change without notice.

Finland–Sweden Via Eurail

The Silja Line has modern passenger terminals in Stockholm, Turku, Helsinki, and TravemŸnde that rival any airport for convenience. Eurailpass, Eurail Flexipass, and ScanRail Pass holders are entitled to discounted rates on Silja Line and may use the food services and rest rooms aboard. They will be provided with sleeping accommodations after cabin space is reserved and paid for. Schedules are shown on the opposite page. Cabins may be reserved in advance by contacting Silja Line's U.S. agent:

> *Bergen Line, Inc.*
> Park Avenue
> New York, NY 10022
> Telephone: (800) 323–7436; (212) 319–1300
> Fax: (212) 319–1390

Crossing between Sweden and Finland, you may select between two routes: Stockholm-Helsinki direct, or Stockholm-Turku with train connections or the Silja Line express bus service between Turku and Helsinki. Our preference is the direct route between the two capital cities because it gives you a few more hours aboard ship to enjoy the scenery, which is spectacular. Both routes traverse the breathtaking archipelago between the two countries.

Although your Eurailpass entitles you to a discounted ticket issued by the Silja Line, you also need to obtain a boarding pass before embarking. If you need a ticket and a boarding pass, you should be at the ferry terminal one and one-half to two hours before ship departure; one-half hour is adequate if you already have your ticket. All terminals have cafeterias, waiting rooms, and baggage lockers.

Silja Terminal—Stockholm: Reached by underground line No. 13 or 14, both running from the city's Central Station to the end of the line—Ropsten. The fare is 12 Swedish kronor. Taxi fare from the train station to the Silja Line terminal is approximately 75 kronor and takes about 15 minutes.

Silja Terminal—Helsinki: Reached by tram No. 3T from the central railway station. Fare is 8.00 Finnish markkaa; journey takes 15 minutes. The taxi between the rail station and Silja terminal costs approximately 35 markkaa and takes 10 minutes.

Silja Terminal—Turku: Reached from Turku central station by train to harbor station (most through trains terminate at harbor). Taxi from central station costs about 30 markkaa and takes about 10 minutes.

Ireland–France Via Eurail

Eurailpass holders may travel between the Continent and the Republic of Ireland aboard the vessels of the Irish Ferries line. Service from the French ports of Cherbourg and Le Havre to the Irish port of Rosslare is available April 1 through September 27, 1998; service to the Irish port of Cork from Le Havre is also available. Ferry service is provided by the line's two ships, the Saint Killian II and the Saint Patrick II. The Saint Killian is a 10,256-ton vessel with a capacity of 2,000 passengers and 380 cars; the Saint Patrick can carry 1,630 passengers and 300 cars.

Eurailpass travelers are entitled to free deck passage (reservations are mandatory even for free deck space July and August), but meals and cabin accommodations are not included. For cabin rates, availability, and reservations, call or write: Scots-American Travel Advisor, 26 Rugen Drive, Harrington Park, New Jersey 07640. Telephone: (201); 768–5505; Fax: (201) 768–3825.

All passages are overnight. Cabin accommodations may also be booked at the ports when presenting your Eurailpass for a boarding pass. The check-in points are usually open two hours prior to sailing times. Passengers are requested to check in not less than one hour before the sailing time.

Rosslare Ferry Terminal: Trains from Dublin and Limerick connect with the Irish Continental ferries on the Rosslare harbor pier. There are no transfer costs.

Cork Ferry Terminal: Trains from the Heuston Station in Dublin connect with the Irish Ferries in Cork. A taxi from the station to the pier is recommended.

Le Havre Ferry Terminal: A bus transfer is available between the ferry terminal and the SNCF rail station. The cost of the transfer is 8 francs. The bus is available for connections with all principal trains to and from Paris.

Cherbourg Ferry Terminal: Bus transfer service from the SNCF rail station is not available. Alternatively, a taxi service is available for about 20 francs. Inquiries should be made because bus-transfer service may be implemented.

Connolly Station: Trains connecting Dublin with the Rosslare ferry terminal use this station. A sign directing visitors to the nearby tourist information office on O'Connell Street is located to the right of the station's cloakroom in the concourse. The train information office is just beyond the cloakroom on the right-hand side. Use the side escalator to the street exit. A taxi stand is located at the station front.

Heuston Station: Board any train outbound from Dublin to Cork but check to be certain that you are in a coach bound for Cork. Some trains serve both Cork and Limerick, splitting at Limerick Junction. Train information is available from any of the ticket windows alongside tracks 1 and 2.

Connolly station is the terminal in Dublin for trains arriving from Northern Ireland. It is also the terminal for boat trains connecting with the Irish Ferries that sail from the port of Rosslare, south of Dublin, to the French ports of Cherbourg and Le Havre.

1998 Irish Ferries Sailing Schedule

Service runs April 1–September 27, 1998

IRELAND TO FRANCE

Rosslare/Le Havre

Departs at 16.00	April 1, 5, 9, 13, 15, 19, 23, 27, 29
	May 3, 5, 11, 17, 19, 25, 31
	June 14, 22, 28
	July 12
Departs at 15.00	July 18, 26
	August 1, 9, 15, 23, 29
	September 6, 12, 20, 26

Rosslare/Cherbourg

Departs at 16.00	April 3, 7, 11, 17, 21, 25
	May 9, 23
	June 6, 8, 20
	July 4, 6, 22, 28
	August 5, 11, 19, 25
	September 2, 8, 16, 22

Cork to Le Havre

Departs at 15.30	July 20
	August 3, 17, 31
	September 14

FRANCE TO IRELAND

Le Havre to Rosslare

Departs at 17.00	April 2, 6, 10, 14, 16, 20, 24, 28, 30
	May 4, 6, 12, 18, 20, 26
	June 1, 15, 23, 29
	July 13, 21, 27
	August 4, 10, 18, 24
	September 1, 7, 15, 21, 27

Cherbourgh to Rosslare

Departs at 19.30	April 4, 8, 12, 18, 22, 26
	May 10, 24
	June 7, 9, 21
	July 5, 7, 23, 29
	August 6, 12, 20, 26
	September 3, 9, 17, 23

Le Havre to Cork

Departs at 16.00	July 19
	August 2, 16, 30
	September 13

Baltic Ferry Crossings

Silja Line Between Finland and Sweden

STOCKHOLM—HELSINKI V.V.		
Stockholm	Depart daily	1800
Helsinki	Arrive following day	0830
Helsinki	Depart daily	1800
Stockholm	Arrive following day	0900

STOCKHOLM—TURKU V.V.	
Depart Stockholm	Arrive Turku
0800	1900
2000	0800 following morning
Depart Turku	Arrive Stockholm
1000	1900
2000	0700 following morning

Sailing From Ireland to Britain

Stena Line, the world's largest international ferry company, operates on 16 routes in northwestern Europe, including the Irish Sea and the English Channel. Stena's HSS (High-speed Sea Service) ships cruise between Belfast in Northern Ireland and Stranraer in Scotland in only 105 minutes. Stena Line's Superferry service offers leisurely crossings with duty-free shopping, meals and even a movie (on some routes). Its Superferry *Koningin Beatrix* on the Rosslare-Fishguard route, capable of carrying 2,100 passengers and 500 automobiles, is the largest and most luxurious ferry to operate on the southern Irish Sea.

Irish Ferries can take you from Dublin to Holyhead and P&O European Ferries serve on the Larne-Cairnryan route.

Coming from London by train requires a transfer to either a Stena Line or Irish Ferries ferry at Holyhead. The Stena Line ferries serve the port of Dun Laoghaire, a suburb of Dublin, where passengers can transfer to the center of the city by the local train service, DART.

IRELAND TO GREAT BRITAIN	
Stena Line To Britain	
ROUTE	**JOURNEY**
Rosslare-Fishguard	three hours twenty minutes Superferry or ninety-nine minutes Stena Lynx
Dun Laoghaire-Holyhead	three hours fifteen minutes Superferry or ninety-nine minutes HSS
Belfast-Stranraer	three hours Superferry or 105 minutes HSS

Irish Ferries Sailing Schedule: Service
January1–December 31, 1998

	DEPARTS	ARRIVES
Dublin to Holyhead	09.45	13.00
	21.45	01.00
Holyhead to Dublin	15.45	19.00
	03.45	07.00
	(Crossing time: three hours and fifteen minutes)	
Rosslare to Pembroke	09.15	13.00
	21.305	01.15
Pembroke to Rosslare	15.00	18.45
	03.15	07.00
	(Crossing time: three hours and fourty-five minutes)	

Note: December 24 at 15.45 is the last sailing before Christmas; and December 27 at 09.45 is the first sailing after Christmas.

INTERNATIONAL CALLING

The following chart provides country codes and city codes that you will need when calling from one country to another. The country codes should be used when dialing to that country from another country. In most cases you will also need to dial a city or area code.

Calling Europe from North America
To use these codes from within North America, dial 011 + country code, city code, and the local number you wish to reach.

Calling North America from Europe with a calling card:
Your local long-distance phone company will have a number for you to dial while in Europe (either a toll-free or a local call) to connect to an operator in your home country. For more information call one of the following:

AT&T Direct Service: (800) 331–1140; from abroad (412) 553–7458
MCI WorldPhone: (800) 996–7535
SprintExpress: (800) 877–4646
Canada Direct: (800) 565–4708

Country/City Code		ATT	MCI	Sprint
AUSTRIA	43	022-903-011	022-903-012	022-903-014
Vienna	1			
Baden	2252/2258			
Innsbruck	512			
Salzburg	662			
BELGIUM	32	0-800-100-10	0-800-100-12	0-800-100-14
Brussels	2			
Antwerp	3			
Bruges	50			
Ghent	9			
Namur	81			
CZECH REPUBLIC	420	00-42-000-101	00-420-00112	00-42-087-187
Prague	2			
Denmark	45	8001-0010	8001-0022	8001-0877
City codes not required.				
Copenhagen	no code required			
Aarhus	no code required			
Helsingor	no code required			
Hillerod	no code required			
Odense	no code required			
Roskilde	no code required			
FINLAND	358	9800-100-10	08001-102-80	9800-102-84
Helsinki	9			
Hanko	19			
Lahti	3			
Tampere	3			
Turku	2			

	Country/City Code	ATT	MCI	Sprint
FRANCE	33	0800 99 00 11	0800 99 00 19	0800 99 00 87
Lyon	no code required			
Annecy	450			
Dijon	380			
Grenoble	476			
Vienne	474			
Nice	no code required			
Cannes	no code required			
Marseilles	491			
Saint-Raphael	494			
Paris	1			
Paris area code:1+9 digits.				
Caen & Normandy Beaches	231			
Chartres	237			
Fountainebleau	1			
Reims	326			
Rennes	299			
Rouen	235			
Versailles	no code required			
Metz	87			
GERMANY	49	0130-0010	0130-0012	0130-0013
Berlin	30			
Dresden	351			
Leipzig	341			
Potsdam	331			
Hamburg	40			
Bremen	421			
Hameln	5151			
Hannover	511			
Lubeck	451			
Munich	89			

Country/City Code		ATT	MCI	Sprint
Berchtesgaden	4			
Garmisch–Partenkirchen	8821			
Nuremberg	911			
Rothenburg (Romantic Road)	9861			
Ulm	731			
Koblenz	261			
Trier	651			
GREECE	30	00-800-1311	00-800-1211	00-800-1411
Athens	1			
Argos	751			
Corinth	741			
Patras	61			
Piraeus	1			
HUNGARY	36	00★★ 800–01111	00★★800–01411	00★★800–01877
Budapest	1			
IRELAND	353	1–800–550–000	1–800–551–001	1–800–552–001
Dublin	1			
Cork	21			
Galway	91			
Kilkenny	56			
Killarney	64			
ITALY	39	172-1011	172-1022	172-1877
Milan	2			
Bologna	51			
Genoa	10			
Venice	41			
Rome	6			
Anzio	6			
Florence	55			

	Country/City Code	ATT	MCI	Sprint
Naples	81			
Pisa	50			
LUXEMBOURG	352	0-800-0111	0800-0112	0800-0115
City codes not required.				
Luxembourg	no code required			
Clervaux	no code required			
MONACO	377	800-90-288	800-90-019	800-90-087
Monte Carlo	92 or 93			
THE NETHERLANDS	31	0800-022-9111	0800-022-9122	0800-022-9119
Amsterdam	20			
Alkmaar	72			
Enkhuizen	228			
Haarlem	23			
Hoorn	299			
NORWAY	47	800-19-011	800-19-912	800-19-877
City codes not required.				
Oslo	no code required			
Bergen and Flam	no code required			
Hamar	no code required			
Larvik and Skien	no code required			
Lillehammer	no code required			
PORTUGAL	351	05017-1-288	05017-1-234	05017-1-877
Lisbon	1			
Cascais & Estoril	1			
Coimbra	39			
Setubal	65			
Sintra	1			

	Country/City Code	ATT	MCI	Sprint
SPAIN	34	900-99-00-11	900-99-00-14	900-99-00-13
When calling in Spain use 9 before dialing city codes.				
Barcelona	3			
Blanes	72			
Lerida	73			
Sitges	3			
Tarragona	77			
Madrid	1			
Aranjuez	1			
Avila	20			
Burgos	47			
El Escorial	1			
Toledo	25			
SWEDEN	46	020-795-611	020-795-922	020-799-011
Stockholm	8			
Eskilstuna	16			
Norrkoping	11			
Uppsala	18			
SWITZERLAND	41	0-800-890011	0-800-890222	0-800-899777
Berne	31			
Interlaken	36			
Lucerne	41			
Lake Lugano	91			
Rheinfelden	61			
Zurich	1			

Key: ★★ = wait second dial tone

TRAIN TERMINOLOGY

English	French	Italian	German	Spanish
On the train:				
aisle	allée	corridoio	gang	pasillo
car	compartiment	vettura	wagen	vagón
couchette	couchette	cuccetta	liegeplatz	couchette
restaurant car	voiture-ristorante	carrozza-restaurante	speisewagen	coche-restaurante
seat	place	posto	sitzplatz	asiento
sleeper	wagon-lit	cabina	bettplätz	cama
sleeping car	voiture-lits	vagone letto	schlafwagen	coche-cama
smoking	fumeur	per fumatori	raucher	fumadores
nonsmoking	non fumeur	non fumatori	nichtraucher	no fumadores
table	tableau	tavolo	tisch	mesa
toilets	toilettes	tolette	toiletten	servicios
window	fenêtre	finestrino	fenster	ventana
In the station:				
entrance	entrée	entrata	eingang	entrada
exit	sortie	uscita	ausgang	salida
Gentlemen	Hommes	Signori	Herren	Caballeros
Information	renseignements	informazioni	information	información
Ladies	Femmes	Signore	Damen	Señoras
left luggage	consigne depositato	bagaglio bewahrung	gepäckauf-	consigna
lost & found	objets trouvés	oggetti smarriti	fundbüro	oficina de objeto/perdidos
luggage	bagages	bagagli	gepäck	equipaje
Luggage lockers	consigne automatique	armadietti per bagagli	schließfächer	consigna automática
station	gare	stazione	bahnhof	estación
subway/underground	Métro	Metropolitana	die U-bahn	Metro
track/platform	quai	binario	bahnsteig	andén
telephone	téléphone	telefono	telefon	teléfono
ticket office	guichet	biglietteria	fahrkarten-sshalter	despacho de billetes
train	train	treno	zug	tren

English	French	Italian	German	Spanish
At the ticket window:				
arrival	arrivée	arrivo	ankunft	llegada
arrives	arrive	arriva	kommt an	llega
change at	changer à	cambiare a	umsteigen in	cambiar en
first class	première classe	prima classe	erste klasse	primera clase
second class	seconde classe	seconda classe	zweite klasse	segunda clase
connection	correspondance	coincidenza	anschluß	conexión
departure	départ	partenza	abfhart	salida
departs	part	parte	fährt ab	sale
domestic tickets	billets	biglietti nazionali	fahrkarten inland	billetes nacionales
earlier	plus tôt	più presto	früher	más temprano
express	express	espresso	schnellzug	expreso
fast	rapid	rapido	schnell	rápido
from Rennes	(en provenance) de Rennes	(proviene) da Rennes	von Rennes	(procede) de Rennes
international tickets	billets internationaux	biglietti internazionali	fahrkarten ausland	billetes internacionales
not available	pas disponible	non disponibile	nicht erhältlich	no disponible
later	plus tard	più tardi	später	más tarde
local service	service local	servizio locale	personenzug	servicio local
next train	prochain train	prossimo treno	nächst zug	próximo tren
reservation	reservation	prenotazione	reservierung	reservación
schedule/ timetable	horaires	orario	fahrplan	horari
supplement payable	avec supplément	con pagamento di supplemento	zuschlagp- flichtig	con pago de suplemento
to *Oslo*	vers Oslo, à destination de Oslo	a Oslo	nach Oslo	a Oslo
via	via	via	über	via

PICTOGRAPHS

. . . symbols used in and around European Rail
Facilities to direct and assist passengers

Rest rooms
Toilettes
Toiletten
Servicios
Toilette

Ladies' rest room
Toilettes (pour dames)
Toiletten (damen)
Senoras
Toilette-signore

Men's rest room
Toilettes (pour hommes)
Toiletten (herren)
Caballeros
Toilette-signori

Bath
Bains
Bader
Bano
Bagni

Shower
Douches
Dusche
Duchas
Docce

Telephone
Telephone public
Offentlicher fernsprecher
Telefono publico
Telefono pubblico

Telegram
Telegraphe
Telegrammannahme
Telegrafo
Telegrafo

Platform
Quai
Bahnsteig
Anden
Marciapiede

Call for porter
Porteur
Gepacktrager
Mozo de equipajes
Facchino

Taxi stand
Station de taxis
Taxistand
Parada de taxis
Posteggio taxi

Rent-a-car
Location de voitures sans chauffeur
Auto am bahnhof
Servicio "tren-auto"
Servizio "treno + auto"

Entrance
Entree
Eingang
Ingreso
Ingresso

Exit
Sortie
Ausgang
Salida
Uscita

INFORMATION

Information
Bureau de renseignements
Information Auskunft
Oficina de informacion
Ufficio informazioni

Tickets
Guichet des billets
Fahrkartenschalter
Taquilla de billetes
Sportello biglietti

RESERVATION

Reservation
Reservation des placos
Platzreservierung
Reserva de plazas
Prenotazione dei posti

Luggage registration office
Enregistrement des bagages
Gepaeckannahme
Facturacion de equipajes
Registrazione dei bagagli

Baggage check room
Consigne des bagages
Gepackaufbewahrung
Consigna de equipajes
Deposito bagali

Locker
Consigne automatique
Gepack-schliessfach
Consigna automatica
Deposito bagali a cassette automatiche

Lost & Found
Bureau des objets perdus
Fundbiiro
Oficina de objetos perdidos
Ufficio oggetti smarriti

Customs
Bureau de douane
Zollamt
Despacho de aduanas
Ufficio doganale

Currency exchange
Bureau de change
Wechselstube
Oficina de cambio
Ufficio cambio

Waiting room
Salle d'attente
Wartesaal
Sala de espera
Sala di attesa

Barber—Beauty Parlor
Coiffeur
Friseur
Peluqueria
Parucchiere

Restaurant
Buffet (restaurant de gare)
Bahnhofswirtshaft
Fonda
Ristoratore

Do Not Drink Water
Eau non potable
Dies ist kein Trinkwasser
Agua no potable
Acqua nonpotabile

Drinking water
Eau potable
Trinkwasser
Agua potable
Acqua potabile

or

Post office
Bureau de poste
Postamt
Oficina de correos
Ufficio postale

Smoking permitted
Fumeurs
Raucher
Fumadores
Fumatori

 No smoking
Non fumeurs
Nichtraucher
Prohibido fumar
Vietato fumare

 Elevator
Ascenseur
Fahrstuhl
Ascensor
Ascensore

 Escalator
Escalier roulant
Rolltreppe
Escalera mecanica
Scala mobile

 Bus
Autobus
Autobus
Autobus
Autobus

 Do Not Enter
Defense d'entrer
Zutritt verboten
Prohibido el paso
Ingresso vietato

RAIL FARES BETWEEN BASE CITIES

First Class one-way fares (*without* a rail pass) between base cities are listed in U.S. dollars, but do not include seat reservations fees or sleeping car accommodations charges. Rates applicable as of press time and subject to change without notice. Second Class fares are approximately one-third less than First Class.

	AMS	ATH	BAR	BAS	BER	BRN	BRU	BUD	COL	CPH	FLO	FRA	GEN	HAM	LIS	LUX	LYN	MAD	MIL	MUC	NCE	OSL	PAR	PRA	ROM	STK	VCE	VEN
Amsterdam																												
Athens	688																											
Barcelona	274	546																										
Basel	232	464	250																									
Berlin	173	756	542	292																								
Berne	284	434	221	52	344																							
Brussels	55	569	227	105	220	157																						
Budapest	391	337	468	259	195	280	402																					
Cologne	76	617	280	164	184	216	53	317																				
Copenhagen	240	833	507	372	162	424	290	357	243																			
Florence	395	321	196	169	362	141	276	193	324	469																		
Frankfurt	140	578	367	117	190	169	117	241	67	278	286																	
Geneva	335	451	147	103	395	74	174	321	267	475	156	220																
Hamburg	132	718	394	272	87	324	182	375	135	113	441	179	375															
Lisbon	336	698	152	402	494	373	292	589	345	564	379	365	299	456														
Luxembourg	89	499	239	68	274	120	44	325	68	309	237	84	171	202	301													
Lyon	176	284	116	68	322	116	124	522	160	404	124	182	39	294	262	95												
Madrid	299	627	81	331	457	302	255	446	308	527	308	328	228	419	71	264	194											
Milan	349	339	183	125	417	95	230	182	278	494	46	239	112	379	264	160	78	264										
Munich	267	435	381	182	244	193	245	157	197	351	118	139	234	251	397	226	359	397	226									
Nice	400	391	132	218	403	189	201	233	329	545	64	290	115	430	284	161	94	213	51	163								
Oslo	402	975	651	529	324	581	439	519	392	162	698	436	632	257	713	459	548	676	654	508	622							
Paris	110	518	164	91	268	133	66	363	119	338	233	139	108	230	226	75	96	189	195	208	135	487						
Prague	288	505	526	299	89	217	253	106	215	251	263	148	379	176	558	232	455	503	371	124	287	433	314					
Rome	430	290	256	206	405	182	311	225	365	512	46	308	187	412	408	247	165	321	87	161	101	669	270	306				
Stockholm	371	944	620	498	293	550	408	488	361	131	667	405	601	226	682	425	517	645	623	477	591	136	451	382	638			
Venice	349	327	221	159	346	135	270	153	318	453	40	279	150	353	373	200	115	302	40	102	89	610	233	178	81	579		
Vienna	331	435	431	199	155	243	307	60	257	460	137	195	284	326	541	274	465	504	137	109	188	583	315	70	180	586	108	
Zurich	282	444	260	53	342	72	158	208	216	425	149	155	113	325	412	88	241	341	105	121	156	582	141	266	186	551	142	171

EURAIL AID OFFICES

Austria

Oesterreichische Bundesbahnen
Innsbruck Hauptbahnhof
A-6010 Innsbruck
Tel: (05222) 33633
Monday-Sunday: 0615-1945

Oesterreichische Bundesbahnen
Salzburg Hauptbahnhof
A-5010 Salzburg
Tel: (0662) 1700
Monday-Sunday: 24 hours a day

Oesterreichische Bundesbahnen
Salzburg Westbahnhof
A-1150 Vienna (Wien)
Tel: (0222) 839574 or 872425
Monday-Friday: 0900-1600

Belgium

Société Nationale des Chemins de fer
belges
Travel center
Service International
Gare de Bruxelles-Midi
B-1070 Brussels (Bruxelles)
Tel: (02) 2248800; Fax: (02) 2245507
Monday-Friday: 0700-2100
Saturday: 0900-1700

Denmark

Danske Statsbaner
DSB Travel Agency
Central Station
Banegärdspladsen
DK-1570 Copenhagen (København)
Tel: (33) 15 0400 ext. 12615
Fax: (33) 15 0400 ext. 17155
Monday-Sunday: 0800-1900

Finland

VR Ltd
Railwaystation
International services
FIN-00100 Helsinki
Tel: (090) 0100 124 or 125
Fax: (090) 707 2111
Monday-Friday: 0830-1630

France

Société Nationale des Chemins de fer
français
Guichet 'Billets Inernationaux'
Gare de Marseille St. Charles
F-13232 Marseille
Tel: 91951403
Monday-Sunday: 0500-1300

Société Nationale de Chemins de fer
français
Gare de Nice-Ville
Bureau Information/reservation
F-06008 Nice
Tel: 93826167
Monday-Saturday: 0800-1200 &
1400-1800

Société Nationale de Chemins de fer
français
Bureau SNCF Orly-sud
F-94543 Orly-Airport (Orly-Aérogare)
Tel: (1) 4884 2674
Monday-Saturday: 0800-2000
Sunday: 0945-1300 & 0245-1830

Société Nationale de Chemins de fer
français
Bureau Information Réserveration
Galerie de Fresques
Gare de Paris-Lyon
F-75012 Paris
Tel: (1) 5333 1991
Monday-Friday: 0545-2300

Société Nationale de Chemins de fer
français
'Espace Grandes Lignes' 1st floor
Garde de Paris-Nord
F-75010 Paris
Tel: (1) 4995 5202; Fax: (1) 4995 5186
Monday-Saturday: 0900-2000

Société Nationale de Chemins de fer
français Service International
Garde de Paris-St. Lazare
F-75008 Paris
Tel: (1) 5342 2762; Fax: (1) 5342 0955
Monday-Friday: 1000-1900
Saturday: 0930-1200 & 1300-1800

Société Nationale de Chemins de fer
français
Bureau SNCF Aéroport Charles de
Gaulle
Terminal 1 – Arrival floor
F-95712 Roissy Airport (Aéroport
Charles de Gaulle)
Tel: (1) 4816 1016; Fax: (1) 4879 6144
Monday-Sunday: 0800-2000

Société Nationale de Chemins de fer
français
Bureau SNCF Aéroport Charles de
Gaulle, Terminal 2
F-95716 Roissy Airport
(Aéroport Charles de Gaulle)
Tel: (1) 4879 6139; Fax: (1) 4879 6135
Monday-Sunday: 0800-2000

Germany

Deutsche Bahn
Fahrkartenausgabe Berlin Zoologischer
Garten Reisenzentrum
Jebenstrae 8-10
D-10623 Berlin
Tel: (030) 297 49 348
Fax: (030) 297 49 161
Monday-Sunday: 0515-2300

Deutsche Bahn
Fahrkartenausgabe Köln Hbf
Trankgasse 11
D-50667 Cologne (Köln)
Tel: (0221) 141 228
Fax: (0221) 141 3241
Monday-Friday: 0600-2300
Saturday/Sunday/Public Holiday:
0600-2030

Deutsche Bahn
Fahrkartenausgabe Dresden Hbf
Reisezentrum/Touristikschalter
Am Hauptbahnhof 4
D-01069 Dresden
Tel: (0351) 461 3656
Fax: (0351) 461 3618
Monday-Friday: 0600-1300 & 1330-
2200; Saturday & Sunday: 0700-1300
& 1330-2000

Deutsche Bahn
Fahrkartenausgabe Frankfurt am Main Hbf
Im Hauptbahnhof

D-60329 Frankfurt am Main
Tel: (069) 265 4470
Fax: (069) 265 4120
Monday-Sunday: 0600-2230

Deutsche Bahn
Fahrkartenausgabe Hamburg Hbf
Hachmannplatz 10
D-20099 Hamburg
Tel: (040) 3918 4313
Fax: (040) 3918 2767
Monday-Friday: 0730-2100
Saturday & Sunday: 1000-1700

Deutsche Bahn
Fahrkartenausgabe Heidelberg Hbf
Kurfürstenanlage 75
D-69115 Heidelberg
Tel: (06221) 525 341
Fax: (06221) 525 494
Monday-Sunday: 0700-2000

Deutsche Bahn
Fahrkartenausgabe Leipzig Hbf
Georgiring 14
D-04103 Leipzig
Tel: (0341) 968 3745
Fax: (0341) 968 3653
Monday-Sunday: 0530-2200

Deutsche Bahn
Fahrkartenausgabe München Hbf
Bahnhofplatz 2
D-80335 Munich (München)
Tel: (089) 1308 5890
Fax: (089) 1308 2485
Monday-Friday: 0715-1800
Saturday/Sunday/Public Holiday:
0830-1600

Deutsche Bahn
Fahrkartenausgabe Stuttgart Hbf
Touristikschalter
Arnulf-Klett-Platz 2
D-70173 Stuttgart
Tel: (0711) 2092 2464
Fax: (0711) 2092 2686
Monday-Friday: 0730-1900
Saturday: 0730-1230
Sunday: closed

Great Britain

French Railways Limited
179 Picadilly
London W1C OBA
Tel: (171) 493 9731
Monday-Friday: 0900-1715
Saturday (from Easter Saturday until
the end of August): 0900-1200

Greece

Chemins de fer Helléniques
Bureau de Voyages et du Tourisme No. 2
1, rue Karolou
Athens 10437
Tel: (01) 522 2491
Monday-Saturday: 0800-1500

Chemins de fer Helléniques
Bureau de Voyages et du tourisme No. 7
17, rue Filellinon - Place de Syntagma
Athens 10557
Tel: (01) 323 6747 0r 6273
Monday-Friday: 0800-1500

Chemins de fer Helléniques
Gare Centrale de Voyageurs
Patras
Tel: (061) 221 311 or 273 694
Fax: (061) 277 441
Summer: Monday-Sunday: 0800-2000
Winter: Monday-Sunday: 0800-1400

Chemins de fer Helléniques
Gare Centrale des Voyageurs
Thessaloniki
Tel: (031) 519 519
Monday-Sunday: 24 hours a day

Hungary

Chemins de fer de l'Etat hongrois
(MAV)
Menetjegyiroda
Andrássy út 35
H-1061 Budapest VI
Tel: (01) 3228405
Monday-Sunday: 0930-1800, April-
September
Monday-Sunday: 0900-1700, October-
March

Ireland (Republic)

Coras Iompair Eireann
International Rail

Travel Centre
35, Lower Abbey Street
Tel: (01) 8363333; Fax: (0l) 8745603
Monday-Friday: 0900-1700

Italy

Ferrovie dello Stato S.p.A.
Stazione Bari Centrale
Biglietteria
Bari
Tel: (080) 5732003/5212202
Fax: (080) 5732611
Monday-Saturday: 0900-1300 &
1600-2000

Ferrovie dello Stato S.p.A.
Stazione Santa Maria Novella-Ufficio
informazioni
Florence (Firenze)
Tel: (055) 235 2595
Fax: (055) 235 2031
Monday-Saturday: 0900-2300

Ferrovie dello Stato S.p.A.
Stazione Centrale-Ufficio informazioni
Milan (Milano)
Tel: (02) 675001
Fax: (02) 67712278
Monday-Sunday: 0730-2140

Ferrovie dello Stato S.P.A.
Stazione Centrale-Ufficio informazioni
Naples (Napoli)
Tel: (081) 5543188
Monday-Sunday: 0700-2100

Ferrovie dello Stato S.p.A.
Stazione Centrale-Ufficio informazioni
Palermo
Tel: (091) 6161806/6164808
Monday-Sunday: 0800-2000

Ferrovie dello Stato S.p.A.
Stazione Termini-Ufficio informazioni
Rome (Roma)
Tel: (06) 4730 6331
Fax: (06) 4730 7617
Monday-Sunday: 0700-2100

Ferrovie dello Stato S.p.A.
Stazione Santa Lucia-Ufficio infor-
mazioni
Venice (Venezia)
Tel: (041) 715555; Fax: (041) 7853038
Monday-Sunday: 0800-2000

Luxembourg

Société Nationale des Chemins de fer
luxembourgeois
Centre d'Accueil et de Vente
Gare de Luxembourg
L-1616 Luxembourg (GD)
Tel: 492424
Monday-Friday: 0800-1200 &
1300-1700

Netherlands

Nederlandse Spoorwegen
Ticket Office-Schiphol Plaza
Amsterdam Schiphol Airport
Tel: (020) 601 0541
Fax: (020) 601 9424
Monday-Sunday: 0800-2000

Nederlandse Spoorwegen
NS Internationaal-Ticket Office
Amsterdam Central Station
Tel: (020) 557 8088
Fax: (020) 557 8235
Monday-Sunday: 0800-2000

Nederlandse Spoorwegen
Customer service
Report to 'Information Desk' in the
hall of Utrech Central Station
Utrech
Tel: (030) 2354480 or 2353735
Fax: (030) 2357157
Monday-Friday: 0830-1630

Norway

Norwegian State Railways
International tickets
Central Station
0048 Oslo
Tel: 23154111; Fax: 23154086
Monday-Sunday: 0700-2300

Portugal

Companhia dos caminhos de ferro
portugueses
Estaçao de caminho de ferro
Largo de estaçao
P-8000 Faro
Tel: (089) 23815
Monday-Sunday: 1000-1800

Companhia dos caminhos de ferro
portugueses
Bilheteira Internacional
Estaçao de Santa Apolonia
Avenida Infante D. Henrique
P-1100 Lisboa
Tel: (01) 888 4181 ext, 189
Fax: (01) 888 4143
Monday-Sunday: 0900-1800

Companhia dos caminhos de ferro por-
tugueses
Estaçao de S. Bento
Praça Almeida Garret
P-4000 Porto
Tel: (02) 2002722 ext. 28
Fax: (02) 2001054
Monday-Sunday: 0630-1600
(until 1800 weekdays during July and
August)

Spain

Red Nacional de los Ferrocarriles
Españoles
Estacion central de Barcelona Sants
Barcelona
Tel: (093) 4910069
Monday-Friday: 0900-1300 &
1600-1800

Red Nacional de los Ferrocarriles
Españoles
avda. Marques de Argentera s/n
Estacion de Barcelona Franca
Barcelona
Tel: (093) 319 6567
Fax: (093) 319 6107
Monday-Friday: 0900-2100

Red Nacional de los Ferrocarriles
Españoles
Alcala 44
Madrid
Tel: (091) 531 4707
Fax: (091) 531 8133
Monday-Saturday: 0930-2000

Red Nacional de los Ferrocarriles
Españoles
Oficina de viajes RENFE
Aeropuerto Internacional Barajas
Madrid
Tel: (091) 2058544
Monday-Saturday: 0800-2000
Sunday: 0800-1400

Red Nacional de los Ferrocarriles
Españoles
Bureau de Vente de billets
Estacion Madrid-Chamartin
Tel: (01) 7330041
Monday-Sunday: 0900-2100

Red Nacional de los Ferrocarriles
Españoles
Calle Zaragoza 29
Sevilla
Tel: (0954) 222693
Monday–Friday" 0900–1315 &
0400–1900
Saturday: 0400–1230

Red Nacional de los Ferrocarriles
Españoles
Taquillas Largo Recorrido
Estacion Renfe-Valencia Termino
Valencia
Tel: (096) 3514 805
Monday-Friday: 0900-1300 & 1600-
1900; Saturday: 0900-1300

Sweden

Statens Järnvägar
Swedish State Railways Ticket Office
Stockholm central Station
S-10550 Stockholm
Tel: (8) 7624855
Fax: (8) 7624899
Monday-Friday: 0900-1900
Saturday: 0800-1600
Sunday: 1000-1700

Switzerland
Schweizerische Bundesbahnen
Banhof Basel SBB
CH-4051 Basel
Tel: (061) 276 2461
Fax: (061) 276 2468
Monday-Friday: 0700-2000
Saturday: 0700-1700
Sunday: 0800-1700

Schweizerische Bundesbahnen
Hauptbahnhof SBB
CH-3000 Bern
Tel: (0512) 204 346
Fax: (0512) 204 192
Monday-Friday: 0800-1900
Saturday: 0800-1700

Chemins de fer fédéraux suisses
Gare de Geneve CFF
CH-1201 Geneva (Geneve)
Tel: (022) 715 2387
Fax: (022) 715 2714
Monday-Friday: 0800-1845
Saturday: 0800-1645

Chemins de fer fédéraux suisses
Garde de Genève Aéroport
CH-1215 Geneva (Genève)
Tel: (022) 7910 250
Fax: (022) 7982 366
Monday-Friday: 0915-1745
Saturday: 0900-1745

BLS - Lötschbergbahn
Bahnhof Interlaken-West
CH-3800 Interlaken
Tel: (033) 826 4750
Fax: (033) 826 4746
Monday-Sunday: 0800-1200
1400-1800

Schweizerische Bundesbahnen
Bahnhof SBB
CH-6002 Lucerne (Luzern)
Tel: (0512) 273 314
Fax: (0512) 273 504
Monday-Friday: 0800-1945
Saturday: 0800-1800
Sunday: 0900-1800

Schweizerische Bundesbahnen
Hauptbahnhof SBB
CH-8021 Zürich
Tel: (0512) 223 364
Fax: (0512) 223 896
Monday-Friday: 0645-2030
Saturday & Sunday: 0645-1930

Schweizerische Bundesbahnen
Bahnhof SBB
Zürich Flughafen (Zürich Airport)
CH-8058 Zürich
Tel: (01) 814 2822; Fax: (01) 813 0330
Monday-Sunday: 0700-1900

Opening hours, phone numbers, and fax
numbers are subject to change.

Passport Offices throughout the U.S.

You may apply for a passport at any passport agency and at many Clerks of Court Offices or Post Offices designated to accept passport applications. The regional offices are as follows:

Boston: Thomas P. O'Neill Federal Building, 10 Causeway Street, Suite 247, Boston, Massachusetts 02222-1094; (617) 565–6990.

Chicago: Kluczynski Office Building, 230 South Dearborn Street, Room 380, Chicago, Illinois 60604-1564; (312) 353–7155.

Honolulu: First Hawaiian Tower, 1132 Bishop Street, Suite 500, Honolulu, HI 96813-2309; (808) 522-8283 or (808) 522-8286.

Houston: Mickey Leland Federal Building, 1919 Smith Street, Suite 1100, Houston, Texas 77002-8049; (713) 209-3153.

Los Angeles: Federal Building, 11000 Wilshire Boulevard, Room 13100, Los Angeles, California 90024-3615; (310) 235–7070.

Miami: Claude Pepper Federal Office Building, 51 Southwest First Avenue, Third Floor, Miami, Florida 33120-1680; (305) 536–4681.

New Orleans: 701 Loyal Avenue, Postal Services Building, T-12005, New Orleans, Louisiana 70113-1931; (504) 589–6728 or (504) 589-6161.

New York: Rockefeller Center, 630 Fifth Avenue, Suite 270, New York, New York 10111-0031; (212) 399–5290.

Philadelphia: U.S. Customs House, 200 Chestnut Street, Room 103, Philadelphia, Pennsylvania 19106-2970; (215) 597–7480.

Portsmouth: 31 Rochester Avenue, Portsmouth, New Hampshire, 03801-2900; (603) 334–0500.

San Francisco: Tishman Speyer Building, 525 Market Street, Room 200, San Francisco, California 94105-2773; (415) 744–4010 or (415) 744-4444.

Seattle: Henry Jackson Federal Building, 915 Second Avenue, Room 992, Seattle, Washington 98174-1091; (206) 220–7788.

Stamford: One Landmark Square, Broad and Atlantic Streets, Stamford, Connecticut 06901-2667; (203) 325–4401 or (203) 325–4402.

Washington, D.C.: 1111 19th Street NW, Washington, D.C. 20522-1705; (202) 647-0518.

Passport Information

The phone number of the passport offices listed above provide a recorded message that describes the documents you need and the application process for obtaining a passport as well as reporting the loss or theft of your passport. It also explains how you can obtain a copy of the report of a birth or death of a U.S. citizen abroad. The message will direct you to the proper agencies for information regarding naturalization, travel advisories, customs regulations, and shots required by various countries. The National Passport Information Center at 1-900-Call NPIC will answer any questions you may have. You can access more passport and travel information via the internet at: http://travel.state.gov.

European Tourist Offices In North America

Austrian National Tourist Office—http://www.anto.com

New York: P.O. Box 1142 Times Square, New York, New York 10108. Tel: (212) 944–6880. Fax: (212) 730–4568.

Montreal: Office National Autrichien du Tourisme, 1010 Ouest Rue Sherbrooke, Suite 1410, Montreal, Quebec H3A 2R7, Canada. Tel: (514) 849–3709. Fax: (514) 849–9577.

Toronto: 2 Bloor Street East, Suite 3330, Toronto, Ontario M4W 1A8, Canada. Tel: (416) 967–3381. Fax: (416) 967–4101.

Vancouver: 200 Granville Street, Suite 1380, Granville Square, Vancouver, British Columbia V6C 1S4, Canada. Tel: (604) 683–5808. Fax: (604) 662–8528.

**Belgium Tourist Office— belinfo@nyxfer.blythe.org
http://www.visitbelgium.com/**

New York: 780 Third Avenue, Suite 1501, New York, New York 10017-7076. Tel: (212) 758–8130. Fax: (212) 355–7675.

British Tourist Authority—http://www.bta.org.uk

New York: 551 Fifth Avenue, Suite 701, New York, New York 10176-0799. Tel: (800) 462–2748 or (212) 986–2200. Fax: (212) 986–1188.

Chicago: 625 N. Michigan Avenue, Suite 1510, Chicago, Illinois 60611.

Czech Service Center

Washington D.C.: 1511 K Street NW, Suite 1030, Washington, D.C. 20005. Tel: (800) Y–Prague; Fax: (202) 638–5308.

French Government Tourist Office—http://www.fgtousa.org

For information on France by telephone, dial (900) 990–0040 in the U.S. (charge is 95 cents per minute).

Chicago: 676 N. Michigan Avenue, Suite 3360, Chicago, Illinois 60611. Tel: (312) 751–7800. Fax: (312) 337–6339.

Los Angeles: 9454 Wilshire Boulevard, Suite 303, Beverly Hills, California 90212. Tel: (310) 271–6665. Fax: (310) 276–2835.

New York: 444 Madison Avenue, 16th Floor, New York, New York, 10022. Tel: (212) 838–7800. Fax: (212) 838–7855.

Montreal: 1981 McGill College Avenue, Suite 490, Montreal, Quebec PQH3A 2W9, Canada. Fax: (514) 845–4868. e-mail: mfrance@passport.com.

Toronto: 30 St. Patrick Street, Suite 700, Toronto, Ontario M5T 3A3, Canada. Fax: (416) 979–7587.

German National Tourist Office—http://www.germany-tourisim.de

Los Angeles: 11766 Wilshire Boulevard, Suite 750, Los Angeles, California 90025. Tel: (310) 575–9799. Fax: (310) 575–1565.

New York: 122 E. 42nd Street, 52nd Floor, New York, New York 10168–0072. Tel: (212) 661–7200. Fax: (212) 661–7174.

Toronto: 175 Bloor Street, East, North Tower, Suite 604, Toronto, Ontario M4W 3R8, Canada. Tel: (416) 968–1570. Fax (416) 968–1986.

Greek National Tourist Organization—gnto@aurora.eexi.gr

Chicago: 168 N. Michigan Avenue, Suite 600, Chicago, Illinois 60601. Tel: (312) 782–1084. Fax: (312) 782–1091.

Los Angeles: 611 West Sixth Street, Suite 2198, Los Angeles, California 90017. Tel: (213) 626–6696. Fax: (213) 489–9744.

New York: 645 Fifth Avenue, Olympic Tower, 5th Floor, New York, New York 10022. Tel: (212) 421–5777. Fax: (212) 826–6940.

Montreal: 1233 rue de la Montagne, Suite 101, Quebec H3G 1Z2, Canada. Tel: (514) 871–1535. Fax: (514) 871–1498.

Toronto: Upper Level, 1300 Bay Street, Toronto, Ontario M5R 3K8, Canada. Tel: (416) 968–2220. Fax: (416) 968–6533.

Hungary Tourist Board—Runtour@gramercy.ios.com

New York:: c/o Embassy of the Republic of Hungary. 150 East 58th Street, 33rd Floor, New York, New York 10155. Tel: (212) 355–0240. Fax: (212) 207–4103.

Irish Tourist Board—http://www.ireland.travel.ie

New York: 345 Park Avenue, New York, New York 10154. Tel: (212) 418–0800, (800) 223–6470. Fax: (212) 371–9052.

Toronto: 160 Bloor Street East, Suite 1150, Toronto, Ontario M4W 1B9, Canada. Tel: (416) 929–2777. Fax: (416) 929–6783.

Italian Government Tourist Board

Chicago: 401 North Michigan Avenue, Suite 3030, Chicago, Illinois 60611. Tel: (312) 644–9448. Fax: (312) 644–3019.

New York: 630 Fifth Avenue, Suite 1565, NY, New York 10111. Tel: (212) 245–4822. Fax: (212) 586–9249.

Los Angeles: 12400 Wilshire Boulevard, Suite 550, Los Angeles, California 90025. Tel: (310) 820–0098. Fax: (310) 820–6357.

Montreal: 1 Place Ville Marie, Suite 1914, Montreal, Quebec, H3B 3M9, Canada. Tel: (514) 866–7667. Fax (514) 392–1429.

Luxembourg National Tourist Office—luxnto@aol.com
New York: 17 Beekman Place, New York, New York 10022. Tel: (212) 935–8888.
Fax: (212) 935–5896.

Malta National Tourist Office—http://www.tourism.org.mt
New York: Empire State Building, 350 Fifth Avenue, Suite 4412, New York, New
York 10118. Tel: (212) 695–9520. Fax: (212) 695–8229. e-mail:
104452.2005@compuserve.com.

**Monaco Government Tourist/Convention Bureau—
http://www.monaco.mc/usa**
New York: 565 Fifth Avenue, New York, New York 10017. Tel: (800) 753–9696
or (212) 286–3330. Fax: (212) 286–9890.

**Netherlands Board of Tourism—http://www.nbt.nl/holland—
e-mail: go2holland@aol.com**
Chicago: 225 N. Michigan Avenue, Suite 1854, Chicago, Illinois 60601. Tel: (888)
GO HOLLAND, Fax: (312) 819–1740.

Portuguese National Tourist Office—http://www.portugal.com.org
Montreal: 500 Sherbrooke Street West, Suite 940, Montreal, Canada, QC H3A
3C6. Tel: (514) 282–1264; Fax: (514) 499–1450.
New York: 590 Fifth Avenue, 4th Floor, New York, New York 10036–4704
Tel: (212) 354–4403; (800) PORTUGAL. Fax: (212) 764–6137.
Toronto: 60 Bloor Street, Suite 1005, Toronto, Ontario M4W 3B8, Canada.
Tel: (416) 921–7376; Fax: (416) 921–1353.

**Scandinavian Tourist Boards of Denmark, Finland, Iceland,
Norway and Sweden**
  Denmark: http://www.deninfo.com/index/htm
  Finland: http://www.travelfile.com/get?finninfo
  Iceland: http://www.arctic.is/ITB/
  Norway: http://www.travelfile.com/get?NORTRA
  Sweden: http://www.travelfile.com/get?swetvl
New York: P.O. Box 4649, Grand Central Station, New York, New York
10163–4649. Tel: (212) 949–2333. Fax: (212) 983–5260.

Tourist Office of Spain—http://www.okspain.org
Chicago: 845 N. Michigan Avenue, Water Tower Place Suite 915 E, Chicago,
Illinois 60611. Tel: (312) 642–1992. Fax: (312) 642–9817.
Los Angeles: San Vicente Plaza Building, 8383 Wilshire Blvd., Suite 960, Beverly
Hills, California 90211. Tel: (213) 658–7188. Fax: (213) 658–1061.
New York: 666 Fifth Avenue, 35th Floor, New York, New York 10103. Tel: (888)
OK SPAIN; (212) 265–8822. Fax: (212) 265–8864.

Toronto: 2 Bloor Street West, 34th Floor, Toronto, Ontario M4W 3E2, Canada. Tel: (416) 961–3131. Fax: (416) 961–1992.

Miami: 1221 Brickell Avenue, Miami, Florida 33131. Tel: (305) 358–1992. Fax: (305) 358–8223.

Switzerland Tourism—http://switzerlandtourism.ch—stnewyork@switzerlandtourism.com

Chicago: 150 North Michigan Avenue, Suite 2930, Chicago, Illinois 60601. Tel: (312) 630–5840.

Los Angeles: 222 N. Sepulveda Blvd., Suite 1570, El Segundo, California 90245. Tel: (310) 335–5980. Fax: (310) 335–5982.

New York: 608 Fifth Avenue, New York, New York 10020. Tel: (212) 757–5944. Fax: (212) 262–6116.

Toronto: 926 The East Mall, Etobicoke, Ontario M9B 6K1, Canada. Tel: (416) 695–2090. Fax: (416) 695–2774

Toll-Free Airline Numbers

(Dialing from U.S.)

Aer Lingus 800–223–6537

Air Canada (AC) 800–776–3000

Air France (AF) 800–237–2747

American Airlines, Inc. (AA) 800–433–7300

Austrian Airlines (OS) 800–843–0002

British Airways (BA) 800–AIRWAYS

Carnival Airlines 800–824–7386

Continental Airlines (CO) . . 800–525–0280

Czech Airlines 800–223–2365

Delta Air Lines, Inc. (DL) . . 800–221–1212

Finnair (AY) 800–950–5000

Icelandair 800–223–5500

KLM Royal Dutch
Airlines (KL) 800–374–7747

Lufthansa German
Airlines (LH) 800–645–3880

Northwest Airlines,
Inc. (NW) 800–225–2525

Olympic Airways 800–223–1226

Sabena Belgian World
Airlines (SN) 800–955–2000

Scandinavian Airlines
System (SAS) 800–221–2350

Swissair (SR) 800–221–4750

TAP Air Portugal (TO) 800–221–7370

Tower Air 800–221–2500

Trans World
Airlines, Inc. (TWA) 800–221–2000

United Air Lines, Inc. (UA) . 800–241–6522

USAir (US) 800–428–4322

Virgin Atlantic
Airways Ltd. (US) 800–862–8621

Toll-Free Hotel Reservations Numbers

(Dialing from U.S.)

Best Western International . 800–528–1234

Choice Hotels
International, Inc. 800–4–CHOICE

Consort Hotels Ltd. . 800–55–CONSORT

Forte & Meridian
Hotels, Inc. 800–225–5843

Golden Tulip International . 800–344–1212

Hilton Reservations
Worldwide 800–HILTONS

Holiday Inn Worldwide . . 800–HOLIDAY

Hyatt Worldwide Reservation
Centres 800–233–1234

Inter–Continental
Hotels Corp 800–327–0200

Inter–Europe Hotels 800–221–6509

ITT Sheraton Corporation 800–325–3535

Kempinski International . . 800–426–3135

Leading Hotels of the World 800–223–6800

Loews Representation
International 800–223–0888

Marriott Corporation 800–228–9290

MinOtels Intl. 800–336 4668

Nikko Hotels International 800–645–5687

Preferred Hotels & Resorts
Worldwide 800–323–7500

Radisson Hotels
International, Inc. 800–333–3333

Ramada International
Hotels & Resorts 800–854–7854

SRS Steigenberger Reservation
Service 800–223–5652

Swissotel 800–63–SWISS

Airport City Connections

Those arriving in many popular European cities will find direct rail service at a growing number of European airports. Rail service between central stations and airport include:

STATION	AIRPORT	DISTANCE	TRANSPORT	BUS #	CITY TERMINAL
Alacant	Alicante	12 km	Bus services daily	13/14	Plaza Chapi
Amsterdam	Schiphol	14 km	Train every 15 mins.	—	Centraal Station
Athinai	Hellenikon	14 km	Bus every 30 mins.	A&B	Syntagma Square/ Amalias Avenue
Barcelona	Prat	10 km	Train every 30 mins.	—	Barcelona Sants
Basel	Basel/Mulhouse/ Freiburg	9 km	Bus every 20–30 mins.	50	SBB Station/ Kannenfeldplatz
Belfast	Belfast International	26 km	Bus every 30 mins.	300 (airbus) Sundays #60	Europa Buscentre, Glengall Street
Berlin	Schönefeld	18 km	S-bahn train every 20 mins.	—	Bahnhof Zoo/Hbf
Berlin	Tegel	7 km	Bus every 10 mins.	X9	Bahnhof Zoo
Bonn	Köln/Bonn	20 km	Bus every 20 mins.	670	Hauptbahnhof
Bordeaux	Merignac	12 km	Bus 15 services daily	—	Gare St. Jean
Bristol	Bristol	13 km	Bus every 2 hrs until 1956	820	Bus station, also Temple Meads Station
Brussels	Nationaal	12 km	Train every 20 mins.	—	Midi/Zuid Station also calls at Central and Nord
Budapest	Ferihegy	16 km	Bus every 30 mins.	—	Bus Station, Erzébet tér
Dublin	Dublin	11 km	Bus 'Airlink' every 20–30 mins.	—	Heuston Station/ Busaras
Düsseldorf	Düsseldorf	7 km	Train (S-Bahn) every 20 mins	—	Hauptbahnhof

STATION	AIRPORT	DISTANCE	TRANSPORT	BUS #	CITY TERMINAL
Firenze (Florence)	Firenze Peretola	7 km	Bus every 25 mins.	ATAF 62	Stazione FS
Frankfurt am Main	Frankfurt/Main	10 km	Train (S-Bahn) 6 times hourly	—	Hauptbahnhof
Gèneve	Cointrin	4 km	Train, 6 times hourly	—	Comavin Station
Genova	Cristoforo Colombo	7 km	"Volabus" services daily	12/14	Brignole & Principe stations; Piazza de Ferrari
Göteburg	Landvetter	25 km	Bus every 15 mins. Monday–Friday; every 20-30 mins. Saturday, Sunday, and holidays	—	City Air Terminal/ Central Station
Grenoble	Lyon Satolas	85 km	Bus (Cars Faure) 9-11 times daily	—	Gare routière (bus station)
Hamburg	Fuhlsbüttel	11 km	Bus (Jasper) every 20 mins.	—	Hauptbahnhof/ Kirchenallee
Hannover	Langenhagen	13 km	Bus every 30 mins.	60	Bus station at Hauptbahnhof
Helsinki	Vantaa	19 km	Bus every 15-20 mins.	—	City Air Terminal/ Rail Station
Kobenhavn (Copenhagen)	Kastrup	9 km	Bus every 10-15 mins.	—	Central Station
Koln (Cologne)	Koln/Bonn	14 km	Bus every 15-20 mins.	170	Dom/Hauptbahnhof
Lisboa (Lisbon)	Portela	7 km	Bus **Aero-Bus**, every 20 mins. 0700–2100	91	Cais do Sodré
London	City	10 km	Bus every 20 mins. 0700-2140 Monday-Friday except holidays	Station	Liverpool Street
London	Gatwick	44 km	Train every 15 mins.	—	Victoria Station
London	Heathrow	24 km	LT train, every 5-10 mins.	—	London Underground

STATION	AIRPORT	DISTANCE	TRANSPORT	BUS #	CITY TERMINAL
Luxembourg	Findel	7 km	Bus every 15-30 mins.	9	Gare Centrale
Lyon	Satolas	25 km	Bus (Navette Aéroport) every 20 mins.	—	Perrache Station, via Part Dieu Station
Madrid	Barajas	12 km	Bus approx. every 10 mins.	—	Plaza Colón
Málaga	Málaga	7 km	Train, every 30 mins.	—	Málaga Station
Marseille	Marseille/Provence	28 km	Bus every 20 mins.	—	Gare St. Charles
Milano (Milan)	Linate	7 km	Bus approx. every 20 mins.	—	Piazza S. Babila/Milano Centrale Station
Milano (Milan)	Milano-Malpensa	45 km	Bus ("Airpullman") for each scheduled flight	—	Centrale & Garibaldi Stations
Munchen (Munich)	Strauss	37 km	S-Bahn Train, every 20 mins.	—	Hauptbahnhof
Napoli	Capodichino	7 km	Bus every 20 mins.	14	Piazza Garibaldi (Central Station)
Nice	Nice-Côte d'Azur	7 km	Bus every 20 mins.	—	Gare Routière Départmentale
Oslo	Fornebu	10 km	Bus every 15/30 mins.	—	Central Station
Palma	Palma	11 km	Bus every 30 mins.	—	Plaza España
Paris	Charles ge Gaulle	25 km	RER train every 15 mins.	—	Gare du Nord/Châtelet les Halles
Paris	Orly	15 km	RER train every 15 mins.	—	Gare du Nord/Châtelet les Halles
Piraeus	Hellinkon	20 km	Bus every 50-60 mins.	—	Central Passenger Terminal & Akti Tzelepi
Pisa	Pisa (Galileo)	2 km	1 per hour	—	Pisa Centrale (trains continue to/from Firenze)

STATION	AIRPORT	DISTANCE	TRANSPORT	BUS #	CITY TERMINAL
Porto	Pedras Rubras	17 km	Bus every 15–30 mins.	—	Praça do Carmo
Praha (Prague)	Ruzyne	17 km	Bus (CSA) every 30 mins.	—	Vltava Terminal/ 25 Ul. Revolucni
Roma (Rome)	Leonardo da Vinci (Fiumicino)	27 km	Train every 20–30 mins.	—	Roma Tiburtina/ Ostiense/Termini
Salzburg	Maxglan	5 km	Bus every 15 mins.	77	Salzburg Bahnhof
Stavanger	Sola	14 km	Bus every 15–20 mins.	—	Sentrum/Hotel Atlantic
Stockholm	Arlanda	44 km	Bus every 10–15 mins.	—	Cityterminalen (close to Central Station)
Strasbourg	Entzheim	12 km	Bus every 30 mins.	—	Place de la Gare (Hôtel Carlton)
Stuttgart	Echterdingen	14 km	Train every 20–30 mins.	—	Hauptbahnhof
Torino	Caselle	16 km	Bus every 45 mins.	—	Corso Inghilterra 3
Toulouse	Blagnac	8 km	Bus every 20 mins. while airport open	—	Gare Routière
València	Manises	9 km	Bus (VASA) 12 times daily except sundays & holidays	—	Central Bus Station, Avenida Menéndez Pidal 13
Venezia (Venice)	Marco Polo	13 km	Bus every 30/60 mins. (Summer/Winter)	5	Pizzale Roma
Wien (Vienna)	Schwechat	17 km	Train every 30 mins.	—	Wien Mitte & Wien Nord Stations
Zürich	Zürich (Kloten)	12 km	Train 5 times hourly	—	Zürich Hauptbahnhof

In addition, rail service to other cities via the Airport Station may be available.

EURAIL PASSES

Eurail Passes entitle you to unlimited travel on Europe's extensive 100,000–mile rail network in the 17 western countries of Europe (England, Scotland, and Wales not included).

Austria • Belgium • Denmark • Finland • France • Germany • Greece
Hungary • Ireland (Rep.) • Italy • Luxembourg • Netherlands • Norway
Portugal • Spain • Sweden • Switzerland

To order, call (800) 722-7151 or (614) 793-7651 or visit the Rail Pass Express website at http://www.eurail.com.

Eurail Pass
Travel on any or all days
for the duration of the pass.
First Class

15 days	$538
21 days	$698
1 month	$864
2 months	$1224
3 months	$1512

Children 4-11 half adult fare. Under 4 free.

Eurail Saverpass
Rail travel for 2-5 people
traveling together at all times.

$458
$594
$734
$1040
$1286

Eurail Flexipass
Choose your travel days and
use them within 2 months.
First Class

10 days in 2 months	$634
15 days in 2 months	$836

Children 4-11 half adult fare. Under 4 free.

Eurail Saver Flexipass
Rail travel for 2-5 people
traveling together at all times.

$540
$710

Eurail Youth Pass*
Second Class

15 days	$376
21 days	$489
1 month	$605
2 months	$857
3 months	$1059

*Available for passengers under 26 on their first date of travel.

Eurail Youth Flexipass*
Second Class

10 days in 2 months	$444
15 days in 2 months	$595

*Available for passengers under 26 on their first date of travel.

EUROPASS

The Europass features unlimited flexible travel in the 5 most frequently visited countries of Europe: France, Germany, Italy, Spain, and Switzerland.

You determine the number of travel days from 5 to 15 travel days in a 2-month period, making the Europass the most flexible rail pass available. In addition you may add zones:

Benelux   Belgium, Luxembourg, & the Netherlands
Danube   Austria & Hungary
Greece Plus Greece & Ferry
Portugal

Europass
Unlimited travel in: France, Germany, Italy, Spain, and Switzerland.

	ADULT 1ST CLASS	ADULT 40% OFF	YOUTH* 2ND CLASS
5 days in 2 months	$326	$196	$216
6 days in 2 months	$368	$221	$245
7 days in 2 months	$410	$246	$274
8 days in 2 months	$452	$271	$303
9 days in 2 months	$494	$296	$332
10 days in 2 months	$536	$321	$361
11 days in 2 months	$578	$346	$390
12 days in 2 months	$620	$371	$419
13 days in 2 months	$662	$396	$448
14 days in 2 months	$704	$421	$477
15 days in 2 months	$746	$446	$506

*Youth price available for passengers under 26. Children 4-11 half adult fare. Under 4 free.

Associate Zones
Zones include: Benelux, Danube, Greece, and Portugal.

	ADULT 1ST CLASS	ADULT 40% OFF	YOUTH* 2ND CLASS
1 Additional Zone	$60	$36	$45
2 Additional Zones	$90	$54	$70
3 Additional Zones	$110	$66	$85
4 Additional Zones	$120	$72	$93

Associate zones extend the geographic area of the pass; they do not extend the pass' length in days. Greece add-on allows ferry crossing from Italy to Greece.

COUNTRY AND REGIONAL PASSES

Austrian Railpass

	ADULT 1ST CLASS	ADULT 2ND CLASS	CHILD 1ST CLASS	CHILD 2ND CLASS
3 days in 15	$145	$98	$73	$49
Additional Days	$21	$15	$11	$8

Children: age 7-15; 6 and under free. 5 day maximum additional rail days. Bonuses include discounts on steamers, local trains, and bicycle rentals.

Balkan Flexipass
Unlimited rail travel in Bulgaria, Greece, Former Yugoslav Republic of Macedonia, Montenegro, Romania, Serbia, and Turkey.

	1ST CLASS ADULT	1ST CLASS YOUTH
5 days in 1 month	$152	$90
10 days in 1 month	$264	$156
15 days in 1 month	$317	$190

Children 4-12 half of the adult fare.

Benelux to Tourrail Pass
Valid for rail travel in Belguim, Luxembourg and the Netherlands.

	1ST CLASS	2ND CLASS
5 days in 1 month	$217	$155
Youth 5 days in 1 month	—	$104

Benelux to Tourrail Pass For Two
Prices are for two people traveling together.

	1ST CLASS	2ND CLASS
5 days in 1 month	$326	$233

Youth for persons age 4-25.

Copenhagen Sightseeing Pass
Valid for trail travel from any German/Danish border crossing to Copenhagen and return within seven days for holders of a Europass or German Railpass.

	1ST CLASS	2ND CLASS
Adult	$100	$70
Youth	$75	$50
Child	$50	$35

Free Canal Sightseeing Tour is included from April 15-October 15. Youth 12-25. Child 4-11. Stop overs are permitted.

Greek Flexipass
Valid for 1st class rail travel in Greece.

	ADULT	CHILD
3 days in 1 month	$86	$58
5 days in 1 month	$120	$85

Child 6-12, under 6 travel free.

German Railpass

	ADULT 1ST CLASS	2ND CLASS	YOUTH* 2ND CLASS
5 days in 1 month	$276	$188	$146
10 days in 1 month	$434	$304	$200
15 days in 1 month	$562	$410	$252

Twinpass–For 2 Adults Traveling Together

	Adult 1st Class	2nd Class	
5 days in 1 month	$414	$282	—
10 days in 1 month	$650	$456	—
15 days in 1 month	$842	$615	—

*Youth ages under 26. Children 4-11 half adult fare.

Bonuses for passholders include free travel on KD River Steamers on certain Rhine, Main, and Moselle River sections and free travel on selected bus lines operated by Deutsche Touring/Europabus.

Holland Railpass

	ADULT		YOUTH*
	1ST CLASS	2ND CLASS	2ND CLASS
3 days in 1 month	$88	$68	$56
5 days in 1 month	$140	$104	$73
10 das in 1 month	$260 $184	$130	

*Youth age 12-25.

Holland Railpass Plus

	ADULT		YOUTH*
	1ST CLASS	2ND CLASS	2ND CLASS
3 days in 1 month	$101	$81	$69
5 days in 1 month	$161	$125	$94

*Youth age 12-25. Entitles the holder to travel free on all buses, metro trains, and trams throughout the Netherlands.

Italy Railcard

Consecutive days

	1ST CLASS	2ND CLASS
8 days	$269	$187
15 days	$335	$228
21 days	$386	$263
30 days	$462	$312

Flexi RailCard

	1ST CLASS	2ND CLASS
4 days in 30	$214	$150
8 days in 30	$306	$204
12 days in 30	$380	$259

Valid for unlimited travel on the entire Italian Rail network including InterCity, EuroCity and Rapido trains with no surcharge. A supplement is required for ETR Pendolino trains. Children age 4-11 half fare; under 4 free. Price includes a $15 non-refundable issuing fee.

Norway Railpass

Consecutive Days

	1ST CLASS	2ND CLASS
7 days (May-Sep)	$250	$195
(Oct-Apr)	$200	$155
14 days (May-Sep)	$335	$255
(Oct-Apr)	$265	$205

Flexipass

	1ST CLASS	2ND CLASS
3/1 month (May-Sep)	$175	$135
(Oct-Apr)	$145	$110

Children 4-16 half fare. Up to 2 children under 4 travel free with one adult. Few trains in Norway offer first class.

Prague Excursion

Valid for rail transportation from any Czech border crossing to Prague and return within seven days.

	1ST CLASS
Adult	$49
Youth	$39
Child	$25

Youth ages 12-25. Child ages 4-11.

Scanrail Pass

Valid for unlimited rail travel in Denmark, Finland, Norway and Sweden.

	1ST CLASS		2ND CLASS	
	ADULT	SENIOR	ADULT	SENIOR
5 days in 15 days	$228	$203	$182	$162
10 days in 1 month	$364	$324	$292	$260
21 days	$422	$376	$338	$301
1 month	$532	$473	$426	$379

	1ST CLASS		2ND CLASS	
	YOUTH	CHILD	YOUTH	CHILD
5 days in 15 days	$171	$114	$137	$91
10 days in 1 month	$273	$182	$219	$146
21 days	$317	$211	$254	$169
1 month	$399	$266	$320	$213

Senior: age 55 and over. Youth: age 12-25. Child: age 4-11.

Spain Flexipass

Unlimited rail travel in Spain.

	1ST CLASS	2ND CLASS
3 days in 1 month	$190	$150
Additional Days	$40	$32

Maximum of 10 days. The AVE and Talgo 200 require an additional supplement. Children 4-11 travel half price.

Sweden Railpass

Unlimited rail travel in Sweden. Special: Two children (under 16) travel free together with one adult.

	ADULT		ADD'L CHILDREN	
CLASS	1ST CLASS	2ND CLASS	1ST CLASS	2ND
7 days	$275	$210	$190	$145
14 days	$365	$280	$255	$200
3 days in 7 days	$170	$130	$120	$90
5 days in 14 days	$215	$160	$150	$110

Please call Rail Pass Express at (800) 722-7151 for information on a variety of other country and regional rail passes or visit: http://www.eurail.com on the world-wide web.

BRITRAIL PASSES

A BritRail consecutive-day or flexipass allows unlimited travel on the entire British rail network spanning England, Scotland, and Wales.

Britrail Classic Pass

Valid for consecutive days of rail travel throughout Britain (England, Wales, and Scotland).

	ADULT		SENIOR		YOUTH
	1ST CLASS	2ND CLASS	1ST CLASS	2ND CLASS	2ND CLASS
8 days	$259	$319	NA	$205	—
15 days	$575	$395	$489	NA	$318
22 days	$740	$510	$630	NA	$410
1 month	$860	$590	$730	NA	$475

Senior age 60+. Youth age 16-25. Children 5-15 half fare. Children under 5 free.

Britrail Flexipass

Valid for unlimited rail travel for the days you choose within a 30-day period.

| | ADULT | | SENIOR | | YOUTH |
	1ST CLASS	2ND CLASS	1ST CLASS	2ND CLASS	2ND CLASS
4 days in 1 month	$315	$219	$269	NA	$175
8 days in 1 month	$459	$315	$390	NA	$253
15 days in 1 month	$699	$480	$590	NA	—
15 days in 2 months	—	—	—	—	$385

Senior age 60+. Youth age 16-25. Children 5-15 half fare. Children under 5 free.

Freedom of Scotland Travelpass

	STANDARD CLASS
8 days	$165
15 days	$235
22 days	$280
8 days within 15	$189

No discounts for children. Includes transportation on most Caledonian MacBrayne ferries to the islands of Scotland. Discounts on several ferry operators and on selected bus companies in Scotland. 20 percent discount on Stena Sealink to Northern Ireland.

BritRail Family Pass

Buy one adult or senior pass and get a free child age 5-15 pass of the same type. Available for the BritRail Classic Pass, BritRail Flexipass, BritRail + Ireland and BritRail + Car. Children under 5 travel free.

London Visitor Travel Card

Valid for unlimited consecutive day travel in the six zones of the London Underground and on the red double-decker buses.

	ADULT	CHILD
3 days	$29	$12
4 days	$39	$15
7 days	$59	$22

Child: age 5-15.

British Heritage Pass

	ADULT
7 days	$45
15 days	$69
1 month	$90

There is a $10 handling fee on all Heritage passes. No discounts for children. The pass is non-refundable/non-returnable.

Airport Transfers

	FIRST	STANDARD
Gatwick Express	$24	$16

Travel by train from Gatwick Airport to London Victoria Station. Children 5-15 half price.

	ADULT	CHILD
Heathrow Airbus	$12	$8

Transfer from Heathrow Airport to one of many Central London hotels.

London Day Tour
Child: age 5-15.

	ADULT	CHILD
	$80	$75

Includes: an experienced guide, a luxury air-conditioned touring coach, pub lunch, cruise of the river Thames with afternoon tea, and all entrance fees. Tour operates daily.

BritRail Pass + Ireland
Valid for travel in England, Scotland, Wales, Northern Ireland and the Republic of Ireland.

	1ST CLASS	2ND CLASS
5 days within 1 month	$473	$359
10 days within 1 month	$698	$511

Children 5-15 half fare. Children under 5 free.
Round-trip Stena Sealink service is included between Holyhead and Dun Laoghaire, Fishguard and Rosslare or Stranraer and Larne via ship, HSS or SeaLynx. NOTE: Reservations are essential for Irish Sea services. No refund on dated or paritally used passes; sea coupons are not refundable if unused.

BritRail Southeast Pass
A Flexipass for a large section of Southern England.

	1ST CLASS		STANDARD CLASS	
	ADULT	CHILD	ADULT	CHILD
3 days within 8 days	$90	$32	$69	$24
4 days within 8 days	$121	$32	$90	$24
7 days within 15 days	$169	$32	$121	$24

Children: age 5-15.

Britrail + Eurostar

	1ST CLASS	STANDARD CLASS
One-Way Eurostar		
4 days in 3 months	$430	$289
8 days in 3 months	$561	$381
Round Trip Eurostar		
4 days in 3 months	$574	$373
8 days in 3 monts	$710	$466

Many local trains in England, Scotland, and Wales have Standard Class accommodations only. This is allowed for in the First-Class price. Eurostar journey must originate in London; Eurostar voucher is only available in Standard Class. There is no reduction for children. There is a $10 process fee charged by the railways for a Eurostar reservation.

BritainShrinker Escorted Tours
Please call for brochure.

DRIVE PASSES

BritRail Pass + Car

Group	Class	3 RAIL & 3 CAR DAYS WITHIN 1 MONTH		6 RAIL & 7 CAR DAYS WITHIN 1 MONTH	
		Adult	Senior	Adult	Senior
Manual Transmission					
Economy	1st	$393	$360	$740	$689
2dr/4st	2nd	$325	—	$634	—
Compact	1st	$440	$407	$852	$801
4dr/5st	2nd	$372	—	$746	—
Intermediate	1st	$484	$451	$954	$903
4dr/5st	2nd	$416	—	$848	—
Automatic Transmission					
Intermediate	1st	$564	$531	$1141	$1090
4dr/4st	2nd	$496	—	$1035	—
Full Size	1st	$644	$457	$1327	$1276
2dr/4st	2nd	$576	—	$1221	—

Additional Person Rail Supplement

	1st	$221	$188	$340	$289
	2nd	$153	—	$234	—

Children 5-15 pay half the adult rail supplement. Children under 5 free. Includes unlimited mileage and free drop-off. Minimum rental age is 25. Many local trains in England, Scotland, and Wales have Standard Class accommodations only. This is allowed for in the First-Class price. Reserve your first car day at least seven days before your departure to Britain by calling Hertz at (800) 654-3001.

German Rail/Drive

Valid for 4 days of unlimited rail travel in Germany and 3 days of car rental. Up to 4 additional rail days.

Car Category	1ST CLASS		2ND CLASS		ADD'L. CAR DAY
	2 ADULTS*	1 ADULT	2 ADULTS*	1 ADULT	
Economy	$268	$338	$208	$278	$53
Compact	$288	$388	$228	$328	$67
Intermed.	$308	$418	$248	$358	$76
Comp. Auto.**	$328	$458	$268	$398	$95

Additional rail days $40 per day First Class, $30 per day Second Class.
*Price per person.
**Automatic available in a few cities only.
Extra person $189 1st class; $129 Second Class.
**Cars with automatic transmision are available at limited locations.

Spanish Rail/Drive

Valid for 4 days of unlimited rail travel in Spain and 3 days of car rental.

Car Category	1ST CLASS 2 ADULTS*	1 ADULT	2ND CLASS 2 ADULTS*	1 ADULT	ADD'L. CAR DAY
Economy	$285	$349	$241	$305	$53
Compact	$305	$399	$261	$355	$67
Intermed.	$325	$429	$281	$385	$76
Comp. Auto.**	$365	$509	$321	$465	$105

Extra Person	1ST CLASS	2ND CLASS
Adult	$220	$176
Child	$110	$88
Add'l. Rail Day Adult	$40	$36
Add'l. Rail Day Child	$20	$16

Scanrail/Drive

Valid for 5 days of unlimited rail travel and 3 days of car rental to be used within 15 days.

Car Category	1ST CLASS 2 ADULTS*	1 ADULT	2ND CLASS 2 ADULTS*	1 ADULT	ADD'L. CAR DAY
Economy	$298	$378	$248	$328	$55
Compact	$318	$428	$268	$378	$70
Intermed.	$338	$458	$288	$408	$80

Car rental not available in Finland. *Price per person.

Europass Drive

Any 6 days (3 rail, 3 car) within 2 months for travel in France, Germany, Italy, Spain, and Switzerland. No 40 percent discount for Rail/Drive program.

Car Category	2 ADULTS* 1ST CLASS	1 ADULT 1ST CLASS	ADD'L. CAR DAY
Economy	$278	$348	$53
Compact	$298	$398	$67
Intermed.	$308	$428	$76
Comp. Auto.**	$338	$468	$95

* Prices per person based on 2 people traveling together. third and fourth person are $199 each. There are no discounts for children.
**Cars with automatic shift are available at selected Hertz rental locations.

Eurail/Drive Pass

Any 7 days (4 rail, 3 car) within 2 months for travel in any of the seventeen Eurail countries (see page 2). Add up to 5 additional rail days and up to 5 more car days.

Car Categories	2 ADULTS* 1ST CLASS	1 ADULT 1ST CLASS	ADD'L. CAR DAY
Economy	$338	$418	$55
Compact	$358	$468	$70
Intermed.	$378	$498	$80
Comp. Auto.**	$398	$548	$99
Add'l. Rail Day	$50	$50	

Third and fourth person sharing car $259 per person. *Prices per person based on 2 people traveling together. **Cars with automatic shift are available at limited Hertz rental locations. Children ages 4-11 = $130. Extra days = $25.

France Rail 'N' Drive

Any 5 days (3 rail, 2 car) within 1 months for travel in France. Add up to 6 additional rail days and car days.

Car Category	1ST CLASS 2 ADULTS*	1 ADULT	2ND CLASS 2 ADULTS*	1 ADULT	ADD'L. CAR DAY
Economy	$179	$259	$159	$239	$45
Small	$199	$299	$179	$279	$65
Medium	$219	$339	$199	$319	$85
Small Auto.	$229	$349	$209	$329	$89
Add'l. Rail Day	$30	$30	$30	$30	

Swiss Rail 'N' Drive

Any 6 days (3 rail, 3 car) within 15 days for travel in Switzerland. Only available 1 May - 31 October.

Car Category	1ST CLASS 2 ADULTS*	1 ADULT	2ND CLASS 2 ADULTS*	1 ADULT	ADD'L. CAR DAY
Economy	$275	$415	$205	$325	$55
Compact	$305	$465	$235	$385	$75
Intermed.	$315	$505	$245	$415	$85

* Prices per person based on 2 people traveling together. Third and fourth person can just buy a regular rail pass

Drive/Pass Protection

This program entitles you to a 100 percent reimbursement on the unused portion of combination Rail Pass/Drive programs if lost or stolen while traveling in Europe.

$15 for the driver
$10 for each additional person

Upon discovery of the loss or theft, please follow these instructions:
1. Report the loss or theft to the local police in Europe within 24 hours and obtain a police report.
2. Mail the following to Rail Pass Express within 30 days of returning home.
   • Notarized written report of the circumstances of loss or theft.
   • Official police report.
   • Receipt for replacement ticket.

Rail Pass Express will reimburse you in full for the unused portion of your rail pass.

Rail Pass Express, Inc.
2737 Sawbury Blvd.
Columbus, OH 43235-4583
USA

Ph: 800/722–7151
Ph: 614/889–9100
Fx: 614/764–0711

http://www.eurail.com

Pass you would like to purchase:_____

Days:_____ Cost:_____

Estimated First Day of Travel:_____

Birthdate:_____

Please indicate whether the pass is 1st or 2nd class, Youth, Adult, Senior, or Child.

Would you like pass protection*: Yes   No
* Covers unused portion of pass if the pass is lost or stolen in Europe. $10 per pass.

Name as it appears on passport:

Mr. / Ms. First:_____Last:_____

Country of Permanent Residence:_____

Billing Address:_____

_____

City:_____ State/Country:_____ Zip/Postal code:_____

Phone:_____

Delivery Address (no P.O. Boxes):_____

_____

City:_____ State/Country:_____ Zip/Postal code:_____

Phone:_____

Please check one:

❏ Visa   ❏ Mastercard   ❏ American Express

Card Number:_____ Expiration Date:_____

Cardholder Name:_____

Signature (Required):_____

Type of shipping (signature is required for all orders):

❏ 2 Business Day FedEx - $10.00
❏ Standard Overnight FedEx (8-5 next business day) - $15.00
❏ Priority Overnight FedEx (by noon next business day) - $25.00
❏ Certified Mail (8-10 days) - $8.50
❏ International FedEx - $30.00*

* Most European countries, other countries may be more.

Eurail is our rail. Eurail is your rail.[TM]

Help Us Keep This Guide Up to Date

Every effort has been made by the author and editors to make this guide as accurate and useful as possible. However, many things can change after a guide is published–establishments close, phone numbers change, facilities come under new management, etc.

We would love to hear from you concerning your experiences with this guide and how you feel it could be made better and be kept up to date. While we may not be able to respond to all comments and suggestions, we'll take them to heart and we'll also make certain to share them with the author. Please send your comments and suggestions to the following address:

The Globe Pequot Press
Reader Response/Editorial Department
P.O. Box 833
Old Saybrook, CT 06475

Or you may e-mail us at:

editorial@globe-pequot.com

Thanks for your input, and happy travels!